AI Governance and Liability in Europe

AI Governance and Liability in Europe

A Primer

Edited by

Ceyhun Necati Pehlivan
Nikolaus Forgó
Peggy Valcke

Wolters Kluwer

Published by:
Kluwer Law International B.V.
PO Box 316
2400 AH Alphen aan den Rijn
The Netherlands
E-mail: lrs-sales@wolterskluwer.com
Website: www.wolterskluwer.com/en/solutions/kluwerlawinternational

Sold and distributed by:
Wolters Kluwer Legal & Regulatory U.S.
920 Links Avenue
Landisville, PA 17538
United States of America
E-mail: customer.service@wolterskluwer.com

ISBN 978-94-035-0549-7

e-Book: ISBN 978-94-035-0559-6
web-PDF: ISBN 978-94-035-0569-5

Editors

Ceyhun Necati Pehlivan is a counsel and head of the technology, media, telecommunications (TMT) and intellectual property (IP) practice group at Linklaters in Madrid. He serves as an adjunct professor of law at IE Law School and a lecturer at the Complutense University of Madrid. He is also the founding editor-in-chief of the Global Privacy Law Review (GPLR) at Wolters Kluwer.

Nikolaus Forgó is full professor of IT and IP law and head of department at the Department of Innovation and Digitalisation in Law, Faculty of Law, University of Vienna. He is also member of Austria's governmental advisory bodies on data protection ('Datenschutzrat') and AI ('KI-Beirat').

Peggy Valcke is full professor of law and technology at the Faculty of Law and Criminology at KU Leuven, co-director of the Centre for IT & IP Law (CiTiP), and principal investigator at Leuven.AI and imec. Since January 2024, she is executive board member at the Belgian Institute for Postal Services and Telecommunications (BIPT – IBPT).

Contributors

Jasper Bellon Managing associate in the Litigation, Arbitration & Investigations (LAI) practice group at Linklaters in Brussels.

Miriam C. Buiten Assistant professor for Law and Economics at the University of St. Gallen.

Joe Cannataci Head of the Department of Information Policy & Governance at the Faculty of Media & Knowledge Sciences of the University of Malta.

Florence Danis Partner in the LAI practice group at Linklaters in Brussels.

Jan De Bruyne Assistant professor of IT law at KU Leuven and at eLaw Leiden. Head of the CiTiP, KU Leuven.

Sonja Dürager Dr. iur. Partner at bpv (Vienna and Salzburg) in IT, IP and data protection law.

Alejandro Ferreres Comella Partner in the LAI practice group at Linklaters in Madrid.

Gert-Jan Hendrix Managing associate in the LAI practice group at Linklaters in Brussels.

Jan Kleijssen Consultant. Lecturer at the Strasbourg University. Member of the ALLAI Advisory Board. Observer to the Council of Europe's Committee on Artificial Intelligence (CAI).

Christof Koolen Postdoctoral researcher at the CiTiP, KU Leuven. Within his postdoctoral project, he critically examines how natural language processing (NLP) techniques can be applied to legal scholarship, with the specific aim of integrating NLP into the methodological toolkit of legal scholars.

Catelijne Muller President of ALLAI. Member of the HLEG. Member of the OECD Expert Group on AI Incidents. Observer to the CAI.

Boris P. Paal Prof. Dr. M.Jur. (Oxford). Chair for Law and Regulation of the Digital Transformation at the Technical University of Munich (TUM), TUM School of Social Sciences and Technology, Department of Governance.

Ceyhun Necati Pehlivan Counsel and head of the TMT and IP practice group at Linklaters in Madrid. Adjunct professor of law at IE Law School and lecturer at the Complutense University of Madrid.

Christabel Randolph Associate director at the Center for AI and Digital Policy (CAIDP).

Marc Rotenberg Executive director and founder of the CAIDP. Adjunct professor at the Georgetown University Law Center.

Quentin B. Schäfer Lecturer (assistant professor) in competition and private law, University of Strathclyde, Glasgow.

Victor Schollaert PhD researcher at the Antwerp Liability Law and Insurance Chair, University of Antwerp.

Nathalie A. Smuha Assistant professor and FWO Fellow at KU Leuven Faculty of Law. Adjunct Professor at NYU School of Law.

Summary of Contents

Editors v

Contributors vii

List of Abbreviations xxvii

Foreword xxxiii

Preface xxxvii

PART I
AI Governance and Regulatory Framework 1

CHAPTER 1
International Frameworks for AI Governance
Marc Rotenberg & Christabel Randolph 3

CHAPTER 2
The Council of Europe's Convention on Artificial Intelligence and Human Rights, Democracy and the Rule of Law
Catelijne Muller & Jan Kleijssen 33

CHAPTER 3
The Work of the High-Level Expert Group on AI as the Precursor of the AI Act
Nathalie A. Smuha 51

CHAPTER 4
Genesis of the Artificial Intelligence Act: When AI Beats the Imitation Game
Christof Koolen 81

Chapter 5
The EU Artificial Intelligence Act: An Introduction
Ceyhun Necati Pehlivan 117

Chapter 6
Economic Regulation and the AI Act: Perspectives from Competition Law, Data Protection, and Intellectual Property
Quentin B. Schäfer 165

Chapter 7
AI Training with Publicly Available Data in Accordance with the GDPR
Boris P. Paal 181

Part II
Proposal for an EU AI Liability Directive: Article-by-Article Commentary 217

Article 1 Subject Matter and Scope
Joe Cannataci 219

Article 2(1) Definition: AI System
Sonja Dürager 257

Article 2(2) Definition: High-Risk AI System
Sonja Dürager 267

Article 2(3) Definition: Provider
Miriam C. Buiten 273

Article 2(4) Definition: User
Miriam C. Buiten 281

Article 2(5) Definition: Claim for Damages
Florence Danis, Gert-Jan Hendrix & Jasper Bellon 287

Article 2(6) Definition: Claimant
Sonja Dürager 295

Article 2(7) Definition: Potential Claimant
Sonja Dürager 299

Article 2(8) Definition: Defendant
Miriam C. Buiten 303

Article 2(9) Definition: Duty of Care
Jan De Bruyne & Victor Schollaert 309

ARTICLE 3 Disclosure of Evidence and Rebuttable Presumption of Non-compliance
Florence Danis, Gert-Jan Hendrix & Jasper Bellon 329

ARTICLE 4 Rebuttable Presumption of a Causal Link in the Case of Fault
Jan De Bruyne & Victor Schollaert 349

ARTICLE 5 Evaluation and Targeted Review
Jan De Bruyne & Victor Schollaert 375

ARTICLE 6 Amendment to Directive (EU) 2020/1828
Alejandro Ferreres Comella 389

ARTICLE 7 Transposition
Ceyhun Necati Pehlivan 397

ARTICLE 8 Entry into Force
Ceyhun Necati Pehlivan 405

ARTICLE 9 Addressees
Ceyhun Necati Pehlivan 411

Index 415

Table of Contents

Editors v

Contributors vii

List of Abbreviations xxvii

Foreword xxxiii

Preface xxxvii

PART I
AI Governance and Regulatory Framework 1

CHAPTER 1
International Frameworks for AI Governance
Marc Rotenberg & Christabel Randolph 3

1 Introduction 3
2 International Frameworks for AI Governance (Excluding the EU AI Act) 3
 2.1 The Universal Guidelines for AI (2018) 3
 2.2 The OECD AI Principles/G20 AI Guidelines (2019/2024) 4
 2.3 The UNESCO Recommendation on AI Ethics (2021) 7
 2.4 The Council of Europe AI Convention (2024) 9
 2.5 The Hiroshima Process 11
3 Role of the United Nations 13
 3.1 High-Level Advisory Board and Internet Governance 13
4 US AI Policy Initiatives 14
 4.1 The White House AI Executive Order (2023) 14
 4.2 The OMB Guidance on AI (2023) 17
 4.3 The Voluntary Commitments of the Tech Companies (2024) 19

4.4 The Joint Statement by Agencies 20
4.5 The Role of the FTC and the CAIDP Complaint 21
5 China Policy Initiatives 22
5.1 Personal Information Protection Law (2021) 23
5.2 Recommendation Algorithm Provisions (2022) 24
5.3 Deep Synthesis Provisions (2022) 24
5.4 Generative AI Measures (2023) 24
6 Conclusion 25
Bibliography 26

CHAPTER 2
The Council of Europe's Convention on Artificial Intelligence and Human Rights, Democracy and the Rule of Law
Catelijne Muller & Jan Kleijssen 33
1 Introduction 33
2 The AI Convention 35
2.1 Objective and Purpose 36
2.1.1 Consistency with Human Rights, Democracy and the Rule of Law 36
2.1.2 Graduated and Differentiated 36
2.1.3 Activities Within the Lifecycle of AI Systems 37
2.1.4 Human Rights, Democracy and Rule of Law Impact Assessment 37
2.1.5 The AI Convention and the AI Act 37
2.2 Scope 38
2.2.1 Definition of AI 38
2.2.2 Public and Private Actors 38
2.2.3 Federal Clause 39
2.2.4 Research and Development 39
2.2.5 National Security 39
2.2.6 National Defence 40
2.3 Human Rights, Democracy and the Rule of Law: General Obligations 40
2.3.1 Human Rights and AI 40
2.4 Democracy, the Rule of Law and AI 40
2.5 Principles Related to Activities Within the Lifecycle of AI Systems 41
2.5.1 Human Dignity and Individual Autonomy 41
2.5.2 Transparency and Oversight 42
2.5.3 Accountability and Responsibility 43
2.5.4 Equality and Non-Discrimination 43
2.5.5 Privacy and Data Protection 44
2.5.6 Reliability 44
2.5.7 Safe Innovation 44
2.5.8 Remedies 45
2.5.9 Procedural Safeguards, Including Bans or Moratoria 45

2.6 Follow-Up Mechanism and Implementation 45
3 Reflections on the Added Value and Shortcomings of the Convention 47
3.1 Added Value 47
3.2 Shortcomings 48
Bibliography 50

CHAPTER 3
The Work of the High-Level Expert Group on AI as the Precursor of the AI Act
Nathalie A. Smuha 51
1 Introduction 51
2 The HLEG in Context 52
2.1 Europe's AI Strategy 52
2.2 The HLEG's Mandate 53
2.3 Broader Context 55
3 The Ethics Guidelines for Trustworthy AI 57
3.1 Core Concepts and Structure 57
3.2 The Guidelines as Inspiration for the High-Risk AI Systems' Requirements 61
3.2.1 Human Agency and Oversight 62
3.2.2 Technical Robustness and Safety 62
3.2.3 Privacy and Data Governance 63
3.2.4 Transparency 63
3.2.5 Diversity, Non-Discrimination and Fairness 65
3.2.6 Societal and Environmental Well-Being 65
3.2.7 Accountability 66
3.3 The Guidelines as Guidance for Voluntary Codes of Conduct 68
3.4 The Guidelines as General Normative Principles 68
4 The Policy and Investment Recommendations for Trustworthy AI 70
4.1 Core Concepts and Structure 70
4.2 A (Different) Risk-Based Approach 71
4.3 Other Relevant Recommendations 73
5 Conclusion 74
Bibliography 76

CHAPTER 4
Genesis of the Artificial Intelligence Act: When AI Beats the Imitation Game
Christof Koolen 81
1 Introduction 81
2 A Brief Look Backwards on AI 82
2.1 Beating the Imitation Game 82
2.2 From AI Winter to AI Summer 83
2.3 Advances in Computing Power and Availability of Data 86

2.3.1 Computing Power 86
2.3.2 Data Availability 89
2.4 The World Wants to Regulate AI 91
2.4.1 Geopolitical Developments 91
2.4.2 Calls for a Pause on AI Development 92
2.4.3 Race to Regulate 92
3 Legislative Journey of the AI Act 93
3.1 2018: AI for Europe 93
3.2 2019: High-Level Expert Group on AI 94
3.3 2020: White Paper on AI 94
3.4 2021: Proposal for a Regulation Laying Down Harmonized Rules on AI 95
3.5 2022-2024: Run-Up to the AI Act 96
3.5.1 The Council's Position 96
3.5.2 The Parliament's Position 97
3.5.3 Trilogue Negotiations 98
4 The AI Act 99
5 A Comprehensive European Digital Framework for AI 101
5.1 Interface Between the GDPR and the AI Act 103
5.2 Interface Between the DGA and the AI Act 105
5.3 Interface Between the DA and the AI Act 106
5.4 Interface Between the DMA and the AI Act 106
5.5 Interface Between the DSA and the AI Act 107
6 Conclusion 109
7 Appendix 110
Bibliography 111

CHAPTER 5
The EU Artificial Intelligence Act: An Introduction
Ceyhun Necati Pehlivan 117
1 AI Is Transforming the World 117
2 Brief Overview of the Legislative Process 120
2.1 Position of the Council 120
2.2 Position of the Parliament 120
2.3 Reconciliation of Positions in the Trilogues 121
3 Scope of Application 123
3.1 Personal Scope: Operators Along the AI Value Chain 123
3.1.1 Provider 123
3.1.2 Deployer 124
3.1.3 Product Manufacturer 124
3.1.4 Importer 125
3.1.5 Distributor 125
3.1.6 Authorized Representative 126
3.2 Extraterritorial Scope 127

3.3 Brussels Effect? 127
3.4 Exemptions 128
4 AI Systems 128
5 Tiered Regulation Based on Risk 131
5.1 Unacceptable Risk: Prohibited Practices 132
5.2 High-Risk AI Systems 133
5.2.1 Classification 133
5.2.1.1 High-Risk: Safety Component 134
5.2.1.2 High-Risk: Standalone AI Systems 134
5.2.1.3 High-Risk: Exceptions 135
5.2.2 Obligations for High-Risk Systems 136
5.2.2.1 Provider's Obligations 136
5.2.2.2 Deployer's Obligations 137
5.2.2.3 Importer's Obligations 139
5.2.2.4 Distributor's Obligations 140
5.3 Specific Transparency Risk 142
5.3.1 Providers 142
5.3.2 Deployers 143
5.3.3 Transparency Requirements 143
5.4 Other AI Systems 144
6 General-Purpose Artificial Intelligence 144
6.1 GPAI Models *Without* Systemic Risk 145
6.1.1 Obligations for Providers 145
6.1.2 Open-Source Licence GPAI Models 147
6.2 GPAI Models *with* Systemic Risk 148
6.2.1 High Impact Capabilities 148
6.2.2 Commission's Role and Technical Evaluation 149
6.2.3 Obligations for Providers 150
7 Interplay with Other Regulations 152
7.1 General Data Protection Regulation 152
7.2 Digital Services Act 153
8 Enforcement and Penalties 154
8.1 AI Systems 154
8.2 GPAI Models 155
9 Entry into Force and Gradual Application 156
10 Conclusion 158
Bibliography 159

CHAPTER 6
Economic Regulation and the AI Act: Perspectives from Competition Law, Data Protection, and Intellectual Property
Quentin B. Schäfer 165
1 Introduction 165
2 The AI Act and Economic Regulation 165

2.1 General Principles in the AI Act 165
2.2 Product Safety Regulation 166
3 The AI Act and Competition Law 167
3.1 Competition Law and Policy in the AI Act 167
3.2 Conflicts Between Competition Law and the AI Act 168
3.3 Specific Interactions: Access Obligations 170
4 The AI Act and Data Protection 171
5 The AI Act and (Intellectual) Property 172
5.1 Obligations in the AI Act Related to IP 172
5.2 Taking into Account IP Rights 174
5.3 The Fundamental Right to Property 175
6 Conclusion 176
Bibliography 177

CHAPTER 7
AI Training with Publicly Available Data in Accordance with the GDPR
Boris P. Paal 181
1 Conflict Between Big Data Needs and Data Protection Law 181
2 Processing Phases Relevant to Data Protection Law in AI Training 183
3 Applicability of the GDPR 184
3.1 Existence of the Personal Identifiers 184
3.2 Elimination of the Personal Identifiers 186
3.2.1 Anonymization 186
3.2.1.1 Definition 186
3.2.1.2 Legal Basis 187
3.2.1.3 Practical Challenges 187
3.2.2 Pseudonymization 188
3.2.3 Privacy Enhancing Technologies 189
3.2.3.1 Synthetic Data 189
3.2.3.2 Homomorphic Encryption 190
3.2.3.3 Differential Privacy 190
3.2.3.4 Interim Result 190
4 Application of the GDPR Requirements to AI Training 190
4.1 Principle of Data Minimization 191
4.2 Principle of Data Accuracy 192
4.3 Purpose Limitation 193
4.4 Principle of Transparency 195
5 Legal Grounds under the GDPR for AI Training 197
5.1 Consent: Article 6(1)(a) of the GDPR 197
5.2 Legitimate Interest: Article 6(1)(f) of the GDPR 198
5.2.1 Legitimate Interests of AI Developers 199
5.2.2 Necessity of the Data Processing 199
5.2.3 Balancing of Interests in the Narrow Sense 200
5.2.3.1 Criteria Against AI Developers 201
5.2.3.2 Criteria in Favour of AI Developers 202

5.3 Interim Result 203
6 Reference to and Effects of the AI Act 203
7 Summary and Outlook 204
Bibliography 206

PART II
Proposal for an EU AI Liability Directive: Article-by-Article Commentary 217

ARTICLE 1 Subject Matter and Scope
Joe Cannataci 219
Related Articles 220
Related Laws 220
Commentary 220
1 Purpose 220
2 Legal Background 220
2.1 International 220
2.2 European Union 221
2.3 National 221
2.4 Case Law 223
2.4.1 Facts of the Case 224
2.4.2 Applicable Law 224
2.4.3 Decision 225
3 Analysis 227
3.1 Scope 227
3.2 High-Risk AI Systems 230
3.2.1 AI System Intended to Be Used as a Safety Component of a Product or Subject to Union Harmonization Legislation 231
3.2.2 Annex III High-Risk Systems 234
3.2.2.1 Biometrics 239
3.2.2.2 Critical Infrastructure 241
3.2.2.3 Education 242
3.2.2.4 Employment, Worker Management and Access to Self-Employment 242
3.2.2.5 Access to and Enjoyment of Essential Private Services and Essential Public Services and Benefits 243
3.2.2.6 Law Enforcement, insofar as Their Use Is Permitted under Relevant Union or National Law 244
3.2.2.7 Migration, Asylum and Border Control 246
3.2.2.8 Administration of Justice and Democratic Processes 249
4 Conclusions 250
Bibliography 253

ARTICLE 2(1) Definition: AI System
Sonja Dürager 257
Related Articles 257
Related Laws 257
Related Case Law 258
Commentary 258
1 Purpose 258
2 Legal Background 258
2.1 International 258
2.2 European Union 259
3 Analysis 259
3.1 Autonomous or Automatic Behaviour of AI Systems? 261
3.2 What Are Different Levels of Autonomy? 262
3.3 Conclusion 264
Bibliography 264

ARTICLE 2(2) Definition: High-Risk AI System
Sonja Dürager 267
Related Articles 267
Related Laws 267
Commentary 268
1 Purpose 268
2 Legal Background 268
2.1 International 268
2.2 European Union 268
3 Analysis 269
Bibliography 271

ARTICLE 2(3) Definition: Provider
Miriam C. Buiten 273
Related Articles 274
Related Laws 275
Commentary 275
1 Purpose 275
2 Analysis 275
2.1 Relation to the AI Act 275
2.2 Developing 276
2.3 Placing on the Market or Putting into Service 276
2.4 Relation to the Product Liability Directive Proposal 277
Bibliography 279

ARTICLE 2(4) Definition: User
Miriam C. Buiten 281
Related Articles 283

Related Laws 283
Commentary 283
1 Purpose 283
2 Analysis 284
Bibliography 285

ARTICLE 2(5) Definition: Claim for Damages
Florence Danis, Gert-Jan Hendrix & Jasper Bellon 287
Related Articles 288
Related Laws 288
Commentary 288
1 Purpose 288
2 Analysis 288
2.1 Introduction 288
2.2 Assessment of the Various Components of the Definition 289
2.2.1 Non-Contractual Claim 289
2.2.2 Fault-Based Civil Law Claim 291
2.2.3 Claim for Compensation of Damage Caused by an Output of an AI System or the Failure of Such a System to Produce an Output 292
Bibliography 293

ARTICLE 2(6) Definition: Claimant
Sonja Dürager 295
Related Article 295
Related Laws 296
Commentary 296
1 Purpose 296
2 Analysis 296
2.1 Damage 296
2.2 Subrogation 296
2.3 Representative Actions 297

ARTICLE 2(7) Definition: Potential Claimant
Sonja Dürager 299
Related Article 299
Related Laws 300
Related Case Law 300
Commentary 300
1 Purpose 300
2 Legal Background 300
2.1 National 300
3 Analysis 301

ARTICLE 2(8) Definition: Defendant
Miriam C. Buiten 303
Related Articles 306
Related Laws 306
Commentary 306
1 Purpose 306
2 Analysis 306
Bibliography 308

ARTICLE 2(9) Definition: Duty of Care
Jan De Bruyne & Victor Schollaert 309
Related Articles 310
Related Laws 311
Related Case Law 311
Commentary 312
1 Purpose 312
2 Legal Background 312
2.1 International 312
2.2 European Union 313
2.3 National 316
2.4 Case Law 316
3 Analysis 317
3.1 Fault in the AILD and the Duty of Care 317
3.2 The Problematic Notion of the 'Duty of Care' 320
3.2.1 The Relationship Between 'Fault' and 'Duty of Care' under the AILD 321
3.2.2 The Remaining Importance and Challenges of National Law 322
3.2.3 What Is Covered by the Fault/Duty of Care under the AILD? 323
3.3 Conclusions 324
Bibliography 325

ARTICLE 3 Disclosure of Evidence and Rebuttable Presumption of Non-compliance
Florence Danis, Gert-Jan Hendrix & Jasper Bellon 329
Related Article 332
Related Laws 332
Related Case Law 333
Commentary 333
1 Purpose 333
2 Analysis 335
2.1 The Right of a (Potential) Claimant to Disclosure 335
2.1.1 The Request for Disclosure Must Be Brought Against the Provider or User of a High-Risk AI System 337

2.1.2 The Request Relates to Relevant Evidence 338
2.1.3 The Request Relates to Evidence at the Disposal of the Defendant 338
2.1.4 The Request Relates to Evidence About a Specific High-Risk AI System That Is Suspected of Having Caused Damage 340
2.1.5 The (Potential) Claimant Has Attempted to Obtain the Evidence from the Defendant 341
2.2 Evidence Preservation Measures 342
2.3 Limits to the Disclosure and Preservation of Evidence 343
2.3.1 The Proportionality and Necessity Test 343
2.3.2 Protective Measures for the Disclosure and Use of Trade Secrets 345
2.3.3 Procedural Remedies for Defendant 345
2.4 Presumption of Defendant's Non-Compliance with a Relevant Duty of Care 345
Bibliography 346

Article 4 Rebuttable Presumption of a Causal Link in the Case of Fault
Jan De Bruyne & Victor Schollaert 349
Related Articles 354
Related Laws 354
Related Case Law 355
Commentary 355
1 Purpose 355
2 Legal Background 356
2.1 International 356
2.2 European Union 357
2.3 National 359
2.4 Case Law 359
3 Analysis 359
3.1 General 360
3.2 Specific Conditions 364
3.3 The Limitations of the Presumption of Causality 366
3.4 Conclusion 369
Bibliography 369

Article 5 Evaluation and Targeted Review
Jan De Bruyne & Victor Schollaert 375
Related Articles 376
Related Laws 376
Commentary 377
1 Purpose 377
2 Legal Background 378
2.1 International 378

2.2 European Union 379
2.3 National 381
2.4 Case Law 381
3 Analysis 381
Bibliography 385

ARTICLE 6 Amendment to Directive (EU) 2020/1828
Alejandro Ferreres Comella 389
Related Articles 389
Related Laws 389
Commentary 390
1 Purpose 390
2 Legal Background 390
2.1 International 390
2.2 European Union 390
2.2.1 Opt-In Versus Opt-Out 391
2.2.2 Qualified Entities 391
2.2.3 Commonality Requirement 392
2.2.4 Protection of Consumers 393
3 Analysis 393
Bibliography 395

ARTICLE 7 Transposition
Ceyhun Necati Pehlivan 397
Related Articles 398
Related Laws 398
Related Case Law 398
Commentary 399
1 Purpose 399
2 Analysis 399
2.1 Transposition of EU Directive 399
2.2 Deadline for Transposition 400
2.3 Communication to the Commission 400
2.4 Failure to Transpose 402
2.5 Protection of Individuals for Incorrect or Lack of Transposition 403
2.6 Reference to the Directive 403
Bibliography 404

ARTICLE 8 Entry into Force
Ceyhun Necati Pehlivan 405
Related Articles 405
Related Laws 405
Related Case Law 405
Commentary 406
1 Purpose 406

2 Analysis 406
2.1 Transposition of EU Directive 406
2.2 Entry into Force 407
2.3 Publication in the Official Journal of the EU 407
Bibliography 409

ARTICLE 9 Addressees
Ceyhun Necati Pehlivan 411
Related Articles 411
Related Laws 411
Related Case Law 411
Commentary 412
1 Purpose 412
2 Analysis 412
2.1 EU Directives Are Addressed to Member State(s) 412
Bibliography 414

Index 415

List of Abbreviations

Accessibility Act	Directive (EU) 2019/882 of the European Parliament and of the Council of 17 April 2019 on the accessibility requirements for products and services, OJ. L. 151 (7 June 2019)
AI	artificial intelligence
AI Act Commission Proposal	European Commission, Proposal for a Regulation of the European Parliament and of the Council laying down harmonised rules on Artificial Intelligence (Artificial Intelligence Act) and Amending Certain Union Legislative Acts, COM(2021) 206 final (21 April 2021)
AI Act Council Proposal	Council of the European Union, Proposal for a Regulation of the European Parliament and of the Council laying down harmonised rules on artificial intelligence (Artificial Intelligence Act) and amending certain Union legislative acts – General approach, 2021/0106(COD) (25 November 2022)
AI Act or AIA	Regulation (EU) 2024/1689 of the European Parliament and of the Council of 13 June 2024 laying down harmonised rules on artificial intelligence and amending Regulations (EC) No. 300/2008, (EU) No. 167/2013, (EU) No. 168/2013, (EU) 2018/858, (EU) 2018/1139 and (EU) 2019/2144 and Directives 2014/90/EU, (EU) 2016/797 and (EU) 2020/1828, OJ. L., 2024/1689 (12 July 2024)
AI Act Parliament Amendments	Amendments adopted by the European Parliament on 14 June 2023 on the proposal for a regulation of the European Parliament and of the Council on laying down harmonised rules on artificial intelligence (Artificial Intelligence Act) and amending certain Union legislative acts (COM(2021)0206 – C9-0146/2021 – 2021/0106(COD) (14 June 2023)
AI Board	European Artificial Intelligence Board

AI Convention	Council of Europe Framework Convention on Artificial Intelligence and Human Rights, Democracy and the Rule of Law, Council of Europe Treaty Series – No. [225] (Vilnius, 9 May 2024)
AI Liability Directive or AILD	Proposal for a Directive of the European Parliament and of the Council on adapting non-contractual civil liability rules to artificial intelligence (AI Liability Directive), COM/2022/496 final (28 September 2022)
AI Office	European Artificial Intelligence Office
AIDP	Artificial Intelligence Development Plan
ALTAI	Assessment List for Trustworthy AI
ANN	artificial neural network
API	application programming interface
Art. 29 WP	Article 29 Data Protection Working Party
BEUC	Bureau Européen des Unions de Consommateurs
CAHAI	Council of Europe's Ad hoc Committee on Artificial Intelligence
CAI	Council of Europe's Committee on Artificial Intelligence
CAIDP	Center for AI and Digital Policy
CCPA	California Consumer Privacy Act
CEDAW	Convention on the Elimination of All Forms of Discrimination Against Women
Charter or CFR	Charter of Fundamental Rights of the EU
CJEU	Court of Justice of the European Union
CLC	International Convention on Civil Liability for Oil Pollution Damage
Commission	European Commission
Commission's White Paper on AI or White Paper on AI	Commission, *White Paper on Artificial Intelligence – A European Approach to Excellence and Trust*, COM(2020) 65 final (Brussels, 19 February 2020)
Convention 108	Convention for the Protection of Individuals with regard to Automatic Processing of Personal Data, Council of Europe, European Treaty Series (ETS) No. 108 (28 January 1981)
Convention 108 +	Modernised Convention for the Protection of Individuals with Regard to the Processing of Personal Data, Council of Europe Treaty Series (CETS) No. 223 (18 May 2018)
Council	Council of the European Union
Data Act or DA	Regulation (EU) 2023/2854 of the European Parliament and of the Council of 13 December 2023 on harmonised rules on fair access to and use of data and amending Regulation (EU) 2017/2394 and Directive (EU) 2020/1828 (Data Act), PE/49/2023/REV/1, OJ. L., 2023/2854 (22 December 2023)

Data Governance Act or DGA	Regulation (EU) 2022/868 of the European Parliament and of the Council of 30 May 2022 on European data governance and amending Regulation (EU) 2018/1724 (Data Governance Act), OJ. L. 152 (3 June 2022)
Digital Content Directive	Directive (EU) 2019/770 of the European Parliament and of the Council of 20 May 2019 on certain aspects concerning contracts for the supply of digital content and digital services, PE/26/2019/REV/1, OJ. L. 136 (22 May 2019)
Digital Copyright Directive or DCD	Directive (EU) 2019/790 of the European Parliament and of the Council of 17 April 2019 on copyright and related rights in the Digital Single Market and amending Directives 96/9/EC and 2001/29/EC, OJ. L. 130 (17 May 2019)
Digital Markets Act or DMA	Regulation (EU) 2022/1925 of the European Parliament and of the Council of 14 September 2022 on contestable and fair markets in the digital sector and amending Directives (EU) 2019/1937 and (EU) 2020/1828, OJ. L. 265 (12 October 2022)
Digital Services Act or DSA	Regulation (EU) 2022/2065 of the European Parliament and of the Council of 19 October 2022 on a Single Market For Digital Services and amending Directive 2000/31/EC, OJ. L. 277 (27 October 2022)
DPIA	data protection impact assessment
DPM	differential privacy method
EACB	European Association of Co-operative Banks
ECHR	European Convention on Human Rights
EDPB	European Data Protection Board
EDPS	European Data Protection Supervisor
EHDS	European Health Data Space
ePrivacy Directive or ePD	Directive 2002/58/EC of the European Parliament and of the Council of 12 July 2002 concerning the processing of personal data and the protection of privacy in the electronic communications sector, OJ. L. 201 (31 July 2002)
ESC	European Social Charter
EU	European Union
EU Institution Data Protection Regulation or EUDPR	Regulation (EU) 2018/1725 of the European Parliament and of the Council of 23 October 2018 on the protection of natural persons with regard to the processing of personal data by the Union institutions, bodies, offices and agencies and on the free movement of such data, and repealing Regulation (EC) No. 45/2001 and Decision No. 1247/2002/EC, OJ. L. 295 (21 November 2018)

Explanatory Memorandum to the AI Act	Explanatory Memorandum to the Proposal for a Regulation of the European Parliament and of the Council laying down harmonised rules on Artificial Intelligence (Artificial Intelligence Act) and Amending Certain Union Legislative Acts, COM(2021) 206 final (21 April 2021)
Explanatory Memorandum to the AI Liability Directive	Explanatory Memorandum to the Proposal for a Directive of the European Parliament and of the Council on adapting non-contractual civil liability rules to artificial intelligence (AI Liability Directive), COM/2022/496 final (28 September 2022)
FLOP	floating point operations per second
FRA	European Union Agency for Fundamental Rights
FRAIA	fundamental rights and algorithm assessment
FRAND	fair, reasonable and non-discriminatory
FRIA	fundamental rights impact assessment
FTC	Federal Trade Commission
G7	The Group of Seven, which is an intergovernmental political and economic forum consisting of Canada, France, Germany, Italy, Japan, the United Kingdom and the United States; additionally, the EU is a 'non-enumerated member'
GAO	Government Accountability Office
GenAI	generative artificial intelligence
General Data Protection Regulation or GDPR	Regulation (EU) 2016/679 of the European Parliament and of the Council of 27 April 2016 on the protection of natural persons with regard to the processing of personal data and on the free movement of such data, and repealing Directive 95/46/EC, OJ. L. 119 (4 May 2016)
GPAI	general-purpose artificial intelligence
GPU	graphics processing unit
HLEG	The High-Level Expert Group on Artificial Intelligence
HLEG Guidelines	The High-Level Expert Group on Artificial Intelligence, *Ethics Guidelines for Trustworthy AI* (8 April 2019)
ICCPR	International Covenant on Civil and Political Rights
ICERD	International Convention on the Elimination of All Forms of Racial Discrimination
ICESCR	International Covenant on Economic, Social and Cultural Rights
ICO	Information Commissioner's Office (UK)
IEC	International Electrotechnical Commission
IoT	internet of things
IP	intellectual property

IP Enforcement Directive	Directive 2004/48/EC of the European Parliament and of the Council of 29 April 2004 on the enforcement of intellectual property rights, OJ. L. 157 (30 April 2004)
ISO	International Organization for Standardization
LAI	Litigation, Arbitration & Investigations
Law Enforcement Directive or LED	Directive (EU) 2016/680 of the European Parliament and of the Council of 27 April 2016 on the protection of natural persons with regard to the processing of personal data by competent authorities for the purposes of the prevention, investigation, detection or prosecution of criminal offences or the execution of criminal penalties, and on the free movement of such data, and repealing Council Framework Decision 2008/977/JHA, OJ. L. 119 (4 May 2016)
LLM	Large Language Model
MAAP	Migration and Asylum Pact
MEP	Member of the European Parliament
Merger Regulation	Council Regulation (EC) No. 139/2004 of 20 January 2004 on the control of concentrations between undertakings, OJ. L. 24 (29 January 2004)
METI	Ministry of Economy, Trade, and Industry
MSA	market surveillance authority
NCA	national competent authority
NDA	National Data Administration
New Legislative Framework or NLF	Decision 768/2008/EC; Market Surveillance Regulation; and Regulation on Accreditation and Market Surveillance
New Product Liability Directive or NPLD	Proposal for a Directive of the European Parliament and of the Council on liability for defective products, COM/2022/495 final (28 September 2022)
NIST	The National Institute of Standards and Technology, an agency of the United States Department of Commerce
NLP	natural language processing
OECD	Organisation for Economic Co-operation and Development
OECD Recommendation	OECD, *Recommendation of the Council on Artificial Intelligence*, OECD/LEGAL/0449 (adopted on 22 May 2019, amended on 3 May 2024)
OEM	original equipment manufacturer
OJEU	Official Journal of the European Union
OMB	Office of Management and Budget, Executive Office of the President of the United States
PETs	privacy-enhancing technologies
PIPL	Personal Information Protection Law
PRC	The People's Republic of China

Product Liability Directive or PLD	Council Directive 85/374/EEC of 25 July 1985 on the approximation of the laws, regulations and administrative provisions of the Member States concerning liability for defective products, OJ. L. 210 (7 August 1985)
RAM	readiness assessment methodology
Representative Actions Directive or RAD	Directive (EU) 2020/1828 of the European Parliament and of the Council of 25 November 2020 on representative actions for the protection of the collective interests of consumers and repealing Directive 2009/22/EC, OJ. L. 409 (4 December 2020)
SDGs	Sustainable Development Goals adopted by the UN in 2015
SMEs	small and medium-sized enterprises
SyRI	System Risk Indication
TEU	Treaty on EU
TFEU	Treaty on the Functioning of the EU
Trade Secrets Directive	Directive (EU) 2016/943 of the European Parliament and of the Council of 8 June 2016 on the protection of undisclosed know-how and business information (trade secrets) against their unlawful acquisition, use and disclosure, OJ. L. 157 (15 June 2016)
UGAI	Universal Guidelines for Artificial Intelligence
UK	United Kingdom
UN	United Nations
UNCRC	UN Convention on the Rights of the Child
UNCRPD	UN Convention on the Rights of Persons with Disabilities
UNESCO	United Nations Educational, Scientific and Cultural Organization
UNESCO Recommendation	UNESCO, *Recommendation on the Ethics of Artificial Intelligence*, SHS/BIO/PI/2021/1 (23 November 2021)
Unfair Commercial Practices Directive	Directive 2005/29/EC of the European Parliament and of the Council of 11 May 2005 on Unfair commercial practices, OJ. L. 149 (11 June 2005)
US	United States
Web Accessibility Directive or WAD	Directive (EU) 2016/2102 of the European Parliament and of the Council of 26 October 2016 on the accessibility of the websites and mobile applications of public sector bodies, OJ. L. 327 (2 December 2016)
Whistleblowing Directive	Directive (EU) 2019/1937 of the European Parliament and of the Council of 23 October 2019 on the protection of persons who report breaches of Union law, PE/78/2019/REV/1, OJ. L. 305 (26 November 2019)

Foreword

How to govern disruptive technologies in the twenty-first century?

Over the past decades, and particularly the last ten years, 'Artificial Intelligence' (AI) has developed from a sci-fi vision into a technology that is all around us every day. Today, algorithms that process data or content to produce new data or content are becoming part of every production process in our economies and societies. The spread of AI does not only affect our communication methods and production chains, but it also challenges our existing governance frameworks, as new questions arise which need to be answered.

However, AI is not the first disruptive technology that has been invented and that we had to learn to cope with. We have seen other disruptive technologies which have created unprecedented opportunities and risks, based on their context of use. And for which we had to develop appropriate governance frameworks. During the Industrial Revolution, the spread of the combustion engine led to disruptions that are in many ways comparable to AI today: Engine-driven machines were used to automate and replace physical labour to produce goods and food and to build automotive vehicles to move people or goods from one place to another. Engines powered by steam, oil or electricity have allowed us to become wealthier than ever before and to travel to the moon. But they have also provided the technology for two world wars, and we are until today trying to find effective ways to minimize the negative effects of engines on our health and the environment.

So how have we tried to govern the enormous potential for good and bad of engines? We have not developed one single 'engine law' or 'engine regulation' that is expected to govern all the aspects of engines. We have developed a system of thousands of technical, legal and sociocultural norms which build a complex governance framework, not only for the engines themselves, but also for the machines that they power, for the infrastructure that these machines use, and for the people that drive the machines and for those that are affected by the operations of the machines.

With AI developing all across our economies and societies, we need to do something similar to what we did with engines. And this is already happening.

Technical norms are being developed at various international and European standardization bodies. In the last five to ten years, numerous soft-law instruments and other forms of guidance have been developed by intergovernmental and European organizations, by tech companies or by other institutions and processes. And in the past few years, binding legal instruments have been and are still being developed at national and regional levels, with the aim to adapt our governance frameworks to AI. While the European Union's (EU's) AI Act is one of the first AI-focused laws in one jurisdiction, the Council of Europe's Framework Convention (Vilnius Convention) is the first international treaty on AI, focusing on the potential impacts of AI on human rights, democracy and the rule of law.

While doing this, we must not forget: not everything is new with AI: We have done statistical analyses and probability calculations before. We have seen mis- and disinformation before. People have used means to exploit and manipulate other people before. We do not have to reinvent our fundamental values and rights because of AI. We need to make sure that the existing principles of human dignity and autonomy and human rights, democracy and the rule of law are also applied to the context of AI. This is what the Vilnius Convention is aiming to achieve. It reaffirms the obligation of states to respect human rights and the rule of law and protect the integrity of democratic processes. It formulates a number of fundamental principles that need to be respected when dealing with AI. It further requires states to have mechanisms in place that allow our societies to properly assess the risks and impacts of AI and identify procedural safeguards and remedies for individuals whose rights may be adversely affected.

When working on these different instruments and on their operationalization, it is important that all relevant actors cooperate in a way that these instruments together form a coherent framework that allows us to find appropriate responses to the opportunities and challenges that AI systems bring about. A good example of such necessary cooperation is the one between technical and legal standardization bodies in order to develop mechanisms to assess and minimize risks and adverse impacts of AI systems in the most practical and least bureaucratic way.

This leads me to a final point. Given the fast and permanent development of technology and its uses, and the increasing interdependence of ecosystems that were more separate previously, we should start thinking about redeveloping our political and legal governance mechanisms, which are currently still built on the procedures developed during the building of nation-states in the wake of the first industrial revolution of the nineteenth century. We should reform these processes and instruments so that they, on the one hand, allow us to have stability and durability on the level of fundamental principles that govern our societies and economies across all sectors, no matter what technologies we use. And on the other hand, we need much more agile and dynamic tools to regulate concrete applications of fast-developing technologies in concrete contexts. For this, we may take inspiration from digital technology itself that is not evolving once every few years, but constantly in small steps. And we may also use AI tools to govern at least certain aspects of AI and its use.

In light of these considerations, *AI Governance and Liability in Europe: A Primer* provides a comprehensive roadmap for navigating the complexities of AI governance and liability. By engaging with current frameworks and proposed regulations, the book provides valuable insights into building a coherent and adaptive governance structure, aiming to align technological advancement with societal and ethical standards.

Thomas Schneider[*]

* Thomas Schneider is an ambassador and director of international relations at the Swiss Federal Office of Communications (OFCOM). In his function as the chair of the CAI, he led the negotiations on the Framework Convention on Artificial Intelligence and Human Rights, Democracy and the Rule of Law.

Preface

Nearly seventy years ago, in 1955, the term 'AI' was coined as a marketing term by computer scientist John McCarthy. He used it in his proposal to the Rockefeller Foundation to fund what would become the famous Dartmouth Summer Research Project on Artificial Intelligence. This '2-month, 10-man study' conducted in 1956 is considered the founding event of AI as a research discipline. The research was based on the premise that 'every aspect of learning or any other feature of intelligence can in principle be so precisely described that a machine can be made to simulate it'.

While AI has been subject to varying interpretations and waves of popularity since its inception (marked by periods known as 'AI winters' and 'AI summers'), recent advances in computing power and the availability of data have fuelled the current AI momentum. As AI systems increasingly permeate various facets of our lives, there are growing concerns about their disruptive effects on society and the risks they pose to human rights, democracy and the rule of law.

Around 2017-2018, several academic and policy initiatives (including the Asilomar AI Principles, Montréal Declaration for Responsible AI, AI4People's Ethical Framework for a Good AI Society, European Commission Communication on Artificial Intelligence for Europe, Organisation for Economic Co-operation and Development (OECD) Principles on AI)[1] started discussing the need to develop ethical and legal guardrails to steer the innovation race in AI (in which broader global power dynamics evidently also play an important role).

Since then, within a relatively short time frame, the AI phenomenon has given rise to numerous governance frameworks at local, regional, national, supra- and international levels of jurisdiction. It cannot be denied, though, that the EU's AI Act is a landmark law on AI. It is the first legislation of its kind with global impact, establishing horizontal rules for the development, market placement, and use of AI systems. The sheer size of the legislation (encompassing 180 recitals, 113 articles, 11

1. For an overview of these early texts, *see* Marc Rotenberg, *The AI Policy Sourcebook*, EPIC (Washington 2020).

annexes, and 144 pages in the Official Journal), combined with the complexity of the topic, makes it a formidable challenge to grasp its subtleties and intricacies.

The aim of our book project is therefore to offer a reference guide and research tool for (legal) professionals – encompassing law practice, policy and academia – who are involved in the design, development and use of AI systems. In addition to providing critical analysis, identifying gaps, and proposing improvements, this book serves as an instrument to enhance the discourse on AI governance and regulation. Although we, as editors, may not necessarily support every viewpoint expressed within, our objective is to facilitate an open forum. Thus, we welcome diverse interpretations and discussions, while maintaining a stance of neutrality with respect to specific perspectives.

Initially, we envisioned this as a *single* book project that would combine an article-by-article commentary of the AI Act with an article-by-article commentary of the AI Liability Directive (AILD), along with several chapters to contextualize these pieces of legislation. However, we eventually had to reconsider this idea. The total number of pages produced by our authors significantly exceeds the physical limits of a single book (and undoubtedly also those of readers who would need to carry such a hefty volume).

After consulting with the publisher, we decided to split the book into two volumes and set 31 July 2024 as the cut-off date for both books. The first volume, titled *The EU Artificial Intelligence (AI) Act: A Commentary*, is dedicated to the AI Act and provides an in-depth, article-by-article commentary based on the text published in the Official Journal of 12 July 2024.

The second volume, which is the present book, aims to place the AI Act in a broader context and consists of two parts:

- Part I: A series of chapters that offer extensive coverage of AI regulatory developments around the world, with a focus on the Council of Europe's Framework Convention on Artificial Intelligence. These chapters discuss key antecedents, such as the work of the High-Level Expert Group on AI, and the genesis of the AI Act. Additionally, they analyse the AI Act's intersection with other significant regulations, such as the General Data Protection Regulation (GDPR) and IP law.
- Part II: An article-by-article commentary on the Commission's 2022 proposal for an AILD.

Regarding Part II, we deemed it useful to publish the commentaries despite the fact that discussions on the draft directive were suspended 'until the adoption of the AI Act' and have yet to resume. On 19 September 2024, the European Parliamentary Research Service published a complementary impact assessment on the proposal for a directive on adapting non-contractual civil liability rules to AI. This study suggests that the AILD should extend its scope to include general-purpose and other 'high-impact AI systems', as well as software. It also proposes a mixed liability framework that balances fault-based and strict liability. Notably, the study recommends transitioning from an AI-focused directive to a software liability regulation to prevent market fragmentation and enhance clarity across the EU.

Therefore, we need to make this disclaimer to the reader: the final text of the AILD – if ever adopted – might differ considerably. However, the insights provided by our authors on the draft directive will undoubtedly prove very useful, not only in the context of the ongoing legislative discussions but also in helping readers better understand the background and rationale behind why certain rules will ultimately (not) be adopted.

While the editing of this book was intense, it was also an immense pleasure. First, because we could rely on a dream team of prestigious scholars and top-tier professionals who are experts in the field. We are extremely grateful to them for delivering their high-quality input in a timely manner.

Second, the professionalism of our publisher made a significant difference. Understanding the time-critical nature of this endeavour, Wolters Kluwer went to great lengths to accommodate our wishes. We are grateful for the efforts of the entire team at Wolters Kluwer, whose support and collaboration were invaluable, and especially to Simon Bellamy for his outstanding support. We are also thankful to the NewGen team, particularly Gayathri Ravi and Udhaya Devi, for their precious efforts in preparing the manuscript.

And finally, the shared feeling of commitment and dedication to this project, along with a sense of humour shared amongst the three of us, made this project particularly enjoyable. Our (almost) weekly calls and numerous emails were lightened up by many jokes and the prospect of 'a European book tour' (if we ever find the time…!). As the book project was Ceyhun's initial idea, he is mentioned as the first editor. The order of appearance of Peggy's and Nikolaus' names was decided through a random ballot by Ceyhun's two-year-old son Íñigo, who became a proud big brother during the making of the book. We dedicate the last words of this preface to express our deepest gratitude to our families for their support, and in particular our spouses David, Birgit, and, above all, Laura, Ceyhun's wife, for her patience and indulgence during all those moments when the book took precedence over baby Jaime.

We hope, dear reader, that you will appreciate the result, and look forward to receiving any comments or feedback you may have.

Peggy, Nikolaus, Ceyhun
24 September 2024

PART I AI Governance and Regulatory Framework

CHAPTER 1

International Frameworks for AI Governance

Marc Rotenberg & Christabel Randolph

1 INTRODUCTION

The adoption of the European Union (EU) AI Act emerges at a time of growing global interest in the governance of artificial intelligence (AI). From national governments to international organizations, new policy guidelines and regulatory frameworks have been set out that establish norms for AI governance. This chapter explores these regulatory frameworks.

2 INTERNATIONAL FRAMEWORKS FOR AI GOVERNANCE (EXCLUDING THE EU AI ACT)

2.1 The Universal Guidelines for AI (2018)

Prior to the creation of the EU High-Level Expert Group on Artificial Intelligence (HLEG) and the circulation of the White Paper, work began on the first global framework for the governance of AI. The Universal Guidelines for Artificial Intelligence (UGAI)[1] were announced at the 2018 International Data Protection and Privacy Commissioners Conference in Brussels, Belgium – one of the most significant meetings of technology leaders and data protection experts in history. The Universal Guidelines have played an influential role in the development of other AI policy frameworks.

1. CAIDP 2018.

'The Guidelines are intended to maximize the benefits of AI, to minimize the risk, and to ensure the protection of human rights,' wrote the drafters.[2] The UGAI incorporate elements of human rights doctrine, data protection law, and ethical guidelines. The UGAI include several well-established principles for AI governance and put forward new principles not previously found in similar policy frameworks.[3] The Explanatory Memorandum states that the guidelines are primarily concerned with those systems that impact the rights of people.

According to the UGAI, the term 'Artificial Intelligence' is both broad and imprecise and encompasses a variety of technological aspects which require some degree of automated decision-making. The UGAI uses the term 'guidelines' as a means of providing directional practices that can be useful for both governments and the private sector and recommends that the application of the guidelines should be incorporated into 'ethical standards, adopted in national law and international agreements, and built into the design of systems'.[4]

The UGAI is structured on twelve fundamental principles: right to transparency, right to human determination, identification obligation, fairness obligation, assessment and accountability obligation, accuracy, reliability and validity obligation, data quality obligation, public safety obligation, cybersecurity obligation, prohibition on secret profiling, prohibition on unitary scoring and a termination obligation. The UGAI also sets out prohibitions for mass surveillance and unitary (or social) scoring and includes a termination obligation when it is no longer possible to maintain control of an AI system. Subsequent to the release of the UGAI, many leading AI scientists have called for a 'pause' on AI development until techniques are established to ensure human control.

The UGAI were widely diffused and formed the basis of several subsequent AI governance frameworks, including the Organisation for Economic Co-operation and Development (OECD) AI Principles, the EU AI Act, and the Hiroshima Process, among others.

2.2 The OECD AI Principles/G20 AI Guidelines (2019/2024)

Shortly after the release of the UGAI, the OECD released the first global framework for AI, endorsed by national governments. The OECD is an international organization that 'works to build better policies for better lives'.[5] The goal of the OECD is to 'shape policies that foster prosperity, equality, opportunity and well-being for all'. The OECD has led the global effort to develop and establish the first framework for AI policy. This is a result of a concerted effort by the OECD and the Member States to develop a coordinated international strategy. The OECD AI Principles also build on earlier OECD initiatives such as the OECD Privacy Guidelines, a widely recognized framework for

2. *Ibid.*
3. *Ibid.*
4. *Ibid.*
5. OECD About.

transborder data flows and the first global framework for data protection.[6] The OECD AI Principles seek to promote AI that is innovative and trustworthy and respects human rights and democratic values.[7] The OECD set out five principles for the responsible stewardship of trustworthy AI:

(1) inclusive growth, sustainable development and well-being;
(2) human-centred values and fairness;
(3) transparency and explainability;
(4) robustness, security and safety; and
(5) accountability.

The OECD also set out five recommendations for national policies and international co-operation for trustworthy AI:

(1) investing in AI research and development;
(2) fostering a digital ecosystem for AI;
(3) shaping an enabling policy environment for AI;
(4) building human capacity and preparing for labour market transformation; and
(5) international co-operation for trustworthy AI.

The OECD AI Principles were subsequently endorsed by the G20 nations in 2019. Consequently, more than fifty countries have endorsed either the OECD AI Principles or the G20 AI Guidelines.

The remarks of the former OECD Secretary-General Angel Gurria at the 2020 G20 Digital Economy Ministers Meeting also provide insight into the initial focus of the OECD's work on AI.[8] Secretary Gurria said:

> AI's full potential is still to come. To achieve this potential, we must advance a human-centred and trustworthy AI, that respects the rule of law, human rights, democratic values and diversity, and that includes appropriate safeguards to ensure a fair and just society. This AI is consistent with the G20 AI Principles you designed and endorsed last year, drawing from the OECD's AI Principles.

In recent years, there has been some concern that the OECD has moved away from the initial focus that the former Secretary-General described. A revised definition of AI systems, adopted in 2023, attempted to align the OECD AI Principles with recent AI developments, such as generative AI (GenAI), but appear also to elevate the concept of autonomous devices while ignoring a large category of AI systems that are rule-based. According to the revised OECD definition:[9]

6. OECD 1981.
7. OECD AI Principles.
8. Rotenberg 2020.
9. OECD Recommendation.

> An AI system is a machine-based system that, for explicit or implicit objectives, infers, from the input it receives, how to generate outputs such as predictions, content, recommendations, or decisions that can influence physical or virtual environments. Different AI systems vary in their levels of autonomy and adaptiveness after deployment.

The definition was also criticized for an unnecessary degree of anthropomorphism, i.e., ascribing agency to machines rather than to the organizations that design, develop, and deploy AI systems.

In 2024, during its planned five-year review, the OECD also revised the AI principles.[10] The OECD cited specific updates aimed at:

- reflecting the growing importance of addressing misinformation and disinformation, and safeguarding information integrity in the context of GenAI;
- addressing uses outside of intended purpose, intentional misuse, or unintentional misuse;
- clarifying the information AI actors should provide regarding AI systems to ensure transparency and responsible disclosure;
- addressing safety concerns, so that if AI systems risk causing undue harm or exhibit undesired behaviour, they can be overridden, repaired, and/or decommissioned safely by human interaction;
- emphasizing responsible business conduct throughout the AI system lifecycle, involving co-operation with suppliers of AI knowledge and AI resources, AI system users, and other stakeholders;
- underscoring the need for jurisdictions to work together to promote;
- interoperable governance and policy environments for AI, against the increase in AI policy initiatives worldwide; and
- introducing an explicit reference to environmental sustainability, of which the importance has grown considerably since the adoption of the Recommendation in 2019.

These updates were generally favourable, though it appears the OECD removed an earlier reference in the 2019 AI Principles that established the right of:[11]

> those adversely affected by an AI system to challenge its outcome based on plain and easy-to-understand information on the factors, and the logic that served as the basis for the prediction, recommendation or decision.

The OECD has also developed companion resources including the OECD.AI Policy Observatory,[12] the OECD AI Incident Monitoring Tool,[13] and the OECD AI Risk Management Framework.[14] The OECD also significantly updated its Guidelines for

10. *Ibid.*
11. *Ibid.*, 1.3, Transparency and explainability (22 May 2019).
12. OECD.AI Policy Observatory.
13. OECD AI Incidents.
14. OECD RMF 2023.

Multinational Enterprises on Responsible Business Conduct[15] to address emerging technology issues.

2.3 The UNESCO Recommendation on AI Ethics (2021)

In November 2021, the 193 Member States of United Nations Educational, Scientific and Cultural Organization (UNESCO) adopted the Recommendation on the Ethics of Artificial Intelligence (UNESCO Recommendation), the most comprehensive global framework to date for the governance of AI.[16] According to UNESCO, the Recommendation will not only protect but also promote human rights and human dignity, and will be an ethical guiding compass and a global normative bedrock allowing to build strong respect for the rule of law in the digital world.[17] UNESCO Director-General Audrey Azoulay stated:

> The world needs rules for artificial intelligence to benefit humanity. The recommendation on the ethics of AI is a major answer. It sets the first global normative framework while giving member states the responsibility to apply it at their level. UNESCO will support its 193 member states in its implementation and ask them to report regularly on their progress and practices.

The UNESCO Recommendation was the outcome of a multi-year process and was drafted with the assistance of more than twenty-four experts.[18] According to UNESCO, the:[19]

> historical text defines the common values and principles which will guide the construction of the necessary legal infrastructure to ensure the healthy development of AI.

UNESCO explained:

> The Recommendation aims to realize the advantages AI brings to society and reduce the risks it entails. It ensures that digital transformations promote human rights and contribute to the achievement of the Sustainable Development Goals, addressing issues around transparency, accountability and privacy, with action-oriented policy chapters on data governance, education, culture, labour, healthcare and the economy.

The UNESCO Recommendation carried forward earlier principles for the governance of AI and also introduced new safeguards such as gender equity and sustainability. The key achievements of the UNESCO Recommendation include:

15. OECD 2023.
16. UNESCO News.
17. UNESCO Recommendation.
18. UNESCO Draft Recommendation.
19. UNESCO News.

(1) *Protecting data:* The UNESCO Recommendation calls for action beyond what tech firms and governments are doing to guarantee individuals more protection by ensuring transparency, agency and control over their personal data.
(2) *Banning social scoring and mass surveillance:* The UNESCO Recommendation explicitly bans the use of AI systems for social scoring and mass surveillance.
(3) *Monitoring and Evaluation:* The UNESCO Recommendation establishes new tools that will assist in implementation, including ethical impact assessments and a readiness assessment methodology (RAM).
(4) *Protecting the environment:* The UNESCO Recommendation emphasizes that AI actors should favour data, energy and resource-efficient AI methods that will help ensure that AI becomes a more prominent tool in the fight against climate change and in tackling environmental issues.

The UNESCO Recommendation aims to provide a basis to make AI systems work for the good of humanity, individuals, societies and the environment and ecosystems, and to prevent harm. It also aims at stimulating the peaceful use of AI systems. The UNESCO Recommendation provides a universal framework of values and principles of the ethics of AI. It sets out four values:

(1) respect, protection and promotion of human rights and fundamental freedoms and human dignity;
(2) environment and ecosystem flourishing;
(3) ensuring diversity and inclusiveness; and
(4) living in peaceful, just and interconnected societies.

Further, the UNESCO Recommendation outlines ten principles – proportionality and do no harm, safety and security, fairness and non-discrimination, sustainability, right to privacy and data protection, human oversight and determination, transparency and explainability, responsibility and accountability, awareness and literacy – backed up by more concrete policy actions on how they can be achieved. The UNESCO Recommendation also introduces red lines to unacceptable AI practices. For example, it states that 'AI systems should not be used for social scoring or mass surveillance purposes.'

The UNESCO Recommendation focuses not only on values and principles but also on their practical realization, with concrete policy actions. The UNESCO Recommendation encourages Member States to introduce frameworks for ethical impact assessments and oversight mechanisms. According to UNESCO, Member States should ensure that harms caused through AI systems are investigated and redressed, by enacting strong enforcement mechanisms and remedial actions, to make certain that human rights and fundamental freedoms and the rule of law are respected.

In 2022, UNESCO announced that it would develop implementation tools for its Recommendation – the Ethical Impact Assessment Tool and the RAM.[20] In 2023,

20. UNESCO Implementation Recommendation.

UNESCO published its Ethical Impact Assessment Tool,[21] primarily designed to help government officials (individuals and teams) involved in the procurement of AI systems and is a general methodology, intended as a set of criteria for how to conduct an ethical impact assessment (EIA).[22]

In 2023, UNESCO also announced the RAM[23] to help countries understand where they stand on the scale of preparedness to implement AI ethically and responsibly for all their citizens, in so doing highlighting what institutional and regulatory changes are needed. The RAM comprises both qualitative and quantitative assessment criteria and recommends that countries':[24]

> regulatory framework should include aspects of effective protection, enforcement, redress, and monitoring of potential harms related to the deployment and use of AI systems.

In 2024, UNESCO presented the AI readiness assessment of Mexico. As UNESCO explained:[25]

> Consolidating and driving a national strategy with an ethical orientation linked to its National Development Plan would position Mexico in AI governance.

2.4 The Council of Europe AI Convention (2024)

The Council of Europe is the continent's leading human rights organization.[26] The Council of Europe is comprised of forty-seven Member States, twenty-seven of which are members of the EU. All Council of Europe Member States have endorsed the European Convention on Human Rights (ECHR), a treaty designed to protect human rights, democracy and the rule of law. Article 8 of the ECHR, concerning the right to privacy, has influenced the development of privacy law around the world.

Several AI initiatives are underway at the Council of Europe, including at the Council of Ministers, and the Council of Europe Parliamentary Assembly. Marija Pejčinović Burić, Secretary-General of the Council of Europe, has said:[27]

> It is clear that AI presents both benefits and risks. We need to ensure that AI promotes and protects our standards. ... The Council of Europe has, on many occasions, demonstrated its ability to pioneer new standards, which have become global benchmarks.

In October 2020, the Parliament Assembly of the Council of Europe adopted a new resolution on the need for democratic governance of AI.[28] The Assembly called for 'strong and swift action' by the Council of Europe. The parliamentarians warned that:

---

21. UNESCO Ethical Impact Assessment.
22. *Ibid.*, at 6.
23. UNESCO RAM.
24. *Ibid.*, at 9.
25. UNESCO Mexico.
26. CoE About.
27. CoE AI.
28. CoE PACE.

> soft-law instruments and self-regulation have proven so far not sufficient in addressing these challenges and in protecting human rights, democracy and rule of law.

In a set of recommendations examining the opportunities and risks of AI for democracy, human rights and the rule of law adopted in October 2020 as well, the Parliamentary Assembly called on the Committee of Ministers to take into account the particularly serious potential impact of the use of AI 'in policing and criminal justice systems'[29] or 'on the enjoyment of the rights to equality and non-discrimination',[30] when assessing the necessity and feasibility of an international legal framework for AI.

In May 2024, the Council adopted the first-ever international legally binding treaty aimed at ensuring the respect of human rights, the rule of law and democracy legal standards in the use of AI systems.[31] The Council of Europe AI Convention, also open to non-European countries, sets out a legal framework that covers the entire lifecycle of AI systems:

- The AI Convention covers AI systems in the public sector – including private actors acting on their behalf. The AI Convention also offers two ways of regulating the private sector: parties may opt to be directly obliged by the AI Convention or take other measures to comply with it.
- The AI Convention establishes transparency and oversight requirements, including identifying content generated by AI systems. Parties must adopt measures to identify, assess, prevent, and mitigate possible risks and also assess the need for a moratorium or a ban on AI systems incompatible with human rights.
- Parties must ensure accountability and responsibility for adverse impacts and ensure that AI systems respect equality, including gender equality, the prohibition of discrimination, and privacy rights. Moreover, parties must ensure legal remedies for victims of human rights violations and establish procedural safeguards, including notifying any persons interacting with AI systems that they are interacting with such systems.
- As regards the risks to democracy, the AI Convention requires parties to adopt measures to ensure that AI systems are not used to undermine democratic institutions and processes.
- Parties to the AI Convention will not be required to apply the treaty's provisions to activities related to the protection of national security interests but will be obliged to ensure that these activities respect international law and democratic institutions and processes.
- The AI Convention will not apply to national defence matters nor to research and development activities, except when the testing of AI systems may have the potential to interfere with human rights, democracy or the rule of law.

29. CoE Recommendation 2182(2020); *See also* CoE Resolution 2342.
30. CoE Recommendation 2183(2020); *See also* CoE Resolution 2343.
31. CoE News.

- In order to ensure its effective implementation, the AI Convention establishes a follow-up mechanism in the form of a Conference of the Parties.
- Finally, the AI Convention requires that each party establishes an independent oversight mechanism to oversee compliance with the convention, and raises awareness, stimulates an informed public debate, and carries out multistakeholder consultations on how AI technology should be used.

The Council of Europe AI Convention will be open for signature on 5 September 2024.

2.5 The Hiroshima Process

Under the leadership of former Prime Minister Shinzo Abe, Japan proposed the first international rules that would make 'AI networks controllable by human beings and respect for human dignity and privacy' at the 2016 G7 Summit in Japan.[32] Work on AI continued at the at the G7. The G7 leaders at the 2021 Summit warned that:[33]

> new forms of decision-making have surfaced examples where algorithms have entrenched or amplified historic biases, or even created new forms of bias or unfairness.

They also called for a 'human centric approach to artificial intelligence'.[34] Civil society organizations have called for the G7 to establish actionable standards to measure progress toward these goals, specifically:[35]

(1) creation of robust mechanisms for independent oversight of AI systems;
(2) transparency and accountability in the procurement and implementation of AI systems for public services;
(3) opportunities for public participation in AI policymaking; and
(4) red lines for technologies that violate fundamental human rights, including facial recognition and biometric surveillance technologies.

The G7 Hiroshima Process, first announced in 2023, had several significant outcomes. The Leaders' Communique[36] emphasizes 'shared principles including the rule of law and democratic values, keeping humankind at the center', 'Safe, secure, and trustworthy AI', and a recognition of the accomplishments at the United Kingdom (UK) AI Safety Summit. The Hiroshima Process produced Guiding Principles for Organizations Developing Advanced AI (Hiroshima Guiding Principles)[37] aimed at:

> organizations developing and using the most advanced AI systems, including the most advanced foundation models and generative AI systems.

32. Japan Times 2016.
33. The White House 2021.
34. CAIDP 2023.
35. *Ibid.*
36. G7 Communique 2023.
37. G7 Guiding Principles 2023.

It sets out eleven key principles:

(1) Taking appropriate measures throughout the development of advanced AI systems, including prior to and throughout their deployment and placement on the market, to identify, evaluate, and mitigate risks across the AI lifecycle.
(2) Identifying and mitigating vulnerabilities, and, where appropriate, incidents and patterns of misuse, after deployment including placement on the market.
(3) Publicly reporting advanced AI systems' capabilities, limitations and domains of appropriate and inappropriate use, to support ensuring sufficient transparency, thereby contributing to increased accountability.
(4) Working towards responsible information sharing and reporting of incidents among organizations developing advanced AI systems including with industry, governments, civil society, and academia.
(5) Developing, implementing, and disclosing AI governance and risk management policies, grounded in a risk-based approach – including privacy policies, and mitigation measures, in particular for organizations developing advanced AI systems.
(6) Investing in and implementing robust security controls, including physical security, cybersecurity and insider threat safeguards across the AI lifecycle.
(7) Developing and deploying reliable content authentication and provenance mechanisms, where technically feasible, such as watermarking or other techniques to enable users to identify AI-generated content.
(8) Prioritizing research to mitigate societal, safety and security risks and prioritize investment in effective mitigation measures.
(9) Prioritizing the development of advanced AI systems to address the world's greatest challenges, notably but not limited to the climate crisis, global health and education.
(10) Advancing the development of and, where appropriate, adoption of international technical standards.
(11) Implementing appropriate data input measures and protections for personal data and intellectual property (IP).

On the basis of the Hiroshima Guiding Principles, the countries participating in the Hiroshima AI Process also adopted the International Code of Conduct for Organizations Developing Advanced AI Systems[38] (Code of Conduct) to promote safe, secure, and trustworthy AI and to provide voluntary guidance for actions by organizations developing advanced AI systems. The Code of Conduct mirrors the eleven principles set out in the Hiroshima Guiding Principles. To complement this, the data protection and privacy authorities adopted the Statement on GenAI.[39]

38. G7 Code of Conduct 2023.
39. OPC 2023.

The G7 Apulia Leaders' Communique[40] commits to building on the Hiroshima Process by launching an action plan on the use of AI in the world of work and supporting the implementation of the Code of Conduct. The Apulia Leaders' Communique emphasizes that:[41]

> efforts to enhance interoperability amongst our AI governance approaches to promote greater certainty, transparency and accountability while recognizing that approaches and policy instruments may vary across G7 members ... deepening coordination between our respective institutes and offices focused on AI, to work towards shared understanding of risk management and advance international standards for AI development and deployment.

The Apulia Summit committed to producing a reporting framework for monitoring the Code of Conduct produced in the Hiroshima Process as well as a toolkit of AI in the public sector.[42]

Following the Hiroshima Process, in January 2024, Japan's Ministry of Internal Affairs and Communications and the Ministry of Economy, Trade and Industry issued Draft AI Guidelines for Businesses.[43] The Guidelines present unified guiding principles in AI governance in Japan to promote the safe and secure use of AI. It is intended to help people who use AI in various businesses to fully recognize AI risks based on international trends and stakeholders' concerns and to voluntarily take the necessary countermeasures across the entire lifecycle.[44]

3 ROLE OF THE UNITED NATIONS

The United Nations (UN) Secretary-General has been vocal about the critical intersection of AI and human rights. In various statements, he has highlighted the potential of AI to contribute to the achievement of the Sustainable Development Goals (SDGs), while cautioning against the risks of exacerbating inequality, discrimination, and other human rights abuses.[45] The Secretary-General has also warned that autonomous weapon systems, 'generally understood as weapon systems that select targets and apply force without human intervention,' pose serious humanitarian, legal, ethical and security concerns.[46]

3.1 High-Level Advisory Board and Internet Governance

The formation of the UN high-level expert group on AI governance carries forward the organization's commitment to ensuring that AI technologies are governed in a manner that prioritizes ethical considerations and human rights. This group is tasked with

40. G7 Communique 2024.
41. *Ibid.*, at 21.
42. *Ibid.*, at 22.
43. Japan Guidelines 2024.
44. *Ibid.*, at 2.
45. Rotenberg 2024.
46. UN 2023.

providing strategic guidance on the ethical development and deployment of AI, bridging the gap between technology and policy to foster a global governance framework that is both inclusive and effective.

A preliminary report from the Advisory Board, *Governing AI for Humanity*, sets out five guiding principles:

(1) AI should be governed inclusively, by and for the benefit of all.
(2) AI must be governed in the public interest.
(3) AI governance should be built in step with data governance and the promotion of data commons.
(4) AI governance must be universal, networked and rooted in adaptive multistakeholder collaboration.
(5) AI governance should be anchored in the UN Charter, International Human Rights Law, and other agreed international commitments such as the SDGs.

There is also the possibility that the UN Advisory Board will recommend the creation of a new global agency, similar to the International Panel on Climate Change, that will bring together scientists specifically to assess risks associated with the development of advanced AI models. Already, new agencies are being set up in the United States (US), the UK, Japan, and elsewhere to help ensure the development of safe, secure, and trustworthy AI.

In March 2024, the UN General Assembly adopted a landmark resolution on AI.[47] The Assembly called on all Member States and stakeholders:[48]

> to refrain from or cease the use of artificial intelligence systems that are impossible to operate in compliance with international human rights law or that pose undue risks to the enjoyment of human rights.

The Assembly also urged all states, the private sector, civil society, research organizations and the media, to develop and support regulatory and governance approaches and frameworks related to safe, secure and trustworthy use of AI. The text was co-sponsored by more than 120 Member States.

4 US AI POLICY INITIATIVES

4.1 The White House AI Executive Order (2023)

In October 2023, President Biden issued an Executive Order on 'Safe, Secure, Trustworthy Development of AI' (Biden EO).[49] President Biden explained:[50]

> Artificial intelligence (AI) holds extraordinary potential for both promise and peril. Responsible AI use has the potential to help solve urgent challenges while making

47. UN News.
48. UN 2024.
49. EO 14110.
50. *Ibid.*, s. 1 ('Purpose').

> our world more prosperous, productive, innovative, and secure. At the same time, irresponsible use could exacerbate societal harms such as fraud, discrimination, bias, and disinformation; displace and disempower workers; stifle competition; and pose risks to national security. Harnessing AI for good and realizing its myriad benefits requires mitigating its substantial risks. This endeavor demands a society-wide effort that includes government, the private sector, academia, and civil society.

The Biden EO is the most extensive in US history and includes new standards for AI safety and security, privacy protection, advances equity and civil rights, safeguards consumers and workers, and promotes innovation and competition.[51] The Biden EO:[52]

> builds on prior work to support the development of responsible AI technologies and policies, including the Office of Science and Technology Policy's (OSTP) *Blueprint for an AI Bill of Rights* and the National Institute of Standards and Technology's (NIST) *AI Risk Management Framework* (AI RMF).

The Biden EO imposes reporting obligations on the private sector by requiring that developers of the most powerful AI systems share their safety test results and other critical information with the US government.[53] The EO invokes the Defense Production Act, to require that companies developing any foundation model that poses a serious risk to national security, national economic security, or national public health and safety must notify the federal government when training the model, and must share the results of all red-team safety tests.[54] Federal agencies have initiated rulemaking to comply with the directives of the Biden EO which will result in regulatory obligations for private actors. The Congressional Research Services summarized the eight over-arching policy areas of the Biden EO as follows:[55]

- *Safety and security.* The EO promotes the development and implementation of repeatable processes and mechanisms to understand and mitigate risks related to AI adoption, including with respect to biosecurity, cybersecurity, national security, and critical infrastructure.
- *Innovation and competition.* The EO compels actions to attract AI talent to the United States, understand novel [IP] questions, protect inventors and creators, and promote AI innovation, including at startups and small businesses.
- *Worker support.* The EO states that AI adoption may be disruptive to the workforce and directs agencies to research and develop potential mitigations against such disruptions.
- *Consideration of AI bias and civil rights.* The EO states that AI models may perpetuate biases and their implementation may lead to civil rights violations. The EO includes a section on equity and civil rights considerations for use of AI in the criminal justice system and the administration of federal government programs and benefits.

51. The White House 2023a.
52. CRS 2024, 1.
53. EO 14110, s. 4.2 ('Ensuring Safe and Reliable AI'), 75197-75199.
54. *Ibid.*, s. 4.2(c).
55. *Ibid.; see also* EO 14110, s. 2 ('Policy and Principles'), 75191-75193.

- *Consumer protection.* The EO instructs agencies to enforce existing, technology-agnostic authorities in an effort to minimize harms to consumers, and to identify needed authorities related to AI.
- *Privacy.* The EO calls for the evaluation and mitigation of privacy risks – potentially exacerbated by AI – associated with the collection, use, and retention of user data.
- *Federal use of AI.* The EO requires the Office of Management and Budget (OMB) to establish an interagency council to coordinate AI use by federal agencies and develop guidance on AI governance and risk management activities for agencies. It acknowledges the ubiquity of generative AI (GenAI) tools and directs agencies to move toward adoption with safeguards in place. The EO also calls for additional agency hiring and training activities to increase the AI workforce capacity across the federal government.
- *International leadership.* The EO declares that the United States should be a global leader in AI development and adoption by engaging with international allies and partners, leading efforts to develop common AI regulatory and accountability principles, and advancing responsible global technical standards for AI.

The Biden-Harris Administration has promoted rapid implementation of the Biden EO and published progress reports through the White House Fact Sheet.[56] Actions already completed under managing 'risks to safety and security' include:[57]

- Using Defense Production Act authorities to compel developers of the most powerful AI systems to report vital information, especially AI safety test results, to the Department of Commerce.
- A draft rule that proposes to compel US cloud companies that provide computing power for foreign AI training to report that they are doing so.
- Completed risk assessments covering AI's use in every critical infrastructure sector.

Agencies have also issued broad statements of principles that apply to the private sector and put companies on notice for unacceptable practices. For example, the Department of Labor issued the Principles for Developers and Employers[58] and the scope of the principles is clearly inclusive as they:

> apply to the development and deployment of AI systems in the workplace, and should be considered during the whole lifecycle of AI – from design to development, testing, training, deployment and use, oversight, and auditing. The principles are applicable to all sectors and intended to be mutually reinforcing, though not all Principles will apply to the same extent in every industry or workplace.

56. The White House 2024a.
57. *Ibid.*
58. DOL (undated).

Prior to the Biden EO, in 2020, the Trump Administration issued Executive Order 13960 (Trump EO) which emphasized that:[59]

> the ongoing adoption and acceptance of AI will depend significantly on public trust ... and AI should be worthy of people's trust.

The Trump EO characterized trustworthy AI as being lawful, respectful of our civil rights, accurate, reliable, safe, understandable, responsible, transparent, accountable and regularly monitored.[60]

4.2 The OMB Guidance on AI (2023)

Pursuant to the Biden EO, the OMB issued a memorandum on *Advancing Governance, Innovation, and Risk Management for Agency Use of Artificial Intelligence* (OMB Guidance).[61] The memorandum:[62]

> directs agencies to advance AI governance and innovation while managing risks from the use of AI in the Federal Government, particularly those affecting the rights and safety of the public.

By 1 December 2024, Federal agencies will be required to implement concrete safeguards when using AI in a way that could impact Americans' rights or safety.[63]

The OMB Guidance has three objectives: (1) strengthening AI governance; (2) advancing responsible AI innovation; and (3) managing risks from the use of AI. The OMB Guidance clarifies that the guidance is:[64]

> scoped to address risks specifically arising from the use of AI, as well as governance and innovation issues that are directly tied to agencies' use of AI.

The OMB Guidance applies to 'new and existing AI that is developed, used, or procured by or on behalf of covered agencies'.[65] The OMB Guidance requires that agencies designate a chief AI officer to improve accountability for AI issues.[66]

The OMB Guidance in section 5 requires agencies to implement 'minimum practices' to manage risks from AI systems. It categorizes AI systems into 'rights-impacting' and 'safety-impacting' and sets out corresponding minimum practices in section 5(c). The OMB Guidance provides certainty and clearly determines 'safety-impacting' and 'rights-impacting' AI systems which are subject to the minimum practices in section 5(c).

59. EO 13960.
60. *Ibid.*
61. OMB Guidance.
62. *Ibid.*, 1.
63. The White House 2024b.
64. OMB AI Guidance, 2, s. 2.
65. *Ibid.*, s. 2(b), at 3.
66. *Ibid.*, s. 3(a), at 4.

According to the OMB Guidance, safety-impacting AI:[67]

> refers to AI whose output produces an action or serves as a principal basis for a decision that has the potential to significantly impact the safety of:
> (1) Human life or well-being, including loss of life, serious injury, bodily harm, biological or chemical harms, occupational hazards, harassment or abuse, or mental health, including both individual and community aspects of these harms;
> (2) Climate or environment, including irreversible or significant environmental damage;
> (3) Critical infrastructure, including the critical infrastructure sectors defined in Presidential Policy Directive 2159 or any successor directive and the infrastructure for voting and protecting the integrity of elections; or,
> (4) Strategic assets or resources, including high-value property and information marked as sensitive or classified by the Federal Government.

Rights-impacting AI refers to:[68]

> AI whose output serves as a principal basis for a decision or action concerning a specific individual or entity that has a legal, material, binding, or similarly significant effect on that individual's or entity's:
> (1) Civil rights, civil liberties, or privacy, including but not limited to freedom of speech, voting, human autonomy, and protections from discrimination, excessive punishment, and unlawful surveillance;
> (2) Equal opportunities, including equitable access to education, housing, insurance, credit, employment, and other programs where civil rights and equal opportunity protections apply; or
> (3) Access to or the ability to apply for critical government resources or services, including healthcare, financial services, public housing, social services, transportation, and essential goods and services.

The OMB Guidance states that 'AI used for one of the purposes identified in Appendix I is automatically presumed to be safety-impacting or rights-impacting.'[69] Appendix I sets out a non-exhaustive list of use-cases that would carry a presumption of being rights-impacting or safety-impacting within the scope of the OMB Guidance.

The minimum practices are described in detail in section 5 of the guidance and require, *inter alia, ex ante* impact assessments, testing performance in real-world contexts, independent evaluations, ongoing monitoring, mitigation of emerging risks, ensuring human training and assessment, providing for human oversight, and providing public notice and plain language documentation.[70] The OMB Guidance states that 'The practices in this section represent an initial baseline for managing risk from the use of AI.'[71] There are additional requirements for 'rights-impacting' AI systems, including, identification and assessment of AI's impact on equity and fairness, and

67. *Ibid.*, s. 6, at 30.
68. *Ibid.*, s. 6, at 29.
69. *Ibid.*, s. 5(b), at 15.
70. *Ibid.*, s. 5(iv), at 17-21.
71. *Ibid.*, s. 5, at 14.

mitigate algorithmic discrimination found, incorporation of feedback from affected communities and public participation.[72]

As a transparency measure, the OMB Guidance requires agencies to implement the risk management practices of section 5 by 1 December 2024 or terminate non-compliant AI.[73] It also requires agencies to certify by 1 December 2024, and annually thereafter, the validity of AI systems under section 5 practices as well as waivers granted and publicly disclose 'each individual determination and waiver, as well as its justification'.[74] However, the section 5 minimum practices of the OMB Guidance does not apply to elements of the intelligence community.[75]

In 2023, the Government Accountability Office (GAO) stated that 'there's no government-wide guidance on how agencies should acquire and use AI'.[76] Following these observations and the mandate of the Biden EO, the OMB has also solicited public comment for the purpose of updating its guidance on procurement of AI systems[77] and privacy impact assessments of AI systems.[78] It is expected that the OMB will issue specific guidance on these areas to fulfil the objectives of the Biden EO.

4.3 The Voluntary Commitments of the Tech Companies (2024)

In July 2023, ahead of the issuance of the Biden EO, tech companies developing and deploying advanced AI systems provided voluntary commitments to the Biden-Harris administration.[79] The companies made these to promote the safe, secure, and transparent development and use of GenAI (foundation) model technology. The 'scope' of the voluntary commitments (Commitments) is limited:[80]

> only to generative models that are overall more powerful than the current most advanced model produced by the company making the commitment.

The Commitments are grouped under three categories: *safety*, *security*, and *trust*. The Commitments are:

(1) Internal and external red-teaming of models or systems in areas including misuse, societal risks, and national security concerns, such as bio, cyber, and other safety areas.
(2) Information sharing among companies and governments regarding trust and safety risks, dangerous or emergent capabilities, and attempts to circumvent safeguards.

72. *Ibid.*, s. 5(c)(v), at 21-22.
73. *Ibid.*, s. 5(a)(i), at 14.
74. *Ibid.*, s. 5(a)(ii), at 14.
75. *Ibid.*, s. 5, at 14.
76. GAO 2023.
77. OMB RFI AI.
78. OMB RFI PIA.
79. The White House AI Commitments 2023.
80. *Ibid.*

(3) Investing in cybersecurity and insider threat safeguards to protect proprietary and unreleased model weights.
(4) Incentivizing third-party discovery and reporting of issues and vulnerabilities.
(5) Developing and deploying mechanisms that enable users to understand if audio or visual content is AI-generated, including robust provenance, watermarking, or both, for AI-generated audio or visual content.
(6) Publicly report model or system capabilities, limitations, and domains of appropriate and inappropriate use, including discussion of societal risks, such as effects on fairness and bias.
(7) Prioritizing research on societal risks posed by AI systems, including on avoiding harmful bias and discrimination, and protecting privacy.
(8) Developing and deploying frontier AI systems to help address society's greatest challenges.

In July 2023, Amazon, Anthropic, Google, Inflection, Meta, Microsoft, and OpenAI provided these Commitments to the administration.[81] Subsequently, in September 2023, a second round of Commitments were made by eight additional tech companies: Adobe, Cohere, IBM, Nvidia, Palantir, Salesforce, Scale AI, and Stability AI.[82]

4.4 The Joint Statement by Agencies

In April 2023, four federal agencies issued a joint statement on enforcement efforts against discrimination and bias in automated systems.[83] The statement does not create any new rights or liabilities but clarifies that agencies' existing enforcement authorities apply to automated systems and automated systems may contribute to unlawful discrimination and otherwise violate federal law.

In April 2024, the Department of Education, Department of Health and Human Services, Department of Homeland Security, Department of Housing and Urban Development and Department of Labor joined in the statement.[84] The updated 2024 joint statement states that agencies:

> pledge to vigorously use our collective authorities to protect individuals' rights regardless of whether legal violations occur through traditional means or advanced technologies.

Assistant Attorney General Kristin Clarke stated:[85]

> Federal agencies are sending a clear message: we will use our collective authority and power to protect individual rights in the wake of increased reliance on artificial intelligence in various aspects of American life.

81. The White House 2023b.
82. The White House 2023c.
83. US Federal Agencies 2023.
84. DOJ 2024.
85. *Ibid.*

The joint statement identifies three sources of 'potential discrimination' and describes the scope of enforcement as follows:[86]

> Data and Datasets: Automated system outcomes can be skewed by unrepresentative or imbalanced datasets, datasets that incorporate historical bias, or datasets that contain other types of errors. Automated systems also can correlate data with protected classes, which can lead to discriminatory outcomes.
>
> Model Opacity and Access: Many automated systems are 'black boxes' whose internal workings are not clear to most people and, in some cases, even the developer of the tool.
>
> This lack of transparency often makes it all the more difficult for developers, businesses, and individuals to know whether an automated system is fair.
>
> Design and Use: Developers do not always understand or account for the contexts in which private or public entities will use their automated systems. Developers may design a system on the basis of flawed assumptions about its users, relevant context, or the underlying practices or procedures it may replace.

4.5 The Role of the FTC and the CAIDP Complaint

The Federal Trade Commission's (FTC's) mission is to protect the public from deceptive or unfair business practices and from unfair methods of competition.[87] The FTC's broad mandate to protect consumers and ensure fair competition allows the agency to 'prosecute any inquiry necessary to its duties in any part of the United States'.[88] The FTC is authorized:[89]

> to gather and compile information concerning, and to investigate from time to time the organization, business, conduct, practices, and management of any person, partnership, or corporation engaged in or whose business affects commerce, excepting banks, savings and loan institutions ... Federal credit unions ... and common carriers ... .

The FTC has the authority to investigate, prosecute, and prohibit 'unfair or deceptive acts or practices in or affecting commerce'.[90]

The Center for AI and Digital Policy (CAIDP) filed a detailed, formal complaint with the FTC about OpenAI, alleging that OpenAI had violated US consumer protection law by releasing a consumer product without sufficient safeguards.[91] In the original complaint, CAIDP explained that OpenAI released a product GPT-4 for the consumer market that is biased, deceptive, and a risk to privacy and public safety. The CAIDP Complaint quoted extensively from the GPT-4 Technical Report in which OpenAI acknowledged the specific dangers of 'Disinformation and influence operations', 'Proliferation of conventional and unconventional weapons', and 'Cybersecurity'. The

86. US Federal Agencies 2024.
87. FTC About.
88. FTC Act, s. 3, 15 U.S.C. s. 43; *See also* FTC 2021.
89. FTC Act, s. 6(a), 15 U.S.C. s. 46(a).83; *See also* FTC 2021.
90. CAIDP 2024, 18.
91. *Ibid.*, at 1.

complaint highlighted that the outputs of ChatGPT cannot be proven or replicated. No independent assessment was undertaken prior to deployment. CAIDP emphasized that there should be independent oversight and evaluation of commercial AI products offered in the US prior to release in the market. CAIDP also highlighted the various enforcement actions initiated in other jurisdictions including Italy, Korea, Japan, Canada, etc.[92] The specific relief sought by CAIDP was an order that would result in baseline guardrails for practices of AI companies and systems, including:[93]

- Independent assessment of GPT products prior to future deployment.
- Compliance with FTC AI Guidance prior to further deployment of GPT.
- Independent assessment throughout the GPT AI lifecycle.
- Publicly accessible incident reporting mechanism for GPT-4 similar to the FTC's mechanisms to report consumer fraud.

In July 2023, both the New York Times and the Wall Street Journal reported that the FTC had launched the investigation sought by CAIDP. The FTC asked OpenAI to provide information about the data practices underlying the training of its large language model (LLM), the pre-release safety and risk assessment measures, the company's consumer marketing and advertising practices, its handling of users' personal information, and how the company offers downstream integrations of its GPT-4 product.[94]

The FTC has issued business guidance in relation to AI products and services[95] and Chair Khan has stated that:[96]

> There is no AI exemption to the laws on the books, and the FTC will vigorously enforce the law to combat unfair or deceptive practices or unfair methods of competition.

In addition to issuing business guidance, the FTC has required firms to destroy algorithms or other work products that were trained on data that should not have been collected.[97] If the FTC concludes the investigation into OpenAI and issues a final order in the terms sought by CAIDP in the complaint, it would establish the first set of guardrails expressly directed to the private sector and business practices.

5 CHINA POLICY INITIATIVES[98]

Since 2013, the Chinese government has published several national-level policies, guidelines, and action plans, which reflect the intention to develop, deploy, and integrate AI in various sectors.

92. *Ibid.*, at 2, 3.
93. *Ibid.*, at 3.
94. *Ibid.*, at 5.
95. *Ibid.*, at 18-22.
96. FTC 2023.
97. US Federal Agencies 2024.
98. Excerpted from CAIDP AIDV 2023.

Most notable of all is the New Generation Artificial Intelligence Development Plan (AIDP) – an ambitious strategy to make China the world leader in AI by 2030 and the most transparent and influential indication of China's AI strategy's driving forces. China's State Council issued the AIDP in 2017. Following the AIDP, the Ministry of Science and Technology published the New Generation Artificial Intelligence Development Code of Ethics (Code of Ethics).[99]

The New Generation AI Governance Professional Committee, consisting of experts from academics and the industry, created the Code of Ethics and is responsible for its implementation. The Code of Ethics aims to:

> thoroughly implement the AIDP, refine the principles of AIDP, enhance society's awareness and behavioural consciousness of AI ethics, actively guide responsible AI research, development, and application activities, as well as promote the healthy development of AI.

The Code of Ethics highlights six fundamental ethical requirements, including: (1) 'improving human well-being'; (2) 'promoting fairness and justice'; (3) 'protecting privacy and security'; (4) 'ensuring controllability, and trustworthiness'; (5) 'strengthening responsibility'; and (6) 'improving ethical literacy', taking into ethical issues of privacy, biases, discrimination, and fairness into consideration. China has started to adopt a comprehensive set of regulations on AI.

5.1 Personal Information Protection Law (2021)

In recent years, China has introduced a number of major data protection laws, including the Personal Information Protection Law (PIPL) (effective from 1 November 2021) and the Data Security Law (DSL) (effective from 1 September 2021), together with a series of implementation regulations and administrative rules. The PIPL establishes a new comprehensive regulatory framework for personal information protection in China, requiring consent as its principal basis for data collection and handling, introducing provisions with extraterritorial effect, restricting cross-border data transfers and imposing significant revenue-based fines for non-compliant conduct. The law is modelled after the EU General Data Protection Regulation (GDPR) however the law places a greater emphasis on how private companies may collect and use data rather than the use of data by authorities. For instance, Article 26 on personal images and facial recognition allows the collection of unlimited amounts of personal data so long as it is done 'for the purpose of safeguarding public security'. That is to say, the law does not limit the government's ability to collect or store biometric data obtained through facial recognition. In contrast, the GDPR sees personal images as sensitive biometric data and requires data protection impact assessment (DPIA) for facial recognition technology. Finally, the law does not assign responsibilities when it comes to government entities that collect personal data, and who will be held responsible when it leaks. This becomes increasingly important with the rise of recent

99. China Code of Ethics 2021; *See also* CJO 2021.

incidents of government leaks of the personal information of its citizens. Nevertheless, as the big data industry has been rapidly growing in China, the law provides more protection to users against unwanted data collection by private companies.

In March 2023, China's Ministry of Science and Technology established the National Data Administration (NDA). The NDA will be:

> responsible for the coordination and advancement of building the data factor system; for overall planning of the integrated sharing and development and use of data resources; for overall planning and advancement of Digital China, digital economy; and digital society plans and construction.

The new regulator will have responsibilities that were previously performed by the Cyberspace Administration of China (CAC) and by the National Development and Reform Commission.

5.2 Recommendation Algorithm Provisions (2022)

The Provisions on the Management of Algorithmic Recommendations in Internet Information Services (Provisions) came into force in March 2022. The Provisions apply to any entity that uses algorithm recommendation technologies to provide internet information services within Mainland China. The Provisions require companies to register algorithms to an online database to the extent that the algorithm has public opinion properties or social mobilization capabilities. Companies shall also complete an algorithm security self-assessment report. Users shall have the right to opt out of recommendation algorithms. The use of recommendation algorithms for illegal or harmful purposes is prohibited.

5.3 Deep Synthesis Provisions (2022)

In January 2023, the CAC introduced new regulations regarding deepfake content. The regulations were formulated in order to 'carry forward the core Socialist value vision, to safeguard national security and the societal public interest'. It prohibits the production of deepfakes without user consent and requires specific identification that the content had been generated using AI. Any content that was created using an AI system must be clearly labelled with a watermark, i.e., text or image visually superimposed on the video indicating that the content had been edited. Deep synthesis services cannot use the technology to disseminate fake news. Content that goes against existing laws is prohibited, as is content that endangers national security and interests, damages the national image or disrupts the economy.

5.4 Generative AI Measures (2023)

The Provisional Administrative Measures of Generative Artificial Intelligence Services (Generative AI Measures) were published by the CAC, together with six other authorities, on 13 July 2023 and took effect on 15 August 2023. The GenAI Measures apply to:

> the use of generative AI technology to provide services for generating text, pictures, sounds, videos and other content within the territory of China.

They will apply to domestic companies and to overseas GenAI service providers offering AI services in China to the public.

In April 2024, a draft AI law was circulated to an AI expert group as a result of the Beijing Forum for soliciting feedback.[100] The draft law specifies various scenarios in which AI developers, providers, or users are liable for misuse of AI tools. It also allows for the use of copyrighted material for model training in most cases and provides IP protections for content created with the assistance of AI technology.[101] In April 2024, China's Information Security Standards Committee solicited public comments on the draft national standard 'Information Security Technology: Specifications for Pre-training and Optimized Training Data for Generative Artificial Intelligence'.[102] The draft standards aim to establish secure and standardized practices for handling pre-training and optimization training data in GenAI technologies, thereby supporting the safe development and use of GenAI services in China. It focuses on the security requirements in pre-training and optimization training data processes for GenAI service developers. Seeks to address issues like data poisoning, malicious prompts, IP infringement, and personal information breaches.

6 CONCLUSION

The rapid emergence of AI governance frameworks alongside the adoption of the EU AI Act raises several questions for policymakers, academics, and journalists going forward. As these new governance frameworks now have legal force, an immediate question is what steps will be taken toward enforcement and implementation. While the EU AI Act has clear mechanisms for oversight and enforcement, it is less clear what the strategy will be for the Biden EO in the US. The OECD AI Principles and the UNESCO Recommendation are both voluntary frameworks, endorsed by governments, that will rely on self-reporting to promote compliance. The Council of Europe AI Convention will require ratification to obtain legal force and then reporting and oversight to promote compliance.

The emergence of multiple governance frameworks also raises questions about convergence and divergence, a familiar consideration for the regulation of the digital economy in a global market. It is likely that a Brussels effect will extend the reach of the AI Act. Moreover, the Commission has worked to make the AI Convention advance the goals of the AI Act. Nonetheless, both the US and China exert significant influence in the global regulatory domain, and it remains to be seen whether the UN will set out an effective strategy for AI governance that will receive support from the nations of the

100. CSET 2024; *see also* China AI Law 2024.
101. *Ibid.*
102. China TC260 2024.

world. One of the authors of this chapter recommends that the UN instead establish a Special Rapporteur for AI and Human Rights to advance the UN's human rights mandate.[103]

Finally, there are the rapid changes in AI technology that are shaping the regulatory responses. The first-generation governance frameworks, such as the UGAI and the OECD AI Principles, focussed on concepts such as fairness, accuracy, and transparency and emphasized 'human-centric' and 'trustworthy' AI. The UNESCO Recommendation introduced governance standards for sustainability and emphasized the need to address gender equity. With the EU AI Act, foundational models and GenAI have now been brought within the ambit of AI governance.

It is too soon to predict which issues will shape AI frameworks over the next few years, but it is clear there will be an increasingly complex and variegated interplay of norms and standards.

BIBLIOGRAPHY

CAIDP 2024: Center for AI & Digital Policy (CAIDP), *ChatGPT and the Federal Trade Commission: Still No Guardrails* (July 2024), www.caidp.org/app/download/8520338863/CAIDP-Still-No-Guardrails-July2024.pdf (accessed 16 July 2024).

CAIDP AIDV 2023: Center for AI & Digital Policy (CAIDP), *Artificial Intelligence and Democratic Values (AIDV) Index* (2023), www.caidp.org/reports/aidv-2023 (accessed 16 July 2024).

CAIDP 2023: Center for AI & Digital Policy (CAIDP), *Statement for the 2023 G7Japan on Artificial Intelligence, Data Protection, and Digital Free Flows with Trust (DFFT)* (24 February 2023), www.caidp.org (accessed 16 July 2024).

CAIDP 2018: Center for AI and Digital Policy (CAIDP), *Universal Guidelines for AI (UGAI)* (2018), www.caidp.org/universal-guidelines-for-ai (accessed 16 July 2024).

China AI Law 2024: *Artificial Intelligence Law of the People's Republic of China (Draft Suggested by Scholars)*, Perma (8 April 2024), perma.cc/L9E4-5K3V (accessed 16 July 2024).

China Code of Ethics 2021: Ministry of Science and Technology, People's Republic of China, *New Generation Artificial Intelligence Development Code of Ethics* (26 September 2021), www.most.gov.cn/kjbgz/202109/t20210926_177063.html (accessed 16 July 2024).

China TC260 2024: National Technical Committee on Cybersecurity Standardization Administration of China (TC260), *Notice on the Exposure Draft of the National Standard 'Information Security Technology Generated Artificial Intelligence Pre-training and Optimization Training Data Security Specification'* (3 April 2024), www.dataguidance.com/news/china-tc260-requests-comments-three-draft-strategies (accessed 16 July 2024).

103. Rotenberg 2024.

CJO 2021: China Justice Observer, *China Issues Code of Ethics for New-Generation AI* (1 November 2021), www.chinajusticeobserver.com/a/china-issues-code-of-ethics-for-new-generation-ai (accessed 16 July 2024).

CoE About: Council of Europe, *Who We Are*, www.coe.int/en/web/about-us/who-we-are (accessed 16 July 2024).

CoE AI: Council of Europe, *Artificial Intelligence and Human Rights*, www.coe.int/en/web/artificial-intelligence/secretary-general-marija-pejcinovic-buric (accessed 16 July 2024).

CoE News: Council of Europe, *Council of Europe Adopts First International Treaty on Artificial Intelligence* (17 May 2024), www.coe.int/en/web/portal/-/council-of-europe-adopts-first-international-treaty-on-artificial-intelligence (accessed 16 July 2024).

CoE PACE: Council of Europe Parliamentary Assembly, *Need for Democratic Governance of Artificial Intelligence* (22 October 2020), pace.coe.int/en/files/28803/html (accessed 16 July 2024).

CoE Recommendation 2182(2020): Council of Europe Parliamentary Assembly, *Recommendation 2182(2020) Justice by Algorithm: The Role of Artificial Intelligence in Policing and Criminal Justice Systems* (22 October 2020), pace.coe.int/en/files/28806/html (accessed 16 July 2024).

CoE Recommendation 2183(2020): Council of Europe Parliamentary Assembly, *Recommendation 2183(2020) Preventing Discrimination Caused by the Use of Artificial Intelligence* (22 October 2020), pace.coe.int/en/files/28809/html (accessed 16 July 2024).

CoE Resolution 2342: Council of Europe Parliamentary Assembly, *Resolution 2342: Justice by Algorithm – The Role of Artificial Intelligence in Policing and Criminal Justice Systems* (22 October 2020) pace.coe.int/en/files/28805 (accessed 16 July 2024).

CoE Resolution 2343: Council of Europe Parliamentary Assembly, *Resolution 2343: Preventing Discrimination Caused by the Use of Artificial Intelligence* (22 October 2020) pace.coe.int/en/files/28807 (accessed 16 July 2024).

CRS 2024: Congressional Research Service (CRS), *Highlights of the 2023 Executive Order on Artificial Intelligence for Congress* (updated 3 April 2024), crsreports.congress.gov/product/pdf/R/R47843 (accessed 16 July 2024).

CSET 2024: Center for Security and Emerging Technologies, *Translation: Artificial Intelligence Law of the People's Republic of China (Draft for Suggestions from Scholars)*, Georgetown University's Walsh School of Foreign Service (2 May 2024), cset.georgetown.edu/publication/china-ai-law-draft (accessed 16 July 2024).

DOL (undated): Department of Labor, *Artificial Intelligence and Worker Well-being: Principles for Developers and Employers*, www.dol.gov/general/AI-Principles (accessed 16 July 2024).

DOJ 2024: US Department of Justice, *Five New Federal Agencies Join Justice Department in Pledge to Enforce Civil Rights Laws in Artificial Intelligence*, Press Release (4 April 2024), www.justice.gov/opa/pr/five-new-federal-agencies-join-justice-department-pledge-enforce-civil-rights-laws (accessed 16 July 2024).

EO 14110: The White House, *Executive Order 14110 of October 30, 2023: Safe, Secure, and Trustworthy Development and Use of Artificial Intelligence*, Presidential Documents, 88 Federal Register (1 November 2023), www.govinfo.gov/content/pkg/FR-2023-11-01/pdf/2023-24283.pdf (accessed 16 July 2024).

EO 13960: The White House, *Executive Order 13960 of December 3, 2020: Promoting the Use of Trustworthy Artificial Intelligence in the Federal Government*, Presidential Documents, 85 Federal Register 78939 (8 December 2020), www.govinfo.gov/content/pkg/FR-2023-11-01/pdf/2023-24283.pdf (accessed 16 July 2024).

FTC About: Federal Trade Commission (FTC), *About the FTC*, www.ftc.gov/about-ftc/mission (accessed 16 July 2024).

FTC 2023: FTC, *FTC Chair Khan and Officials from DOJ, CFPB and EEOC Release Joint Statement on AI*, Press Releases (25 April 2023), www.ftc.gov/news-events/news/press-releases/2023/04/ftc-chair-khan-officials-doj-cfpb-eeoc-release-join t-statement-ai (accessed 16 July 2024).

FTC 2021: FTC, *A Brief Overview of the Federal Trade Commission's Investigative, Law Enforcement, and Rulemaking Authority* (May 2021), www.ftc.gov/about-ftc/mission/enforcement-authority (accessed 16 July 2024).

G7 Code of Conduct 2023: Group of Seven (G7), *Hiroshima Process International Code of Conduct for Organizations Developing Advanced AI Systems*, Ministry of Foreign Affairs of Japan (2023), www.mofa.go.jp/files/100573473.pdf (accessed 16 July 2024).

G7 Communique 2024: Group of Seven (G7), *Apulia G7 Leaders' Communiqué*, Council of the EU (2024), www.consilium.europa.eu/media/fttjqncg/apulia-g7-leaders-communique.pdf (accessed 16 July 2024).

G7 Communique 2023: Group of Seven (G7), *G7 Hiroshima Leaders' Communique*, Ministry of Foreign Affairs of Japan (20 May 2023), www.mofa.go.jp/policy/economy/summit/hiroshima23/documents/pdf/Leaders_Communique_01_en.pdf?v20231006 (accessed 16 July 2024).

G7 Guiding Principles 2023: Group of Seven (G7), *Hiroshima Process International Guiding Principles for Organizations Developing Advanced AI System*, Ministry of Foreign Affairs of Japan (2023), www.mofa.go.jp/files/100573471.pdf (accessed 16 July 2024).

GAO 2023: *Government Accountability Office (GAO), Artificial Intelligence: Agencies Have Begun Implementation But Need to Complete Key Requirements*, Report, GAO-24-105980 (12 December 2023), www.gao.gov/products/gao-24-105980 (accessed 16 July 2024).

Japan Guidelines 2024: Ministry of Internal Affairs and Communications, Ministry of Economy, Trade and Industry, Japan, *AI Guidelines for Business, Ver. 1.0* (19 April 2024), www.meti.go.jp/shingikai/mono_info_service/ai_shakai_jisso/pdf/20240419_9.pdf (accessed 16 July 2024).

Japan Times 2016: Japan Times, *Japan Pushes for Basic AI Rules at G-7 Tech Meeting* (29 April 2016), www.japantimes.co.jp/news/2016/04/29/national/japan-push es-basic-ai-rules-g-7-tech-meeting (accessed 16 July 2024).

OECD 2023: OECD, *OECD Guidelines for Multinational Enterprises on Responsible Business Conduct* (2023), www.oecd-ilibrary.org/finance-and-investment/oecd-guidelines-for-multinational-enterprises-on-responsible-business-conduct_81f92357-en (accessed 16 July 2024).

OECD 1981: OECD, *OECD Guidelines on the Protection of Privacy and Transborder Flows of Personal Data* (1981), www.oecd-ilibrary.org/science-and-technology/oecd-guidelines-on-the-protection-of-privacy-and-transborder-flows-of-personal-data_9789264196391-en (accessed 16 July 2024).

OECD About: OECD, *About* (undated), www.oecd.org/en/about.html (accessed 16 July 2024).

OECD AI Incidents: OECD.AI, *OECD AI Incidents Monitor*, www.oecd.org/en/topics/ai-risks-and-incidents.html (accessed 16 July 2024).

OECD AI Policy Observatory: OECD.AI, *Policy Observatory*, oecd.ai/en (accessed 16 July 2024).

OECD AI Principles: OECD.AI, *OECD AI Principles Overview* (2024), oecd.ai/en/ai-principles (accessed 16 July 2024).

OECD Recommendation.

OECD RMF 2023: OECD, *Artificial Intelligence Risk Management Framework (AI RMF 1.0)*, Catalogue of Tools & Metrics for Trustworthy AI (26 October 2023), oecd.ai/en/catalogue/tools/artificial-intelligence-risk-management-framework-%28ai-rmf-1.0%29 (accessed 16 July 2024).

OMB Guidance: Office of Management and Budget (OMB), *Memorandum for the Heads of Departments and Agencies, Advancing Governance, Innovation, and Risk Management for Agency Use of Artificial Intelligence*, M-24-10 (28 March 2024), www.whitehouse.gov/wp-content/uploads/2024/03/M-24-10-Advancing-Governance-Innovation-and-Risk-Management-for-Agency-Use-of-Artificial-Intelligence.pdf (accessed 16 July 2024).

OMB RFI AI: Office of Management and Budget (OMB), *Request for Information: Responsible Procurement of Artificial Intelligence in Government*, 89 FR 22196 (29 March 2024), www.federalregister.gov/documents/2024/03/29/2024-06547/request-for-information-responsible-procurement-of-artificial-intelligence-in-government#footnote-4-p22197 (accessed 16 July 2024).

OMB RFI PIA: Office of Management and Budget (OMB), *Request for Information: Privacy Impact Assessments*, 89 FR 5945 (30 March 2024), www.federalregister.gov/documents/2024/01/30/2024-01756/request-for-information-privacy-impact-assessments (accessed 16 July 2024).

OPC 2023: The Office of the Privacy Commissioner of Canada (OPC), *Statement on Generative AI: Roundtable of G7 Data Protection and Privacy Authorities* (21 June 2023), www.priv.gc.ca/en/opc-news/speeches/2023/s-d_20230621_g7 (accessed 16 July 2024).

Rotenberg 2024: Marc Rotenberg, *The Imperative for a UN Special Rapporteur on AI and Human Rights*, 1 Journal of AI Law and Regulation 110-112 (2024), doi.org/10.21552/aire/2024/1/13.

Rotenberg 2020: Marc Rotenberg, Center for AI and Digital Policy, *Center for AI Policy Update: OECD's Gurria Underscores AI Fairness at G-20 Meeting*, The Michael

Dukakis Institute For Leadership And Innovation (25 July 2020), dukakis.org/center-for-ai-and-digital-policy/center-for-ai-policy-update-oecds-gurria-underscores-ai-fairness-at-g-20-meeting (accessed 16 July 2024).

The White House 2024a: The White House, *Fact Sheet: Biden-Harris Administration Announces Key AI Actions Following President Biden's Landmark Executive Order*, Briefing Room: Statements and Releases (29 January 2024), www.whitehouse.gov/briefing-room/statements-releases/2024/01/29/fact-sheet-biden-harris-administration-announces-key-ai-actions-following-president-bidens-landmark-executive-order (accessed 16 July 2024).

The White House 2024b: The White House, *Fact Sheet: Vice President Harris Announces OMB Policy to Advance Governance, Innovation, and Risk Management in Federal Agencies' Use of Artificial Intelligence*, Briefing Room: Statements and Releases (28 March 2024), www.whitehouse.gov/briefing-room/statements-releases/2024/03/28/fact-sheet-vice-president-harris-announces-omb-policy-to-advance-governance-innovation-and-risk-management-in-federal-agencies-use-of-artificial-intelligence/ (accessed 16 July 2024).

The White House 2023a: The White House, *Fact Sheet: President Biden Issues Executive Order on Safe, Secure, and Trustworthy Artificial Intelligence*, Briefing Room: Statements and Releases (30 October 2023), www.whitehouse.gov/briefing-room/statements-releases/2023/10/30/fact-sheet-president-biden-issues-executive-order-on-safe-secure-and-trustworthy-artificial-intelligence (accessed 16 July 2024).

The White House 2023b: The White House, *Fact Sheet: Biden-Harris Administration Secures Voluntary Commitments from Leading Artificial Intelligence Companies to Manage the Risks Posed by AI, Statements and Releases*, Briefing Room: Statements and Releases (21 July 2023), www.whitehouse.gov/briefing-room/statements-releases/2023/07/21/fact-sheet-biden-harris-administration-secures-voluntary-commitments-from-leading-artificial-intelligence-companies-to-manage-the-risks-posed-by-ai (accessed 16 July 2024).

The White House 2023c: The White House, *Fact Sheet: Biden-Harris Administration Secures Voluntary Commitments from Eight Additional Artificial Intelligence Companies to Manage the Risks Posed by AI, Statements and Releases*, Briefing Room: Statements and Releases (12 September 2023), www.whitehouse.gov/briefing-room/statements-releases/2023/09/12/fact-sheet-biden-harris-administration-secures-voluntary-commitments-from-eight-additional-artificial-intelligence-companies-to-manage-the-risks-posed-by-ai (accessed 16 July 2024).

The White House 2021: The White House, *Carbis Bay G7 Summit Communiqué*, Briefing Room: Statements and Releases (13 June 2021), www.whitehouse.gov/briefing-room/statements-releases/2021/06/13/carbis-bay-g7-summit-communique (accessed 16 July 2024).

The White House AI Commitments 2023: The White House, *Voluntary AI Commitments* (2023), www.whitehouse.gov/wp-content/uploads/2023/09/Voluntary-AI-Commitments-September-2023.pdf (accessed 16 July 2024).

UN 2024: United Nations General Assembly, *Resolution A/78/L. 49: Seizing the Opportunities of safe, Secure and Trustworthy Artificial Intelligence Systems for*

Sustainable Development, documents.un.org/doc/undoc/ltd/n24/065/92/pdf/n2406592.pdf?token = bsXPX2A9F9iXTK6fDR&fe = true (accessed 16 July 2024).

UN 2023: United Nations, Secretary-General, *Note to Correspondents: Joint Call by the United Nations Secretary-General and the President of the International Committee of the Red Cross for States to Establish New Prohibitions and Restrictions on Autonomous Weapon Systems*, Statements (5 October 2023), www.un.org/sg/en/content/sg/note-correspondents/2023-10-05/note-correspondents-joint-call-the-united-nations-secretary-general-and-the-president-of-the-international-committee-of-the-red-cross-for-states-establish-new (accessed 16 July 2024).

UN News: United Nations, *General Assembly Adopts Landmark Resolution on Artificial Intelligence* (21 March 2024), news.un.org/en/story/2024/03/1147831 (accessed 16 July 2024).

UNESCO Draft Recommendation: UNESCO, *Preparation of a Draft Text of the Recommendation: Ad Hoc Expert Group*, en.unesco.org/artificial-intelligence/ethics#aheg (accessed 16 July 2024).

UNESCO Ethical Impact Assessment: UNESCO, *Ethical Impact Assessment: A Tool of the Recommendation on the Ethics of Artificial Intelligence* (2023), unesdoc.unesco.org/ark:/48223/pf0000386276 (accessed 16 July 2024).

UNESCO Implementation Recommendation: UNESCO, *Implementation of the Recommendation on the Ethics of Artificial Intelligence (AI)* (2022), unesdoc.unesco.org/ark:/48223/pf0000382931 (accessed 16 July 2024).

UNESCO Mexico: UNESCO, *UNESCO Presents the Artificial Intelligence Readiness Assessment of Mexico* (4 July 2024), www.unesco.org/en/articles/unesco-presents-artificial-intelligence-readiness-assessment-mexico (accessed 16 July 2024).

UNESCO News: UNESCO, *UNESCO Member States Adopt the First Ever Global Agreement on the Ethics of Artificial Intelligence*, Press Release (25 November 2021, updated 20 April 2023), www.unesco.org/en/articles/unesco-member-states-adopt-first-ever-global-agreement-ethics-artificial-intelligence (accessed 16 July 2024).

UNESCO RAM: UNESCO, *Readiness Assessment Methodology: A Tool of the Recommendation on the Ethics of Artificial Intelligence* (2023), unesdoc.unesco.org/ark:/48223/pf0000385198 (accessed 16 July 2024).

UNESCO Recommendation.

US Federal Agencies 2024: US Federal Agencies (Equal Employment Opportunity Commission (EEOC), Consumer Financial Protection Bureau (CFPB), Department of Justice (DOJ), the Federal Trade Commission (FTC), Department of Education, Department of Health and Human Services, Department of Homeland Security, the Department of Housing and Urban Development, and Department of Labor), *Joint Statement on Enforcement of Civil Rights, Fair Competition, Consumer Protection, and Equal Opportunity Laws in Automated Systems* (2024), www.dol.gov/sites/dolgov/files/OFCCP/pdf/Joint-Statement-on-AI.pdf (accessed 16 July 2024).

US Federal Agencies 2023: US Federal Agencies (Equal Employment Opportunity Commission (EEOC), Consumer Financial Protection Bureau (CFPB), Department of Justice (DOJ), and the Federal Trade Commission (FTC)), *Joint Statement on Enforcement Efforts Against Discrimination and Bias in Automated Systems* (2023), www.justice.gov/crt/page/file/1581491/dl?inline (accessed 16 July 2024).

CHAPTER 2

The Council of Europe's Convention on Artificial Intelligence and Human Rights, Democracy and the Rule of Law

Catelijne Muller & Jan Kleijssen

1 INTRODUCTION

The Council of Europe is the pan-European human rights organization. It has forty-six Member States and is based in Strasbourg, France. The Council was established in 1949, on the initiative of leading European statesmen, such as Sir Winston Churchill, to promote and protect human rights, democracy and the rule of law. This was to ensure that the horrors of the Second World War would not be repeated. The organization deals with all matters of government, with the exception of national defence. It has established some 200 international treaties, called conventions, ranging from human rights, data protection, gender equality, and cultural diversity to combating racism, cybercrime, child abuse, domestic violence and terrorism.

Although the work of the European Union (EU) or international organizations, such as United Nations Educational, Scientific and Cultural Organization (UNESCO) or Organisation for Economic Co-operation and Development (OECD), sometimes seems to overshadow the Council of Europe in terms of artificial intelligence (AI) governance, its role in legal harmonization should not be underestimated.

The Council of Europe realized already a long time ago that new technologies can have a massive impact on human rights, rule of law and democracy. Hence, they have been on the agenda of the organization since the 1980s. Consider, for example, the first-ever treaty on the protection of personal data, adopted about forty years ago. The

Convention 108, as it became known, can be considered the grandmother of today's General Data Protection Regulation (GDPR). It was established at a time when virtually no country in the world had any legislation on data privacy and protection in place. The Convention now has fifty-five state parties, with some twenty more regularly participating in the work of its Consultative Committee (T-PD). Or take the Budapest Convention on Cybercrime established just over twenty years ago, which remains the only international treaty on cybercrime to date and has seventy state parties from all continents.

As it became clear that the development and use of AI did not only bring benefits but also posed risks to human rights, democracy and the rule of law, the Council gradually began to address AI governance. The *Toeslagenaffaire* in the Netherlands is a telling and dramatic example of what can go wrong when governments use AI systems without proper governance. The *Toeslagenaffaire* refers to the scandal (or tragedy) in which the Dutch tax authorities used an algorithmic decision-making system to predict fraud with social benefits. This system turned out to be heavily biased and discriminatory against parents of foreign origin leading to some thirty thousand people being falsely accused of fraud and forced to pay back allocations received over long periods. The results were devastating, with livelihoods and families destroyed, and some three thousand children being taken away from their families. The Courts dramatically failed to protect the victims, as did the authorities; a parliamentary enquiry resulted in a report entitled 'Unprecedented Injustice', and the fall of the government in 2021. At the request of the Dutch parliament, the Council of Europe's Venice Commission also investigated and published its highly critical report on 18 October 2021.

On the basis of proposals made by the then Director of Information Society and Action against Crime, Jan Kleijssen, in September 2019, the Council of Europe's Committee of Ministers established the Council of Europe's Ad Hoc Committee on Artificial Intelligence (CAHAI), an intergovernmental committee with a two-year mandate from 2019-2021. The CAHAI was mandated to examine the feasibility of a new legal framework for the development, design and application of AI within the boundaries of human rights, democracy and the rule of law as guiding standards. In December 2021, the CAHAI unanimously decided that there was indeed a need for such additional binding legal instrument on AI. In its final report, that was among others based on an analysis of the impact of AI on human rights, democracy and the rule of law by this chapter's co-author Catelijne Muller,[1] the CAHAI set out a checklist of useful elements that should ideally be included in a new binding instrument.

Following CAHAI's feasibility study,[2] the Council of Europe's Committee of Ministers established the Council of Europe's Committee on Artificial Intelligence (CAI), with a mandate running from 1 January 2022 to 31 December 2024. It gave CAI

1. Muller 2020.
2. CAHAI 2020.

an extremely ambitious mandate, namely, to elaborate a transversal legally binding instrument on AI, human rights, democracy and the rule of law.

It should be noted that, from the outset, the negotiations involved not only (then forty-seven) Member States of the Council of Europe, the EU, and five observer states (Canada, Japan, Mexico, the USA, and the Holy See), but that the Committee of Ministers also accepted the requests by Argentina, Australia, Costa Rica, Israel, Peru, and Uruguay to be admitted to the negotiations sending a clear signal about the global vocation of the future AI Convention. In addition, and in line with the Council of Europe's practice, relevant non-state actors were involved as observers to the development of the AI Convention, including civil society organizations, companies and representatives of international organizations and agencies such as the OECD, UNESCO, European Union Agency for Fundamental Rights (FRA), and the European Data Protection Supervisor (EDPS).

In early 2023, the CAI delivered its first draft of a convention on AI, human rights, democracy and the rule of law, the so-called Zero Draft.[3] Following intensive negotiations, parties provisionally agreed upon the draft AI Convention – at close to midnight – on 14 March 2024. The Parliamentary Assembly adopted its opinion on 18 April 2024, and the adoption by the Committee of Ministers took place on 17 May 2024. The AI Convention was opened for signature in Vilnius on 5 September 2024. Already on the opening date, it was signed by ten states (or thirty-six, as the European Union signed on behalf of its twenty-seven Member States), including also the United Kingdom, the United States of America, and Israel.

2 THE AI CONVENTION

The AI Convention aims to address the potential risks governments face when AI is being deployed, either by public or private actors. As will be discussed in detail below, it sets out general obligations regarding the protection of human rights, integrity of democratic processes and respect for the rule of law, against the risk of harm from AI. Moreover, it establishes specific principles such as human dignity and autonomy, equality and non-discrimination, privacy and personal data protection, accountability and responsibility, transparency and oversight, reliability and safe innovation, which must be ensured within the lifecycle of AI systems. Negotiations are continuing on a complementary, non-binding human rights, democracy and rule of law impact assessment system (HUDERIA).

As AI does not (and never did) operate in a lawless world, while preparing the AI Convention, existing global and regional legal instruments, prepared by the Council of

3. CAI 2023.

Europe,[4] the EU,[5] as well as by other international organizations were taken into account.[6]

2.1 Objective and Purpose

2.1.1 Consistency with Human Rights, Democracy and the Rule of Law

The AI Convention aims to ensure that activities within the lifecycle of AI are fully consistent with human rights, democracy and the rule of law (Articles 1 and 2 of the AI Convention). It seeks full alignment with existing human rights protection systems of the parties but neither creates new human rights nor, obviously, undermines existing human rights protection provisions. Its main objective is to reinforce the role of international human rights law and relevant domestic legislation in view of AI's potential impact. Hence, for many obligations it allows the parties to adopt or maintain measures to acknowledge that either of these options suffices.

2.1.2 Graduated and Differentiated

It further provides that measures should be graduated and differentiated depending on the severity and probability of adverse impacts of an AI system on human rights,

4. *Council of Europe and EU instruments include*: The ECHR and its Protocols; the 1961 European Social Charter (ESC) and its protocols and the 1996 Revised European Charter; the 1981 Convention for the Protection of Individuals with Regard to Automatic Processing Personal Data (Convention 108 +), as amended and its Protocols; the 1987 European Convention for the Prevention of Torture and Inhuman or Degrading Treatment or Punishment and its Protocols; the 1997 Convention for the Protection of Human Rights and Dignity of the Human Being with regard to the Application of Biology and Medicine: Convention on Human Rights and Biomedicine (the Oviedo Convention) and its Protocols; and the 1998 AI Convention for the Protection of National Minorities.
5. The Charter of Fundamental Rights of the EU (CFR), recognized with the same legal value as the treaties pursuant to Treaty on EU (TEU), Art. 6(1); the 2005 Council of Europe Convention on Action against Trafficking in Human Beings; the 2007 Council of Europe Convention on the Protection of Children against Sexual Exploitation and Sexual Abuse (the Lanzarote Convention); and the 2011 Council of Europe Convention on Preventing and Combating Violence Against Women and Domestic Violence (the Istanbul Convention).
6. *Global instruments include*: The 1965 UN International Convention on the Elimination of All Forms of Racial Discrimination (ICERD); the 1966 UN International Covenant on Civil and Political Rights (ICCPR) and its Optional Protocols; the 1966 UN International Covenant on Economic, Social and Cultural Rights (ICESCR) and its Optional Protocol; the 1979 UN Convention on the Elimination of All Forms of Discrimination Against Women (CEDAW) and its Optional Protocol; the 1984 UN Convention against Torture and Other Cruel, Inhuman or Degrading Treatment or Punishment and its Optional Protocol; the 1989 UN Convention on the Rights of the Child (UNCRC) and its Optional Protocols; the 2006 UN Convention for the Protection of All Persons from Enforced Disappearance; and the 2006 UN Convention on the Rights of Persons with Disabilities (UNCRPD) and its Optional Protocol. *Other regional instruments*: The 1969 American Convention on Human Rights (Pact of San José) and its first additional Protocols; the 1985 Inter-American Convention to Prevent and Punish Torture; the 1994 Inter-American Convention on the Forced Disappearance of Persons; the 1994 Inter-American Convention on the Prevention, Punishment and Eradication of Violence against Women; the 1999 Inter-American Convention on the Elimination of All Forms of Discrimination against Persons with Disabilities; the 2013 Inter-American Convention against Racism, Racial Discrimination, and Related Forms of Intolerance; and the 2015 Inter-American Convention on Protecting the Human Rights of Older Persons.

democracy and the rule of law. The authors of this chapter however are of the opinion that adverse human rights impacts, as well as the measures to protect against these, are to be interpreted and applied based on all relevant circumstances, without pre-established thresholds or limits for what can be considered a relevant criterion for the adverse impact. This is even more important because the current criteria are open to interpretation and can contradict each other, e.g., an adverse impact that is improbable can still be severe, making a graduated measure ineffective.

2.1.3 *Activities Within the Lifecycle of AI Systems*

It includes the concept of 'activities within the lifecycle of AI systems', to ensure that the AI Convention applies not only to the AI system in isolation but rather to all stages of activities that are relevant to AI systems as well as to all actors that are involved in these stages at one time or another. These stages could include: (1) planning and design; (2) data collection and processing; (3) system development (including fine-tuning); (4) testing, verification, and validation; (5) deployment; (6) operation and monitoring; and (7) retirement.

2.1.4 *Human Rights, Democracy and Rule of Law Impact Assessment*

In order to enable the parties to decide whether existing domestic human rights protection is adequate, an assessment of the human rights, democracy and rule of law impact should be carried out. When performing the assessment, parties to the AI Convention should take into consideration not only the AI system's context but also the broader societal context, including power asymmetries, social justice, the relationship and trust between citizens and government and the integrity of democratic processes.

2.1.5 *The AI Convention and the AI Act*

The AI Convention and the AI Act, the two main legislative instruments from Europe, respectively the EU, while having certain overlaps, differ significantly.

First of all, the AI Convention lays down obligations for Council of Europe Member States and any other state that decides to sign and ratify it. While the AI Act focuses on the EU and only binds the EU's twenty-seven Member States, the Council of Europe's AI Convention has been negotiated by fifty-seven states and aims to have a global impact.

Second, the AI Convention approaches AI from a human rights, democracy and rule of law perspective, laid down in various Council of Europe legal instruments.[7] Its principles are hence overarching. The AI Convention does directly bind states, and only indirectly public or private entities, meaning that states that ratify the AI Convention have the obligation to ensure compliance with the AI Convention through domestic regulation or other appropriate measures.

7. *See* CAHAI, *supra* n. 2.

The AI Act is to be seen as a 'hybrid' instrument. It holds many characteristics of a regular EU product (safety) regulation; however, it is also explicitly aimed at protecting fundamental rights (and health and safety) from the potential ill effects of AI. It binds public and private parties directly, provided that they bring an AI system onto the EU internal market or their AI system affects EU citizens.

2.2 Scope

2.2.1 Definition of AI

The AI Convention uses the same definition of AI as the revised definition developed by the OECD[8] and further explained by its accompanying 'Explanatory memorandum on the updated OECD definition of an AI system'.[9] This decision was made in view of the need to enhance international co-operation and alignment of international AI governance. It was also decided that while the OECD definition aims to ensure legal precision and certainty, it remains sufficiently abstract to cover those systems that actually pose a risk of harm to human rights, democracy and the rule of law. It should be noted that the definition should always be read in light of the other relevant provisions of the AI Convention. This means that even if a system would fall within the scope of the definition, its potential to adversely impact human rights, democracy and the rule of law determines the actual reach of the AI Convention.

2.2.2 Public and Private Actors

The AI Convention obliges the parties to ensure that AI systems developed or used by public actors, or private actors on their behalf, comply with the provisions of the convention (Article 3(1)). The range of these types of private actors is wide and includes those that develop or use AI systems pursuant to a public actor's delegated responsibility but also through a contract with a public authority, private provision of public services, public procurement and contracting.

Much has been said and speculated about the reach of the AI Convention to the actions of other private actors. It should be noted that the AI Convention does oblige the parties to ensure that AI systems developed or used by private actors (other than those mentioned above) comply with the AI Convention. It does however provide the parties with two options: (1) they can choose to apply the convention directly to private parties; or (2) they can choose to make use of other appropriate measures, which could include administrative or voluntary measures to ensure protection. When choosing the second option, the AI Convention prescribes that those measures should in any event not undermine existing human rights, democracy and rule of law protections. Upon

8. AI system means a machine-based system designed to operate with varying levels of autonomy, that may exhibit adaptiveness after deployment and that, for explicit for explicit or implicit objectives, infers, from the input it receives, how to generate outputs such as predictions, content, recommendations, or decisions that can influence physical or virtual environments.
9. OECD 2024.

signature, ratification, acceptance, approval or accession, parties must declare how they intend to apply the AI Convention to private parties, i.e., if they choose option (1) or (2).

The authors of this chapter would like to point out that this compromise was the result of lengthy negotiations predominantly between European and non-European states, the latter pointing out national constitutional barriers to direct application of the convention to private parties. Hence, we do expect all Council of Europe (or at the least all EU Member and Candidate) States to choose option (1), as is common practice for Council of Europe instruments, and apply the AI Convention directly to private parties.

2.2.3 *Federal Clause*

An important goal of the Council of Europe is to enable the largest possible number of states to become parties to the AI Convention. However, not all states are in a position to do so, due to federal law restrictions or power distributions between national and regional authorities. For that reason, Article 33 allows for a reservation which is intended to accommodate any restrictions federal states may face when implementing the AI Convention.[10]

2.2.4 *Research and Development*

As long as AI systems have not been made available for use, and testing or similar activities do not have the potential to interfere with human rights, democracy and the rule of law, AI used in research and development remains excluded from the AI Convention (Article 3(3)). It should however be noted that human rights compliance often requires that technical and non-technical measures are already taken during the research and innovation phase. If research and innovation are aimed at the eventual use of the AI system, taking the AI Convention into consideration could be the most appropriate route. Moreover, the exemption is without prejudice to the principle of 'safe innovation' (Article 13) and exchange of risks and positive and negative effects (Article 25(2)).

2.2.5 *National Security*

Parties may, but are not obliged to, apply the AI Convention to AI systems (including activities within its lifecycle) related to the protection of national security interests, as long as these activities are in line with international and domestic laws, respecting the parties' democratic processes and institutions. The focus on national security interests ensures that dual use of AI systems that are not related to national security remains within the scope of the AI Convention. The same goes for all regular law enforcement

10. Precedents exist for federal declarations or reservations to other international agreements including, within the framework of the Council of Europe, the Convention on Cybercrime of 23 Nov. 2001, Art. 41. *See, as examples*: The 1951 UN Convention Relating to the Status of Refugees of 28 Jul. 1951, Art. 41; the 1954 UN Convention Relating to the Status of Stateless Persons, Art. 37; the 1958 UN Convention on the Recognition and Enforcement of Foreign Arbitral Awards, Art. 11; The 1972 UN Convention for the Protection of World Cultural and Natural Heritage, Art. 34.

activities, including regarding threats to public security. As long as national security is not at stake, these activities fall within the scope of the AI Convention. The future Conference of the Parties will have an important role in providing guidance on this issue.

2.2.6 *National Defence*

AI systems (including activities within its lifecycle) developed or used for matters of national defence are excluded from the scope of the AI Convention. The parties considered this exemption based on Article 1(d) of the Statute of the Council of Europe (European Treaty Series (ETS) No. 1), stating that 'matters relating to national defence do not fall within the scope of the Council of Europe'.

2.3 Human Rights, Democracy and the Rule of Law: General Obligations

2.3.1 *Human Rights and AI*

Because almost all human rights could potentially be adversely affected by AI,[11] the first general obligation of the AI Convention is to ensure that AI systems are consistent with human rights (as laid down in both international and domestic law) (Article 4). This obliges the parties to take stock of their existing human rights obligations and mechanisms in their domestic legal system to determine whether these suffice against infringement by AI systems (including activities during its lifecycle). This stocktaking exercise includes all global, Council of Europe or EU instruments that a state may be a party to.[12] These include not only instruments that deal with non-discrimination and data privacy but also those that deal with the rights of children, elderly and persons with disabilities, human trafficking or dignity of humans in biology and medicine, to name but a few. In addition, Article 4 also refers to domestic human rights legislation, including not only constitutional norms but also mechanisms for supervision and enforcement, as a source.

2.4 Democracy, the Rule of Law and AI

There is ample concern regarding the adverse impact of AI on democratic processes and institutions. AI-powered or -enabled dissemination of dis- and misinformation could undermine information integrity, including through AI-generated content or AI-enabled manipulation of authentic content, jeopardizing the right of access to information. AI-tools could make prejudiced decisions about individuals, potentially leading to segregation and inequality. AI-tools used in the judiciary could have implications for the integrity of the justice system. AI-driven illegal or arbitrary surveillance leads to restrictions on the freedom of assembly or freedom of expression, and privacy. At the same time, the AI Convention acknowledges the potential of AI

11. Muller, *supra* n. 1.
12. *See supra* nn 1, 2 and 3.

systems to improve democracy and enhance democratic institutions and processes. The AI Convention aims to ensure that AI systems are not used to undermine the integrity, independence and effectiveness of democracy and its institutions.

It considers democratic institutions and processes particularly sensitive contexts that require a careful consideration of whether the use of a particular AI system poses a risk to democracy and the rule of law. As such, parties could focus on the protection of the separation of powers (both horizontal and vertical), the system of checks and balances, political pluralism, democratic participation, free and fair elections, the political majority rule and the rights of political minorities access and proper administration of justice and judicial independence.

In other words, the AI Convention acknowledges the broad and deep impact of AI on human rights, democracy and the rule of law and provides an 'umbrella' to protect these (Article 5).

2.5 Principles Related to Activities Within the Lifecycle of AI Systems

2.5.1 Human Dignity and Individual Autonomy

Article 7 prescribes the parties to adopt or maintain measures to respect human dignity because the dignity of the human person is universally agreed to constitute the basis of human rights.[13] Respect for human dignity in the AI Convention refers to AI's potential to dehumanize individuals, undermine their agency, reduce them to mere data points, or manipulate or coerce them through anthropomorphizing. It also implies respect for the inherent value and worth of each individual. This inherent value and worth is reflected in the European Convention on Human Rights (ECHR) in various rights, such as the right to liberty and security, the right to a fair trial, the right to no punishment without law and the right to a private life and physical and mental integrity (the latter two are dealt with in a separate provision of the AI Convention).[14]

The fact that AI can perpetuate or amplify existing biases, is particularly pertinent when used in law enforcement and the judiciary. In situations where physical freedom or personal security is at stake, such as with predictive policing, recidivism risk determination and sentencing, the right to liberty and security combined with the right to a fair trial can become vulnerable. When it is a 'black box', it becomes impossible for legal professionals, such as judges, lawyers and district attorneys to understand the reasoning behind the outcomes of the system and thus complicate the motivation and appeal of the judgment. AI-applications used for predictive policing, that merely seek correlations based on shared characteristics with other 'cases' can lead to biased and inaccurate predictions. Suspicion in these instances is not based on actual suspicion of a crime or misdemeanour by the particular suspect, but merely on shared characteristics of the suspect with others (such as address, income, nationality, debts, employment,

13. *See*, as the most prominent examples, the preambles of the Universal Declaration of Human Rights (UDHR), the ICCPR and the ICESCR; the Pact of San José, Arts 5, 6 and 11; Protocol No. 13 to the ECHR; CFR, Art. 1.
14. ECHR, Arts 5, 6, 7 and 8.

behaviour, behaviour of friends and family members and so on), jeopardizing the right to a reasonable suspicion and the prohibition of arbitrary arrest.

The AI Convention includes respect for individual autonomy as an important aspect of human dignity in the realm of AI. Individual autonomy refers to a person's self-determination, to freely make choices and decisions and to live freely. Given the ability of AI systems to influence, coerce, manipulate and imitate people, the AI Convention considers human autonomy as particularly appropriate to reference.

2.5.2 Transparency and Oversight

The fact that many AI systems are complex, opaque, adaptable and to a smaller or larger extent autonomous, makes them particularly vulnerable to human rights impacts. For that reason, transparency and oversight are introduced in the AI Convention as safeguards. Both safeguards involve various elements. Transparency (Article 8) refers to openness and clarity about AI governance, including about the system itself (e.g., purpose(s), known limitations, assumptions and engineering choices made during design, features, details of the underlying models or algorithms, data, training methods and quality assurance processes), as well as about risk mitigation efforts, understanding of how the AI system's outputs are derived and how the system could impact human rights, democracy and the rule of law.

Transparency also includes informing persons concerned about the processing of information, the types and levels of automation used to make consequential decisions, and the risks associated with the use of the AI system. Providing this kind of transparency could facilitate the possibility for parties with legitimate interests, including copyright holders, to exercise and enforce their rights. It furthermore includes measures to identify AI-generated content.

Transparency finally includes the notions of explainability ('why') and interpretability ('how'). The term 'explainability' refers to information about why an AI system provides information and produces predictions, content, recommendations or decisions, which is particularly crucial in sensitive domains where understanding the reasoning behind decisions produced or assisted by an AI system is essential. Interpretability is aimed at understanding *how* an AI system reaches predictions or decisions. The internal workings, logic, and decision-making processes of AI systems need to be understandable and accessible to human users, including developers, stakeholders, end-users, and persons affected.

The principle of oversight involves a wide variety of mechanisms aimed at monitoring, evaluating and guiding activities within the lifecycle of AI systems. These mechanisms could include legal, policy and regulatory frameworks, ethics guidelines, codes of practice, certification programmes, oversight bodies, competent authorities, and auditing schemes, to name but a few. Particularly because of the complexity of AI systems, the AI Convention encourages the parties to ensure that AI systems are designed and developed in such a way that effective and reliable oversight, including human oversight, is possible.

2.5.3 *Accountability and Responsibility*

The principles of accountability and responsibility (Article 9) are aimed at ensuring that individuals and organizations can be held accountable for the adverse effects of AI systems. The parties have a wide variety of mechanisms at their disposal to effectuate these requirements, for example, liability and other civil law regimes, administrative procedures, and criminal law regimes. These principles require clear lines of responsibility in order to trace outcomes back to specific individuals or organizations, in order to attribute responsibility correctly. Obviously, these principles are closely linked to the principle of transparency, as they cannot exist without the other.

Importantly, the principle requires states to ensure that those responsible for AI systems consider the potential impact of their system on human rights, democracy and the rule of law in an anticipatory manner.

2.5.4 *Equality and Non-Discrimination*

One of the most reported impacts of AI on human rights is the impact on the prohibition of discrimination and the right to equal treatment. In many cases, AI has shown to perpetuate and amplify and possibly enshrine discriminatory or otherwise unacceptable biases. Also, AI can enlarge the group of impacted people, when it groups them based on shared characteristics. Moreover, AI systems can obscure the existence of biases, marginalizing the social control mechanisms that govern human behaviour.[15] As the right to non-discrimination is laid down in a vast body of international and domestic human rights law, which provides a solid legal foundation, Article 10 of the AI Convention refers to this body specifically.[16]

The provision however also requires that parties take into account the broader concept of bias. This includes the many instances where discrimination or bias can enter the lifecycle of an AI system: the bias of the algorithm's developers; bias built into the model; biases inherent in the use of training data sets or in the aggregation or evaluation of data; biases introduced when AI systems are implemented in real-world settings or as they evolve; human automation or confirmation biases; social bias,

15. *See supra* n. 8.
16. At the global level, articles relevant to each party may include the following provisions: ICCPR, Arts 2, 24 and 26; ICESCR, Arts 2, 3 and 7; and the specialized legal instruments such as the ICERD, the CEDAW, the UNCRC and the UNCRPD. At the regional level, rules relevant to each party may include ECHR, Art. 14 and its Protocol No. 12; ESC, paras 20 and 27 of Part I, Art. 20 of Part II, and Art. E of Part V; specialized legal instruments of the Council of Europe such as the Framework Convention for the Protection of National Minorities, Art. 4 and the Istanbul Convention, Art. 4; CFR, Title III, EU treaties (e.g., TEU, Art. 2; Treaty on the Functioning of the EU (TFEU), Art. 10), EU secondary legislation and the relevant case law of the Court of Justice of the European Union (CJEU); the Pact of San José, Art. 24; and the specialized legal instruments, such as the 1999 Inter-American Convention on the Elimination of All Forms of Discrimination against Persons with Disabilities; the 2013 Inter-American Convention against Racism, Racial Discrimination, and Related Forms of Intolerance; and the 2015 Inter-American Convention on Protecting the Human Rights of Older Persons.

where historical or current inequalities in society are not properly accounted for within the lifecycle of an AI system.

It is important to note that the tackling of discrimination, bias and inequality in AI systems should not be limited to ensure that an individual is not treated less favourably. It should also lead to the adoption of measures to overcome historical and structural barriers to gender equality and fair and just treatment of people of certain groups, that tend to be replicated and amplified by AI systems.

2.5.5 Privacy and Data Protection

Many AI systems and uses have a broad and deep impact on the right to privacy. Privacy discussions around AI often tend to focus primarily on data privacy and the indiscriminate processing of personal data. In view of the key role that the protection of personal data plays in safeguarding privacy rights and other human rights in the digital world, the AI Convention makes a specific mention of the domestic and international laws, standards, and rules in the sphere of personal data protection.

It should however be noted that, while data privacy is indeed an important element, the impact of AI on our privacy goes well beyond our data. Article 8 of the ECHR encompasses the protection of a wide range of elements of our private lives, which can be grouped into three broad categories namely: (1) a person's (general) privacy; (2) a person's physical, psychological or moral integrity; and (3) a person's identity and autonomy. Different applications and uses of AI can have an impact on these categories. The AI Convention considers this obligation to require parties to take measures to protect this broader concept of privacy as well.

2.5.6 Reliability

AI systems, as any software system, should be relied upon in terms of security, safety, accuracy, robustness and performance. Hence, this provision aims to ensure that it leaves open the way in which reliability is achieved, for example, through standards, technical specifications, transparent documentation, cybersecurity measures, protocols, end-to-end accountability structures, assurance and compliance schemes. The ultimate goal of this provision is to achieve justified confidence in the trustworthiness of AI systems.

2.5.7 Safe Innovation

The AI Convention further seeks to promote and foster innovation in line with human rights, democracy and the rule of law. This is especially important as certain risks associated with AI systems can only be effectively addressed at the design stage.

Approaches that can be considered are 'regulatory sandboxes' under the supervision of relevant authorities.

2.5.8 Remedies

Given the particular characteristics of AI systems such as complexity, opaqueness, and information asymmetry, the exercise of rights to remedies has proven to be difficult if not impossible for those whose human rights are adversely affected. That is why this provision recalls the principle that a remedy needs to be both effective and accessible. Consistent with the principles in Articles 8 (Principle of transparency and oversight) and 9 (Principle of accountability and responsibility), this provision requires proper availability of information to affected persons, that is context-appropriate, sufficiently clear and meaningful, and critically, provides the person concerned with an effective ability to exercise their rights.

Additionally, an effective right of complaint is established, that can be exercised both by individuals as well as public interest organizations, as provided for within a state's legal system.

Impactful AI systems should be surrounded by procedural safeguards such as human oversight and *ex ante* and *ex post* review of decisions by humans that have the necessary competence, training and authority to carry out that role.

AI systems that directly interact with humans should notify that they are interacting with a system.

2.5.9 Procedural Safeguards, Including Bans or Moratoria

States need to take appropriate measures to ensure the identification, assessment, prevention and mitigation of risks posed by AI systems to human rights, democracy and the rule of law. While not imposing direct bans or moratoria on certain AI systems, the AI Convention obligates states to consider bans or moratoria whenever an AI system is deemed incompatible with human rights, the functioning of democracy or the rule of law. The authors of this chapter would like to stress that certain AI systems already in use could be deemed incompatible, such as AI systems that (supposedly) predict a person's thoughts through the interpretation of brain activity or other biometric features or behaviours. While it remains scientifically unclear whether this is in fact possible, we find such AI use incompatible with human dignity, which is the basis of all human rights, as well as with the human right to mental integrity and privacy. Our thoughts are our ultimate barrier to the outside world. Breaking that barrier would pose indiscernible risks and challenges that we cannot even oversee at this point.

2.6 Follow-Up Mechanism and Implementation

In line with well-established Council of Europe practice, the Convention provides for the setting up of a Conference of the Parties, composed of representatives of the parties.

The setting up of this body will ensure equal participation of all the parties in the decision-making process and in the AI Convention follow-up procedure and will also strengthen co-operation between the parties to ensure proper and effective implementation of the AI Convention.

It will be convened by the Secretary-General of the Council of Europe (paragraph 3) as appropriate and periodically (paragraph 2). However, it can only be convened at the request of the majority of the parties or at the request of the Committee of Ministers of the Council of Europe (paragraph 3).

With respect to this AI Convention, the Conference of the Parties has the traditional follow-up competencies and plays a role in respect of:

(1) the effective implementation of the AI Convention, by making proposals to facilitate or improve the effective use and implementation of this AI Convention, including the identification of any problems therein, and the effects of significant legal, policy or technological developments pertaining to the activities within the lifecycle of AI systems, as well as the effects of any declaration or reservation made under this AI Convention;
(2) the amendment of the AI Convention, by making proposals for amendment in accordance with Article 28, paragraph 1 and formulating its opinion on any proposal for amendment of the AI Convention, which is referred to in Article 28, paragraph 3;
(3) a general advisory role in respect of the AI Convention by expressing specific recommendations on any question concerning its interpretation or application, including, for instance, suggesting interpretations of legal terms contained in the AI Convention. Although not legally binding in nature, these recommendations may be seen as a joint expression of opinion by the parties on a given subject which should be taken into account in good faith by the parties in their application of the AI Convention;
(4) serving as a forum for facilitating the exchange of information on significant legal, societal, policy or technological developments in relation to the application of the provisions of the AI Convention, including in relation to the international co-operation activities described in Article 25;
(5) in accordance with Article 29 of the AI Convention, facilitating, where necessary, the friendly settlement of disputes related to the application of its provisions, in a non-binding, consultative capacity; and
(6) facilitating co-operation with stakeholders, including non-governmental organizations, and other bodies which can improve the effectiveness of the follow-up mechanism. In view of the highly technical subject matter of the AI Convention, paragraph 6 of Article 23 expressly points at the possibility for the Conference of the Parties to seek, where appropriate, the relevant expert advice.

Following an amendment proposed by ALLAI, it was agreed, at quite literally the very last minutes of the negotiations, to include an obligation for the Conference of the Parties to adopt its own rules of procedure 'within 12 months of the entry into force of the Convention' (Article 23(4)). This will greatly facilitate the implementation of the reporting obligation by the first states having ratified the AI Convention, as they will need to present their first report within the first two years after becoming a party. The reporting obligation enshrined in Article 24 (as part of the compromise reached on the scope of application of Article 3) will be key to the interpretation, implementation and development of the AI Convention, including with regard to the private sector.

The Conference of the Parties should also play its part and conduct a proper assessment of how state parties comply with Article 3(1)(b), including with respect to those states that decide to take 'other appropriate measures' as an alternative to applying the AI Convention to private sector activities. Every effort should be made to ensure that a progressive interpretation of this provision by the follow-up mechanism will foster advances over time, through reporting requirements and peer pressure.

As the Assembly pointed out in its opinion,[17] it would have been preferable:

> to see an explicit reference in Article 23.2 to the power to *review* or *monitor* the implementation of the Convention by the Conference of the Parties, but ... the power to identify any problems in the effective use and implementation (Article 23.2 (a)) and the power to make 'specific recommendations concerning the interpretation and application' of the Convention (Article 23.2 (c)) give a sufficient legal basis for the review or assessment needed for an effective reporting system.

In this context, it should be noted that the Explanatory Report clarifies that:

> although not legally binding in nature, these recommendations may be seen as a joint expression of opinion by the Parties on a given subject which should be taken into account in good faith by the Parties in their application of the AI Convention.

Moreover, the Conference of the Parties will be tasked with facilitating co-operation with 'relevant stakeholders' (Article 23(2)(f)) and the latter may also be involved in the exchanges of information and co-operation envisaged between the parties 'as/where appropriate' (Article 25(2) and (3)). According to the Explanatory report 'relevant stakeholders' should include NGOs, non-state actors (academics, industry representatives), as well as other bodies that can improve the effectiveness of the follow-up mechanism.

3 REFLECTIONS ON THE ADDED VALUE AND SHORTCOMINGS OF THE CONVENTION

It is well known that politics is the art of the possible. Therefore, it is no surprise that the draft AI Convention falls short of the high ambitions set out in the final report of CAHAI.

3.1 Added Value

Most importantly the AI Convention will be the first global treaty on AI based on standards of human rights, democracy and the rule of law. As the Assembly[18] points out:

17. PACE 2024.
18. *Ibid.*

> The fact that it is a convention open to non-member States that have participated in the negotiations and other non-European countries which might join from all over the world at a later stage is crucial. The challenges and risks posed by AI are transnational and need to be tackled in a global instrument. For this reason, the AI convention has been drafted in such a way that it will facilitate ratification or accession by States having different legal and political traditions, allowing for a sufficient level of flexibility and margin of discretion in its implementation.

Furthermore, the fact that the first international treaty regulating AI will be based on a human-rights approach and the *acquis* of the Council of Europe (human rights, democracy and the rule of law) must be acknowledged as a very important achievement for the Council of Europe and as a sign of its global leadership in setting standards in emerging areas. We have seen this before with previous open Council of Europe conventions such as Convention 108 and the Budapest Convention on Cybercrime.

Another important aspect of the Convention is that in addition to protecting human rights in the context of AI, it also aims to safeguard the two other core values of the Council of Europe, namely democracy and the rule of law (*see* Article 5, as reflected in the title of the convention itself).

AI technologies have the potential to disrupt the functioning of democratic institutions and processes, for instance, through interference in electoral processes, disinformation and manipulation of public opinion. They can also interfere with the functioning of the rule of law, including the independence and integrity of the judiciary and access to justice.

While there is no common definition of 'democratic institutions and processes' in the text of the Convention, the Explanatory Report gives a non-exhaustive list of principles that can be potentially threatened by AI: separation of powers, political pluralism, judicial independence, free and fair elections, rule of law, etc. In our opinion, the interpretation of Article 5 should also be based on the interdependent notions of democracy and the rule of law as developed over the years by different Council of Europe bodies, particularly the ECHR (notions of 'democratic society' and 'the principle of the rule of law' underpinning the ECHR), the Venice Commission (the Rule of Law Checklist).

Further valuable elements are the explicit reference to gender equality (Article 10) and women (Preamble) in the context of non-discrimination, as well as the obligation to take due account of the vulnerabilities of the rights of persons with disabilities and children (Article 18).

3.2 Shortcomings

It has been pointed out by civil society organizations that some language and qualifiers used throughout the text may raise difficulties with regard to the enforceability and uniform application of the AI Convention. For instance, the use of 'seek to ensure' instead of 'ensure' (for instance, Articles 5(1) and 15(2)), 'where appropriate' or 'as appropriate' (e.g., Articles 16(2)(g) and 19), 'where practicable' (Article 26(3) and (4)) and the frequent references to 'domestic law/legal system' (e.g., Articles 6, 14(1),

15(1), and 18) have a negative impact on the legal certainty and foreseeability in the interpretation of the Convention.

As regards the use of expressions such as 'seek to ensure', there is no reason, for instance, to distinguish between the general obligation to ensure the respect for human rights (Article 4) and the general obligation to protect democratic institutions and processes (Article 5). Both obligations should be read in the light of the object and purpose of the Convention which is to '*ensure* that activities within the lifecycle of AI systems are fully consistent with human rights, democracy and the rule of law' (*emphasis added*).

With regard to the multiple references to 'domestic law', the Explanatory Report states that (commentary to Article 21):

> all references to domestic law in this AI Convention should be read as limited to cases where domestic law provides for a higher standard of human rights protection than applicable international law.

Consequently, international (human rights) obligations should always be the minimum standard applicable.

Regrettably, the text refers to some internationally established rights as 'principles' and not as 'rights' (Chapter III). For example, the right to non-discrimination and equality or the right to privacy should have been formulated as positive rights of individuals. This would not have implied creating new human rights, as negotiating States are already bound by international treaties which recognize them as individual rights. In the authors' opinion, a better option would have been to refer in the heading of Chapter III to 'fundamental principles and rights'.

More generally, the CAI missed an opportunity to include new rights, rights that could flow from already existing rights (human dignity, personal autonomy, right to respect for private life) but adapted or specifically tailored to an AI context.

For instance, when examining the brain-computer interface technology, certain organizations and experts,[19] as well as the Parliamentary Assembly have called on Member States to consider establishing new 'neurorights', such as cognitive liberty, mental privacy and mental integrity.

Also, the recent developments in AI have shown an ever stronger capability of AI to manipulate and deceive us without us knowing. There are many examples where people are tricked by AI systems into behaviour or decisions they would not have made otherwise. The CAI could have addressed this by introducing a right of non-manipulation by AI.

The second challenge is agency. If we are to believe some of the people who build ever-stronger systems, there is a risk of losing control or agency over these systems. The CAI could have addressed this by introducing a right of human agency over AI.

The third is experimentation. Many of the latest generative AI systems are, according to their deployers, experimental. Nevertheless, they are introduced into services and products that affect the entire society and even children. The CAI could have addressed this by introducing a 'right of non-experimentation with AI'. The

19. ALLAI (undated).

authors of this chapter believe that the tech practice of rolling out imperfect systems and then fixing them later on based on user experience might work for some tools, but it should not be the modus operandi for AI.

Again, regrettably, some negotiating states were not ready to accept a horizontal scope in order to have the AI Convention cover equally public and private entities. This is far from ideal for legal certainty and predictability of the obligations imposed by the Convention vis-à-vis private actors. The authors of this chapter are of course aware of the constraints of the final stages of the negotiations and the enormous pressure to reach a compromise, however, we do expect all Council of Europe (or at the least all EU) Member and Candidate States to choose option (1), as is common practice for Council of Europe instruments, and apply the AI Convention directly to private parties.

It must also be noted that the process as it developed, and quite contrary to the terms of reference given by the Committee of Ministers, did not allow for timely and in-depth analysis and consultation with all stakeholders, in particular civil society and other observers participating in the CAI.

As always, the proof of the pudding is in the eating, and the jury on the actual effectiveness of the Convention is still out. The verdict will depend both on the actual number of ratifications and, very importantly, the determination and effectiveness of the Conference of the Parties.

BIBLIOGRAPHY

ALLAI (undated): ALLAI, *ALLAI Calls for New Fundamental Principles in the AI Treaty* (undated), allai.nl/allai-calls-for-new-fundamental-principles-to-be-included-in-the-ai-treaty (accessed 23 June 2024).

CAHAI 2020: CAHAI, *Feasibility Study*, Council of Europe, CAHAI(2020)23, (2020), rm.coe.int/cahai-2020-23-final-eng-feasibility-study-/1680a0c6da (accessed 23 June 2024).

CAI 2023: CAI, *Revised Zero Draft [Framework] Convention on Artificial Intelligence, Human Rights, Democracy and the Rule of Law*, Council of Europe, CAI(2023)01 (6 January 2023), rm.coe.int/cai-2023-01-revised-zero-draft-framework-conven tion-public/1680aa193f (accessed 23 June 2024).

Muller 2020: Catelijne Muller, *The Impact of Artificial Intelligence on Human Rights, Democracy and the Rule of Law*, Council of Europe, CAHAI(2020)06-fin (2020).

OECD 2024: OECD, *Explanatory Memorandum on the Updated OECD Definition of an AI System*, OECD Artificial Intelligence Papers, No. 8, OECD Publishing (2024), doi: 10.1787/623da898-en.

PACE 2024: Parliamentary Assembly of the Council of Europe, Opinion 303 (2024)1: *Draft Framework Convention on Artificial Intelligence, Human Rights, Democracy and the Rule of Law*, Council of Europe (2024), pace.coe.int/en/files/33517/html (accessed 23 June 2024).

CHAPTER 3

The Work of the High-Level Expert Group on AI as the Precursor of the AI Act

Nathalie A. Smuha[*]

1 INTRODUCTION

On 25 April 2018, the Commission published a Communication titled 'Artificial Intelligence for Europe', setting out a comprehensive artificial intelligence (AI) strategy for the European Union (EU).[1] As part of that strategy, it appointed an independent High-Level Expert Group on AI (HLEG) with the instruction to draft voluntary AI ethics guidelines titled Ethics Guidelines for Trustworthy AI (HLEG Guidelines), and policy recommendations for EU institutions and Member States, titled Policy and Investment Recommendations for Trustworthy AI (Policy Recommendations). These documents, and the HLEG Guidelines in particular, on which the Policy Recommendations build, have proven to be foundational for the subsequent proposal and adoption of the AI Act.[2] In this contribution, I will therefore retrace how EU institutions shifted their attention from soft law to hard law, and discuss the way in which the former influenced the latter.

To do so, I start by introducing the HLEG and its context, against a background of other (international) initiatives (section 2). Subsequently, I provide an overview of the

* This contribution was written during my time as an Emile Noël Fellow and BAEF Fellow at the Jean Monnet Center, NYU School of Law. For reasons of transparency, it should also be mentioned that I was the coordinator of the HLEG until July 2019, and in this capacity contributed to both the HLEG Guidelines and its Policy Recommendations.

1. Commission 2018.
2. While the role of the HLEG Guidelines as a precursor of the AI Act is primarily implicit, at several instances, the regulation also explicitly refers to the HLEG Guidelines or to the concept of 'trustworthy AI' which the HLEG coined. *See, for instance,* AIA, Recs 2, 7, 27 and 165; and Arts 1 and 95. Interestingly, the AI Act does not explicitly refer to the Policy Recommendations, despite their clear influence.

HLEG Guidelines and discuss the three-pronged role they play in the AI Act: (1) they inspired the requirements imposed on high-risk AI systems as well as other provisions of the regulation; (2) they act as a basis for voluntary codes of conduct that the AI Act seeks to foster; and (3) they serve as a more general normative framework underlying the AI Act's rationale (section 3). I then move to the Policy Recommendations and explain to which extent the advice which the members of the HLEG formulated therein found its way to the AI Act (section 4), before concluding (section 5).

2 THE HLEG IN CONTEXT

2.1 Europe's AI Strategy

When the Commission adopted an AI strategy for the EU in April 2018, this occurred against the background of a global race to AI.[3] China and the United States (US) – along with other countries and regions – had started asserting and bolstering their technological prowess by adopting policies and action plans to harness AI's benefits and enable their economies to reap its advantages. At the same time, the promulgation of national AI strategies could also be seen as a vindication of digital sovereignty, both in the economic and the normative sense.[4] Indeed, given the technology's societal impact, AI strategies also reflected the idea that jurisdictions should be able to keep on protecting their (public) interests within a context of increased technological dependency. Importantly, however, the focus of these strategies lay on AI's benefits. At that time, even in Europe, identifying and mitigating AI's ethical, legal and social risks was often an afterthought. Granted, in the late 2010s, the growing instances of (large-scale) AI-related harms started appearing more prominently on policymakers' radars and elicited increased citizen concerns.[5] Yet many believed that existing legislative frameworks, such as general non-discrimination laws and the General Data Protection Regulation (GDPR) which had just come into force, would be able to address these.[6]

That said, the Commission did aim to pursue a 'third way' of AI governance. It sought to distinguish itself from the Chinese state-driven approach and the American market-driven approach by explicitly embracing an approach based on 'values'. In its AI strategy, the Commission described Europe's embrace of values as the way in which 'the EU can make a difference – and be the champion of an approach to AI that benefits people and society as a whole'.[7] It, however, still framed this as a 'competitive advantage', thereby implying that values are treated as instrumental to promote Europe's competitiveness.[8]

The AI strategy consisted of three pillars, reflecting the aims of the Union's AI approach as well as its order of priorities: (1) boosting the EU's technological and

3. Lee 2018; Harari 2019.
4. *See in this regard also* Smuha 2023.
5. *See, e.g.*, Allen & Castro 2017; *see also* the Cambridge Analytica scandal's impact, as, e.g., discussed in Wylie 2019.
6. *See also* Smuha & Yeung 2024.
7. *See* HLEG Guidelines, 2.
8. *See also* Bradford 2020.

industrial capacity and AI uptake across the economy, both by the private and public sectors; (2) preparing for socio-economic changes brought about by AI; and (3) ensuring an appropriate ethical and legal framework, based on the Union's values and in line with the Charter. As part of the third pillar, the Commission proposed the development of 'draft AI ethics guidelines' in cooperation with 'all relevant stakeholders'.[9] According to the strategy's document, these guidelines would:[10]

> address issues such as the future of work, fairness, safety, security, social inclusion and algorithmic transparency. More broadly, they will look at the impact on fundamental rights, including privacy, dignity, consumer protection and non-discrimination. ... Companies, academic institutions, and other organisations from civil society bodies will be invited to contribute.

The announcement of the Commission's decision to develop ethics guidelines clearly marked a preference for a soft law approach to AI governance. This decision received quite some criticism, especially from those who believed that the GDPR and other existing rules showed too many legal gaps and did not offer sufficient protection against AI-related harms. It should, however, be pointed out that the Commission did leave the door open for future binding rules. Indeed, the strategy acknowledged that:[11]

> while self-regulation can provide a first set of benchmarks against which emerging applications and outcomes can be assessed, public authorities must ensure that the regulatory frameworks for developing and using of AI technologies are in line with these values and fundamental rights.

The Commission therefore proclaimed that it:[12]

> will monitor developments and, if necessary, review existing legal frameworks to better adapt them to specific challenges, in particular to ensure the respect of the Union's basic values and fundamental rights.

2.2 The HLEG's Mandate

While the strategy remained vague about the way in which the 'draft AI ethics guidelines' would be developed, the Commission's Directorate-General in charge of AI policy (DG Connect) did publish a call for applications for a new HLEG, explicitly referring to the HLEG Guidelines.[13] Pursuant to the call for applications, the HLEG's mandate consisted of three tasks:

(1) proposing 'AI ethics guidelines' to the Commission;
(2) advising the Commission on addressing AI-related mid to long-term challenges and opportunities through recommendations; and

9. *See supra* n. 1, at 14.
10. *Ibid.*, at 15.
11. *Ibid.*
12. *Ibid.*
13. DG Connect 2018a.

(3) supporting the Commission with further engagement and outreach mechanisms to interact with a broader set of stakeholders in the context of the European AI Alliance.[14]

A subsequent concept note that was published by DG Connect further specified these tasks as well as their respective timeline.[15]

To avoid the HLEG reinventing the wheel or starting its drafting exercise from scratch, the call for applications specified that the guidelines should build on the work of the European Group on Ethics in Science and New Technologies[16] and the EU Fundamental Rights Agency. It also warned that 'the content of these deliverables will not bind the Commission to any specific follow up'.[17] This formulation, rather standard with expert groups, sought to clarify that the Commission had no obligation to actually implement the HLEG's proposed guidelines or recommendations. In theory, the Commission thus retained discretion to decide *not* to endorse or use the deliverables, or at least to amend them or set them aside, depending on the output's quality or the way in which it would be received. In practice, however, the idea of letting stakeholders draft AI ethics guidelines and then ignoring or revising them would have been politically somewhat difficult, since it was the Commission itself who chose the group's composition.

While the call for applications specified that the HLEG would consist of thirty members, the group was ultimately comprised of fifty-two experts, encompassing representatives from industry, academia, and civil society (with industry being most represented).[18] To facilitate the drafting process of the two documents, the HLEG divided its work among two sub-groups. This working methodology was specified in the concept note as follows:

> Working Group 1 will focus on the draft AI ethics guidelines, and Working Group 2 will focus on the policy & investment strategy. ... All members will be able to provide input on both deliverables, either during the regular meetings of the full AI HL[E]G (where both deliverables will always be discussed), or in writing. The final documents prepared by each working [group] will be adopted by the AI HL[E]G as a whole, after all members of the group have had the opportunity to comment thereon.

The two groups worked in parallel, yet the timeline of their work was staggered, enabling the experts to focus on each deliverable in turn. The HLEG's first meeting took place in June 2018, and by December 2018 it had published a first draft of the HLEG

14. The European AI Alliance is an online multistakeholder platform through which the HLEG and the Commission could gather input and feedback, engage in discussions with a broader set of people, and have exchanges on AI policy.
15. DG Connect 2018b.
16. The European Group on Ethics in Science and New Technologies (EGE) is an independent advisory body established by the President of the Commission. *See also* EGE 2018.
17. DG Connect 2018a.
18. This has been a point of criticism. *See, e.g.*, Simonite 2019.

Guidelines, which it subjected to a public consultation to gather stakeholder feedback. After the feedback's implementation, the final version of the HLEG Guidelines was published in April 2019 (alongside a Commission Communication endorsing its content),[19] while the Policy Recommendations were published at the end of June 2019 and presented at the first Assembly of the European AI Alliance.

2.3 Broader Context

The Commission was not the only policymaker with the idea to draft normative principles for the responsible use of AI.[20] One of the reasons why the Commission felt the need to establish an expert group at the European level was the fact that some EU Member States planned to launch their own AI ethics initiatives, as a response to increased concerns from citizens and civil society. For instance, in March 2018, France's President Emmanuel Macron presented a five-year national AI strategy, which included the goal to 'develop an ethical framework for a transparent and fair use of AI applications'.[21] In September 2018, Germany established a 'Data Ethics Commission' to provide an opinion with recommendations for action and suggestions for possible legislation.[22] The appointment of the HLEG can hence also be seen as an attempt to counter the fragmentation of AI ethics principles in the Single European (AI) Market. Yet also beyond the EU, AI ethics gained traction.[23] Around the same time as the launch of the HLEG, several governmental and intergovernmental organizations set up their own AI expert groups for similar purposes. In January 2019, Singapore published the first edition of its 'Model Artificial Intelligence Governance Framework',[24] followed by the release of AI principles by Japan in March 2019,[25] and by the Beijing Academy of AI in May 2019.[26] Singapore and Japan were also observers in the HLEG, alongside Quebec and several international organizations that were developing AI policies.

Indeed, in September 2018, the Organisation for Economic Co-operation and Development (OECD) set up an informal group of AI experts (AIGO) to 'provide guidance in scoping principles for artificial intelligence in society'.[27] This work formed the basis of a subsequent 'Recommendation of the Council on Artificial Intelligence' which put forward a set of OECD principles that 'aim to ensure AI systems are designed

19. Commission 2019.
20. For an overview of the global AI ethics landscape at the time of the HLEG's work, *see also* Jobin et al. 2019. *See also* Hickok 2021.
21. *See in this regard* AI Watch 2021.
22. *See also* Data Ethics Commission 2019.
23. *See also* Hagendorff 2020; Whittlestone et al. 2019.
24. An updated version of the Framework was published in 2020 and can be seen at PDPC 2019.
25. These principles, called the 'Social Principles of Human-centric AI' were adopted by Japan's Integrated Innovation Strategy Promotion Council, which also contributed to the formulation of the OECD Recommendations.
26. Beijing AI Academy 2019.
27. OECD 2018. The group was comprised of experts from OECD member countries and think tanks, business, civil society and labour associations, and other international organizations.

to be robust, safe, fair and trustworthy'.[28] These principles subsequently formed the basis of the G20 'AI Principles for responsible stewardship of Trustworthy AI', adopted as part of the G20 Ministerial Statement on Trade and Digital Economy in June 2019.[29] Since some of the AIGO's members were also part of the HLEG, this resulted in a cross-fertilization of perspectives and a more common vocabulary. In November 2019, United Nations Educational, Scientific and Cultural Organization (UNESCO) followed suit, when its 193 Member States mandated the creation of 'the first global normative instrument on the ethics of AI', resulting in the adoption of a 'Recommendation on the Ethics of Artificial Intelligence' in November 2021.[30] While the non-binding nature of these various initiatives was criticized by some, others considered it a necessary first step to work towards a more universal consensus around the principles that should govern AI's development and use.

The Council of Europe went one step further though, by setting up an Council of Europe's Ad hoc Committee on Artificial Intelligence (CAHAI) with the explicit mandate to examine:[31]

> the feasibility and potential elements on the basis of broad multi-stakeholder consultations, of a legal framework for the development, design and application of artificial intelligence, based on Council of Europe's standards on human rights, democracy and the rule of law.

Building on this work, the CAHAI's successor, the Council of Europe's Committee on AI (CAI), ultimately proposed a new Framework Convention on AI, which was adopted by the Council of Europe's Committee of Ministers in May 2024.[32] All these international organizations – including the EU as the supranational organization – liked to emphasize their unique and pioneering role in establishing norms for AI governance, seeking a first-mover advantage to set the global standard. In other words, the race to AI was also accompanied by a race to AI regulation,[33] with regulatory competition taking place not only among different countries but also among different international organizations.[34]

Importantly, the HLEG was also seen as an answer to the ever-growing proclamation of ethics principles by private actors. Indeed, companies like IBM (in May 2018),[35] Google (in June 2018),[36] and many others started publishing their own perspective of what the ethical use of AI entails, and the principles they would uphold in this context. Many critics depicted these initiatives as insufficient,[37] or even as a form of 'ethics-washing', or the deliberate reliance on ethics to stall or divert efforts to

28. OECD 2019. The OECD Council adopted the Recommendation at its meeting at Ministerial level on 22-23 May 2019, and updated in 2024.
29. G20 2019.
30. UNESCO Recommendation.
31. *See* CAHAI 2020; CAHAI 2021.
32. CAI 2024.
33. *See* Smuha 2021b.
34. *See also* Ala-Pietilä & Smuha 2021.
35. IBM 2018. *See* Rossi 2020.
36. Pichai 2018.
37. *See, e.g.*, Mittelstadt 2019.

impose binding legislation.[38] The same scholars also considered the HLEG's mandate to 'draft ethics guidelines' rather than to 'propose legislation' as a sign of the Commission's appeasement of companies who wished to avoid new legal obligations. While this reading is an overly reductionist interpretation of the role that ethics (guidelines) can play in society, not only as a precursor but also as a complement to law,[39] it is important to acknowledge the limitations of an approach whereby those who need guidance and control essentially adopt their own principles, with limited stakeholder input, no accountability or enforcement mechanism, nor any underlying democratic public deliberation, despite the impact of their actions on society. This is one of the reasons why the Commission sought to involve a larger group of stakeholders beyond companies in the guidelines' drafting process and to keep the imposition of binding rules as a stick behind the door in case of need.[40]

Ultimately, this stick was used. Instances of AI-related harm kept piling up, and it became increasingly untenable to relegate the responsibility of interpreting and adopting responsible AI practices to the very companies that needed to be kept in check. By mid-2019, both the Council and the Parliament had already adopted several resolutions calling for an EU approach to AI governance, including the incorporation of ethics principles into potential regulation. Accordingly, one month after the HLEG published its Policy Recommendations, the Commission's then President-Elect Ursula Von Der Leyen proclaimed that:[41]

> in my first 100 days in office, I will put forward legislation for a coordinated European approach on the human and ethical implications of Artificial Intelligence.

This was followed by the Commission's adoption of a White Paper on AI in 2020, which referred to the HLEG's work and set out several options for a future AI-specific regulation. As a next step, the Commission published a proposal for an AI Act in April 2021,[42] which after three years of negotiations led to the AI Act's formal adoption in the spring of 2024. In what follows, I elaborate on the structure and content of the HLEG's deliverables, and the way in which they influenced the AI Act.

3 THE ETHICS GUIDELINES FOR TRUSTWORTHY AI

3.1 Core Concepts and Structure

The HLEG opened the Guidelines with a description of what it meant with the term 'Trustworthy AI', of which the advancement and promotion is considered the

38. *See also* Wagner 2019. Note, however, that the HLEG explicitly stated in the HLEG Guidelines that 'These Guidelines do not intend to substitute any form of current or future policymaking or regulation, nor do they aim to deter the introduction thereof. They should be seen as a living document to be reviewed and updated over time to ensure their continuous relevance as the technology, our social environments, and our knowledge evolve.' *See* HLEG Guidelines, 3.
39. *See also* Smuha 2024a.
40. *See in this regard also* Smuha 2019.
41. von der Leyen 2019.
42. AI Act Commission Proposal.

document's main aim. While the Commission requested the preparation of 'ethics guidelines for AI', it did not suggest the use of the term 'Trustworthy'. This term was deliberately chosen by the HLEG after internal deliberations on what the most suitable concept would be, and subsequently also added to the document's title. As the group stated in the Guidelines:[43]

> we ... identify Trustworthy AI as our foundational ambition, since human beings and communities will only be able to have confidence in the technology's development and its applications when a clear and comprehensive framework for achieving its trustworthiness is in place.

To clarify that the term 'Trustworthy' should not be seen as merely referring to AI systems without the human beings behind it, they further specified that:[44]

> trust in the development, deployment and use of AI systems concerns not only the technology's inherent properties, but also the qualities of the socio-technical systems involving AI applications. Analogous to questions of (loss of) trust in aviation, nuclear power or food safety, it is not simply components of the AI system but the system in its overall context that may or may not engender trust. Striving towards Trustworthy AI hence concerns not only the trustworthiness of the AI system itself, but requires a holistic and systemic approach, encompassing the trustworthiness of all actors and processes that are part of the system's socio-technical context throughout its entire life cycle.

According to the HLEG Guidelines, Trustworthy AI consists of three components, which should be met throughout the entire life cycle of an AI system. First, it should be *lawful*, complying with all applicable laws and regulations. The HLEG thus explicitly incorporated the need to respect all existing rules, including human rights law, into the concept of Trustworthy AI. Second, it should be *ethical*, which entails adherence to ethical principles and values, which is a non-exhaustive normative framework that can change over time. Third, it should be *robust*, both from a technical and social perspective. This is because, even with good intentions, the development and use of AI can cause unintentional harm. While each of these three components is necessary to speak of Trustworthy AI, the HLEG clarified that none of them are sufficient to achieve it. Moreover, ideally, all components work in harmony and overlap in their operation. Yet if 'in practice, tensions arise between these components, society should endeavor to align them'.[45]

The term Trustworthy AI has been highly influential in other EU policies on AI and is repeated in the AI Act in several instances. Most notably, Article 1(1) of the regulation states that its purpose:

> is to improve the functioning of the internal market and promote the uptake of human-centric and trustworthy artificial intelligence.

43. *See* HLEG Guidelines, 4.
44. *See ibid.*, at 5.
45. *See ibid.*, at 2.

Importantly, however, the HLEG Guidelines themselves do not explicitly deal with the first component of Trustworthy AI (lawful AI) but only offer guidance on how to achieve the second and third components. They note that:[46]

> while the two latter are to a certain extent often already reflected in existing laws, their full realisation may go beyond existing legal obligations.

These sentences were included to ensure that the HLEG Guidelines are not mistakenly seen as a replacement for legal guidance (and hence of legal obligations).[47] In the same breath, the group also made explicit that these Guidelines 'do not intend to substitute any form of current or future policymaking or regulation, nor do they aim to deter the introduction thereof', to counter the risk that the document would be used for the purpose of ethics-washing.[48]

To attain the ambition of Trustworthy AI (at least as regards its ethical and robustness components), the Guidelines are structured as offering guidance:[49]

> in three layers of abstraction, from the most abstract in Chapter I to the most concrete in Chapter III, closing with examples of opportunities and critical concerns raised by AI systems.

Chapter I deals with the 'foundations' of Trustworthy AI, which sets out the normative basis on which the guidance is developed. The group debated different ethical theories and frameworks, and the HLEG Guidelines contain elements associated with Kantian ethics ('AI is not an end in itself, but rather a promising means to increase human flourishing'),[50] utilitarianism (suggesting the goal of 'seeking to maximise the benefits of AI systems while at the same time preventing and minimising their risks'),[51] and virtue ethics (stressing, e.g., the importance of 'training and education to help developing accountability practices').[52]

Ultimately, however, the HLEG recommended a 'fundamental rights-based approach', explicitly grounding the Guidelines in the EU Treaties, the Charter, and international human rights law. Indeed:[53]

> respect for fundamental rights, within a framework of democracy and the rule of law, provides the most promising foundations for identifying abstract ethical principles and values, which can be operationalised in the context of AI.

It can be noted that this approach significantly differs from the AI Act's market-based approach, a point to which I will return in subsequent sections. Based on this fundamental rights-oriented framework, the HLEG then described four ethical principles that are

46. *See ibid.*, at 6.
47. *See in this regard also* Smuha et al. 2021.
48. *See* HLEG Guidelines, 3.
49. *See ibid.*, at 2.
50. *See ibid.*, at 4.
51. *Ibid.*
52. *See ibid.*, at 31.
53. *See ibid.*, at 9.

especially relevant to ensure ethical and robust AI, namely: (1) respect for human autonomy; (2) prevention of harm; (3) fairness; and (4) explicability. The Guidelines also acknowledged that:

> tensions may arise between the above principles, for which there is no fixed solution. In line with the EU fundamental commitment to democratic engagement, due process and open political participation, methods of accountable deliberation to deal with such tensions should be established.

After this foundational setting, Chapter II of the HLEG Guidelines deals with the 'realization' of Trustworthy AI, by translating the rather abstract ethical principles into seven more concrete 'key requirements for Trustworthy AI' that should be implemented and met throughout AI's entire life cycle, and suggesting both technical and non-technical methods that can be used for this purpose. This chapter forms the core part of the HLEG Guidelines and has arguably been the key inspirer of the AI Act: the seven requirements are included in Recital 27 of the AI Act, they are mentioned as the basis for future voluntary codes of conduct for which the AI Act creates a framework, and they have also been imported into the regulation's substantive articles.

There are two more parts of the Ethics Guidelines that impacted the AI Act in an essential way and that merit being highlighted here. Chapter III of the Guidelines – titled 'Assessing Trustworthy AI' – operationalizes the key requirements for Trustworthy by offering practical guidance to AI practitioners on how they should fulfil them. To this end, the HLEG prepared an 'Assessment list for Trustworthy AI' (ALTAI), which provides a set of (non-exhaustive) questions for AI practitioners to guide them towards concrete actions. Since these action-oriented questions concretize the key requirements, the ALTAI has indirectly also given body to the AI Act's requirements for high-risk AI systems. After the HLEG Guidelines publication in April 2019, the ALTAI has been subjected to a piloting process, enabling stakeholders to provide feedback through dedicated workshops and a large public consultation. A revised version of the ALTAI, prepared on the basis of that feedback, was published in July 2020. This feedback was also explicitly considered by the Commission in its preparatory work on the AI Act.[54]

Finally, the HLEG Guidelines close with a set of examples of beneficial opportunities and critical concerns raised by AI systems, 'which should serve to stimulate further debate'.[55] Of most relevance to the AI Act, the 'critical concerns' identified by the HLEG constitute domains or applications in which 'one of the components of Trustworthy AI is violated', such as 'identifying and tracking individuals with AI' (which needs to happen in a proportionate and legitimate manner, especially when biometric data is involved), 'covert AI systems' (which should only be used if human beings are made aware of the fact that they are interacting with a non-human), 'citizen scoring in violation of fundamental rights' (a problematic practice which is significantly facilitated by AI), as well as 'lethal autonomous weapons systems' and 'potential

54. *See in this regard* Explanatory Memorandum to the AI Act, s. 3.2 at 8.
55. *See* HLEG Guidelines, 7.

longer-term concerns' (both of which fall outside the AI Act's scope).[56] While some people deplored the fact that these domains were not identified as *red lines* but merely as *critical concerns*, many of these examples nevertheless found their way to the AI Act, either in the category of prohibited AI practices (e.g., AI-driven generalized social scoring in Article 5), the category of high-risk systems (e.g., AI-driven biometric identification in Annex III) or the category of systems requiring additional transparency (e.g., chatbots in Article 50).

In sum, the HLEG Guidelines play a three-pronged role in the AI Act, which I will respectively discuss in the next three sections:

(1) they inspired the requirements for high-risk AI systems and for other risk-categories;
(2) they act as normative guidance for the development of voluntary codes of conduct; and
(3) they act as general normative principles for all AI practitioners, regardless of the system's risk level.

3.2 The Guidelines as Inspiration for the High-Risk AI Systems' Requirements

As noted above, Chapter II of the HLEG Guidelines sets out seven interrelated 'key requirements' that should be met for AI systems to be deemed trustworthy.[57] Almost all these requirements were incorporated in Chapter III, section 2 of the AI Act ('requirements for high-risk systems'). In what follows, I hence provide a brief overview of how these requirements were defined in the HLEG Guidelines and describe how they are reflected in the AI Act. I should, however, point out that whereas the Guidelines clearly state that the list of requirements is open-ended and principle-based, the AI Act maintains a closed set of exhaustively listed obligations that are more legalistic in nature.

56. The latter refer to 'Artificial General Intelligence, Artificial Consciousness, Artificial Moral Agents, Super-intelligence or Transformative AI' which are considered by some as examples of such long-term concerns (currently non-existent), while others believe these to be unrealistic. This was a contentious point in the debates of the HLEG, yet the HLEG Guidelines ultimately state that 'a risk-based approach suggests that these concerns should be kept into consideration in view of possible unknown unknowns and "black swans." The high-impact nature of these concerns, combined with the current uncertainty in corresponding developments, calls for regular assessments of these topics'. *See* HLEG Guidelines, 35.

57. Different groups of stakeholders are assigned different roles to ensure their attainment: AI developers should implement and apply the requirements to design and development processes; AI deployers should ensure that the systems they use and the products and services they offer meet the requirements; and end-users and society at large (meaning all those directly or indirectly affected by AI systems) should be informed about the requirements and able to request that they are upheld. *See* HLEG Guidelines, at 14.

3.2.1 *Human Agency and Oversight*

The first requirement concerns 'human agency and oversight' and implies that:[58]

> AI systems should support human autonomy and decision-making, as prescribed by the principle of respect for human autonomy. This requires that AI systems should both act as enablers to a democratic, flourishing and equitable society by supporting the user's agency and foster fundamental rights, and allow for human oversight.

To ensure this, the HLEG suggests that in situations where the risk of a fundamental rights violation exists, 'a fundamental rights impact assessment should be undertaken'. Conversely, pursuant to Article 27, the AI Act only mandates such assessment for a limited set of deployers of high-risk systems, namely bodies governed by public law, private entities providing public services, and deployers of high-risk AI systems used for creditworthiness assessments as well as risk and pricing assessments in life and health insurance.

The HLEG Guidelines also state that users should be protected against forms of unfair manipulation and that they should be given the knowledge and tools to comprehend and interact with AI systems to a satisfactory degree (and, where possible, be enabled to reasonably self-assess or challenge the system). While the former practice is to some extent banned under the AI Act's Article 5 list of prohibited practices,[59] the latter point is reflected in the AI Act's transparency requirements.

Finally, the Guidelines emphasize the importance of human oversight, including the capability to oversee the overall activity of the AI system (including its broader economic, societal, legal and ethical impact) and the ability to decide when and how to use the system in any particular situation. According to the HLEG:[60]

> this can include the decision not to use an AI system in a particular situation, to establish levels of human discretion during the use of the system, or to ensure the ability to override a decision made by a system.

Article 14 of the AI Act now transposed this requirement into law, by listing several requirements to ensure 'human oversight' over the AI system.

3.2.2 *Technical Robustness and Safety*

The second requirement of the HLEG Guidelines concerns 'technical robustness and safety', which is closely linked to the principle of prevention of harm. According to the HLEG, this:[61]

58. *See ibid.*, at 15.
59. *See, e.g.*, AIA, Art. 5(1)(a).
60. *See* HLEG Guidelines, at 16.
61. *Ibid.*

> requires that AI systems be developed with a preventative approach to risks and in a manner such that they reliably behave as intended while minimising unintentional and unexpected harm, and preventing unacceptable harm.

Moreover, the physical and mental integrity of humans should be ensured. The requirement is split into four sub-themes, covering the need to ensure the system's resilience to attack and security; setting up a fallback plan and considering general safety; ensuring the system's accuracy; and setting up mechanisms to secure the system's reliability and the reproducibility of its outcomes. This requirement is largely mirrored in the AI Act's Article 15 titled 'accuracy, robustness and cybersecurity', which addresses these different sub-themes and gives them legal expression.

3.2.3 Privacy and Data Governance

The third requirement pertains to 'privacy and data governance'. While it includes respect for privacy (which is already broadly covered in privacy legislation),[62] it also implies due consideration for the quality and integrity of data, and for mechanisms to govern data access. For instance:[63]

> to allow individuals to trust the data gathering process, it must be ensured that data collected about them will not be used to unlawfully or unfairly discriminate against them.

Furthermore, to avoid:[64]

> socially constructed biases, inaccuracies, errors and mistakes ... processes and data sets used must be tested and documented at each step such as planning, training, testing and deployment.

Finally:[65]

> only duly qualified personnel with the competence and need to access individual's data should be allowed to do so.

These requirements, particularly as regards data quality, representativeness, integrity and testing against bias, are now largely reflected in Article 10 of the AI Act, titled 'data and data governance'.

3.2.4 Transparency

The fourth requirement, 'transparency', is closely linked with the principle of explicability and 'encompasses transparency of elements relevant to an AI system: the data,

62. In addition to the GDPR, one can also think of the Law Enforcement Directive (LED), EU Institution Data Protection Regulation (EUDPR), and ePrivacy Directive (ePD).
63. HLEG Guidelines, at 17.
64. *Ibid.*
65. *Ibid.*

the system and the business models'.[66] The HLEG Guidelines list three strands of this requirement, namely traceability, explainability and communication. The first requires the documentation 'to the best possible standard' of the data sets and processes that yield the AI system's decision, including those of data gathering and data labelling practices, as well as the algorithms used, to facilitate the system's auditability and explainability.[67] This sub-requirement is reflected in Articles 11 and 12 of the AI Act. Article 11 compels the drawing up of technical documentation before the system is placed on the market or put into service, while Article 12 requires high-risk systems to 'technically allow for the automatic recording of events (logs) over the lifetime of the system'. Annex IV of the AI Act further clarifies which information the technical documentation should contain.

The second strand of the transparency requirement concerns explainability, requiring 'that the decisions made by an AI system can be understood and traced by human beings' and that 'whenever an AI system has a significant impact on people's lives, it should be possible to demand a suitable explanation of the AI system's decision-making process'.[68] The HLEG also suggested that:[69]

> explanations of the degree to which an AI system influences and shapes the organisational decision-making process, design choices of the system, and the rationale for deploying it, should be available (hence ensuring business model transparency).

This requirement can be found, at least to some extent, in Article 86 of the AI Act, which establishes a right to an explanation of individual decision-making. Indeed, according to this article:

> any affected person subject to a decision which is taken by the deployer on the basis of the output from a high-risk AI system listed in Annex III, with the exception of systems listed under point 2 thereof, and which produces legal effects or similarly significantly affects that person in a way that they consider to have an adverse impact on their health, safety or fundamental rights shall have the right to obtain from the deployer clear and meaningful explanations of the role of the AI system in the decision-making procedure and the main elements of the decision taken.

It should, however, be noted that this right only applies to a very narrow set of AI systems (unlike what the HLEG had in mind) and that the AI Act also provides that the right can be restricted.[70]

Finally, the HLEG Guidelines require clear 'communication', noting that 'humans have the right to be informed that they are interacting with an AI system', that 'the option to decide against this interaction in favour of human interaction should be provided where needed to ensure compliance with fundamental rights', and that 'the

66. *See ibid.*, at 18.
67. *Ibid.*
68. *Ibid.*
69. *Ibid.*
70. *See* AIA, Art. 86(2).

AI system's capabilities and limitations should be communicated to AI practitioners or end-users in a manner appropriate to the use case at hand'.

The AI Act primarily provides for transparency towards deployers of high-risk AI systems, such as in Article 13 ('Transparency and provision of information to deployers'), and barely contains information rights for those who are subjected to the systems. The regulation does establish that one should be informed about the fact that one interacts with an AI system, but it does not do so in terms of a right - rather, this is an obligation imposed on providers in Article 50 of the AI Act.[71] Pursuant to Article 71, the regulation also establishes an EU database of (standalone) high-risk systems which somewhat enhances transparency, yet it remains to be seen to which extent this will be helpful for those subjected to the systems.

3.2.5 *Diversity, Non-Discrimination and Fairness*

The fifth key requirement of the HLEG Guidelines focuses on 'diversity, non-discrimination and fairness' and includes guidance on: (1) the avoidance of unfair bias; (2) ensuring the accessibility and universal design of AI systems (especially for people with disabilities); and (3) involving stakeholders in the systems' life cycle.[72] The first point is covered in Article 10 of the AI Act on 'data and data governance', while the second point is addressed by Article 16 of the AI Act which obliges providers of high-risk systems to 'ensure that the high-risk AI system complies with accessibility requirements in accordance with Directives (EU) 2016/2102 and (EU) 2019/882' which seek to improve the accessibility of certain products and services for people with a disability.[73] Note, however, that these provisions only apply to the limited category of systems that have been designated as 'high-risk' in the AI Act.

As to the third point, the AI Act arguably falls dolefully short of its potential, as stakeholders have only been allocated a marginal role in the regulation. In Article 67, the AI Act did set up an AI Advisory Forum which 'shall represent a balanced selection of stakeholders, including industry, start-ups, SMEs, civil society and academia',[74] but its functions are relatively limited. Other provisions on stakeholder inclusion primarily pertain to the standardization process and to the creation of voluntary codes of conduct.[75]

3.2.6 *Societal and Environmental Well-Being*

The sixth requirement of the HLEG Guidelines concerns 'societal and environmental well-being', addressing the need to ensure: (1) 'sustainable and environmentally

71. For a critique on the AI Act's focus on obligations rather than rights, and its limited transparency requirements, *see also* Smuha et al. 2021, 50.
72. HLEG Guidelines, at 18.
73. *See respectively* Web Accessibility Directive (WAD); and Accessibility Act.
74. *See* AIA, Art. 67(2).
75. *See, e.g.*, AIA, Arts 40 and 56(3).

friendly AI'; (2) to deal with AI's effects 'on institutions, democracy and society at large'; and (3) to tackle AI's social impact and the way in which it can affect people's physical and mental wellbeing.[76] While the third point is to some extent reflected in certain provisions of the AI Act (such as the prohibition in Article 5 of subliminal manipulation and the exploitation of vulnerabilities in a way that distorts a person's behaviour), the first point is virtually absent. During the AI Act's negotiations, the Parliament did seek to include some provisions to address AI's environmental footprint, yet this was not retained in the regulation's final version (except in the context of voluntary codes of conduct).

As to the second point, it can be noted that Annex III of the AI Act, which provides a list of high-risk systems, includes a heading on systems affecting the 'administration of justice and democratic processes'. Systems falling under this heading can hence potentially be considered high-risk and thus be subjected to the high-risk requirements. Currently, however, the heading only includes two applications, namely systems used by a judicial authority to assist it in researching and interpreting facts and the law; and systems used to influence the outcome of an election or referendum or the voting behaviour of natural persons when voting.[77] As explained elsewhere, this is not nearly enough to address the systemic and institutional risks that the scaled use of AI entails, for instance, to the rule of law,[78] and hence falls short of the HLEG Guidelines' requirements.

3.2.7 Accountability

The HLEG Guidelines' final key requirement, 'accountability', affirms the need to ensure that responsibility is taken for the implementation of all the other requirements. This need is reflected most clearly in the AI Act's obligation to set up a risk-management system for high-risk systems, enshrined in Article 9. The risk-management system consists of several steps to anticipate and mitigate risks, and:

> shall be understood as a continuous iterative process planned and run throughout the entire lifecycle of a high-risk AI system, requiring regular systematic review and updating.

As discussed elsewhere, this risk-mitigation approach is significantly flawed, yet it stems from the Commission's decision to base the AI Act on a market-oriented New Legislative Framework (NLF), which is typically used for product safety legislation, but entirely inapt to deal with fundamental rights concerns.[79]

76. *See* HLEG Guidelines, at 19.
77. *See* AIA, Annex III, point 8.
78. *See* Smuha 2024b, Ch. 5.4.
79. *See, e.g.*, Smuha & Yeung 2024. *See also* the critique in Smuha 2024b, Ch. 5.4; and in Veale & Zuiderveen Borgesius 2021.

The Guidelines' accountability requirement also entails the need to document and justify the trade-offs that are made when striving to implement the key requirements, which are likewise meant to be covered by the AI Act's risk-management system. Importantly, the HLEG added that:[80]

> in situations in which no ethically acceptable trade-offs can be identified, the development, deployment and use of the AI system should not proceed in that form.

Unfortunately, due to the AI Act's legalistic approach, it is rather unlikely for this conclusion to ever be reached, given that the AI Act enables these trade-offs to be made by the very providers whom the AI Act empowers with the decision to judge which risk is 'acceptable'.[81] And while, in theory, human rights law could still be invoked to prevent the development or use of a system that violates a fundamental right, in practice, the AI Act's risk-categorization (which already pre-emptively decided which systems are prohibited, high-risk, or uncovered by the regulation) makes it difficult to argue this, especially in light of the presumption of conformity that all high-risk system providers can benefit from when they adopt harmonized standards or common specifications.[82]

In addition, the HLEG Guidelines point out the need to minimize and report AI systems' negative impact, and to protect whistle-blowers, NGOs, trade unions or other entities when reporting legitimate concerns about an AI system.[83] In this regard, the AI Act contains an obligation for (certain) AI providers to report serious incidents.[84] Moreover, Recital 172 of the regulation provides that:

> persons acting as whistleblowers on the infringements of this Regulation should be protected under the Union law. Directive (EU) 2019/1937 of the European Parliament and of the Council[85] should therefore apply to the reporting of infringements of this Regulation and the protection of persons reporting such infringements.

Finally, the HLEG also defined the accountability requirement as encompassing the need to ensure the auditability of AI systems, noting that:

> in applications affecting fundamental rights, including safety-critical applications, AI systems should be able to be independently audited.

The AI Act, however, does not establish the need to conduct *ex ante* external audits of AI systems – neither when it concerns a high-risk system nor when it concerns a (systemic risk-posing) general-purpose artificial intelligence (GPAI) model. It does,

80. *See* HLEG Guidelines, 20.
81. *See* AIA, Art. 9(5).
82. *See* the critique on this point in Smuha 2024c.
83. *See* HLEG Guidelines, 20.
84. *See, e.g.,* AIA, Art. 73.
85. [Whistleblowing Directive].

however, facilitate *ex post* audits in case something goes wrong, based on the technical documentation and record-keeping requirements of Articles 11 and 12.

3.3 The Guidelines as Guidance for Voluntary Codes of Conduct

Beyond the requirements imposed on high-risk systems pursuant to Chapter III, section 2 of the AI Act, the regulation also refers to the HLEG Guidelines' seven key requirements in Article 95, which deals with 'codes of conduct for the voluntary application of specific requirements'. For systems that do not fall under the high-risk category, the EU legislator sought to incentivize the voluntary implementation of the requirements it imposes on high-risk systems by drawing up codes of conduct, which will be facilitated by the newly established European Artificial Intelligence Office (AI Office) and the Member States. These codes of conduct should take:

> into account the available technical solutions and industry best practices allowing for the application of such requirements.

Article 95(2) sets out the elements that can be taken into account when drawing up the voluntary codes of conduct. Among these elements are those 'provided for in Union ethical guidelines for trustworthy AI', by which the legislator presumably intended to denote the HLEG Guidelines. It is also in this context that the assessment and minimization of AI systems' impact on the environment (covered by the HLEG Guidelines' sixth requirement) can play a role.

Other elements listed in Article 95(2) which echo the Guidelines are the facilitation of inclusive and diverse design teams, 'including through the establishment of inclusive and diverse development teams and the promotion of stakeholders' participation in that process'; and an assessment of the 'negative impact of AI systems on vulnerable persons or groups of vulnerable persons, including as regards accessibility for persons with a disability, as well as on gender equality'. In other words, some aspects of the HLEG Guidelines' key requirements that were not taken up in the AI Act's legal requirements, have nevertheless found their way to the AI Act through the voluntary codes of conduct it seeks to promote.

3.4 The Guidelines as General Normative Principles

Finally, the fact that Recital 27 of the AI Act is specifically dedicated to the role and content of the Guidelines' key requirements also affirms their position as the more general normative backbone of the regulation. At the same time, the recital also acknowledges the way in which the AI Act diverges from the Guidelines. Indeed, it notes that:

> while the risk-based approach is the basis for a proportionate and effective set of binding rules, it is important to recall the 2019 Ethics guidelines for trustworthy AI developed by the independent HLEG appointed by the Commission. In those guidelines, the HLEG developed seven non-binding ethical principles for AI which are intended to help ensure that AI is trustworthy and ethically sound.

This statement seems to contrast the HLEG Guidelines' rights and principles-based approach with the AI Act's risk and list-based approach – and rightfully so.

While the HLEG Guidelines do mention that certain high-risk contexts require more stringent measures in proportion to the risk posed thereby, they start from the assumption that the key requirements for Trustworthy AI should apply, to a greater or lesser extent, to *all* AI systems. This is also clear from HLEG Guidelines' statement that:[86]

> while all requirements are of equal importance, context and potential tensions between them will need to be taken into account when applying them across different domains and industries. Implementation of these requirements should occur throughout an AI system's entire life cycle and depends on the specific application. While most requirements apply to all AI systems, special attention is given to those directly or indirectly affecting individuals. Therefore, for some applications (for instance in industrial settings), they may be of lesser relevance.

In other words, while context certainly plays a role when it comes to the way in which the key requirements for Trustworthy AI should be implemented, they must always be taken into consideration when designing, developing or deploying AI systems.

This is also why, as already noted above, the Guidelines state that:[87]

> in situations in which no ethically acceptable trade-offs can be identified, the development, deployment and use of the AI system should not proceed in that form.

In essence, the Guidelines propose that AI systems should always undergo a tailored assessment to verify whether the trade-offs that are made in the system's context are acceptable, meaning, in line with fundamental rights, democracy and the rule of law, and that they should not be used if this is not the case. The AI Act, instead, carefully delineates the (high-risk) systems upon which the requirements are imposed, in an exhaustive and *ex ante* manner. If an application is not listed in the high-risk Annex, the requirements for Trustworthy AI simply do not apply, even if the system is deeply problematic and does not allow for a trade-off that does not infringe fundamental rights.

The fact that Recital 27 of the AI Act invokes the Guidelines in a more general fashion and that it describes each of the seven key requirements in turn, can hence be seen as a way to at least acknowledge their underlying normative role in the regulation, by stating that (regardless of any risk-level) the Guidelines' principles 'should be translated, when possible, in the design and use of AI models'. While this is a rather weak formulation, it is arguably nevertheless of symbolic value as it explicitly anchors the HLEG Guidelines' substantive framework within the AI Act.

86. HLEG Guidelines, 15.
87. *Ibid.*, 20.

4 THE POLICY AND INVESTMENT RECOMMENDATIONS FOR TRUSTWORTHY AI

4.1 Core Concepts and Structure

Before concluding this contribution, I should also briefly discuss the influence of the HLEG's second deliverable, the Policy Recommendations. Though less known, these recommendations likewise contributed to the Union's AI policy: they enabled the HLEG to move beyond non-binding guidelines and also suggested the need for new binding rules. To ensure consistency across its deliverables, and to link both documents with each other, the HLEG purposely decided to keep the emphasis on 'Trustworthy AI' as a compass towards which EU policy and investment decisions should be oriented. As the group stated in the introduction of the Policy Recommendations, the HLEG Guidelines:[88]

> constituted a first important step in identifying the type of AI that we want and do not want for Europe, but that is not enough to ensure that Europe can also materialise the beneficial impact that Trustworthy AI can bring. Taking the next step, this document contains our proposed Policy and Investment Recommendations for Trustworthy AI, addressed to EU institutions and Member States.

In terms of structure, the Policy Recommendations consist of eight chapters. The first four discuss the areas in which AI can have a beneficial impact, while the last four discuss the enablers that can help achieve this potential. One of the identified enablers is 'appropriate governance and regulation'. Indeed, the HLEG considered that:[89]

> ensuring Trustworthy AI necessitates an appropriate governance and regulatory framework. By appropriate, we mean a framework that promotes socially valuable AI development and deployment, ensures and respects fundamental rights, the rule of law and democracy, while safeguarding individuals and society from unacceptable harm.

The group conceded that establishing such a framework, and ensuring the protection of EU values while maintaining its global competitiveness is not an easy task, especially given that:[90]

> little evidence is available to inform policy-making, due to the novelty of the technology, the lack of thorough and systematic understanding of its impacts and associated business models, and the unpredictability of its uptake, development and evolution even in the short term.

Notwithstanding this concession, the group put forward four general action-categories that EU institutions and Member States should pursue when developing AI regulation: (1) adopt a risk-based and multi-stakeholder approach; (2) evaluate and potentially revise EU laws; (3) consider the need for new regulation to protect against adverse

88. Policy Recommendations, 6.
89. *Ibid.*, at 37.
90. *Ibid.*

impacts; and (4) consider whether existing institutional structures, competences and capacities require revision to ensure proportionate and effective protection. Under each of those action-categories, the HLEG listed a set of concrete recommendations to promote their achievement. In what follows, I will focus on the recommendations that are most relevant to the context of the AI Act, without being exhaustive.

4.2 A (Different) Risk-Based Approach

The HLEG's most characteristic recommendation was to adopt a 'risk-based approach' to AI regulation, which is ultimately the approach adopted in the AI Act. However, as already pointed out above, there are many different ways in which a risk-based approach can be implemented, and the one adopted by the EU legislator does not appear to align with what the HLEG had in mind. Granted, when proposing a risk-based approach, the Policy Recommendations noted that:[91]

> the character, intensity and timing of regulatory intervention should be a function of the type of risk created by an AI system. In line with an approach based on the proportionality and precautionary principle, various risk classes should be distinguished as not all risks are equal. The higher the impact and/or probability of an AI-created risk, the stronger the appropriate regulatory response should be.

Yet the HLEG's reference to the precautionary principle and the recommendations that accompany its suggestion for a 'risk-based approach' made it clear that it did not suggest a product-safety-based, prescriptive and legalistic take on this approach like the one taken in the AI Act.

First, the group clarified that 'risk' should be broadly defined to encompass adverse impacts of all kinds, both individual and societal, including:[92]

> not only tangible risks to human health or the environment, but also includes intangible risks to fundamental rights, democracy and the rule of law, and other potential threats to the cultural and socio-technical foundations of democratic, rights-respecting, societies.

In other words, the HLEG's concept of risk is far broader than the one used in the AI Act.[93]

Second, rather than proposing a rigid checklist of requirements that would apply to a priorly identified category of high-risk systems, the Policy Recommendations suggested to 'foster a principle-based approach to regulation'.[94] Indeed:[95]

> unnecessarily prescriptive regulation should be avoided. In contexts characterised by rapid technological change, it is often preferable to adopt a principled-based approach, as well as outcome-based policies, subject to appropriate monitoring and enforcement.

91. *See ibid.*, at 38.
92. *Ibid.*
93. *See also* the discussion thereof in Smuha 2024c, Ch. 5.4; and more generally in Smuha 2021a.
94. Policy Recommendations, 38.
95. *Ibid.*

A principle-based approach could have limited the risk that compliance with the AI Act would turn into a red-taped ticking-the-box exercise. While templates and technical standards certainly make it easier for companies to comply with the AI Act's requirements, they are notoriously loopholed and do not necessarily ensure that the EU's values are protected, or that the risks identified by the HLEG are duly addressed.[96]

Third, the HLEG recommended that:[97]

> for specific AI applications that generate 'unacceptable' risks or pose threats of harm that are substantial, a precautionary principle-based approach should be adopted instead.

Granted, the AI Act does include a category of prohibited AI systems in Article 5. To some extent, this also corresponds to the HLEG's suggestion that the EU legislator should:[98]

> examine the need for new regulation to address the critical concerns listed in our Ethics Guidelines for Trustworthy AI. ... In particular, individuals should not be subject to unjustified personal, physical or mental tracking or identification, profiling and nudging through AI powered methods of biometric recognition such as: emotional tracking, empathic media, DNA, iris and behavioural identification, affect recognition, voice and facial recognition and the recognition of micro-expressions. Exceptional use of such technologies, such as for national security purposes, must be evidence based, necessary and proportionate, as well as respectful of fundamental rights.

However, the prohibited practices listed in Article 5 of the AI Act constitute an exhaustive and non-amendable category, which is already under-inclusive and does not correspond to the idea of adopting a precautionary and principle-based approach that allows for the future integration of new problematic practices. While it is not unthinkable that in the next few years novel AI applications will arise that are incompatible with the EU's values and pose an unacceptable risk, the AI Act's architecture does not provide a good solution for this problem.[99]

Fourth, the Policy Recommendations also suggested that:[100]

> questions about the kinds of risks deemed unacceptable must be deliberated and decided upon by the community at large through open, transparent and accountable deliberation, taking into account the EU's legal framework and obligations under the Charter of Fundamental Rights.

However, the AI practices which are deemed unacceptable are already exhaustively listed in the AI Act, and this list cannot be altered without re-opening the legislative procedure.[101] Moreover, also beyond the prohibited practices, stakeholder participation

96. *See also* the critique on the AI Act's approach in Smuha & Yeung 2024.
97. *Ibid.*
98. Policy Recommendations, 40.
99. *See in this regard also* the criticism in Smuha & Yeung 2024.
100. Policy Recommendations, 38.
101. Indeed, contrary to the systems designated as 'high-risk', which are listed in the AI Act's Annexes, the prohibitions of Art. 5 cannot be periodically amended by the Commission.

in the AI Act is rather limited. As noted above, the establishment of the AI Advisory Forum in Article 67 did facilitate, to some extent, the HLEG's recommendation to:[102]

> institutionalise a dialogue on AI policy with affected stakeholders to define red lines and discuss AI applications that may risk generating unacceptable harms, including applications that should be prohibited and/or tightly regulated or in specific situations where the risk for people's rights and freedoms would be too high and the impact of this technology would be detrimental to individuals or society as a whole.

Yet the role that was assigned to the AI Advisory Forum is far more limited than what the HLEG recommended, and it remains to be seen which role this Forum will play in practice.

4.3 Other Relevant Recommendations

The HLEG Guidelines only focused on the 'ethical' and 'robust' components of Trustworthy AI. However, in the Policy Recommendations, the HLEG strongly emphasized that ensuring the 'lawful' component of Trustworthy AI is as important. As regards AI systems used by the public sector, the group suggested making the implementation of the key requirements for Trustworthy AI always mandatory (particularly through the ALTAI's concrete action-questions).[103] This did not happen, as only systems explicitly included in the 'high-risk' category of the AI Act are subject to those requirements.

For AI systems deployed by the private sector that 'have the potential to have a significant impact on human lives, for example by interfering with an individual's fundamental rights at any stage of the AI system's life cycle and for safety-critical applications',[104] the HLEG recommended the EU legislator to consider the need to introduce:

(1) an obligation to conduct a trustworthy AI assessment (including a fundamental rights impact assessment (FRIA) which also covers, for example, the rights of children, the rights of individuals in relation to the state, and the rights of persons with disabilities);
(2) an obligation to conduct stakeholder consultations, including a consultation with relevant authorities;
(3) traceability, auditability and *ex ante* oversight requirements; and
(4) an obligation to ensure appropriate by default and by design procedures to enable effective and immediate redress in case of mistakes, harms and/or other rights infringements.

102. Policy Recommendations, 41.
103. *Ibid.*, at 20.
104. *Ibid.*, at 40.

To what extent have these rather concrete suggestions been mirrored in the AI Act? While providers of high-risk systems (which can roughly be equated with 'systems that have a significant impact on human lives') have an obligation to set up a risk and quality management system, this is not the same as the obligation to conduct an assessment of the way in which their system can affect fundamental rights. As noted previously, the AI Act does include, in Article 27, a provision on mandatory FRIAs, but this is only limited to a subset of (mainly public) AI deployers. The AI Act also does not mandate high-risk system providers to carry out stakeholder consultations (regardless of their private or public nature).

As discussed above, the regulation does impose, however, traceability, auditability and *ex ante* oversight requirements. Moreover, it does not explicitly mandate high-risk AI providers or deployers to establish redress mechanisms for those adversely affected by the system, but it does establish a public enforcement mechanism which not only facilitates compliance monitoring but also enhances the possibility of redress. In fact, while this right was absent in the AI Act's original proposal, Article 85 of the regulation's final version now explicitly includes a 'right to lodge a complaint with a market surveillance authority' whenever someone has grounds to consider there was an infringement of the regulation, and this without prejudice to existing administrative or judicial remedies.

Finally, anticipating that AI governance would become ever more important and complex, the HLEG suggested that:[105]

> the European Union should consider the setting up [of] an institutional structure for Trustworthy AI to fill an existing governance gap.

Wary of the possible national fragmentation of AI rules, which would not only weaken the Union's single market but could also undermine the protection of people's rights, the HLEG recommended that such an institutional structure be created at the EU level, and suggested several tasks for it to take on.[106] Conversely, the Commission's original proposal of the AI Act exclusively attributed enforcement competences to national supervisory authorities, with the 'European AI Board' merely bringing national representatives together to exchange best practices. Yet this changed under the impetus of both the Council and the Parliament, who envisaged a much stronger role for the EU. They not only bolstered the European Artificial Intelligence Board's (AI Board's) role in Article 66, but they also set up an AI Office in Article 64, which has been granted specific enforcement tasks for highly impactful AI applications, thus resulting in more alignment with the HLEG's Policy Recommendations.

5 CONCLUSION

In this contribution, I analysed the impact of the HLEG's work on the AI Act. I explained how the HLEG Guidelines for Trustworthy AI served as the regulation's

105. *Ibid.*, at 42.
106. *See ibid.*, particularly under point 30.5.

precursor, and discussed the role that these Guidelines still play within the EU's regulatory framework for AI. The AI Act's explicit reference to the Guidelines' key requirements evokes their role as a normative compass for Europe's AI regulation, as a basis for future soft law through the establishment of voluntary codes of conduct, and as inspiration for many of the AI Act's substantive provisions.

The impact of the HLEG Guidelines' key requirements is most visible when looking at the *legal* requirements that the AI Act imposes on high-risk AI systems in Chapter III, section 2, but can also be seen in the list of prohibited AI practices in Article 5, and in the list of AI systems that require additional transparency measures in Article 50. At the same time, despite these similarities, I discussed the numerous instances in which the AI Act deviated from both the letter and the spirit of the Guidelines, reflecting some dissonances between both approaches.

I also reflected on the role played by the HLEG's Policy Recommendations, which offered concrete advice on the need for new binding legislation and likewise contributed to EU AI policymaking. While some of the recommendations – in one form or another – do seem to have influenced the regulation's structure and content, others were clearly not taken up by the legislator. Moreover, I pointed out the discrepancies between the regulatory methodology suggested by the HLEG, and the choices that the EU legislator ultimately made. Unlike the HLEG Guidelines, the Policy Recommendations are not explicitly mentioned in the AI Act and received less attention from stakeholders,[107] making the exact impact they had uncertain. That said, the HLEG Guidelines and the Policy Recommendations are complementary to each other,[108] and their relevance and meaning can hence best be understood by considering them holistically and interconnectedly.

Furthermore, in addition to the direct influence of these deliverables on the AI Act, it should be pointed out that the HLEG's work sparked a broader debate on Europe's AI policy, and particularly on who should contribute thereto, on which terms, through which medium, and with which result. The public consultation organized by the HLEG both on the HLEG Guidelines and the ALTAI also fed into the Commission's preparatory work on the regulation and further ignited reflection on the most adequate position for Europe to take in the global regulatory arena for AI. Only time will tell what the societal impact of this position will be, and whether Europe's new AI regulation will live up to its aims. Undoubtedly, however, this position has been co-shaped by the HLEG's work, and the group's legacy will continue to live on, in one way or another, through the AI Act.

107. That said, the Policy Recommendations did receive occasional scholarly scrutiny. *See, e.g.*, Veale 2020.
108. *See in this regard also* Smuha 2019, 102.

BIBLIOGRAPHY

Guidelines of Authorities

Beijing AI Academy 2019: Beijing Academy of Artificial Intelligence, *Beijing Artificial Intelligence Principles* (2019), ai-ethics-and-governance.institute/beijing-artificial-intelligence-principles (accessed 14 May 2024).

Data Ethics Commission 2019: Data Ethics Commission of the Federal Government Federal Ministry of the Interior, Building and Community, *Opinion of the Data Ethics Commission* (Berlin, December 2019), www.bmi.bund.de/SharedDocs/downloads/EN/themen/it-digital-policy/datenethikkommission-abschlussgutachten-lang.pdf (accessed 14 May 2024).

EGE 2018: European Group on Ethics in Science and New Technologies (EGE), *Statement on Artificial Intelligence, Robotics and 'Autonomous' Systems*, Commission – Directorate-General for Research and Innovation (9 March 2018), op.europa.eu/en/publication-detail/-/publication/dfebe62e-4ce9-11e8-be1d-01aa75ed71a1 (accessed 14 May 2024).

G20 2019: G20, *AI Principles for Responsible Stewardship of Trustworthy AI*, Ministerial Statement on Trade and Digital Economy (2019), wp.oecd.ai/app/uploads/2021/06/G20-AI-Principles.pdf (accessed 14 May 2024).

HLEG Guidelines.

HLEG Policy Recommendations: HLEG, *Policy and Investment Recommendations for Trustworthy AI* (Commission, 26 June 2019), digital-strategy.ec.europa.eu/en/library/policy-and-investment-recommendations-trustworthy-artificial-intelligence (accessed 14 May 2024).

Japan Council 2019: Japan Integrated Innovation Strategy Promotion Council, *Social Principles of Human-Centric AI* (2019), www.cas.go.jp/jp/seisaku/jinkouchinou/pdf/humancentricai.pdf (accessed 14 May 2024).

PDPC 2019: Singapore Personal Data Protection Commission, *Model Artificial Intelligence Governance Framework* (2019), www.pdpc.gov.sg/-/media/files/pdpc/pdf-files/resource-for-organisation/ai/sgmodelaigovframework2.pdf (accessed 14 May 2024).

UNESCO Recommendation.

Reports and Recommendations

AI Watch 2021: AI Watch, *National Strategies on Artificial Intelligence: A European Perspective – 2021 Edition*, European Commission Joint Research Centre (September 2021), ai-watch.ec.europa.eu/countries/france/france-ai-strategy-report_en (accessed 14 May 2024).

CAHAI 2021: Council of Europe's Ad Hoc Committee on Artificial Intelligence (CAHAI), *Possible Elements of a Legal Framework on Artificial Intelligence, Based on the Council of Europe's Standards on Human Rights, Democracy and the Rule of Law*, Council of Europe (Strasbourg, 3 December 2021), rm.coe.int/possible-elements-of-a-legal-framework-on-artificial-intelligence/1680a5ae6b (accessed 14 May 2024).

CAHAI 2020: Council of Europe's Ad Hoc Committee on Artificial Intelligence (CAHAI), *Feasibility Study on a Legal Framework on AI Design, Development and Application Based on Council of Europe's Standards* Council of Europe (Strasbourg, 17 December 2020), rm.coe.int/cahai-2020-23-final-eng-feasibility-study-/1680a0c6da (accessed 14 May 2024).

CAI 2024: Council of Europe's Committee on AI (CAI), *Draft Framework Convention on Artificial Intelligence, Human Rights, Democracy and the Rule of Law*, Council of Europe Committee of Ministers (Strasbourg, 2024), rm.coe.int/-1493-10-1b-committee-on-artificial-intelligence-cai-b-draft-framework/1680aee411 (accessed 14 May 2024).

Commission 2019: Commission, *Building Trust in Human-Centric Artificial Intelligence* (Brussels, 8 April 2019), COM(2019) 168 final.

Commission 2018: Commission, *Artificial Intelligence for Europe* (Brussels, 25 April 2018), COM/2018/237 final.

Commission's White Paper on AI.

von der Leyen 2019: Ursula von der Leyen, *A Union That Strives for More: My Agenda for Europe, Political Guidelines for the Next European Commission 2019-2024* (July 2019), www.europarl.europa.eu/resources/library/media/20190716RES57231/20190716RES57231.pdf (accessed 14 May 2024).

Academic Writings

Ala-Pietilä & Smuha 2021: Pekka Ala-Pietilä & Nathalie A. Smuha, *A Framework for Global Cooperation on Artificial Intelligence and Its Governance, in Reflections on Artificial Intelligence for Humanity*, 237-265 (Bertrand Braunschweig & Malik Ghallab eds, Springer International Publishing 2021).

Bradford 2020: Anu Bradford, *The Brussels Effect: How the European Union Rules the World* (Oxford University Press, 2020).

Hagendorff 2020: Thilo Hagendorff, *The Ethics of AI Ethics: An Evaluation of Guidelines*, 30 Minds and Machines 99-120 (2020), doi.org/10.1007/s11023-020-09517-8.

Hickok 2021: Merve Hickok, *Lessons Learned from AI Ethics Principles for Future Actions*, 1 AI Ethics 41-47 (2021), doi.org/10.1007/s43681-020-00008-1.

Jobin et al. 2019: Anna Jobin, Marco Ienca & Effy Vayena, *The Global Landscape of AI Ethics Guidelines*, 1 Nature Machine Intelligence 389-399 (2019), doi.org/10.1038/s42256-019-0088-2.

Lee 2018: Kai-Fu Lee, *AI Superpowers: China, Silicon Valley, and the New World Order* (1st ed., Boston, Houghton Mifflin Harcourt 2018).

Mittelstadt 2019: Brent Mittelstadt, *Principles Alone Cannot Guarantee Ethical AI*, 1 Nature Machine Intelligence 501-507 (2019), doi.org/10.1038/s42256-019-0114-4.

Smuha 2024a: Nathalie A. Smuha, *Vijf(Tig) Tinten AI-Ethiek*, Karakter – Tijdschrift van de Wetenschap 85 (2024), www.tijdschriftkarakter.be/vijftig-tinten-ai-ethiek (accessed 14 May 2024).

Smuha 2024b: Nathalie A. Smuha, *Algorithmic Rule by Law: How Algorithmic Regulation in the Public Sector Erodes the Rule of Law* (Cambridge University Press 2025).

Smuha 2024c: Nathalie A. Smuha, *The Paramountcy of Data Protection Law in the Age of AI (Acts), in Two Decades of Personal Data Protection. What Next?* (European Data Protection Supervisor, Brussels, 2024).

Smuha 2023: Nathalie A. Smuha, *Digital Sovereignty in the European Union: Five Challenges from a Normative Perspective*, Social Science Research Network (SSRN) (July 2023), ssrn.com/abstract=4501591 (accessed 14 May 2024), doi.org/10.2139/ssrn.4501591.

Smuha 2021a: Nathalie A. Smuha, *Beyond the Individual: Governing AI's Societal Harm*, 10 Internet Policy Review No. 3 (2021), doi.org/10.14763/2021.3.1574.

Smuha 2021b: Nathalie A. Smuha, *From a 'Race to AI' to a 'Race to AI Regulation': Regulatory Competition for Artificial Intelligence*, 13 Law, Innovation and Technology 57-84 (2021), doi.org/10.1080/17579961.2021.1898300.

Smuha 2019: Nathalie A. Smuha, *The EU Approach to Ethics Guidelines for Trustworthy Artificial Intelligence*, 20 Computer Law Review International 97-106 (2019), doi.org/10.9785/cri-2019-200402.

Smuha & Yeung 2024: Nathalie A. Smuha & Karen Yeung, *The European Union's AI Act: Beyond Motherhood and Apple Pie*, in *The Cambridge Handbook of the Law, Ethics and Policy of Artificial Intelligence* (Nathalie A. Smuha ed., Cambridge University Press forthcoming), Social Science Research Network (SSRN) (June 2024), ssrn.com/abstract=4874852 (accessed 15 July 2024).

Smuha et al. 2021: Nathalie A. Smuha et al., *How the EU Can Achieve Legally Trustworthy AI: A Response to the European Commission's Proposal for an Artificial Intelligence Act*, Social Science Research Network (August 2021), ssrn.com/abstract=3899991 (accessed 14 May 2024), doi.org/10.2139/ssrn.3899991.

Veale 2020: Michael Veale, *A Critical Take on the Policy Recommendations of the EU High-Level Expert Group on Artificial Intelligence*, 11 European Journal of Risk Regulation 1-10 (2020), doi.org/10.1017/err.2019.65.

Veale & Zuiderveen Borgesius 2021: Michael Veale & Frederik Zuiderveen Borgesius, *Demystifying the Draft EU Artificial Intelligence Act*, 22 Computer Law Review International 97-112 (2021), doi.org/10.31235/osf.io/38p5f.

Wagner 2019: Ben Wagner, *Ethics As an Escape From Regulation. From 'Ethics-Washing' To Ethics-Shopping?*, in *Being Profiled*, Cogitas Ergo Sum 84-89 (Emre Bayamlioglu et al. eds, Amsterdam University Press 2018).

Whittlestone et al. 2019: Jess Whittlestone et al., *The Role and Limits of Principles in AI Ethics: Towards a Focus on Tensions. In Proceedings of the 2019 AAAI/ACM Conference on AI, Ethics, and Society*, Association for Computing Machinery 195-200 (New York, 2019).

Others

Allen & Castro 2017: Doug Allen & Daniel Castro, *Why So Sad? A Look at the Change in Tone of Technology Reporting From 1986 to 2013*, Information Technology and

Innovation Foundation (February 2017), www2.itif.org/2017-why-so-sad.pdf? (accessed 14 May 2024).

DG Connect 2018a: DG Connect, *Call for Applications for the Selection of Members of the High-Level Expert Group on Artificial Intelligence* (Brussels, 9 March 2018), ec.europa.eu/transparency/expert-groups-register/core/api/front/calls-application/11665/download (accessed 14 May 2024).

DG Connect 2018b: DG Connect, *Concept Note on the High-Level Expert Group on AI* (Brussels, 27 July 2018), ec.europa.eu/futurium/en/system/files/ged/concept_note_on_the_ai_hlg_0.pdf (accessed 14 May 2024).

Harari 2019: Yuval Noah Harari, *Who Will Win the Race for AI?*, Foreign Policy Blog (2019), foreignpolicy.com/gt-essay/who-will-win-the-race-for-ai-united-states-china-data (accessed 14 May 2024).

IBM 2018: IBM, *IBM's Principles for Trust and Transparency* (2018), www.ibm.com/policy/wp-content/uploads/2018/06/IBM_Principles_SHORT.V4.3.pdf (accessed 14 May 2024).

OECD 2019: OECD, *Forty-Two Countries Adopt New OECD Principles on Artificial Intelligence* (22 May 2019), www.oecd.org/science/forty-two-countries-adopt-new-oecd-principles-on-artificial-intelligence.htm (accessed 14 May 2024).

OECD 2018: OECD, *OECD Creates Expert Group to Foster Trust in Artificial Intelligence* (Paris, 13 September 2018), www.oecd.org/innovation/oecd-creates-expert-group-to-foster-trust-in-artificial-intelligence.htm (accessed 14 May 2024).

Pichai 2018: Sundar Pichai, *AI at Google: Our Principles*, Google Blog (7 June 2018), blog.google/technology/ai/ai-principles (accessed 14 May 2024).

Rossi 2020: Francesca Rossi, *How IBM Is Working Toward a Fairer AI*, Harvard Business Review (5 November 2020), hbr.org/2020/11/how-ibm-is-working-toward-a-fairer-ai (accessed 14 May 2024).

Simonite 2019: Tom Simonite, *How Tech Companies Are Shaping the Rules Governing AI*, Wired (16 May 2019), www.wired.com/story/how-tech-companies-shaping-rules-governing-ai (accessed 14 May 2024).

Wylie 2019: Christopher Wylie, *Mindf*ck: Cambridge Analytica and the Plot to Break America* (Random House, 2019).

CHAPTER 4

Genesis of the Artificial Intelligence Act: When AI Beats the Imitation Game

Christof Koolen

1 INTRODUCTION

Only a few phenomena have triggered legal and ethical questions quite like the development of artificial intelligence (AI). What began as simple constructs designed to solve number-crunching problems has evolved into complex and intricate systems capable of interacting with speech, language, and vision. From generating images to writing code and solving logic puzzles: the current sentiment surrounding AI models is a blend of both excitement and fear.[1] On the positive end of the spectrum, AI promises to profoundly impact our lives, whether by aiding in drug development,[2] designing new materials,[3] or helping to combat climate change.[4] On the negative end of the spectrum, however, these very same AI systems can just as easily contribute to the spread of misinformation, aid in the design of deadly pathogens, and play a role in military applications.

If anything, AI is poised to transform our relationship with technology. Its recent resurgence therefore raises a pertinent question: *how to ensure that AI neither evolves into a tool of wrongdoing nor poses a threat to humanity?* While doomsday scenarios may be exaggerated, the question should nonetheless be taken seriously, as the capabilities of AI models are clearly outrunning those of their human creators. With AI increasingly mimicking human skills to an eerie degree, and with fundamental human

1. The Economist 2023, 9-10.
2. Mock et al. 2023, 468.
3. Henshall 2023.
4. Cowls et al. 2023, 284-285; Stein 2020, 898-900.

rights and values hanging in the balance, a serious discussion about the regulation of AI is necessary. While calls for regulatory action were voiced across the globe, the governance of AI has proven challenging, in part due to the speed of AI developments, ambivalence about the precise nature of AI, and uncertainty about how AI should be regulated. As a result, questions linger as to how lawmakers should address AI, its uses, and its consequences.

In Europe, efforts were launched as early as 2018 to find appropriate answers to these questions. Six years later, on 13 March 2024, these questions were finally answered with the adoption of the AI Act. Together with, among others, the General Data Protection Regulation (GDPR), the Digital Markets Act (DMA) and Digital Services Act (DSA), the Data Governance Act (DGA) and Data Act (DA), the adoption of the AI Act is expected to further cement the European Union's (EU's) position as a global leader in setting rules for the digital world.

It is against this backdrop that this book sets out to contribute to a better understanding of the regulation of AI in Europe. By way of introduction, this chapter seeks to contextualize the topic of AI, provide further background information on some of the main AI developments and, more importantly, relate the AI Act to several other ongoing or completed legislative initiatives in the EU.

To attain these objectives, the chapter is divided into six sections. Following this introductory section, section 2 takes a brief look back on the development of AI and sheds light on the advances in computer power and the availability of data. Section 3 then touches on the legislative history of the AI Act. Section 4 subsequently expands on the core underpinnings and main principles of the AI Act. Section 5 then frames the AI Act in relation to several other legal instruments, notably the GDPR (subsection 5.1), the DGA (subsection 5.2), the DA (subsection 5.3), the DMA (subsection 5.4), and the DSA (subsection 5.5). Section 6 concludes the chapter.

2 A BRIEF LOOK BACKWARDS ON AI

2.1 Beating the Imitation Game

The origins of AI date back to the 1950s and the research of British mathematician Alan Turing. In the opening sentences of his seminal article entitled Computing Machinery and Intelligence, he poses the following fundamental question: 'Can machines think?'[5] Throughout the article, Turing elaborated on a methodological thought framework that could be used to determine whether AI is distinguishable from human intelligence. Fundamentally, he proposed playing a game with three different players placed in different rooms: a human, a machine, and an interrogator.[6] The goal of the interrogator is to pose questions to the other two players in order to determine who is human and

5. Turing 1950, 433.
6. *Ibid.*, at 434.

who is machine. At the same time, both the human and the machine are tasked with trying to convince the interrogator that they are the human respondent. This test became known as the Turing Test, or more colloquially, the *Imitation Game.*[7]

Anno 2024, AI is capable of convincingly beating this Imitation Game. In many respects, the output of AI models is completely indistinguishable from human-generated output. What is more, the capabilities of AI models have even surpassed those of humans in several domains, notably in relation to reading comprehension, language understanding,[8] and image recognition.[9] In other words, in terms of quality, AI is capable of producing output that is at least as good as human output. More importantly, AI is currently also capable of engaging in behaviour that attracts legal consequences. A befitting example in this respect is the conclusion of contracts.[10] More macabre are situations where AI systems cause personal injury or even death.[11]

2.2 From AI Winter to AI Summer

While Alan Turing fairly accurately predicted that, in due time, machine intelligence would be able to convince its interrogator of its human-esque capabilities,[12] the journey of AI has not been without its problems. In fact, the history of AI has been defined by ups and downs, and by booms and busts: periods marked by high levels of optimism, followed by the realization that much-anticipated progress did not materialize.[13] Two particular periods – the 1974-1980 era[14] and the 1987-1994 era[15] – have been described in literature as *AI winters*, representing stretches of time when AI research went into hibernation for the better half of a decade (*see Figure 4.1*).[16]

7. In 2022, discussions about the Turing Test resurfaced in the press following (unsubstantiated) claims that Google's LaMDA (Language Model for Dialog Applications) chatbot had achieved 'sentience': Dave 2022; Reuters 2022; for an academic analysis of the Turing Test, *consider* Saygin et al. 2000.
8. Regarding AI benchmarks for language understanding, *see* Wang et al. 2018; Wang et al. 2019.
9. Kiela et al. 2024; Kiela et al. 2023.
10. *See, for example,* Herbosch 2023, 66-67, para. 79; and the references cited therein.
11. Consider, for instance, Atkinson 2023; Tesla 2016.
12. Turing 1950, at 442: 'I believe that in about fifty years' time it will be possible to programme computers … to make them play the imitation game so well that an average interrogator will not have more than 70 per cent, chance of making the right identification after five minutes of questioning. The original question, "Can machines think?" I believe to be too meaningless to deserve discussion.'
13. Duan et al. 2019, 63.
14. After an initial wave of excitement, it became clear that many of the problems that AI promised to solve could not yet be adequately framed from a computational point of view. The resulting pullback in funding for AI research was termed the first AI winter, which stretched from 1974 to 1980.
15. Interest in AI was renewed following the emergence of so-called expert systems, which replicated human decision-making in an 'if … then … else' format. However, the limitations of this type of conditional reasoning soon became apparent, leading to the second AI winter from 1987 to 1994.
16. Nilsson 2009, 408-409.

Figure 4.1 Evolution of AI Popularity over Time[17]

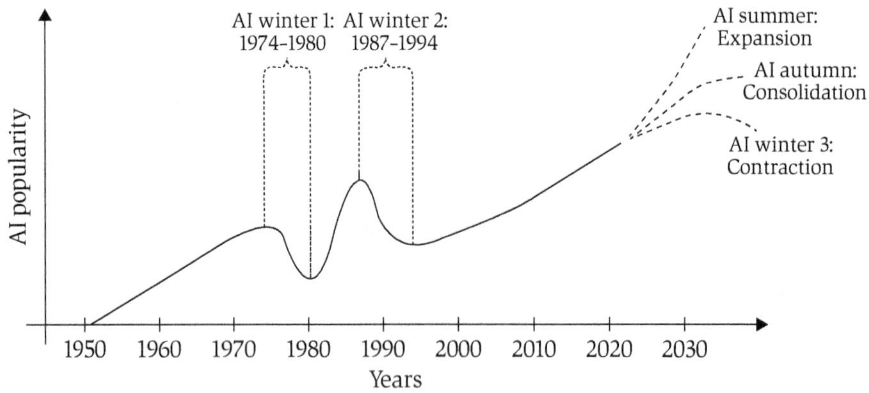

Over time, however, it became clear that problems previously thought impossible to solve with AI – whether due to a lack of computational power or due to challenges of computationally framing logic and reasoning – were slowly but surely coming within our grasp. As a result, the excitement surrounding AI rekindled during the late 1990s, with the famous defeat of Garry Kasparov by the computer chess-playing system Deep Blue in 1997 serving as one of the key highlights.[18]

During the 2010s, AI research branched out exponentially. Long gone are the times when AI systems rely on rule-based logic and the simple indexing and retrieval of knowledge. AI systems now have the ability to learn and improve their performance over time for certain tasks, they can interact with the intricate nuances of language, and convert complex inputs – such as speech and vision – into numerical representations. Currently, the state-of-the-art is focused on *deep learning*, a class of machine learning algorithms that uses artificial neural networks (ANNs) with multiple layers of 'depth' to extract high-level features from unstructured input data (*see Figure 4.2*).[19]

17. The visual is the author's own work, but was based on EPRS 2020, 5. Note, however, that the visual is primarily intended to illustrate how interest in AI has fluctuated over time, rather than to provide an accurate measure of AI's popularity.
18. Campbell et al. 2002, 57; readers interested in learning more about the development of Deep Blue may also consider Hsu 2002.
19. Foster & Friston 2023, 23; Kelleher 2019, 68; Goodfellow et al. 2016, 5-6.

Figure 4.2 Artificial Neural Network Consisting of Three Hidden Layers[20]

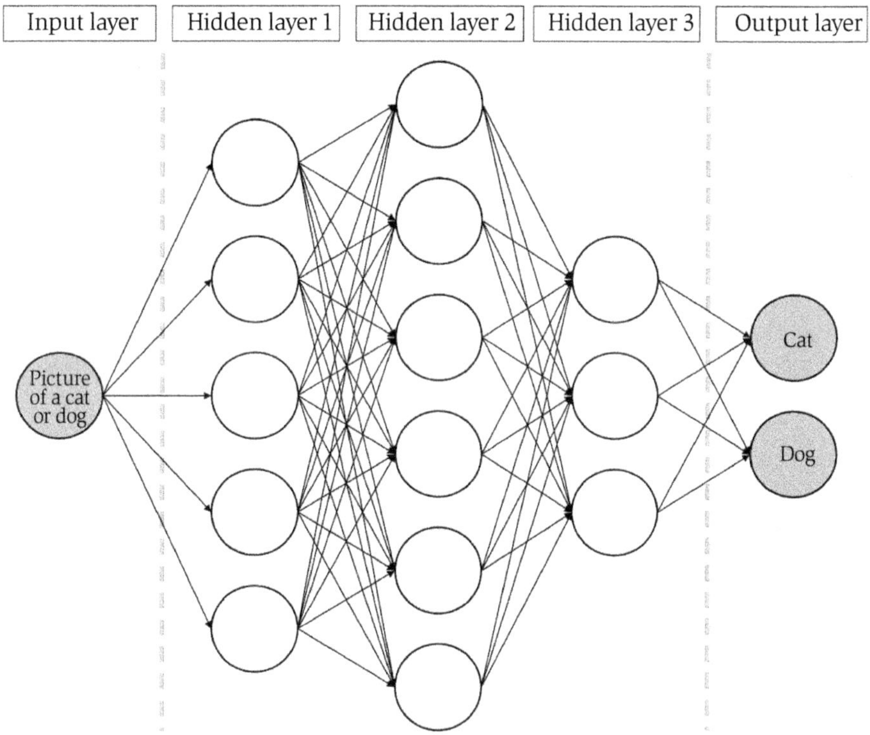

A key characteristic of these neural networks is their ability to independently learn which features are most relevant based on a given set of training data. The learning done by the neural network essentially involves optimizing its internal parameters (or *weights*) to maximize the probability of correctly treating new, unseen input data (e.g., classifying pictures of cats and dogs).[21] Over time, the field of deep learning has evolved into assorted subdisciplines, each of which focuses on a specific type of problem or application.[22]

20. The visual is the author's own work. When classifying images of cats and dogs using an ANN, the network automatically learns to identify features important for distinguishing between these two animals. In the early stages of training, the initial hidden layers (e.g., hidden layer 1) learn to recognize simple visual elements (e.g., colours, edges, lines). As the network passes through deeper hidden layers (e.g., hidden layer 3), these features are combined into more complex patterns specific to cats and dogs (e.g., shape and placement of the eyes and ears, texture of the hair coat, proportions of the animal's body). Ultimately, the network synthesizes all the extracted features from the different hidden layers to accurately classify an image as either a cat or a dog.
21. Kelleher 2019, 49-51.
22. For example, *autoencoders* are a particular type of ANN used to process unlabelled data, where the network learns to represent input data in a compressed manner and with fewer dimensions (i.e., encode) and then reconstruct the data as close as possible to the original input data (i.e.,

2.3 Advances in Computing Power and Availability of Data

Before delving into the legal developments, it is fair to ask what has caused the sudden resurgence of interest in AI. In this respect, the Commission points to two key drivers fuelling the current AI momentum: exponential increases in computing power and the increased availability of data.[23] Combined, these two dynamics create an ideal climate for AI to flourish and for AI systems to be applied to various facets of our lives.[24] To better understand this, it is worth taking a closer look at each of these factors individually.

2.3.1 *Computing Power*

When assessing computing power, the discussion quickly shifts to so-called *graphics processing units* (GPUs). While originally designed to render computer graphics, these chips are now increasingly being used for their general-purpose computing capabilities.[25] In essence, GPUs are architecturally optimized to be extremely efficient at performing calculations. When describing the computational capabilities of a GPU, the unit of measurement typically used is floating point operations per second (FLOPs). Fundamentally, floating point arithmetic involves applying basic arithmetic functions - such as additions, subtractions, multiplications, or divisions - to *floating point numbers*. Consider, for instance, the number 481, which can be re-expressed as a floating point number by rewriting it as a combination of an integer that is scaled by an exponent of a fixed base:[26]

$$481 = 48.1 \times 10^1 = 4.81 \times 10^2 = 0.481 \times 10^3$$

A single floating point operation could then look as follows:

$$0.481 \times 10^3 + 7.947 \times 10^3 = 8.428 \times 10^3$$

decode). *Generative adversarial networks* (GANs) are another type of ANN, where two different neural networks (a generator and a discriminator) are pitted against each other another in an effort to generate new data with the same statistical patterns as the training data. Also well-known are *convolutional neural networks* (CNNs), which are suited to grid-like data such as images, and *recurrent neural networks* (RNNs), which are used to process sequential data where the directional flow of information is important, such as natural language. *Transformers*, a deep learning architecture where text is represented in a numerical format called 'tokens', have also received a lot of attention recently and have seen widespread application in the context of training LLMs.

23. White Paper on AI, 2.
24. AIA, Rec. 3: 'AI systems can be easily deployed in a large variety of sectors of the economy and many parts of society, including across borders, and can easily circulate throughout the Union'.
25. The term general-purpose graphics processing unit (GPGPU) is often mentioned in this context.
26. In this sense, 'floating-point' refers to the simple fact that a number can be expressed in a decimal floating point form and that the decimal can quite literally float by changing the exponent of the fixed base.

The advantage of using floating point numbers instead of integers is that very small numbers and very large numbers can be expressed in a very compact and consistent format. As such, floating point numbers represent a good balance between, on the one hand, numerical precision and, on the other hand, numerical stability when dealing with a wide range of values.[27]

When looking at the evolution of GPUs, the number of FLOPs that a GPU chip can perform has increased exponentially over time (*see Figure 4.3*).

Figure 4.3 Evolution of Single GPU Computing Power over Time in Consumer-Grade GPUs[28]

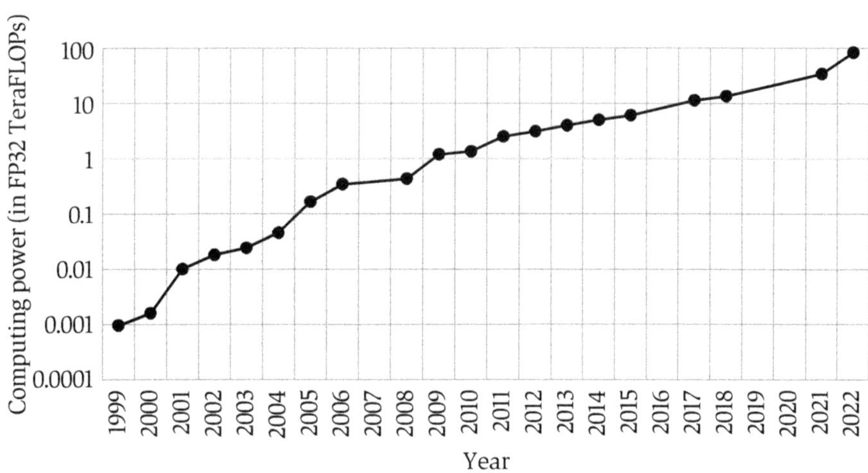

Consider, for example, the information taken up in *Table 4.1*: the most advanced enterprise-level chips currently available on the market – Nvidia's H100 GPUs – are capable of performing a staggering 51,220,000,000,000 floating point operations *every second*. What is even more remarkable is that this represents a ~53,354x increase in computing power between 1999 and 2023.

27. Floating point arithmetic typically uses a limited number of 'significant digits' compared to integer arithmetic. For example, the integer value 849,058 has six significant digits, whereas the floating point value 0.849×10^6 has only three significant digits. Note, therefore, that these two different notation methods represent a trade-off between precision and range.
28. The visual is the author's own work, but was based on numbers from TechPowerUp (undated) and Nvidia GPU specification sheets. *See also* Table 4.3 in s. 7 (Appendix).

Table 4.1 Evolution of GPU Computing Power over Time[29]

	Nvidia GeForce 256	*Nvidia Tesla K20X*	*Nvidia H100*
Release date	1999	2012	2023
Transistor count	17 million (0.24%)	7,080 million (100%)	80,000 million (1,130%)
Memory size	0.032 GB (0.53%)	6 GB (100%)	80 GB (1,333%)
Memory bus	128-bit (33%)	384-bit (100%)	5,120-bit (1,333%)
Bandwidth	4.8 GB/s (0.48%)	1,008 GB/s (100%)	2,039 GB/s (202%)
32-bit Floating Point	0.00096 teraFLOPs (0.01%)	9,935 teraFLOPs (100%)	51.22 teraFLOPs (516%)
MSRP at release	USD 249	USD 7,699	USD 30,000

Figure 4.4 also illustrates that the cost of acquiring a computing capacity of one teraFLOP per second (i.e., 1,000,000,000,000 floating point operations per second) has fallen from USD 259,375.00 in 1999 to just USD 19.36 in 2022.

Figure 4.4 Evolution of Single GPU Price per teraFLOP Computing Power over Time in Consumer-Grade GPUs[30]

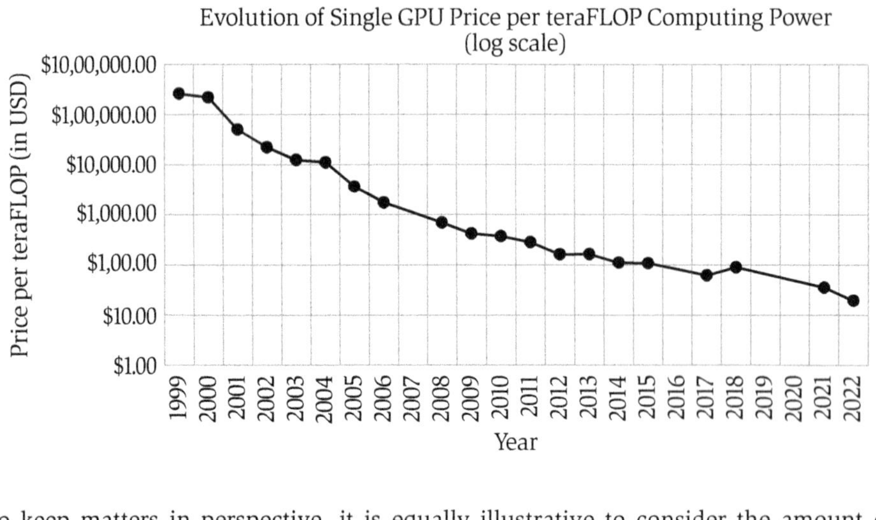

To keep matters in perspective, it is equally illustrative to consider the amount of computation required to train an AI model. For example, the technical documentation provided with GPT-3 175B – a large language model released by OpenAI in 2020 – states that a staggering 3.14×10^{23} floating point operations were needed to train the

29. Numbers adopted from *ibid.*
30. *See supra* n. 29.

model.[31] If we were to train GPT-3 175B using just a single Nvidia H100 GPU with a processing power of 51.22 teraFLOPs, it would take 6,013,021,831 seconds or about 191 years of continuous computing.[32,33&34]

While no official information is available about GPT-4 – OpenAI's successor to GPT-3 released in 2023 – leaked details suggest that it is approximately ten times the size of GPT-3, with 1.8 trillion parameters compared to GPT-3's 175 billion parameters.[35] When using GPT-4, the cost of generating a single token[36] is about 560 teraFLOP.[37] Training GPT-4 required $\sim 2.15 \times 10^{25}$ floating point operations and was performed on 25,000 Nvidia A100 GPUs over 90-100 days at a total computational cost of about USD 63 million.[38] While these numbers have never been officially confirmed by OpenAI, they are corroborated by other news articles and, more importantly, also explain why tech conglomerates such as Meta are spending an inordinate amount of money to acquire bulk quantities of Nvidia H100 GPUs to parallelize AI model training.[39]

2.3.2 Data Availability

Beyond the raw computational capabilities of GPUs, floating point operations ultimately need to be applied to data. In this respect, it is relevant to note that data come in all forms and shapes. For the purposes of this chapter, a distinction is made between numerical data, textual data, and visual data.

When it comes to *numerical data*, vast amounts of data are being generated as a by-product of using IT systems.[40] For example, large quantities of information are collected via the internet (e.g., search queries and search behaviour, e-commerce

31. Brown et al. 2020, 46; writing this number out in full amounts to 314,000,000,000,000,000,000,000,000 floating point operations.
32. Note that these calculations assume that a 32-bit single-precision floating point format is used (i.e., FP32). There are other formats, notably 16-bit floating point (FP16; half-precision), 64-bit floating point (FP64; double-precision) and 8-bit floating point (FP8; minifloat). Lowering the 'precision' is associated with performance gains during both model training and inference, but comes at the expense of accuracy in terms of the model's output. It should be noted that proprietary computational formats also exist (e.g., TensorFloat-32; TF32).
33. Note that there exists a unit for expressing total computation time, which is PF-days or petaFLOP per second-days. The number of PF-days refers to the total number of days required to train an AI model at a rate of one petaFLOP per second for a full day. The training of GPT-3 175B required 3,640 PF-days: Brown et al. 2020, 46.
34. Note that AI model training is not performed at the theoretical maximum capacity of the GPU to better address thermal limitations and limit power consumption. Real-world model FLOPs utilization (MFU) typically ranges from 60% to 30%.
35. While the official leak has been scrubbed from the internet, the relevant information is still accessible via web archiving websites: Peleg 2023.
36. In the context of large language models, 'tokens' represent the basic unit of text processed by an AI model. Tokens are best thought of as parts of a word, such as the stem, prefix, or suffix of a word. For instance, the word 'unbelievable' could be tokenized in 'un', 'believ' and 'able'. Note, however, that there are different types of tokenizers that break down text differently.
37. Peleg 2023.
38. *Ibid.*
39. Kan 2024.
40. EPRS 2020, 16.

transactions, or social networking activities). Similarly, with the proliferation of smart devices, the amount of data generated by these devices has also increased, ranging from heart rate sensor data from smartwatches to productivity metrics from a manufacturing plant. Other economic activities, such as banking and transportation, also contribute to a steady flow of numerical data. Taken together, this readily available influx of information can be used for data modelling purposes, whether in the context of detecting heart arrhythmia or building complete virtual, true-to-life representations of manufacturing plants (i.e., digital twins).

Also of interest are sources of *textual data*. In this respect, it is worth noting that language datasets are becoming increasingly available.[41] Arguably the best-known textual dataset is the Common Crawl:[42] a public repository of web crawl data that is available for anyone to use. Its most recent archive contains 3.16 billion web pages, as well as trillions of contextual URLs that link those pages together.[43] The dataset represents an impressive 424.7 terabytes (TB) of uncompressed text data,[44] making the Common Crawl arguably the most impactful dataset when it comes to training language-based AI models. Also noteworthy is The Pile, a curated and open-source dataset consisting of data taken from PubMed, ArXiv, GitHub, Project Gutenberg, Wikipedia, and seventeen other sources.[45] Many other, more topical text-based datasets are also available online (e.g., news articles, wine reviews, movie plots, Twitter tweets).[46]

Several repositories also host *visual data*, consisting of image-text pairs that can be used to train image-generating AI systems. For example, the training of text-to-image model Stable Diffusion relied on LAION-5B, which is essentially a dataset derived from the Common Crawl and consists of over five billion pairs of images and their corresponding captions.[47] DALL•E 2 – a text-to-image model developed by OpenAI – was trained based on images from publicly available sources as well as several licensed sources.[48]

In addition to well-known collections of data, there are several aggregator websites – such as *Hugging Face*,[49] *Papers with Code*,[50] and *Kaggle*[51] – that list numerous other datasets. Beyond the three main data types mentioned above, there are open-source datasets available for download relating to video, audio, 3D visuals, dialog data, graphs, tabular data, medical data (e.g., MRIs or EEGs), financial data (e.g., stock prices), LiDAR data, and so on. Combined, these datasets can serve as training data for a wide variety of AI systems and AI models, ranging from image classification, text,

41. By way of illustration, consider the datasets used to train GPT-3: Brown et al. 2020, 9.
42. Common Crawl 2024.
43. Vaughan 2024.
44. *Ibid.*
45. For the relevant underlying academic paper, *see* Gao et al. 2020.
46. *See, for instance,* Kaggle (undated), which lists 3,462 datasets suitable for natural language processing.
47. Beaumont 2022; Schuhmann et al. 2022.
48. Ramesh et al. 2022; OpenAI 2022.
49. Hugging Face 2024.
50. Papers with Code (undated).
51. Kaggle (undated).

image, or music generation, object recognition, anomaly detection, speech recognition, autonomous driving, facial recognition, machine translation, recommendation systems, emotion recognition systems, image upscalers, fake news detectors, handwriting recognition, grammatical error correction, and literally hundreds of other applications.

2.4 The World Wants to Regulate AI

The realization that AI systems can easily be applied to a very wide range of economic sectors and parts of society has brought up questions about the regulation of AI applications as well as access to AI technology.[52] Given the disruptive effects of AI, this is not entirely unsurprising: AI-related concerns extend not only to individual human rights and values but also to broader global power dynamics.

2.4.1 Geopolitical Developments

The growing recognition that AI offers both broad economic benefits and poses significant threats has led to a twofold dynamic. On the one hand, both the EU and the United States (US) have launched legislative packages – the Chips Act[53] and the CHIPS Act of 2022,[54] respectively – aimed at boosting the local recreation of *semiconductor infrastructure* to secure the production of advanced computer chips. In doing so, these jurisdictions are signalling their intention to reduce their dependence[55] on Taiwan, which currently produces approximately 90% of the world's state-of-the-art microchips.[56]

On the other hand, the heavy reliance on Taiwan to maintain leadership in both civilian and military technology has led the US to tighten export controls on China.[57] Among others, the US has banned semiconductor firm Nvidia from exporting its most cutting-edge GPUs, thereby putting China at a competitive disadvantage in terms of the availability of computing power to train AI systems.[58] Similarly, the US has sought to further cripple China's ability to build and expand its own semiconductor industry by

52. AIA, Recs 4-5.
53. Chips Act.
54. CHIPS and Science Act, Public Law (US) 117-167.
55. Chips Act, Rec. 2: 'A framework for increasing the Union's resilience in the field of semiconductor technologies should be established, reinforcing the Union's semiconductor ecosystem by reducing dependencies, enhancing digital sovereignty, stimulating investment, strengthening the capabilities, security, adaptability and resilience of the Union's semiconductor supply chain.'
56. Lee et al. 2021.
57. Bureau of Industry and Security, Implementation of Additional Export Controls: Certain Advanced Computing Items; Supercomputer and Semiconductor End Use; Updates and Corrections, 88 Federal Register 73458 (2023); for an overview of the relevant press releases, *see* BIS 2023.
58. As disclosed in an investor report: Nvidia 2023: 'The Interim Final Rule amends ECCN 3A090 and 4A090 and imposes additional licensing requirements for exports to China and Country Groups D1, D4, and D5 ... of the Company's integrated circuits exceeding certain performance thresholds.'

barring the Netherlands-based company ASML[59] from selling its extreme ultraviolet (EUV) lithography systems – machines needed to mass-produce microchips – to China.[60] In doing so, the US is further kneecapping China's ability to develop computationally intensive AI systems.

2.4.2 *Calls for a Pause on AI Development*

Aside from the geopolitical developments mentioned above, parts of the AI industry itself have called for a temporary pause on AI development. This particular movement culminated in 2023 with the publication of an open letter by the Future of Life Institute, signed by prominent AI researchers, academics, and industry players.[61] Their core argument is that unfettered competition will force AI companies to behave recklessly, potentially unleashing AI models that pose serious threats to society and humanity.[62] This argument rests on two premises: first, that AI regulation is lagging behind, and second, that developers can no longer fully control their own AI models once they are released on the market. As a result, the open letter argues that an AI development freeze is needed. Ultimately, the proposed AI development freeze did not materialize, and firms have continued their AI research efforts.

When considering the market for AI, this outcome is not entirely unexpected. With the release of several notable open-source[63] and closed-source[64] AI models, the proverbial genie may already be out of the bottle, and it will be nearly impossible to put it back in.[65] Especially since firms such as OpenAI,[66] Anthropic,[67] and Google[68] operate on a for-profit basis and charge a subscription fee for access to their models. As a result, these firms face strong incentives to be first-to-market with the next-generation frontier model – with an even higher number of parameters – making it unrealistic to expect them to stop improving their AI models. And that leaves only one way forward: AI regulation.

2.4.3 *Race to Regulate*

The concerns about AI outlined earlier in this chapter are not entirely unfounded, and recent AI developments have indeed prompted a race to regulate AI. This, of course, raises an important preliminary question: *what to regulate?* Perhaps only the so-called

59. ASML is the only firm in the world that manufactures EUV lithography systems (i.e., chip-making equipment) capable of producing microchips with transistor sizes in the range of 2-3 nanometer (nm).
60. ASML 2024.
61. Future of Life Institute 2023.
62. *Ibid.*
63. E.g., Llama 3.1 405B (Meta), Command R+ (Cohere), Mixtral-8x22b-Instruct-v0.1 (Mistral).
64. E.g., GPT-4o (OpenAI), Claude 3.5 Sonnet (Anthropic), Gemini 1.5 Pro (Google).
65. In the realm of large language models, AI developments have even spawned chatbot leaderboards: LMSYS 2024; *see also* the relevant research paper: Chiang et al. 2024.
66. OpenAI 2023.
67. Anthropic 2024.
68. Google 2023.

frontier models that represent the state of the art, such as GPT-4o (OpenAI), Claude 3.5 Sonnet (Anthropic), Llama 3.1 405B (Meta), and Gemini 1.5 Pro (Google), should become subject to regulation? Or perhaps AI models should be regulated on the basis of certain performance thresholds – such as a maximum amount of computation required to operate the model – or that AI models must perform their task within a certain energy budget? Alternatively, perhaps the emphasis should be on regulating specific AI use cases rather than AI models themselves, suggesting, for example, that more intrusive AI applications (e.g., facial recognition) should be subject to more stringent rules.

While many of these questions remain open to discussion today, the world has witnessed multiple efforts around the globe to reign in AI.[69] In the US, the Biden administration adopted Executive Order 14110 on a Safe, Secure, and Trustworthy AI.[70] In turn, China has enacted rules governing specific applications of AI, such as recommender systems and generative AI (GenAI).[71] India is also in the process of drafting new legislation, in the form of the Digital India Act, to regulate high-risk AI systems. However, on 13 March 2024, the first comprehensive AI regulatory instrument of its kind was adopted by the EU: the *AI Act*. The Act was published in the Official Journal of the EU as Regulation (EU) 2024/1689 on 12 July 2024.

3 LEGISLATIVE JOURNEY OF THE AI ACT

3.1 2018: AI for Europe

The first tentative steps towards the regulation of AI in Europe were already taken in 2018 when the Commission published a communication entitled *AI for Europe*.[72] In this document, the Commission not only sets out its ambition to embrace AI but also states that the European way forward on AI should be aligned with the following three objectives:[73]

(1) boosting the EU's technological and industrial capacity and AI uptake;
(2) preparing for the socio-economic changes brought about by AI; and
(3) ensuring that an ethical and legal framework is in place to align AI developments with European values and fundamental rights.

The publication was followed by the creation of a High-Level Expert Group on Artificial Intelligence (HLEG),[74] tasked with drafting ethical guidelines for the development of trustworthy AI, and the publication of a twenty-three-page *Coordinated Plan on AI*,[75]

69. Several AI regulation trackers are available online. *Consider, for instance*, IAPP 2024; Sun 2024.
70. Safe, Secure, and Trustworthy Development and Use of Artificial Intelligence, 88 Federal Register 75191 (2023).
71. For an English translation, *see* Creemers et al. 2022.
72. Commission Communication 2018.
73. *Ibid.*, at 3.
74. Commission 2018a.
75. Commission 2018b, 1.

which outlines a more detailed strategy for maximizing the benefits of AI for all Europeans. Specifically, the action plan puts forward the idea of 'AI made in Europe', which should be implemented by pursuing strategic investments, focussing on AI talent development, creating a common European data space, and establishing an appropriate ethical and regulatory framework.[76]

3.2 2019: High-Level Expert Group on AI

In 2019, the HLEG published its *Ethics Guidelines for Trustworthy AI*.[77] The approach of the HLEG Guidelines is threefold.

First, it identifies a set of four ethical principles – respect for human autonomy, prevention of harm, fairness, and explicability – that must be considered during the development, deployment, and use of AI systems.[78]

Second, these principles are expanded into seven[79] key ethical requirements for AI systems:[80]

(1) human agency and oversight;
(2) technical robustness and safety;
(3) privacy and data governance;
(4) transparency;
(5) diversity, non-discrimination and fairness;
(6) environmental and societal well-being; and
(7) accountability.

Third, the Guidelines also present both technical and non-technical methods for operationalising these ethical requirements.[81] This is achieved by means of an AI assessment list, which provides specific questions to assess compliance with the seven requirements outlined above.

3.3 2020: White Paper on AI

The Commission, now fully equipped with a detailed action plan and having received extensive input from the HLEG, released a *White Paper on AI* in February 2020.[82] The document, entitled 'A European approach to excellence and trust', reiterates many of the findings of previous reports and uses ambitious language such as 'seizing the opportunity' and 'building an ecosystem of excellence'. As a prelude to the proposal text of the AI Act, the Commission's White Paper dedicates specific attention to

76. *Ibid.*, at 2.
77. HLEG Guidelines.
78. *Ibid.*, at 11-12.
79. The list of seven ethical requirements is intended to be 'non-exhaustive' and there is no particular hierarchy among these requirements: *ibid.*, at 14.
80. *Ibid.*
81. *Ibid.*, at 26-31.
82. White Paper on AI.

delineating the scope of potential future EU rules on AI. Among other things, attention is paid to how AI should be defined and that any definition should be sufficiently flexible to accommodate technological progress.[83]

It is also noteworthy that the Commission is mindful of interactions with other legal instruments, such as consumer protection rules and data protection legislation. In this respect, the Commission clearly states that all existing provisions of EU law will apply in relation to AI, although certain updates may be necessary.[84]

The White Paper subsequently refers to a *risk-based approach* to AI.[85] To ensure effectiveness, the Commission proposes to differentiate whether AI systems are 'high risk' or not. Without going into details, the Commission suggests that the qualification as high risk should depend on the specific sector in which the AI system is used and the significance of the risks that can be expected in light of the activities performed by the AI system.

3.4 2021: Proposal for a Regulation Laying Down Harmonized Rules on AI

Over time, the Commission's vision for AI regulation continued to take shape, culminating in the production of an updated *Coordinated Plan on AI*,[86] a proposal text for an *Artificial Intelligence Act*,[87] as well as an *Impact Assessment*[88] accompanying the proposed AI Act. The explanatory memorandum included in the proposed AI Act not only reiterates much of the information contained in earlier documents but also expands on it in several respects. Among others, the text takes the time to emphasize that AI can have a positive impact on society, but that it is of the utmost importance to also address any risks.[89] Ultimately, the proposed AI act seeks to create a single European market for trustworthy AI. It aims to do this by ensuring that the development of AI can take place on the basis of a framework of European values, while at the same time providing much-needed legal certainty to encourage AI innovation.

There are two important takeaways from the text of the proposal. First, the proposed AI Act seeks to establish a *definition of an AI system* that would apply across the EU. The proposed (but now outdated) definition[90] refers to a dedicated Annex to further elaborate on what is to be considered an AI system. In the Annex, three different approaches are mentioned that qualify as AI: (1) machine learning approaches; (2) logic- and knowledge-based approaches; and (3) statistical approaches.[91]

83. *Ibid.*, at 16.
84. *Ibid.*
85. *Ibid.*, at 17.
86. Commission 2021, 1.
87. AI Act Commission Proposal.
88. Commission SWD Impact Assessment.
89. AI Act Commission Proposal, 1.
90. AI Act Commission Proposal, Art. 3(1): '"artificial intelligence system" (AI system) means software that is developed with one or more of the techniques and approaches listed in Annex I and can, for a given set of human-defined objectives, generate outputs such as content, predictions, recommendations, or decisions influencing the environments they interact with'.
91. AI Act Commission Proposal, Annex I.

Second, the proposal text further refines the *risk-based approach* mentioned in the 2020 White Paper. Among others, the proposal differentiates between:

(1) *Prohibited AI systems*, which pose an unacceptable risk to EU values and therefore cannot be placed on the EU market.
(2) *High-risk AI systems*, which pose a serious risk to EU values, and therefore must be subject to a set of strict requirements before being allowed to circulate in the EU.
(3) *Low-risk AI systems*, which pose only a minimal risk to EU values and are therefore subject only to limited transparency requirements.

3.5 2022-2024: Run-Up to the AI Act

3.5.1 The Council's Position

As part of the ordinary legislative procedure, discussions took place in the Council and its preparatory bodies in 2022.[92] On 6 December 2022, the Council published its common position on the AI Act.[93] Compared to the original text of the proposal, several notable changes and deviations were found:[94]

(1) The *definition of an AI system* has been redrafted in a narrower manner.[95] The definition also no longer refers to Annex I of the proposed AI Act to delineate the techniques and approaches that fall within its scope. Instead, the relevant language is now entirely contained within the definition itself. Unlike Annex I, however, the revised definition no longer mentions 'statistical approaches', retaining only machine learning and logic-based approaches.
(2) Regarding the *scope of application* of the proposed AI Act, several exclusion criteria have now been explicitly added to the proposal (e.g., military purposes).[96] In the same vein, the revised text now also clarifies that the obligations of the AI Act should not apply to AI systems that are used for research purposes.[97]
(3) On the topic of *prohibited AI practices*, the Council's position extends the prohibition on social scoring to private actors, while also inscribing an exemption for real-time remote biometric identification systems for law enforcement purposes in exceptional circumstances.[98]

92. For a further analysis of the position of the Council, *see* Chapter 5, Pehlivan, in this volume, s. 2.1.
93. AI Act Council Proposal.
94. Council 2022.
95. AI Act Council Proposal, Art. 3(1).
96. *Ibid.*, Art. 2(3).
97. *Ibid.*, Art. 2(6).
98. *Ibid.*, Art. 5.

(4) Apropos *high-risk AI systems*, the Council provides for a new carve-out within the high-risk AI system categorization when the AI system's output is merely ancillary to the action or decision to be taken, with the effect being that no significant risks to the health, safety or fundamental rights arise.[99] In effect, this derogation entails that some AI systems may now escape the classification as high risk. Staying on the topic of high-risk AI systems, many of the substantive obligations have also been slightly redrafted and further refined.

(5) The Council added a number of new provisions that apply when AI systems can be used for a wide variety of different purposes, so-called *general purpose AI*.[100] In essence, the Council's position reflects that some requirements applicable to high-risk AI systems should also apply to general purpose AI.

(6) Concerned about the implications of the proposed AI Act on innovation, the Council proposed to amend the provisions on *measures in support of innovation*.[101] In particular, the aim was to be more innovation-friendly and to encourage evidence-based learning. As a result, AI regulatory sandboxes should allow for the testing of AI systems under real-world conditions.

3.5.2 *The Parliament's Position*

Following the adoption of a common position by the Council, the Parliament was next to take action.[102] A joint committee procedure was launched under the auspices of the Committee on Internal Market and Consumer Protection (IMCO) and the Committee on Civil Liberties, Justice and Home Affairs (LIBE). The resulting joint report, dated 16 May 2023, introduces further changes to the Commission's proposal.[103] These changes mainly revolve around the following six topics:[104]

(1) The *definition of an AI system* remained a subject of contention and inevitably saw further amendments. While some Members of the European Parliament (MEPs) preferred a more broadly worded definition to ensure future proofing, the rapport eventually settled on aligning the AI Act's definition of an AI system with the definition used by the Organisation for Economic Co-operation and Development (OECD).[105]

(2) The *list of prohibited AI practices* was substantially revised to include biometric categorization systems, AI systems intended for risk assessments,

99. *Ibid.*, Art. 6(3).
100. *Ibid.*, Art. 4a, 4b, and 4c.
101. *Ibid.*, Arts 53-55a.
102. For a further analysis of the position of the Parliament, *see* Chapter 5, Pehlivan, in this volume, s. 2.2.
103. AI Act Parliament Amendments.
104. European Parliament, *Parliament's Negotiating Position on the Artificial Intelligence Act*, 1 (2023).
105. AI Act Parliament Amendments, Art. 3.

emotion recognition systems, and a blanket ban on AI systems that create facial recognition databases through untargeted scraping from the internet.[106]

(3) New substantive requirements were added for *high-risk AI systems*: to qualify as a high-risk AI system, these AI systems must pose a 'significant risk' to the health, safety, or fundamental rights of natural persons.[107] The assessment of high risk entails a self-assessment procedure.

(4) Additional rules were added regarding the regulation of *General-Purpose Artificial Intelligence (GPAI) systems*, including a new definition of a 'foundation model', the extension of existing provisions to foundation models, as well as some new specific substantive obligations.[108]

(5) Under the governance section of the AI Act, it was proposed to establish a *European Artificial Intelligence Office (AI Office)* in order to strengthen the enforcement of the Act.[109] The proposed role of the AI Office would be to support, advise, and cooperate with Member States, and also monitor the effective application of the Regulation.

(6) The introduction of a generous, albeit not complete, exemption for *free and open-source* AI systems.[110]

3.5.3 Trilogue Negotiations

Trilogue negotiations between the Parliament, the Council, and the Commission took place next. Between June and December 2023, the provisional text of the AI Act was further amended to arrive at a compromise text. Notable topics of discussion revolved around the definition of AI systems, the list of banned AI systems, requirements for high-risk AI systems, obligations pertaining to GPAI, measures in support of innovation and small and medium-sized enterprises (SMEs), and the enforcement of the AI Act.[111]

Ultimately, it took a thirty-six-hour ultramarathon of negotiations to fully hammer out the final details of the AI Act and resolve any outstanding issues. On 9 December 2023, EU policymakers announced that they had reached a political agreement on what would become the first global instrument of AI regulation.[112] The provisional text of the AI Act was subsequently endorsed by the Parliament on 13 March 2024, with the roll call showing 523 votes in favour, 46 against, and 49 abstentions.[113]

106. *Ibid.*, Art. 5.
107. *Ibid.*, Art. 6.
108. *Ibid.*, Arts 3 and 28b.
109. *Ibid.*, Art. 56.
110. *Ibid.*, Art. 2.
111. Fazlioglu 2023.
112. Bertuzzi 2023.
113. Parliament 2024.

4 THE AI ACT

While a detailed analysis is beyond the scope of this chapter,[114] it is nonetheless illustrative to provide a high-level overview of the finalized AI Act. In terms of the overall structure, the Act consists of 180 Recitals, 113 Articles, and 13 Annexes. Seven key issues surrounding the AI Act deserve attention before proceeding.

A closer look at the definitions taken up in Article 3 indicates that the European *definition of an AI system* reads as follows:[115]

> 'AI system' means a machine-based system that is designed to operate with varying levels of autonomy and that may exhibit adaptiveness after deployment, and that, for explicit or implicit objectives, infers, from the input it receives, how to generate outputs such as predictions, content, recommendations, or decisions that can influence physical or virtual environments.

Assessing whether a specific AI system falls within the definition will certainly pose its fair share of challenges, and will certainly spark much scholarly debate about what words such as 'autonomy' and 'adaptiveness' mean or how they should be applied.

It is also necessary to draw attention to the *scope of application* of the AI Act. Article 2 is quite clear in this respect, stipulating that it is mainly applicable to: (1) providers who place AI systems or GPAI models on the EU market or put those systems or models into service in the EU; (2) deployers of AI systems that are located in the EU and that use an AI system under their authority;[116] (3) providers and deployers of AI systems located in a third country, but where the output produced by the AI system is used in the EU; and (4) importers and distributors of AI systems in the EU.

The *risk-based approach* should also be further contextualized.[117] As the term suggests, the specific requirements applicable to an AI system will vary depending on the intensity and scope of risks posed by that AI system to the values and rights enshrined in EU law. To that end, the AI Act classifies AI systems into four different risk categories. The first category is *prohibited AI practices* which, due to their harmful impact, cannot be deployed in the EU. The second category concerns *high-risk AI systems*, which potentially pose significant risks to EU citizens' health, safety, and fundamental rights and must comply with an extensive set of mandatory requirements. The third category encompasses *limited-risk AI systems*, which are subject to transparency obligations due to their ability to shape false impressions (e.g., synthetic content or artificially generated text, images, or video). The fourth category encapsulates *minimal-risk AI systems*, which can be used freely albeit while still complying with other applicable rules (e.g., the GDPR).

---

114. For a more detailed analysis of the provisions of the AI Act, the reader is referred to the relevant article-by-article commentaries contained *in* Ceyhun Necati Pehlivan, Nikolaus Forgó & Peggy Valcke (eds), *The EU Artificial Intelligence (AI) Act* (Kluwer Law International 2025).
115. AIA, Art. 3(1).
116. *Ibid.*, Art. 3(4) *in fine*: an exception applies when the AI system is deployed in the course of a personal, non-professional activity.
117. *Ibid.*, Rec. 26.

Some comments should be added on the topic of *GPAI*. In this respect, the AI Act sets out two relevant definitions: a definition for GPAI model[118] and one for GPAI system.[119] In essence, the 'general purposeness' of an AI model refers to the ability to build different AI systems - each with different use cases - on the basis of the GPAI model. In this respect, the 'generality' of the AI model depends on (among others) the number of parameters included in the model (*see* GPT-3 with 175 billion parameters and GPT-4 with 1.8 trillion parameters). In turn, the number of parameters has a significant impact on the amount of computation required to use the AI model, both during the training and inference phases. In light of this, EU policymakers opted to use the amount of computing power required as a criterion for determining whether a GPAI model should qualify as 'high-risk' or not. This measure is expressed in FLOPs: if more than 10^{25} FLOPs are required to train the AI model, a presumption applies that the AI model poses a systemic risk.[120] In addition, Annex XIII sets out several criteria on which the Commission can rely to designate GPAI as a model with systemic risk on an ad hoc basis. It should also be noted that a generous exemption applies to free and open-source AI models.[121]

The AI Act contains a dedicated chapter on measures in support of innovation. In this context, Member States face an obligation to operationalize so-called *AI regulatory sandboxes*,[122] to be understood as controlled environments where developers can train, test, and validate new AI systems under regulatory supervision but with certain relaxations.[123] This regime also extends to the possibility of testing AI systems under real-world circumstances. In this respect, the AI Act accommodates the specific needs of SMEs by providing an easier compliance procedure for market entry.[124]

With regard to *enforcement*, the approach taken in the AI Act is multi-layered. A first anchor point is that the AI Act mandates Member States to designate at least one market surveillance authority to oversee the correct application of the AI Act. This market surveillance authority possesses extensive enforcement powers, ranging from investigative powers to the ability to impose sanctions for non-compliance, including the imposition of administrative fines of up to 7% of the worldwide turnover or EUR 35 million, whichever is higher.[125] Market surveillance authorities and the Commission can also launch joint investigations. The AI Office can play a supporting role.

The AI Act will have a staggered *entry into force*, spread over a two-year window (*see Figure 4.5*).[126] Six months after publication in the Official Journal, the provisions

118. *Ibid.*, Art. 3(63).
119. *Ibid.*, Art. 3(66).
120. *Ibid.*, Art. 51(2); Note that GPT-4 - with an estimated 2.15×10^{25} floating point operations required for its training - exceeds this threshold.
121. *Ibid.*, Art. 2(12).
122. *Ibid.*, Art. 57.
123. Regarding these relaxations, *see, for instance, ibid.*, Art. 57(12): 'provided that the prospective providers observe the specific plan and the terms and conditions for their participation and follow in good faith the guidance given by the national competent authority, no administrative fines shall be imposed by the authorities for infringements of this Regulation'.
124. *Ibid.*, Art. 57(9)(e).
125. *Ibid.*, Art. 99.
126. *Ibid.*, Art. 113.

on prohibited AI systems will come into force (2 February 2025). At the twelve-month mark, the rules on GPAI will take effect (2 August 2025). After twenty-four months, most of the other obligations of the AI Act come into force (2 August 2026). Lastly, at thirty-six months, the rules on high-risk AI systems enter into force (2 August 2027).

Figure 4.5 Timeline of the Entry into Force and Application of the AI Act[127]

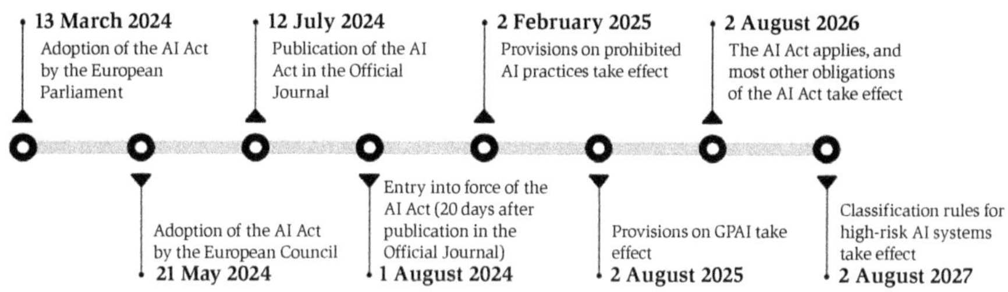

5 A COMPREHENSIVE EUROPEAN DIGITAL FRAMEWORK FOR AI

The AI Act does not exist in a vacuum but is part of a larger body of legal instruments dealing with digitization in the EU. In this respect, the AI Act itself devotes attention to clarifying how its provisions are consistent with other EU instruments. Reading Recital 9 of the AI Act, it is posited that EU rules on AI should be:[128]

> without prejudice to existing Union law, in particular on data protection, consumer protection, fundamental rights, employment, and protection of workers, and product safety.

This effectively suggests that the *lex specialis* principle[129] will be relevant to consider in situations where two EU instruments apply to the same factual circumstances. As shown in *Table 4.2*, sometimes the scope of application of the AI Act may indeed overlap with other instruments of EU law. In such cases, specific rules should take precedence over general rules, and the more general rules should be disapplied to the extent that they conflict with the more specific rules. In addition, whenever possible, different legal instruments should be applied concurrently to provide the most comprehensive level of protection. While not intended to be exhaustive, this section provides an initial overview of the intersections between the AI Act and other EU instruments related to digitization.

127. The visual is the author's own work, and is based on the information contained in *ibid.*
128. *Ibid.*, Rec. 9.
129. Based on the Latin maxim *lex specialis derogat legi generali*: more specific rules prevail over more general rules.

Table 4.2 The AI Act as Part of the EU Digital Acquis[130]

Regulatory Instrument	*Actors*	*Rightsholders*	*Objective*	*Material Scope*
AI Act	- Providers of AI systems and AI models - Deployers of AI systems - Importers of AI systems - Distributors of AI systems	- Individuals - Society - Democracy	Promoting the uptake of human-centric and trustworthy AI, while ensuring a high level of protection of health, safety, fundamental rights[131]	Placing on the market or putting into service AI systems or AI models[132]
GDPR	- Data controllers - Data processors	- Data subjects	Protecting natural persons with regard to the processing of personal data[133]	Processing of personal data wholly or partly by automated means[134]
DGA	- Public sector bodies - Data intermediation services - Data altruism organizations	- Data subjects - Data holders	Creating a harmonized framework for data exchanges and laying down certain basic requirements for data governance[135]	Re-using, within the Union, of certain categories of data[136]
DA	- Manufacturers of connected products - Data holders - Data recipients - Public sector bodies - Providers of data processing services - Participants in data spaces	- Users of connected products or related services	Ensuring fairness in the allocation of value from data among actors in the data economy and fostering fair access to and use of data[137]	Making available product data and related service data and their subsequent use[138]

130. The tabular overview is the author's own work and is based on the wording used in the different legal instruments.
131. AIA, Art. 1.
132. *Ibid.*, Art. 2.
133. GDPR, Art. 1.
134. *Ibid.*, Art. 2.
135. DGA, Rec. 3.
136. *Ibid.*, Art. 1.

Regulatory Instrument	*Actors*	*Rightsholders*	*Objective*	*Material Scope*
DMA	- Undertakings designated as gatekeepers[139]	- End users - Business users	Laying down harmonized rules ensuring for all businesses, contestable and fair markets in the digital sector across the Union where gatekeepers are present[140]	Provision of core platform services[141] by gatekeepers to business users or end users in the Union[142]
DSA	- Providers of intermediary services, including: - very large online platforms; and - very large online search engines	- Recipients of intermediary services	Setting out harmonized rules for a safe, predictable and trusted online environment that facilitates innovation and in which fundamental rights are effectively protected[143]	Provision of intermediary services in the internal market[144]

5.1 Interface Between the GDPR and the AI Act

The first relevant area of attention concerns the interplay between the AI Act and the GDPR. As recalled, the GDPR is concerned with the protection of data subjects with respect to the processing of their personal data.[145] It is important to note that the GDPR is *technologically neutral*;[146] its only anchor point is the processing of personal data, regardless of how or by what means this is done.

As evidenced by Article 4(2) of the GDPR, the definition of 'processing' is very broad and covers virtually any activity involving personal data. The implication thereof is that the GDPR can find application to AI systems, to the extent that personal data is processed by the AI system. Such situations are likely to arise either because AI systems process personal data during the training phase (i.e., personal data is processed as

137. DA, Rec. 119.
138. *Ibid.*, Art. 1.
139. DMA, Art. 2(1) *juncto* Art. 3.
140. *Ibid.*, Art. 1.
141. *Ibid.*, Art. 2(2).
142. *Ibid.*, Art. 1.
143. DSA, Art. 1.
144. *Ibid.*
145. GDPR, Art. 1.
146. *Ibid.*, Rec. 15.

input data) or because AI systems process personal data during the inference phase (i.e., personal data is processed as output data). In these circumstances, both the AI Act and the GDPR will apply, which in practice means that a firm can hold a dual qualification. Consider, for instance, the following three situations:[147]

(1) *Qualification as a* provider *under the AI Act and as a* data controller *under the GDPR*: a firm processes personal data for the purpose of training a new AI system, that is intended to be placed on the Union market.
(2) *Qualification as a* deployer *under the AI Act and as a* data controller *under the GDPR*: a firm acquires an AI system from another entity and subsequently uses that AI system under its authority to process personal data (e.g., for staff recruitment purposes).
(3) *Qualification as a* provider *under the AI Act and as a* data processor *under the GDPR*: a firm sells an AI system to another firm, but remains involved in the second firm's processing of personal data (e.g., because the AI system is hosted on the vendor's servers).

When such circumstances arise, the principles of both instruments must be respected. This is also reflected as such in Recital 10 of the AI Act:[148]

> [i]t also does not affect the obligations of providers and deployers of AI systems in their role as data controllers or processors.

To streamline these interactions, the text of the AI Act also aligns itself with several definitions used in the GDPR.[149]

Now that the AI Act has been formally adopted, there is also, in some ways, a greater alignment between the substantive principles of the two instruments. In some respects, there is a clear *complementarity* between the AI Act and the GDPR. For instance, some of the principles of the GDPR also correspond to the principles of the AI Act. Befitting examples in this respect are the provisions on transparency,[150] data governance,[151] data protection impact assessments (DPIAs),[152] and human oversight.[153] In other respects, however, there are also *tensions* between both instruments. For instance, AI systems typically require the processing of large amounts of data during the training phase, which could conflict with the principle of data minimization and storage limitation.[154] Similarly, AI systems can sometimes be used for a variety of different purposes, making it difficult to clearly delineate the purpose of data processing and potentially putting these AI systems at odds with the principle of purpose

147. Clark & Muhammed Demircan 2024, 9.
148. AIA, Rec. 10.
149. This is the case for 'biometric data', 'special categories of personal data', 'personal data', and 'non-personal data', and 'profiling'.
150. AIA, Art. 50 *juncto* GDPR, Art. 5(1)(a).
151. AIA, Art. 10 *juncto* GDPR, Art. 5(1)(d)-(f).
152. AIA, Art. 27 *juncto* GDPR, Art. 35.
153. AIA, Art. 14 *juncto* GDPR, Art. 22.
154. GDPR, Art. 5(1)(c).

limitation. More broadly, the strict application and compliance with the data processing principles of the GDPR may have the effect of limiting the functionality of AI systems.

Prior to the adoption of the AI Act, there have already been a number of cases involving AI systems brought before national data protection authorities. Two cases in particular are worth mentioning: the banning of ChatGPT in Italy[155] and the fining of Clearview AI.[156] If anything, these cases indicate that this is an area of law to monitor.

5.2 Interface Between the DGA and the AI Act

The intersection between the EU's DGA and the AI Act is also worth analysing. At its core, the DGA is designed to facilitate the re-use of certain categories of data held by public sector bodies, and its main objective is to provide a coherent framework to facilitate the sharing of data in a secure and efficient manner.[157] Thus, while the DGA is not specifically focused on AI, it serves as a prerequisite for placing high-quality AI systems on the Union market by ensuring that data that could be used for training AI systems is handled with due care. In this respect, there exists some overlap between the AI Act and the DGA. Three elements in particular are worth highlighting.

First, there is the *data sharing* dimension. The DGA is primarily concerned with sharing data in a trustworthy manner, while the AI Act is concerned with the use of this data.[158] In that way, the DGA acts as an enabler for the training of AI systems on the basis of high-quality datasets. Second, there is the *data governance* aspect: both instruments draw attention to data governance and the need to properly manage data.[159] As such, the requirements of the DGA align well with those of the AI Act. A final element to highlight is the *risk management* angle. While the DGA seeks to manage possible risks associated with data sharing, the AI Act seeks to ensure that once data is used by AI systems, the resulting risks by deploying those AI systems are also appropriately administered.[160]

Ultimately, the DGA is aimed at developing a borderless digital internal market and a human-centric, trustworthy and secure data society, while the AI Act is intended to improve the functioning of the single market by promoting the deployment of human-centric and trustworthy AI.[161] In this sense, there is an element of linkage between the two instruments. Only when trustworthy and secure data sharing is enabled under the DGA, can human-centric AI systems be developed under the AI Act. Therefore, both legal instruments together are an integral part of shaping a comprehensive data ecosystem within the EU.

155. Garante 2023.
156. CNIL 2022.
157. DGA, Rec. 3 and Art. 3.
158. *Ibid.*, Art. 5(1) *juncto* AIA, Art. 10.
159. DGA, Art. 5(3) *juncto* AIA, Art. 10.
160. DGA, Art. 5(4)-(7) *juncto* AIA, Art. 10.
161. DGA, Rec. 3 *juncto* AIA, Rec. 1.

5.3 Interface Between the DA and the AI Act

Another area of note is the intersection between the DA and the AI Act. The premise of the DA is that, due to the proliferation of smart devices and the widespread availability of internet connectivity, the volume and value of data have increased tremendously since the 2010s.[162] At the same time, the DA also identifies barriers to data sharing that prevent much of the value of that data from being unlocked.[163] In light of this, the DA sets out rules to remove the barriers to sharing data from connected products and their ancillary services. Essentially, the DA operates in two ways. First, it creates new obligations for businesses to make data from connected products and related services available to users.[164] Second, it empowers those users to share their data with third parties.[165]

At this point, the analysis of the intersection between the DA and the AI Act shows some similarities to the findings made under the DGA, namely that data from connected devices and their ancillary services can serve as useful input data for training AI systems. In that sense, the element of linkage between the DA's data-sharing obligations and the ability to train AI systems is also present here. The key aspect is that the DA is an enabler of the provisions of the AI Act, in particular the data and data governance requirements that are taken up in Article 10 of the AI Act.

It is worth looking at a concrete example to illustrate this. Consider a smart speaker that collects audio data from interactions with its owner. The collected data – voice commands and other spoken input – is primarily used by the smart speaker to provide some sort of functionality to the user (e.g., the ability to control a smart lighting system through voice commands). However, the potential utility of the voice data goes beyond the immediate functionality of the smart speaker. For example, the voice data could also be used to develop an AI language learning application: the same voice excerpts could also be relied upon to identify pronunciation errors, suggest corrections, and tailor language learning exercises to the user's language proficiency level. The data sharing obligations of the DA make this kind of value realization possible.

Of particular interest is the DA's attention to the importance of structured and machine-readable data for users.[166] This suggests that the DA recognizes the value of data volume and the necessity for AI systems to be trained on large datasets. When data is structured in a well-defined and organized manner, this makes the data ingestion process considerably more straightforward.

5.4 Interface Between the DMA and the AI Act

When the attention turns to digital ecosystems, the discussion quickly gravitates to the EU's DMA. At the heart of the DMA is the observation that a select number of

162. DA, Rec. 1.
163. *Ibid.*, Rec. 2.
164. *Ibid.*, Art. 3.
165. *Ibid.*, Art. 5.
166. E.g., *ibid.*, Art. 3.

undertakings have emerged with considerable economic power, enabling them to exercise a great deal of control over digital markets and the digital economy as a whole.[167] Pursuant to the DMA, these actors are called gatekeepers[168] and it is accepted that the presence of gatekeeper firms on a market may hinder the contestability of that market.[169] Therefore, in order to remedy these situations as well as phenomena such as lock-in effects and data network effects, the DMA imposes a set of rules on gatekeepers to ensure the contestability and fairness of digital markets.

A closer reading of the DMA reveals that the primary focus is on the regulation of core platform services provided or offered by gatekeepers to business users established in the Union.[170] At first glance, this seems to suggest that AI is not directly covered by the DMA. While it is true that AI technology is not (currently) included in the list of 'core platform services' explicitly referred to in Article 2(2) of the DMA, it is nonetheless true that services that are included in this list, such as online search engines, virtual assistants, and online advertising, rely on some form of AI. Therefore, an overlap may exist between the application of the DMA and the AI Act to the extent that AI is used by gatekeepers in the process of competition. In these circumstances, the DMA exists to ensure that AI-driven core platform services do not enhance monopoly power or impede the competitive process - for example, by prohibiting algorithmic self-preferencing in the context of online search engines or online advertising - while the AI Act imposes extensive obligations on the functioning of the AI systems themselves.

Within the domain of competition law, particular attention has been paid to GenAI and whether GenAI models should be included in the list of core platform services. Calls to this effect were made by the Parliament in 2024 when it asked the Commission to launch a market investigation into GenAI and raised the question of whether a gatekeeper's possession of a state-of-the-art GenAI model could further solidify that gatekeeper's market position.[171] In this context, concerns seem to focus in particular on the ability of gatekeepers to leverage immense amounts of data and computing power that are typically only available to a few undertakings. This in turn could lead to new bottlenecks in the development of AI systems. Thus, while the DMA is concerned with keeping markets contestable, the nature of AI introduces some barriers to market entry - in terms of data availability and computing power - that would arguably make it difficult for smaller AI firms to compete with large gatekeepers.

5.5 Interface Between the DSA and the AI Act

Moving from the DMA to the DSA, it is clear that the main objective of the DSA is to create a safe, predictable, and trustworthy online environment.[172] It does so by

167. DMA, Rec. 3.
168. *Ibid.*, Recs 2-3; Art. 2(1).
169. *Ibid.*, Recs 2-3.
170. *Ibid.*, Art. 1.
171. European Parliament, *Competition Policy: Annual Report 2023*, 11 (2024).
172. DSA, Rec. 3.

targeting so-called providers of intermediary services – including (very large) online platforms and search engines – by imposing a number of obligations on them, in particular, to address the spread of illegal content, the risks associated with the spread of disinformation, and transparency in online advertising.[173]

When considering the interplay with the AI Act, it becomes clear that the goals are markedly different but clearly compatible: while the DSA regulates the online platforms on which AI systems can be deployed, the AI Act regulates the AI systems themselves and ensures that their deployment on online platforms is in accordance with fundamental rights obligations.[174] In this regard, two particular facets are worth highlighting.

The first relevant aspect to note is that both the DSA and the AI Act put a lot of emphasis on *transparency*. For the DSA, much of the attention is focused on the transparency of recommender systems that online platforms use to push products or content to their users. The DSA requires, among other things, disclosure of the criteria used to determine what particular information is displayed to end users, as well as the reasons why certain parameters are of relative importance to those users.[175] This element of transparency is also found in the AI Act, for example, through the wording of Recital 27.[176] In relation to AI systems that are considered 'high risk', it is relevant to draw attention to Article 13 of the AI Act, which requires transparency regarding the design and development of AI systems and mandates that AI systems must be accompanied by comprehensive documentation – including on the characteristics, capabilities, and limitations of the AI system – in order to properly explain or interpret their output. For low-risk AI systems, the relevant transparency requirements are taken up in Article 50 of the AI Act. Although these are somewhat relaxed compared to Article 13, they remain relevant, for example, to clearly inform users when they interact with AI systems[177] or when they are confronted with artificially generated/manipulated content. Thus, at the intersection of the DSA and the AI Act, both instruments contain provisions aimed at improving users' understanding of the AI systems with which they interact. Importantly, these transparency requirements may overlap, for example, when AI systems are used to personalize or recommend content on an online platform that falls within the scope of the DSA.

The second key interaction to consider between the DSA and the AI Act is the phenomenon of *AI-driven compliance*. Essentially, this refers to situations where substantive compliance with the DSA can be achieved through the implementation of an AI system. Good examples of this are content moderation requirements[178] and

173. *Ibid.*, Art. 2; Arts 11 et seq.
174. *Ibid.*, Rec. 70 *juncto* AIA, Rec. 3.
175. DSA, Art. 27.
176. *Ibid.*, Rec. 27: 'Transparency means that AI systems are developed and used in a way that allows appropriate traceability and explainability, while making humans aware that they communicate or interact with an AI system, as well as duly informing deployers of the capabilities and limitations of that AI system and affected persons about their rights.'
177. This requirement does not apply when it is obvious to individuals that they are interacting with an AI systems.
178. I.e., DSA, Art. 14.

notice-and-action mechanisms[179] for dealing with illegal content. Of course, the use of such AI systems can raise concerns in their own right, for example, in relation to the right to freedom of expression. Therefore, while AI-driven compliance is an emerging theme that is likely to attract more attention in the future when AI systems are used for regulatory compliance purposes, those AI systems will need to be subjected to a rigorous assessment under both the DSA and the AI Act to consider whether they impact any fundamental rights.

Overall, while the DSA and the AI Act cover different aspects of the digital economy, they both seek to contribute to a safer and more transparent digital environment, albeit each in its own way. It is clear that AI systems have a role to play in the DSA, whether for product/content recommendation purposes or content moderation. At the same time, the use of AI systems by providers of intermediary services and online platforms requires careful consideration in light of the extensive transparency requirements and potential negative impact on fundamental rights.

6 CONCLUSION

The purpose of this introductory chapter was to provide some background context regarding the development of AI and the adoption of the AI Act in the EU. With the AI Act, the EU is the first jurisdiction to take a clear stance on the future direction of AI growth, steering towards AI that is human-centric and trustworthy. Given the groundbreaking nature of the AI Act, there is little doubt that it will become the subject of extensively legal scholarly writing in the coming years. At the same time, the many interpretative issues surrounding the AI Act will likely require the Commission to issue various implementing acts, delegated instruments, and guidelines.

At the beginning of this chapter, it was mentioned that early developments in the field of AI took place as early as the 1950s. The graph depicting the AI development curve is characterized by ups and downs. From this perspective, it is fair to ask what this curve will look like in ten, twenty, or thirty years' time, and many questions remain about the future of AI. Is the writing on the wall now that the AI Act has been adopted? Will there be a third AI winter? Will AI technology reach a ceiling? What happens when there is no more data to consume? There are no clear answers to any of these questions, nor is it possible to make any firm assertions about them either.

Based on what we know, AI momentum is high in 2024 and there seems to be room for further growth in the coming years. Can the current high level of growth be sustained? Presumably not, and readers should be reminded of the S-curved pattern of innovation: a new technology trend requires some time to gain momentum, then experiences a period of rapid growth and feature expansion, before slowing down in terms of meaningful further improvements, only to be trumped by a whole new technology trend. At the time of writing, however, not a week goes by without another, more powerful, AI model being released to the public. AI applications also seem to be becoming more complex and intricate, with text-to-video generation tools representing

179. I.e., *ibid.*, Art. 16.

the latest example.[180] In addition, the archival website arXiv.org receives several hundred preprint paper submissions on AI and machine learning developments every day. However, it remains healthy to view AI developments with a certain degree of scepticism. For example, the phenomenon of so-called ChatGPT wrapper start-ups has begun to emerge: new start-ups that claim to be pioneers of an innovative AI-driven product, but that in reality only rely on the AI model of OpenAI behind the scenes. Against this backdrop, it remains important to be wary of overly presumptuous AI claims.

As this chapter draws to a close, I would like to invite you – the reader of this book – to reflect on three critical developments that are likely to shape the future of AI technology and society:

(1) *The commodification of computing power.* As AI technology advances, the value of computing power may transform it into a key economic asset, potentially serving as a currency in its own right. This shift could redefine how resources are allocated and valued across industries.
(2) The *rise of data markets.* The increasing reliance on data is not only shaping the capabilities of AI but is also likely to encourage the further growth of specialized markets for data. In the future, these markets may play a central role in governing how data is valued and exchanged.
(3) The *ongoing demand for AI expertise.* Despite advances in automation, the need for human expertise in AI will likely remain irreplaceable. Even over time, talent in this field will continue to be in high demand and serve as a driving factor in AI innovation.

Combined, these three developments allow us to envision a future where technology, society, and human expertise are increasingly intertwined. It is our task, as humans, to navigate this evolving landscape, to effectively adapt, and to continue to thrive.

7 APPENDIX

Table 4.3 Evolution of teraFLOPs and Prices per teraFLOP over Time in Consumer-Grade GPUs[181]

Year	*GPU*	*teraFLOPs*	*MSRP (in USD)*	*Price per teraFLOP (in USD)*
1999	GeForce 256	0.00096	249.00	259,375.00
2000	GeForce2 GTS	0.0016	349.00	218,125.00
2001	GeForce3	0.01	499.00	49,900.00
2002	GeForce4 Ti4600	0.018	399.00	22,166.67

180. OpenAI 2024.
181. *See supra* n. 29.

Year	*GPU*	*teraFLOPs*	*MSRP (in USD)*	*Price per teraFLOP (in USD)*
2003	GeForce FX 5800	0.024	299.00	12,458.33
2004	GeForce 6800 Ultra	0.045	499.00	11,088.89
2005	GeForce 7800 GTX	0.165	599.00	3,630.30
2006	GeForce 8800 GTX	0.345	599.00	1,736.23
2008	GeForce 9800 GTX	0.432	299.00	692.13
2009	GeForce GTX 295	1.1923	499.00	418.52
2010	GeForce GTX 480	1.3449	499.00	371.01
2011	GeForce GTX 590	2.4883	699.00	280.91
2012	GeForce GTX 680	3.0904	499.00	161.47
2013	GeForce GTX 780	3.9767	649.00	163.20
2014	GeForce GTX 980	4.9807	549.00	110.23
2015	GeForce GTX 980 Ti	6.0544	649.00	107.19
2017	GeForce GTX 1080 Ti	11.3397	699.00	61.64
2018	GeForce RTX 2080 Ti	13.4476	1,199.00	89.16
2021	GeForce RTX 3080 Ti	34.1	1,199.00	35.16
2022	GeForce RTX 4090	82.6	1,599.00	19.36

BIBLIOGRAPHY

Guidelines of Authorities

BIS 2023: Bureau of Industry and Security, *Public Information on Export Controls Imposed on Advanced Computing and Semiconductor Manufacturing Items to the People's Republic of China (PRC)*, US Department of Commerce (2023), www.bis.doc.gov/index.php/documents/about-bis/newsroom/press-releases/3158-2022-10-07-bis-press-release-advanced-computing-and-semiconductor-manufacturing-controls-final/file (accessed 22 April 2024).

Commission 2021: European Commission, *Coordinated Plan on Artificial Intelligence: 2021 Review* (2021).

Commission 2018a: Commission, *Commission Appoints Expert Group on AI and Launches the European AI Alliance*, Digibyte (2018), digital-strategy.ec.europa.eu/en/news/commission-appoints-expert-group-ai-and-launches-european-ai-alliance (accessed 2 May 2024).

Commission 2018b: Commission, *Coordinated Plan on Artificial Intelligence*, Policies (2018), digital-strategy.ec.europa.eu/en/policies/plan-ai (accessed 2 May 2024).

Commission Communication 2018: Commission, *Communication from the Commission to the European Parliament, the European Council, the Council, the European Economic and Social Committee and the Committee of the Regions: Artificial Intelligence for Europe*, COM/2018/237 final (Brussels, 25 April 2018).

Commission SWD Impact Assessment.

CNIL 2022: Commission nationale de l'Informatique et des Libertés (CNIL), *Délibération de la formation restreinte n° SAN-2022-019 du 17 octobre 2022 concernant la société CLEARVIEW AI* (2022) [for the press release in English, CNIL, *Facial Recognition: 20 Million Euros Penalty against CLEARVIEW AI*, CNIL (2022), www.cnil.fr/en/facial-recognition-20-million-euros-penalty-against-clearview-ai (accessed 6 May 2024)].

Garante 2023: Garante per la protezione dei dati personali, *Provvedimento del 30 marzo 2023*, doc. web n. 9870832.

HLEG Guidelines.

Reports and Recommendations

EPRS 2020: European Parliamentary Research Service (EPRS), *The Impact of the General Data Protection Regulation (GDPR) on Artificial Intelligence* (2020), data.europa.eu/doi/10.2861/293 (accessed 1 April 2024).

White Paper on AI.

Academic Writings

Brown et al. 2020: Tom B. Brown et al., *Language Models Are Few-Shot Learners*, arXiv (2020), doi.org/10.48550/arXiv.2005.14165 (accessed 7 May 2024).

Campbell et al. 2002: Murray Campbell, A. Joseph Hoane & Feng-hsiung Hsu, *Deep Blue*, 134 Artificial Intelligence 57 (2002), doi.org/10.1016/s0004-3702(01)00129-1.

Chiang et al. 2024: Wei-Lin Chiang et al., *Chatbot Arena: An Open Platform for Evaluating LLMs by Human Preference*, arXiv (2024)

Schuhmann et al. 2022: Christoph Schuhmann et al., *LAION-5B: An Open Large-Scale Dataset for Training Next Generation Image-Text Models*, arXiv (2022).

Clark & Muhammed Demircan 2024: James Clark & Muhammed Demircan (DLA Piper), *EU AI Act: Data Protection Aspects (EU)*, 2024 Practical Law 1 (2024).

Cowls et al. 2023: Josh Cowls et al., *The AI Gambit: Leveraging Artificial Intelligence to Combat Climate Change: Opportunities, Challenges, and Recommendations*, 38 AI & Society 283 (2023), doi.org/10.1007/s00146-021-01294-x.

Duan et al. 2019: Yanqing Duan, John S. Edwards & Yogesh K Dwivedi, *Artificial Intelligence for Decision Making in the Era of Big Data: Evolution, Challenges and Research Agenda*, 48 International Journal of Information Management 63 (2019), doi.org/10.1016/j.ijinfomgt.2019.01.021.

Fazlioglu 2023: Müge Fazlioglu, *Contentious Areas in the EU AI Act Trilogues*, IAPP (2023), iapp.org/news/a/contentious-areas-in-the-eu-ai-act-trilogues/ (accessed 7 May 2024).

Foster & Friston 2023: David Foster & Karl Friston, *Generative Deep Learning: Teaching Machines to Paint, Write, Compose, and Play* (O'Reilly 2nd ed. 2023).

Gao et al. 2020: Leo Gao et al., *The Pile: An 800GB Dataset of Diverse Text for Language Modeling*, arXiv 1 (2020).

Goodfellow et al. 2016: Ian Goodfellow, Yoshua Bengio & Aaron Courville, *Deep Learning* (The MIT Press 2016).

Herbosch 2023: Maarten Herbosch, *Intelligent contracteren: Het precontractueel gebruik van systemen op basis van artificiële intelligentie* (Wolters Kluwer 2023).

Hsu 2002: Feng-hsiung Hsu, *Behind Deep Blue: Building the Computer That Defeated the World Chess Champion* (Princeton University Press 2002).

Kan 2024: Michael Kan, *Zuckerberg's Meta Is Spending Billions to Buy 350,000 Nvidia H100 GPUs*, PCMag (2024), www.pcmag.com/news/zuckerbergs-meta-is-spending-billions-to-buy-350000-nvidia-h100-gpus (accessed 6 April 2024).

Kelleher 2019: John D. Kelleher, *Deep Learning* (The MIT Press 2019).

Mock et al. 2023: Marissa Mock et al., *AI Can Help to Speed up Drug Discovery: But Only If We Give it the Right Data*, 621 Nature 467 (2023), doi.org/10.1038/d41586-023-02896-9.

Nilsson 2009: Nils J. Nilsson, *The Quest for Artificial Intelligence* (Cambridge University Press 2009).

Ramesh et al. 2022: Aditya Ramesh et al., *Hierarchical Text-Conditional Image Generation with CLIP Latents*, arXiv (2022).

Saygin et al. 2000: Ayse Pinar Saygin, Ilyas Cicekli & Varol Akman, *Turing Test: 50 Years Later*, 10 Minds and Machines 463 (2000), doi.org/10.1007/978-94-010-0105-2_2.

Stein 2020: Amy L. Stein, *Artificial Intelligence and Climate Change*, 37 Yale Journal on Regulation 890 (2020).

Turing 1950: Alan Turing, *Computing Machinery and Intelligence*, 59 Mind 433, 433 (1950).

Wang et al. 2019: Alex Wang et al., *SuperGLUE: A Stickier Benchmark for General-Purpose Language Understanding Systems*, 33rd Conference on Neural Information Processing Systems 1 (2019).

Wang et al. 2018: Alex Wang et al., *GLUE: A Multi-Task Benchmark and Analysis Platform for Natural Language Understanding*, Proceedings of the 2018 EMNLP Workshop BlackboxNLP: Analyzing and Interpreting Neural Networks for NLP 353 (2018).

News

Atkinson 2023: Emily Atkinson, *Man Crushed to Death by Robot in South Korea, BBC News* (2023), www.bbc.com/news/world-asia-67354709 (accessed 16 January 2024).

Bertuzzi 2023: Luca Bertuzzi, *European Union Squares the Circle on the World's First AI Rulebook*, Euractiv (2023), www.euractiv.com/section/artificial-intelligence/news/european-union-squares-the-circle-on-the-worlds-first-ai-rulebook (accessed 7 May 2024).

Dave 2022: Paresh Dave, *It's Alive! How Belief in AI Sentience Is Becoming a Problem*, Reuters (2022), www.reuters.com/technology/its-alive-how-belief-ai-sentience-is-becoming-problem-2022-06-30 (accessed 1 April 2024).

Henshall 2023: Will Henshall, *Google DeepMind AI Breakthrough Could Help Battery and Chip Development*, Time (2023), www.time.com/6340681/deepmind-gnome-ai-materials (accessed 19 January 2024).

Lee et al. 2021: Yimou Lee, Norihiko Shirouzu & David Lague, *Taiwan Chip Industry Emerges as Battlefront in U.S.-China Showdown*, Reuters (2021), www.reuters.com/investigates/special-report/taiwan-china-chips/ (accessed 9 April 2024).

Reuters 2022: Reuters, *Google Fires Software Engineer Who Claimed Its AI Chatbot Is Sentient*, Reuters (2022), www.reuters.com/technology/google-fires-software-engineer-who-claimed-its-ai-chatbot-is-sentient-2022-07-23 (accessed 1 April 2024).

The Economist 2023: The Economist, *How to Worry Wisely About Artificial Intelligence*, 447 The Economist, Technology and Society 9 (London, 22 April 2023), www.economist.com/leaders/2023/04/20/how-to-worry-wisely-about-artificial-intelligence (accessed 7 May 2024).

Other

Anthropic 2024: Anthropic, *Claude 3 Pricing* (2024), www.anthropic.com/api (accessed 22 April 2024).

ASML 2024: ASML, *Statement Regarding Partial Revocation Export License*, ASML Press Releases (2024), www.asml.com/en/news/press-releases/2023/statement-regarding-partial-revocation-export-license (accessed 22 April 2024).

Beaumont 2022: Romain Beaumont, *LAION-5B: A New Era of Open Large-Scale Multi-Modal Datasets*, LAION (2022), www.laion.ai/blog/laion-5b (accessed 6 April 2024).

Common Crawl 2024: Common Crawl, *Open Repository of Web Crawl Data* (2024), www.commoncrawl.org/ (accessed 6 April 2024).

Council 2022: Council of the European Union, *Artificial Intelligence Act: Council Calls for Promoting Safe AI That Respects Fundamental Rights*, Press Release (6 December 2022), www.consilium.europa.eu/en/press/press-releases/2022/12/06/artificial-intelligence-act-council-calls-for-promoting-safe-ai-that-respects-fundamental-rights/ (accessed 3 May 2024).

Creemers et al. 2022: Rogier Creemers, Graham Webster & Helen Toner, *Translation: Internet Information Service Algorithmic Recommendation Management Provisions*, Stanford University: DigiChina (2022), www.digichina.stanford.edu/work/translation-internet-information-service-algorithmic-recommendation-management-provisions-effective-march-1-2022 (accessed 23 April 2024).

Future of Life Institute 2023: Future of Life Institute, *Pause Giant AI Experiments: An Open Letter* (2023), www.futureoflife.org/wp-content/uploads/2023/05/FLI_Pause-Giant-AI-Experiments_An-Open-Letter.pdf (accessed 22 April 2024).

Google 2023: Google, *Gemini API Pricing, Google AI for Developers* (2023), ai.google.dev/pricing (accessed 22 April 2024).

Hugging Face 2024: *Hugging Face: The AI Community Building the Future*, Hugging Face (2024), huggingface.co (accessed 6 April 2024).

IAPP 2024: IAPP, *Global AI Law and Policy Tracker, International Association of Privacy Professionals* (2024), iapp.org/media/pdf/resource_center/global_ai_law_policy_tracker.pdf (accessed 23 April 2024).

Kaggle (undated): Kaggle, *Find Open Datasets and Machine Learning Projects*, www.kaggle.com/datasets (accessed 6 April 2024).

Kiela et al. 2024: Kiela et al., *Test Scores of AI Systems on Various Capabilities Relative to Human Performance*, Our World in Data (2023, updated on 2 April 2024), ourworldindata.org/grapher/test-scores-ai-capabilities-relative-human-performance (accessed 6 April 2024).

Kiela et al. 2023: Kiela et al., *Plotting Progress in AI, Contextual AI (2023)*, contextual.ai/plotting-progress-in-ai (accessed 6 April 2024).

LMSYS 2024: LMSYS, *Chatbot Arena Leaderboard* (2024), chat.lmsys.org/?leaderboard (accessed 23 April 2024).

Nvidia 2023: Nvidia Corporation, *Form 8-K*, SEC (2023), www.sec.gov/Archives/edgar/data/1045810/000104581023000217/nvda-20231017.htm (accessed 22 April 2024).

OpenAI 2024: OpenAI, *Sora: Creating Video from Text*, OpenAI (2024), openai.com/index/sora (accessed 7 May 2024).

OpenAI 2023: OpenAI, *Pricing* (2023), openai.com/pricing (accessed 22 April 2024).

OpenAI 2022: OpenAI, *DALL•E 2 Preview: Model Training Data*, GitHub, github.com/openai/dalle-2-preview/blob/main/system-card.md (accessed 6 April 2024).

Papers with Code (undated): *Papers with Code: The Latest in Machine Learning, Papers with Code*, paperswithcode.com/ (accessed 6 April 2024).

Parliament 2024: Parliament, *Results of Roll-Call Votes 13-03-2024: Artificial Intelligence Act*, 1 (2024).

Peleg 2023: Yam Peleg, *GPT-4's Details Are Leaked*, X, Archive.Today (2023), archive.ph/2RQ8X (accessed 6 April 2024).

Sun 2024: Raymond Sun, *Global AI Regulation Tracker*, TechieRay (2024), www.techieray.com/GlobalAIRegulationTracker (accessed 23 April 2024).

TechPowerUp (undated): TechPowerUp, www.techpowerup.com (accessed 7 May 2024).

Tesla 2016: Tesla, *A Tragic Loss*, Tesla Blog (2016), www.tesla.com/blog/tragic-loss (accessed 16 January 2024).

Vaughan 2024: Thom Vaughan, *February/March 2024 Crawl Archive Now Available, Common Crawl*, Common Crawl Blog (2024), commoncrawl.org/blog/february-march-2024-crawl-archive-now-available (accessed 6 April 2024).

Chapter 5

The EU Artificial Intelligence Act: An Introduction

Ceyhun Necati Pehlivan[*]

1 AI IS TRANSFORMING THE WORLD

Artificial intelligence (AI) is no longer a futuristic idea. It is already here and being used across a variety of sectors: investment and financial services,[1] healthcare,[2] pharmaceuticals,[3] transportation and smart cities,[4] national security,[5] and criminal justice,[6] among others.[7]

AI analyses large volumes of market data and makes investment decisions, improves healthcare research and treatments by producing more accurate diagnoses, develops personalized medicines, drives cars autonomously, predicts traffic congestion and optimizes sailing routes. It anticipates criminal activity and assists judges in determining appropriate sentences and evaluating the likelihood of recidivism. In short, AI is augmenting human capabilities, reshaping industries, and transforming our lives in ways that were previously unimaginable.

Nonetheless, despite such significant benefits, it also raises challenges for our societies and economies. For example, it can perpetuate and exacerbate biases bias in

* This chapter is an updated and enhanced version of a report originally published in 5 Global Privacy Law Review 31 (Kluwer Law International 2024). It builds on the analysis and ideas presented in the original piece and includes several additional chapters.

1. Venkataramakrishnan 2023.
2. Capoot 2023.
3. Grover & Coulter 2023.
4. Hever 2023.
5. Fung & Lyngaas 2023.
6. Dement & Inglis 2023.
7. Marr 2023.

employment decision-making,[8] increase the spread of misinformation and deepfakes,[9] and develop more sophisticated cyber threats.[10] It may lead to job losses,[11] social surveillance,[12] and lethal autonomous weapons powered by AI.[13]

Concerns about AI systems surpassing human intelligence have further intensified with the rise of highly capable generative AI (GenAI) systems such as OpenAI's ChatGPT.[14] Researchers and industry leaders have even warned that AI could become impossible to control and eventually pose an existential risk to humanity.[15]

These threats have prompted governments worldwide to scramble for effective AI regulation. Nevertheless, the global regulatory landscape on AI is far from uniform.

While some countries like Singapore and the United Kingdom (UK) have adopted a light-touch strategy to promote safe and responsible AI and drive innovation, the United States (US) has signalled its aim to assert international influence over AI regulation through the Biden Administration's Executive Order on the safe, secure, and trustworthy development and use of AI.[16] Additionally, certain states in the US are adopting new laws, such as the facial recognition bill in California,[17] comprehensive state AI legislation in Colorado,[18] and AI hiring law in New York.[19]

China has also released several rules to establish an algorithm registry and issued some of the world's first mandatory rules on GenAI. The Chinese State Council is also expected to submit a draft national AI law later this year.

The European Union (EU) is however the forerunner in the comprehensive legal regulation of AI across the globe. It has adopted the world's first Al-specific regulation, featuring an extensive regulatory framework, and aims to lead the world on AI regulation.[20]

With its 180 Recitals, 113 Articles, and 13 Annexes, the AI Act aims to regulate the development and use of AI systems in the EU and address the aforementioned threats of AI.

This chapter provides an in-depth examination of the AI Act, offering organizations and stakeholders a detailed understanding of its critical components and their implications. While the AI Act's scope is extensive and far-reaching, this overview is designed to focus on the most pertinent aspects, acknowledging the practical limits of our discussion due to space constraints.

Throughout this chapter, we will explore the legislative background of the AI Act, providing context to its inception and development (section 2). We will then delve into

8. Malik 2023.
9. Verma 2023.
10. Krishnan 2023.
11. Napolitano 2023.
12. Herbert 2023.
13. Dresp-Langley 2023.
14. El País 2023.
15. Roose 2023.
16. The White House 2023.
17. Gutierrez 2024.
18. Colorado AI Act.
19. Weber 2024.
20. Chan 2023.

the personal and territorial scope, defining the regulatory perimeters and identifying the entities it governs, alongside applicable exemptions (section 3). The material scope of the Act, particularly the definition of an 'AI system,' which lies at the core of the legislation, will be thoroughly examined (section 4). We will discuss the Act's risk-based and tiered approach to regulating AI, including prohibited practices, high-risk AI systems, and the obligations imposed on operators of such systems (section 5).

Further, the chapter will cover the specific rules pertaining to general-purpose artificial intelligence (GPAI) models, addressing the unique challenges and regulatory requirements associated with them (section 6). We will investigate the interplay between the AI Act and other significant regulations such as the General Data Protection Regulation (GDPR) and the Digital Services Act (DSA), to highlight regulatory convergence and divergence (section 7). Enforcement mechanisms and penalties for non-compliance will be analysed to provide a clear picture of the consequences of non-adherence (section 8). Additionally, we will outline the timelines pertaining to the entry into force and gradual application of the AI Act, ensuring organizations are well-informed about when and how they need to comply (section 9). Finally, we will conclude with a summary of key insights (section 10).

However, because of the substantial breadth and depth of the AI Act, this chapter does not aim to cover every aspect of the legislation. Certain areas, though important, are beyond the scope of this overview due to the need for conciseness and focus. For instance, we will not delve into the roles of notifying authorities and notified bodies, nor will we examine standards, conformity assessments, or certification processes in detail. Furthermore, topics such as registration protocols and measures designed to support innovation, including regulatory sandboxes, will be briefly mentioned or omitted.

In addition, the governance structure at the Union level, including the establishment of the European Artificial Intelligence Office (AI Office) and the European Artificial Intelligence Board (AI Board), their respective tasks, and related advisory forums and scientific panels, will not be covered extensively. Similarly, we will not include in-depth discussions on post-market monitoring, information sharing, and market surveillance mechanisms.

By honing in on specific elements, this chapter aims to provide a coherent and practical overview of the AI Act. This focus ensures that the coverage is detailed yet accessible, concentrating on the most significant regulations and requirements that will directly impact businesses. Such an approach aims to equip readers with essential insights needed to navigate the forthcoming AI regulatory landscape effectively. While this chapter does not constitute an exhaustive analysis of the AI Act, it endeavours to highlight the key areas of immediate relevance and practical importance, ensuring that stakeholders are well-prepared for the changes ahead.[21]

21. For a detailed commentary of the AI Act, *see* Ceyhun Necati Pehlivan, Nikolaus Forgó & Peggy Valcke (eds), *The EU Artificial Intelligence (AI) Act* (Kluwer Law International 2025).

2 BRIEF OVERVIEW OF THE LEGISLATIVE PROCESS[22]

As part of its digital strategy, the Commission proposed the first-ever comprehensive legal framework on AI in April 2021.[23]

2.1 Position of the Council

The Council adopted the negotiating mandate on the proposal on 25 November 2022.[24] Among other things, the Council proposed to:[25]

- narrow down the definition of AI system to distinguish AI from simpler software systems;[26]
- extend to private actors the prohibition on using AI for social scoring;
- prohibit the use of AI systems to exploit the vulnerabilities of persons who are vulnerable due to their social or economic situation;
- allow real-time remote biometric identification systems in publicly accessible spaces by law enforcement authorities where such use is strictly necessary for law enforcement purposes;
- add a horizontal layer on top of the high-risk classification to ensure that AI systems that are not likely to cause serious fundamental rights violations or other significant risks are not captured;
- add new provisions on GPAI and on integrating GPAI into a high-risk system;
- provide for explicit exclusions of national security, defence, and military purposes from the scope of the AI Act[27] and additional provisions relating to the use of AI systems for law enforcement purposes;
- increase transparency regarding the use of high-risk AI systems and allow users to file complaints with the market surveillance authorities; and
- modify the provisions concerning measures in support of innovation (e.g., AI regulatory sandboxes should allow for testing of innovative AI systems in real-world conditions).

2.2 Position of the Parliament

Later, the Parliament confirmed its position in a plenary vote on 14 June 2023.[28] In this version, Parliament proposed to, among others:[29]

22. For additional information on the legislative process, *see* Koolen, in this volume, ch. 4, s. 3.5.
23. AI Act Commission Proposal.
24. AI Act Council Proposal.
25. *Ibid.*; Madiega 2024.
26. *See* s. 4.
27. *See* s. 3.3.
28. AI Act Parliament Amendments; Pehlivan & Valín 2023a.
29. *Ibid.*; Madiega 2024.

- amend the definition of AI systems to align it with the definition agreed by the Organisation for Economic Co-operation and Development (OECD);[30]
- substantially amend the list of AI systems prohibited in the EU, including banning the use of both real-time and *ex post* biometric identification systems in the EU (except in cases of severe crime and pre-judicial authorization for *ex post* use);[31]
- add the requirement that AI systems must pose a 'significant risk' to qualify as high risk and impose in certain cases to carry out a fundamental rights impact assessment (FRIA);
- categorize as high risk those AI systems used to influence voters in political campaigns and AI systems used in recommender systems displayed by social media platforms designated as very large online platforms under the DSA;
- include in the AI Act a layered approach to regulate GPAI systems, including imposing stringent obligations on providers of GenAI models (foundation models) to: (1) ensure robust protection of fundamental rights, health, safety, the environment, democracy and the rule of law; (2) assess and mitigate the risks their models entail, comply with some design, information and environmental requirements, and register such models in an EU database; and (3) comply with transparency obligations for models that use large language models to generate art, music and other content;
- enable national authorities to request access to both the trained and training models of the AI systems, including foundation models;
- establish an AI Office to support the harmonized application of the AI Act, provide guidance and coordinate joint cross-border investigations; and
- agree that research activities and the development of free and open-source AI components would be largely exempt from the scope of the AI Act.

2.3 Reconciliation of Positions in the Trilogues

On 1 July 2023, Spain took over the Presidency of the Council and announced that it would make the adoption of the AI Act one of its main priorities, with the aim of reaching a final text by the end of 2023.[32]

However, negotiations broke down on 10 November 2023 after France, Germany, and Italy opposed the Parliament's stringent approach to the regulation of foundation models[33] and offered 'an innovation-friendly approach'.[34] Accordingly, the Council

30. *See* s. 4.
31. *See* s. 5.1.
32. Pehlivan & Valín 2023b; Bertuzzi 2023a.
33. In relation to the regulation of GPAI, the Parliament's negotiating position in June 2023 was to: 'enshrine a layered approach in the AI act to regulate general-purpose AI systems. Parliament wants to impose an obligation on providers of foundation models to ensure robust protection of fundamental rights, health, safety, the environment, democracy and the rule of law. They would be required to assess and mitigate the risks their models entail, comply with some design, information and environmental requirements and register such models in an EU database. Furthermore, generative foundation AI models (such as ChatGPT) that use large language

proposed lighter-touch mandatory self-regulation through codes of conduct, allowing developers of foundation models to adopt a voluntary compliance mechanism.[35] The Parliament and the Council eventually reportedly agreed on a tiered approach introducing a stricter regime for 'high impact' foundation models and GPAI systems.[36]

Another significant controversy was around the use of AI in law enforcement and specifically remote biometric identification and facial recognition.[37] The Commission proposed to ban real-time remote biometric identification in public spaces for law enforcement purposes unless certain substantive and procedural conditions are met.[38] The Council's general approach also aligned with the Commission's position to strike a balance between law enforcement and human rights protection. Conversely, the Parliament proposed a complete ban on both real-time and post-remote (based on recorded video data) remote biometric identification in publicly accessible spaces.[39] Nevertheless, as a compromise, the Parliament eventually agreed to provide for exceptions to the real-time remote biometric identification ban and to categorize post-remote identification as high risk instead of a prohibited practice.[40]

After such intense negotiations, the Parliament and Council negotiators reached a provisional agreement on the final text on 9 December 2023.[41]

The Parliament adopted the AI Act with a large majority (523 votes in favour, 46 against and 49 abstentions) in March 2024.[42] Subsequently, in the final stage of the legislative process, the Council also endorsed it in May 2024.[43] The AI Act was formally signed into law on 13 June 2024.

On 12 July 2024, what is claimed to be the world's first-ever comprehensive legal framework on AI was published in the Official Journal of the EU as 'Regulation (EU) 2024/1689 of the European Parliament and of the Council of 13 June 2024 laying down harmonised rules on artificial intelligence'.[44] It entered into force on 1 August 2024, twenty days after its publication in the Official Journal.

The AI Act aims to ensure that health, safety, and fundamental rights enshrined in the Charter, including democracy, the rule of law and environmental protection are

models to generate art, music and other content would be subject to stringent transparency obligations. Providers of such models and of generative content would have to disclose that the content was generated by AI not by humans, train and design their models to prevent generation of illegal content and publish information on the use of training data protected under copyright law. Finally, all foundation models should provide all necessary information for downstream providers to be able to comply with their obligations under the AI act'. Madiega 2023.

34. France, Germany, and Italy joint non-paper; Bertuzzi 2023b; Rinke 2023.
35. Bertuzzi 2023c.
36. Council 2023; Parliament 2023; *see* s. 6.
37. *See* AI Act Parliament Amendments.
38. *See* AI Act Commission Proposal. For: (1) search for potential crime victims, e.g., missing minors; (2) prevention of threats to the life and physical safety of individuals or a terrorist incident; and (3) detection, identification, or prosecution of a perpetrator or a suspect of a criminal offence.
39. *See* AI Act Parliament Amendments.
40. Bertuzzi 2023d.
41. Council 2023; Parliament 2023.
42. Parliament 2024.
43. Council 2024.
44. OJ. L. 2024/1689 (12 Jul. 2024).

safeguarded from the harmful effects of AI systems.[45] However, some stakeholders remain concerned and argue that the AI Act fails to strike a sensible balance between regulating risk and promoting innovation.[46]

3 SCOPE OF APPLICATION

3.1 Personal Scope: Operators Along the AI Value Chain

The AI Act will apply to all operators along the AI value chain, namely:[47]

- providers;[48]
- deployers;[49]
- product manufacturers;[50]
- importers;[51]
- distributors;[52] and
- authorized representatives.[53]

The qualification of an operator's role under the AI Act is key, as each operator is subject to different levels of compliance obligations under the AI Act.

3.1.1 Provider

At the centre of the AI Act, providers are subject to the most stringent obligations under the AI Act. A provider is a person who *develops* an *AI system* or a *GPAI model* under its own name or trademark.[54] The AI Act applies to such developers where they:

- *place it on the market*, which means to first make available an *AI system* or a *GPAI model* in the EU;[55]
- *put it into service*, which means to supply the *AI system* for first use directly to the deployer or for own use in the EU market;[56] or
- *produce*, through an *AI system*, *output* that is used in the EU.[57]

45. AIA, Rec. 176.
46. *See, e.g.*, Crenshaw 2023.
47. AIA, Art. 3(8).
48. *Ibid.*, Art. 3(3).
49. *Ibid.*, Art. 3(4).
50. *Ibid.*, Arts 2(e) and 3(8).
51. *Ibid.*, Art. 3(6).
52. *Ibid.*, Art. 3(7).
53. *Ibid.*, Art. 3(5).
54. *Ibid.*, Art. 3(3).
55. *Ibid.*, Art. 2(1)(a).
56. *Ibid.*
57. *Ibid.*, Art. 2(1)(c).

Where a provider meets any of these three criteria, it will be required to comply with the AI Act, regardless of its place of establishment and location, and regardless of whether such provision is for payment or free of charge.[58]

Providers are subject to most of the obligations under the AI Act, such as implementing risk and quality management,[59] carrying out conformity assessment,[60] as well as extensive documentation obligations, as further discussed below.[61]

In case of high-risk AI systems, other operators will also be deemed providers, and will need to comply with the related requirements, where they: (1) put their name or trademark on a high-risk AI system already on the market or in service; (2) make a 'substantial modification' to a high-risk AI system already on the market or in service and it remains high risk; or (3) modify the 'intended purpose' of an AI system in such a way that it becomes high risk.[62]

3.1.2 Deployer

Deployers are, in essence, business users of AI systems. They (any individual or entity) use an *AI system* (but not *GPAI models*) under their own authority except where the *AI system* is used within their professional scope, excluding personal and non-professional activities.[63]

Deployers are subject to the AI Act where: (1) they are established or located in the EU; or (2) they operate an *AI system* that produces output used in the EU.[64]

This expansive definition captures many organizations that utilize AI, whether as part of their core operations or for ancillary activities such as human resource management and recruitment.

Deployers are uniquely positioned to observe AI systems in action, identifying risks that may not have been apparent during the development phase, and thus are tasked with monitoring the operation of high-risk AI systems.[65] Deployers must also take appropriate technical and organizational measures in order to ensure that they use AI systems in accordance with the instructions for use.[66]

3.1.3 Product Manufacturer

Product manufacturers are also under the scope of applicability of the AI Act, where they place on the market or put into service an AI system *together with their products* and under their own name or trademark.[67]

58. *Ibid.*, Art. 2(1)(a) and (c).
59. *Ibid.*, Art. 17.
60. *Ibid.*, Art. 43.
61. *Ibid.*, e.g., Art. 11. *See* s. 5.2.2.1.
62. *Ibid.*, Art. 25.
63. *Ibid.*, Art. 3(4).
64. *Ibid.*, Art. 2(1)(b) and (c).
65. *Ibid.*, Art. 26(5).
66. *Ibid.*, Art. 26(1).
67. *Ibid.*, Art. 2(1)(e).

Accordingly, where manufacturers incorporate an AI system into their product design, they will be subject to the AI Act, regardless of its establishment or location.

For instance, where an automotive original equipment manufacturer (OEM), regardless of its location, incorporates an AI system to monitor battery health or provide self-driving functionalities such as decision-making, sensing and perception, and navigation, and commercializes the vehicle under its own name or trademark in the EU, such OEM is a product manufacturer subject to the AI Act.

Also, as further discussed below, where such an AI system is classified as a high-risk AI system as a safety component of a vehicle, the OEM will be considered a provider subject to applicable compliance obligations.[68]

3.1.4 Importer

Any person qualifies as an importer where: (1) it is located or established in the EU; and (2) places an *AI system* (not GPAI models) on the EU market that bears the name or trademark of a person established in a third country.[69]

Accordingly, the AI Act aims to ensure that AI systems developed by non-EU providers also comply with the requirements set forth by the AI Act.

Importers must comply with rigorous due diligence and record-keeping obligations before placing a high-risk AI system on the EU market.[70]

These obligations include, among others, the verification that a provider has completed the conformity assessment,[71] prepared the necessary technical documentation,[72] the system bears the required CE marking and is accompanied by the EU declaration of conformity,[73] appointed an authorized representative,[74] and fulfilled other required criteria.[75]

3.1.5 Distributor

Organizations qualify as distributors when they make an *AI system* available on the EU market.[76] Accordingly, the definition of the distributor includes any person in the supply chain other than the *provider* or the *importer*, and thus serves as a 'catch-all provision'.

In a similar way to importers, the categorization of a distributor is only relevant with regard to *AI systems*, but not *GPAI models*.

68. *See* s. 5.2.1.1.
69. AIA, Art. 3(6).
70. *Ibid.*, Art. 23.
71. *Ibid.*, Art. 23(1)(a).
72. *Ibid.*, Art. 23(1)(b).
73. *Ibid.*, Art. 23(1)(c).
74. *Ibid.*, Art. 23(1)(d).
75. *Ibid.*, Art. 23.
76. *Ibid.*, Art. 3(7).

3.1.6 Authorized Representative

An authorized representative is: (1) located or established in the EU; and (2) serves as a contact person between (a) a non-EU provider of an *AI system* or a *GPAI model* and (b) supervisory authorities and consumers.[77]

In case of high-risk *AI systems*, non-EU providers must, prior to making their systems available on the EU market and by written mandate (or agreement), appoint an authorized representative that is established in the EU.[78] Recital 82 of the AI Act further states that:

> This authorised representative plays a pivotal role in ensuring the compliance of the high-risk AI systems placed on the market or put into service in the Union by those providers who are not established in the Union and in serving as their contact person established in the Union.

Similarly, non-EU providers of *GPAI models* must appoint in writing an authorized representative in the EU before launch.[79]

The providers (of both AI systems and GPAI models) must enable their authorized representative to perform the obligations specified in the written mandate received from the provider.[80] The obligations of the authorized representative include:

- keeping all relevant compliance documentation for ten years after the high-risk AI system or GPAI model has been placed on the market or put into service;[81]
- verifying that the EU declaration of conformity[82] and the technical documentation[83] have been drawn up and that an appropriate conformity assessment procedure[84] has been carried out by the provider of high-risk AI systems;
- providing a copy of the mandate to the market surveillance authorities[85] or the AI Office[86] upon request; and
- registering itself and its relevant high-risk AI system[87] with the EU database.[88,89]

The role and responsibility of the authorized representative are generally comparable to those of a 'representative' under the GDPR,[90] in the sense that non-EU organizations

77. *Ibid*. Art. 3(5).
78. *Ibid*., Art. 22(1).
79. *Ibid*., Art. 54(1).
80. *Ibid*., Art. 22(2) for high-risk AI systems; and Art. 54(2) for GPAI models.
81. *Ibid*., Art. 22(3)(b) for high-risk AI systems; and Art. 54(3)(b) for GPAI models.
82. *Ibid*., Art. 22(3)(a) and Art. 47.
83. *Ibid*., Arts 22(3)(a) and 11 for high-risk AI systems; and Art. 54(3)(a) and Annex XI for GPAI models.
84. *Ibid*., Art. 22(3)(a).
85. *Ibid*., Art. 22(3), para. 1, for high-risk AI systems.
86. *Ibid*., Art. 54(3), para. 1, for GPAI models.
87. In particular, high-risk AI system listed in AIA, Annex III, with the exception of high-risk AI systems referred to in point 2 of Annex III, *see* AIA, Art. 49(1).
88. EU database referred to in *ibid*., Art. 71.
89. AIA, Arts 22(3)(e) and 49(1).
90. GDPR, Arts 4(1) and 27; Rec. 80.

falling within its extraterritorial scope must designate a representative under the jurisdiction of the EU regulators. In the next section, we will further analyse this extraterritorial scope.

3.2 Extraterritorial Scope

The territorial scope of the AI Act is exceptionally broad. It will not only apply to operators that are established or located within the EU but also to non-EU *providers* of *AI systems* and *GPAI models* that have an effect on the EU - either by placing such *systems* and *models* on the EU market or putting the *AI system* into service in the EU.[91]

Further, the AI Act will apply to *providers* and *deployers* of *AI systems* (again, not *GPAI models*) to the extent that the output produced by such *systems* is used in the EU.[92]

The AI Act therefore has 'extraterritorial' reach and so could potentially capture a wide array of organizations with only a minor connection to the EU.

This extraterritorial reach tracks the similar approach of other EU legislation, such as the GDPR that applies to both EU-based organizations and to non-EU entities that offer goods and services to individuals in the EU or monitor their behaviour.[93]

This has significant consequences for businesses established outside of the EU. For instance, providers or deployers of AI systems located in third countries, such as the US, will have to comply with the AI Act where the output of their AI system is used in the EU.

Accordingly, where the AI Act applies, organizations outside the EU will face enforcement actions for non-compliance with its provisions.

3.3 Brussels Effect?

In addition to the *direct* application of the AI Act to organizations established outside of the EU falling within its extraterritorial scope discussed in the previous section, the AI Act will also have an *indirect* effect. This is because the AI Act is expected to make a significant impact on global standards through the 'Brussels Effect' and influence the development of AI regulations in other countries.[94]

As a result, other countries outside of the EU may consider the EU's regulatory approach as a model for their own national AI laws, as again has been the case with the GDPR, or seek to align their laws with the EU's standards in order to facilitate cross-border trade and cooperation.[95]

The AI Act's focus on 'ethical and trustworthy AI' and fundamental rights, freedoms, and democracy may therefore set a precedent for global AI governance.

91. AIA, Art. 2(1)(a).
92. *Ibid.*, Art. 2(1)(c).
93. GDPR, Art. 3(2)(a) and (b). *See also* s. 7.
94. Siegmann & Anderljung 2023.
95. Rzeszucinski 2022.

3.4 Exemptions

As discussed above, the AI Act has an exceptionally broad personal and territorial scope. Nevertheless, the AI Act sets out a number of *general* exemptions from its scope.

First, the AI Act will also not affect Member States' competences in national security nor apply to AI systems that are used exclusively for military or defence purposes, regardless of the type of entity entrusted by the Member States with carrying out tasks in relation to those competences.[96]

The uses of AI systems or models for 'purely personal non-professional' activities,[97] and for the sole purpose of scientific research and development[98] are also excluded from the scope of the AI Act. Similarly, the AI Act does not apply to any research, testing or development activity regarding AI systems or models prior to their being placed on the market or put into service (excluding testing in real-world conditions).[99]

Further, the AI Act does not apply to public authorities in a third country nor to international organizations, where they use AI systems in the framework of international cooperation or agreements for law enforcement and judicial cooperation with the EU or with one or more Member States, provided that such a third country or international organization provides adequate safeguards with respect to the protection of fundamental rights and freedoms of individuals.[100]

There are also specific exclusions with respect to certain AI systems or GPAI models, such as the systems offered under free and open-source licences.[101] Such systems are exempt from the AI Act unless they are placed on the market as high-risk[102] or prohibited AI practices,[103] or as certain AI systems that are subject to transparency obligations,[104] such as medical devices or AI systems used in law enforcement.

These exceptions are very specific and subject to conditions, and applying them can be complex and require careful consideration.

4 AI SYSTEMS

What does it mean to be artificially intelligent? This question has been subject to philosophical debate for a long time.[105] The term 'AI' is often used as a generic term for various computer applications that simulate human intelligence and problem-solving capabilities.[106] This involves the development of AI algorithms, modelled after the decision-making processes of the human brain, that can 'learn' from available data and

96. AIA, Art. 2(3).
97. *Ibid.*, Art. 2(10).
98. *Ibid.*, Art. 2(6).
99. *Ibid.*, Art. 2(8).
100. *Ibid.*, Art. 2(4).
101. *Ibid.*, Art. 2(12).
102. *Ibid.*, Arts 2(12) and 6.
103. *Ibid.*, Arts 2(12) and 5.
104. *Ibid.*, Arts 2(12) and 50.
105. Bringsjord & Govindarajulu 2018.
106. CAHAI 2020.

make increasingly more accurate classifications or predictions over time.[107] There is however no single, universally agreed definition of AI.[108]

On the legal front, the AI Act provides a definition of 'AI systems', which was also heavily debated and underwent several changes throughout the legislative process.[109]

At first, the Commission proposed a broad definition based on a number of techniques and approaches listed in an annex to the AI Act, so that it could be updated through delegated acts as the technology developed.[110]

Annex I of the AI Act had listed such techniques and approaches as part of an AI system, as follows:[111]

- machine learning approaches, including supervised, unsupervised, and reinforcement learning, using a wide variety of methods including deep learning;
- logic- and knowledge-based approaches, including knowledge representation, inductive (logic) programming, knowledge bases, inference and deductive engines, (symbolic) reasoning and expert systems; and
- statistical approaches, Bayesian estimation, search and optimization methods.

Following concerns that such a broad definition could sweep into traditional computational processes or software, the Council and Parliament later agreed to move the definition to the body of the text and proposed a narrower definition with additional conditions.

Finally, the AI Act defines an 'AI system' as:[112]

> a machine-based system that is designed to operate with varying levels of autonomy and that may exhibit adaptiveness after deployment, and that, for explicit or implicit objectives, infers, from the input it receives, how to generate outputs such as predictions, content, recommendations, or decisions that can influence physical or virtual environments.

This definition mirrors the OECD's recently updated definition of an AI system:[113]

> a machine-based system that, for explicit or implicit objectives, infers, from the input it receives, how to generate outputs such as predictions, content, recommendations, or decisions that can influence physical or virtual environments. Different AI systems vary in their levels of autonomy and adaptiveness after deployment.

In Table 5.1 below, we compare the different versions of the definition of 'AI system' proposed along the legislative process and used by the AI Act and the OECD.

107. IBM 2024.
108. OECD 2019.
109. Bertuzzi 2023e.
110. AI Act Commission Proposal, Art. 3(1).
111. *Ibid.*, Annex I.
112. AIA, Art. 3(1).
113. OECD Recommendation, Rec. I.

Table 5.1 Comparison of the Definitions of 'AI System'

Commission 2021 Proposal[114]	*Council 2022 Mandate*[115]	*Parliament 2023 Mandate*[116]	*AI Act (2024 Final Version)*[117]	*OECD Recommendation (Revised 2023 Definition)*[118]
software	a system	a machine-based system	a machine-based system	a machine-based system
that is developed with one or more of the techniques and approaches listed in Annex I and	that is designed to operate	that is designed to operate	that is designed to operate	
	with elements of autonomy and that, based on machine and/or human-provided data and inputs,	with varying levels of autonomy and	with varying levels of autonomy and that may exhibit adaptiveness after deployment, and	[Different AI systems vary in their levels of autonomy and adaptiveness after deployment.]
can, for a given set of human-defined objectives,	infers how to achieve a given set of objectives using machine learning and/or logic- and knowledge-based approaches,	that can, for explicit or implicit objectives,	that, for explicit or implicit objectives, infers, from the input it receives,	that, for explicit or implicit objectives, infers, from the input it receives,
generate outputs	and produces system-generated outputs	generate outputs	how to generate outputs	how to generate outputs

114. AI Act Commission Proposal, Art. 3(1).
115. AI Act Council Proposal, Art. 3(1).
116. AI Act Parliament Amendments, Art. 3(1).
117. AIA, Art. 3(1).
118. OECD Recommendation, Rec. I.

Commission 2021 Proposal[114]	*Council 2022 Mandate*[115]	*Parliament 2023 Mandate*[116]	*AI Act (2024 Final Version)*[117]	*OECD Recommendation (Revised 2023 Definition)*[118]
such as content, predictions, recommendations, or decisions influencing the environments they interact with.	such as content (generative AI systems), predictions, recommendations or decisions, influencing the environments with which the AI system interacts.	such as predictions, recommendations, or decisions, that influence physical or virtual environments.	such as predictions, content, recommendations, or decisions that can influence physical or virtual environments.	such as predictions, content, recommendations, or decisions that can influence physical or virtual environments.

In a similar vein, in the US, the definition used in the Executive Order (EO) on Safe, Secure, and Trustworthy AI, signed by President Biden, reads:[119]

> machine-based system that can, for a given set of human-defined objectives, make predictions, recommendations, or decisions influencing real or virtual environments.

The final definition set forth in the AI Act is a positive change in my view. The Commission's earlier proposal was indeed too broad in scope and could potentially include any software that uses data to predict, including statistical models, thereby creating legal uncertainty as to the material scope of the AI Act. The semantic alignment at the international level is also welcome.

However, from a technological perspective, it may not be entirely clear what an 'AI system' means in practice. For instance, there remains significant room for discussion as to whether or not a system operates with 'autonomy'.

The Commission is expected to provide guidance on the interpretation of this definition early in 2025.[120]

5 TIERED REGULATION BASED ON RISK

The obligations under the AI Act are tiered based on the type of AI system and, notably, the purposes for which it is intended to be used. The AI Act classifies AI systems by risk level. In this regard, Recital 26 states:

> In order to introduce a proportionate and effective set of binding rules for AI systems, a clearly defined risk-based approach should be followed. That approach should tailor the type and content of such rules to the intensity and scope of the

119. The White House 2023, s. 3(b).
120. Linklaters 2024, 24.

> risks that AI systems can generate. It is therefore necessary to prohibit certain unacceptable AI practices, to lay down requirements for high-risk AI systems and obligations for the relevant operators, and to lay down transparency obligations for certain AI systems.

Accordingly, some AI practices are deemed to pose an unacceptable risk and are banned outright, while systems classified as high risk are subject to stringent requirements.

The AI Act also sets specific rules relating to GPAI, with additional obligations for the most advanced GPAI models deemed to present systemic risk. All providers of human-facing AI systems are subject to transparency obligations.

In short, the higher the risk that an AI system poses to fundamental rights and freedoms, health and safety, the stricter the rules.

This will require organizations to be particularly careful when classifying their AI systems for the purposes of the AI Act's risk-based approach.

5.1 Unacceptable Risk: Prohibited Practices

As mentioned, certain AI practices are outright banned, as they are deemed to pose an unacceptable risk to individuals and violate EU fundamental rights and values.

The list initially proposed by the Commission in 2021 has been expanded in the final version of the AI Act, which now includes those AI systems that, in summary:

(1) apply subliminal, manipulative or deceptive techniques to distort their behaviour or cause harm;[121]
(2) exploit vulnerable individuals by distorting their behaviour in a manner that causes harm;[122]
(3) carry out certain social scoring;[123]
(4) predict the commission of criminal offences;[124]
(5) create facial recognition databases based on web scraping;[125]
(6) infer emotions in work or education (except where the AI system is intended to be used for medical or safety reasons);[126]
(7) create biometric categorization for race, political opinions, trade union membership, religious or philosophical beliefs, sex life or sexual orientation;[127] and
(8) are used by law enforcement for *real-time* remote biometric identification (with exceptions).[128]

121. AIA, Art. 5(1)(a).
122. *Ibid.*, Art. 5(1)(b).
123. *Ibid.*, Art. 5(1)(c).
124. *Ibid.*, Art. 5(1)(d).
125. *Ibid.*, Art. 5(1)(e).
126. *Ibid.*, Art. 5(1)(f).
127. *Ibid.*, Art. 5(1)(g).
128. *Ibid.*, Art. 5(1)(h).

The Parliament had initially proposed a longer list of prohibited applications, including a complete ban on real-time biometric identification systems in publicly accessible spaces.[129] However, as discussed above, upon opposition from the Council, the Parliament eventually dropped the prohibition on using real-time biometric identification in exchange for certain law enforcement exceptions.[130]

The use of real-time biometric identification systems for law enforcement purposes is allowed in limited circumstances and is subject to necessary and proportionate safeguards and conditions.[131] It should only be authorized if the law enforcement authority has completed an FRIA[132] and has registered the system in the corresponding EU database (except in duly justified cases of urgency).[133] Also, such use must be subject to a prior authorization granted by a judicial or independent administrative authority issued upon a reasoned request and in accordance with the detailed rules of the applicable national law.[134] It will also be limited in time and location[135] and only allowed for the purposes of:[136]

- targeted searches of victims of abduction, trafficking, sexual exploitation, and search for missing people;
- prevention of a specific, substantial and imminent threat; or
- the localization or identification of a person suspected of having committed a serious crime[137] (e.g., terrorism, trafficking in human beings, sexual exploitation of children and child pornography, trafficking in drugs and weapons, murder, kidnapping and rape).

5.2 High-Risk AI Systems

5.2.1 Classification

The AI Act mostly focusses on high-risk AI systems, which are permitted but need to comply with stricter requirements and obligations.

AI systems are classified as high risk due to their significant potential harm to health, safety, fundamental rights (as protected by the Charter), the environment, democracy and the rule of law.

There are broadly two categories of high-risk AI systems under the AI Act.

129. *See* s. 2; AI Act Parliament Amendments; Pehlivan & Valín 2023a; Pehlivan 2023.
130. Bertuzzi 2023f.
131. AIA, Art. 5(2), para. 2; and Rec. 34.
132. *Ibid.*, Art. 5(2), para. 2 and Art. 27; and Rec. 34.
133. *Ibid.*, Art. 5(2), para. 2 and Art. 49.
134. *Ibid.*, Art. 5(3).
135. *Ibid.*, Art. 5(2), para. 2.
136. *Ibid.*, Art. 5(2).
137. Criminal offences listed in *ibid.*, Annex II (List of criminal offences referred to in Art. 5(1), first subparagraph, p. (h)(iii)).

5.2.1.1 High-Risk: Safety Component

The first category refers to those AI systems that are:[138]

(1) used as a safety component of a product covered by specific sectorial legislation (EU harmonization legislation); and
(2) where that product is required to undergo a third-party conformity assessment under such EU legislation with a view to placing it on the market or putting it into service.

Such EU harmonization legislation (based on the New Legislative Framework (NLF) and other legislation) relates to among others:[139]

- machinery;
- toys;
- radio equipment;
- medical devices;
- civil aviation;
- marine equipment;
- motor vehicles;
- agricultural vehicles; and
- railway interoperability.

For instance, this category includes AI systems used as a safety component in:

- cars, planes, trains, boats, motor vehicles, drones, forestry equipment and quadricycles; and
- certain medical devices, machinery, toys, watercraft, lifts, protected equipment, radio equipment, pressure equipment, cable cars and gas appliances.

5.2.1.2 High-Risk: Standalone AI Systems

The second category of high-risk AI systems refers to standalone AI systems intended to be used in eight specific areas for very specific purposes (insofar as their use is permitted under the AI Act, i.e., they are not considered prohibited practices as discussed in section 5.1, and relevant EU or national law). They are listed in Annex III of the AI Act:

(1) *Biometrics:* systems intended to be used for remote identification, categorization, or emotion recognition.
(2) *Critical infrastructure:* systems intended to be used as safety components in the management and operation of critical digital infrastructure, road traffic, or in the supply of water, gas, heating or electricity.

138. AIA, Art. 6(1).
139. *Ibid.*, Annex I (List of Union harmonization legislation).

(3) *Education and vocational training:* systems intended to be used for determining access or admission, evaluating learning outcomes, assessing the appropriate level of education, or monitoring cheating.
(4) *Employment, workers' management and access to self-employment:* systems intended to be used for the recruitment or selection of natural persons or to make decisions affecting terms of work-related relationships.
(5) *Access to and enjoyment of essential private services and essential public services and benefits:* systems intended to be used to evaluate the eligibility of individuals for essential public assistance benefits and services, evaluate the creditworthiness, risk assessment and pricing for life and health insurance, or to evaluate and classify emergency calls.
(6) *Law enforcement*: systems intended to be used to assess the risk of a person becoming the victim of criminal offences, be used as polygraphs or similar tools, evaluate the reliability of evidence in the course of the investigation or prosecution of criminal offences, assess the risk of a person (re)offending not solely on the basis of the profiling, assess personality traits and characteristics or past criminal behaviour of persons or groups, or to provide support for the profiling of individuals in the course of the detection, investigation or prosecution of criminal offences.
(7) *Migration, asylum and border control management:* systems intended to be used as polygraphs or similar tools, assess the risk of security, irregular migration, or health, assist competent authorities for the examination of applications for asylum, visa or residence permits, and systems for the purpose of detecting, recognizing or identifying individuals in this context.
(8) *Administration of justice and democratic processes*: systems intended to be used for assisting a judicial authority in researching and interpreting facts and the law, and influencing the outcome of an election or referendum or the voting behaviour of natural persons.

5.2.1.3 High-Risk: Exceptions

Those standalone high-risk AI systems, as discussed in the previous section 5.2.1.2, will lose their 'high-risk' classification if they do not pose a significant risk of harm to the health, safety or fundamental rights of natural persons, 'including by not materially influencing the outcome of decision-making'.[140] The Commission and AI Board will provide practical guidance on this exception.[141]

This could be the case where the presumably high-risk AI system is *intended to:*[142]

140. *Ibid.*, Art. 6(3), para. 1.
141. *Ibid.*, Art. 6(5).
142. *Ibid.*, Art. 6(3), para. 2.

- perform narrow procedural tasks, such as transforming unstructured into structured data;[143]
- improve the result of a previously completed human activity, such as merely providing an additional layer to human activity;[144]
- detect decision-making patterns and deviations, and does not replace or influence human decisions, such as identifying potential inconsistencies;[145] or
- perform a preparatory task to an assessment relevant to the purposes of the high-risk use cases discussed in the previous section 5.2.1.2, such as file handling.[146]

Nonetheless, an AI system must always be considered high risk if it performs profiling of natural persons.[147]

A provider who considers that a presumably high-risk AI system is not high risk under these exceptions must document its assessment before that system is placed on the market or put into service.[148] The provider will also be subject to the registration obligations.[149]

5.2.2 Obligations for High-Risk Systems

As discussed, the AI Act sets out significant obligations for high-risk AI systems, with different responsibilities depending on the role of the operator.

5.2.2.1 Provider's Obligations

Unsurprisingly, most obligations fall on the providers of high-risk AI systems. Providers are generally required to ensure that these AI systems are designed, developed, and deployed with the highest standards of safety, transparency, and accountability.[150]

Providers must establish a risk management system that continuously assesses potential hazards associated with their AI technologies.[151] This involves conducting thorough pre-market evaluations and ongoing post-market surveillance to identify and mitigate any emerging risks during the deployment and operational phases of the AI systems.[152]

The AI Act mandates that providers implement robust data governance measures to ensure the quality, accuracy, and relevance of the datasets used for training and

143. *Ibid.*, Art. 6(3)(a).
144. *Ibid.*, Art. 6(3)(b).
145. *Ibid.*, Art. 6(3)(c).
146. *Ibid.*, Art. 6(3)(d).
147. *Ibid.*, Art. 6(3), last paragraph.
148. *Ibid.*, Art. 6(4).
149. *Ibid.*; *see also* Art. 49(2).
150. *Ibid.*, Arts 8 and 16.
151. *Ibid.*, Arts 9 and 17(1)(g).
152. *Ibid.*, Arts 9(2) and 61.

testing AI systems.[153] This includes adopting procedures to prevent bias and discrimination and guaranteeing that data is processed lawfully and ethically.[154] Moreover, providers must document their AI systems meticulously, detailing the design, development processes, and algorithms to facilitate traceability and accountability.[155]

To build trust and provide transparency to users and affected parties, providers are also obliged to ensure that their high-risk AI systems are accompanied by clear and comprehensive information, including instructions for use, safety precautions, and the intended purpose of the systems.[156] When incidents or malfunctions occur, providers must have mechanisms in place for swift and effective reporting and corrective action.[157]

In essence, the AI Act enforces a proactive and comprehensive approach to managing the lifecycle of high-risk AI systems, requiring providers to uphold the highest standards of diligence and responsibility.

5.2.2.2 Deployer's Obligations

Deployers of high-risk AI systems have clearly defined obligations to ensure the safe and effective use of such high-risk AI systems.

Primarily, deployers must take appropriate technical and organizational measures to use high-risk AI systems in accordance with the instructions for use provided by the system's provider.[158] This includes ensuring human oversight by assigning sufficiently competent, trained, and authorized personnel to monitor the system's operations.[159]

One key responsibility of deployers involves the proper management and monitoring of input data used by the AI system.[160] If the deployer has control over the input data, they must ensure that it is relevant and sufficiently representative of the intended purpose of the AI system.[161]

Additionally, deployers are required to monitor the operation of the AI system based on the instructions for use and inform providers if there is any risk or serious incident related to the system's functioning.[162] In situations where deployers detect that the use of the high-risk AI system may result in significant risks, they are required to inform the provider, distributor, and relevant market surveillance authority without undue delay.[163] If the deployer identifies a serious incident, immediate notification to the provider and relevant authorities is mandated.[164]

153. *Ibid.*, Art. 10(1).
154. *Ibid.*, Art. 10(2).
155. *Ibid.*, Art. 11.
156. *Ibid.*, Arts 13 and 14.
157. *Ibid.*, Arts 17(1)(i) and 73.
158. *Ibid.*, Art. 26(1).
159. *Ibid.*, Art. 26(2).
160. *Ibid.*, Art. 26(4).
161. *Ibid.*
162. *Ibid.*, Art. 26(5).
163. *Ibid.*
164. *Ibid.*

Deployers of high-risk AI systems are also obliged to keep the logs automatically generated by those systems to the extent that such logs are under their control.[165] These logs must be maintained for an appropriate period relevant to the intended purpose of the AI system, which should be at least six months, unless stipulated otherwise by Union or national law, particularly regarding data protection regulations.[166] This obligation underscores the importance of maintaining comprehensive records to facilitate traceability, monitoring, and regulatory compliance.

There are also important transparency requirements for deployers. For instance, deployers must inform workers and their representatives about the deployment and use of high-risk AI systems in the workplace.[167] This ensures that employees and their representatives are kept informed about new technologies impacting their working conditions.

Deployers also have a duty to inform natural persons whenever decisions made by these systems have direct implications for them.[168] Deployers are required to disclose the use of high-risk AI systems, detailing the intended purpose and the type of decisions being made.[169] This requirement promotes transparency and facilitates trust in the deployment of AI technologies by ensuring individuals are aware of the systems' impacts on their lives.

In cases involving high-risk AI systems used for remote biometric identification or emotion recognition, deployers must notify the affected individuals about the operation of these systems.[170] Such disclosures help maintain compliance with data protection standards, underscoring the importance of transparency in AI system usage (Articles referenced in general biometrics context).

For stand-alone high-risk AI systems discussed in section 5.2.1.2 (with the exception of AI systems intended to be used in critical infrastructure), certain deployers must conduct an FRIA to evaluate the potential consequences of the system's use.[171] This assessment should include a detailed description of how the system will be used, the categories of individuals affected, and measures to mitigate identified risks.[172]

Where the deployer is required to carry out a data protection impact assessment (DPIA) under the GDPR,[173] the FRIA will be conducted in conjunction with the DPIA.[174]

Deployers of high-risk AI systems, in certain circumstances, such as those used by public authorities or in the public sector, must comply with registration obligations and ensure the AI system is duly registered in the EU database before usage.[175]

165. *Ibid.*, Art. 26(6).
166. *Ibid.*
167. *Ibid.*, Art. 26(7).
168. *Ibid.*, Art. 26(11).
169. *Ibid.*
170. *Ibid.*, Art. 50(3).
171. *Ibid.*, Art. 27(1).
172. *Ibid.*, Art. 27(2).
173. GDPR, Art. 35. *See also* s. 7.
174. AIA, Art. 26(9).
175. *Ibid.*, Art. 26(8).

In summary, the obligations of deployers of high-risk AI systems encompass ensuring the use of these systems according to provided instructions, maintaining adequate logs, monitoring system operations, informing relevant authorities and affected individuals, and cooperating with competent authorities. These measures aim to ensure high-risk AI systems are deployed ethically, transparently, and with due regard for safety and fundamental rights.

5.2.2.3 Importer's Obligations

The obligations of importers of high-risk AI systems under the AI Act aim to ensure that these systems meet the necessary regulatory standards before reaching the EU market.[176] Importers play a crucial role in the AI Act's compliance system, acting as gatekeepers who verify that high-risk AI systems conform to the prescribed requirements.

Before an importer places a high-risk AI system on the market, they must ensure the system conforms to the AI Act's regulations.[177] This entails verifying that the relevant conformity assessment procedure has been conducted by the provider of the AI system.[178] The provider must have drawn up the technical documentation.[179] Additionally, the system must bear the CE marking and be accompanied by the EU declaration of conformity articulated,[180] along with instructions for use. Importers also need to confirm that the provider has appointed an authorized representative.[181] These requirements collectively ensure that the AI system is rigorously assessed and documented before entering the market.

Should an importer have sufficient reason to consider that a high-risk AI system is not compliant with the AI Act or is accompanied by falsified documentation, they are prohibited from placing the system on the market until it has been brought into conformity.[182] This includes situations where the system is suspected to be falsified. If the high-risk AI system presents a risk to the health or safety, or to fundamental rights, of persons,[183] the importer must inform the provider of the AI system, the authorized representative, and the market surveillance authorities.[184] This obligation underscores the importer's role in preventing non-compliant or dangerous AI systems from reaching the market, thereby protecting end-users and maintaining public trust in AI technologies.

Importers are also required to indicate their name, registered trade name or registered trademark, and the address at which they can be contacted on the high-risk

176. *Ibid.*, Art. 23.
177. *Ibid.*, Art. 23(1).
178. *Ibid.*, Arts 23(1)(a) and 43.
179. *Ibid.*, Arts 23(1)(b) and 11; and Annex IV.
180. *Ibid.*, Arts 23(1)(c) and 47.
181. *Ibid.*, Arts 23(1)(d) and 22(1).
182. *Ibid.*, Art. 23(2).
183. Within the meaning of as defined in *ibid.*, Art. 79(1).
184. *Ibid.*, Art. 23(2).

AI system and its packaging or accompanying documentation, where applicable.[185] This requirement ensures traceability and accountability, facilitating communication and regulatory checks throughout the AI system's lifecycle.

While a high-risk AI system is under the importer's responsibility, they must ensure that storage or transport conditions do not compromise the system's compliance with the requirements of the Act.[186] Maintaining appropriate storage and transport conditions is key to preserving the integrity and functionality of the AI system, thereby upholding its conformity to regulatory standards.

Importers must retain, for a period of ten years after the high-risk AI system has been placed on the market or put into service, a copy of the certificate issued by the notified body, where applicable, of the instructions for use, and the EU declaration of conformity.[187]

Importers are further obligated to provide relevant competent authorities, upon a reasoned request, with all necessary information and documentation to demonstrate the conformity of a high-risk AI system with the requirements.[188]

Finally, importers must cooperate with relevant competent authorities in any actions taken concerning a high-risk AI system they have placed on the market, particularly actions aimed at reducing and mitigating risks posed by the AI system.[189] This cooperation is necessary for effective market surveillance and for addressing any emergent issues related to the AI system's safety or compliance, further illustrating the importers' integral role in the regulatory framework.

The obligations of importers under Article 23 of the AI Act are comprehensive and detailed, ensuring that high-risk AI systems undergo rigorous scrutiny before entering the market. These responsibilities encompass verifying conformity assessments, maintaining documentation, ensuring proper labelling and storage, and cooperating with regulatory authorities. Through these measures, importers significantly contribute to the overall safety, reliability, and trustworthiness of high-risk AI systems in the market.

5.2.2.4 Distributor's Obligations

The obligations of distributors of high-risk AI systems aim to ensure that these systems comply with regulatory standards throughout the supply chain. Distributors are pivotal in maintaining the integrity and compliance of high-risk AI systems before they reach the final user.

Before making a high-risk AI system available on the market, distributors are mandated to verify that the system bears the requisite CE marking.[190] It must also be accompanied by a copy of the EU declaration of conformity and by instructions for

185. *Ibid.*, Art. 23(3).
186. *Ibid.*, Art. 23(4).
187. *Ibid.*, Art. 23(5).
188. *Ibid.*, Art. 23(6).
189. *Ibid.*, Art. 23(7).
190. *Ibid.*, Art. 24(1).

use.[191] Additionally, distributors need to ensure that both the provider and the importer of the system have fulfilled their respective obligations.[192] This preliminary verification is essential to guarantee that the high-risk AI system conforms to the established regulatory standards even before it is presented to potential users.

If a distributor has reason to believe that a high-risk AI system does not meet the requirements, they are prohibited from making the system available on the market until it has been brought into conformity.[193] Additionally, if the high-risk AI system poses a risk to the health or safety, or to fundamental rights, of persons,[194] the distributor must inform the provider or the importer accordingly.[195] This provision emphasizes the distributor's role in acting as a checkpoint, preventing non-compliant or risky AI systems from entering the market, thereby protecting users and maintaining trust in AI technologies.

Distributors must also ensure that during their responsibility period, storage or transport conditions do not jeopardize the system's compliance with the requirements.[196] Proper storage and transport are needed to maintain the system's integrity and ensure that it remains compliant with regulatory standards throughout its lifecycle.

When a distributor has reason to believe that a high-risk AI system they have made available on the market is not in conformity with the requirements, they are required to take corrective actions.[197] These actions could include bringing the system into compliance, withdrawing or recalling it.[198] Furthermore, the distributor must ensure that the provider, importer, or any other relevant operator takes necessary corrective measures.[199] If the system presents a certain risk, the distributor must immediately inform the provider or importer and the relevant competent authorities, detailing the non-compliance and any corrective actions taken.[200] This responsibility underscores the distributor's role in ensuring ongoing compliance and addressing any issues that arise post-market deployment.

Upon a reasoned request from a competent authority, distributors must provide all necessary information and documentation to demonstrate the system's conformity with the requirements.[201] Distributors must be prepared to present detailed records, ensuring transparency and accountability in their compliance activities.

Distributors are also required to cooperate with relevant competent authorities in any actions taken concerning a high-risk AI system they have placed on the market.[202] This cooperation is particularly focussed on reducing or mitigating risks posed by the system. The distributor's willingness and ability to cooperate with authorities are key

191. *Ibid.*
192. *Ibid.*
193. *Ibid.*, Art. 24(2).
194. Within the meaning of as defined in *ibid.*, Art. 79(1).
195. *Ibid.*, Art. 24(2).
196. *Ibid.*, Art. 24(3).
197. *Ibid.*, Art. 24(4).
198. *Ibid.*
199. *Ibid.*
200. *Ibid.*
201. *Ibid.*, Art. 24(5).
202. *Ibid.*, Art. 24(6).

for effective market surveillance and for addressing any emergent compliance or safety issues.

The obligations of distributors under Article 24 of the EU AI Act play an important role in maintaining the regulatory compliance of high-risk AI systems throughout the supply chain. These responsibilities include verifying CE marking and accompanying documentation, ensuring proper storage and transport conditions, taking corrective actions when necessary, and cooperating with competent authorities.

5.3 Specific Transparency Risk

The AI Act sets out specific transparency requirements for certain AI systems.

Such requirements are articulated in Article 50 of the AI Act and aim to mitigate risks associated with impersonation and deception when AI systems interact with natural persons or generate synthetic content. They are designed to ensure that users and those impacted understand they are interacting with an AI system, thereby safeguarding the integrity and trustworthiness of the digital ecosystem.

5.3.1 Providers

Providers developing AI systems intended for direct interaction with humans must ensure that these systems are designed to inform users that they are engaging with AI.[203] This transparency requirement applies unless it is patently clear to a reasonably informed, observant, and circumspect individual, considering the context of use.[204]

Notably, this disclosure obligation does not extend to AI systems authorized by law for law enforcement purposes, such as the detection, prevention, investigation, or prosecution of criminal activities, unless such systems are publicly available for reporting crimes.[205] This exception acknowledges the sensitive nature of such applications while balancing the necessity for public transparency where feasible.

Providers of AI systems that generate synthetic audio, image, video, or text content must ensure that this content is clearly marked, indicating its artificial origin in a machine-readable format.[206] The marking should be detectable, reliable, and state-of-the-art, incorporating technical standards and cost considerations.[207] This marking obligation is exempt for systems performing assistive functions for standard editing or those which do not substantially alter the input data, thereby maintaining editorial integrity.[208] Specific techniques for marking may include watermarks, cryptographic methods, or fingerprints, ensuring robust traceability.[209] This requirement addresses

203. *Ibid.*, Art. 50(1).
204. *Ibid.*
205. *Ibid.*
206. *Ibid.*, Art. 50(2).
207. *Ibid.*
208. *Ibid.*
209. *Ibid.*

the proliferation of AI-generated content and its potential to misinform, manipulate, or deceive, thereby bolstering trust and transparency in information dissemination.

5.3.2 *Deployers*

Deployers of emotion recognition or biometric categorization systems are also required to inform individuals of the system's operation and process personal data in accordance with European data protection regulations (the GDPR, Law Enforcement Directive, and EU Institution Data Protection Regulation).[210] This disclosure obligation does not apply where such systems are legally authorized for law enforcement purposes.[211] Again, this provision recognizes the critical balance between operational efficiency and the protection of individual rights and freedoms, ensuring that sensitive biometric data is processed transparently and ethically, balancing operational efficiency with the protection of individual rights and freedoms. This addresses potential concerns regarding the intrusive nature of such technologies.

Deployers of AI systems that generate deep fakes - synthetic content that authentically resembles real people, objects, or events - must disclose the artificial nature of such content to prevent fraud, manipulation, and misinformation.[212] However, this obligation is mitigated for creative, satirical, or analogous works, where disclosure should not impede the normal use or enjoyment of the work.[213] For AI-generated text purporting to inform the public on matters of interest, disclosure is required unless the content has undergone editorial control or human review, thereby ensuring accountability.[214] This balances transparency with creative freedom, addressing the potential ethical and legal implications of misinforming the public.

5.3.3 *Transparency Requirements*

The information must be clear, accessible, and distinguishable, and provided at the first interaction or exposure to the AI system.[215] Accessibility requirements ensure that all individuals, including those with disabilities, can understand and engage with the information seamlessly.[216] This inclusive approach is emphasized, considering the diverse demographic interacting with AI systems.

The AI Office is encouraged to facilitate the creation of EU-level codes of practice to enhance the implementation of transparency obligations.[217] The Commission may adopt implementing acts to endorse these codes or establish common rules if they are deemed inadequate.[218] This collaborative effort aims to establish clear, harmonized

210. *Ibid.*, Art. 50(3).
211. *Ibid.*
212. *Ibid.*, Art. 50(4).
213. *Ibid.*
214. *Ibid.*, para. 2.
215. *Ibid.*, Art. 50(5).
216. *Ibid.*
217. *Ibid.*, Art. 50(7).
218. *Ibid.*

practices across the EU, fostering consistency and reliability in detecting and labelling AI-generated content.

In conclusion, Article 50's transparency obligations aim to ensure ethical AI deployment, fostering trust and integrity in interactions between AI systems and humans. Through specific requirements, the AI Act seeks to preemptively address the challenges posed by AI technologies, thereby promoting responsible innovation.

5.4 Other AI Systems

All other AI systems that are neither prohibited (as per section 5.1) nor classified as high risk (as per section 5.2) and are not subject to transparency requirements (as per section 5.3) are not subject to further regulation under the AI Act, other than AI literacy requirements imposed on providers and deployers.[219]

The Commission observes that 'the vast majority' of AI systems will fall into this category.[220] However, the Commission may need to provide further clarifications to achieve this regulatory balance, particularly in light of the swift transition from traditional, rule-based program designs to sophisticated trained models.

As trained models become more prevalent, replacing older, rule-based systems, the complexity and diversity of their use cases expand. Consequently, the need for precise and updated regulatory guidance may grow to ensure that stakeholders fully understand their obligations and the implications of these advanced AI technologies.

This proactive approach will also help manage the evolving landscape of AI development and application, mitigating risks while fostering innovation.

6 GENERAL-PURPOSE ARTIFICIAL INTELLIGENCE

GPAI models are those AI models that display significant generality and versatility of output, which can perform a wide range of distinct tasks across multiple domains (such as generating video, text, images, conversing in lateral language, or generating computer code), rather than being specialized for a single specific task. They can serve either as independent systems or as foundational elements for numerous specialized AI systems to perform a variety of tasks.

These models are typically characterized by their ability to understand and generate human-like text, make decisions, recognize patterns, and learn from diverse sets of data. They leverage advanced machine learning techniques, particularly deep learning and neural networks, to achieve their versatile functionality.

Examples of GPAI models include: OpenAI's GPT (known for its capability to understand and generate human-like text across various contexts and tasks); Google's BERT (primarily used for natural language understanding tasks); and Meta's LLaMA (designed to be versatile and effective across a range of natural language processing tasks).

219. *Ibid.*, Art. 4.
220. Commission 2023.

The Commission's proposal for the AI Act was launched in 2021, prior to the rise of such GenAI tools.[221] The initial draft did not therefore include any specific requirements for GenAI.

However, their meteoric rise in 2023 and potential impact on the fundamental rights and freedoms of individuals have disrupted the debate,[222] pushing the Parliament and the Council to propose specific obligations for the providers of GPAI.[223]

As a result, the AI Act provides for a two-tiered regulation of GPAI models. The first tier of obligations applies horizontally to all GPAI models, while the second tier only applies to the most advanced GPAI models deemed to present *systemic risk.*

All GPAI models are in-scope of the regulation, with an additional set of obligations for the second layer of GPAI models.

6.1 GPAI Models *Without* Systemic Risk

6.1.1 Obligations for Providers

The AI Act sets out a number of horizontal obligations that apply to *all* GPAI models, regardless of whether they carry systemic risk. Such obligations are outlined to ensure the responsible development, deployment, and integration of AI technologies. They are underpinned by the principles of transparency, accountability, and cooperation with governing authorities, aiming to foster a trustworthy AI ecosystem across the EU.

Providers of GPAI models must draw up and keep up-to-date technical documentation pertaining to the model.[224] This documentation encompasses the training and testing processes as well as the evaluation results of the AI model.[225] At a minimum, the documentation must include the information set out in Annex XI.[226] This ensures that, upon request, the AI Office and national competent authorities can access all necessary details to evaluate the model's compliance and risk profiles.[227]

In addition to technical documentation, providers are required to gather and make available comprehensive information and documentation to AI system providers who intend to integrate the GPAI model into their own systems.[228] This requirement will allow these system providers to thoroughly understand the capabilities and limitations of the AI model, enabling them to meet their specific regulatory obligations.[229] However, the dissemination of this information must strike a balance between transparency and the protection of intellectual property (IP) rights, confidential

221. *See* AI Act Commission Proposal.
222. Pehlivan 2023.
223. *See* s. 2 and AI Act Parliament Amendments; Bertuzzi 2023g.
224. AIA, Art. 53(1)(a).
225. *Ibid.*
226. *Ibid.*
227. *Ibid.*
228. *Ibid.*, Art. 53(1)(b).
229. *Ibid.*, para. (i).

business information, and trade secrets, as protected under Union and national laws.[230] The included documentation must align with the elements specified in Annex XII.[231]

Another significant obligation is the enforcement of policies that comply with the EU copyright and related rights laws.[232] Providers must identify and uphold reservations of rights as expressed in Article 4(3) of the Digital Copyright Directive, using state-of-the-art technologies.[233] This underscores the ethical dimension of AI development, ensuring that the rights of creators and content owners are respected.

Furthermore, providers are obliged to prepare and publish a detailed summary regarding the content used for training the GPAI model.[234] This summary must adhere to a template prescribed by the AI Office, thus standardising the information made available to the public and ensuring consistency and comprehensibility.[235]

In their operations, providers must cooperate with the Commission and national competent authorities, facilitating the smooth exercise of their regulatory competences.[236] Moreover, providers can rely on approved codes of practice to demonstrate compliance with their obligations until harmonized standards are published.[237] Compliance with these European standards offers providers a presumption of conformity to the extent that the standards encapsulate the outlined obligations.[238] Should providers choose not to adhere to an approved code of practice or a harmonized standard, they must present alternative, adequate means of compliance for the Commission's assessment.[239]

To aid in the compliance with Annex XI (technical documentation for providers of GPAI models), the Commission is empowered to adopt delegated acts.[240] These acts detail methodologies for measurement and calculation, thereby facilitating the production of comparable and verifiable documentation.[241] Furthermore, the Commission can amend Annexes XI and XII (technical documentation for providers of GPAI models to downstream providers that integrate the model into their AI system) to reflect technological advancements through delegated acts, ensuring that regulations stay current with evolving technological landscapes.[242]

Lastly, any information or documentation obtained under these obligations, including trade secrets, is subject to confidentiality rules.[243] This provision guarantees the protection of sensitive business information while maintaining regulatory transparency.

230. *Ibid.*
231. *Ibid.*, para. (ii).
232. *Ibid.*, Art. 53(1)(c).
233. *Ibid.*
234. *Ibid.*, Art. 53(1)(d).
235. *Ibid.*
236. *Ibid.*, Art. 53(3).
237. *Ibid.*, Art. 53(4).
238. *Ibid.*
239. *Ibid.*
240. *Ibid.*, Art. 53(5).
241. *Ibid.*
242. *Ibid.*, Art. 53(6).
243. *Ibid.*, Arts 53(7) and 78.

6.1.2 Open-Source Licence GPAI Models

A distinct provision of the AI Act acknowledges the unique nature of open-source GPAI models.

Open-source GPAI models, characterized by their free accessibility, usage, modification, and distribution, represent a collaborative approach to AI development. The openness and transparency inherent in their design allow for widespread innovation and community-driven improvements. Recognizing this, the AI Act provides certain exemptions to these models, distinguishing them from commercially developed AI systems, while still maintaining necessary regulatory oversight to ensure safety and compliance.

Primarily, the obligations set out in Article 53 – requiring providers to maintain up-to-date technical documentation and to provide comprehensive information and documentation to AI system providers – are waived for open-source AI models.[244] This exemption applies on the condition that the models are released under a free and open-source licence, ensuring that all parameters, including weights, architecture details, and usage information, are publicly accessible.[245] This provision acknowledges the transparent nature of open-source projects, where community-led scrutiny and continuous improvement are integral components of development and deployment.

However, this exemption has significant boundaries. It does not apply whenever open-source GPAI models are categorized as having 'systemic risks'.[246] For these high-impact models, the same stringent obligations apply to ensure that the potential for widespread and unpredictable consequences is addressed. The rationale here is clear: the systemic risks posed by certain powerful AI models necessitate robust safeguards, regardless of their open-source nature, to protect societal interests and ensure public safety.

Importantly, providers of open-source GPAI models are still required to ensure compliance with EU copyright laws and related rights.[247] This includes identifying and adhering to reservations of rights as specified under the Digital Copyright Directive.[248] This obligation safeguards the IP rights of content creators and maintains ethical standards in the utilization of training data.

Additionally, providers are obligated to cooperate with the Commission and national competent authorities as required.[249] This cooperation ensures that open-source models align with overarching regulatory frameworks and facilitate the exchange of crucial information between developers and authorities.

As discussed above, the AI Act also accommodates the dynamic nature of the AI field by allowing providers to rely on codes of practice to demonstrate compliance until harmonized standards are established. This flexibility helps open-source providers

244. *Ibid.*, Art. 53(2).
245. *Ibid.*
246. *Ibid.*, last sentence.
247. *Ibid.*, Art. 53(2) and 53(1)(c).
248. *Ibid. See also* s. 6.1.1.
249. *Ibid.*, Art. 53(3). *See also* s. 6.1.1.

adhere to regulatory expectations while contributing to an evolving repository of best practices within the community.

6.2 GPAI Models *with* Systemic Risk

The AI Act imposes additional stringent obligations on providers of GPAI models classified as having systemic risk.[250] These are models that, due to their capabilities and widespread applicability, have potentially far-reaching impacts necessitating heightened regulatory scrutiny and control.

6.2.1 High Impact Capabilities

The cornerstone of this classification is the model's 'high impact capabilities'.[251] A GPAI model is deemed to possess high-impact capabilities when evaluated via appropriate technical tools and methodologies.[252] This includes indicators and benchmarks designed to rigorously assess the model's potential effects.[253] High impact here is not simply a measure of performance; rather, it delves into the model's capacity to influence or disrupt various domains at scale. For instance, an AI model capable of significantly influencing stock markets or manipulating public opinion on social media can be classified as high impact under these criteria.

One critical metric is the computational effort invested in training a model, measured in floating-point operations (FLOP).[254] If a model's training requires more than 10^{25} FLOPs, it is presumed to have high-impact capabilities.[255] This threshold serves as a quantitative measure to pre-emptively identify models that, by virtue of the resources invested in their creation, are likely to exert significant influence.

The 10^{25}-FLOP threshold captures the currently most advanced GPAI models, such as OpenAI's GPT-4.[256] The Commission may update this threshold considering technological advances and designate other models based on further criteria, such as the number of users or degree of autonomy of the model.[257]

In comparison, under the US Executive Order on AI, only models using more than 10^{26} FLOPS (or more than 10^{23} FLOPS with biological sequence data) will come under scrutiny and trigger reporting obligations.[258] This computational power threshold is

250. *Ibid.*, Art. 55(1).
251. *Ibid.*, Art. 51(1)(a).
252. *Ibid.*
253. *Ibid.*
254. *Ibid.*, Art. 3(67): '"floating-point operation" means any mathematical operation or assignment involving floating-point numbers, which are a subset of the real numbers typically represented on computers by an integer of fixed precision scaled by an integer exponent of a fixed base'.
255. *Ibid.*, Art. 51(2).
256. Mcguinness 2023: 'OpenAI's pre-training for GPT-4 required about 2.15 x 10^25 FLOPS. This meant running on 25,000 A100s for 90 to 100 days, with a total pre-training hardware cost of $63 million. They also estimated the cost of pre-training compute on H100s to be around $22 million.'
257. AIA, Art. 51(3) and Rec. 111.
258. The White House 2023.

higher than any model available in the market, including advanced models like GPT-4.[259] This means that no commercially available AI model currently meets these thresholds and, therefore, none are subject to the scrutiny or reporting requirements outlined in the Executive Order. The regulation appears to be targeting future, more powerful AI models rather than burdening the current generation with these requirements.

6.2.2 Commission's Role and Technical Evaluation

The Commission holds the authority to make these classifications based on its own assessments or following an alert from a qualified scientific panel.[260] Specifically, if a GPAI model matches the high-impact criteria outlined in Annex XIII of the Act, it can be classified accordingly.[261] The Commission's decision-making process is not only proactive but also reactive, ensuring that emergent risks are swiftly addressed.

Annex XIII provides a detailed enumeration of criteria that the Commission considers to determine whether an AI model has capabilities or impacts akin to those with 'high impact capabilities'.[262] The criteria include the number of parameters in the model, the quality or size of the dataset measured through tokens, and the amount of computation used for training the model – often quantified in floating-point operations.[263] Alternatively, computation can also be indicated by other variables such as the estimated cost, time, or energy consumed during training.[264]

Further, the input and output modalities of the model, such as text-to-text (large language models), text-to-image, or multi-modality approaches, are critically assessed against state-of-the-art thresholds for determining high-impact capabilities.[265] The benchmarks and evaluations of the model's capabilities, including its adaptability to learn new tasks without additional training, its autonomy, scalability, and the tools it could access, also play an essential role.[266]

Moreover, the criteria consider whether the model significantly affects the internal market, presumed if it has at least ten thousand registered business users within the EU.[267] The number of registered end-users serves as an additional metric to gauge the reach and impact of the AI model.

Understanding the dynamic nature of AI technology, Article 51 also empowers the Commission to adapt and evolve these benchmarks and thresholds via delegated acts.[268] This adaptive approach ensures that the regulatory framework remains state-of-the-art, taking into account continual improvements in algorithms and hardware

259. CRS 2023.
260. *Ibid.*, Art. 51(3).
261. *Ibid.*, in connection with Art. 51(1)(b).
262. *Ibid.*, 51(1)(b).
263. *Ibid.*, Annex XIII.
264. *Ibid.*
265. *Ibid.*
266. *Ibid.*
267. *Ibid.*
268. *Ibid.*, Art. 51(3).

efficiency. As the landscape of AI technology changes, so do the parameters that define systemic risk, ensuring ongoing relevance and efficacy in regulation.

6.2.3 Obligations for Providers

Providers have elevated obligations when it comes to GPAI models with systemic risk, driven by the rationale that these models, due to their extensive capabilities and broad applicability, possess the potential to cause widespread and unpredictable impacts across various domains. This heightened potential for both positive and negative outcomes necessitates a more rigorous regulatory framework to ensure that any risks, particularly those that could permeate and disrupt societal, economic, or technological systems, are meticulously identified, assessed, and mitigated.

Primarily, providers of these AI models must conduct evaluations based on standardized protocols and tools reflecting current state-of-the-art practices.[269] This includes conducting and documenting adversarial testing aimed at uncovering and mitigating systemic risks.[270] This evaluation process ensures that vulnerabilities are identified and addressed proactively, thus safeguarding against possible adverse outcomes.[271]

In tandem with model evaluation, providers are obligated to assess and mitigate possible systemic risks at the EU level.[272] This risk assessment must account for all sources of potential risks that may emanate from the model's development, its market deployment, or its usage.[273] By having a broad and proactive risk management strategy, providers can ensure that their models do not inadvertently contribute to systemic disruptions within the EU.

A critical aspect of these obligations is the requirement to monitor, document, and report serious incidents without undue delay.[274] Providers must communicate relevant information about such incidents and any corrective measures undertaken to the AI Office and, when appropriate, to national competent authorities.[275]

Moreover, ensuring an adequate level of cybersecurity protection for the AI model and its physical infrastructure is another significant obligation.[276] Given the potential systemic risks these models pose, robust cybersecurity measures are key to preventing malicious attacks or breaches that could lead to widespread harm.

Providers of systemic risk GPAI models may also rely on codes of practice to demonstrate compliance until harmonized standards are published.[277] Compliance with European harmonized standards grants providers a presumption of conformity

269. *Ibid.*, Art. 55(1)(a).
270. *Ibid.*
271. *Ibid.*
272. *Ibid.*, Art. 55(1)(b).
273. *Ibid.*
274. *Ibid.*, Art. 55(1)(c).
275. *Ibid.*
276. *Ibid.*, Art. 55(1)(d).
277. *Ibid.*, Art. 55(2).

provided that these standards encompass the set obligations.[278] For providers who opt out of adhering to approved codes of practice or harmonized standards, they must demonstrate alternative adequate means of compliance for the Commission's assessment.[279]

Furthermore, any information or documentation obtained under these obligations, including trade secrets, is protected under the confidentiality provisions detailed in Article 78.[280] This confidentiality ensures that sensitive business information is safeguarded while maintaining necessary regulatory oversight.

Thus, the EU AI Act meticulously outlines a dual-layered structure of obligations for providers of general-purpose AI models, with an added emphasis on those models posing systemic risks. These comprehensive obligations ensure that high-impact AI models are developed and deployed responsibly, with adequate safeguards to protect societal interests and maintain market integrity. In Table 5.2 below, we provide a comparative overview of the obligations applicable to different types of GPAI models.

Table 5.2 GPAI Model Requirements

Requirements	*With Systemic Risk*	*Without Systemic Risk*	*Without Systemic Risk (Open Source)*
Model evaluation and adversarial testing[281]	✓		
Systemic risk assessment and mitigation[282]	✓		
Documenting and reporting serious incidents[283]	✓		
Cybersecurity and physical security of AI models[284]	✓		
Technical documentation[285]	✓	✓	
Documentation for downstream AI system providers[286]	✓	✓	
Appointment of an authorized representative for non-EU providers[287]	✓	✓	
Copyright and rights reservation policy[288]	✓	✓	✓
Public detailed summary of training data and content[289]	✓	✓	✓

278. *Ibid.*
279. *Ibid.*
280. *Ibid.*, Art. 55(3).
281. *Ibid.*, Art. 55(1)(a).
282. *Ibid.*, Art. 55(1)(b).
283. *Ibid.*, Art. 55(1)(c).
284. *Ibid.*, Art. 55(1)(d).
285. *Ibid.*, Art. 53(1)(a) and 53(2).
286. *Ibid.*, Art. 53(1)(b) and 53(2).
287. *Ibid.*, Art. 54(6).
288. *Ibid.*, Art. 53(1)(c).

Requirements	*With Systemic Risk*	*Without Systemic Risk*	*Without Systemic Risk (Open Source)*
Cooperation and coordination with regulatory authorities[290]	✓	✓	✓

7 INTERPLAY WITH OTHER REGULATIONS

7.1 General Data Protection Regulation

While both the AI Act and the GDPR share the underlying principle of extensive regulatory reach, their scopes are tailored to their specific objectives.

The GDPR's scope is primarily concerned with the protection and processing of personal data, extending its application to any entity that processes the personal data of individuals in the EU.[291] This includes both EU-based entities and those outside the EU offering goods or services to,[292] or monitoring the behaviour of, individuals within the EU.[293] The GDPR's broad territorial reach ensures comprehensive data protection across a range of activities, adopting a rights-based approach focused on individuals' privacy and data security.

Conversely, the AI Act's scope is more focused, regulating the development, deployment, and use of AI systems within the EU market. Article 2 delineates its broad yet targeted coverage, encompassing providers, deployers, importers, distributors, and manufacturers of AI systems, irrespective of their geographical location, provided their AI systems impact the EU market or its citizens.[294] The AI Act classifies AI systems into different risk categories, imposing rigorous obligations on high-risk AI systems to ensure safety, transparency, and ethical usage.[295]

In terms of compliance requirements, many of the risk management and governance obligations set out under the AI Act are similar to those under the GDPR, albeit the provisions of the former are more detailed and wider in scope as they apply to all categories of data.

For example, the AI Act's requirement to establish and implement a risk management system in relation to high-risk AI systems is similar to the GDPR's requirement to carry out a DPIA, a process designed to identify risks arising out of the processing of personal data and to minimize these risks as much as possible.[296]

Another significant differentiation is the AI Act's alignment with product regulatory frameworks, such as the CE marking, which is fundamentally different from the

289. *Ibid.*, Art. 53(1)(d).
290. *Ibid.*, Art. 53(3).
291. GDPR, Art. 2.
292. *Ibid.*, Art. 3(2)(a).
293. *Ibid.*, Art. 3(2)(b).
294. *See* s. 3.2.
295. *See* s. 5.
296. GDPR, Art. 35. *See also* DPC (undated).

GDPR's data protection paradigm. The AI Act draws heavily from product safety regulations, implementing standards and conformity assessments for high-risk AI systems to ensure they meet predefined safety and performance criteria before entering the market. This approach echoes traditional product regulation models, focussing on the operational reliability and safety of AI technologies rather than purely on the data they process.

Despite the AI Act's focused regulatory approach, the GDPR remains profoundly significant in the AI landscape for several reasons. Many AI systems, especially those not classified as high risk, are virtually unregulated by the AI Act but likely to fall under the GDPR's comprehensive domain due to their processing of personal data. This means that even AI systems developed for less critical applications must adhere to stringent data protection standards, ensuring individual data rights are preserved.

For regulated high-risk AI systems and GPAI models, the GDPR applies in parallel. The dual application necessitates that such AI systems not only meet the AI Act's operational and safety requirements but also comply with GDPR's personal data protection mandates. This intersection underscores the GDPR's foundational role in managing data privacy across all types of AI systems, irrespective of their risk classification.

Notably, data protection regulators exhibit a marked focus on AI technologies, driven by the complexities and potential privacy implications inherent in AI systems.[297] Regulators are keen to ensure that AI deployments do not compromise data protection principles. This persistent regulatory scrutiny highlights the GDPR's pivotal role in overseeing AI systems, reinforcing its relevance alongside the AI Act's specific regulatory provisions.

In summary, while the GDPR provides a comprehensive framework for data protection applicable to all entities processing EU residents' data, the AI Act introduces a tailored approach to regulating AI systems, emphasizing safety, transparency, and ethical considerations. The AI Act's product regulation alignment and the GDPR's extensive data protection scope complement each other, creating a robust, multifaceted regulatory environment that addresses both the operational and ethical dimensions of AI technologies in the EU. Together, these regulations ensure that technological advancements are harnessed responsibly, safeguarding both societal interests and individual rights.

7.2 Digital Services Act

An intriguing aspect of the AI Act's scope is its intersection with other significant regulations, notably the DSA. For instance, Recital 118 of the AI Act highlights this relationship, detailing how the AI Act's requirements complement those of the DSA, particularly for very large online platforms and search engines. The DSA imposes a risk-management framework on these platforms, requiring them to assess systemic

297. *See, e.g.*, AEPD 2020.

risks and implement appropriate mitigation measures.[298] This includes evaluating how algorithmic systems may contribute to these risks and addressing potential misuses.[299]

The AI Act builds on this by presuming that if AI systems or models are embedded within very large online platforms or search engines governed by the DSA, their corresponding obligations under the AI Act are considered fulfilled unless significant systemic risks emerge that the DSA does not cover.[300] This layered regulatory approach ensures that AI systems integrated into widespread and influential digital services are scrutinized not only for their AI-specific risks under the AI Act but also for broader digital service implications under the DSA.[301] By requiring these platforms to identify and mitigate potential systemic risks from AI models, the EU enhances the comprehensive oversight of technologies that significantly impact the public and the market.

This convergence with the DSA's risk management protocols reflects the EU's holistic regulatory strategy, which integrates multiple regulatory domains to address complex technological landscapes effectively. The risk assessments mandated by the DSA for very large online platforms and search engines take into account the design, functioning, and potential misuse of AI systems, ensuring that risks to fundamental rights and societal impacts are systematically mitigated. This demonstrates an alignment and reinforcement between AI-specific regulations and broader digital service frameworks, facilitating a cohesive regulatory environment.

8 ENFORCEMENT AND PENALTIES

8.1 AI Systems

The AI Act entrusts Member States with the responsibility of laying down rules and enforcing penalties for infringements.[302] This includes both monetary and non-monetary measures, such as warnings, designed to ensure compliance across various stakeholders involved in the AI ecosystem.[303] The penalties are designed to be adaptable, taking into account the specific circumstances, and interests of small and medium-sized enterprises (SMEs), and start-ups, thus ensuring their economic viability while maintaining rigorous compliance standards.[304]

Economic considerations are paramount when determining penalties. For non-compliance with practices prohibited under Article 5, the AI Act stipulates severe fines. Operators found in violation can face administrative fines of up to EUR 35,000,000 or up to 7% of their total worldwide annual turnover for the preceding financial year, whichever amount is higher.[305] This stringent measure aims to deter operators from engaging in harmful AI practices that could have widespread adverse effects.

298. Church & Pehlivan 2023.
299. AIA, Rec. 118.
300. *Ibid.*
301. *Ibid.*
302. *Ibid.*, Art. 99(1).
303. *Ibid.*
304. *Ibid.*, last sentence.
305. *Ibid.*, Art. 99(3).

Enforcement extends to various obligations under the Act. For instance, providers, authorized representatives, importers, distributors, and deployers of AI systems face fines of up to EUR 15,000,000 or 3 % of their total worldwide annual turnover for failures to meet their respective obligations.[306] These obligations include the duties outlined in Articles 16 (for providers), 22 (for authorized representatives), 23 (for importers), 24 (for distributors), and 26 (for deployers), as well as the requirements for notified bodies and transparency obligations for providers and deployers of AI systems. These comprehensive provisions ensure that all actors within the AI supply chain adhere to the regulations, thereby fostering an ecosystem of accountability and ethical AI deployment.

Further, entities that provide incorrect, incomplete, or misleading information to notified bodies or national competent authorities are subject to administrative fines of up to EUR 7,500,000 or 1 % of their total worldwide annual turnover.[307]

The AI Act also includes considerations for mitigating factors when determining the imposition and size of fines. Factors such as the nature, gravity, and duration of the infringement, consequences, number of affected persons, and previous fines or legal actions are considered.[308] Additionally, the financial benefits gained from the infringement, the degree of cooperation with authorities, and measures taken to remedy the infringement or to mitigate harm are also evaluated.[309]

Public authorities and bodies within Member States have to comply with specific rules regarding administrative fines.[310] While the application of fines may differ based on national legal systems, Member States must ensure that these fines have an equivalent deterrent effect.[311] Furthermore, procedural safeguards, including the right to effective judicial remedies and adherence to due process, are pivotal in the enforcement of penalties, aligning with the broader EU legal framework to ensure fairness and justice.[312]

A vital part of maintaining transparency and oversight is the requirement for Member States to annually report to the Commission the administrative fines issued, along with related litigation or judicial proceedings.[313] This reporting mechanism facilitates a harmonized and coordinated enforcement approach across the EU.

8.2 GPAI Models

The Commission is empowered to impose fines on providers of GPAI models for intentional or negligent infringements of the AI Act.[314] These fines can reach up to 3 % of the provider's annual total worldwide turnover for the preceding financial year or

306. *Ibid.*, Art. 99(4).
307. *Ibid.*, Art. 99(5).
308. *Ibid.*, Art. 99(7).
309. *Ibid.*
310. *Ibid.*, Art. 99(8).
311. *Ibid.*, Art. 99(9).
312. *Ibid.*, Art. 99(10).
313. *Ibid.*, Art. 99(11).
314. *Ibid.*, Art. 101(1).

EUR 15,000,000, whichever is higher.[315] The scope of infringements that attract these fines includes non-compliance with key provisions of the AI Act, failure to adhere to requests for documents or information, providing incorrect or misleading information, and failing to grant access to the AI model for evaluation purposes.[316] This robust penalty framework underscores the EU's commitment to maintaining stringent oversight over GPAI models, given their potential impacts.

In determining the severity of the fines, the Commission considers factors such as the nature, gravity, and duration of the infringement, ensuring that the penalties are proportionate and appropriate.[317] The principles of proportionality and appropriateness are vital in ensuring that the fines are not excessively punitive but rather serve as an effective deterrent to non-compliance.[318] Additionally, the Commission takes into account any commitments made by providers in relevant codes of practice and the level of cooperation exhibited by the providers.[319]

Before finalizing any decision to impose fines, the Commission ensures due process by communicating its preliminary findings to the GPAI provider and offering an opportunity to be heard.[320] This procedural fairness is crucial in maintaining the legitimacy and acceptance of the enforcement measures.

To maintain a transparent and consistent enforcement environment, the Commission will adopt implementing acts detailing procedural safeguards and arrangements for imposing fines.[321]

In summary, the AI Act's enforcement and penalty mechanisms are designed to ensure compliance across the AI ecosystem. By imposing significant fines and considering multiple mitigating factors, the Act seeks to balance deterrence with fairness. The specific provisions for GPAI models highlight the EU's proactive approach to addressing the unique challenges posed by these versatile and high-impact AI technologies.

9 ENTRY INTO FORCE AND GRADUAL APPLICATION

On 12 July 2024, the AI Act was published in the Official Journal of the EU, marking the final step in the AI Act's legislative journey.[322] Following this milestone, the Act will formally enter into force on 1 August 2024, which is the twentieth day after its publication.[323] This initiation date signifies the official adoption and recognition of the AI Act as binding legislation across the EU.

While the AI Act technically comes into force on 1 August 2024, its practical application is designed to be gradual, giving stakeholders sufficient time to adapt to the

315. *Ibid.*
316. *Ibid.*
317. *Ibid.*, para. 2.
318. *Ibid.*
319. *Ibid.*
320. *Ibid.*, Art. 101(2).
321. *Ibid.*, Art. 101(6).
322. *See supra* n. 43.
323. *Ibid.*, Art. 113(1).

new regulatory requirements. The initial provisions, found in Chapters I and II, will apply from 2 February 2025.[324]

Chapter I sets out the scope and objectives of the regulation, establishing a guiding framework that outlines the regulatory intent. This early application is essential as it sets the foundational principles that inform the rest of the Act.

Chapter II, which provides definitions and categorizations, is equally important, offering terminological clarity and consistency necessary for the proper interpretation and application of the subsequent chapters. By implementing these chapters early, the EU ensures that all stakeholders have a clear and uniform understanding of the basic principles and definitions underpinning the regulation.

Subsequently, an expanded set of provisions will come into effect on 2 August 2025.[325] This includes Chapter III, section 4; Chapter V; Chapter VII; Chapter XII; and Article 78.[326] Chapter III, section 4 addresses specific requirements for certain AI systems, particularly those related to transparency and human oversight, which are vital for building public trust in AI technologies. Chapter V focuses on conformity assessment and the documentation and quality management systems that AI providers must implement to ensure compliance with the Act's rigorous standards. The early application of these chapters in 2025, a year before the general application date, allows businesses and regulatory bodies to establish the necessary processes and infrastructures to adhere to the new regulations.

Chapter VII deals with post-market monitoring and vigilance, highlighting the need for ongoing oversight even after AI systems have been deployed. Chapter XII delineates the penalty framework, essential for enforcing the Act and deterring non-compliance. Article 78, which addresses the confidentiality and processing of personal data, is also included in this phase, underscoring the importance of data protection within the regulatory framework. However, Article 101, concerning fines for providers of GPAI models, is subject to the general application deadline of August 2026, reflecting a strategic phased application.[327]

The comprehensive application of the AI Act is set to begin on 2 August 2026, marking the date when the majority of the Act's provisions will become fully effective.[328] This timeline affords stakeholders a balanced period to adapt, implement necessary changes, and ensure compliance with the new regulatory requirements. The phased approach recognizes the complexities involved in transitioning to such a comprehensive regulatory framework, especially given the diverse and expansive nature of the AI ecosystem.

Additionally, Article 6(1) and the corresponding obligations will only apply from 2 August 2027.[329] This specific provision pertains to high-risk AI systems and their associated requirements, warranting a longer adaptation period due to the stringent measures and thorough assessments involved. By allowing additional time for these

324. *Ibid.*, para. 3(a).
325. *Ibid.*, para. 3(b).
326. *Ibid.*
327. *Ibid.*
328. *Ibid.*, para. 2.
329. *Ibid.*, para. 3(c).

high-stakes components, the EU ensures that stakeholders can fully comprehend and integrate the detailed compliance mechanisms required for high-risk AI systems.

In conclusion, the staggered application of the AI Act shows a prudent and strategic regulatory approach. It allows for phased adaptation, enabling stakeholders to progressively meet the demands of the regulation.

10 CONCLUSION

The introduction of the EU's comprehensive regulatory framework has prompted a spectrum of reactions from different stakeholders, reflecting the complex and evolving nature of the AI ecosystem.

On one side, supporters of the AI Act argue that rigorous regulations are necessary to harness the benefits of AI while mitigating potential risks. Proponents argue that the Act's stipulations on transparency, accountability, and human oversight are crucial for building public trust in AI technologies. By mandating conformity assessments, quality management systems, and post-market monitoring, they believe the Act will establish a robust framework that safeguards fundamental rights and prevents harmful practices. They cite instances of AI misuse and bias as evidence of the need for stringent controls, asserting that the regulation will foster a responsible AI landscape that encourages innovation within a safe and ethical framework.

Conversely, critics of the AI Act express concerns that the regulation may stifle innovation and hinder the rapid growth of AI technology within the EU. They argue that the stringent requirements and potential financial penalties could impose significant burdens on AI developers, particularly SMEs and start-ups, which are crucial drivers of technological innovation. The need to comply with extensive documentation, conformity assessments, and continuous monitoring could divert resources away from research and development, potentially slowing down progress in the AI sector.

Moreover, some industry experts highlight the risk of regulatory fragmentation, where different interpretations and implementations of the Act by Member States could create barriers to a cohesive European AI market. This concern underscores the importance of harmonized standards and guidelines to ensure consistency and clarity in the application of the Act.

Recognizing these challenges, businesses that develop and deploy AI systems are strongly recommended to begin preparing for regulatory compliance well in advance of the AI Act's enforcement dates. Taking proactive measures now will ensure they are fully prepared to meet the stringent requirements of the Act when it takes effect.

The AI Act also intersects with other regulatory frameworks, such as the GDPR and the DSA, adding another layer of complexity. Proponents see this as an advantage, creating an integrated approach to digital and AI governance. However, critics warn that navigating multiple overlapping regulations could pose additional compliance challenges for businesses.

In conclusion, the AI Act embodies the EU's ambition to lead in the ethical and safe development of AI technologies. The regulation aims to balance the promise of AI with the necessity of protecting public interests and upholding fundamental rights.

While it presents a model for responsible AI governance, its potential impact on innovation and technological progress remains a subject of debate. The diverse reactions to the AI Act reflect the broader discourse on how best to regulate rapidly evolving technologies in a way that fosters both innovation and public trust. As the Act comes into force and stakeholders adapt to its requirements, the ongoing dialogue between regulators, industry players, and civil society will be crucial in shaping a dynamic and balanced AI ecosystem in the EU. This discourse will help ensure that the regulation evolves in tandem with technological advancements, maintaining the delicate balance between promoting innovation and safeguarding societal values.

Ultimately, only time will tell whether the AI Act strikes the right balance between protecting public welfare and encouraging the ongoing innovation and advancement of AI technologies.

BIBLIOGRAPHY

Guidelines of Authorities

AEPD 2020: Agencia Española de Protección de Datos (AEPD), *Adecuación al RGPD de tratamientos que incorporan Inteligencia Artificial. Una introducción*, www.aepd.es/guias/adecuacion-rgpd-ia.pdf (accessed 10 January 2024).

DPC (undated): Data Protection Commission (Ireland), *Data Protection Impact Assessments* (undated), www.dataprotection.ie/en/organisations/know-your-obligations/data-protection-impact-assessments (accessed 10 January 2024).

Reports and Recommendations

CRS 2023: Congressional Research Service, *Highlights of the 2023 Executive Order on Artificial Intelligence for Congress*, R47843 6 (17 November 2023), crsreports.congress.gov/product/pdf/R/R47843 (accessed 11 January 2024).

Szczepański 2024: Marcin Szczepański, *United States Approach to Artificial Intelligence*, European Parliamentary Research Service (EPRS) (January 2024), www.europarl.europa.eu/RegData/etudes/ATAG/2024/757605/EPRS_ATA(2024)757605_EN.pdf (accessed 20 July 2024).

Madiega 2024: Tambiama Madiega, *Legislative Train Schedule: Commission 2019-24: A Europe Fit for the Digital Age: Artificial intelligence Act*, European Parliamentary Research Service (EPRS) (20 June 2024), www.europarl.europa.eu/legislative-train/theme-a-europe-fit-for-the-digital-age/file-regulation-on-artificial-intelligence (accessed 20 July 2024).

Madiega 2023: Tambiama Madiega, *At a Glance: Parliament's Negotiating Position on the Artificial Intelligence Act*, European Parliamentary Research Service (EPRS) (June 2023), www.europarl.europa.eu/RegData/etudes/ATAG/2023/747926/EPRS_ATA(2023)747926_EN.pdf (accessed 20 July 2024).

OECD 2019: OECD, *Artificial Intelligence in Society* (11 June 2019), doi:10.1787/eedfee77-en.

Academic Writings

Church & Pehlivan 2023: Peter Church & Ceyhun Necati Pehlivan, *The Digital Services Act (DSA): A New Era for Online Harms and Intermediary Liability*, 4 Global Privacy Law Review 53-59 (2023), doi.org/10.54648/gplr2023005.

Dresp-Langley 2023: Birgitta Dresp-Langley, *The Weaponization of Artificial Intelligence: What the Public Needs to Be Aware of*, 6 Frontiers in Artificial Intelligence (8 March 2023), doi.org/10.3389/frai.2023.1154184 (accessed 21 December 2023).

Lee & Dews 2023: Nicol Turner Lee & Fred Dews, *Unpacking President Biden's Executive Order on Artificial Intelligence*, Brookings (3 November 2023), www.brookings.edu/articles/unpacking-president-bidens-executive-order-on-artificial-intelligence (accessed 20 July 2024).

Rotenberg & Randolph 2024: Marc Rotenberg & Christabel Randolph, *International Frameworks for AI Governance*, in this volume (2024).

Blogs

Bringsjord & Govindarajulu 2018: Selmer Bringsjord & Naveen Sundar Govindarajulu, *Artificial Intelligence*, Stanford Encyclopedia of Philosophy (12 July 2018), plato.stanford.edu/entries/artificial-intelligence (accessed 21 December 2023).

Dement & Inglis 2023: Carl Dement & Melissa Inglis, *AI Can Be Used to Write Better Criminal Justice Reports, But Professionals in the Field Still Have Reservations About Its Use*, London School of Economics Blog (20 July 2023), blogs.lse.ac.uk/usappblog/2023/07/20/ai-can-be-used-to-write-better-criminal-justice-reports-but-professionals-in-the-field-still-have-reservations-about-its-use (accessed 21 December 2023).

Küspert et al. 2023: Sabrina Küspert, Nicolas Moës & Connor Dunlop, *The Value Chain Of General-Purpose AI*, Ada Lovelace Institute Blog (10 February 2023), www.adalovelaceinstitute.org/blog/value-chain-general-purpose-ai (accessed 10 January 2024).

Mcguinness 2023: Patrick Mcguinness, *GPT-4 Details Revealed*, Patrick Mcguinness Substack (12 July 2023), patmcguinness.substack.com/p/gpt-4-details-revealed (accessed 10 January 2024).

Pehlivan 2023: Ceyhun Necati Pehlivan, *European Parliament Reaches Deal on AI Act*, Linklaters TechInsights (28 April 2023), techinsights.linklaters.com/post/102idss/european-parliament-reaches-deal-on-ai-act (accessed 10 January 2024).

Pehlivan & Valín 2023a: Ceyhun Necati Pehlivan & Elena Valín, *EU's AI Act Moves to the Final Stage of Adoption*, Linklaters TechInsights (14 June 2023), techinsights.linklaters.com/post/102igwm/eus-ai-act-moves-to-the-final-stage-of-adoption (accessed 11 January 2024).

Pehlivan & Valín 2023b: Ceyhun Necati Pehlivan & Elena Valín, *Spanish EU Presidency and the AI Act*, Linklaters TechInsights (6 July 2023), techinsights.linklaters.com/post/102iip4/spanish-eu-presidency-and-the-ai-act (accessed 11 January 2024).

Siegmann & Anderljung 2023: Charlotte Siegmann & Markus Anderljung, *The Brussels Effect and AI: How EU Regulation will Impact the Global AI Market*, Montreal AI Ethics Institute (1 June 2023), montrealethics.ai/the-brussels-effect-and-ai-how-eu-regulation-will-impact-the-global-ai-market (accessed 21 December 2023).

News

Bertuzzi 2023a: Luca Bertuzzi, *AI Act: Spanish Presidency Sets Out Options on Key Topics of Negotiation*, Euractiv (3 July 2023), www.euractiv.com/section/artificial-intelligence/news/ai-act-spanish-presidency-sets-out-options-on-key-topics-of-negotiation (accessed 11 January 2024).

Bertuzzi 2023b: Luca Bertuzzi, *EU's AI Act Negotiations Hit the Brakes Over Foundation Models*, Euractiv (10 November 2023), www.euractiv.com/section/artificial-intelligence/news/eus-ai-act-negotiations-hit-the-brakes-over-foundation-models (accessed 21 December 2023).

Bertuzzi 2023c: Luca Bertuzzi, *France, Germany, Italy Push For 'Mandatory Self-Regulation' for Foundation Models in EU's AI Law*, Euractiv (19 November 2023), www.euractiv.com/section/artificial-intelligence/news/france-germany-italy-push-for-mandatory-self-regulation-for-foundation-models-in-eus-ai-law (accessed 21 December 2023).

Bertuzzi 2023d: Luca Bertuzzi, *AI Act: MEPs Mull Narrow Facial Recognition Technology Uses in Exchange for Other Bans*, Euractiv (6 November 2023), www.euractiv.com/section/artificial-intelligence/news/ai-act-meps-mull-narrow-facial-recognition-technology-uses-in-exchange-for-other-bans/ (accessed 10 January 2024).

Bertuzzi 2023e: Luca Bertuzzi, *AI Act Moves Ahead in EU Parliament with Key Committee Vote*, Euractiv (11 May 2023), www.euractiv.com/section/artificial-intelligence/news/ai-act-moves-ahead-in-eu-parliament-with-key-committee-vote (accessed 21 December 2023).

Bertuzzi 2023f: Luca Bertuzzi, *MEPs Seal the Deal on Artificial Intelligence Act*, Euractive (27 April 2023), www.euractiv.com/section/artificial-intelligence/news/meps-seal-the-deal-on-artificial-intelligence-act/ (accessed 24 January 2024).

Bertuzzi 2023g: Luca Bertuzzi, *Leading EU Lawmakers Propose Obligations for General Purpose AI*, Euractive (14 March 2023), www.euractiv.com/section/artificial-intelligence/news/leading-eu-lawmakers-propose-obligations-for-general-purpose-ai (accessed 10 January 2024).

Capoot 2023: Ashley Capoot, *Google Is Rolling Out New AI Models for Health Care. Here's How Doctors Are Using Them*, CNBC (13 December 2023), www.cnbc.com/2023/12/13/how-doctors-are-using-googles-new-ai-models-for-health-care.html (accessed 21 December 2023).

Chan 2023: Kelvin Chan, *Europe Was Set to Lead the World on AI Regulation. But Can Leaders Reach a Deal?*, ABC News (6 December 2023), abcnews.go.com/Technology/wireStory/europe-set-lead-world-ai-regulation-leaders-reach-105413389 (accessed 21 December 2023).

Chee & Hummel 2024: Foo Yun Chee & Tassilo Hummel, *Europe Sets Benchmark for Rest of the World with Landmark AI Laws*, Reuters (22 May 2024), www.reuters.com/world/europe/eu-countries-back-landmark-artificial-intelligence-rules-2024-05-21 (accessed 20 July 2024).

El País 2023: El País, *Artificial Intelligence Poses 'Risk of Extinction,' Experts Say in New Warning* (30 May 2023), english.elpais.com/science-tech/2023-05-30/artificial-intelligence-poses-risk-of-extinction-experts-say-in-new-warning.html (accessed 21 December 2023).

Fung & Lyngaas 2023: Brian Fung & Sean Lyngaas, *The US Government Plans to Go All-In on Using AI. But It Lacks a Plan, Says A Government Watchdog*, CNN (12 December 2023), edition.cnn.com/2023/12/12/tech/gao-ai-report/index.html (accessed 21 December 2023).

Grover & Coulter 2023: Natalie Grover & Martin Coulter, *Insight: Big Pharma Bets on AI to Speed Up Clinical Trials*, Reuters (22 September 2023), www.reuters.com/technology/big-pharma-bets-ai-speed-up-clinical-trials-2023-09-22 (accessed 21 December 2023).

Gutierrez 2024: Hannah Gutierrez, *California Bill Seeks to Regulate Law Enforcement's Use of Facial Recognition Technology*, KRCR (21 January 2024), krcrtv.com/news/local/proposed-california-bill-seeks-to-regulate-law-enforcements-use-of-facial-recognition (accessed 11 January 2024).

Herbert 2023: Nick Herbert, *Intelligent Surveillance as a Tool for Social Good*, Forbes (2 November 2023), www.forbes.com/sites/forbestechcouncil/2023/11/02/intelligent-surveillance-as-a-tool-for-social-good (accessed 21 December 2023).

Hever 2023: Amir Hever, *How AI Is Helping to Improve Transportation Safety on a Global Scale*, Forbes (12 May 2023), www.forbes.com/sites/forbestechcouncil/2023/05/12/how-ai-is-helping-to-improve-transportation-safety-on-a-global-scale (accessed 21 December 2023).

Krishnan 2023: Ashwin Krishnan, *Generative AI Is Making Phishing Attacks More Dangerous*, TechTarget (18 December 2023), www.techtarget.com/searchsecurity/tip/Generative-AI-is-making-phishing-attacks-more-dangerous (accessed 21 December 2023).

Malik 2023: Aditya Malik, *AI Bias in Recruitment: Ethical Implications and Transparency*, Forbes (25 September 2023), www.forbes.com/sites/forbestechcouncil/2023/09/25/ai-bias-in-recruitment-ethical-implications-and-transparency (accessed 21 December 2023).

Marr 2023: Bernard Marr, *15 Amazing Real-World Applications of AI Everyone Should Know About*, Forbes (10 May 2023), www.forbes.com/sites/bernardmarr/2023/05/10/15-amazing-real-world-applications-of-ai-everyone-should-know-about/ (accessed 21 December 2023).

Napolitano 2023: Elizabeth Napolitano, *AI Eliminated Nearly 4,000 Jobs in May, Report Says*, CBS News (2 June 2023), www.cbsnews.com/news/ai-job-losses-artificial-intelligence-challenger-report (accessed 21 December 2023).

Rinke 2023: Andreas Rinke, *Exclusive: Germany, France and Italy Reach Agreement on Future AI Regulation*, Reuters (20 November 2023), www.reuters.com/tech

nology/germany-france-italy-reach-agreement-future-ai-regulation-2023-11-18 (accessed 21 December 2023).

Roose 2023: Kevin Roose, *AI Poses 'Risk of Extinction,' Industry Leaders Warn*, New York Times (30 May 2023), www.nytimes.com/2023/05/30/technology/ai-threat-warning.html (accessed 21 December 2023).

Rzeszucinski 2022: Pawel Rzeszucinski, *Be Ready for the Brussels Effect: It's Coming to Data and AI*, Forbes (26 May 2022), www.forbes.com/sites/forbestechcouncil/2022/05/26/be-ready-for-the-brussels-effect---its-coming-to-data-and-ai (accessed 21 December 2023).

Venkataramakrishnan 2023: Siddharth Venkataramakrishnan, *AI in Investment and Financial Services*, Financial Times (20 July 2023), www.ft.com/content/da0f4df3-72bd-481d-a3c1-222a406e7ba2 (accessed 21 December 2023).

Verma 2023: Pranshu Verma, *The Rise of AI Fake News Is Creating a 'Misinformation Superspreader'*, Washington Post (17 December 2023), www.washingtonpost.com/technology/2023/12/17/ai-fake-news-misinformation (accessed 21 December 2023).

Weber 2024: Lauren Weber, *New York City Passed an AI Hiring Law. So Far, Few Companies Are Following It*, The Wall Street Journal (22 January 2024), www.wsj.com/business/new-york-city-passed-an-ai-hiring-law-so-far-few-companies-are-following-it-7e31a5b7 (accessed 24 July 2024).

Other

CAHAI 2020: Council of Europe's Ad Hoc Committee On Artificial Intelligence (CAHAI), *Feasibility Study*, Council of Europe (17 December 2020), CAHAI(2020)23, rm.coe.int/cahai-2020-23-final-eng-feasibility-study-/1680a0c6da (accessed 10 January 2024).

Colorado AI Act: *Consumer Protections for Interactions with Artificial Intelligence*, Colorado General Assembly (2024), leg.colorado.gov/sites/default/files/2024a_205_signed.pdf (accessed 24 July 2024).

Commission 2023: Commission, *Commission Welcomes Political Agreement on Artificial Intelligence Act*, Press Release (9 December 2023), https://ec.europa.eu/commission/presscorner/detail/%20en/ip_23_6473 (accessed 10 January 2024).

Council 2024: Council, *Artificial Intelligence (AI) Act: Council Gives Final Green Light to the First Worldwide Rules on AI*, Press Release (21 May 2024), www.consilium.europa.eu/en/press/press-releases/2024/05/21/artificial-intelligence-ai-act-council-gives-final-green-light-to-the-first-worldwide-rules-on-ai/ (accessed 24 July 2024).

Council 2023: Council, *Artificial Intelligence Act: Council and Parliament Strike a Deal on the First Rules for AI in the World*, Press Release (9 December 2023), www.consilium.europa.eu/en/press/press-releases/2023/12/09/artificial-intelligence-act-council-and-parliament-strike-a-deal-on-the-first-worldwide-rules-for-ai (accessed 21 December 2023).

Crenshaw 2023: Jordan Crenshaw, *Future of AI: EU AI Act Fails to Strike Sensible Balance*, US Chamber of Commerce (17 November 2023 and updated 12 December 2023), www.uschamber.com/technology/future-of-ai-latest-updates (accessed 21 December 2023).

France, Germany, and Italy joint non-paper, *An Innovation-Friendly Approach Based on European Values for the AI Act*, Politico (14 April 2021).

IBM 2024: IBM, *What Is Artificial Intelligence (AI)?* (2024), www.ibm.com/topics/artificial-intelligence (accessed 21 December 2023).

Linklaters 2024: Linklaters, *Ethical, Safe, Lawful: A Toolkit for Artificial Intelligence Projects* (2024), www.linklaters.com/en/client-services/artificial-intelligence (accessed 24 July 2024).

Parliament 2024: Parliament, *Artificial Intelligence Act: MEPs Adopt Landmark Law*, Press Release (13 March 2024), www.europarl.europa.eu/news/en/press-room/20240308IPR19015/artificial-intelligence-act-meps-adopt-landmark-law (accessed 24 July 2024).

Parliament 2023: Parliament, *Artificial Intelligence Act: Deal on Comprehensive Rules for Trustworthy AI*, Press Release (9 December 2023), www.europarl.europa.eu/news/en/press-room/20231206IPR15699/artificial-intelligence-act-deal-on-comprehensive-rules-for-trustworthy-ai (accessed 21 December 2023).

The White House 2023: The White House, *Executive Order on the Safe, Secure, and Trustworthy Development and Use of Artificial Intelligence* (30 October 2023), www.whitehouse.gov/briefing-room/presidential-actions/2023/10/30/ executive-order-on-the-safe-secure-and-trustworthy-development-and-use-of-artificial-intelligence (accessed 11 January 2024).

CHAPTER 6

Economic Regulation and the AI Act: Perspectives from Competition Law, Data Protection, and Intellectual Property

Quentin B. Schäfer[*]

1 INTRODUCTION

The AI Act is an unprecedented piece of sectoral regulation applicable to a rapidly evolving and highly dynamic field of technology capable of producing significant economic benefits. Obviously, the use of artificial intelligence (AI) may also create harmful effects on a number of legitimate aims of a liberal democratic society, such as health, safety and fundamental rights.[1] The AI Act is an attempt to balance these competing considerations.

In addition to the AI Act, residually or generally applicable legal norms continue to apply to undertakings creating, implementing, and using AI. Legal regulatory norms frequently overlap and sometimes pursue contradictory policies. This is especially true in relation to regimes that apply residually and complementarily to sectoral regulation. This chapter focuses on the interaction of the AI Act with such regimes, namely the competition law, data protection, and intellectual property (IP) protection.

2 THE AI ACT AND ECONOMIC REGULATION

2.1 General Principles in the AI Act

The general principle emanating from Recital 9 of the AI Act is that it does not displace obligations for compliance with applicable laws and regulations. Recital 45 further

---

* The author has no conflict of interest to disclose.
1. AIA, Rec. 1.

notes explicitly that prohibited practices in Union law, 'including data protection, non-discrimination, consumer protection, and competition law' are not affected by the AI Act. As a result, conflicts between applicable laws and regulations and the AI Act cannot be resolved by reference to an overriding norm included in the AI Act.

Rather, the AI Act generally adopts the principles of 'concurrency' that has also dominated the intersection between competition law and economic regulation[2] and 'complementarity' which has largely governed the IP-competition interface.[3] The principles of concurrency and complementarity do not resolve conflicts by themselves. They express the ideas that: (1) both specific and residual economic regulation apply unless specific economic regulation excludes the possibility of the application of the residual; and (2) the goals and functions of the concurrently applicable forms of regulation are complementary in the long term. Economic regulation forms a regime that sets parameters for the application of competition law and determines the scope of competition on the merits.[4]

Neither concurrency nor complementarity rules out conflicts in marginal cases. In reality, such conflicts will be more than an exception. The AI Act's ambit is wide-ranging, encroaching on a number of different regulatory fields. Those fields include IP, privacy and data protection, fundamental rights, as well as competition policy.

Both the text and the spirit of the AI Act accord some regulatory objectives more attention than others. The *Ethics Guidelines for Trustworthy AI* of the High-Level Expert Group on Artificial Intelligence (HLEG Guidelines) set out seven key requirements explicitly, among them 'technical robustness and safety', 'privacy and data governance', 'diversity' and 'non-discrimination and fairness', and 'environmental and societal well-being'. The AI Act itself makes plentiful mention of these matters, in addition to respect for fundamental rights, and copyright and related rights. Other regulatory objectives find only scant expression, in particular the protection of other IP rights and competition policy.

2.2 Product Safety Regulation

There is sectoral regulation applicable to the products that AI is likely to be implemented in. The regulations establishing the product safety regime are listed in Annex I. The AI Act governs the interaction between it and applicable sectoral (product safety) regulation with more detail than the interaction between it and any other type of regulation.

The AI Act confers powers and responsibility for the enforcement of the AI Act onto the market surveillance authorities (MSAs). MSAs are responsible, *inter alia*, for the supervision of testing under Article 76. Examples of the powers of MSAs can be found, *inter alia*, in Article 88(2), allowing MSAs to request the Commission to exercise its enforcement powers; Article 85, providing for the right to lodge a complaint with a

2. *See* Dunne 2015.
3. Schäfer 2024.
4. *See* Wiedemann 2023, 602.

MSA; and Article 83, prescribing the result of formal non-compliance with the high-risk AI system obligations.

The AI Act also provides for strong interaction between the European Artificial Intelligence Office (AI Office) and the MSAs. Examples are found, *inter alia*, in Article 79, prescribing procedures of cooperation between the Commission and the MSAs; Article 76(5), prescribing communication between MSAs in relation to testing; and Article 75(3) on requests for information to the AI Office.

Overall, the scheme envisioned by the AI Act places the MSAs in the role of national champions of the AI Act. It is also worth noting that the 'without prejudice' clause in Article 2(9) only applies to consumer protection and product safety, despite the general principle in Recital 9 that the AI Act does not displace obligations for compliance with all applicable laws and regulations. It might be reasoned that the legislator intended a broader degree of deference to product safety regulation than to other types of regulations.

3 THE AI ACT AND COMPETITION LAW

Competition law protects the interest of a fair and efficient competitive process as well as the aim of consumer welfare.[5] Harm to consumers can be prima facie inferred from an impairment of the competitive process.[6]

The public's interest in competition is a rarely mentioned interest in legal instruments, hard and soft, on the regulation of AI. China and Japan have so far been alone in incorporating competition interests explicitly.[7] International or Union instruments, for example, the Council of Europe's AI Convention or the HLEG Guidelines, generally do not mention the intersection between AI regulation and competition.

3.1 Competition Law and Policy in the AI Act

The AI Act is largely silent on its interaction with the economic and political interest in competition and the competition laws. Recital 9 notes the AI Act's 'complementarity' with data protection, consumer protection, fundamental rights, employment, protection of workers, and product safety. Given that the Recital mentions employment, which is, as opposed to, e.g., product safety, only of marginal relevance to the AI Act more generally, it may be suspected that omissions of other areas are intentional rather than mere oversights. The term 'competition' appears only three times in the AI Act, in neither context in an explicit exhortation of 'complementarity' or 'concurrency':

(1) Article 66(h) allows the European Artificial Intelligence Board (AI Board) to cooperate with Union institutions, bodies, offices, agencies, and relevant

5. *Servizio* (Case C-377/20), para. 44.
6. *Ibid.*, para. 47.
7. *See* Social Principles for Human-Centric AI (Japan) *and* White Paper on Standardization in AI (China).

Union expert groups and networks, in particular, *inter alia*, in the field of competition.

(2) Article 74(2) requires MSAs to report annually to the Commission and relevant national competent authorities (NCAs) on issues relevant to the competition laws.

(3) Under Recital 45, '[p]ractices that are prohibited by Union law, including data protection law, non-discrimination law, consumer protection law, and competition law, should not be affected by this Regulation'.

The AI Act therefore does not govern either the substantive relationship between the AI Act and the competition laws nor the procedural relationship between the bodies implementing and enforcing the AI Act and the bodies enforcing the competition laws.

3.2 Conflicts Between Competition Law and the AI Act

These provisions do not exhaustively set out the relevance of the competition laws in relation to the exercise of powers by the AI Office nor of the relevance of the AI Act in the Commission's and the NCA's powers to enforce the competition laws. Four types of conflicts can be foreseen:

(1) explicit derogations in the AI Act may form part of anti-competitive conduct;
(2) explicit prohibitions in the AI Act may form part of anti-competitive conduct;
(3) competition law enforcement may be contrary to the aims of the AI Act more generally, and vice versa; and
(4) institutional conflicts where a course of conduct is contrary to both the AI Act and the competition laws.

First, a defendant in a competition matter may plead the existence of an explicit derogation in the AI Act as the cause and justification for its behaviour. As a general matter, such arguments will not be successful, certainly in relation to restraints clearly capable of harming competition. In *Valve*, the derogation in Article 6 of the Copyright and Information Society Directive 2001 was insufficient to justify geo-blocking restraints.[8] In *Google Shopping*, improvement of the search experience for consumers was not a sufficient pro-competitive justification on the evidence.[9] In *AstraZeneca*, the withdrawal of a marketing authorization which would allow generic manufacturers to enter the market without business justification constituted an abuse.[10] But, it is also clear that, where regulation offers no alternative but to act in a certain manner, this is likely to preclude competition law liability.[11] Therefore, while derogations are unlikely to be accepted as justifications for anti-competitive behaviour, the good faith fulfilment of affirmative obligations with business justification may constitute a justification for

8. *Valve* (Case T-172/21).
9. *Google Shopping* (Case T-612/17).
10. *AstraZeneca* (Case C-457/10 P).
11. *Deutsche Telekom* (Case C-280/08 P), paras 80-84.

the conduct at issue where it removes the undertaking's ability to choose a course of action (the 'State action defence'); it is nonetheless worth noting that this justification has been construed narrowly.[12]

Second, the AI Act prohibits certain conduct; anti-competitive behaviour may, in whole or in part, be constituted of such behaviour. We can infer the applicable principles from the case of *Meta v. BKA*, which concerned a breach of data privacy law being taken into account in finding an abuse under Article 102 of the Treaty on the Functioning of the EU (TFEU). While *Meta* arose in the context of the intersection between the General Data Protection Regulation (GDPR) and competition law, there is no reason to suspect that the principles would differ in the context of the AI Act and competition law. In March, the French Autorité de la Concurrence fined Google for a breach of an IP licensing agreement in the context of 'related rights'.[13]

After *Meta*, a breach of the GDPR does not in itself establish unlawfulness under Article 102 TFEU, though it may help to establish a failure to compete on the merits.[14] There is no reason for this principle not to apply to the relationship between competition law and AI Act. A failure to comply with the AI Act will accordingly be 'an important hint' in the context of Article 102 TFEU enforcement.[15] In line with *Meta*, competition authorities will likely be required to consider the existence of breaches of the AI Act, as they are required to consider GDPR breaches.[16]

Third, more broadly, the enforcement of competition law may contravene the policy aims of the AI Act more generally. There is no general answer to this in the case law, owed mainly to the fact that this is an issue of principle rather than one capable of resolution in individual cases. A number of disparate issues fall into this category. One of them is the enforcement of the merger rules against AI firms that have relied on 'acquihires' and partnerships to vertically integrate rather than mergers and acquisitions that can more straightforwardly be assessed under the Merger Regulation. Such vertical integration may contravene the implicit aim of the AI Act to create a vertically differentiated 'AI value chain'. The broad policy of complementarity dictates that both areas pursue complementary goals but it is apparent that conflicts may arise nonetheless. Such conflicts are best resolved not through law but through communication, organization, and politics. Conversely, the enforcement of the AI Act may be contrary to the aims of the competition laws. This seems to largely be an intentional consequence of the AI Act. Similarly to the above, broader policy conflicts are best resolved through co-operation and co-ordination rather than through legal norms.

Fourth, who enforces which norms and when can be inferred from *Meta*. Enforcement by a competition authority under the competition laws which it is authorized to enforce remains an assessment along the lines of the regulatory objectives of the competition laws and using the tools developed in the context of competition enforcement because competition regulators exercise different powers for

12. *See* Dunne 2015, 212-228.
13. *Google* (ADLC Decision 22-D-13).
14. *Meta* (Case C-252/21), para. 23, *and see generally* Wiedemann 2023.
15. *See Meta* (Case C-252/21), para. 47.
16. *Meta* (Case C-252/21), para. 43.

different objectives when establishing breaches of the GDPR.[17] Just as competition regulators have a duty to co-operate with data protection supervision authorities[18] and not to depart from their decisions,[19] they will be subject to a duty to co-operate with the AI Office and must not depart from its decisions.[20] When in doubt, competition authorities are to consult the more specialized regulator.[21] Conversely, GDPR compliance may be a relevant circumstance, i.e., to determine competition on the merits, and NCAs may examine compliance.[22] Nonetheless, legality in non-competition regulation does not prevent a conclusion of a violation of the competition laws.[23] Competition authorities have a primacy of enforcement where there is a breach of competition law.[24]

3.3 Specific Interactions: Access Obligations

There are several further issues of overlap between the competition laws and the AI Act that are worth discussing specifically: I focus here on the interaction between the provisions in the AI Act enabling complaints by downstream provers and the duty to provide interoperability obligations, and the competition laws imposing duties to deal and enforcing fair, reasonable and non-discriminatory (FRAND) commitments.

A further key obligation related tangentially to the competition laws is the possibility in Article 89(2) for downstream providers to make complaints to the AI Office in relation to the infringement of the AI Act by general-purpose artificial intelligence (GPAI) providers. Under Article 89(2), downstream providers shall have the right to lodge a complaint alleging an infringement by a GPAI model provider to the AI Office.[25] In addition, Article 85 allows 'any natural or legal person' to submit complaints to the relevant MSA. The obligation in Article 89(2) operates separately from the competition jurisdiction under Article 102 TFEU imposing duties to deal in 'exceptional circumstances'.[26] Overlap should, in particular, be expected in relation to downstream providers who may complain under Articles 89(2) and 53(1)(b), as well as under Article 102 TFEU prohibiting refusals to supply and refusals to license.

As I note in a commentary associated with Article 89, the right to complaint only attaches to downstream providers; customers may have recourse under Article 102 TFEU instead.[27] Obviously, downstream providers may avail themselves of Article 102 TFEU as well. The subject matter covered by complaints under Article 89(2) is an 'infringement', best read as an infringement of an obligation within the AI Act and not an infringement of another legal norm outside the AI Act. Accordingly, the subject

17. *Ibid.*, paras 42-49.
18. *Ibid.*, paras 42, 52-54.
19. *Ibid.*, para. 56.
20. *See analogous also* AIA, former Art. 58(h).
21. *Meta* (Case C-252/21), paras 55-59.
22. *Ibid.*, paras 47-48.
23. *AstraZeneca* (Case C-457/10 P); *Meta* (Case C-252/21); *and Valve* (Case T-172/21).
24. Wiedemann 2023, 602.
25. *See* Schäfer 2025.
26. *RTE* (Cases C-241/91 and C-242/91 P), para. 39.
27. Schäfer 2025.

matter covered by Article 89(2) may overlap with an infringement of the competition rules but should not extend to an exclusive infringement of the competition rules.

Nonetheless, there is some overlap in the duties that may be imposed under competition law and the duties under the AI Act. Under Article 102, refusals to supply or refusals to license IP are subject to the tests in *Bronner*,[28] and *Magill*,[29] respectively. Implicit refusals to supply are subject not the *Bronner* rules.[30] Further, discriminatory access to a platform is subject to Article 102 TFEU.[31] It seems that such duties will run concurrently with obligations under the AI Act.

In some cases, the AI Act may imply a lower barrier to the imposition of duties to deal. For example, Article 53(1)(b) imposes duty of providing interoperability information, though no clear duty to deal. Notably, in *Microsoft*, the General Court held that Microsoft's refusal to supply interoperability information constituted an abuse under Article 102 TFEU.[32] Duties to deal under Article 102 TFEU will be more readily imposed where the obligation in Article 53(1)(b) applies.

Further, where a dominant upstream provider commits to licensing on FRAND terms, Article 102 TFEU will likely enforce the framework for negotiations of licences set out in *Huawei*.[33] Recital 90 further allows (but does not exhort) the Commission to develop voluntary model contractual terms for AI value chains with respect to high-risk AI systems.[34] The Commission's voluntary model contractual terms are likely to have an impact on the definition of FRAND and the imposition of access obligations by the courts where the model terms are not implemented by the parties.[35]

Where a complaint by a downstream provider also alleges a violation of the competition laws, or a private or private competition law enforcement action alleges a violation of the AI Act, the principles set out in the previous section on the division of competences apply.

4 THE AI ACT AND DATA PROTECTION

In comparison to the competition laws, the AI Act is much more vocal about the interaction between it and the data protection rules. The application of the GDPR in the context of AI is discussed by Boris Paal elsewhere in this volume.[36] Accordingly, I only cover data protection briefly.

There is a clear scope for conflict between the GDPR and the AI Act. Hervey and Lavy note that GDPR principles may restrict the availability of data and thereby affect

28. *Bronner* (Case C-7/97).
29. *RTE* (Cases C-241/91 and C-242/91 P).
30. *Google Shopping* (Case T-612/17).
31. *Ibid.*
32. *Microsoft* (Case T-201/04).
33. *Huawei* (Case C-170/13).
34. *See* Schäfer 2025.
35. *See ibid.*
36. *See* Paal, *AI Training with Publicly Available Data in Accordance with the GDPR*, ch. 7 in this volume.

the use of AI.[37] They also point to the obligations under GDPR of providing explanations for and a right to object to certain decisions made by AI. The right to object under Article 22(1) GDPR may often be triggered as AI decision-making may constitute 'automated processing' under the Article.[38] The right to an explanation under Articles 13-15 GDPR may conflict with the black box nature of AI systems.[39]

The *Meta v. BKA* judgment addressed the intersection between data protection and competition law. I showed in the previous section that the principles expressed in the judgment can be applied to the interaction between competition law and the AI Act. The relationship stated in the case law laid out above pertaining to competition law should apply more broadly to other fields of regulation, including data protection. If anything, the data protection regime and the AI Act are more akin in their goals and character than the AI Act and the competition laws.

In light of the complementarity thesis, conflicts are generally to be resolved towards the complementary application of concurrently applicable AI Act and GDPR norms and therefore in favour of the less permissive regime. Yet, in some contexts, the AI Act may assist in the interpretation of a GDPR in a permissive way, since the strict application of the GDPR may frustrate the regulatory objectives of the AI Act or vice versa.

5 THE AI ACT AND (INTELLECTUAL) PROPERTY

IP fuels the AI industry. AI models and AI outputs are, to differing extents, capable of protection through copyright and patent law. Arguably, IP protection is essential to the provision of incentives to invent in the AI field as it stands today.

The interaction between AI and IP law remains largely unsettled. *Inter alia*, whether the training of AI models using copyrighted works or the replication of content in the style of copyrighted content constitutes copyright infringement under European Union (EU) law or national law are, at the time of writing, questions subject to active litigation. The practical extent of prejudice by the AI Act to rightholders' interests will depend on whether actions taken by providers of AI models infringe copyright and related rights. If, in particular, the training of AI models using copyrighted works constitutes copyright infringement, the publication of summaries of training data used is likely to be of substantial utility in pinpointing infringements by providers of AI models.

5.1 Obligations in the AI Act Related to IP

The AI Act does not displace existing Union IP law under the without prejudice clause in Recital 9. Yet, it imposes a number of novel obligations on providers of GPAI models in respect of copyright and related rights. These obligations support the private

37. Hervey & Lavy 2021, para. [4-004].
38. *Ibid.*, paras [4-005]-[4-013].
39. *Ibid.*, paras [4-018]-[4-020].

enforcement of existing IP law. These obligations are found in Article 53 and Recitals (104)-(108).[40]

Under Article 53(1)(b), providers of GPAI models shall 'draw up, keep up-to-date and make available information and documentation to providers of AI systems who intend to integrate the general-purpose AI model into their AI systems'; the minimum content of this information and documentation is:

> [w]ithout prejudice to the need to observe and protect intellectual property rights and confidential business information or trade secrets in accordance with Union and national law.

Under Article 53(1)(c), providers of GPAI models shall:

> put in place a policy to comply with Union law on copyright and related rights, and in particular to identify and comply with, including through state-of-the-art technologies, a reservation of rights expressed pursuant to Article 4(3) of Directive (EU) 2019/790.

Under Article 53(1)(d), providers of GPAI models shall:

> draw up and make publicly available a sufficiently detailed summary about the content used for training of the general-purpose AI model, according to a template provided by the AI Office.

Under Articles 52(6) and 78 and Recital 167, authorities are to protect IP rights when applying the AI Act. Under Article 53(7):

> information or documentation obtained pursuant to this Article, including trade secrets, shall be treated in accordance with the confidentiality obligations set out in Article 78.

As Recital 106 notes, Article 4(3) of Directive 2019/790 reserves certain rights to rightholders. Recital 105 notes that the Copyright Directive includes exceptions and limitations for purposes of text and data mining, allowing rightholders to opt out and reserve their rights, which requires the providers of GPAI models to obtain licences. Under Recital 108, the AI Act 'does not affect the enforcement of copyright rules as provided for under Union law'. Outside the confidentiality obligation in Article 78, there is no mention of trade secrets or confidential information. There is no mention at all of patent rights in the AI Act. This includes a lack of any 'without prejudice' clauses outside the requirement to comply with existing laws and regulations. Despite the lack of such language, inevitably, the Act will restrict the ability of providers of GPAI models to exploit their IP rights, including but not limited to copyright, patents, and trade secrets.

Further, the effect of Recital 106 is to extend the ambit of Union law on copyright and related rights extraterritorially beyond its application in the legislation. This is contrary to the general principle that IP rights are as territorially bounded, applying in the jurisdiction that granted them. It is unclear whether a limiting doctrine on

40. *See* Vellinga & Mifsud Bonnici 2025.

extraterritorial effect akin to the one employed in competition law will be applied by the courts.[41]

5.2 Taking into Account IP Rights

Article 53 protects IP rights from being rendered ineffective in the context of providing interoperability information, copyright policies, and training data summaries.[42] The existence of an applicable IP right clearly constitutes a justification for the redaction of such information.

Outside the narrow issue of confidentiality, IP rights may come into conflict with the AI Act when the AI Act prohibits certain conduct that is protected by an IP right. The simplest example of such a conflict would be an IP right covering one of the prohibited practices in Article 5. Given that IP law is permissive, and the AI Act is prohibitive, it seems clear that the AI Act would take precedence; in any event, the IP right itself may be invalid as contrary to public policy.

A more difficult example of a conflict is IP rights covering the components or outputs of high-risk AI systems covered by Articles 6-49 of the AI Act, or GPAI models covered by Articles 50-56 of the AI Act. Where the AI Act prohibits aspects of the use of IP rights, would this deprive the IP right holder of the essence of IP protection and entitle the IP right holder to deference, i.e., render the legal norm in the AI Act inapplicable or reduce its scope?

While it is theoretically conceivable that enforcement of the AI Act may take into account the existence of IP rights when evaluating conduct related to the exploitation of those rights, it seems highly unlikely that owners of IP rights will be owed any substantial deference on this basis when infringements of the AI Act are alleged. The obligations to 'protect IP rights' seem to apply only to the receipt and publication of information related to fulfilling obligations under the AI Act rather than the substance of IP rights.

Rather, the primary policy goal emanating from the AI Act in relation to IP rights seems to be the discovery of infringements of the IP laws as extant, particularly of copyright infringements in the context of AI model training and Article 53. The obligation of public disclosure of training data for GPAI models under Article 53(1)(d) and Recital 107 prejudices the interest of GPAI models in favour of the owners of infringed IP rights. It is in the public interest that infringements of IP rights are discovered and sanctioned. This mirrors the policy expressed elsewhere by the European courts that it is beneficial that invalid IP rights are declared invalid.[43]

In broad terms, the European courts see economic regulation in different areas as complementary rather than conflicting. This broad statement has been subject to study most extensively in the context of the interaction between IP rights and competition law enforcement. Under the jurisprudence of the Court of Justice of the European

41. *See Intel* (Case T-286/09).
42. *See also* AIA, Rec. 107.
43. *Windsurfing* (Case 193/83), para. 92.

Union (CJEU), the existence of IP rights does not prevent the enforcement of competition law in respect of conduct that exercises such rights.[44] In addition, remedies granting licensing access to private property rights, including IP rights, may be granted as remedies to violations of competition law associated with those property rights.[45] Even explicit authorizations seem insufficient to displace the complementary application of different regulatory regimes.[46]

Legal scholarship has described this approach as the 'complementarity' of EU competition law and IP law, in light of common goals being pursued by both areas.[47] While these common goals are commonly exaggerated, the core principle that other economic regulation does not stand in the way of competition law enforcement remains true.

The AI Act and IP protection arguably do not pursue the common long-term goal of economic efficiency and innovation. The goal of the AI Act is the encouragement of human-centric and trustworthy AI[48] and *responsible* innovation.[49] Outside limits to IP protection on the basis of public policy, IP law generally leaves the market to determine the path of innovation. In other words, the position here is likely a different one from that on the IP-competition interface.

This is supported by the different operation of the competition laws and the AI Act. Whereas competition law operates on an economic assessment and may balance incentives to invent provided by the exclusivity of IP rights against the anti-competitive effects of anti-competitive conduct. Nothing in the AI Act obliges the enforcing authority to engage in a similar assessment of balancing the positive economic effects of IP rights protecting GPAI models and breaches of obligations under the AI Act. While there is nothing explicit in the AI Act that would prevent an authority from taking such matters into account, given the stated goals of the AI Act in Article 1(1), such an economic assessment is likely to frustrate the legislative intent of the Act, despite the mention of 'supporting innovation' as an aim in Article 1(1).

Accordingly, the AI Act provides little room for deference to IP rights in the course of its enforcement, outside the obligations relating to confidentiality and publication of information.

5.3 The Fundamental Right to Property

As noted above, most conflicts of the AI Act with IP rights (outside the confidentiality obligations), are likely to be resolved in favour of the AI norm. Yet, more substantive interferences with IP rights may be subject to fundamental rights objections.[50]

44. *CICRA and Maxicar* (Case C-53/87); *AB Volvo* (Case C-238/87); and *AstraZeneca* (Case C-457/10 P).
45. *RTE* (Cases C-241/91 and C-242/91 P); *Bronner* (Case C-7/97); *IMS Health* (Case C-418/01); and *Microsoft* (Case T-201/04).
46. *Valve* (Case T-172/21).
47. Régibeau & Rockett 2007.
48. *See* AIA, Rec. 1.
49. *See ibid.*, Rec. 138.
50. *See* Schmidt-Kessen 2019.

Article 17(1) of the Charter protects the right to property, subject to regulation as necessary for the public interest. Article 17(2) states merely that 'Intellectual property shall be protected'. Under the Explanatory Note to Article 17(2), the guarantees under Article 17(1) 'shall apply as appropriate to intellectual property'. The AI Act accordingly has to be interpreted consistently with the Charter. The main principle emanating from Article 17 is that once granted, an IP right may not be deprived of its core content in relation to its core elements (ownership, use, assignment) outside the strict limitations set out in Article 17(1).[51] Recital 48 explicitly enumerates IP rights as fundamental rights that may be impacted negatively by AI systems. Similarly, the indirect protection provided to IP rights by the regulatory aims of boosting innovation and Union leadership in trustworthy AI in Recitals (1)-(3), and the beneficial economic effects of AI in Recital 4 should be noted. Recital 12 may provide more robust protection since it enumerates innovation, freedom of science and not undermining R&D (though it caveats this last aim strongly) as aims of the AI Act. Moreover, Article 345 TFEU arguably also expresses some protection against interference with property rights by the state,[52] which may have influenced CJEU case law which governs the extent to which competition law interference with IP rights is legitimate.[53]

What the fundamental right to property in the Charter means in practice remains unclear. IP rights have a 'relatively weak status as fundamental rights'.[54] Regulation, where necessary, is stated by Article 17(1) to be consistent with the fundamental right to property. Some of the ways in which a public authority could act inconsistently with the fundamental right to IP are covered by the confidentiality obligations in the AI Act. But, conceivably, there are other ways in which a public authority may infringe the fundamental right to IP, particularly where the public authority, under the powers granted by the AI Act, enjoins the exercise of IP rights vis-à-vis third parties. Infringements of the core right to exclude others have been permitted in the past in the refusals to license cases in EU competition law but have been subject to the limits of the *Magill/Bronner* conditions. It is suggested that, at minimum, equally stringent limits ought to apply in the context of the AI Act under the Charter.

6 CONCLUSION

The AI Act is not exhaustive in relation to the conflicts that may arise between it and other economic regulations, at least outside the rules on product safety. Nonetheless, a good deal of jurisprudence surrounding the complementarity of regulation in EU law allows us to infer a great deal of principles for the application of the AI Act in its early days. This chapter has elucidated some of these principles.

The general argument presented here is that the AI Act will affect the enforcement of other economic regulations both positively and negatively, though mostly in an

51. Hilty & Jaeger 2016, 23.
52. *See* Akkermans & Ramaekers 2010; and Losada Fraga et al. 2012.
53. *Consten and Grundig* (Case C-56/64); *Deutsche Grammophon* (Case C-78/70); and *Valve* (Case T-172/21); *see also* Schäfer 2024.
54. Torremans 2014.

oblique fashion: Obligations under the competition rules run concurrently with the obligations under the AI Act, but may well be affected in their extent by the AI Act. I have noted the impact of the duty to provide interoperability information, as well as voluntary model contractual terms on findings of refusals to license and FRAND terms. Deference to IP rights is likely to be minimal, but extensive interference with IP rights may be subject to fundamental rights objections.

There is a larger conceptual question apparent between the lines that I have not attempted to resolve: In how far will enforcement of the AI Act depend on or be frustrated by the enforcement of other economic regulations, in particular in relation to the three areas of regulation covered here? It remains to be seen how successful the coordination of policy will be in the future between different regulatory regimes and regulators.

BIBLIOGRAPHY

Policy Documents

Social Principles for Human-Centric AI (Japan): Government Cabinet Office (Japan), *Social Principles for Human-Centric AI*, www.cas.go.jp/jp/seisaku/jinkouchinou/pdf/humancentricai.pdf (accessed 13 July 2024).

White Paper on Standardization in AI (China): National Standardization Management Committee, Second Ministry of Industry (China), *White Paper on Standardization in AI* (18 January 2018), www.cesi.cn/images/editor/20180124/20180124135528742.pdf (accessed 13 July 2024).

Case Law

AB Volvo (Case C-238/87): Case C-238/87, *AB Volvo v. Erik Veng (UK) Ltd.*, 5 October 1988, ECLI:EU:C:1988:477.

AstraZeneca (Case C-457/10 P): Case C-457/10 P, *AstraZeneca AB and AstraZeneca plc v. European Commission*, 6 December 2012, ECLI:EU:C:2012:770.

Bronner (Case C-7/97): Case C-7/97, *Oscar Bronner GmbH & Co. KG v. Mediaprint Zeitungs-und Zeitschriftenverlag GmbH & Co. KG, Mediaprint Zeitungsvertriebsgesellschaft mbH & Co. KG and Mediaprint Anzeigengesellschaft mbH & Co. KG*, 26 November 1998, ECLI:EU:C:1998:569.

CICRA and Maxicar (Case C-53/87): Case C-53/87, *Consorzio italiano della componentistica di ricambio per autoveicoli and Maxicar v. Régie nationale des usines Renault*, 5 October 1988, ECLI:EU:C:1988:472.

Consten and Grundig (Case C-56/64): Case C-56/64, *Établissements Consten S.à.R.L. and Grundig-Verkaufs-GmbH v. Commission of the European Economic Community*, 13 July 1966, ECLI:EU:C:1966:41.

Deutsche Grammophon (Case C-78/70): Case C-78/70, *Deutsche Grammophon Gesellschaft mbH v. Metro-SB-Großmärkte GmbH & Co. KG*, 8 June 1971, ECLI:EU:C:1971:59.

Deutsche Telekom (Case C-280/08 P): Case C-280/08 P, *Deutsche Telekom AG v. European Commission*, 14 October 2010, ECLI:EU:C:2010:603.

Google Shopping (Case T-612/17): Case T-612/17, *Google LLC, formerly Google Inc. and Alphabet v. European Commission*, 10 November 2021, ECLI:EU:T:2021:763.

IMS Health (Case C-418/01): Case C-418/01, *IMS Health GmbH & Co. OHG v. NDC Health GmbH & Co. KG.*, 29 April 2004, ECLI:EU:C:2004:257.

Intel (Case T-286/09): Case T-286/09, *Intel Corp. v. European Commission*, 12 June 2014, ECLI:EU:T:2014:547.

Microsoft (Case T-201/04): Case T-201/04, *Microsoft Corp. v. Commission of the European Communities*, 17 September 2007, ECLI:EU:T:2007:289.

Meta (Case C-252/21): Case C-252/21, *Facebook Inc. and Others v. Bundeskartellamt*, 22 April 2021, ECLI:EU:C:2023:537.

Microsoft (Case T-201/04): Case T-201/04, *Microsoft Corp. v. Commission of the European Communities*, 17 September 2007, ECLI:EU:T:2007:289.

RTE (Cases C-241/91 and C-242/91 P): Cases C-241/91 and C-242/91 P, *Radio Telefis Eireann (RTE) and Independent Television Publications Ltd (ITP) v. Commission of the European Communities*, ECLI:EU:C:1995:98.

Servizio (Case C-377/20): Case C-377/20, *Servizio Elettrico Nazionale SpA and Others v. Autorità Garante della Concorrenza e del Mercato and Others*, 12 May 2022, ECLI: EU:C:2022:379.

Valve (Case T-172/21): Case T-172/21, *Valve Corporation v. European Commission*, 27 September 2023, ECLI:EU:T:2023:587.

Windsurfing (Case 193/83): Case 193/83, *Windsurfing International Inc. v. Commission of the European Communities*, 25 February 1986, ECLI:EU:C:1986:75.

France: *Google* (ADLC Decision 22-D-13): *Autorité de la Concurrence*, Decision 22-D-13 of 21 June 2022 regarding practices implemented in the press sector.

Academic Writings

Akkermans & Ramaekers 2010: Bram Akkermans & Eveline Ramaekers, *Article 345 TFEU (Ex Article 295 EC), Its Meanings and Interpretations*, 16 European Law Journal 292 (2010), doi.org/10.1111/j.1468-0386.2010.00509.x.

Dunne 2015: Niamh Dunne, *Competition Law and Economic Regulation: Making and Managing Markets* (Cambridge University Press 2015).

Hilty & Jaeger 2016: Reto M. Hilty & Thomas Jaeger, *Europäisches Immaterialgüterrecht: Funktionen und Perspektiven* (Springer 2016).

Losada Fraga et al. 2012: Fernando Losada Fraga et al., *Property and European Integration: Dimensions of Article 345 TFEU*, Helsinki Legal Studies Research Paper 17 (2012).

Régibeau & Rockett 2007: Pierre Régibeau & Katharine Rockett, *The Relationship Between Intellectual Property Law and Competition Law: An Economic Approach*, in *The Interface Between Intellectual Property Rights and Competition Policy* (Steven D. Anderman ed., Cambridge University Press 2007).

Schäfer 2024: Quentin B. Schäfer, *Case T-172/21 Valve v. Commission: Revisiting the Territorial Character and Probabilistic Nature of Intellectual Property Rights in Competition Enforcement*, 45 European Competition Law Review 233 (2024).

Schäfer 2025: Quentin B. Schäfer, *Article 89, in The EU Artificial Intelligence (AI) Act: A Commentary* (Ceyhun Necati Pehlivan, Nikolaus Forgó & Peggy Valcke eds, Kluwer Law International 2025).

Schmidt-Kessen 2019: Maria José Schmidt-Kessen, *The Future of IP-Competition Conflicts in EU Law*, Copenhagen Business School Law Research Paper No. 24 (2019).

Torremans 2014: Paul Torremans, *Article 17(2), in The EU Charter of Fundamental Rights: A Commentary* (Steve Peers et al. eds, Hart 2014).

Vellinga & Mifsud Bonnici 2025: Nynke Vellinga & Jeanne Mifsud Bonnici, *Article 53, in The EU Artificial Intelligence (AI) Act: A Commentary* (Ceyhun Necati Pehlivan, Nikolaus Forgó & Peggy Valcke eds, Kluwer Law International 2025).

Wiedemann 2023: Klaus Wiedemann, *Datenschutz- und Kartellrecht auf Facebook und Andernorts: Anmerkung zu EuGH in Sachen Meta Platforms u.a./Bundes kartellamt*, 11 Neue Zeitschrift für Kartellrecht (NZKart) 601 (2023).

CHAPTER 7

AI Training with Publicly Available Data in Accordance with the GDPR

*Boris P. Paal**

1 CONFLICT BETWEEN BIG DATA NEEDS AND DATA PROTECTION LAW

Since the market launch of OpenAI's ChatGPT 3.5 (ChatGPT) in November 2022, the topic of artificial intelligence (AI) has prudently received special and ever-increasing attention. New AI-based technologies are constantly emerging around the world, research and development in the field of AI is progressing rapidly and the importance of AI for science and business is growing dynamically.[1] As a foundational technology, AI affects many (potential) application areas with enormous disruption potential for numerous economic and industrial sectors, such as the medical and healthcare sectors, the automotive and transport industries, manufacturing and agriculture.[2]

The development of AI systems is accompanied by a pronounced 'data hunger' due to the technology involved.[3] The success of an AI model is crucially determined by training data, particularly their quality and accessibility. The basic principle is that the more data available and usable for AI training, the better.[4] The AI Act defines such training data as 'data used to training an AI system through fitting its learnable parameters' (Article 3(29)). To access the vast amounts of data required (Big Data), the

* This chapter continues and elaborates ideas and deliberations published by the author in German in 2 Zeitschrift für Digitalisierung und Recht (ZfDR) 129-157 (2024). This chapter is based on a legal study independently prepared by the author, commissioned by the Computer & Communications Industry Association (CCIA).

1. *See* Maslej et al. 2023, 23 et seq., chs 1.1 et seq.; Novelli et al. 2024, 1 et seq.
2. With an overview of the social impact and an outlook for the future: Beck et al. 2020, 126 et seq.
3. Paal 2020, Ch. 8.7, 427.
4. *See* Vogel 2022, 49. In addition to the quantity, the quality of the data is also crucial. However, the principle remains that 'more' is always 'better'.

use of freely accessible public data from the internet is of central importance for the training of AI applications in practice. For example, when asked about the data used to train the underlying algorithm and data privacy measures on it, ChatGPT's response is:[5]

> I was trained on a diverse range of internet text, which includes websites, books, articles, and other written material to develop a broad understanding of human language. The specific datasets used by OpenAI to train me are extensive and cover various domains to ensure a wide breadth of knowledge. Regarding data privacy measures, OpenAI takes several precautions to protect user data and privacy: Data Anonymization, Secure Data Handling, Ethical Use, User Control and Transparency. These measures are part of a broader effort to ensure that AI technologies are developed and deployed in a way that respects user privacy and aligns with ethical standards.

By emphasizing the importance of anonymizing the training data used - without prejudice to the question of whether the anonymization claimed by ChatGPT has actually occurred or is even feasible - the focus is immediately on the fact that AI training with personal data harbours considerable potential for conflict with regard to data protection regulations and, in particular, the General Data Protection Regulation (GDPR) regulatory regime. According to Article 6(1) GDPR,[6] the processing of personal data is subject to a preventive measures with a reservation of permission. In addition, due to the need for Big Data in AI training, data protection principles such as the principle of data minimization (Article 5(1)(c) of the GDPR)[7] or the principle of transparency (Article 5(1)(a),[8] section 3 of the GDPR) lead to structural tension. This finding, in turn, raises (follow-up) questions of legal and economic policy regarding the balancing of the promotion of innovation and data protection, competitive data economy, and fundamental rights-compliant data sovereignty.

In this context, the requirements of the GDPR constitute the core of such importance.[9] It will therefore be discussed below which data protection requirements must be observed when training AI within the scope of the GDPR.[10] For the purpose of differentiated legal consideration, the characteristic phases of AI training and AI development are first identified below (section 2). The prerequisites for the applicability of the GDPR are then dealt with, focussing on the characteristics of the personal identifiers of the training data and the possibilities of eliminating these personal identifiers (section 3). This is followed by an examination of the unique features that must be taken into account when applying the GDPR principles in the context of AI

5. Web Archive (23 Jul. 2024), web.archive.org/web/20240723163154/https://ibb.co/30DVJMP (accessed 23 Jul. 2024).
6. Spiecker et al. 2023, Art. 6, paras 14 et seq.; Kotschy 2020, 329 et seq.
7. Spiecker et al. 2023, Art. 5, paras 89 et seq.; Terwangne 2020, 317.
8. Spiecker et al. 2023, Art. 5, paras 22 et seq.; Terwangne 2020, 314, 315.
9. This is illustrated not least by a recent decision by the Italian data protection authority *Garante per La Protezione dei Dati Personali* (Garante). After ChatGPT was already temporarily banned by the Garante last year, the Italian data protection authority has now announced in a press release that it has once again informed OpenAI of violations of the GDPR by ChatGPT. Pollina & Mukherjee 2023; Reuters 2024.
10. On copyright issues, *see, for example,* Pesch & Böhme 2023a, 917; Pesch & Böhme 2023b, 997.

training (section 4) before the chapter turns to the required legal basis in the various data processing phases of AI training (section 5). Finally, the effects of the AI Act (section 6) and the implications of the results found at the output level are summarized and an outlook is provided (section 7).

2 PROCESSING PHASES RELEVANT TO DATA PROTECTION LAW IN AI TRAINING

As a starting point, it should be briefly mentioned that, web crawlers or web scrapers extract data from publicly available data, such as websites. Then, they process and use it for AI training for specific AI applications.[11] Moreover, using their own or third-party licensed data(sets) is possible. In addition, corresponding data may be obtained from publicly accessible internet sources via application programming interfaces (APIs) provided by the online platforms specifically for this purpose.[12] From a data protection perspective, it should be emphasized that this publicly available data may potentially include personal data. In this context, it should also be noted that with web scraping and web crawling, the – possibly unintentional – collection of personal data shall not be completely ruled out given the current state-of-the-art.[13] Finally, it should be emphasized that personal data is regularly indispensable for training large language models (LLMs). Moreover, it significantly influences the quality and functionality of such models. This is because LLMs also and especially require access to data about people to learn how language includes and presupposes possible concepts about relationships between people and the world. A model that is supposed to generate text about a historical or current event must be able to identify and use the correct names of individuals involved and places affected.

When dealing with the development of AI systems, a distinction must be made between different relevant processing phases under data protection law.[14] The first phase concerns the collection and collation of data. If the data is freely available in the public domain, it is usually collected – as already mentioned – via web scraping, web crawling or a correspondingly provided API.[15] Once the data has been collected, the raw data is transformed into usable training data by means of cleansing and validation.[16] In a further phase, the AI training data is structured and categorized.[17] The actual training and testing of the AI model using the prepared training data only takes place after these preparatory measures have been completed.[18]

11. Khder 2021, 145; for technical details on scraping, *see* Solove & Hartzog 2024, 7 et seq.
12. *Ibid.*
13. Dieker 2024, 132, 133. For the historical and technological overview on the datasets and its relationship with the AI training, *see* Lee et al. 2023, 6 et seq.
14. For the typical life cycle of an AI system, *see* OECD 2020; less detailed: OECD 2019. Also illustrated by LfDI Ba-Wü 2023, 7 et seq.
15. *See* Khder 2021, 145; for technical details on scraping, *see* Solove & Hartzog 2024, 7 et seq.
16. Marmy-Brändli & Oehri 2023, 655, 657.
17. Apel & Kaulartz 2020, 24 (25).
18. For the various types of training using supervised or unsupervised, reinforcement learning and other machine learning methods: Marsland 2014, 5 et seq.; Russell & Norvig 2021, 670 et seq.

3 APPLICABILITY OF THE GDPR

Considering the broad definition of 'processing' under GDPR, it could generally be assumed that the processing of personal data regarding data protection regulations (may) take place in each phase of AI training. This means that the collection and recording of training data already constitutes 'processing' in accordance with Article 4(2),[19] sections 1 and 2 of the GDPR. If and to the extent that the collected data is personal data within the meaning of Article 4(1)[20] of the GDPR, requirements the AI training must fulfil to comply with the GDPR must be clarified.

According to Articles 1(1)[21] and 2(1)[22] of the GDPR, the material scope of the application requires the processing of personal data. The question therefore arises as to when a reference to a person exists, how this reference to a person can be removed or at least limited and what special features need to be taken into account in the context of Big Data analyses. In this regard, in addition to referring to the literature, particular attention shall also be given to the relevant case law of the Court of Justice of the European Union (CJEU).

3.1 Existence of the Personal Identifiers

According to Article 4(1) of the GDPR, personal data is defined as 'any information' that 'relates' to an 'identified or identifiable' natural person. According to case law, the term 'all information' is to be interpreted broadly, which includes, in addition to sensitive and private information, all other types of objective and subjective information.[23] Opinions and judgments may therefore also be considered personal data.[24] The reference of the information to a specific natural person results from the fact that the information is linked to the person due to its content, purpose or effects.[25]

A person is deemed as 'identified' if s/he is specifically named and may be clearly distinguished from other persons in a group.[26] This identification could be direct or indirect. Indirect identification can be achieved in particular by association with an identifier or other specific characteristic that expresses the identity of the data subject.[27] According to Recital 26 of the GDPR, all means that are likely to be used by the controller or another person, in particular with regard to the costs and the time required, to realize the identification should, in principle, be taken into account.[28]

---

19. Spiecker et al. 2023, Art. 4(2), paras 16 et seq.; Bygrave & Tosoni 2020, Art. 4(2), 119 et seq.
20. Spiecker et al. 2023, Art. 4(1), paras 8 et seq.; Bygrave & Tosoni 2020, Art. 4(1), 108 et seq.
21. Spiecker et al. 2023, Art. 1, paras 23 et seq.; Hijmans 2020, 53 et seq.
22. Spiecker et al. 2023, Art. 2, paras 17 et seq.; Kranenborg 2020, Arts 2, 66 et seq.
23. *See SRB v. EDPS* (Case T-557/20), ECJ ECLI:EU:T:2023:219, 7 Zeitschrift für Datenschutz 399, para. 68 (2023).
24. *See ibid.*
25. *See Nowak* (Case C-434/16), ECJ ECLI:EU:C:2017:994, 3 Zeitschrift für Datenschutz 113, para. 35 (2018).
26. Article 29 WP 2007, 14; Gola 2022, Art. 4, para. 7.
27. Schild 2018, GDPR, Art. 4, para. 14.
28. *Ibid.*, para. 15.

In certain cases, it was disputed whether an absolute or relative standard should be applied for identifiability.[29] One (relative) view - which deviates from the wording of Recital 26 of the GDPR - considers identifiability to be possible in principle, only if the specific data controller is able to establish the link between the date and the data subject.[30] According to this relative view, only the possibilities and knowledge of the specific data controller may be taken into account. According to an opposing view, however, it should be sufficient for identifiability if the controller or any third party can establish the link between the information in question and the data subject (absolute standard).[31]

In the *Breyer* decision from 2016, the CJEU opted for a mediating, but in principle relative approach.[32] According to this approach, identifiability should be affirmed if the controller has the legal means that reasonably allow the identification of the data subject.[33] This is not the case if the identification of the data subject is prohibited by law or is not practically feasible, for example, because the identification would require a disproportionate effort and the risk of identification therefore remains negligible as a result.[34] If special additional information - possibly only available to a third party - is required for identification, it must be accessible and achievable for the data processor with reasonable effort in order to establish the relevant personal reference within the meaning of the GDPR.[35] The CJEU thus clarifies that if additional information is required for the identification of the data subject, which is not all held by the same person, this alone does not exclude the possibility that the data qualifies as personal data.[36] This outcome should also be applicable in the case when this additional information is retrieved from a third party or source other than the data controller.[37] If the additional information required for identification is in the possession of a third party, the CJEU has recently ruled that the data can be considered 'indirectly' as personal data, even for those who do not directly possess the relevant additional information themselves.[38] However, in this respect, the possibility of combining the data in question with the additional information must constitute a means likely to be used by the third party to identify the natural person, considering all the circumstances.[39]

29. Bergt 2015, 365 et seq. provides a comprehensive overview of the dispute.
30. *See, for example,* Roßnagel & Scholz 2000, 723; Kühling & Klar 2013, 3615; Meyer 2002, 1030; Krüger & Maucher 2011, 436.
31. Pahlen-Brandt 2008, 38.
32. *See* Vogel 2022, 82-83.
33. *Patrick Breyer* (Case C-582/14), 19 Oct. 2016, ECJ ECLI:EU:C:2016:779, 49 Neue Juristische Wochenschrift (NJW) 3581 (2016).
34. *Ibid.* with reference to the Opinion of the Advocate General, *see* Beck-Rechtsprechung (BeckRS) 81027, para. 68 (2016).
35. Ernst 2021, para. 11.
36. *See Patrick Breyer, supra* n. 33, Neue Juristische Wochenschrift (NJW) 3581, paras 43, 44 (2016).
37. *See European Commission v. Slovak Republic* (Case C-342/21), 9 Feb. 2023, ECJ ECLI: EU:C:2023:87, para. 55.
38. *See Gesamtverband Autoteile-Handel (Accès aux informations sur les véhicules)* (Case C-319/22), 9 Nov. 2023, ECLI:EU:C:2023:837, para. 49.
39. *Patrick Breyer, supra* n. 33, paras 55, 61. With this case law, the CJEU seems to be moving towards an absolute understanding of the reference to a person.

According to all of the above, the determination of the personal reference is not just a purely academic and abstract theoretical dispute.[40] Rather, this issue is of certain practical relevance for the requirements and conditions for eliminating the personal reference, which in turn would render the GDPR provisions inapplicable.

3.2 Elimination of the Personal Identifiers

In the following section, measures that fundamentally eliminate or at least limit existing personal identifiers are presented to avoid the GDPR's applicability or to reduce the intensity of the GDPR regulatory regime's intervention.[41]

3.2.1 Anonymization

According to Recital 26, the provisions of the GDPR do not apply to anonymous data. This raises the question of whether and how such anonymity can be technically implemented and achieved, whether a legal basis for anonymization is required and what challenges arise for anonymization through Big Data analyses. Possible anonymization must be examined directly in connection with the various phases of AI training. As training data collection generally precedes any anonymization, anonymization is likely to only become relevant in practice for later stages of AI training.

3.2.1.1 Definition

The GDPR defines anonymous data as any information that does not relate to an identified or identifiable natural person or personal data that has been altered so that the data subject cannot or can no longer be identified.[42] Anonymization is, therefore, intended to ensure that the value of the information is preserved without making it possible to attribute the information to an underlying natural person.[43]

Anonymous data is to be understood conceptually as the opposite of personal data, which is why the two pairs of terms must be negatively differentiated from each other.[44] If a personal reference is given due to the identifiability of the person concerned, taking into account the previously discussed relative definition, the information is not anonymous. At the same time, information can only be regarded as anonymous until at least the relative identifiability of the person concerned has been restored. Effective anonymization must be based on the current state-of-art,[45] which

40. *See vividly*: Vogel 2022, 80.
41. *See in detail* Paal 2020, Ch. 8.7, 437 et seq.
42. GDPR, Rec. 26.
43. Ernst 2021, para. 49.
44. Roßnagel 2021, 189; Klar & Kühling 2018, para. 32; Hofmann & Johannes 2017, 223.
45. For detailed information on the various anonymization techniques of randomization, generalization: Art. 29 WP 2014, 13 et seq.; also detailed on common anonymization techniques: Valkanova 2020, 346 et seq.

excludes (re-)identification according to ordinary life experience or at least subjects it to a disproportionately high or unreasonable effort.[46]

3.2.1.2 Legal Basis

The elimination of personal identifier processing in accordance with Article 4(4) of the GDPR has long been disputed.[47] Until 2016, the Federal Commissioner for Data Protection and Freedom of Information (BfDI) assumed that anonymization was not considered processing under data protection law and was therefore always permissible.[48] It was only in 2020 that the BfDI adopted the more convincing and widely prevailing view in the literature[49] that anonymization (also) constitutes a relevant data protection processing.[50] This legal classification in turn leads to the controversial follow-up question of the appropriate legal basis for anonymization.

According to one view, anonymization is a form of erasure, which is why Article 6(1)(c)[51] of the GDPR in conjunction with Article 17 GDPR[52] should apply.[53] According to another view, anonymization should be based on the legal basis of Article 6(1)(c) of the GDPR in conjunction with the statutory erasure obligation under Article 5(1)(e) of the GDPR.[54] Others stand for Article 6(1)(f) of the GDPR as the legal basis for anonymization and argue that the data controller has an overriding interest in anonymization.[55] Some suggest solving the problem by means of a teleological reduction of the scope of application or at least of Article 9(1) of the GDPR (concerning sensitive data categories).[56] The BfDI derives the legality of anonymization from Article 6(4) of the GDPR in conjunction with the original legal basis.[57] The issue can ultimately remain open for the scenario under investigation, as the anonymization can be reliably based on a GDPR legal basis according to all opinions.

3.2.1.3 Practical Challenges

Particular practical challenges regarding the potential re-identifiability of natural persons arise in the course of Big Data analyses, in which large and unstructured data volumes from various data sources are analysed at high processing speeds in order to

46. Roßnagel & Geminn 2021, 488; Roßnagel 2021, 189; Ernst 2021, para. 50; Brisch & Pieper 2015, 727.
47. Spiecker et al. 2023, Art. 4(4), paras 2 et seq.; Bygrave 2020, 129 et seq.
48. BfDI 2017, 170.
49. *See* Gierschmann 2021, 484 with further references.
50. *DfBI*, Position paper on anonymization under the GDPR with special consideration of the telecommunications industry, 2020, p. 5.
51. Spiecker et al. 2023, Art. 6, paras 41, 42; Kotschy 2020, 332 et seq.
52. Spiecker et al. 2023, Art. 17, paras 20 et seq.; Kranenborg 2020, Art. 17, 479 et seq.
53. *Stürmer*, ZD 2020, 626 (630).
54. *See* Gierschmann 2021, 484 with reference to Hornung & Wagner 2020, 226.
55. *See* Gierschmann 2021, 585.
56. Hornung & Wagner 2020, 228; *for details, see* Spiecker et al. 2023, Art. 9, paras 7 et seq.; Georgieva & Kuner 2020, 373 et seq.
57. *See* Gierschmann 2021, 485; BfDI 2020, ss 6 et seq.

automatically extract patterns and correlations from the data.[58] The combination of quantity and quality of data processing and the dynamic increase in computing power give rise to considerable re-identifiability potential and risks.[59] This is because by linking data from different data sources, relevant characteristics can be combined in such a way that a personal reference can be (re-)established, and thus, re-identifiability shall be achieved.[60] The temporal component plays an important role in assessing the risk of re-identifiability. In addition, the assessment of the re-identifiability risk must not only be based on the *status quo* over time but a risk forecast[61] must also be made for the entire duration of the data analysis; this must include anticipating future newly uploaded data records and potential access by third parties to existing data records.[62]

Whether effective anonymization may (still) be used as a reliable measure to eliminate personal references in the future can by no means be considered certain, especially in the context of Big Data analyses.[63] Overall, it is a significant challenge across the industry to effectively remove or delete personal data from AI training sets.

3.2.2 Pseudonymization

According to Article 4(5) of the GDPR, pseudonymization is defined as the processing of personal data in such a way that the personal data cannot (or can no longer) be attributed to a data subject without the use of additional information. It is necessary that this additional information is stored separately and is subject to technical or organizational measures that ensure that the data subject cannot be directly identified.[64] For an effective pseudonymization of personal data, the informational characteristics of the datasets are usually modified in such a way that an assignment to the data subject can only be made with the help of specific assignment information/rules.[65] As a result, this leads to a separation of functions: the data owner can no longer directly assign the information content to a natural person due to a lack of access to the assignment information or rule, and the owner of the assignment information or rule cannot access the personal data in question.[66]

While anonymization aims to completely remove the personal identifiers and thereby exclude the scope of application of the GDPR, pseudonymized data is considered personal data according to Recital 26 and, therefore, continues to fall within the scope of the GDPR.[67] Pseudonymization cannot, therefore, completely avoid the

58. Gola 2022, Art. 4, para. 151; Ohrtmann & Schwierig 2014, 2984; Schefzig 2014, 774; Hoffmann-Riem 2018, 19 et seq. The characteristics of volume, variety and velocity are also known as the 3Vs of big data analysis and go back to Laney 2001.
59. *See* Paal 2020, ch. 8.7, 438, para. 27.
60. *See* Roßnagel & Scholz 2000, 728 et seq.; Schefzig 2014, 775.
61. On planning and assessing the risks of anonymization, *see also* Gierschmann 2021, 482 et seq.
62. *See* Schefzig 2014, 775 et seq.
63. To summarize: *see* Vogel 2022, 225 et seq.
64. *See also ibid.*, at 218; *for details, see* Spiecker et al. 2023, Art. 4(5), paras 4 et seq.; Tosoni 2020, 135 et seq.
65. Roßnagel 2018, 243.
66. Schleipfer 2020, 285.
67. *See also* Hermann 2021, para. 22.

data protection requirements of the GDPR. Nevertheless, there are considerable incentives for the controller to pseudonymize personal data in order to comply with the basic mandate to minimize risks for the data subject.[68] As pseudonymization generally has a beneficial effect on the rights of the data subject and is also in line with the principle of data minimization, the GDPR contains various privileges regarding the processing of pseudonymous data.[69] Of particular importance for the training of AI systems is the fact that pseudonymization has a positive effect on the assessment of the lawfulness of processing in the context of a balancing of interests pursuant to Article 6(1)(f) of the GDPR.[70]

3.2.3 Privacy Enhancing Technologies

In addition to anonymization and pseudonymization, other data protection-friendly technologies are used in practice to ensure the lawfulness of data processing.[71] Specifically, privacy-enhancing technologies (PETs) play an essential role in the data protection-compliant design of AI systems and are continuously evolving.[72] Three critical PETs are: (1) synthetic data generation; (2) homomorphic encryption; and (3) the differential privacy method (DPM).

3.2.3.1 Synthetic Data

Synthetic data means wholly or partially artificially created data that abstractly reproduces the statistical characteristics of a real dataset.[73] The synthesized data does not (or no longer) contain any personal identifier, which excludes the applicability of the GDPR and, therefore, facilitates data processing in the context of AI training in terms of data protection law.[74] The synthetization of data becomes particularly relevant where a dataset for AI training already exists but is still too small in quantitative terms. In this case, new, statistically comparable, artificial data without personal identifiers can be generated using synthetization based on the existing data to increase the data set for effective and GDPR-compliant AI training.[75] However, it must be considered that the creation and utilization of synthetic data entail increased efforts, mainly because human involvement (human in the loop) is regularly required.

68. Paal 2020, Ch. 8.7, 439, para. 27; Gola 2022, Art. 4, para. 55.
69. *See* Paal 2020, ch. 8.7, 439; Eßer 2022; Gola 2022, Art. 5, para. 24.
70. Klar & Kühling 2018, paras 13 et seq.; *for details, see* Spiecker et al. 2023, Art. 6, paras 69 et seq.; Kotschy 2020, 337 et seq.
71. A fundamental overview of the role of PET in connection with the assessment of data protection risks when using AI systems can be found in Schaff & Dujak 2023, 445.
72. *See* OECD 2023; major economic players are also involved in the development of PET: Apple 2022; Rogers et al. 2020; Brill 2021; and the Commission is also explicitly in favour of using PET: Commission 2023, para. 30, Art. 13(3)(b), para. 4 and Art. 14(1)(e).
73. Hense 2023, para. 75; Wagner 2020.
74. Lukas 2023, 322.
75. *See* Hense 2023, para. 75.

3.2.3.2 Homomorphic Encryption

Another central PET is homomorphic encryption.[76] This encryption technique aims to perform arithmetic operations on encrypted data and extract relevant knowledge from the dataset without having to decrypt the personal data.[77] This approach enables third parties to access the information content of the encrypted dataset in a way that protects data privacy and to process and utilize it for AI training.[78] Homomorphic encryption tends to be more aligned with the advanced state of science rather than the present state of technology.[79]

3.2.3.3 Differential Privacy

Finally, the DPM should be mentioned as a practical PET. 'Differential privacy' is an anonymization technique in which additional information is added to a data set to achieve a random data falsification.[80] This type of data manipulation creates a technical noise, and the individual data points are disguised or blurred so that the statistical characteristics of the dataset can still be utilized. Still, certain persons in the data set can no longer be identified.[81] One of the criticisms of DPM is that it regularly results in a loss of informational precision due to the random falsification of the dataset.[82] When DPM is applied to the training data of AI systems, this loss of precision can cause considerable disadvantages at the output level, for example, leading to an increased risk of indirectly discriminatory output results.[83]

3.2.3.4 Interim Result

Overall, it shall therefore be stated at this point that both the classic methods of anonymization and pseudonymization, as well as novel PETs that are still under development, are essential instruments for eliminating or at least reducing the personal identifiers of data and thereby allowing for GDPR-compliant AI training systems. After this background, the situations in which personal identifiers cannot be eliminated, and thus GDPR requirements apply, will be examined in the following section.

4 APPLICATION OF THE GDPR REQUIREMENTS TO AI TRAINING

According to Recital 15, the GDPR is a technology-neutral set of rules. However, the actual and technical characteristics of AI systems raise fundamental questions about

76. Detailed and fundamental information on homomorphic encryption: Gentry 2009, 5 et seq.; Salem et al. 2018, 5.
77. *See* Lukas 2023, 322 et seq.; Schur 2021.
78. Schaff & Dujak 2023, 451 et seq.
79. Martini 2021, para. 34a; Dressel 2019, 282.
80. Schaff & Dujak 2023, 450; Valkanova 2020, 347.
81. *See* Lukas 2023, 323; Martini 2021, paras 34 et seq.
82. *See* Hense 2023, para. 74; Bambauer et al. 2020, 701; Hu 2015, 1692; Ji et al. 2014.
83. Hense 2023; Bagdasaryan et al. 2019.

almost all processing principles.[84] In this context, it is necessary to analyse how AI training can be reliably reconciled with the GDPR requirements.

4.1 Principle of Data Minimization

According to the principle of data minimization, Article 5(1)(c) of the GDPR[85] – also applicable in the AI context[86] – personal data must be adequate, relevant and limited to what is necessary for the purposes of processing. At first glance, this principle seems difficult, if not impossible, to reconcile with the considerable need for large amounts of data for AI training. The tension between the principle of data minimization and the 'data hunger' characteristic of AI training is thus evident, with compatibility being completely denied in some cases due to a supposed fundamental incompatibility.[87] However, upon closer examination, there are robust arguments in favour of the compatibility of AI training with the principle of data minimization: the terms 'appropriate', 'substantial' and 'necessary', for example, are undefined legal terms that are fundamentally open to interpretation and open up considerable leeway in the interpretation and application of legal provisions.[88]

Therefore, Article 5(1)(c) of the GDPR does not result in any rigid requirements for data processing. Instead, the wording of the standard is inherently dependent on the individual case. This interpretation is also supported by Recital 39 of the GDPR, according to which the permissibility of data processing depends on whether it is reasonable for the controller to resort to other means to achieve the purpose. In this respect, a relative and not an absolute understanding of the principle of data minimization is appropriate.[89] Article 5(1)(c) of the GDPR, therefore, does not impose an obligation on the controller to process fewer data in general but to ensure using only necessary data for achieving the purpose. However, how much data will be required for which purpose is a case-by-case issue.

Which process could apply to data processing constitutes one of the critical questions in this case. In principle, each piece of personal information must be analysed to determine whether and to what extent the processing of this data is necessary to achieve the purpose. However, if – as in the case of AI training – a critical mass of data has to be processed, a separate examination of the necessity for each piece of data is neither practical nor practicable. The quality of an AI system depends not on the individual piece of information but on the totality of all the data to be processed. Accordingly, it may be argued that almost every piece of information is not required to

84. Paal 2020, Ch. 8.7, 428, para. 4; *see* Vogel 2022, 89; Hessel & Dillschneider 2023, 459; Baumgartner et al. 2023, 543.
85. Spiecker et al. 2023, Art. 5, paras 89 et seq.; Terwangne 2020, 317.
86. DSK has deemed it necessary to once again explicitly emphasize the applicability of the principle of data minimization to AI systems: DSK 2019a, 4. For the US approach, *see* Solove & Hartzog 2024, 35 et seq.
87. *See* Hoffmann-Riem 2018, 89, which considers big data applications to be unlawful if the processing principles are applied consistently.
88. *See* Vogel 2022, 162.
89. *See in this sense ibid.*, at 170.

achieve the purpose. However, according to the wording of Article 5(1)(c) of the GDPR, the application of the data minimization principle should not mean that no more data processing takes place at all. Therefore, when applying the principle of data minimization in the context of AI, a teleological perspective should be taken to avoid preventing innovation, which is neither legislatively intended nor teleologically desirable.

Since AI training relies on large amounts of training data and processing such data is technically a 'must', processing these large datasets can, therefore, be reasonably categorized as 'necessary'.[90] In addition, technical measures can be taken to limit the amount of personal data processed.[91] In this sense, extensive anonymization or pseudonymization and consistent data protection-friendly default settings within the meaning of Article 25 GDPR (privacy by design), for example, contribute to improving AI systems' compatibility with the data minimization principle.[92] It should, therefore, be noted that, by the principle of data minimization and under certain conditions, it may indeed be compatible with processing large amounts of personal data to enhance AI training (and, ultimately, AI output).

4.2 Principle of Data Accuracy

According to the principle of data accuracy set out in Article 5(1)(d) of the GDPR, personal data must be accurate and up to date; furthermore, appropriate measures must be taken to erase or rectify inaccurate data without undue delay.[93] The principle of data accuracy plays a vital role in AI training, especially for generative AI (GenAI) models, as these models generate their own output.[94] Since the quality of the output depends mainly on the quality of the preceding input,[95] the principle of data accuracy could be of particular importance for AI training data to prevent incorrect, discriminatory[96] or biased[97] results at the output level.[98] At the same time, the relevance and influence of the principle of data accuracy are always highly context-dependent (also) in the context of AI training.

However, if the AI training data originates from freely accessible public (internet) sources, a comprehensive *ex ante* accuracy check will generally be almost impossible

90. *See ibid.*, at 162 et seq.
91. *See also* Baumgartner et al. 2023, 545 et seq.
92. *See* Pötters 2022, para. 24.
93. Spiecker et al. 2023, Art. 5, paras 107 et seq.; Terwangne 2020, 317, 318.
94. Pesch & Böhme 2023a, 917.
95. Vogel 2022, 50.
96. On the fundamental problem of discriminatory results of AI systems, *see* Hüger 2023, 298 et seq.; Lauscher & Legner 2022, 376.
97. For detailed information on the issues involved in biased training, *see* Solove 2024, 42 et seq.; Gillis 2022, 1177 et seq.
98. For the output level, which is not the focus of this consideration, lower requirements are to be set and only 'statistical accuracy' is required, Baumgartner et al. 2023, 543. This takes into account the fact that the output of an AI model is often only a forecast based on statistical probability calculations, Paal 2020, Ch. 8.7, 434; Pesch & Böhme 2023a, 918 et seq.

to implement.[99] Suppose training data subsequently turns out to be incorrect or inherently biased, discriminative or based on relative facts. In that case, the targeted deletion of individual data is also often practically impossible, disproportionately costly or ineffective due to the particular technological features of AI systems.[100] This is because when AI systems 'remember' data, the AI model may reconstruct personal training data that has already been deleted or modified later when generating an output.[101] As a far-reaching compliance measure, it could be considered that AI models trained with incorrect data (and thus contaminated, so to speak) must be deleted entirely and then redeveloped and retrained.[102] However, this approach is associated with high costs and, moreover, does not guarantee comprehensive data accuracy for the newly trained AI model in itself, which is why it should only be used as a last resort.[103]

As a result, a risk-based approach should be applied, focussing on a data protection-friendly technical design of AI training to ensure compatibility with the principle of data accuracy.[104]

4.3 Purpose Limitation

According to the principle of purpose limitation, the collection (and further processing) of personal data is only permitted for predetermined, explicit and legitimate purposes, Article 5(1)(b) of the GDPR. The purpose limitation principle is primarily intended to ensure that the data subjects have an overview of and can check the data processing.[105] Accordingly, the controller's purpose specification must effectively limit the possibility of further processing. To this end, the purposes must be defined as precisely as possible or necessary. There is, therefore, a consensus that overly abstract[106] purposes are incompatible with Article 5(1)(b) of the GDPR.[107]

In this context, the development of AI applications appears prima facie to conflict with the requirement of purpose limitation. This is because AI training is also primarily intended to develop AI systems that first 'discover' new information or application potential. In these cases, the purposes of the processing cannot yet be concretely determined at the beginning of the training. Instead, the use cases of the AI systems will only (or can only) be reliably developed during the AI training. A restrictive interpretation of the purpose limitation principle, therefore, threatens to limit AI technologies'

99. *See* Baumgartner et al. 2023, 546.
100. Pesch & Böhme 2023a, 921 et seq.
101. *See ibid.*, at 920; Novelli et al. 2024, 7; Brown et al. 2022, 2282 et seq.
102. Determann 2024, ch. 1, 25 et seq.; Pesch & Böhme 2023a, 922.
103. Determann 2024, ch. 1, 25 et seq.
104. Pesch & Böhme 2023a, 922.
105. Herbst 2020, para. 22; *see* Roßnagel 2019, Art. 5, para. 77; Solove & Hartzog 2024, 34.
106. For example, the use of data for 'advertising purposes', 'IT security', 'big data applications' is too abstract, Schantz 2016, 1844; Mantz & Marosi 2019, Part A, s. 3, para. 86.
107. Reimer 2022, Art. 5, para. 22; Herbst 2020, para. 35; Kramer 2020, Art. 5, para. 27; *for details, see* Spiecker et al. 2023, Art. 5, paras 45 et seq.; Terwangne 2020, 315 et seq.

innovation and development potential.[108] Thus, meticulous consideration and discussion may be warranted regarding the separation of AI system establishment processes, such as coding, development, and deployment.

In this respect, it should be emphasized that Article 5(1)(b) of the GDPR is not intended to restrict data processing in a preventive and prohibitive manner. Instead, the purpose limitation requirement merely requires controllers to define the purposes as precisely as is possible and necessary at the time of processing. However, if and to the extent that a specification of the purposes can be considered during the processing procedure, the controller must also carry out this specification. According to the wording and the telos of Article 5(1)(b) GDPR, a 'subsequent insertion or adding' of purposes is not permitted.[109] However, if the purposes are subsequently specified, the data processing options are limited, which increases the desired transparency of the processing. This corresponds to the meaning and purpose of the requirements of the said principle and is therefore not only permissible but also necessary. Suppose it is not possible to specify the purposes, but only a change of purpose is possible. In that case, the permissibility of further AI training is governed by the provisions of Article 6(4) of the GDPR.

Article 6(4) of the GDPR specifies the requirements for a permissible change of purpose for scenarios in which data processing is carried out for a purpose other than the original purpose for which the data was collected. Since, according to the correct interpretation, Article 6(4) of the GDPR does not establish an independent authorization for processing for another purpose, the permissibility of further processing requires a justification from Article 6(1) of the GDPR for the other purpose as well.[110] The controller must, therefore, check whether the processing for the new purpose is compatible with the original purpose and also determine the legal basis for the processing for this new purpose. Scenarios in which new, initially unknown contexts are generated, which are then assigned to new purposes of personal data processing, are particularly prone to conflict. It should also be noted that in the event of a change of purpose, the exact requirements for determining the purpose must be met as when the data was initially collected.

According to the view expressed here, the purpose limitation requirement is not incompatible with the objectives of AI training. Nevertheless, the limitation of purpose poses considerable challenges for data controllers in this context. Particularly in cases where the purposes of processing cannot be clearly defined at the beginning of AI training, data controllers must consistently monitor and support the processing operations to concretize the purposes if necessary. Failure to do so may result in severe fines, *see* Article 83(5)(a) of the GDPR.

Finally, it should be noted that the draft version of a European Health Data Space (EHDS) Regulation[111] for the establishment of an EHDS explicitly mentions AI training

108. *See* Conrad 2018, 742; Frenzel 2020, Art. 6, para. 49: 'can ... only have a restrictive effect', which is subsequently followed by Roßnagel 2019, Art. 6 paras 4, 58; Datatilsynet 2018, 18.
109. Kramer 2020, Art. 5, para. 23; Heberlein 2018, Art. 5, para. 13.
110. Albers & Veit 2023, para. 108; Reimer 2022, Art. 5, para. 26; Schantz 2016, 1844.
111. Commission EHDS 2022.

in Article 34(1)(g) as a purpose for which electronic health data can be processed by way of secondary use. The European legislator is therefore in favour of enabling AI training that complies with data protection regulations and ensuring that this is covered by standards. At the same time, it remains to be seen how the EHDS and the other planned data spaces will be organized legislatively.

4.4 Principle of Transparency

Article 5(1)(a),[112] section 3, of the GDPR contains the principle of transparency, which raises various practical questions concerning AI training. Personal data must be 'processed in a manner that is transparent to the data subject'. This requirement is specified in Recital 39 of the GDPR, according to which all information on data processing must be easily accessible, understandable and written in clear and plain language; at the same time. It is also emphasized that the transparency obligation extends to information on the controller's identity, the processing's purposes and all other circumstances that ensure fair and transparent processing with regard to the data subject. The principle of transparency is normatively supplemented and concretized by the information obligations set out in Articles 12 et seq. GDPR and the data subjects' rights to information.[113] Following Recital 39 of the GDPR, these transparency obligations apply to future processing operations and data processing that has already occurred.[114]

In AI training, compliance with the principle of transparency is essential in several respects. First, a high level of transparency positively affects other processing principles, such as the principle of data accuracy. In this sense, a transparent AI system regularly enables or facilitates the accuracy check of training data.[115] Furthermore, the level of transparency is also taken into account in the legality check. It is included, in particular, in the practical balancing of interests under Article 6(1)(f) of the GDPR.[116] Furthermore, the principle of transparency is essential for promoting the general social acceptance of AI systems and can help strengthen general trust in AI technologies.[117] It is, therefore, all the more important to resolve (as far as possible) the various potential conflicts regarding the normative transparency requirements.

Article 12(1), sentence 1 of the GDPR stipulates that all relevant information must be provided in a concise, transparent, intelligible and easily accessible form, using clear and plain language. This obligation also includes information about the specific processing procedure, the logic involved, and the training data used.[118] Concerning the responsibility to provide information about the processing procedures, it is problematic

112. *For details, see* Spiecker et al. 2023, Art. 5, paras 22 et seq.; Terwangne 2020, 314, 315.
113. On the basic transparency requirements, *see* Art. 29 WP 2018.
114. *See* Frenzel 2020, Art. 32, para. 21.
115. Brink et al. 2020, Ch. 8.11, 501.
116. Gola 2022, Art. 6, para. 68; *for details, see* Spiecker et al. 2023, Art. 6, paras 69 et seq.; Kotschy 2020, 337 et seq.
117. *See* Müller-Quade et al. 2023, 20 et seq.
118. At least according to DSK 2019a, 3; *for details, see* Spiecker et al. 2023, Art. 12, paras 9 et seq.; Polcak 2020, 406 et seq.

that the functioning of AI systems is regularly highly complex and cannot be explained in simple and easily understandable terms.[119] In many cases, autonomous and self-learning processes in the context of AI training, particularly concerning GenAI models and neural networks, are not fully comprehensible even to the developers, which is why AI systems are also referred to as 'black box' phenomena.[120] This finding implies a fundamental, technology-induced transparency deficit.[121]

However, it is questionable whether the principle of transparency actually requires that the data subjects be able to understand the exact functioning of the AI model. To answer this question, the requirements of Article 13(2)(f) of the GDPR[122] shall be used as a guide. According to this provision, the data subject must provide reliable information about the 'involved logic' in automated individual case decisions. The standard aims to create transparency in using algorithm-based data processing systems. Such systems – even if not AI models – are usually so complex that disclosure of the source code, for example, would ultimately not provide the average data subject with any real insight.[123] This applies, in particular, to self-learning AI models.[124] To ensure that the principle of transparency from Article 5(1)(a), section 3 of the GDPR is applied as effectively as possible, it should therefore be considered sufficient if the information about the logic involved in the AI system is limited to the abstract functionality and orientation. Furthermore, protecting business secrets may stand in the way of a comprehensive information obligation regarding the functioning of the AI system, notably the specific AI algorithm.[125]

Furthermore, it should be noted that the training data is collected from publicly accessible sources in the present situation. This does not constitute data collection from the data subject within the meaning of Article 14 of the GDPR.[126] According to Article 14(5)(b) of the GDPR, the transparency requirement is restricted if and to the extent that the provision of information is impossible or involves a disproportionate effort. If large amounts of data are collected in the context of web scraping or web crawling, it is hardly feasible to inform all data subjects at the time of data collection. In addition, it should be noted that the considerable research effort required to identify the data subjects in a way that enables the provision of information may even intensify and deepen the impairment of fundamental rights. In this context, a careful examination must be conducted to determine whether and to what extent the provision of information is dispensable in individual cases following Article 14(5)(b) of the GDPR.

119. Solove 2024, 55; Paal 2020, Ch. 8.7, 430, para. 8.
120. *See ibid.*; LfDI Ba-Wü 2023, 12; Datenethikkommission 2019, 169 et seq.; Skistims 2020, 358, para. 19; fundamental on the black box issue Tschider 2021, 700 et seq.
121. Paal 2020, Ch. 8.7, 430, para. 8.
122. *For details, see* Spiecker et al. 2023, Art. 13, paras 7 et seq.; Zanfir-Fortuna 2020, Art. 13, 425 et seq.
123. *See also* Steinrötter 2023, Art. 13, para. 53.
124. *Ibid.*
125. Schürmann 2022, 318; Hennemann 2020, para. 31b; *in detail* Tschider 2021, 710 et seq.; on the tension between data protection obligations to provide information and conflicting business secrets *also* Paal 2014.
126. Bäcker 2024, para. 9; *for details, see* Spiecker et al. 2023, Art. 14, paras 3 et seq.; Zanfir-Fortuna 2020, Art. 14, 443 et seq.

Given the above, the principle of transparency must be interpreted and applied in a way that takes appropriate account of the unique features of AI systems so that developers and operators of AI systems are not subject to practically unfulfillable transparency obligations.[127] However, as far as legally and technically possible, extensive precautions must be taken to ensure a high level of transparency (as far as possible). Depending on the addressee and target group, differentiated and graduated information provisions with different content and focal points are necessary to cover the respective information needs of the parties involved as comprehensively as possible.[128] While superficial information without technical depth is often sufficient for the data subjects, controllers and supervisory authorities regularly require more comprehensive and in-depth information on the functioning of the AI model.[129]

According to all of the above, a risk-based interpretation can reconcile the processing procedures in the context of AI systems with both the transparency principle from Article 5(1)(a), section 3 of the GDPR and the information obligations and rights to information from Articles 12 et seq. GDPR.

5 LEGAL GROUNDS UNDER THE GDPR FOR AI TRAINING

According to Article 6(1) of the GDPR, the processing of personal data is subject to a preventive prohibition subject to authorization, which is why the existence of one of the six *numerus clausus* legal bases from Article 6(1)(a)-(f) of the GDPR is required for lawful processing.[130] It is recognized that the process of collecting publicly available personal training data in advance of the actual AI training already constitutes data processing relevant under data protection law. In this context, consent (Article 6(1)(a) of the GDPR) and the legitimate interest (Article 6(1)(f) of the GDPR) could be deemed as justifying legal grounds.

5.1 Consent: Article 6(1)(a) of the GDPR

The legal basis of consent under Article 6(1)(a) of the GDPR encounters legal and practical hurdles, not least when collecting AI training data from publicly accessible internet sources. According to Article 4(11) of the GDPR, the data subject's consent under data protection law according to Article 6(1)(a) of the GDPR must be given

127. Baumgartner et al. 2023, 544. A corresponding restriction of the transparency obligation also corresponds to the assessment of GDPR, Art. 15(5)(b), which contains an exclusion of the information obligation in cases of impossibility or disproportionality. *See in more detail* Paal 2020, Ch. 8.7, 431, para. 11.
128. *See* DSK 2019b, 11 et seq.
129. *See ibid.*
130. Solove & Wartzog 2024, 24. This is different in United States (US) data protection law, for example. There, no legal basis is generally required for the processing of personal data. In the California Consumer Privacy Act (CCPA), however, data subjects can at least make use of opt-out rights and refuse the processing of their personal data, *see* Solove 2024, 47. Interestingly, however, publicly available data falls outside the scope of the CCPA, which is why its provisions do not apply to the collection of training data from freely accessible internet sources, *see* Determann 2024, Ch. 1, 23 et seq.; Solove 2024, 24; Solove & Wartzog 2024, 26 et seq.

voluntarily, for the specific case, in an informed and unambiguous manner in the form of a declaration or other unambiguous, affirmative act.[131]

Even the criterion of 'consent given in an informed manner' is challenging in AI training data, as the data controller would have to provide the data subject with comprehensive information about the specific processing and its purposes to obtain sufficiently informed consent.[132] Due to the technology-related lack of transparency and the difficulty of explaining AI systems, developers are often unable to explain the relevant processing procedures precisely and comprehensibly, so informed consent is hardly possible in practice.[133] In addition, consent can be freely withdrawn by the data subject at any time following Article 7(3), sentence 1 of the GDPR. In this case, the relevant data must be deleted immediately at the request of the data subject by Article 17(1)(b) of the GDPR. Suppose the AI model has already been trained with the data. Therefore, the (follow-up) question arises as to whether and to what extent subsequent erasure is still possible or appropriate.[134]

Finally, consent is often not considered a legal basis because it is impossible to identify and inform all data subjects in advance and obtain the corresponding consent.[135] Larger companies with significant numbers of users could, under certain conditions, obtain prior consent from their users for the further processing of data for the purpose of AI training. However, in individual cases, such a procedure risks violating the prohibition of coupling under Article 7 of the GDPR[136] and also raises fundamental questions about the value of the corresponding consent as an adequate legal basis. Such a practice could lead to consent fatigue due to general desensitization of the data subjects due to a lack of factual choice options and, in some cases, non-transparent or overly extensive information provision.[137] In some cases, it is therefore feared that a corresponding consent could be degraded to a mere 'fictitious consent' by simply clicking on an 'Accept' button.[138]

5.2 Legitimate Interest: Article 6(1)(f) of the GDPR

Under Article 6(1)(f) of the GDPR, the processing is lawful if it is necessary for the legitimate interests pursued by the controller or a third party, except where such interests are overridden by the interests or fundamental rights and freedoms of the data subject. Therefore, the lawfulness of data processing can be established using a comprehensive balancing of interests on a case-by-case basis.[139] Despite the legal

131. Publication by the data subject does not in itself constitute implied consent, as the mere publication of the personal data by the data subject does not qualify as a clearly affirmative act within the meaning of GDPR, Art. 4(11); *see* Franke 2023, 567; Bernzen 2023, 8; Solove & Wartzog 2024, 24.
132. LfDI Ba-Wü 2023, 12.
133. *See* Dieker 2024, 133 et seq.
134. *See also* Pesch & Böhme 2023a, 920; Trigo Kramcsák 2023, 5.
135. CEDPO 2023, 10; Novelli et al. 2024, 8; Dieker 2024, 133.
136. *See in more detail* Paal 2020, Ch. 8.2, 356 et seq., paras 14 et seq.
137. *See* Trigo Kramcsák 2023, 6.
138. *See* Solove 2024, 28 et seq. who sees consent as a 'blank check to do almost anything'.
139. Gola 2022, Art. 6, paras 59, 69.

uncertainty associated with justification through balancing of interests, Article 6(1)(f) of the GDPR is currently considered by both the data protection authorities[140] and prevailing opinions of the literature[141] as the most relevant and robust legal basis for the lawful collection and processing of AI training data. This is justified above all by the flexibility of the assessment process, which enables comprehensive consideration of the particular technological features of AI systems.[142]

The examination of the lawfulness of data processing under Article 6(1)(f) of the GDPR occurs in three steps:[143] First, it is necessary to establish a legitimate interest of the data controller before proceeding to the second step, where the necessity of the specific processing to safeguard this interest must be examined. Third and finally, a comprehensive assessment is conducted considering the data subject's opposing interests, fundamental rights, or freedoms.

5.2.1 Legitimate Interests of AI Developers

The legitimate interest of the AI developer (natural or legal person) in data processing for the purpose of AI training can be of a factual, economic or non-material nature. It must be compatible with the legal system.[144] AI developers regularly have a financial interest in data processing for the purpose of AI training to offer the corresponding AI system on the market.[145] In addition to the purely economic interest in commercially developed AI systems, other interests, mainly non-profit, public welfare-related interests, can be taken into account if the AI system is intended to provide social or societal added value in the medical and healthcare sectors, for example.[146] AI developers in the field of research may be able to invoke freedom of science and freedom of information as relevant non-material interests.[147]

5.2.2 Necessity of the Data Processing

Furthermore, specific data processing is also necessary. The necessity is affirmed when the purpose of the data processing and:[148]

> the legitimate data processing interests pursued cannot reasonably be achieved just as effectively by other means less restrictive of the fundamental rights and freedoms of data subjects, in particular the rights to respect for private life and to

140. ICO 2023; LfDI Ba-Wü 2023, 7 et seq.; Commission Nationale de l'Informatique et des Libertés (CNIL); Datatilsynet; CEDPO 2023.
141. *Among others*: Franke 2023, 567; Werry 2023, 912 et seq.; Bernzen 2023, 9 et seq.; Solove 2024, 30; Novelli et al. 2024, 8; Dieker 2024, 134 et seq.
142. LfDI Ba-Wü 2023, 16; Trigo Kramcsák 2023, 7.
143. *See in detail* Skistims 2020, 365 et seq., paras 39 et seq.
144. Schulz 2022, Art. 6, para. 61.
145. Bernzen 2023, 9; due to entrepreneurial freedom, the economic interest of the AI operator must be interpreted broadly.
146. Novelli et al. 2024, 8; Werry 2023, 912 et seq.
147. Dieker 2024, 134.
148. *Meta Platforms* (Case C-252/211), 4 Jul. 2023, ECLI:EU:C:2023:537, para. 108.

> the protection of personal data guaranteed by Articles 7 and 8 of the Charter (*see*, to that effect, judgment of 22 June 2021, *Latvijas Republikas Saeima (Penalty points)*, C-439/19, EU:C:2021:504, paragraph 110 and the case-law cited).

Thus, it is crucial to undertake a differentiated view of the various processing phases.

Collecting and collating training data is essential for successful AI training.[149] This is because an AI system cannot be developed without training data. The scope of the data collection and the amount of training data used must also be considered part of the necessity test.[150] In this respect, the principle of data minimization from Article 5(1)(c) of the GDPR must – once again – be taken into account, according to which the training data may not be processed beyond what is necessary.[151] This becomes particularly problematic when a 'basis' of training data is fundamentally required for AI training, and additional data is collected that only contributes to marginal quality improvements.[152] If a strict scrutiny standard is applied, the necessity could be denied in these cases.[153]

However, it is probably more convincing to affirm the necessity of more extensive data collection, even in the case of only minor increases in quality. One of the views posits in favour of this argument and states that the necessity depends on whether other means are 'equally effective' in realizing the legitimate interest. If a more extensive training dataset leads to an increase in quality, even only a small one, not using this 'more' data would not be 'equally effective'. Commercially marketed AI systems are particularly exposed to intense and dynamic competition,[154] which is why even small increases in quality can be of great importance. However, a pervasive collection of data can also be taken into account at a later stage when balancing interests.

Furthermore, storing training data, which constitutes independent data processing, is also subject to a strict necessity test. Suppose external providers can be used to store the training data. In that case, permanent internal storage is generally unnecessary and, therefore, does not (or no longer) fulfil the requirements of the necessity test.[155]

5.2.3 Balancing of Interests in the Narrow Sense

Finally, the legitimate interests of the AI developer shall be assessed comprehensively against the potentially conflicting interests and rights of the data subjects. This is a case-by-case assessment that considers all circumstances of the specific processing.[156]

149. Dieker 2024, 134.
150. *See* Skistims 2020, 368, para. 48.
151. *See* LfDI Ba-Wü 2023.
152. *See* Skistims 2020, 368.
153. LfDI Ba-Wü clarifies, for example, that in this context not 'a lot helps a lot', but rather 'only what is necessary' should apply, *see* LfDI Ba-Wü 2023, 17.
154. *See* Ferràs-Hernández & Nylund 2023, 73 et seq.; Devlin 2023.
155. Bernzen 2023, 9.
156. *Rīgas satiksme* (Case C-13/16), 4 May 2017, ECLI:EU:C:2017:336, Beck-Rechtsprechung (BeckRS) 108615, para. 31 (2017); Albers & Veit 2023, para. 71.

In addition to the relevant fundamental rights and freedoms of the data subject and the respective intensity of the interference, the main criteria for assessment include the type of data and the data subject, the compatibility of the processing with the processing principles, the technical and organizational security measures taken and the affected sphere of interference.[157]

5.2.3.1 Criteria Against AI Developers

First, it should be taken into account that the data subjects often have no positive knowledge that their personal data has been collected for the purpose of AI training. When comparing the interests, this circumstance generally works in favour of the AI developers, as the data subjects cannot use their data subject rights in the absence of knowledge. However, AI developers can counter this adverse finding by implementing technical measures that allow data subjects to check whether personal data concerning them has been collected for AI training.[158]

Similarly, the risk of so-called model inversion attacks must be considered to the detriment of AI developers.[159] These reverse engineering techniques can be used to reconstruct and disclose training data at the output level, possibly including personal[160] data.[161] To counter this threat to the privacy and data security of the data subjects, AI developers can take technical and organizational security precautions to reduce the risk of such attacks.[162]

Furthermore, 'profiling' may also be included in comparing interests. Article 4(4) of the GDPR defines profiling as any form of automated processing of personal data in which the data is used to evaluate, analyse or predict certain personal aspects. Although the collection of AI training data does not constitute profiling,[163] it may lead to the creation of comprehensive personality profiles in the further course of the preparation or training of AI models. Particularly in scenarios where the personality profiles are extensive and cover several areas of life, the interests of the persons concerned are particularly worthy of protection. Also, in this case, AI operators must use technical protective measures to reduce the risks associated with profiling the data subjects, for example, by technically separating specific categories of data to prevent the creation of overarching personality profiles.[164]

Finally, the fact that special categories of personal data may be collected and processed for AI training must be considered when balancing interests. These sensitive categories of data are generally subject to a processing ban based on and under Article

157. *See* Schulz 2022, Art. 6, para. 63; Dieker 2024, 134.
158. Bernzen 2023, 10.
159. Franke 2023, 568.
160. This contrasts with so-called membership inference attacks, which can only be used to determine whether certain data was part of the training data set or not. Personal data is not directly generated with this method. *See* Kaulartz 2020, 466, para. 11.
161. Novelli et al. 2024, 8 et seq.
162. Franke 2023, 568.
163. *See* Dieker 2024, 136.
164. Skistims 2020, 370, para. 52.

9(1) of the GDPR. It should be noted that, according to recent case law from the CJEU, the scope of application of sensitive data categories under Article 9(2) of the GDPR is already triggered 'when such data processing enables the disclosure of information falling within one of these categories'.[165] Exceptionally, Article 9(2)(e) of the GDPR allows processing if the data subject has made the data public. This is because a data subject who voluntarily discloses their sensitive data and thereby waives their protection is generally considered less worthy of protection.[166] However, this exception requires that the data subject has made the data public.[167] This criterion must be interpreted restrictively, and the mere presence of personal data in freely accessible public sources is not in itself sufficient.[168] Instead, an independent publication by the data subject himself must emerge from the overall context.[169] To avoid the risk of potentially prohibited processing of sensitive personal data, filter systems, in particular, can be used; in addition, AI developers should check the collected data as comprehensively as possible.[170]

The lack of knowledge of the data subject, data security-specific processing risks, profiling, and the processing of sensitive data are criteria that, from the perspective of AI developers, can negatively impact the balancing of interests. However, AI developers can counteract these negative delimitation criteria with targeted technical protective measures, thus substantially influencing the balancing of interests in their favour.

5.2.3.2 Criteria in Favour of AI Developers

The next step is to elaborate on the circumstances that could be favourable in terms of AI developers' interests. According to the previous explanations, the processing principles and the specific technical and organizational measures implemented to safeguard the rights of data subjects can be of decisive importance.[171] Comprehensive and effective anonymization or pseudonymization, high transparency standards and privacy-by-design requirements enable data protection-friendly design of AI training and thus reduce the individual intensity of interference for the data subjects.[172] The less intrusive the measures taken are for the data subjects, the more likely it is that the balance of interests will be in favour of the AI developers.

According to Recital 47 GDPR, the data subject's reasonable expectations about the specific processing should be considered when balancing interests. Suppose personal data is collected from freely accessible public (internet) sources for the purpose of AI training. Here, the question arises as to whether the data subject could reasonably expect their data to be used for this purpose, for example, through web

165. *EuGH*, ECLI:EU:C:2023:537, 41 Neue Juristische Wochenschrift (NJW) 3002, para. 73 (2023).
166. *See* Albers & Veit 2023, para. 74.
167. Schulz 2022, Art. 9, para. 33.
168. *See* Dieker 2024, 135; Weichert 2020, para. 82.
169. *See* Albers & Veit 2023, para. 79; Weichert 2020, para. 82.
170. *See* Dieker 2024, 136.
171. Hessel & Dillschneider 2023, 461, Gola 2022, Art. 5, paras 59, 63.
172. Franke 2023, 568.

scraping.[173] A mixed subjective-objective standard shall be used to determine reasonable expectations.[174] The decisive factor in this respect is whether an objective third party can expect further processing in question, considering the 'common knowledge (of the average society)'.[175] It should be noted here that an increasing number of companies use web scraping or web crawling methods for AI training in their privacy policies or guidelines.[176] This allows these companies to influence user expectations to a certain extent, at least indirectly, in their favour.[177]

Finally, in the situation discussed here, it should be noted that the training data is publicly accessible from the internet. This can have a decisive effect in favour of the AI developers when weighing up interests.[178] If the data subjects have published the data themselves, they are generally considered less worthy of protection. This assessment is based on the legal concept of Article 9(2)(e) of the GDPR, which contains a privilege for processing self-published sensitive data, which can also be transferred to non-sensitive data by way of a first conclusion of law.[179]

5.3 Interim Result

In light of the above explanations, Article 6(1)(f) of the GDPR seems the most reliable and, therefore, preferable legal basis for processing personal data for AI training. The balancing of interest clause may not be used to make a generalized statement about the lawfulness of data processing; instead, it must be decided on a case-by-case basis. Nevertheless, the balancing of interests offers sufficient leeway for AI developers to influence the relevant balancing criteria in their favour positively and essentially minimize the attack surface(s) to determine unlawfulness. To this end, it is recommended that the GDPR processing principles, in particular, be observed, and technical and organizational measures be implemented when designing the AI training that enables data protection-friendly processing and safeguards the rights of data subjects.

6 REFERENCE TO AND EFFECTS OF THE AI ACT

Based on previous outcomes, the latest developments in implementing the AI Act by the European legislator must now be considered. Conceptually, the regulation primarily focuses on the output of AI systems and defines different regulatory requirements for various risk categories.[180] With the risk-based AI Act, the European legislator logically recognizes and addresses the potential risks posed by AI technologies on the

173. *Ibid.*, 567; for technical details on scraping, *see* Solove & Hartzog 2024, 7 et seq.
174. *See* Schulz 2022, Art. 6, para. 67; Skistims 2020, 369, para. 50.
175. *See* DSK 2022, 4; Gola 2022, Art. 6, para. 67; Franke 2023, 567.
176. *See* Meta (undated); Southern 2023.
177. Skistims 2020, 369 et seq., para. 51, on the question of whether and to what extent over-mandatory provision of information by companies can expand expectations and what limits must be observed.
178. Schulz 2022, Art. 6, para. 63.
179. Dieker 2024, 135; Dallmann & Busse 2019, 395 et seq.; Schwarz 2022, 355.
180. *See* Hacker & Berz 2023, 226.

output side.[181] In contrast, the AI Act only makes (very) few statements about the input level and the training of AI systems. It only stipulates certain quality and transparency requirements for the AI training data.[182] From this, it can be reliably concluded that the legislator did not see an urgent need to answer the data protection issues discussed above in the course of enacting the AI Act. For the governance and enforcement of the AI Act, the European Artificial Intelligence Office (AI Office) (Article 64 of the AI Act) and the European Artificial Intelligence Board (Article 65 of the AI Act) will be established, whereby Member States may consider establishing specialized AI authorities – including existing (data protection) supervisory authorities. The European Data Protection Board (EDPB) will also be involved at the coordination level.

Furthermore, as referred to in Recitals 10 and 63, the European Union (EU) legislator expressly clarifies that the AI Act does not affect the GDPR. Namely, it does not, in principle, provide a legal basis 'for the processing of personal data, including, where appropriate, special categories of personal data'. An exception may apply if 'this Regulation ... expressly provides otherwise'. Such an exception is provided for the use of personal data collected for other purposes for the development of specific AI systems in the public interest within an AI laboratory (Article 59 of the AI Act; Recital 140); however, the AI Act does not provide for such an exception for the purpose of AI training; instead, even in the aforementioned real-world laboratory context, it is only a matter of further processing, not a legal basis for the upstream collection and storage of (training) data.[183]

However, according to Article 10(3) of the AI Act, training data used by high-risk systems must be 'relevant, sufficiently representative and, as far as possible, accurate and complete concerning the intended purpose'. Regarding the issues under investigation concerning the tension between the GDPR and AI training, questions may arise in legal practice about whether and to what extent a GDPR violation during the training phase leads to an error within the meaning of the AI Act.[184]

In the future, further EU legislative initiatives are also likely to make selective additions and extensions to the legal bases for data processing; for instance – once again – Article 34(1)(g) of the EHDS Regulation,[185] which states that AI training is expressly to be a purpose for which electronic health data can be processed by way of secondary use.

7 SUMMARY AND OUTLOOK

AI training using publicly available data raises numerous data protection issues given the characteristic factual and technological framework conditions. At first glance, the tension between AI training and the GDPR data processing principles and the need for

181. *See ibid.*; detailed information on the categorization of AI systems according to risk groups in the AI Act, Novelli et al. 2024, 3 et seq.
182. *See* AIA, Rec. 67, Arts 10 and 13.
183. *See also* Dieker 2024, 136 et seq.
184. In this sense *also ibid.*, at 137, with appropriate reference to the previous draft versions regarding the requirements for accuracy.
185. Commission EHDS 2022.

a robust legal basis for personal data processing may appear to prevent AI training from being compatible with the GDPR regulatory regime. However, by taking a differentiated approach, AI training can regularly be harmonized with the GDPR on closer inspection by recourse to various suitable instruments and measures. This is a reassuring and welcome interim finding, as the human-centred development of AI applications is in the interests of society as a whole. However, the collection and processing of personal data during AI training cannot be ruled out given the current state-of-the-art.

The technology-neutral design of the GDPR is of central importance.[186] Concerning AI technologies, which were not yet foreseeable in their current form at the time the GDPR was adopted and were therefore not included in the legal concept, this results in the requirement of an innovation-promoting interpretation based on and in line with the risk-based approach of the GDPR.[187] This risk-based approach is a guiding principle of the GDPR[188] and requires a risk assessment in each individual case, which therefore contradicts the assumption of an absolute 'zero-risk approach'.[189] In this sense, the enforcement and application of data protection principles should focus primarily on areas and scenarios where the most significant dangers and risks to the rights of data subjects are imminent.[190] The data protection risks for AI systems will mainly be located on the output side rather than the input side concerning AI training data. In addition, at the application level, there are various opportunities for protective measures against disseminating personal data and inappropriate, offensive, or harmful content. These include establishing usage guidelines, restricting the application's interaction with personal data, using watermarks, and fine-tuning models and classifiers.

For accessibility and thus the availability of AI training data, the recently adopted Data Act, which also contains comprehensive regulations on data access (both personal and non-personal data) for users and third parties on the Internet of Things, can make an essential contribution to access to and thus the availability of AI training data. However, the practical effectiveness of the Data Act is especially limited in terms of AI developments, as aggregated data is not covered by the scope of the newly created data access claim. The Data Act also refers to the European Data Innovation Board (EDIB) to be established under Article 29 of the Data Governance Act, which is intended to strike a balance between innovation and the protection of the legal positions concerned. Therefore, EU policymakers have recognized that the different objectives can and must be reconciled for the benefit of society.

The fact that the legislator did not take the enactment of the AI Act as an opportunity to address the data protection issues relating to AI training separately and instead predominantly regulated the output level must first be assessed so that the legal admissibility of AI training is assumed. Furthermore, it can be stated that the EU

186. *See* GDPR, Rec. 15.
187. In this sense *also* Baumgartner et al. 2023, 547.
188. For more details on the fundamentally risk-based design of the GDPR, *see* Jungkind & Koch 2022, 656.
189. *See ibid.*, at 662.
190. Piltz 2022, para. 24; GDPR, Rec. 74.

legislator did not intend to impose any significant additional hurdles for the input level. Therefore, it assumes that the GDPR, as a central set of rules, is suitable for adequately covering the data protection implications of AI training. This legislative guiding principle appears convincing and logical based on the results and deductions from the overall consideration of the normative framework.

Finally, it should be noted that, in light of the GDPR, corresponding announcements by supervisory authorities, in particular the EDPB,[191] can significantly contribute to (accelerating) the achievement of legal certainty in the field of AI training, which is of great practical importance for the future of innovation.

BIBLIOGRAPHY

Guidelines of Authorities

Art. 29 WP 2018: Article 29 Working Party, *Guidelines on Transparency under Regulation 2016/679*, WP 260 rev.01 (2018), ec.europa.eu/newsroom/article29/items/622227 (accessed 24 July 2024).

Art. 29 WP 2014: Article 29 Working Party, *Opinion 5/2014 on Anonymization Techniques*, WP 216 (2014), ec.europa.eu/justice/article-29/documentation/opinion-recommendation/files/2014/wp216_en.pdf (accessed 24 July 2024).

Art. 29 WP 2007: Article 29 Working Party, *Opinion 4/2007 on the Term 'Personal Data' 260 rev.01*, WP 136 (2007), www.lda.bayern.de/media/wp136_en.pdf (accessed 24 July 2024).

BfDI 2020: Federal Commissioner for Data Protection and Freedom of Information (BfDI), *Positionspapier zur Anonymisierung unter der DSGVO* (2020), www.bfdi.bund.de/SharedDocs/Downloads/DE/Konsultationsverfahren/1_Anonymisierung/Positionspapier-Anonymisierung.pdf?__blob=publicationFile&v=6 (accessed 24 July 2024).

BfDI 2017: Federal Commissioner for Data Protection and Freedom of Information (BfDI), *Tätigkeitsbericht zum Datenschutz für die Jahre 2015 und 2016* [Activity report on data protection for the years 2015/2016] (2017), www.bfdi.bund.de/SharedDocs/Downloads/DE/Taetigkeitsberichte/26TB_15_16.pdf;jsessionid=7484FA36CA2BB24DB760F6EADE3E5B6F.2_cid329?__blob=publicationFile&v=3 (accessed 24 July 2024).

CEDPO 2023: Confederation of European Data Protection Organisations (CEDPO), *Generative AI: The Data Protection Implications* (2023), cedpo.eu/generative-ai-the-data-protection-implications (accessed 24 July 2024).

Commission 2023: Proposal for a Regulation of the European Parliament and of the Council on European statistics on population and housing, amending Regulation (EC) No. 862/2007 and repealing Regulations (EC) No. 763/2008 and (EU) No. 1260/2013, 2023/0008/COD, COM (2023) 31.

191. EDPB – like the German DSK (DSK 2023) – has set up a working group on ChatGPT: EDPB 2023.

Commission EHDS 2022: Commission, *Proposal for a Regulation of the European Parliament and of the Council on the European Health Data Space* (2022), eur-lex.europa.eu/legal-content/DE/TXT/HTML/?uri=CELEX:52022PC0197 (accessed 24 July 2024).

Datatilsynet 2018: Datatilsynet, *Artificial Intelligence and Privacy: Report* (2018), www.datatilsynet.no/globalassets/global/english/ai-and-privacy.pdf (accessed 24 July 2024).

Datenethikkommission 2019: Datenethikkommission, *Gutachten der Datenethikkommission* (2019), www.bmi.bund.de/SharedDocs/downloads/DE/publikationen/themen/it-digitalpolitik/gutachten-datenethikkommission.pdf?__blob=publicationFile&v=6 (accessed 24 July 2024).

DSK 2023: Datenschutzkonferenz (DSK), *105. Konferenz der unabhängigen Datenschutzaufsichtsbehörden des Bundes und der Länder am 10. und 11. Mai 2023: Protokoll* (2023), www.datenschutzkonferenz-online.de/media/pr/Protokoll_105_DSK_2023.pdf (accessed 24 July 2024).

DSK 2022: Datenschutzkonferenz (DSK), *Orientierungshilfe der Aufsichtsbehörden zur Verarbeitung von personenbezogenen Daten für Zwecke der Direktwerbung unter Geltung der Datenschutz-Grundverordnung* (2022), www.datenschutzkonferenz-online.de/media/oh/OH-Werbung_Februar%202022_final.pdf (accessed 24 July 2024).

DSK 2019a: DSK, *Hambach Declaration on Artificial Intelligence* (2019), www.datenschutz-berlin.de/fileadmin/user_upload/pdf/publikationen/DSK/2019/2019-DSK-Hambach_Declaration_AI-en.pdf (accessed 24 July 2024).

DSK 2019b: DSK, *Positionspapier der DSK zu empfohlenen technischen und organisatorischen Maßnahmen bei der Entwicklung und dem Betrieb von KI-Systemen* (2019), www.datenschutzkonferenz-online.de/media/en/20191106_positionspapier_kuenstliche_intelligenz.pdf (accessed 24 July 2024).

EDPB 2023: EDPB, *EDPB Resolves Dispute on Transfers by Meta and Creates Task Force on Chat GPT*, EDPB News (2023), www.edpb.europa.eu/news/news/2023/edpb-resolves-dispute-transfers-meta-and-creates-task-force-chat-gpt_en (accessed 24 July 2024).

ICO 2023: Information Commissioner's Office (ICO), *Guidance on AI and Data Protection* (2023), ico.org.uk/for-organisations/uk-gdpr-guidance-and-resources/artificial-intelligence/guidance-on-ai-and-data-protection (accessed 24 July 2024).

ICO 2017: Information Commissioner's Office (ICO), *Big Data, Artificial Intelligence, Machine Learning and Data Protection* (Version 2.2, 2017), ico.org.uk/media/for-organisations/documents/2013559/big-data-ai-ml-and-data-protection.pdf (accessed 24 July 2017).

LfDI Ba-Wü 2023: Landesbeauftragter für den Datenschutz und die Informationsfreiheit Baden-Württemberg (LfDI Ba-Wü), *Rechtsgrundlagen im Datenschutz beim Einsatz von KI*, www.baden-wuerttemberg.datenschutz.de/rechtsgrundlagen-datenschutz-ki (accessed 24 July 2024).

Reports and Recommendations

OECD 2023: OECD, *Emerging Privacy Enhancing Technologies*, OECD Digital Economy Papers No. 351 (2023), www.oecd.org/en/publications/2023/03/emerging-privacy-enhancing-technologies_a6bdf3cb.html (accessed 24 July 2024).

OECD 2020: OECD, *Künstliche Intelligenz in der Gesellschaft, Technische Grundlagen, Lebenszyklus eines KI-Systems* (2020), www.oecd-ilibrary.org/sites/64ae49f7-de/index.html?itemId=/content/component/64ae49f7-de (accessed 24 July 2024).

OECD 2019: OECD, *Empfehlung des Rats zu künstlicher Intelligenz* (2019), legalinstruments.oecd.org/en/instruments/OECD-LEGAL-0449 (accessed 24 July 2024).

Academic Writings

Albers & Veit 2023: Marion Albers & Raoul-Darius Veit, *Art. 9*, BeckOK DatenschutzR (Heinrich Amadeus Wolff, Stefan Brink & Antje von Ungern-Sternberg eds, 44th edn, C.H. Beck 2023).

Apel & Kaulartz 2020: Simon Apel & Markus Kaulartz, *Rechtlicher Schutz von Machine Learning-Modellen*, Recht Digital (RDi) 24 (2020).

Bäcker 2024: Matthias Bäcker, *Art. 14*, in *Datenschutz-Grundverordnung, Bundesdatenschutzgesetz: DS-GVO/BDSG* (Jürgen Kühling & Benedikt Buchner eds, 4th ed. C.H. Beck 2024).

Bagdasaryan et al. 2019: Eugene Bagdasaryan, Omid Poursaeed & Vitaly Shmatikov, *Differential Privacy Has Disparate Impact on Model Accuracy*, 32 Advances in Neural Information Processing Systems (NeurIPS 2019).

Bambauer et al. 2020: Jane Bambauer et al., *Fool's Gold: An Illustrated Critique of Differential Privacy*, 16 Vanderbilt Journal of Entertainment and Technology Law (JETLaw) 701 (2020).

Baumgartner et al. 2023: Ulrich Baumgartner, Jonas H. Brunnbauer & Samuel Cross, *Anforderungen der DS-GVO an den Einsatz von Künstlicher Intelligenz*, 107 Multimedia und Recht (MMR) 543 (C.H. Beck 2023).

Beck et al. 2020: Susanne Beck et al., *Digitalisierung, Automatisierung, KI und Recht* (Nomos 2020).

Bergt 2015: Matthias Bergt, *Die Bestimmbarkeit als Grundproblem des Datenschutzrechts: Überblick über den Theorienstreit und Lösungsvorschlag*, Zeitschrift für Datenschutz (ZD) (2015).

Bernzen 2023: Anna K. Bernzen, *Fruit of the poisonous KI? Welche Rechte beim KI-Training zu beachten sind*, 10 Kommunikation & Recht (K&R) 6-11 (2023).

Brink et al. 2020: Stefan Brink et al., *Sicht der Datenschutzaufsichtsbehörden, in Rechtshandbuch Artificial Intelligence und Machine Learning*, Ch. 8.11 (Markus Kaulartz & Tom Braegelmann eds, C.H. Beck 2020).

Brisch & Pieper 2015: Klaus Brisch & Fritz Pieper, *Das Kriterium der 'Bestimmbarkeit' bei Big Data-Analyseverfahren*, 11 Computer und Recht (CR) 724 (2015), doi.org/10.9785/cr-2015-1109.

Brown et al. 2022: Hannah Brown et al., *What Does It Mean for a Language Model to Preserve Privacy?*, FAccT '22: ACM Conference on Fairness, Accountability, and Transparency (2022).

Bygrave & Tosoni 2020, Art. 4(1): Lee A. Bygrave & Luca Tosoni, *Article 4(1). Personal Data, in the EU General Data Protection Regulation (GDPR): A Commentary* (Christopher Kuner et al. eds, Oxford 2020).

Bygrave & Tosoni 2020, Art. 4(2): Lee A. Bygrave & Luca Tosoni, *Article 4(2). Processing, in the EU General Data Protection Regulation (GDPR): A Commentary* (Christopher Kuner et al. eds, Oxford 2020).

Bygrave 2020: Lee A. Bygrave, *Article 4(4). Profiling, in The EU General Data Protection Regulation (GDPR): A Commentary* (Christopher Kuner et al. eds, Oxford 2020).

Conrad 2018: Conrad Sebastian Conrad, *Künstliche Intelligenz und die DSGVO*, 12 Kommunikation & Recht (K&R) 741 (2018).

Dallmann & Busse 2019: Michael Dallmann & Philipp Busse, *Die Datenschutz-Folgenabschätzung: Ausnahme oder Regelfall?*, Zeitschrift für Datenschutz (ZD) 390 (2019).

Determann 2024: Lothar Determann, *Determann's Field Guide to Artificial Intelligence Law* (Edward Elgar Publishing 2024).

Devlin 2023: Kieran Devlin, *Who Has Pole Position in the AI Race Ahead of 2024?*, UC Today (13 December 2023), www.uctoday.com/collaboration/who-has-pole-position-in-the-ai-race-ahead-of-2024 (accessed 24 July 2024).

Dieker 2024: Amon Dieker, *Datenschutzrechtliche Zulässigkeit der Trainingsdatensammlung*, Zeitschrift für Datenschutz (ZD) 132 (2024).

Dressel 2019: Christian Dressel, *Detailtiefe der Darstellung technisch-organisatorischer Maßnahmen nach Art. 32 DSGVO in der betrieblichen Datenschutzdokumentation*, 12 IT-Rechtsberater (ITRB) 279 (2019).

Ernst 2021: Stefan Ernst, *Art. 32, in Datenschutz-Grundverordnung Bundesdatenschutzgesetz* (Boris P. Paal & Daniel A. Pauly eds, C.H. Beck 2021).

Eßer 2022: Martin Eßer, *Pseudonymisierung*, in *Rechtswörterbuch* (Klaus Weber ed., C.H. Beck 2022).

Ferràs-Hernández & Nylund 2023: Xavier Ferràs-Hernández & Petra Nylund, *The Emergence of Dominant Designs in AI*, 65 California Management Review 73-91 (2023), doi.org/10.1177/00081256231164362.

Franke 2023: Lucia Franke, *Datenschutzrechtskonformes Training von KI-Systemen mit öffentlich verfügbaren personenbezogenen Daten*, Recht Digital (RDi) 565 (2023).

Frenzel 2020, Art. 32: Eike Michael Frenzel, *Art. 6,* in *Datenschutz-Grundverordnung Bundesdatenschutzgesetz* (Boris P. Paal & Daniel A. Pauly eds, 3rd ed., C.H. Beck 2020).

Frenzel 2020, Art. 6: Eike Michael Frenzel, *Art. 6,* in *Datenschutz-Grundverordnung Bundesdatenschutzgesetz* (Boris P. Paal & Daniel A. Pauly eds, 3rd ed., C.H. Beck 2020).

Gentry 2009: Craig Gentry, *A Fully Homomorphic Encryption Scheme*, (Stanford University 2009).

Georgieva & Kuner 2020: Ludmila Georgieva & Christopher Kuner, *Article 9. Processing of Special Categories of Personal Data,* in *The EU General Data Protection Regulation (GDPR): A Commentary* (Christopher Kuner et al. eds, Oxford 2020).

Gierschmann 2021: Sibylle Gierschmann, *Gestaltungsmöglichkeiten durch systematisches und risikobasiertes Vorgehen: Was ist schon anonym?*, Zeitschrift für Datenschutz (ZD) 482 (2021).

Gillis 2022: Talia B. Gillis, *The Input Fallacy,* 106 Minnesota Law Review 1175 (2022).

Gola 2022, Art. 4: Peter Gola, *Art. 4,* in *Datenschutz-Grundverordnung, Bundesdatenschutzgesetz: DS-GVO/BDSG* (Peter Gola & Dirk Heckmann eds, C.H. Beck 2022).

Gola 2022, Art. 5: Peter Gola, *Art. 5,* in *Datenschutz-Grundverordnung, Bundesdatenschutzgesetz: DS-GVO/BDSG* (Peter Gola & Dirk Heckmann eds, C.H. Beck 2022).

Gola 2022, Art. 6: Peter Gola, *Art. 6,* in *Datenschutz-Grundverordnung, Bundesdatenschutzgesetz: DS-GVO/BDSG* (Peter Gola & Dirk Heckmann eds, C.H. Beck 2022).

Hacker & Berz 2023: Philipp Hacker & Amelie Berz, *Der AI Act der Europäischen Union: Überblick, Kritik und Ausblick*, Zeitschrift für Rechtspolitik (ZRP) 226 (2023).

Heberlein 2018: Horst Heberlein, *Art. 5,* in *DS-GVO Kommentar* (Eugen Ehmann & Martin Selmayr eds, 2nd ed., C.H. Beck 2018).

Hennemann 2020: Moritz Hennemann, *Art. 32,* in *Datenschutz-Grundverordnung Bundesdatenschutzgesetz* (Boris P. Paal & Daniel A. Pauly eds, 3rd ed., C.H. Beck 2020).

Hense 2023: Peter Hense, *Projektspezifischer Datenschutz,* in *Computerrechts-Handbuch,* s. 33.2 (Jürgen Taeger & Jan Pohle eds, C.H. Beck 2023).

Herbst 2020: Tobias Herbst, *Art. 5,* in *Datenschutz-Grundverordnung, Bundesdatenschutzgesetz: DS-GVO/BDSG* (Jürgen Kühling & Benedikt Buchner eds, C.H. Beck 2020).

Hermann 2021: Maximilian Hermann, *Anonymisation/Pseudonymisation,* in *IT-Recht,* Part 10.5, B.II.5 (Andreas Leupold, Andreas Wiebe & Silke Glossner eds, C.H. Beck 2021).

Hessel & Dillschneider 2023: Stefan Hessel & Jeanne Dillschneider, *Datenschutzrechtliche Herausforderungen beim Einsatz von Künstlicher Intelligenz,* Recht Digital (RDi) 458 (2023).

Hijmans 2020: Hielke Hijmans, *Article 1. Subject-Matter and Objectives,* in *The EU General Data Protection Regulation (GDPR): A Commentary* (Christopher Kuner et al. eds, Oxford 2020).

Hoffmann-Riem 2018: Wolfgang Hoffmann-Riem, *Big Data: Regulative Herausforderungen* (Nomos 2018).

Hofmann & Johannes 2017: Johanna M. Hofmann & Paul C. Johannes, *Anleitung zur autonomen Auslegung des Personenbezugs*, Zeitschrift für Datenschutz (ZD) 221 (2024).

Holzinger et al. 2022: Andreas Holzinger et al., *Explainable AI Methods: A Brief Overview,* in *exAI: Beyond Explainable AI* (Holzinger et al. eds, International Workshop, Held in Conjunction with ICML 2020, 18 July 2020).

Hornung & Wagner 2020: Gerrit Hornung & Bernd Wagner, *Anonymisierung als datenschutzrelevante Verarbeitung?*, Zeitschrift für Datenschutz (ZD) 223 (2020).

Hu et al. 2015: Xueyang Hu et al., *Differential Privacy in Telco Big Data Platform*, 8 Proceedings of the VLDB Endowment 1692 (2015).

Hüger 2023: Jakob Hüger, *Künstliche Intelligenz und Diskriminierung* (Nomos 2023).

Ji et al. 2014: Zhanglong Ji, Zachary C. Lipton & Charles Elkan, *Differential Privacy and Machine Learning: A Survey and Review*, arXiv (2014).

Jungkind & Koch 2022: Vera Jungkind & Susanne Koch, *The Risk-Based Approach in the GDPR*, Zeitschrift für Datenschutz (ZD) 650 (2022).

Kaulartz 2020: Markus Kaulartz, *Personenbezug von KI-Modellen,* in *Rechtshandbuch Artificial Intelligence und Machine Learning,* Ch. 8.9 (Markus Kaulartz & Tom Braegelmann eds, C.H. Beck 2020).

Khder 2021: Moaiad Khder, *Web Scraping or Web Crawling: State of Art, Techniques, Approaches and Application,* 13 International Journal of Advances in Soft Computing and Its Applications 145-168 (2021), doi.org/10.15849/ijasca.211128.11.

Klar & Kühling 2018: Manuel Klar & Jürgen Kühling, *Art. 4,* in *Datenschutz-Grundverordnung, Bundesdatenschutzgesetz: DS-GVO/BDSG* (Jürgen Kühling & Benedikt Buchner eds, C.H. Beck 2020).

Kotschy 2020: Waltraut Kotschy, *Article 6. Lawfulness of Processing,* in *The EU General Data Protection Regulation (GDPR): A Commentary* (Christopher Kuner et al. eds, Oxford 2020).

Kramer 2020: Philipp Kramer, *Art. 5,* in *DSGVO/BDSG* (Herbert Auernhammer ed., 7th ed., 2020).

Kranenborg 2020, Art. 2: Herke Kranenborg, *Article 2. Material Scope,* in *The EU General Data Protection Regulation (GDPR): A Commentary* (Christopher Kuner et al. eds, Oxford 2020).

Kranenborg 2020, Art. 17: Herke Kranenborg, *Article 17. Right to Erasure ('Right to Be Forgotten'),* in *The EU General Data Protection Regulation (GDPR): A Commentary* (Christopher Kuner et al. eds, Oxford 2020).

Krüger & Maucher 2011: Stefan Krüger & Svenja-Ariane Maucher, *Ist die IP-Adresse wirklich ein personenbezogenes Datum?: Ein falscher Trend mit großen Auswirkungen auf die Praxis,* Multimedia und Recht (MMR) 433 (C.H. Beck 2023).

Kühling & Klar 2013: Jürgen Kühling & Manuel Klar, *Unsicherheitsfaktor Datenschutzrecht: Das Beispiel des Personenbezugs und der Anonymität,* Neue Juristische Wochenschrift (NJW) 3611 (2013).

Laney 2001: Doug Laney, *3D Data Management: Controlling Data Volume, Velocity, and Variety,* Gartner, File No. 949 (2001).

Lauscher & Legner 2022: Anne Lauscher & Sarah Legner, *Künstliche Intelligenz und Diskriminierung,* Zeitschrift für Digitalisierung und Recht (ZfDR) 367 (2022).

Lee et al. 2023: Katherine Lee et al., *AI and Law: The Next Generation,* SSRN (2023), ssrn.com/abstract=4580739 (accessed 24 July 2024), doi.org/10.2139/ssrn.4580739.

Lukas 2023: Arnold J.F. Lukas, *Privacy Enhancing Technologies im Zusammenspiel mit der DS-GVO,* Zeitschrift für Datenschutz (ZD) 321 (2023).

Mantz & Marosi 2019: Reto Mantz & Johannes Marosi, *Vorgaben der Datenschutz-Grundverordnung*, in *Handbuch Europäisches und deutsches Datenschutzrecht* (Louisa Specht & Reto Mantz eds, C.H. Beck 2019).

Marmy-Brändli & Oehri 2023: Sanra Marmy-Brändli & Isabelle Oehri, *Sic! Zeitschrift für Immaterialgüter-, Informations- und Wettbewerbsrecht*, Heft 12 (2023).

Marsland 2014: Stephen Marsland, *Machine Learning: An Algorithmic Perspective* (Chapman & Hall 2014).

Martini 2021: Mario Martini, *Art. 32*, in *Datenschutz-Grundverordnung Bundesdatenschutzgesetz* (Boris P. Paal & Daniel A. Pauly eds, C.H. Beck 2021).

Maslej et al. 2023: Nestor Maslej et al., *The AI Index 2023 Annual Report*, AI Index Steering Committee, IHCAI (Stanford University, 2023).

Meyer 2002: Sebastian Meyer, *Cookies & Co.: Datenschutz und Wettbewerbsrecht*, Wettbewerb in Recht und Praxis (WRP) 1028 (2002).

Müller-Quade et al. 2023: Jörn Müller-Quade et al., *Datenschatz für KI nutzen, Datenschutz mit KI wahren*, Plattform Lernende Systeme Whitepaper (2023).

Novelli et al. 2024: Claudio Novelli et al., *Generative AI in EU Law: Liability, Privacy, Intellectual Property, and Cybersecurity*, SSRN (2024), ssrn.com/abstract=4694565 (accessed 24 July 2024), doi.org/10.2139/ssrn.4694565.

Ohrtmann & Schwierig 2014: Jan-Peter Ohrtmann & Sebastian Schwiering, *Big Data und Datenschutz: Rechtliche Herausforderungen und Lösungsansätze*, Neue Juristische Wochenschrift (NJW) 2984 (2014).

Paal 2014: Boris P. Paal, *BGH, 28.1.2014*, 69 Juristen Zeitung (JZ) 1002 (2014).

Paal 2020: Boris P. Paal, *Spannungsverhältnis von KI und Datenschutzrecht*, in *Rechtshandbuch Artificial Intelligence und Machine Learning* (Markus Kaulartz & Tom Braegelmann eds, C.H. Beck 2020).

Pahlen-Brandt 2008: Ingrid Pahlen-Brand, *Datenschutz braucht scharfe Instrumente Beitrag zur Diskussion um 'personenbezogene Daten'*, 32 Datenschutz und Datensicherheit (DuD) 34-40 (2008), doi.org/10.1007/s11623-008-0009-8.

Pesch & Böhme 2023a: Paulina Jo Pesch & Rainer Böhme, *Verarbeitung personenbezogener Daten und Datenrichtigkeit bei großen Sprachmodellen*, 26 Multimedia und Recht (MMR) 917 (C.H. Beck 2023).

Pesch & Böhme 2023b: Paulina Jo Pesch & Rainer Böhme, *Artpocalypse Now? Generative KI und die Vervielfältigung von Trainingsbildern [Generative AI and the reproduction of training images]*, GRUR 997 (2023).

Piltz 2022: Carlo Piltz, *Art. 24*, in *Datenschutz-Grundverordnung, Bundesdatenschutzgesetz: DS-GVO/BDSG* (Peter Gola & Dirk Heckmann eds, C.H. Beck 2022).

Polcak 2020: Radim Polcak, *Article 12. Transparent Information, Communication and Modalities for the Exercise of the Rights of the Data Subject*, in *The EU General Data Protection Regulation (GDPR): A Commentary* (Christopher Kuner et al. eds, Oxford 2020).

Pötters 2022: Stephan Pötters, *Art. 5*, in *Datenschutz-Grundverordnung, Bundesdatenschutzgesetz: DS-GVO/BDSG* (Peter Gola & Dirk Heckmann eds, C.H. Beck 2022).

Reimer 2022: Philipp Reimer, *Art. 5*, in *DS-GVO/BDSG* (Gernot Sydow & Nikolaus Marsch eds, C.H. Beck 2022).

Rogers et al. 2020: Ryan Rogers et al., *LinkedIn's Audience Engagements API: A Privacy Preserving Data Analytics System at Scale*, 11 Journal of Privacy and Confidentiality 1 (2020), doi.org/10.29012/jpc.782.

Roßnagel & Geminn 2021: Alexander Roßnagel & Christian L. Geminn, *Vertrauen in Anonymisierung*, Zeitschrift für Datenschutz (ZD) 487 (2021).

Roßnagel & Scholz 2000: Alexander Roßnagel & Philip Scholz, *Datenschutz durch Anonymität und Pseudonymität, Rechtsfolgen der Verwendung anonymer und pseudonymer Daten*, Multimedia und Recht (MMR) 721 (2000).

Roßnagel 2018: Alexander Roßnagel, *Pseudonymisierung personenbezogener Daten*, Zeitschrift für Datenschutz (ZD) 243 (2018).

Roßnagel 2019: Alexander Roßnagel, *in Datenschutzrecht* (Spiros Simitis, Gerrit Hornung & Indra Spiecker genannt Döhmann eds, Nomos 2019).

Roßnagel 2021: Alexander Roßnagel, *Datenlöschung und Anonymisierung*, Zeitschrift für Datenschutz (ZD) 188 (2021).

Russell & Norvig 2021: Stuart J. Russell & Peter Norvig, *Artificial Intelligence: A Modern Approach* (Pearson 2021).

Salem et al. 2018: Milad Salem et al., *Utilizing Transfer Learning and Homomorphic Encryption in a Privacy Preserving and Secure Biometric Recognition System*, Computer Science (2018).

Schaff & Dujak 2023: Nadia Schaff & Andrea Dujak, *Privacy Enhancing Technologies: Ein Ansatz zur Minimierung datenschutzrechtlicher Risiken beim Einsatz Künstlicher Intelligenz*, Deutsche Stiftung für Recht und Informatik Tagungsband (DSRITB) 445 (2023).

Schantz 2016: Peter Schantz, *Die Datenschutz-Grundverordnung: Beginn einer neuen Zeitrechnung im Datenschutzrecht*, Neue Juristische Wochenschrift (NJW) 1841-1847 (2016).

Schefzig 2014: Jens Schefzig, *Big Data = Personal Data? Der Personenbezug von Daten bei Big Data-Analysen*, 12 Kommunikation & Recht (K&R) 772 (2014).

Schild 2018: Hans-Hermann Schild, *Art. 4 GDPR*, in *BeckOK Datenschutzrecht* (Stefan Brink & Heinrich Amadeus Wolff eds, C.H. Beck 2018).

Schleipfer 2020: Stefan Schleipfer, *Pseudonymität in verschiedenen Ausprägungen*, Zeitschrift für Datenschutz (ZD) 284 (2020).

Schulz 2022, Art. 6: Sebastian Schulz, *Art. 6*, in *Datenschutz-Grundverordnung, Bundesdatenschutzgesetz: DS-GVO/BDSG* (Peter Gola & Dirk Heckmann eds, C.H. Beck 2022).

Schulz 2022, Art. 9: Sebastian Schulz, *Art. 9*, in *Datenschutz-Grundverordnung, Bundesdatenschutzgesetz: DS-GVO/BDSG* (Peter Gola & Dirk Heckmann eds, C.H. Beck 2022).

Schur 2021: Nico Schur, *Know-how und Geheimnisschutz von Daten*, in *IT-Recht*, Part 6.8 (Andreas Leupold, Andreas Wiebe & Silke Glossner eds, C.H. Beck 2021).

Schürmann 2022: Kathrin Schürmann, *Datenschutz-Folgenabschätzung beim Einsatz Künstlicher Intelligenz*, Zeitschrift für Datenschutz (ZD) 316 (2022).

Schwarz 2022: Lea-Christina Schwarz, *Datenschutzrechtliche Zulässigkeit des Pre-Employment Screening*, Zeitschrift für Datenschutz (ZD) 353 (2022).

Skistims 2020: Hendrik Skistims, *Rechtsgrundlagen für datenverarbeitende KI, in Rechtshandbuch Artificial Intelligence und Machine Learning,* Ch. 8.2 (Markus Kaulartz & Tom Braegelmann eds, C.H. Beck 2020).

Solove & Hartzog 2024: Daniel J. Solove & Woodrow Hartzog, *The Great Scrape: The Clash Between Scraping and Privacy* (2024).

Solove 2024: Daniel J. Solove, *Artificial Intelligence and Privacy*, 77 Florida Law Review (forthcoming January 2025).

Spiecker et al. 2023: Indra Spiecker gen. Döhmann et al., *General Data Protection Regulation Article-by-Article Commentary* (2023).

Steinrötter 2023: Björn Steinrötter, *Art. 13 in BeckOK IT-Recht* (Georg Borges & Marc Hilber eds, 13th ed., C.H. Beck 2023).

Terwangne 2020: Cecile de Terwangne, *Article 5. Principles Relating to Processing of Personal Data,* in *The EU General Data Protection Regulation (GDPR): A Commentary* (Christopher Kuner et al. eds, Oxford 2020).

Tosoni 2020: Luca Tosoni, *Article 4(5). Pseudonymisation*, in *The EU General Data Protection Regulation (GDPR): A Commentary* (Christopher Kuner et al. eds, Oxford 2020).

Trigo Kramcsák 2023: Pablo Trigo Kramcsák, *Can Legitimate Interest Be an Appropriate Lawful Basis for Processing Artificial Intelligence Training Datasets?*, 48 Computer Law & Security Review 105765 (2023), doi.org/10.1016/j.clsr.2022.105765.

Tschider 2021: Charlotte Tschider, *Beyond the Black Box*, 98 Denver Law Review 683 (2021).

Valkanova 2020: Monika Valkanova, *Trainieren von KI-Modellen,* in *Rechtshandbuch Artificial Intelligence und Machine Learning,* Ch. 8.1 (Markus Kaulartz & Tom Braegelmann eds, C.H. Beck 2020).

Vogel 2022: Paul Vogel, *Künstliche Intelligenz und Datenschutz* (Nomos 2022).

Wagner 2020: Paul Wagner, *Privacy Enhancing Technologies and Synthetic Data,* SSRN (2020), papers.ssrn.com/sol3/papers.cfm?abstract_id = 3762686 (accessed 24 July 2024), doi.org/10.2139/ssrn.3762686.

Weichert 2020: Thilo Weichert, *Art. 9,* in *Datenschutz-Grundverordnung, Bundesdatenschutzgesetz: DS-GVO/BDSG* (Jürgen Kühling & Benedikt Buchner eds, C.H. Beck 2020).

Werry 2023: Susanne Werry, *Generative KI-Modelle im Visier der Datenschutzbehörden,* Multimedia und Recht (MMR) 911 (C.H. Beck 2023).

Zanfir-Fortuna 2020, Art. 13: Gabriela Zanfir-Fortuna, *Article 13. Information to be Provided Where Personal Data are Collected from the Data Subject,* in *The EU General Data Protection Regulation (GDPR): A Commentary* (Christopher Kuner et al. eds, Oxford 2020).

Zanfir-Fortuna 2020 Art. 14: Gabriela Zanfir-Fortuna, *Article 14. Information to be Provided Where Personal Data Have Not Been Obtained from the Data Subject,* in *The EU General Data Protection Regulation (GDPR): A Commentary* (Christopher Kuner et al. eds, Oxford 2020).

News

Pollina & Mukherjee 2023: Elvira Pollina & Supantha Mukherjee, *Italy Curbs ChatGPT, Starts Probe over Privacy Concerns*, Reuters (31 March 2023), www.reuters.com/technology/italy-data-protection-agency-opens-chatgpt-probe-privacy-concerns-2023-03-31 (accessed 24 July 2024).

Reuters 2024: Reuters, *OpenAI's ChatGPT Breaches Privacy Rules, Says Italian Watchdog*, Reuters (30 January 2024), www.reuters.com/technology/cybersecurity/italy-regulator-notifies-openai-privacy-breaches-chatgpt-2024-01-29 (accessed 24 July 2024).

Southern 2023: Matt G. Southern, *Google Updates Privacy Policy to Collect Public Data for AI Training*, Search Engine Journal (3 July 2023), www.searchenginejournal.com/google-updates-privacy-policy-to-collect-public-data-for-ai-training/490715 (accessed 24 July 2024).

Other

Apple 2022: Apple, *Apple Privacy-Preserving Machine Learning Workshop 2022*, Machine Learning Research (2022), machinelearning.apple.com/updates/ppml-workshop-2022 (accessed 24 July 2024).

Brill 2021: Julie Brill, *Protecting Our Data Infrastructure Through Some New Approaches to Privacy*, Microsoft On The Issues (2021), blogs.microsoft.com/on-the-issues/2021/12/06/protecting-data-infrastructure-privacy (accessed 24 July 2024).

Meta (undated): Meta, *How Meta Uses Information for Generative AI Models and Features*, Meta Privacy Centre, www.facebook.com/privacy/genai (accessed 24 July 2024).

Part II Proposal for an EU AI Liability Directive: Article-by-Article Commentary

ARTICLE 1 Subject Matter and Scope

Joe Cannataci

Article 1. Subject matter and scope

1. This Directive lays down common rules on:
   (a) the disclosure of evidence on high-risk artificial intelligence (AI) systems to enable a claimant to substantiate a non-contractual fault-based civil law claim for damages;
   (b) the burden of proof in the case of non-contractual fault-based civil law claims brought before national courts for damages caused by an AI system.
2. This Directive applies to non-contractual fault-based civil law claims for damages, in cases where the damage caused by an AI system occurs after [the end of the transposition period].
   This Directive does not apply to criminal liability.
3. This Directive shall not affect:
   (a) rules of Union law regulating conditions of liability in the field of transport;
   (b) any rights which an injured person may have under national rules implementing Directive 85/374/EEC;
   (c) the exemptions from liability and the due diligence obligations as laid down in [the Digital Services Act] and
   (d) national rules determining which party has the burden of proof, which degree of certainty is required as regards the standard of proof, or how fault is defined, other than in respect of what is provided for in Articles 3 and 4.
4. Member States may adopt or maintain national rules that are more favourable for claimants to substantiate a non-contractual civil law claim for damages caused by an AI system, provided such rules are compatible with Union law.

Recitals

(1) Artificial Intelligence ('AI') is a set of enabling technologies which can contribute to a wide array of benefits across the entire spectrum of the economy and society. It has a large potential for technological progress and allows new business models in many sectors of the digital economy.

RELATED ARTICLES

Article 2 (Definitions); Article 3 (Disclosure of evidence and rebuttable presumption of non-compliance); Article 4 (Rebuttable presumption of a causal link in the case of fault); Article 5 (Evaluation and targeted review); and Article 6 (Amendment to Directive (EU) 2020/1828).

RELATED LAWS

AI Act; New Product Liability Directive; Product Liability Directive.

COMMENTARY

1 Purpose

Article 1 deals with the scope of the AI Liability Directive (AILD). A scope section is a key part of any legal instrument, whether a regulation, a directive, a recommendation or a convention or other multilateral or bilateral treaty since it sets the boundaries of the situations to which the legal provisions may apply. Bringing something into the scope of a law or deliberately leaving something outside it is normally one of the most carefully undertaken and sometimes the longest discussions in the legislative process to which the legislator returns again and again to re-evaluate the inclusion or exclusion of situations and actors in the scope of the law. The purpose of the scope section is to provide a civil law remedy to citizens adversely affected by artificial intelligence (AI) through the application of fault-based liability rules to high-risk AI systems (as defined separately within the AI Act).

2 Legal Background

2.1 International

If and when finalized and adopted, the AILD would not be the first international legal instrument dealing with AI. Within the European Union (EU) itself, it was preceded by the AI Act.

Outside the EU, and open to signature by all 193 United Nations (UN) Member States, in May 2024 the Council of Europe launched the first-ever international legally binding treaty aimed at ensuring the respect of human rights, the rule of law and democracy legal standards in the use of AI systems. While similar in legal effect to an EU directive, i.e., it would require transposition of its provisions by the national parliament into national law, the AI Convention is far more ambitious in scope than the AILD, which pursues much narrower objectives insofar as the latter seeks only to provide civil law remedies to citizens by providing fault-based liability rules to high-risk AI systems. The AI Convention is far more wide-ranging in scope and attempts to cover all or most activities within the lifecycle of AI systems that have the potential to interfere with human rights, democracy and the rule of law.

While the AI Act is already in effect at the time of writing, the AI Convention will come into force (Article 30) on the first day of the month following the expiration of a period of three months after the date on which five signatories, including at least three Member States of the Council of Europe, have expressed their consent to be bound by this Convention (through ratification, acceptance, or approval). Given that the AI Act has provisions that are largely compatible with the AI Convention, it is possible that the latter will quickly garner enough signatures to come into force, possibly even before the AILD.[1] All of the three legal instruments mentioned so far are binding, upon the signatories in the case of the AI Convention and on EU Member States in the case of the AI Act and the AILD.

The Organisation for Economic Co-operation and Development (OECD) AI principles are, by contrast, a typical piece of non-binding 'soft law' typical of the OECD. They were initially adopted in 2019 and updated in May 2024. The principles are intended to guide AI actors in their efforts to develop trustworthy AI and provide policymakers with recommendations for effective AI policies. Since the OECD principles are non-binding they can at best have some impact by way of moral authority but similar OECD legal instruments have, in the past, usually had far less visible impact than Council of Europe conventions or EU regulations and directives.

2.2 European Union

Taken together with the AI Act, the AILD largely supersedes the High-Level Expert Group on Artificial Intelligence (HLEG) Guidelines published by the Commission in 2019, now adding the force of law to less detailed guidelines which were not binding upon EU Member States.

2.3 National

Apart from the AI Act, as of 31 July 2024, only nine instances can be traced of nation-states attempting to regulate AI. Of these, we can include the United States (US) where we can note a significant initiative at the federal level in the form of President Biden's 2022 Blueprint for an AI Bill of Rights.[2] On 30 October 2023, President Biden further articulated US policy in this area through his Executive Order 14110 on the Safe, Secure, and Trustworthy Development and Use of Artificial Intelligence.[3] This notable policy guidance from the US Executive has not yet been translated into overarching law

1. On 5 Sep. 2024, the date of opening for signatures, already ten countries (or thirty-six, if we count the European Union's signature as twenty-seven countries), signed the Convention in Vilnius, including also the United States and Israel. *See* Council of Europe, *Council of Europe Opens First Ever Global Treaty on AI for Signature* (5 Sep. 2024), www.coe.int/en/web/portal/-/council-of-europe-opens-first-ever-global-treaty-on-ai-for-signature (accessed 24 Sep. 2024).
2. The White House 2022.
3. The White House 2023.

at the federal level but the situation regulating AI in the US is actually quite complex with a patchwork of federal and state regulation covering certain sectors (as opposed to an omnibus approach) which has grown organically over the last several years. These can cover areas as diverse as US export control laws and regulations, outbound as well as inbound investment and AI.[4] When examining developments in those approximately forty US states out of fifty enacting regulation at the state level, it is interesting to note that, of all human rights, in the US legislation at the state level, privacy would seem to be the one garnering the most attention, with most state-level regulation indicating legislative concern about the use of AI in customer profiling.[5]

Japan had, in 2019, published its Social Principles for Human-Centric AI[6] creating a Council for Social Principles of Human-Centric AI. To date, it has been true to state that:[7]

> Japan takes a risk-based and soft-law approach to regulation on AI while actively advancing legislative reform from the perspective of regulation for AI.

Five years is a long time in technology law and, by February 2024, one could follow reports in the Japanese media that 'The Liberal Democratic Party of Japan is set to present new legislation to regulate generative AI technologies in 2024.'[8] This would seem to reflect a rapid turnaround on the official position of Japan's ruling party which, as recently as 2021, was stating quite the opposite. In the AI Governance in Japan, report published by the Ministry of Economy, Trade, and Industry (METI) in July 2021 – which comprehensively describes Japan's AI regulatory policy (AI Governance Report) – one reads that the official position less than three years ago was that 'legally-binding horizontal requirements for AI systems are deemed unnecessary at the moment'.[9]

Australia, Brazil, Canada, China, India, Switzerland, and the United Kingdom are the only other countries in the world apart from those mentioned above, which, at the time of writing, have attempted significant forms of AI regulation.

The Dutch government was an early adopter of AI-related governance tools[10] and, as of 1 January 2023, is requiring Dutch public institutions to carry out a fundamental rights and algorithm assessment (FRAIA):[11]

> This fundamental rights and algorithm impact assessment ('FRAIA') is a discussion and decision-making tool for government organisations. The tool facilitates an interdisciplinary dialogue by those responsible for the development and/or use

4. For a useful brief overview of the regulation of AI in the USA *see* Rotenberg & Randolph, in this volume, s. 4; and Plotinski & Cinelli 2024.
5. *See* Freedman 2024.
6. Japan 2019.
7. Habuka 2023.
8. Digital Watch 2024.
9. Habuka 2023.
10. With some commentators attributing this early adopter status to 'a large-scale scandal because of a flawed algorithm that led the tax authorities to falsely accuse thousands of fraud related to a childcare benefit scheme'. *See, for example,* Bertuzzi 2022.
11. Netherlands 2021, 2.

> of an algorithmic system. The commissioning client is primarily responsible for the (delegated) implementation of the FRAIA.

Thus, since January 2023, any law enforcement or intelligence agency in the Netherlands which may be interested in AI-based tools is by definition a public institution. It has therefore been bound to use FRAIA:[12]

> in any instance where a government organisation considers developing, delegating the development of, buying, adjusting and/or using an algorithm (hereinafter for the sake of brevity: the use of or using an algorithm). Even when an algorithm is already being used, the FRAIA may serve as a tool for reflection.

The Dutch example, as consistent with the AI Act, thus puts obligations on the part of the commissioning authority and thereby indirectly on the developers of AI systems, with various other new requirements in place.[13] While the application of FRAIA is currently restricted to public bodies,[14] it is not inconceivable that this and similar fundamental rights assessment tools will become part of emerging de facto standards that systems developers and others in the academic and private sectors will be expected to observe. To a considerable extent, the Dutch initiative of 2023 is both reinforced and superseded by Article 27 of the AI Act.

In summary, globally we only have ten separate instances overall of some form of legislation at the national level. If the metric to be applied were to be nation-state membership of the UN, and one were thus to count the EU's Member States individually, one would arrive at a grand total of thirty-six countries or 18.6% which have as yet taken significant regulatory action regarding AI. Put differently, nearly 82% of the UN's Member States have yet to take decisions as to how best to use law or some other form of regulatory mechanism to control AI's impact on society.

2.4 Case Law[15]

On 5 February 2020, the District Court of The Hague (Rechtbank Den Haag) held that the System Risk Indication (SyRI) algorithm system, a legal instrument that the Dutch government uses to detect fraud in areas such as benefits, allowances, and taxes, violates Article 8 of the European Convention on Human Rights (ECHR) (right to respect for private and family life).

12. *Ibid.*
13. 'A new supervisory body, starting on 1 January 2023, will enforce a set of new rules that essentially anticipate the EU's upcoming rules regarding transparency obligations, compliance marking and the right to complain. Similarly, next month, the Dutch government will introduce a mandatory algorithm register for AI used by public bodies, from the central administration to the local authorities. The idea is that citizens cannot enjoy the right to redress unless they know that an AI is being used'. Bertuzzi 2022.
14. 'In the original version of the AI Act, only providers of high-risk AI systems were obliged to register on an EU-wide database. However, following pressure from countries like the Netherlands, the obligation was also extended to public authorities who use an AI system'. *Ibid.*
15. This s. 2.4 has been reproduced from Gesley 2020 and edited to fit the article format.

2.4.1 *Facts of the Case*

The case was brought by several civil rights organizations, including the Netherlands Committee of Jurists for Human Rights (*Nederlands Juristen Comité voor de Mensenrechten*, NJCM), and two natural persons against the Dutch government. The Federation of Trade Unions in the Netherlands (*Federatie Nederlandse Vakbeweging*, FNV) intervened on behalf of the plaintiffs. The NJCM works to protect and strengthen fundamental human rights and freedoms. The FNV is a trade union that acts in the interests of its members and 'is guided in part by the fundamental values of equality of all people, of freedom, justice and solidarity'.[16] The UN special rapporteur on extreme poverty and human rights, Philip Alston, submitted an amicus brief.

The SyRI system is an algorithm used by the government:

> to prevent and combat fraud in the fields of social security and income-related schemes, tax and social insurance contributions, and labor laws.

It links and analyses data from various government or public agencies and generates a risk report if a person is suspected of fraud. In 2003, these agencies, which include, among others, municipalities, the Employee Insurance Agency (UWV), the Social Insurance Bank (SVB), the national tax authorities, the Immigration and Naturalization Service (IND), and the Inspectorate SZW, concluded a Cooperation Agreement and formed a National Steering Committee on Intervention Teams (LSI). The Cooperation Agreement was updated in 2017. The LSI is chaired by a representative of the Ministry of Social Affairs and Employment. The SyRI is deployed by the minister of social affairs and employment (the minister) upon request of these agencies.[17]

In 2004, a provision was inserted into the Work and Social Assistance Act (*Wet werk en bijstand*, WWB) that allowed the linking of data of the agencies. One hundred sixty projects were undertaken under the supervision of the LSI to prevent and detect fraud between 2008 and 2014. The SyRI or its predecessors were used for twenty-two of them. Nineteen of the twenty-two projects used a 'neighborhood-oriented approach', meaning they targeted specific neighbourhoods in which the linked data indicated an increased risk of welfare fraud.

The plaintiffs alleged that the use of the SyRI system violates the right to respect for privacy codified in Article 8 of the ECHR, Article 17 of the International Covenant on Civil and Political Rights (ICCPR), and Articles 7 and 8 of the Charter, as well as in data protection law.

2.4.2 *Applicable Law*

The SyRI was given a legal basis in 2014 with an amendment of the SUWI Act (*Wet structuur uitvoeringsorganisatie werk en inkomen*, Wet SUWI). Further details are

16. District Court 2020, paras 2.2, 2.4 & 2.5.
17. *Ibid.*, paras 3.1-3.7.

provided in the SUWI Decree (Besluit SUWI).[18] The terms 'data', 'processor', and 'controller' are defined in accordance with the General Data Protection Regulation (GDPR). Article 64, paragraph 1 of the SUWI Act provides for the cooperation of a number of designated government bodies to:

> prevent and combat the unlawful use of government funds and government provisions in the field of social security and income-related schemes, prevent and combat tax and premium fraud, and non-compliance with labor laws.

Article 65 authorizes the minister to process data in the SyRI for risk analysis at the request of the designated government bodies for the purposes referred to in Article 64(1). The start of a SyRI project must be published in the government gazette.

The data processing consists of two phases: the processing (phase 1) and the analysis (phase 2). In the first phase, the processor brings the files together and pseudonymizes them. After this, the source file is automatically checked against the risk model with all indicators, which generates potential hits, meaning an indication of an increased risk of fraud. All data associated with these increased risks is passed on to the minister for phase 2, in which it is further analysed, and assessed. A definitive risk selection follows. The minister makes the risk reports on the basis of the definitive risk selection. The SyRI legislation contains retention periods (two years) and restrictions with regard to the inspection and use of risk reports, and confidentiality and evaluation obligations.[19]

Article 8 of the ECHR guarantees the right to respect for private and family life. Paragraph 2 requires that any interference be in accordance with the law and necessary in a democratic society in the interests of national security, public safety, or the economic well-being of the country, for the prevention of disorder or crime, for the protection of health or morals, or for the protection of the rights and freedoms of others. The public authority must strike a fair balance between the violation of the right to private life and the social interest that the legislation serves.

2.4.3 Decision

The court first stated that social security is one of the pillars of Dutch society and contributes significantly to prosperity in the Netherlands. The fight against fraud, which is the stated aim of the SyRI legislation, is therefore crucial. It agreed with the government that new technologies such as the SyRI, which offer more possibilities to prevent and combat fraud, should be utilized and generally serve a legitimate purpose. However, the court pointed out that the development of new technologies means that the right to respect for private life, which includes the right to the protection of personal data, is increasingly important and that the absence of sufficient and transparent protection of it might have a 'chilling effect' among the population.[20]

18. *Ibid.*, paras 3.8-4.1.
19. *Ibid.*, paras 4.28-4.31.
20. *Ibid.*, paras 6.3-6.5.

The court reiterated that the Netherlands has an obligation under Article 8 of the ECHR to strike a fair balance between the interference with the right to respect for private life and the benefits of the use of new technologies to prevent and combat fraud. It held that the SyRI legislation fails to comply with that requirement because it is 'insufficiently clear and verifiable'. It therefore declared Article 65 of the SUWI Act and Chapter 5a of the SUWI Decree incompatible with Article 8(2) of the ECHR.[21]

The court focused its remarks on Article 8 of the ECHR but took the general principles of data protection codified in the Charter and the GDPR into account because they offer the same level of protection.[22] According to the court, it is undisputed that the SyRI legislation interferes with the right to respect for private life and that the court must decide whether it is justified. The court held that it cannot determine what exactly the SyRI is because the government has neither publicized the risk model and the indicators that make up the risk model nor submitted them to the court.[23] It ruled that the implementation of the SyRI legislation currently does not involve deep learning, data mining, and risk profile development but that it might in the future.[24] Even though there is no random data collection, a large amount of data is collected, in the opinion of the court.[25] Finally, the court stated that people whose data is collected and included in a risk report are not automatically informed. There is only a legal requirement to announce the start of a SyRI project.[26]

The court reiterated the case law of the ECHR that states that any interference with the right to respect for private life must be provided for by law. It explained that it does not have to be a law in the formal sense, but that 'some basis in domestic law' is sufficient. The legal basis must be sufficiently accessible and foreseeable, meaning it must be so clear that it is possible for an individual to adjust his or her behaviour accordingly. In the case at issue, the court left open the question of whether the SyRI legislation is sufficiently accessible and foreseeable and concentrated on whether it was necessary in a democratic society.[27]

The court held that in light of the margin of discretion provided to national authorities under the ECHR, the damage caused by welfare fraud justified the conclusion of the legislator that there was a compelling social need to take measures in the interest of the economic well-being of the Netherlands as provided for under the SyRI legislation. However, it ruled that the way the SyRI was operated and the associated procedures and safeguards were insufficient and that the SyRI legislation did not strike a fair balance as the ECHR requires. In the view of the court, the principle of transparency was not observed, because there is no insight into the risk indicators and the operation of the risk model. Finally, the court stated that it cannot be ruled out that the deployment of the SyRI in 'problem areas' will discriminate and stigmatize the

21. *Ibid.*, paras 6.6 & 6.7.
22. *Ibid.*, para. 6.41; CFR, Art. 52(3).
23. District Court 2020, para. 6.49.
24. *Ibid.*, para. 6.63.
25. *Ibid.*, para. 6.50.
26. *Ibid.*, paras 6.54 and 6.65.
27. *Ibid.*, paras 6.66-6.72.

citizens in such areas. Due to the lack of transparency, the court cannot assess how these risks have been addressed.[28]

3 Analysis

3.1 Scope

The AILD has been long-awaited in some circles. In one of the earliest works on liability for AI-based systems (1988), there was already some discussion on strict product liability and even a nod to the then EEC Product Liability Directive (PLD)[29] but perhaps it is best to discuss the scope of the AILD by first identifying that which it is not and that which it does *not* cover.

The first major point to take into account when trying to understand the scope of the Directive is to bear in mind that the AILD was *never* intended to be a stand-alone instrument that would solve *all* the possible liability issues arising out of the deployment of AI-based technologies. Instead, the AILD has been negotiated on the understanding that it is part of a package which also includes the upgrade[30] of pre-existing law such as the PLD and brand-new law such as the AI Act[31] adopted in March 2024. The AILD should therefore not be taken out of context but rather it needs to be understood in terms of being a set of safeguards dovetailed and devised concurrently with a number of other very relevant pieces of legislation including (but not exhaustively) the AI Act and the New Product Liability Directive (NPLD) which was also adopted by the Parliament on 12 March 2024. Put simply, one cannot understand the AILD without also properly understanding the full implications and the intricate details of the AI Act and the NPLD.

Which is why the AILD's short title is possibly a bit misleading. Looking at the full title, i.e., 'Proposal for a directive of the European Parliament and of the Council on adapting non-contractual civil liability rules to artificial intelligence (AI liability directive)' would far more easily help the reader to understand that this particular piece of EU law is not about *all* of AI but is just about part of it. Indeed, as will emerge more clearly in this commentary, a less snappy, but more accurate 'shortish' title would have possibly been 'Non-contractual fault-based liability for high-risk AI'.

The key phrase to help one understand better is to be found in the following section of the AILD:

28. *Ibid.*, paras 6.76, 6.79, 6.83, 6.87, 6.92-6.95.
29. *See* Cannataci 1988.
30. NPLD: Parliament, *Liability for defective products European Parliament legislative resolution of 12 Mar. 2024 on the proposal for a directive of the European Parliament and of the Council on liability for defective products (COM(2022)0495 – C9-0322/2022 – 2022/0302(COD))*, P9_TA(2024)0132.
31. Published in the EU Official Journal on 12 Jul. 2024 and therefore coming into effect on 1 Aug. 2024 and coming into force as of 2 Feb. 2025.

1. This Directive lays down common rules on:
   (a) the disclosure of evidence on high-risk artificial intelligence (AI) systems to enable a claimant to substantiate a non-contractual fault-based civil law claim for damages;

The first test to determine whether an action comes within scope for the AILD is therefore logically that of correctly identifying whether a system is AI or not. An 'AI system' is defined under the AI Act as:[32]

> a machine-based system designed to operate with varying levels of autonomy and that may exhibit adaptiveness after deployment and that, for explicit or implicit objectives, infers, from the input it receives, how to generate outputs such as predictions, content, recommendations, or decisions that can influence physical or virtual environments.

The second step is to establish whether the AI system is one which the EU legislator has deliberately taken out of scope of the AI Act and consequently also the AILD. A good first indication of these limitations of scope are to be found in Article 2(3)[33] and Recital 24 of the AI Act:

> If, and insofar as, AI systems are placed on the market, put into service, or used with or without modification of such systems for military, defence or national security purposes, those should be excluded from the scope of this Regulation regardless of which type of entity is carrying out those activities, such as whether it is a public or private entity. As regards military and defence purposes, such exclusion is justified both by Article 4(2) Treaty on EU (TEU) and by the specificities of the Member States' and the common Union defence policy covered by Chapter 2 of Title V of the TEU that are subject to public international law, which is therefore the more appropriate legal framework for the regulation of AI systems in the context of the use of lethal force and other AI systems in the context of military and defence activities. As regards national security purposes, the exclusion is justified both by the fact that national security remains the sole responsibility of Member States in accordance with Article 4(2) TEU and by the specific nature and operational needs of national security activities and specific national rules applicable to those activities. Nonetheless, if an AI system developed, placed on the market, put into service or used for military, defence or national security purposes is used outside those temporarily or permanently for other purposes, for example, civilian or humanitarian purposes, law enforcement or public security purposes, such a system would fall within the scope of this Regulation.

32. AIA, Art. 3(1).
33. *Ibid.*, Art. 2(3): 'This Regulation does not apply to areas outside the scope of Union law, and shall not, in any event, affect the competences of the Member States concerning national security, regardless of the type of entity entrusted by the Member States with carrying out tasks in relation to those competences.

    This Regulation does not apply to AI systems where and in so far they are placed on the market, put into service, or used with or without modification exclusively for military, defence or national security purposes, regardless of the type of entity carrying out those activities.

    This Regulation does not apply to AI systems which are not placed on the market or put into service in the Union, where the output is used in the Union exclusively for military, defence or national security purposes, regardless of the type of entity carrying out those activities'.

The Commission's concern, endorsed by both the Parliament and the Council is clear. It does not wish to legislate *ultra vires* by straying into reserved matters excluded by Article 4(2) of the Treaty of the Union such as military, defence or national security yet, however, if an AI system designed primarily for purposes which are military, defence or national security is deployed in a civilian context outside those purposes, then that system comes into scope. This reflects the legislators' concern that:[34]

> Aside from the many beneficial uses of AI, it can also be misused and provide novel and powerful tools for manipulative, exploitative and social control practices. Such practices are particularly harmful and abusive and should be prohibited because they contradict Union values of respect for human dignity, freedom, equality, democracy and the rule of law and fundamental rights enshrined in the Charter, including the right to non-discrimination, to data protection and to privacy and the rights of the child.

Now this is just one of one hundred and three separate mentions of fundamental rights to be found in the AI Act, which indeed opened with its stated aim of promoting:[35]

> the uptake of human centric and trustworthy artificial intelligence (AI) while ensuring a high level of protection of health, safety, fundamental rights as enshrined in the Charter of Fundamental Rights of the European Union.

The Charter however has its limitations and unlike the mother ship to which it defers, the ECHR, it cannot extend its reach into matters which are reserved to Member States in terms of EU law.

Many AI systems will not be subject to the regulatory framework the AI Act and the AILD will otherwise establish. Other AI systems which are not in scope for the AI Act and thus neither for the AILD, are those systems and models including their output, specifically developed and put into service for the sole purpose of scientific research and development.[36] Likewise excluded from scope is any research, testing and development activity regarding AI systems or models prior to being placed on the market or put into service.[37] Deployers who are individuals and use the AI systems in a purely personal non-professional activity are also excluded from scope.[38]

The third and fourth basic steps are to:

(1) identify those AI systems which are in scope of the AILD (since some AI systems could be out of scope of the AILD but in scope of another separate piece of EU law such as the NPLD or caught in a grey area currently not explicitly regulated by any piece of EU law); and
(2) emphasize that the AILD is intended to be used principally in those instances where a claimant suffers a harm but cannot seek a remedy based on a contractual clause and instead must litigate on the basis of a non-contractual

34. *Ibid.*, Rec. 28.
35. *Ibid.*, Rec. 1.
36. *Ibid.*, Art. 2(6).
37. *Ibid.*, Art. 2(8) and Rec. 25.
38. *Ibid.*, Art. 2(10).

fault-based[39] civil law claim. Put differently, if somebody suffers a harm arising from a system procured from a supplier or used by a service provider with whom the person suffering the harm has a direct contractual relationship which foresees and establishes remedies or excludes harms caused by faults in the AI system in question, then it is probable that this fact would be raised as a first defence to argue to a judge that such a contractual provision would exclude the AILD-based national law as a basis for litigation. Moreover, if the potential claimant would be unable to prove fault then the case would fall out of scope for the AILD. Where litigation would not be possible on a fault-based-liability legal regime then the main alternative would be that of recourse to strict liability law which NPLD may notionally provide. As will be seen, however, bringing harms caused by an AI system into scope of the NPLD, as an alternative to AILD, is not necessarily a straightforward business.

3.2 *High-Risk AI Systems*

Any potential claimant under a national law transposing the AILD, having first established that the system by which he or she has been adversely impacted meets the foregoing statutory description of an AI-based system *and* is not deliberately excluded by the EU legislator in Article 2 of the AI Act, next needs to consider whether the system further qualifies as a 'high-risk' AI system, in line with the provisions of the AI Act. The latter envisages three ways for AI systems to be considered 'high-risk':

- when the AI system is itself a certain type of product;
- when the AI system is a safety component of a certain type of product; and
- when the AI system meets the description of listed 'high-risk' AI systems.

These three categories of high-risk AI systems are specifically identified in Article 6 of the AI Act as follows:

> Article 6. Classification rules for high-risk AI systems
> 1. Irrespective of whether an AI system is placed on the market or put into service independently from the products referred to in points (a) and (b), that AI

39. The notion of fault-based (as opposed to strict liability) actions will be familiar to most lawyers. A defendant subject to strict liability must pay damages irrespective of whether she has met, or failed to meet, an applicable standard of conduct. Action that causes harm is all that is required. By contrast, fault-based liability is conceived as liability predicated on some sort of wrongdoing. Following Goldberg & Zipursky 2016, the AILD conceives of this aspect of scope in the following way: 'Article 1 indicates the subject matter and scope of this Directive: it applies to non-contractual civil law claims for damages caused by an AI system, where such claims are brought under fault-based liability regimes. This means namely regimes that provide for a statutory responsibility to compensate for damage caused intentionally or by a negligent act or omission. The measures provided in this Directive can fit without friction in existing civil liability systems, since they reflect an approach that does not touch on the definition of fundamental concepts like "fault" or "damage", given that the meaning of those concepts varies considerably across the Member States. Thus, beyond the presumptions it establishes, this Directive does not affect Union or national rules determining, for instance, which party has the burden of proof, what degree of certainty is required as regards the standard of proof, or how fault is defined'.

system shall be considered high-risk where both of the following conditions are fulfilled:

(a) the AI system is intended to be used as a safety component of a product, or is itself a product, covered by the Union harmonisation legislation listed in Annex I;

(b) the product whose safety component is the AI system, or the AI system itself as a product, is required to undergo a third-party conformity assessment with a view to the placing on the market or putting into service of that product pursuant to the Union harmonisation legislation listed in Annex I.

2. In addition to the high-risk AI systems referred to in paragraph 1, AI systems referred to in Annex III shall also be considered high-risk.

Thus, the fifth stage of the scoping test for the AILD is whether the AI system at the basis of litigation is covered by Article 6(1), i.e., being a safety component or the AI system is itself a product required to undergo a third-party conformity assessment as mandated by EU legislation in any of the fields as identified in Annex I of the AI Act. The latter Annex I consists of several pages of the titles of various EU harmonized legislation listing eleven regulations and nine directives. An AI system is therefore also in scope of the AILD if it were to come within the scope of any of those legal instruments covering areas ranging from the safety of marine equipment to in vitro diagnostic equipment and, at first glance, most everything in between that the EU has had occasion to legislate about for the best part of the last two decades with a view to promoting safety standards and avoiding harm to citizens in various sectors, especially through a requirement to undergo a third-party conformity assessment.

3.2.1 *AI System Intended to Be Used as a Safety Component of a Product or Subject to Union Harmonization Legislation*

Through the notion of high-risk as defined in the AI Act and the list of sectors identified in Annex I, the AILD brings within scope AI systems used as safety components for medical devices, industrial machinery, toys, aircraft, and cars, as well as other AI systems used as safety components for rail infrastructure, lifts, or appliances burning gaseous fuels, among other examples.

This raises the question as to what happens when an AI system is itself the product but is *not* subject to the EU harmonization legislation mentioned above as listed in Annex I. For example, rather than being a safety component in a medical device such as an in vitro diagnostic medical device, the AI system would be part or all of a decision-support medical diagnosis system which does not fall within the scope of Annex I but may now possibly, but not necessarily, fall within the scope of the NPLD. Except that, even the NPLD may have liability gaps. The NPLD defines 'product' very broadly to include stand-alone software,[40] including AI software, although free and

40. NPLD, Rec. 13: 'Products in the digital age can be tangible or intangible. Software, such as operating systems, firmware, computer programs, applications or AI systems, is increasingly common on the market and plays an increasingly important role for product safety. Software is capable of being placed on the market as a standalone product or can subsequently be integrated

open-source software developed or supplied outside the course of a commercial activity is excluded. There is however considerable doubt as to the way NPLD covers the whole of an AI system since in Recital 13 of the NPLD one reads specifically that:

> Information is not, however, to be considered a product, and product liability rules should therefore not apply to the content of digital files, such as media files or e-books or the source code of software.

Now this makes for a tricky situation since an AI-based system used, say, in medical decision-support, is per force also based on propositional and heuristic knowledge structured as information elicited from domain experts by a knowledge engineer. A strict interpretation of Recital 13 would therefore suggest that where an AI-based system causes harm on the basis of the information or knowledge fed into it as opposed to the way it was coded, then it falls outside the scope of the NPLD as well as the AILD.

Moreover, when one examines the Commission's concerns as publicly expressed, further basic queries arise. In the explanatory memorandum, one notes the Commission's awareness of so-called black-box AI:[41]

> the specific characteristics of AI, including complexity, autonomy and opacity (the so-called 'black box' effect), may make it difficult or prohibitively expensive for victims to identify the liable person and prove the requirements for a successful liability claim.

That statement is correct. The Commission's concern is well placed but do either the AILD or NPLD resolve this issue by properly bringing such matters into scope? Limitations of space mean that it is not possible to here examine examples from every form of AI system but, for the sake of convenience, let's remain in the field of medical AI:[42]

> while black-box medical AI models such as deep learning models provide greater accuracy, they are considered noninterpretable, and thus their output can be unpredictable and not amenable to independent assessment by human healthcare providers.

Put differently, most stand-alone AI medical systems primarily providing diagnostics would not be within scope of AILD and, if ever considered to be within scope of NPLD (despite the fact that the medical information inside the system would be out of scope

---

into other products as a component, and it is capable of causing damage through its execution. In the interest of legal certainty, it should be clarified in this Directive that software is a product for the purposes of applying no-fault liability, irrespective of the mode of its supply or usage, and therefore irrespective of whether the software is stored on a device, accessed through a communication network or cloud technologies, or supplied through a software-as-a-service model. Information is not, however, to be considered a product, and product liability rules should therefore not apply to the content of digital files, such as media files or e-books or the source code of software. A developer or producer of software, including AI system providers within the meaning of Regulation (EU) 2024/ ... of the European Parliament and of the Council *, should be treated as a manufacturer'.

41. Explanatory Memorandum to the AILD, s. 1.
42. Babic et al. 2021 and Hosanagar 2020, as cited in Duffourc & Gerke 2023, 77.

in terms of Recital 13) how could one successfully prosecute even a strict liability claim in the case of harm induced by black-box medical AI? To the legislator and policy maker this is a particularly thorny question. The notion of scope is intimately linked to that of adequate remedies for the citizen. Prior to the arrival of AI on the scene, lawyers, judges and legislators had spent decades putting together a legal framework which afforded protection to medical patients where standards of care were built into the legal system such that, in the hopefully less likely possibility that medical treatment would go wrong, then a measure of remedy was available through rules on either or both fault-based liability and strict liability, which rules governed responsibility for damages. With the advent of AI systems, the objective of the legislator is explicitly that of ensuring that victims would not have had more legal protection without AI involvement in their medical care:[43]

> With this proposal, the Commission aims to ensure that victims of damage caused by AI have an equivalent level of protection under civil liability rules as victims of damage caused without the involvement of AI. The proposal will enable effective private enforcement of fundamental rights and preserve the right to an effective remedy where AI-specific risks have materialised.

If this is the metric that the Commission has set itself, then it would appear that it may not have totally succeeded since it would appear that it may have failed in bringing all commercially available or legally deployed AI systems within the scope of either the AILD or NPLD.[44] For example, in some cases, as in those of, e.g., black-box systems,[45]

43. AILD, s. 3.
44. The Parliament's version of the NPLD, adopted on 12 Mar. 2024, nevertheless simplifies the burden of proof requirements for those claiming compensation. In particular, NPLD, Art. 10(4) introduces the rebuttable presumption of the product's defectiveness and/or the causal link between the defect of the product and the damage where (1) 'the claimant faces excessive difficulties, in particular due to technical or scientific complexity, in proving' the defectiveness and/or the causal link between its defectiveness and the damage; and (2) the claimant proves that it is 'likely' that the product is defective and/or that there is a causal link between the defect and the damage. Similarly, AILD, Art. 4(1) sets out a rebuttable presumption of causality where: (1) the claimant has demonstrated that the damage was caused by non-compliance with a certain EU or national obligation relevant to the AI system; (2) it can be considered reasonably likely, based on the circumstances of the case, that the fault has influenced the output produced by the AI system or the failure of the AI system to produce an output; and (3) the claimant has demonstrated that the output produced by the AI system or the failure of the AI system to produce an output gave rise to the damage. However, in accordance with AILD Art. 4(5), in the case of a claim for damages concerning an AI system that is *not* a high-risk AI system under the AIA, this presumption will only apply where 'the national court considers it excessively difficult for the claimant to prove the causal link'. For a detailed analysis of AILD, Art. 4, *see* De Bruyne & Victor Schollaert, in this volume.
45. Duffourc & Gerke 2023 formulate an analysis based on two types of black box AI systems: 'The first type is a non-autonomous black-box AI that predicts the origin of metastatic cancer of unknown primary (CUP) by "utilis[ing] [a] large number of genomic and transcriptomic features". As cancer origin "can be a significant indicator of how the cancer will behave clinically," a human physician might rely on the AI's prediction to develop a treatment plan. The second type is an autonomous black-box AI that uses a deep learning algorithm to evaluate X-rays without the input of a radiologist. This AI can generate final radiology reports for X-rays that reveal no abnormalities, while those with suspected abnormalities will be referred to a human radiologist for final evaluation and reporting'.

as will be briefly outlined below, it would seem that the victim would have less legal protection than had there been only human specialists involved.

Duffourc and Gerke provide two examples of liability gaps for such black box systems, one for non-autonomous medical AI systems:[46]

> Potential Liability Gap 1 will manifest for the first hypothetical black-box system when the non-autonomous AI provides an incorrect CUP prediction that causes a patient injury. This liability gap occurs because while a human physician oversaw and relied upon the AI's prediction to maximize the patient's chance for successful treatment, they could not independently assess the accuracy of the AI's output. As a result, the physician's reliance on the output of a system used in accordance with its EU CE marking will likely not violate an applicable duty of care for the physician who could not have known that the AI's prediction was incorrect. This gap in liability is remarkable because the AI is making a medical recommendation that would have otherwise been made by a human physician, who the patient could have sued for fault (or medical malpractice). For example, had a human pathologist misclassified the CUP, the patient would likely succeed in a lawsuit against the human pathologist if their misclassification violated the standard of care or medical lege artis. However, this path to liability becomes unavailable under national law even with the proposed AILD when a non-autonomous black-box AI, rather than a human pathologist, predicts the CUP origin, undermining the EC's goal of providing the same level of protection for victims of AI-caused damage.

and the other for autonomous medical AI systems:[47]

> Potential Liability Gap 2 will manifest for the second hypothetical black-box AI system when the autonomous AI reports no abnormality for an X-ray film with remarkable findings, which leads to a missed diagnosis and patient injury. This gap in liability is remarkable because the AI is making a medical decision that would have otherwise been made by a human physician, who the patient could have sued for fault (or medical malpractice). For example, if a human radiologist missed an abnormality in the X-ray film, the patient would likely succeed in a lawsuit against the radiologist if the missed abnormality violated the standard of care or *medical lege artis*. However, this path to liability becomes unavailable under national law even with the proposed AILD when an autonomous black-box AI, rather than a human radiologist, evaluates the X-ray, thus again undermining the EC's goal of providing the same level of protection for victims of AI-caused damage.

It should be borne in mind that prima facie the two conditions for Article 6(1) of the AI Act are cumulative ones, i.e., *both* of the conditions laid out in them have to be met for a system to be categorized as high-risk.

3.2.2 Annex III High-Risk Systems

The AI systems identified in Article 6(1) of the AI Act are not the only ones which come into scope of the AILD. This brings us to the sixth stage of the AILD scoping test since, in addition to the instances identified above, an AI system is also categorized as

46. *Ibid.*
47. *Ibid.*

high-risk under EU law if it is one of those covered by Article 6(2) which refers us to Annex III of the AI Act and which, in turn, reads:

> High-risk AI systems pursuant to Article 6(2) are the AI systems listed in any of the following areas:
>
> 1. Biometrics, in so far as their use is permitted under relevant Union or national law:
>   (a) remote biometric identification systems. This shall not include AI systems intended to be used for biometric verification the sole purpose of which is to confirm that a specific natural person is the person he or she claims to be;
>   (b) AI systems intended to be used for biometric categorisation, according to sensitive or protected attributes or characteristics based on the inference of those attributes or characteristics;
>   (c) AI systems intended to be used for emotion recognition.
> 2. Critical infrastructure: AI systems intended to be used as safety components in the management and operation of critical digital infrastructure, road traffic, or in the supply of water, gas, heating or electricity.
> 3. Education and vocational training:
>   (a) AI systems intended to be used to determine access or admission or to assign natural persons to educational and vocational training institutions at all levels;
>   (b) AI systems intended to be used to evaluate learning outcomes, including when those outcomes are used to steer the learning process of natural persons in educational and vocational training institutions at all levels;
>   (c) AI systems intended to be used for the purpose of assessing the appropriate level of education that an individual will receive or will be able to access, in the context of or within educational and vocational training institutions at all levels;
>   (d) AI systems intended to be used for monitoring and detecting prohibited behaviour of students during tests in the context of or within educational and vocational training institutions at all levels.
> 4. Employment, workers management and access to self-employment:
>   (a) AI systems intended to be used for the recruitment or selection of natural persons, in particular to place targeted job advertisements, to analyse and filter job applications, and to evaluate candidates;
>   (b) AI systems intended to be used to make decisions affecting terms of work-related relationships, the promotion or termination of work-related contractual relationships, to allocate tasks based on individual behaviour or personal traits or characteristics or to monitor and evaluate the performance and behaviour of persons in such relationships.
> 5. Access to and enjoyment of essential private services and essential public services and benefits:
>   (a) AI systems intended to be used by public authorities or on behalf of public authorities to evaluate the eligibility of natural persons for essential public assistance benefits and services, including healthcare services, as well as to grant, reduce, revoke, or reclaim such benefits and services;
>   (b) AI systems intended to be used to evaluate the creditworthiness of natural persons or establish their credit score, with the exception of AI systems used for the purpose of detecting financial fraud;
>   (c) AI systems intended to be used for risk assessment and pricing in relation to natural persons in the case of life and health insurance;

(d) AI systems intended to evaluate and classify emergency calls by natural persons or to be used to dispatch, or to establish priority in the dispatching of, emergency first response services, including by police, firefighters and medical aid, as well as of emergency healthcare patient triage systems.

6. Law enforcement, in so far as their use is permitted under relevant Union or national law:
   (a) AI systems intended to be used by or on behalf of law enforcement authorities, or by Union institutions, bodies, offices or agencies in support of law enforcement authorities or on their behalf to assess the risk of a natural person becoming the victim of criminal offences;
   (b) AI systems intended to be used by or on behalf of law enforcement authorities or by Union institutions, bodies, offices or agencies in support of law enforcement authorities as polygraphs or similar tools;
   (c) AI systems intended to be used by or on behalf of law enforcement authorities, or by Union institutions, bodies, offices or agencies, in support of law enforcement authorities to evaluate the reliability of evidence in the course of the investigation or prosecution of criminal offences;
   (d) AI systems intended to be used by law enforcement authorities or on their behalf or by Union institutions, bodies, offices or agencies in support of law enforcement authorities for assessing the risk of a natural person offending or re-offending not solely on the basis of the profiling of natural persons as referred to in Article 3(4) of Directive (EU) 2016/680, or to assess personality traits and characteristics or past criminal behaviour of natural persons or groups;
   (e) AI systems intended to be used by or on behalf of law enforcement authorities or by Union institutions, bodies, offices or agencies in support of law enforcement authorities for the profiling of natural persons as referred to in Article 3(4) of Directive (EU) 2016/680 in the course of the detection, investigation or prosecution of criminal offences.
7. Migration, asylum and border control management, in so far as their use is permitted under relevant Union or national law:
   (a) AI systems intended to be used by or on behalf of competent public authorities or by Union institutions, bodies, offices or agencies as polygraphs or similar tools;
   (b) AI systems intended to be used by or on behalf of competent public authorities or by Union institutions, bodies, offices or agencies to assess a risk, including a security risk, a risk of irregular migration, or a health risk, posed by a natural person who intends to enter or who has entered into the territory of a Member State;
   (c) AI systems intended to be used by or on behalf of competent public authorities or by Union institutions, bodies, offices or agencies to assist competent public authorities for the examination of applications for asylum, visa or residence permits and for associated complaints with regard to the eligibility of the natural persons applying for a status, including related assessments of the reliability of evidence;
   (d) AI systems intended to be used by or on behalf of competent public authorities, or by Union institutions, bodies, offices or agencies, in the context of migration, asylum or border control management, for the purpose of detecting, recognising or identifying natural persons, with the exception of the verification of travel documents.
8. Administration of justice and democratic processes:
   (a) AI systems intended to be used by a judicial authority or on their behalf to assist a judicial authority in researching and interpreting facts and the law

> and in applying the law to a concrete set of facts, or to be used in a similar way in alternative dispute resolution;
>
> (b) AI systems intended to be used for influencing the outcome of an election or referendum or the voting behaviour of natural persons in the exercise of their vote in elections or referenda. This does not include AI systems to the output of which natural persons are not directly exposed, such as tools used to organise, optimise or structure political campaigns from an administrative or logistical point of view.

The above lists are politico-legal compromises reached after lengthy negotiations and are being reproduced in full in order to give the reader as clear as possible a picture of the intentions of the legislator. For the Parliament, the Commission and the Council were not legislating in a vacuum. They were involved in a long debate which was heavily charged by the fears of anything and everything that could go wrong if an AI system produced an undesired result. Annex III reproduced above is therefore a pre-emptive risk-management exercise whose scope should be evaluated in line with the AI Act's stated intentions that:[48]

> AI systems identified as high-risk should be limited to those that have a significant harmful impact on the health, safety and fundamental rights of persons in the Union and such limitation should minimise any potential restriction to international trade.

What the AILD seeks to provide in terms of Article 6(2) of the AI Act therefore are *non-contractual fault-based remedies* in eight distinct fields:

(1) Biometrics.
(2) Critical infrastructure.
(3) Education and vocational training.
(4) Employment, worker's management and access to self-employment.
(5) Access to and enjoyment of essential private services and essential public services and benefits.
(6) Law enforcement.
(7) Migration, asylum and border control management.
(8) Administration of justice and democratic processes.

It should be stressed that the current list in Annex III of the AI Act is not the EU's last word on the subject. Indeed the entire AI Act has been structured in such a way so as to enable the Commission to expand and otherwise amend this list in an expedited manner through delegated acts. So a seventh step should be added to the AILD scoping test: check whether the list in Annex III has been expanded since this commentary was finalized in July 2024.

The scope-relevant thrust of the AI Act's Annex III is best understood in light of the explanation provided in its Recital 48:

48. AIA, Rec. 46.

> The extent of the adverse impact caused by the AI system on the fundamental rights protected by the Charter is of particular relevance when classifying an AI system as high risk. Those rights include the right to human dignity, respect for private and family life, protection of personal data, freedom of expression and information, freedom of assembly and of association, the right to non-discrimination, the right to education, consumer protection, workers' rights, the rights of persons with disabilities, gender equality, intellectual property rights, the right to an effective remedy and to a fair trial, the right of defence and the presumption of innocence, and the right to good administration. In addition to those rights, it is important to highlight the fact that children have specific rights as enshrined in Article 24 of the Charter and in the United Nations Convention on the Rights of the Child, further developed in the UNCRC General Comment No 25 as regards the digital environment, both of which require consideration of the children's vulnerabilities and provision of such protection and care as necessary for their well-being. The fundamental right to a high level of environmental protection enshrined in the Charter and implemented in Union policies should also be considered when assessing the severity of the harm that an AI system can cause, including in relation to the health and safety of persons.

Recital 48 of the AI Act therefore provides an insight into why the EU came up with eight different high-risk categories listed in the order of biometrics, critical infrastructure, education and vocational training, employment, worker's management and access to self-employment, access to and enjoyment of essential private services and essential public services and benefits, law enforcement, migration, asylum and border control management, and administration of justice and democratic processes. Why, precisely they are listed in that order, starting off alphabetically at B, continuing with C and E, jumping to W in mid-stream and then returning to A in the middle of the list, is not formally explained and perhaps more than anything reflects stages in the drafting process as the drafters took note and discussed the various concerns raised to them. As things stand, the categories are not cumulative conditions for an AI system coming into scope of the AILD and all have equal legal standing: it is enough for an AI system to meet the conditions under one category and one is not being presented as being more important than another. What is important is that they have been classified as high risk and thus brought into scope of the AILD since each one tackles one dimension or another of an AI system that could impact fundamental rights. Of interest too when considering scope 'past, present and future' is the rather tautological thinking expressed in Recital 52 of the AI Act:

> As regards stand-alone AI systems, namely high-risk AI systems other than those that are safety components of products, or that are themselves products, it is appropriate to classify them as high risk if, in light of their intended purpose, they pose a high risk of harm to the health and safety or the fundamental rights of persons, taking into account both the severity of the possible harm and its probability of occurrence and they are used in a number of specifically pre-defined areas specified in this Regulation. The identification of those systems is based on the same methodology and criteria envisaged also for any future amendments to the list of high-risk AI systems that the Commission should be empowered to adopt, via delegated acts, to take into account the rapid pace of technological development, as well as the potential changes in the use of AI systems.

From this one learns that the Commission claims a methodology and criteria to extend the AILD/AI Act scope by identifying new systems for inclusion in Annex III and inserting them through the power of amendment 'via delegated acts',[49] with the basis of the criteria being AI systems posing:

> a high risk of harm to the health and safety or the fundamental rights of persons, taking into account both the severity of the possible harm and its probability of occurrence.

Restrictions on space do not permit an in-depth analysis of the implications on scope of each of the eight sectors indicated above but a brief evaluation of some of the salient points may be useful.

3.2.2.1 Biometrics

The notion of biometrics was clearly a vexing one for the legislators who, interestingly enough, started off by indirectly bringing into scope of the AI Act, AI systems:

> which deploy subliminal components such as audio, image, video stimuli that persons cannot perceive, as those stimuli are beyond human perception, or other manipulative or deceptive techniques that subvert or impair person's autonomy, decision-making or free choice in ways that people are not consciously aware of those techniques or, where they are aware of them, can still be deceived or are not able to control or resist them.

Now this may not prima facie appear relevant to scope since this is presented in the AI Act as an absolute prohibition in terms of Article 5, immediately preceding Article 6 cited above. This approach to some AI-facilitated techniques harks back to concerns stemming from the possibility of unfair commercial practices contemplated nearly two decades previous in Directive 2005/29/EC[50] but what is more remarkable is perhaps the conscious or unconscious nod to the right to free development of personality. This is strongly implied in the concern expressed in Recital 29:

> AI-enabled manipulative techniques can be used to persuade persons to engage in unwanted behaviours, or to deceive them by nudging them into decisions in a way that subverts and impairs their autonomy, decision-making and free choices. The placing on the market, the putting into service or the use of certain AI systems with

49. *See, for example*, AIA, Art. 7 is entirely dedicated to when and how the Commission will have the power to amend Annex III as well as Art. 6(6) which provides: 'The Commission shall adopt delegated acts in accordance with Article 97 to amend the conditions laid down in paragraph 3, first subparagraph, of this Article. The Commission may adopt delegated acts in accordance with Article 97 in order to add new conditions to those laid down in paragraph 3, first subparagraph, or to modify them, only where there is concrete and reliable evidence of the existence of AI systems that fall under the scope of Annex III but do not pose a significant risk of harm to the health, safety or fundamental rights of natural persons'.
50. Directive 2005/29/EC of the European Parliament and of the Council of 11 May 2005 concerning unfair business-to-consumer commercial practices in the internal market and amending Council Directive 84/450/EEC, Directives 97/7/EC, 98/27/EC and 2002/65/EC of the European Parliament and of the Council and Regulation (EC) No 2006/2004 of the European Parliament and of the Council ('Unfair Commercial Practices Directive'), OJ. L. 149 (11 Jun. 2005).

> the objective to or the effect of materially distorting human behaviour, whereby significant harms, in particular having sufficiently important adverse impacts on physical, psychological health or financial interests are likely to occur, are particularly dangerous and should therefore be prohibited.

This reference to autonomy, decision-making and free choices is extremely interesting since it picks up some vibes from a small number of cases of the European Court of Human Rights referring explicitly to the development of self and thus implicitly to the overarching right to free unhindered development of personality, a right enunciated in the UN Declaration of Human Rights of 1948 but not explicitly in the ECHR nor in the EU Charter of Fundamental Rights.[51] Notionally therefore, by extension, one has here the seeds for extending the scope of AILD by eventually inserting into Annex III of the AI Act any AI-system not yet indicated therein which could reasonably be held to risk negatively impacting 'autonomy, decision-making and free choices'.

Although in several places, the AI Act presents itself as being complementary to the GDPR and in no way intended to substitute it, it is interesting to note that, in addition to unfair commercial practices and protection of autonomy, decision-making and free choices, it predicates its concern about biometrics on it also constituting sensitive data:[52]

> As biometric data constitutes a special category of personal data, it is appropriate to classify as high-risk several critical-use cases of biometric systems, insofar as their use is permitted under relevant Union and national law.

The drafters do not explain further but immediately jump to their next point of concern, i.e., remote biometric identification:[53]

> Technical inaccuracies of AI systems intended for the remote biometric identification of natural persons can lead to biased results and entail discriminatory effects. The risk of such biased results and discriminatory effects is particularly relevant with regard to age, ethnicity, race, sex or disabilities. Remote biometric identification systems should therefore be classified as high-risk in view of the risks that they pose.

So it is not biometric identification in front of a passport officer or an e-gate at the border or in a normal 1:1 direct transactional environment that is in scope of the AILD or AI Act here but rather remote biometric identification defined by AI Act as an:[54]

> AI system for the purpose of identifying natural persons, without their active involvement, typically at a distance through the comparison of a person's biometric data with the biometric data contained in a reference database.

This is of such grave concern to the legislator that biometrics also figures prominently in Article 5 of the AI Act, i.e., prohibited AI practices, but, reading between the lines,

51. For a more detailed evolution of the right to free development of personality and its historical relationship to other fundamental rights such as privacy and freedom of speech *see* Cannataci 2022.
52. AIA, Rec. 54.
53. *Ibid.*
54. *Ibid.*, Art. 3(41).

it is easy to see that most sensible uses of AI by law enforcement for a number of specified purposes are explicitly excluded from this prohibition and thus, to all intents and purposes, are permitted rather than prohibited. For example, in practice, provided that some safeguards are introduced and observed, one can still use biometrics at the border or in a public space for law enforcement purposes such as the targeted search for specific victims of abduction, trafficking in human beings or sexual exploitation of human beings, as well as searching for missing persons and counter-terrorism purposes. Almost needless to add neither AILD nor AI Act speak about the use of biometrics and remote biometric identification for national security purposes as distinct from law enforcement purposes since that would be *ultra vires*.

The logic of the AI Act with regard to biometrics may appear to some to be slightly convoluted: first, it makes what appears to be a blanket prohibition in Article 5 while within that very same article creating several possibilities for derogation of this prohibition and then it returns to biometrics as the first category of high-risk systems in Annex III to which Article 6(2) of the AI Act defers. Recognizing that the derogations to its own Article 5 allow the Member States quite a degree of flexibility in approach to deploying biometric systems, the AI Act uses Annex III to impose further safeguards and constraints in those cases where biometric systems are actually permitted under national law and this by the simple expedient of classifying them as high-risk systems. Apart from (a) remote biometric identification already addressed in Article 5, Annex III.1 adds (b) AI systems intended to be used for biometric categorization, according to sensitive or protected attributes or characteristics based on the inference of those attributes or characteristics; as well as (c) AI systems intended to be used for emotion recognition, thus bringing these systems into scope for AILD.

3.2.2.2 Critical Infrastructure

The second category found in Annex II, critical infrastructure is also one of those instances where useful insights may be obtained from the recitals of the AI Act:[55]

> As regards the management and operation of critical infrastructure, it is appropriate to classify as high-risk the AI systems intended to be used as safety components in the management and operation of critical digital infrastructure as listed in point (8) of the Annex to Directive (EU) 2022/2557, road traffic and the supply of water, gas, heating and electricity, since their failure or malfunctioning may put at risk the life and health of persons at large scale and lead to appreciable disruptions in the ordinary conduct of social and economic activities. Safety components of critical infrastructure, including critical digital infrastructure, are systems used to directly protect the physical integrity of critical infrastructure or the health and safety of persons and property but which are not necessary in order for the system to function. The failure or malfunctioning of such components might directly lead to risks to the physical integrity of critical infrastructure and thus to risks to health and safety of persons and property. Components intended to be used solely for cybersecurity purposes should not qualify as safety components. Examples of

55. AIA, Rec. 55.

safety components of such critical infrastructure may include systems for monitoring water pressure or fire alarm controlling systems in cloud computing centres.

3.2.2.3 Education

The systems identified in Annex III as being high risk in the educational sector suggest a deep underlying mistrust of the ability of AI systems to get things right and a strong preference for the final decision to be left in the hands of a human being. Thus one reads that:[56]

> AI systems used in education or vocational training, in particular for determining access or admission, for assigning persons to educational and vocational training institutions or programmes at all levels, for evaluating learning outcomes of persons, for assessing the appropriate level of education for an individual and materially influencing the level of education and training that individuals will receive or will be able to access or for monitoring and detecting prohibited behaviour of students during tests should be classified as high-risk AI systems, since they may determine the educational and professional course of a person's life and therefore may affect that person's ability to secure a livelihood.

The EU legislator holds that:[57]

> When improperly designed and used, such systems may be particularly intrusive and may violate the right to education and training as well as the right not to be discriminated against and perpetuate historical patterns of discrimination, for example against women, certain age groups, persons with disabilities, or persons of certain racial or ethnic origins or sexual orientation.

While appreciating the higher standards and the stricter safeguards that such systems will be subjected to before deployment by the mere act of classifying them as high-risk systems, it should be noted that the utility of bringing them into scope of AILD may probably be rather limited. The time, effort, money and energy involved in using civil law-based fault liability law to sue the educational authority or the school which deployed an AI system which could be held responsible for, e.g., denying access or admission as well as correctly evaluating learning outcomes, are such that launching such a court action would not normally be the first or indeed the second course of action of an adolescent or a young adult keen to get on with his or her life. Conceptually correct but its value in practice is yet to be seen. Only time will tell whether it being brought into scope of the AILD served more as a deterrent than as a genuinely useful remedy.

3.2.2.4 Employment, Worker Management and Access to Self-Employment

AI systems used in employment, workers management and access to self-employment, in particular for the recruitment and selection of persons, for making decisions

56. *Ibid.*, Rec. 56.
57. *Ibid.*

affecting terms of the work-related relationship, promotion and termination of work-related contractual relationships, for allocating tasks on the basis of individual behaviour, personal traits or characteristics and for monitoring or evaluation of persons in work-related contractual relationships are classified as high risk by the EU legislator since they may have 'an appreciable impact on future career prospects, livelihoods of those persons and workers' rights'.[58]

Once again, one of the main benefits of such classification as high risk would be that 'prevention is better than cure' with the deployment of more reliable and accurate AI systems *a priori*. In terms of scoping these also within AILD, it is probable that these would have more take up in civil law-based fault liability than those in the educational sector since the claimant would often have moved to another employer or would still be employed, in each case having more funds and time and often the sufficient level of motivation to engage in the litigation required to obtain a remedy.

3.2.2.5 Access to and Enjoyment of Essential Private Services and Essential Public Services and Benefits

Spurred on no doubt by developments in certain EU Member States, not least the Dutch scandal where 'the Dutch tax authority ruined thousands of lives after using an algorithm to spot suspected benefits fraud',[59] the EU legislator has made it a point to afford extra protection when:[60]

> natural persons applying for or receiving essential public assistance benefits and services from public authorities namely healthcare services, social security benefits, social services providing protection in cases such as maternity, illness, industrial accidents, dependency or old age and loss of employment and social and housing assistance, are typically dependent on those benefits and services and in a vulnerable position in relation to the responsible authorities.

With the recent Dutch experience graphically in mind, the EU legislator has determined that since:[61]

> AI systems are used for determining whether such benefits and services should be granted, denied, reduced, revoked or reclaimed by authorities, including whether beneficiaries are legitimately entitled to such benefits or services, those systems may have a significant impact on persons' livelihood and may infringe their fundamental rights, such as the right to social protection, non-discrimination, human dignity or an effective remedy and should therefore be classified as high-risk.

The contrast between the concern about access to healthcare and other services and the actual harm that may be caused once the citizen actually obtains access to the service is stark. If one were to continue with the examples of a black-box AI-based medical

58. *Ibid.*, Rec. 57.
59. Heikkla 2024.
60. AIA, Rec. 58.
61. *Ibid.*

decision support system given above, one can here distinguish between the AILD's concern about the impact of AI on the *access* to healthcare and what then happens if, once healthcare is accessed to, an AI-based system actually used in healthcare results in harm to the patient. Thus the AILD brings within scope AI systems used in determining access to healthcare or housing services or for access to maternity benefits or systems determining price and risk for health insurance. EU legislators have said such systems should be classed as high risk as they 'may have a significant impact on persons' livelihood and may infringe their fundamental rights, such as the right to social protection, non-discrimination, human dignity or an effective remedy. However, if a medical decision support system results in a wrong treatment of a patient the AILD does not provide a remedy, though possibly the NPLD may conceivably but not overwhelmingly, in some instances, do so.

Annex III of the AI Act seems to deliberately leave some things out of scope for itself and hence the AILD while providing an explanation as to why other systems are brought into scope by being classified as high-risk systems. AI systems intended to be used to evaluate a person's creditworthiness or to establish their credit score are also among those that could be regulated as high-risk AI systems unless those systems are used for detecting financial fraud:

> However, AI systems provided for by Union law for the purpose of detecting fraud in the offering of financial services and for prudential purposes to calculate credit institutions' and insurance undertakings' capital requirements should not be considered to be high risk under this Regulation. Moreover, AI systems intended to be used for risk assessment and pricing in relation to natural persons for health and life insurance can also have a significant impact on persons' livelihood and if not duly designed, developed and used, can infringe their fundamental rights and can lead to serious consequences for people's life and health, including financial exclusion and discrimination. Finally, AI systems used to evaluate and classify emergency calls by natural persons or to dispatch or establish priority in the dispatching of emergency first response services, including police, firefighters and medical aid, as well as emergency healthcare patient triage systems, should also be classified as high-risk since they make decisions in very critical situations for the life and health of persons and their property.[62]

3.2.2.6 Law Enforcement, insofar as Their Use Is Permitted under Relevant Union or National Law

This part of Annex III is reminiscent of the approach taken towards biometrics. The use of AI and especially face recognition by police forces has been a source of public controversy for many years both outside and inside Europe. The EU legislator justifies the AI Act's approach to this sector by considering that:[63]

> Given their role and responsibility, actions by law enforcement authorities involving certain uses of AI systems are characterised by a significant degree of power

62. *Ibid.*
63. *Ibid.*, Rec. 59.

> imbalance and may lead to surveillance, arrest or deprivation of a natural person's liberty as well as other adverse impacts on fundamental rights guaranteed in the Charter.

This concern then leads to the bringing into scope of a long list of examples cited in which AI systems used in a law enforcement context could be considered 'high-risk' AI. The list includes AI systems intended to be used to assess individuals' risk of becoming a victim of crime – or of offending or re-offending – as well as those used as polygraphs or similar tools. It also covers AI systems used to evaluate the reliability of evidence in criminal investigations or prosecutions, or for profiling individuals in the course of detection, investigation or prosecution of criminal offences. Those persons who could reasonably claim a significant harm arising from the use of any the AI systems identified in Annex III.6 would doubtless need to look for evidence of whether in particular:[64]

> the AI system is not trained with high-quality data, does not meet adequate requirements in terms of its performance, its accuracy or robustness, or is not properly designed and tested before being put on the market or otherwise put into service.

as a result of which they may have been singled out 'in a discriminatory or otherwise incorrect or unjust manner'.[65] Another defect that could be tested for in terms of AILD-inspired national law is one which could possibly hamper 'the exercise of important procedural fundamental rights, such as the right to an effective remedy and to a fair trial as well as the right of defence and the presumption of innocence'[66] ... 'in particular, where such AI systems are not sufficiently transparent, explainable and documented'.[67]

Deliberately taken out of scope are:[68]

> AI systems specifically intended to be used for administrative proceedings by tax and customs authorities as well as by financial intelligence units carrying out administrative tasks analysing information pursuant to Union anti-money laundering law ... AI systems used by law enforcement authorities for the purpose of prevention, detection, investigation and prosecution of criminal offences.

The exclusion of anti-money laundering AI systems is an interesting one and may sometime in future be usefully studied together with allegations that EU money-laundering law has been allowed to go too far[69] and significantly breaches the right to private and family life entrenched in Article 8 of the ECHR and Article 7 of the Charter.

64. *Ibid.*
65. *Ibid.*
66. *Ibid.*
67. *Ibid.*
68. *Ibid.*
69. For an in-depth examination of this subject *see* Kaiser 2018.

3.2.2.7 Migration, Asylum and Border Control

While the EU legislator was making the right noises as recently as March 2024 by identifying that:[70]

> AI systems used in migration, asylum and border control management affect persons who are often in particularly vulnerable position and who are dependent on the outcome of the actions of the competent public authorities.

the reality on the ground by July 2024 may be turning out to be quite different. Inclusion in scope of migration-relevant AI systems as high-risk systems will doubtless help improve the quality of such systems before they are deployed but the practical utility of AILD in such cases may need to be revisited. The migration sector provides us with an interesting use-case of the complexity of a situation into which real-life AI systems are being, designed tested and launched.[71]

Since 'the accuracy, non-discriminatory nature and transparency of the AI systems used in those contexts are therefore particularly important to guarantee respect for the fundamental rights of the affected persons',[72] Annex III classifies as high-risk and thus within scope of the AILD:[73]

> those AI systems intended to be used by or on behalf of competent public authorities or by Union institutions, bodies, offices or agencies charged with tasks in the fields of migration, asylum and border control management as polygraphs and similar tools, for assessing certain risks posed by natural persons entering the territory of a Member State or applying for visa or asylum, for assisting competent public authorities for the examination, including related assessment of the reliability of evidence, of applications for asylum, visa and residence permits and associated complaints with regard to the objective to establish the eligibility of the natural persons applying for a status, for the purpose of detecting, recognising or identifying natural persons in the context of migration, asylum and border control management, with the exception of verification of travel documents.

As ever, and as in other sectors too, the AILD should not be taken out of context and a lot has been happening recently in the migration sector. On 10 April 2024, the Parliament voted in favour of the new rules on migration, followed by their formal adoption by the Council, on 14 May 2024, 'allowing the EU to tackle complex issues with determination and ingenuity'.[74] The Commission states that:[75]

> this will ensure that the Union has strong and secure external borders, that people's rights are guaranteed, and that no EU country is left alone under pressure.

70. AIA, Rec. 60.
71. Including at least three major EU-supported research projects: IT Flows, Mirror and Criteria.
72. AIA, Rec. 60.
73. *Ibid.*
74. Commission 2024.
75. *Ibid.*

Many NGOs disagree with this perspective[76] and some are launching court actions to challenge the outcomes of this latest development which has been additionally designated as the Migration and Asylum Pact (MAAP).

The situation on the ground as of end July 2024 after the signature of the MAAP may be summarized as follows:

- Border agencies across Europe will not necessarily be in a position to take identical approaches to the respect of human rights despite recent attempts to improve matters.
- The EU approach to border management has again recently formally shifted with effect from the MAAP of May 2024, which is a key part of the EU's strategy to deal with hybrid threats.
- *All* border agencies will have to apply the new Screening Regulation which is intended to impede the entry of 'bogus' asylum seekers, in other words, those whose main motivation for migration is economic (the vast majority of those who cross the Mediterranean border), who tie up national asylum-processing systems and consume considerable public resources.
- All border agencies will have to be on the lookout for people who 'pose a security risk, who mislead the authorities by providing false information or withhold information, or who are coming from countries with a low recognition rate'. These persons will be subjected to a 'border procedure' with the result that they will not remain at liberty in the country while their claim is being examined, but be obliged to remain at specific facilities at or near the border, for a maximum period of twelve weeks until it is decided whether they will move on to the 'in-territory' asylum procedure – the normal asylum procedure – or to expulsion.
- Much as it tries the MAAP does not create a level playing field. The pact enables border procedures and standards at the reception centres to be harmonized, but there will continue to be major national differences in terms of:
  - the levels of state assistance given to asylum seekers and refugees (housing and social support);
  - the various nationalities' acceptance rates; and
  - the likelihood of being sent back in the event of rejection.

Moreover, the MAAP does not create a single refugee status valid throughout the EU: anyone obtaining this status in one Member State may not reside in another:

- Meanwhile, the MAAP does not address many of the main shortcomings in the way irregular immigration and asylum are currently managed:
  - the return or repatriation of failed applicants continues to depend on agreements with the countries of origin, which are often non-existent or weak. Only 20% of those due to be returned actually are, and most remain

76. *See, for example,* Statewatch 2024; Grammatikou 2024.

in a sort of limbo on European soil pending some form of regularization. The MAAP is unable to solve this problem, which depends on the EU's foreign policy and that of each Member State. Although the MAAP includes mentions of the external aspects of migration policies (relations with the countries of origin), the signature of agreements will obviously depend on bilateral agreements (initiated by the Commission, such as those sealed with Egypt and Tunisia, or by Member States, such as those agreed between Spain and Morocco). In this regard, the MAAP suggests that immigration be systematically included in the EU's foreign relations with countries of origin, including in trade agreements;
  - that the fight against human trafficking be stepped up with specific programmes in certain countries;
  - that cooperation on readmission be improved (exerting pressure through, for example, the awarding of visas to the countries of origin that do not collaborate on such readmission); and
  - that more channels be opened to facilitate legal migration through the EU Talent Partnerships.
- While having to deal with the new MAAP, border agencies will also have to deal with the introduction of at least two major pieces of new EU law pertinent to the AI-based technologies that border control personnel will probably increasingly be using to do their jobs not only for cases of regular and irregular migration but also for human trafficking, drug smuggling and countering organized crime.
- The AI Act will require border agencies to carry out intensive impact assessments *before* deploying AI technologies since use in this context is now categorized as high-risk in terms of Article 6 of the AI Act. Yet, the volume of work will make such AI systems an increasingly attractive proposition for border agencies with the promise of lightening the workload and expediting the processing of migrants and asylum seekers.
- Against the scenario provided by these latest developments, once they have deployed AI-based systems, border agencies will have to be doubly careful as to how they use them since, in terms of the AILD, they will also be liable for non-contractual fault-based liability payable as a result of civil law claims by persons adversely affected by the use of such systems.

Within this context, the inclusion of AI systems used at the border in the scope of AILD could serve some use if the claims were to be supported by relatively well-resourced NGOs assisting the migrants. Absent this assistance, the AILD provisions would in practice be mostly useless and unused since the vast majority of vulnerable people wrongly caught up in AI-facilitated migration and/or asylum procedures would not have the know-how or resources or the opportunity to engage in long-drawn-out civil law non-contractual liability claims.

3.2.2.8 Administration of Justice and Democratic Processes

Fundamental rights are again at the forefront of the *raison d'être* for classifying certain AI systems in the justice system as being high-risk and thus bringing them into scope for the AILD. The motivation given by the EU Legislator is their:[77]

> potentially significant impact on democracy, the rule of law, individual freedoms as well as the right to an effective remedy and to a fair trial.

The concern of the legislator with the need to 'to address the risks of potential biases, errors and opacity',[78] thus brought into scope:

> AI systems intended to be used by a judicial authority or on its behalf to assist judicial authorities in researching and interpreting facts and the law and in applying the law to a concrete set of facts.

The EU legislator went further and held that:[79]

> AI systems intended to be used by alternative dispute resolution bodies for those purposes should also be considered to be high-risk when the outcomes of the alternative dispute resolution proceedings produce legal effects for the parties.

The underlying approach of the legislator is even more explicit than in the case of education referred to above:[80]

> The use of AI tools can support the decision-making power of judges or judicial independence, but should not replace it: the final decision-making must remain a human-driven activity.

What the legislator understandably takes out of scope are:

> AI systems intended for purely ancillary administrative activities that do not affect the actual administration of justice in individual cases, such as anonymisation or pseudonymisation of judicial decisions, documents or data, communication between personnel, administrative tasks.

Although they also come into scope for the AILD, it is probably the 'prevention dimension', which figured most prominently in the mind of the EU legislator when it was determined through the AI Act, Annex III that:

> in order to address the risks of undue external interference with the right to vote enshrined in Article 39 of the Charter, and of adverse effects on democracy and the rule of law, AI systems intended to be used to influence the outcome of an election or referendum or the voting behaviour of natural persons in the exercise of their vote in elections or referenda should be classified as high-risk AI systems with the exception of AI systems whose output natural persons are not directly exposed to, such as tools used to organise, optimise and structure political campaigns from an administrative and logistical point of view.

77. AIA, Rec. 61.
78. *Ibid.*
79. *Ibid.*
80. *Ibid.*

The Cambridge Analytica saga would appear to have influenced the EU legislation in this direction since the exception taking out of scope 'tools used to organise, optimise and structure political campaigns from an administrative and logistical point of view' would seem to be coming right out of that particular playbook.

In summary, with regard to the impact of Annex III of the AI Act on scope, if somebody is, for example, unjustifiably denied access to the EU at the EU border or asylum within the EU on the basis of an AI-assisted decision, or unfairly denied a promotion on the basis of a wrong assessment of an AI-based system, or is negatively impacted by a wrongful court decision significantly influenced by an AI-based decision support system, then the claimant may seek fault-based damages for the harm suffered especially in terms of a system identified in Annex III of the AI Act. However, there are entire categories of cases which are excluded from the AILD. If a patient suffers from the wrong or late diagnosis because a black-box stand-alone AI-based system used by his or her local hospital got it wrong, then there is probably no remedy under AILD. Neither would there be a remedy through the AILD if a lawyer were to give wrong advice because of reliance on a well-coded AI-based system.

Additionally to all of the foregoing, there are ways to claim that an AI system is out of scope for the purposes of the AILD in any or all of the eight categories contemplated in Annex III by considering the following Article 6(3):

> By derogation from paragraph 2, an AI system shall not be considered to be high-risk if it does not pose a significant risk of harm to the health, safety or fundamental rights of natural persons, including by not materially influencing the outcome of decision making. This shall be the case where one or more of the following conditions are fulfilled:
>
> (a) the AI system is intended to perform a narrow procedural task;
> (b) the AI system is intended to improve the result of a previously completed human activity;
> (c) the AI system is intended to detect decision-making patterns or deviations from prior decision-making patterns and is not meant to replace or influence the previously completed human assessment, without proper human review; or
> (d) the AI system is intended to perform a preparatory task to an assessment relevant for the purposes of the use cases listed in Annex III.

Notwithstanding the first subparagraph, an AI system referred to in Annex III shall always be considered to be high-risk where the AI system performs profiling of natural persons.

4 Conclusions

The discussion on scope of the AILD should be extended in conjunction with the discussion on scope of the NPLD since, when a citizen is seeking a legal remedy, the main concern that one may have is whether there may exist a gap in liability laws covering AI. Typically, four main categories of interested parties[81] would be impacted and hopefully involved in such a discussion:

(1) the citizen who may suffer harm and is seeking a remedy;
(2) the AI system manufacturer or producer;
(3) the service provider which may be using an AI-based system; and
(4) the policymakers and legislators who may be concerned about 'getting it right' when it comes to AI policy and law-making.

Some of the problems with medical AI have already been identified above and here again, medical AI can be used to illustrate the existence of possible gaps in liability law even when taking the AILD and the NPLD together, something which can also be understood better when examining two tables produced in the relevant above-cited study[82] by Duffourc & Gerke.

While some improvements in the text of the NPLD in the period September 2022-March 2024 may possibly have altered some of the likelihood of liability indicated since their article was published in May 2023, the conclusion provided by Duffourc & Gerke regarding what comes into scope and what remains out of scope, even when taking the AILD and the PLD together, is a sobering one:[83]

> While these proposed Directives provide some uniform liability rules for AI-caused harm, they fail to fully accomplish the EU's goal of providing clarity and uniformity for liability for injuries caused by AI-driven goods and services. Instead, the Directives leave potential liability gaps for injuries caused by some black-box medical AI systems, which use opaque and complex reasoning to provide medical decisions and/or recommendations. Patients may not be able to successfully sue manufacturers or healthcare providers for some injuries caused by these black-box medical AI systems under either EU Member States' strict or fault-based liability laws. Since the proposed Directives fail to address these potential liability gaps, manufacturers and healthcare providers may have difficulty predicting liability risks associated with creating and/or using some potentially beneficial black-box medical AI systems.

The AILD does not, as currently drafted – and this may, of course, change if and when the AILD is finally adopted and comes into force – address situations where an AI system causes damage but there is no obvious defective product or fault by either the provider or user. There is however the intention that the Commission will assess the need for no-fault strict liability rules five years after the entry into force of the AILD.

The next point to be established by any lawyer examining the possibility of a claim under the AILD as transposed into a particular Member State is whether when

81. Properly speaking the technical terms used by the AIA and AILD are 'provider', 'deployer' and 'importer', 'distributor' but the use of more reader-friendly terms here may hopefully make the reasoning behind this text more accessible.
82. Duffourc & Gerke 2023.
83. *Ibid.*

transposing the AILD, that state's parliament more or less stuck to the letter of the AILD or made it stricter or more comprehensive in coverage. For the AILD generally allows the national parliaments to adopt stricter national laws to govern non-contractual liability for AI-caused damages that fall outside of the PLD's scope (Article 1(4),[84] Recital 11). Thus EU Member States still have considerable discretion in developing national rules to govern liability for injuries caused by AI systems.

In conclusion, when discussing scope of the AILD one must consider the possible impact of the fact that the development and finalization of the NPLD has outpaced that of the AILD. When examining the version of NPLD currently[85] in front of the Council for approval, one notes that its scope now explicitly encompasses software and software developers and addresses damages resulting from data destruction or corruption. This expansion in scope raises concerns about whether the AILD offers a route for redress that, in fact, overlaps with the one provided by the PLD despite the grey areas identified earlier in this commentary. This is one of the reasons why the Parliament has called for a thorough impact assessment of the draft proposal to evaluate its relevance and effectiveness in the current legislative landscape.[86] It is expected that this assessment will be completed by the end of September 2024 and will possibly consider the existence of any legislative gaps that the AILD could still address following the adoption of the AI Act and the PLD. Coupled with uncertainty about scope, *inter alia*, that exists at the Council level,[87] if the impact assessment finds, as has this commentary, that significant gaps still exist then it is not unlikely that the Parliament would recommend[88] that the Commission withdraws the September 2022 AILD proposal and goes back to the drawing board in order to plug the gaps and reduce overlap between AILD and NPLD.

84. 'Member States may adopt or maintain national rules that are more favourable for claimants to substantiate a non-contractual civil law claim for damages caused by an AI system, provided such rules are compatible with Union law.'
85. As at the time of writing in Jul. 2024.
86. AILD is currently at Committee stage in the Parliament: 'The responsible committee is Legal Affairs (JURI), with Internal Market and Consumer Protection (IMCO) and Civil Liberties, Justice and Home Affairs (LIBE) also giving opinions. The Industry, Research and Energy (ITRE) committee decided not to opine on the directive. The legal affairs committee has commissioned a study from the European Parliament's Research Service, who in turn hired an external contractor to determine whether there is a legal gap left by the AI Act and PLD for the AILD to fill, Kai Zenner, digital policy adviser for MEP Axel Voss, who leads work on the AILD at the JURI committee, told Euractiv', Gkritsi 2024.
87. 'At the Council level, there is uncertainty about the AILD's usefulness. Two member states have argued against the file, while others have asked for more time, a look at the Parliament's study, and workshops with the Commission, which will be conducted over the summer, Zenner said'. *Ibid.*
88. Given the time required for the newly constituted (Jun. 2024) Parliament to settle down, the apparent lack of priority that the AILD will be accorded by the Hungarian Presidency incumbent until end 2024, it is not expected that such a decision and recommendation would be formally finalized before 2025.

BIBLIOGRAPHY

Academic Writings

Babic et al. 2021: Boris Babic et al., *Beware Explanations from AI in Health Care*, 373 Science 284-286 (2021).

Cannataci 2022: Joe Cannataci, *Private & Family Life, in Elgar Encyclopedia of Human Rights* 72-81 (Christina Binder et al. eds, Elgar 2022).

Cannataci 1988: Joe Cannataci, *Liability and Responsibility for Expert Systems* (Oslo, Norway 1988).

Duffourc & Gerke 2023: Mindy Nunez Duffourc & Sara Gerke, *The Proposed EU Directives for AI liability Leave Worrying Gaps Likely to Impact Medical AI*, 6 npj Digital Medicine 77 (2023), doi.org/10.1038/s41746-023-00823-w.

Goldberg & Zipursky 2016: John C.P. Goldberg & Benjamin C. Zipursky, *The Strict Liability in Fault and the Fault in Strict Liability*, 85 Fordham Law Review 743 (2016), doi.org/10.2139/ssrn.2871328.

Hosanagar 2020: Kartik Hosanagar, *A Human's Guide to Machine Intelligence: How Algorithms Are Shaping Our Lives and How We Can Stay in Control* (Penguin, New York 2020).

Kaiser 2018: Carolin Kaiser, *Privacy and Identity Issues in Financial Transactions: The Proportionality of the European Anti-Money Laundering Legislation*, Thesis University of Groningen (The Netherlands 2018).

Blogs

Freedman 2024: Robert Freedman, *16 States Have AI laws, Most of Them to Curb Profiling*, Legal Dive (20 March 2024), www.legaldive.com/news/16-states-have-ai-laws-curb-profiling-BCLP-interactive-compilation-state-AI-laws/710878 (accessed 18 April 2024).

Gesley 2020: Jenny Gesley, *Netherlands: Court Prohibits Government's Use of AI Software to Detect Welfare Fraud*, Law Library of Congress (13 March 2020), www.loc.gov/item/global-legal-monitor/2020-03-13/netherlands-court-prohibits-governments-use-of-ai-software-to-detect-welfare-fraud (accessed 30 July 2024).

Habuka 2023: Hiroki Habuka, *Japan's Approach to AI Regulation and Its Impact on the 2023 G7 Presidency*, Center for Strategic and International Studies (14 February 2023), www.csis.org/analysis/japans-approach-ai-regulation-and-its-impact-2023-g7-presidency (accessed 18 April 2024).

Plotinski & Cinelli 2024: David Plotinski & Giovanna M. Cinelli, *Existing and Proposed Federal AI Regulation in the United States*, Morgan Lewis Insight (9 April 2024), www.morganlewis.com/pubs/2024/04/existing-and-proposed-federal-ai-regulation-in-the-united-states (accessed 18 April 2024).

News

Bertuzzi 2022: Luca Bertuzzi, *Once Bitten, Netherlands Wants to Move Early on Algorithm Supervision*, Euractiv (14 November 2022), www.euractiv.com/

section/digital/news/once-bitten-netherlands-wants-to-move-early-on-algorithm-supervision (accessed 30 July 2024).

Digital Watch 2024: Digital Watch, *Japan Joins Global AI Regulation Race with Comprehensive 2024 Legislative Push* (18 February 2024), dig.watch/updates/japan-joins-global-ai-regulation-race-with-comprehensive-2024-legislative-push (accessed 18 April 2024).

District Court 2020: District Court of The Hague (Rechtbank Den Haag), Judgment of 5 February 2020, C-09-550982-HA ZA 18-388, perma.cc/DS89-K477 (accessed 30 July 2024).

Gkritsi 2024: Eliza Gkritsi, *Picking Up the AI Liability Directive after the Tech Policy Spree*, Euractiv (19 July 2024), www.euractiv.com/section/digital/news/picking-up-the-ai-liability-directive-after-the-tech-policy-spree (accessed 21 July 2024).

Grammatikou 2024: Spyridoula Grammatikou, *EU Migration and Asylum Pact Will Violate Key Rights, NGOs Warn*, Balkan Insight (11 June 2024), balkaninsight.com/2024/06/11/eu-migration-and-asylum-pact-will-violate-key-rights-ngos-warn (accessed 21 July 2024).

Heikkla 2024: Melissa Heikkla, *Dutch Scandal Serves as a Warning for Europe over Risks of Using Algorithms*, Politico (29 March 2022), www.politico.eu/article/dutch-scandal-serves-as-a-warning-for-europe-over-risks-of-using-algorithms (accessed 21 July 2024).

Others

Commission 2024: Commission, *What is the Pact on Migration and Asylum* (21 May 2024), home-affairs.ec.europa.eu/policies/migration-and-asylum/pact-migration-and-asylum_en (accessed 21 July 2024).

Criteria, www.project-criteria.eu (accessed 21 July 2024).

Netherlands 2021: Government of the Netherlands, *Fundamental Rights and Algorithms Impact Assessment (FRAIA)* (31 July 2021), www.government.nl/documents/reports/2021/07/31/impact-assessment-fundamental-rights-and-algorithms (accessed 30 July 2024).

IT Flows, www.itflows.eu (accessed 21 July 2024).

Japan 2019: Council for Social Principles of Human-centric AI, *Social Principles for Human-Centric AI*, Japan Cabinet Secretariat (2029), www.cas.go.jp/jp/seisaku/jinkouchinou/pdf/humancentricai.pdf (accessed 21 July 2024).

Mirror, h2020mirror.eu (accessed 21 July 2024).

Statewatch 2024: Statewatch, *The EU Migration Pact: A Dangerous Regime of Migrant Surveillance* (10 April 2024), www.statewatch.org/news/2024/april/the-eu-migration-pact-a-dangerous-regime-of-migrant-surveillance (accessed 21 July 2024).

The White House 2023: The White House, *Executive Order on the Safe, Secure, and Trustworthy Development and Use of Artificial Intelligence*, Briefing Room (30 October 2023), www.whitehouse.gov/briefing-room/presidential-actions/2023/10/30/executive-order-on-the-safe-secure-and-trustworthy-development-and-use-of-artificial-intelligence (accessed 30 July 2024).

The White House 2022: The White House, *Blueprint for an AI Bill of Rights: Making Automated Systems Work for the American People*, Office of Science and Technology Policy (2022), www.whitehouse.gov/ostp/ai-bill-of-rights (accessed 30 July 2024).

ARTICLE 2(1) Definition: AI System

Sonja Dürager

Article 2. Definitions

For the purposes of this Directive, the following definitions shall apply:
(1) 'AI system' means an AI system as defined in [Article 3(1) of the AI Act]; ...

Recitals

(15) Consistency with [the AI Act] should also be ensured. It is therefore appropriate for this Directive to use the same definitions in respect of AI systems, providers and users. In addition, this Directive should only cover claims for damages when the damage is caused by an output or the failure to produce an output by an AI system through the fault of a person, for example the provider or the user under [the AI Act]. There is no need to cover liability claims when the damage is caused by a human assessment followed by a human act or omission, while the AI system only provided information or advice which was taken into account by the relevant human actor. In the latter case, it is possible to trace back the damage to a human act or omission, as the AI system output is not interposed between the human act or omission and the damage, and thereby establishing causality is not more difficult than in situations where an AI system is not involved.

RELATED ARTICLES

Article 3 (Disclosure of evidence and rebuttable presumption of non-compliance); Article 4 (Rebuttable presumption of a causal link in the case of fault).

RELATED LAWS

AI Act.

RELATED CASE LAW

Austria

Austrian Supreme Court 2007: Austrian Supreme Court, of 22 November 2007, 8 ObA 70/07p; Arb 12.716 = SZ 2007/182.

COMMENTARY

1 Purpose

The starting point for the question of liability is the damage caused by an artificial intelligence (AI) system. The legislator himself mentions as reason for the new liability rules, *inter alia*, the autonomy of such systems. In his view, characteristics of AI systems such as opacity/lack of transparency and explainability, autonomous behaviour, complexity, continuous adaptation and lack of predictability, make the application of existing liability rules uncertain or more difficult. The definition of the term AI system is therefore central to the effectiveness of the AI Liability Directive (AILD). In order to create consistency with the regulatory framework in the AI Act, the AILD refers to the AI Act with regard to the definition of AI system and high-risk AI system.[1]

2 Legal Background

2.1 International

The Organisation for Economic Co-operation and Development (OECD) Recommendation was the first intergovernmental standard on AI and was adopted by the OECD's Council at the Ministerial level on 22 May 2019 on the proposal of the Committee on Digital Economy Policy (CDEP). It included the following definition of an AI system:[2]

> An AI system is a machine-based system that can, for a given set of human-defined objectives, make predictions, recommendations, or decisions influencing real or virtual environments. AI systems are designed to operate with varying levels of autonomy.

In order to ensure the OECD Recommendation continues to be technically accurate and reflect technological developments, including with respect to generative AI (GenAI), the OECD AI Principles, however, adapted the definition of AI system on 8 November 2023. Compared to the original Council's definition it is now more comprehensive:

> An AI system is a machine-based system that, for explicit or implicit objectives, infers, from the input it receives, how to generate outputs such as predictions, content, recommendations, or decisions that can influence physical or virtual

1. *See* Explanatory Memorandum to the AILD, s. 5., *Other Elements, 2. Definitions.*
2. *See* OECD Recommendation.

> environments. Different AI systems vary in their levels of autonomy and adaptiveness after deployment.

In particular, this reference to interdependencies with autonomy has been taken for the AI Act from the OECD definition by the European Union (EU). The OECD definition posits that systems can have varying levels of autonomy, a sentiment that is shared by the AI Act, which uses the same words in the definition of AI systems (Article 3).

2.2 European Union

Article 2(1) of the AILD refers for the sake of consistency to the definition of 'AI system' as defined in the AI Act. Article 3(1) of the AI Act defines 'AI system' as:

> a machine-based system that is designed to operate with varying levels of autonomy and that may exhibit adaptiveness after deployment, and that, for explicit or implicit objectives, infers, from the input it receives, how to generate outputs such as predictions, content, recommendations, or decisions that can influence physical or virtual environments.

The definition of AI systems has evolved since the discussions about regulating AI started; now it is very close to the definition that has been prepared by the OECD and considers, as mentioned under Article 2(1), the latest update of the definition.[3]

It is important to mention that the AI Act also applies to general-purpose AI (GPAI) models,[4] and in particular stipulates certain obligations on providers of such models.[5] The original text of the regulation did not provide for this classification for AI models at all, in contrast, the compromise text of the Council Mandate still provided for requirements for GPAI systems and obligations for providers of such systems. It was clarified that GPAI systems are AI systems that are intended by the provider to perform generally applicable functions, such as image/speech recognition, and in a plurality of contexts. They may be used as high-risk AI systems by themselves or be components of other high-risk AI systems.[6] However, the term 'GPAI models' was not explicitly mentioned. This compromise addressed the regulation surrounding foundation models.

3 Analysis

'AI' is not a clearly defined homogenous technology, but rather a method for solving specific tasks depending on the area of application. Finding a definition is therefore not

3. Russell et al. 2023.
4. AIA, Art. 51 lays down the definition for GPAI model, what means an AI model, including when trained with a large amount of data using self-supervision at scale, that displays significant generality and is capable to competently perform a wide range of distinct tasks regardless of the way the model is placed on the market and that can be integrated into a variety of downstream systems or applications.
5. *See ibid.*, Art. 53.
6. *Ibid.*, Rec. 12.

only difficult for legal scholars; the term AI is not even clearly defined among experts.[7] According to a much-cited definition, AI describes a branch of computer science that deals with methods and technologies that enable a computer to solve tasks that, when solved by humans, require intelligence.[8] This makes a definition by the European legislator all the more important. Legal definitions fulfil a linguistic-economic function because if a certain term is used several times in law, it only has to be defined once how this term is to be understood.[9] Legal definitions determine in a binding manner how a certain legal term is to be understood. They preclude recourse to general usage or to a deviating understanding of a technical language.[10]

One of the main focuses of the EU legislator with the determination of legal terms was to distinguish AI from simpler traditional software systems or programming approaches. It says that the AI Act:[11]

> should not cover systems that are based on the rules defined solely by natural persons to automatically execute operations.

This is important because for traditional software products that only perform an 'if-then' link, the question of responsibility for safeguarding against security risks or for liability in the event of errors in programming or in the application can be answered from existing security regulations and liability regimes. The EU legislator only sees a need for regulation in such autonomous systems that are only slightly deterministic, which should mean that the actual behaviour of such a system can deviate significantly from the initial conditions and is therefore unpredictable.

For this characteristic of an AI system, the legislator uses the term autonomy. The definition in Article 2(1) of the AILD in conjunction with Article 3(1) of the AI Act therefore determines 'AI systems' and prescribes as the main feature for differentiating AI systems from software programs (which do not use AI) autonomy and adaptiveness after deployment. Recital 6 of the AI Act explains that AI systems are designed to operate with varying levels of autonomy, meaning that they have some degree of independence of actions from human involvement and of capabilities to operate without human intervention. Hence, according to Recital 6, the concept of autonomy of an AI system relates to the degree to which such a system functions without human involvement.[12] The adaptiveness that an AI system could exhibit after deployment, refers to self-learning capabilities, allowing the system to change while in use.[13]

In addition to autonomy or autonomous behaviour, the legislator also sees in opacity and complexity the specific characteristics of certain AI systems, which may make it excessively difficult, if not impossible, for the injured person to meet this burden of proof.[14] This topic is also mentioned in the AI Act, and in order to address

7. *See also* Reinisch 2019, 298, 299.
8. Siepermann (undated).
9. *See* Kodek 2015, Rz 76 mwN.
10. *See, e.g.*, Austrian Supreme Court 2007.
11. AIA, Rec. 12.
12. Commission 2018.
13. AIA, Rec. 6.
14. AILD, Rec. 3.

these criteria of AI systems transparency should be required for high-risk AI systems before they are placed on the market or put into service.[15]

3.1 *Autonomous or Automatic Behaviour of AI Systems?*

Autonomy is neither defined in the AILD nor is it based on a general understanding of the term that requires no further interpretation, and it is also unclear what the different levels of autonomy are supposed to mean and how they are to be differentiated. It is moreover unclear whether this reference to autonomy means that systems can be fully or partly autonomous or whether AI can exist at all without autonomy.

The AI Act seemingly proposes that AI systems can only be partially autonomous, not fully, and that a human must always be in the loop, and if this does not apply the system is qualified as high-risk system (*see* Articles 6 and 7(2) of the AI Act),[16] with the consequence that it must be ensured that the system shall be designed and developed in such a way, that they can be effectively overseen by natural persons during the period in which the AI system is in use.[17] As a consequence, it seems that an AI system under the AI Act never acts fully 'autonomously', because a human always has the possibility to override a decision or recommendations (either *ex ante* or *ex post*). But what is the difference compared to ordinary software?

The way 'autonomy' is described varies between the legal acts and the technical standard issued by International Organization for Standardization (ISO) about AI defines AI systems[18] differently. It says that AI systems are designed to operate with varying levels of automation,[19] but not autonomy. By contrast, the AI Act as well as the OECD guidelines refer to autonomy. 'Autonomy' means a characteristic of a system that is capable of modifying its operating domain or goal without external intervention, control or oversight.[20] 'Automation' is pertaining to a process or system that, under specified conditions, functions without human intervention.[21] From a technical point of view, it is obvious that autonomy is not equivalent to automation, and that these two terms refer to different technical features.

Autonomy is defined in the technical standard about 'Information technology – Artificial intelligence – Artificial intelligence concepts and terminology'[22] as 'characteristic of a system that is capable of modifying its intended domain of use or goal without external intervention, control or oversight'. Hence, the technical standard recognizes autonomy as a feature of technical systems in general, and further, such systems are not necessarily automated. However, as already mentioned, the term

15. *See* AIA, Rec. 47.
16. The AIA opens the possibility for provider to document that an AI system referred to in Annex III is not high-risk on the basis of certain criteria demonstrating that the systems do not materially influence the decision-making or do not harm those interests substantially (*see* Rec. 53).
17. *See ibid.*, Art. 14.
18. ISO/IEC DIS 22989(en).
19. ISO, Art. 3, No. 3.1.4.
20. *Ibid.*, Art. 3, No. 3.1.5.
21. *Ibid.*, Art. 3, No. 3.1.7.
22. *Ibid.*, No. 3.1.5.

autonomy must be distinguished from the term automation, and if you analyse the technical definition of automation more closely – a process or system that, under specified conditions, functions without human intervention – this term certainly seems to describe the dreaded risk.

For these reasons, the AI Act might have meant 'automation',[23] but used the more popular term autonomous/autonomy to describe automation. However, this wording might, unfortunately, suggest that AI is equated with autonomous systems, which would be wrong, because on the one hand, AI systems also exist without autonomy, and on the other hand varying digital systems could also have this ability to produce decisions/actions.

It shall be noted that, prior to the proposal of the AI Act, the Commission did not equate AI system with autonomy. It was moreover the intention to revise the concept of liability with regard to emerging digital technologies (e.g., advanced robots or devices empowered by AI and internet of things (IoT)) and their characteristics, which includes the feature of autonomy.[24] The exact technical distinction between technologies with and without an AI system will pose considerable practical difficulties. Even the technical standard of ISO refers to this misconception in the AI Act; it makes a note under No. 7.1.5. mentioning that in jurisprudence, autonomy refers to the capacity for self-governance, and that in this sense, also, 'autonomous' is a misnomer as applied to automated AI systems, because even the most advanced AI systems are not self-governing. The ISO standard further explains that rather, AI systems operate based on algorithms and otherwise obey the commands of operators.

3.2 What Are Different Levels of Autonomy?

Further, it remains unclear what should be understood under 'levels of autonomy' and which levels exist. It is questionable, whether it refers to a quantitative or a qualitative threshold, and if quantitative, how much autonomy constitutes one element, or which level is required to pass the threshold.

The OECD had discussed the autonomy levels,[25] however, the AI Act does not include this explanation. According to the OECD, the acting human or machine uses the outcome from the AI system (more specifically, the outcome from the inferencing

23. It should be mentioned that also the General Data Protection Regulation (GDPR) refers in Art. 22, which deals with systems that act to a certain extent without human intervention, to 'automated' decision-making.
24. Furthermore, these technologies will encompass more and more the feature of autonomy. Advanced robots or devices empowered by AI and IoT will have increased capabilities to interpret the environment (via sensing, actuating, cognitive vision, machine learning, etc.), to interact with humans, to cooperate with other artefacts, to learn new behaviours and execute actions autonomously without human intervention. The more autonomous systems are, the less they depend on other actors (e.g., the manufacturer, the owner, the user) and the greater is their impact on their environment and on third parties. Combined with self-learning and autonomy, the behaviour of these technologies may be difficult to predict. This could raise questions regarding liability, in situations where the damage caused by a machine operating with a certain degree of autonomy cannot be linked to a defect or a human wrongdoing (Commission 2018, 16).
25. OECD 2022.

process) to perform an action - prescribed by humans - that influences the environment in which the system operates. The way in which this action is performed determines the autonomy level of an AI system; that is, the degree to which a system can act without human involvement. The OECD has referred to a typology with four levels:[26]

(1) No-action autonomy (System cannot act on its recommendations or output. The human uses or disregards the AI system's recommendations or output at will).
(2) Low-action autonomy (System evaluates input and acts upon its recommendations or output if the human agrees).
(3) Medium-action autonomy (System evaluates input and acts upon its recommendations or output unless the human vetoes).
(4) High-action autonomy (System evaluates input and acts upon its recommendations or output without human involvement).

A very well-known standard on autonomy levels comes from the Platform Industry 4.0.[27] According to Platform Industry 4.0, autonomy level 0 would mean the operation of industrial production without AI-based automation. Humans have full control and responsibility, and even extensive, simple automation may be present. Level 5, however, describes the fully autonomous operation of production under AI guidance. In this case, the AI system takes over the entire decision-making and execution. Levels 1 to 4 accordingly describe the gradations in between, whereby AI does not necessarily have to be used at every level. Autonomy levels define the system limits of the AI technologies used, and which tasks may be performed. In relation to AI, the degree of autonomy specifies the general system limits within which AI is allowed to operate, i.e., also non-technical limits of the AI technology used, such as legal or ethical limits.[28]

The AILD itself does not solve this topic; in particular, it is also unclear whether the legislator is referring to the autonomy levels proclaimed by the OECD or the Platform Industry 4.0, or whether a different demarcation is meant. It only says that it is not intended to regulate cases in which damage occurs as a result of a person using AI to assist them in their actions or omissions; however, this would apply to almost all levels of autonomy, even if humans can only monitor the tasks listed or set reactions, e.g., if the machine refers a decision back to the human under certain circumstances. The usual rules on damages shall apply in such scenarios, as it is no more difficult to prove causality than in other factual constellations in which software is used instead of the AI system for support.[29] However, this does not explain what other gradations there are in the degree of autonomy, apart from the levels at which either the human or the AI system alone sets the action.

26. *Ibid.*, at 53.
27. Federal Ministry 2021.
28. *Ibid.*, at 20.
29. *See* AIA, Rec. 6.

3.3 *Conclusion*

The application of the presumption of causality depends on it being proven that a technically produced decision originates from a system that utilizes autonomy. However, as already mentioned, autonomy occurs in a large number of complex digital systems that use rule-based algorithms designed to automatically execute rules encoded by their programmers (e.g., robots),[30] which is why the AILD almost appears to be an unobjective overregulation, especially since the danger recognized by the legislator is more likely to come from systems that supplement its knowledge base purely on the basis of empirical data and observations without outside help and derive conclusions from it ('deep learning') and is therefore even inappropriate in terms of content. AI systems not having more autonomy than other types of software could as a consequence of the definition in Article 3 of the AI Act be dealt with under the new liability rules. Such algorithms, which then normally follow the classical 'if- then logic', normally, do not put victims of harm in a fundamentally more difficult situation than other types of software.

Overall, the intention to protect humans from incorrect decisions by AI systems is understandable, but it should not be prematurely concluded that we are dealing with a degenerate technology that acts independently and leads to previously unknown risks. In this respect, it is questionable whether the approach chosen by the legislator of constituting liability rules for operators of AI systems using (a certain level of) autonomy is the optimal approach, and moreover adequate for drawing a sharp line to software programs that work with different automated functions.

BIBLIOGRAPHY

Reports and Recommendations

Commission 2018: Commission, *Commission Staff Working Document, Liability for Emerging Digital Technologies Accompanying the Document Communication from the Commission to the European Parliament, the European Council, the Council, the European Economic and Social Committee and the Committee of the Regions Artificial intelligence for Europe* (25 April 2018), SWD(2018) 137 final, eur-lex.europa.eu/legal-content/DE/ALL/?uri=CELEX%3A52018SC0137 (accessed 5 May 2024).

OECD 2022: OECD, *Framework for the Classification of AI Systems* (published on 22 February 2022), www.oecd.org/publications/oecd-framework-for-the-classification-of-ai-systems-cb6d9eca-en.htm (accessed 5 May 2024).

OECD Recommendation.

30. ISO 8373:2021(en), Robot: programmed actuated mechanism with a degree of autonomy (3.2) to perform locomotion, manipulation or positioning.

Academic Writings

Kodek 2015: Georg Kodek, *§ 6 in Austrian Civil Law Code Act* (Peter Rummel & Meinhard Lukas eds, Stand 1 July 2015).

Reinisch 2019: Fabian Reinisch, *Artificial Intelligence: Questions on Liability 4.0 and Other Civil Law Considerations on Autonomous Systems*, ÖJZ 2019/37.

Russell et al. 2023: Stuart Russell, Karine Perset & Marko Grobelnik, *Updates to the OECD's Definition of an AI System Explained*, OECD.AI Policy Observatory (29 November 2023), oecd.ai/en/wonk/ai-system-definition-update (accessed 7 April 2024).

Siepermann (undated): Markus Siepermann, *Künstliche Intelligenz (KI)*, Gabler Wirtschaftslexikon (Springer undated), wirtschaftslexikon.gabler.de/definition/kuenstliche-intelligenz-ki-40285 (accessed 10 December 2023).

Others

Federal Ministry 2021: Federal Ministry for Economic Affairs and Energy Germany, *Working Paper: Technology Scenario 'Artificial Intelligence in Industry 4.0'* (13 June 2021), www.plattform-i40.de/IP/Redaktion/DE/Downloads/Publikation/KI-industrie-40.html (accessed 5 May 2024).

ISO/IEC 22989:2022(E): ISO, *Information Technology: Artificial Intelligence: Artificial Intelligence Concepts and Terminology*.

ISO 8373:2021(E): ISO, *Robotics: Vocabulary*.

ARTICLE 2(2) Definition: High-Risk AI System

Sonja Dürager

Article 2. Definitions

For the purposes of this Directive, the following definitions shall apply: ...
(2) 'high-risk AI system' means an AI system referred to in [Article 6 of the AI Act] ...

Recitals

(15) Consistency with [the AI Act] should also be ensured. It is therefore appropriate for this Directive to use the same definitions in respect of AI systems, providers and users. In addition, this Directive should only cover claims for damages when the damage is caused by an output or the failure to produce an output by an AI system through the fault of a person, for example the provider or the user under [the AI Act]. There is no need to cover liability claims when the damage is caused by a human assessment followed by a human act or omission, while the AI system only provided information or advice which was taken into account by the relevant human actor. In the latter case, it is possible to trace back the damage to a human act or omission, as the AI system output is not interposed between the human act or omission and the damage, and thereby establishing causality is not more difficult than in situations where an AI system is not involved.

RELATED ARTICLES

Article 3 (Disclosure of evidence and rebuttable presumption of non-compliance); Article 4 (Rebuttable presumption of a causal link in the case of fault).

RELATED LAWS

AI Act (Article 6).

COMMENTARY

1 Purpose

This Directive aims to provide persons seeking compensation for damage caused by high-risk artificial intelligence (AI) systems with effective means to identify potentially liable persons and relevant evidence for a claim. In this respect, Article 3(1) of the AI Liability Directive (AILD) provides that a court may order the disclosure of relevant evidence about specific high-risk AI systems that are suspected of having caused damage.[1] Article 3 refers to high-risk AI systems and Article 4 distinguishes between high-risk AI systems and non-high-risk AI systems, and applies the presumption of causality which is introduced in Article 3 to a different extent. Hence, the reference to the definition of high-risk AI systems in Article 6 of the AI Act is of great importance.

2 Legal Background

2.1 International

The Organisation for Economic Co-operation and Development (OECD) published in 2022, a classification framework[2] which describes key aspects of an applied AI system, including the various contexts in which it impacts the real world, the nature and type of data and input, the various AI models, and the types of tasks it executes and output it produces. Information derived from this framework for a specific use case, augmented by information on governance and risk mitigation processes, could be useful in assessing the associated ethical and societal risks of an applied AI system, which may have considerable practical significance for stakeholders in numerous contexts – policymaking, business, etc. The risks of using any AI system strongly depend on the application. Since it is difficult to anticipate and assess every possible use case, applied AI systems should be grouped into a small collection of risk levels.

The framework was meant to provide the basis for developing a future risk-assessment framework to help with diminishing and mitigating risks.

2.2 Council of Europe

The Council of Europe is also working on rules for the use of AI systems. The Council of Europe's Committee on Artificial Intelligence (CAI) had been asked by the Council of Europe to create a suitable legal instrument for the use of AI systems by November 2023. The AI Convention sets out principles and obligations aimed at ensuring that the design, development, use and decommissioning of AI systems are fully consistent with respect for human dignity and individual autonomy, human rights and fundamental freedoms, the functioning of democracy and the observance of the rule of law. It also

1. *See* Explanatory Memorandum to the AILD, s. 5., *Other Elements, 3. Disclosure of Evidence.*
2. OECD 2022.

adopted a risk-based approach,[3] which has its basis in the recommendations of the Council of Europe's Ad hoc Committee on Artificial Intelligence (CAHAI),[4] where it was said that the legal requirements for the design, development and use of AI systems should be proportionate to the nature of the risk they pose to human rights, democracy and the rule of law.

3 Analysis

The AILD aims to provide persons seeking compensation for damage caused by (high-risk) AI systems and prescribes presumption rules if the defendant is the provider of a high-risk AI system. Hence, the concept of the AI Act to qualify AI systems as high-risk or not is of great importance for the AILD. The limitation of disclosure of evidence, as regards high-risk AI systems, was justified by the AILD with the structure of the AI Act, which provides certain specific documentation, record keeping and information obligations for operators involved in the design, development and deployment of high-risk AI systems (Recital 18). Considering that, with the final AI Act, a number of principles were introduced, that have to be adhered to by operators that develop and use general-purpose AI (GPAI) models[5] and GPAI systems,[6] and further, GPAI models with systemic risks, it is questionable if this distinction still maintains the necessary proportionality between operators of AI systems posing higher or lower risk considering that now even providers of GPAI models (Article 53) or providers of GPAI models with systemic risks (Article 55) are obliged to document certain information.

The AI Act distinguishes between two different types of GPAI models, and outlines obligations into two tiers:[7]

(1) several uniformed obligations for all GPAI models; and
(2) an additional set of obligations for GPAI models with systemic risks.

All GPAI model providers must adhere to transparency requirements, which require developing technical documentation with detailed summaries about the content used for training. Additionally, these organizations must comply with the European Union (EU) copyright law to ensure ethical use of content. Further, GPAI models encompassing systemic risk will be subjected to more stringent obligations, including evaluating AI model evaluations, assessing and mitigating risk, using adequate security measures, reporting severe incidents, ensuring proper security measures, and reporting on energy

3. AI Convention, Art. 2: In order to give full effect to the principles and obligations set out in this Convention, each Party shall maintain and take such graduated and differentiated measures in its domestic legal system as may be necessary and appropriate in view of the severity and probability of occurrence of adverse impacts on human rights and fundamental freedoms, democracy and the rule of law during design, development, use and decommissioning of AI systems.
4. CAHAI 2022.
5. *See* AIA, Art. 53.
6. *See ibid.*, Art. 50.
7. *Ibid.*, Annex XI lists the required technical documentation referred to in Art. 53(1)(a) for providers of GPAI models (s. 1) and additional documentation for providers of GPAI model with systemic risk (s. 2).

efficiency. In particular, GPAI models with systemic risks could also affect individuals if such models, e.g., propagate harmful biases in the downstream applications they are integrated into. However, according to the current wording of the AILD, these would not be taken into account.

Another classification made in the final AI Act is relevant to the scope of the AILD. Article 3(63) of the AI Act stipulates the definition of a GPAI system, which means an AI system which is based on a GPAI model, that has the capability to serve a variety of purposes, both for direct use as well as for integration in other AI systems. Such systems can be used directly or as components of an AI system, hence these types of AI systems are also relevant to define the scope of the AILD. The wording of the AILD must be clarified if such GPAI models, which are by definition AI systems, shall also be covered by the AILD. This could be relevant in supply chain structures, where the failure of the AI system is caused by the GPAI model.

Also, the list of AI systems to be classified as high-risk were expanded, e.g.:

- AI systems intended for remote biometric identification of natural persons;
- AI systems intended to be used for biometric categorization, according to sensitive or protected attributes or characteristics based on the inference of those attributes or characteristics;
- AI systems intended to be used for emotion recognition; and
- AI systems intended to be used for risk assessment and pricing in relation to natural persons in the case of life and health insurance.

Many AI systems that only prepare human decisions would then also fall under Annex III of the AI Act. However, this excessive scope of application is now restricted again in Article 6(3). Namely, AI systems shall not be considered high risk if they do not pose a significant risk of harm, to the health, safety or fundamental rights of natural persons, including by not materially influencing the outcome of decision-making (Article 6(3)),[8] what gives providers the opportunity to self-exempt (Article 6(4)).

Hence, Article 6(4) provides for this, that where providers falling under one or more of the critical areas and use cases referred to in Annex III of the AI Act consider that their AI system does not pose a significant risk as described in Article 6(3), they shall submit a notification reasoning why they are not subject to the requirements to the national supervisory authority (e.g., if an AI systems intended to be used for recruitment or selection of natural persons[9] does only provide preparatory output for a decision that must be made by a human). Apart from this documentation providers of such systems with a reduced risk, only have to register their system in the EU

8. This shall be the case if one or more of the following criteria are fulfilled, 'if the AI system is intended to (merely) perform a narrow procedural task'; 'if the AI system improves the result of a previously completed human activity'; 'if the AI system is intended to detect decision-making patterns or deviations from prior decision-making patterns and is not meant to replace or influence the previously completed human assessment, without proper human review'; or 'if the AI system performs a preparatory task to an assessment relevant for the purpose of the use cases listed in Annex III'.
9. *See* AIA, Annex III (4)(a).

database.[10] Even if the supervisory authority could make objections against this classification within three months after notification, and the AI system may not be put on the market before the deadline has expired unused, this, however, might call into question the effectiveness of the reversal of the burden of proof for AI systems with high risk. Thus, it can be assumed that in particular, the large AI providers have the expertise and resources to justify why a system does not pose a risk that is significant as a result of the combination of its severity, intensity, probability of occurrence, and duration of its effects, and its ability to affect an individual, a plurality of persons or to affect a particular group of persons (*see* the definition of significant risk in Article 6(3)).

In the end, this possibility for providers to be exempt as well as the introduction of systemic risk with GPAI models make it more difficult[11] for consumers to find out whether the AI system that caused the damage falls under the AILD or not.

BIBLIOGRAPHY

Reports and Recommendations

AI Convention.

CAHAI 2022, CAHAI, *Recommendations on Possible Elements of a Legal Framework on Artificial Intelligence*, CM(2021)173-add, 1425th meeting (16 February 2022), search.coe.int/cm/Pages/result_details.aspx?ObjectId=0900001680a4e8a5 (accessed 5 May 2024).

Commission 2018: Commission, *Commission Staff Working Document, Liability for Emerging Digital Technologies Accompanying the Document Communication from the Commission to the European Parliament, the European Council, the Council, the European Economic and Social Committee and the Committee of the Regions Artificial intelligence for Europe*, SWD(2018) 137 final (25 April 2018), eur-lex.europa.eu/legal-content/DE/ALL/?uri=CELEX%3A52018SC0137 (accessed 5 May 2024).

OECD 2022: OECD, *Framework for the Classification of AI Systems* (22 February 2022), www.oecd.org/publications/oecd-framework-for-the-classification-of-ai-systems-cb6d9eca-en.htm (accessed 5 May 2024).

Academic Writings

Bomhard & Siglmüller 2024: David Bomhard & Jonas Siglmüller, *AI Act: das Trilogergebnis*, 45 RDi 24 (2024).

10. *Ibid.*, Art. 49(2) in conjunction with Art. 71.
11. *See, e.g.*, Bomhard & Siglmüller 2024.

ARTICLE 2(3) Definition: Provider

Miriam C. Buiten

Article 2. Definitions

For the purposes of this Directive, the following definitions shall apply: ...
(3) 'provider' means a provider as defined in [Article 3(3) of the AI Act]; ...

Recitals

(15) Consistency with [the AI Act] should also be ensured. It is therefore appropriate for this Directive to use the same definitions in respect of AI systems, providers and users. In addition, this Directive should only cover claims for damages when the damage is caused by an output or the failure to produce an output by an AI system through the fault of a person, for example the provider or the user under [the AI Act]. There is no need to cover liability claims when the damage is caused by a human assessment followed by a human act or omission, while the AI system only provided information or advice which was taken into account by the relevant human actor. In the latter case, it is possible to trace back the damage to a human act or omission, as the AI system output is not interposed between the human act or omission and the damage, and thereby establishing causality is not more difficult than in situations where an AI system is not involved.

(17) The large number of people usually involved in the design, development, deployment and operation of high-risk AI systems, makes it difficult for injured persons to identify the person potentially liable for damage caused and to prove the conditions for a claim for damages. To allow injured persons to ascertain whether a claim for damages is well-founded, it is appropriate to grant potential claimants a right to request a court to order the disclosure of relevant evidence before submitting a claim for damages. Such disclosure should only be ordered where the potential claimant presents facts and information sufficient to support the plausibility of a claim for damages and it has made a prior request to the provider, the person subject to the obligations of a provider or the user to disclose such evidence at their disposal about specific high-risk AI systems that are suspected of having caused damage which has been refused. Ordering disclosure should lead to a reduction of unnecessary litigation and avoid costs for the possible litigants caused by claims which are unjustified or likely to be unsuccessful. The refusal of the provider, the person subject to the obligations of a provider or

the user prior to the request to the court to disclose evidence should not trigger the presumption of non-compliance with relevant duties of care by the person who refuses such disclosure.

(19) National courts should be able, in the course of civil proceedings, to order the disclosure or preservation of relevant evidence related to the damage caused by high-risk AI systems from persons who are already under an obligation to document or record information pursuant to [the AI Act], be they providers, persons under the same obligations as providers, or users of an AI system, either as defendants or third parties to the claim. There could be situations where the evidence relevant for the case is held by entities that would not be parties to the claim for damages but which are under an obligation to document or record such evidence pursuant to [the AI Act]. It is thus necessary to provide for the conditions under which such third parties to the claim can be ordered to disclose the relevant evidence.

(26) This Directive covers the fault constituting non-compliance with certain listed requirements laid down in Chapters 2 and 3 of [the AI Act] for providers and users of high-risk AI systems, the non-compliance with which can lead, under certain conditions, to a presumption of causality. The AI Act provides for full harmonisation of requirements for AI systems, unless otherwise explicitly laid down therein. It harmonises the specific requirements for high-risk AI systems. Hence, for the purposes of claims for damages in which a presumption of causality according to this Directive is applied, the potential fault of providers or persons subject to the obligations of a provider pursuant to [the AI Act] is established only through a non-compliance with such requirements. Given that in practice it may be difficult for the claimant to prove such non-compliance when the defendant is a provider of the AI system, and in full consistency with the logic of [the AI Act], this Directive should also provide that the steps undertaken by the provider within the risk management system and the results of the risk management system, i.e. the decision to adopt or not to adopt certain risk management measures, should be taken into account in the determination of whether the provider has complied with the relevant requirements under the AI Act referred to in this Directive. The risk management system put in place by the provider pursuant to [the AI Act] is a continuous iterative process run throughout the lifecycle of the high-risk AI system, whereby the provider ensures compliance with mandatory requirements meant to mitigate risks and can, therefore, be a useful element for the purpose of the assessment of this compliance. This Directive also covers the cases of users' fault, when this fault consists in non-compliance with certain specific requirements set by [the AI Act]. In addition, the fault of users of high-risk AI systems may be established following non-compliance with other duties of care laid down in Union or national law, in light of Article [26(2)] of [the AI Act].

RELATED ARTICLES

Article 3 (Disclosure of evidence and rebuttable presumption of non-compliance); Article 4 (Rebuttable presumption of a causal link in the case of fault).

RELATED LAWS

AI Act; Draft Compromise AI Act 2021: Draft Compromise Amendments on the Proposal for a Regulation (EU) 2021/0106(COD) of the European Parliament and of the Council on harmonized rules on Artificial Intelligence (Artificial Intelligence Act) and amending certain Union Legislative Acts, COM(2021)0206; New Product Liability Directive.

COMMENTARY

1 Purpose

Article 2(3) of the AI Liability Directive (AILD) aims to clarify the definition of 'provider' that should apply under the Directive, as part of the Directive's aim to harmonize non-contractual civil liability for damages caused by artificial intelligence (AI) systems.[1]

2 Analysis

The AILD addresses both users and providers of AI.[2] The AILD speaks of providers, operators and users of AI systems but does not define 'operators'. This approach diverges from the Parliament's proposal for AI liability, which focused on holding 'operators', or 'backend developers' liable for AI-related harm.[3] The Parliament proposed strict liability for operators or 'backend developers' of AI systems.[4]

By including providers next to users, the AILD recognizes the central role of AI producers in ensuring the safe design of AI and the limited control users may have over AI.[5]

Relevant to the scope of the AILD are both the AI Act, to which it refers and the Product Liability Directive, including its review, which the AILD aims to complement.[6]

2.1 Relation to the AI Act

The AILD aims to harmonize specific aspects of fault-based liability rules for claims involving AI-related harm against either providers or users of AI systems. The AILD

1. AILD, 11.
2. Operators are mentioned in AILD, Art. 5(2) and Rec. 31, as well as at 5-6 and 18.
3. Parliament Resolution 2020; Parliament Report 2020. *See also* Wagner 2022. *Consider further* Parliament Draft Report 2020, Annex Rec. 7.
4. Parliament Resolution 2020; Parliament Report 2020.
5. Geistfeld 2017; Buiten et al. 2023; Buiten 2024; Zech 2020; Wagner 2019.
6. AILD, 3.

follows the definitions of provider and user in the AI Act,[7] aiming to ensure consistency.[8]

The AI Act defines 'provider' in Article 3(3) as:[9]

> a natural or legal person, public authority, agency or other body that develops an AI system or a general-purpose AI model or that has an AI system or a general-purpose AI model developed and places it on the market or puts the AI system into service under its own name or trademark, whether for payment or free of charge.

Compared to the initial proposal, the final text excludes AI systems merely intended to be placed on the market[10] while explicitly adding general-purpose AI models to the definition.

2.2 Developing

The AI Act distinguishes the development of an AI system from its deployment. 'Developing' AI involves designing, coding or producing the AI system. This meaning can be inferred from the definition of AI system in the AI Act, which refers to an AI system as:[11]

> a machine-based system that is designed to operate with varying levels of autonomy and that may exhibit adaptiveness after deployment, and that, for explicit or implicit objectives, infers, from the input it receives, how to generate outputs such as predictions, content, recommendations, or decisions that can influence physical or virtual environments.

The AI developer is presumed to wield control over design decisions, while the deployer assumes control over the subsequent uses of the AI system.[12]

2.3 Placing on the Market or Putting into Service

The AI Act defines 'placing on the market' as the first making available of an AI system or a general-purpose AI model on the European Union (EU) market.[13] 'Making available on the market' means any supply of an AI system or a general-purpose AI

7. *Ibid.*, Art. 2(3) notes that 'provider' means a provider as defined in AIA, Art. 3(3).
8. *Ibid.*, Rec. 15.
9. Moreover, AIA, Art. 2(1)(a) states that the Regulation applies to 'providers placing on the market or putting into service AI systems in the Union, irrespective of whether those providers are established within the Union or in a third country'.
10. Earlier versions defined 'provider' as 'a natural or legal person, public authority, agency or other body that develops an AI system or that has an AI system developed *with a view to placing it on the market* or putting it into service under its own name or trademark, whether for payment or free of charge' (*emphasis added*). *See* Draft Compromise AI Act 2021.
11. AIA, Art. 3(1).
12. BSA 2023.
13. AIA, Art. 3(9).

model for distribution or use on the EU market in the course of a commercial activity, whether in return for payment or free of charge.[14]

The term provider also includes those who put the system into service, meaning the supply of an AI system for first use directly to the deployer or for own use on the EU market for its intended purpose.[15] The AI Act also states that the provider is responsible for placing on the market or putting into service a high-risk AI system, 'regardless of whether that natural or legal person is the person who designed or developed the system'.[16] These provisions make clear that developing or designing is not the dividing line between being a provider or a deployer; what matters is the responsibility for placing the system on the market or putting it into service, regardless of who produced it. This interpretation is confirmed by Article 25(1)(b) of the AI Act, which stipulates that a deployer may become a user if they 'make a substantial modification to a high-risk AI system that has already been placed on the market or has already been put into service'.[17]

In practice, the line between developers and deployers of AI may be difficult to draw. Providers include entities who put an AI system into service for their own use, while deployers use an AI system under their own authority.[18] This ambiguity may introduce legal uncertainty for those regulated by the AI Act, raising questions about whether they qualify as providers or deployers for a specific system.[19] This uncertainty is particularly significant due to the substantial implications for the obligations associated with being classified as a provider or deployer.

2.4 Relation to the Product Liability Directive Proposal

The AILD complements the New Product Liability Directive (NPLD) by delineating the allocation of liability for AI-related harm between manufacturers and users. The NPLD defines a manufacturer as:[20]

> any natural or legal person who develops, manufactures or produces a product or has a product designed or manufactured, or who markets that product under its name or trademark or who develops, manufactures or produces a product for its own use.

14. *Ibid.*, Art. 3(10).
15. *Ibid.*, Art. 3(11). According to Art. 3(12) 'intended purpose' means the use for which an AI system is intended by the provider, including the specific context and conditions of use, as specified in the information supplied by the provider in the instructions for use, promotional or sales materials and statements, as well as in the technical documentation.
16. *Ibid.*, Rec. 79.
17. *See also ibid.*, Art. 3(23), which defines a 'substantial modification' as 'a change to an AI system after its placing on the market or putting into service which is not foreseen or planned in the initial conformity assessment carried out by the provider'.
18. *Ibid.*, Art. 3(3) and (4).
19. *See, e.g.*, regarding the classification of researchers, Smuha et al. 2021; Ebers et al. 2021. AIA, Art. 2(12) excludes AI systems released under a free and open-source license under certain conditions.
20. NPLD, Art. 4(11).

Consequently, a provider assumes liability as a manufacturer under the NPLD for specific types of damage arising from defective AI systems. The provisions outlined in the AILD extend beyond product defects, addressing liability claims and damages not explicitly recognized by the NPLD.[21] This includes any damage defined by national law and claims brought forth by both natural and legal persons.[22] Notably, claims against providers related to harm resulting from discrimination or violations of fundamental rights, such as privacy, fall within the ambit of the AILD, as the NPLD does not cover them.

While the NPLD incorporates the term 'provider' within the definition of 'manufacturer', uncertainty remains regarding the allocation of roles.[23] The NPLD explicitly includes AI system providers, as defined in the AI Act, under the classification of a manufacturer.[24] Accordingly, some have concluded that the 'provider' in the AI Act is identical to the 'manufacturer' in the NPLD.[25]

However, the NPLD introduces a nuanced distinction by stating that 'the *developer or producer* of software, including AI system providers' (emphasis added) should be treated as a manufacturer.[26] Considering that the AI Act's term 'provider' encompasses individuals or entities who did not necessarily develop or design the AI system, it becomes challenging to reconcile how all AI Act providers could fit under the NPLD definition of a manufacturer, which places emphasis on designing, developing, or manufacturing the product. If the two terms were meant to overlap perfectly, this also raises questions about the intention behind these variations in terminology and definitions between the NPLD and the AI Act.

The correlation between AI Act providers and NPLD manufacturers holds significance for the AILD, as the AILD seeks to address liability gaps not covered by the NPLD while aligning with the provisions of the AI Act. The NPLD and the AILD complement the AI Act's product safety purpose but do not share identical goals with the AI Act. Attempting to establish horizontal definitions may pose challenges, as it could either significantly broaden the concept of manufacturer in the NPLD or result in interpretation issues and gaps within the liability framework of the NPLD and the AILD. Overall, it may be more beneficial to align the AILD scope with the term 'manufacturer' as defined in the NPLD directly, as this will not affect the AILD scope (which also includes users anyway).

21. AILD, Rec. 11.
22. *See also* Explanatory Memorandum, under 1: 'The Product Liability Directive covers producer's no-fault liability for defective products, leading to compensation for certain types of damages, mainly suffered by individuals. This proposal covers national liability claims mainly based on the fault of any person with a view of compensating any type of damage and any type of victim.'
23. *See, e.g.*, Smuha et al. 2021; *see also* Dheu et al. 2022.
24. AILD, Rec. 12: 'The developer or producer of software, including AI system providers within the meaning of [the AI Act], should be treated as a manufacturer.'
25. *See, e.g.*, Wagner, *supra* n. 3.
26. NPLD, Rec. 12.

BIBLIOGRAPHY

Reports and Recommendations

Parliament Draft Report 2020: Parliament, *Draft Report with Recommendations to the Commission on a Civil Liability Regime for Artificial Intelligence* (2020/2014(INL)), PE650.556v01-00 (27 April 2020).

Parliament Report 2020: Parliament, *Report with Recommendations to the Commission on a Civil Liability Regime for Artificial Intelligence* (2020/2014(INL)), A9-0178/2020.c (5 October 2020).

Parliament Resolution 2020: *Parliament, Resolution with Recommendations on a Civil Liability for Artificial Intelligence* (2020/2014(INL)), P9_TA-PROV(2020)0276 (20 October 2020).

Academic Writings

BSA 2023: BSA The Software Alliance, *AI Developers and Deployers: An Important Distinction*, Position Paper (16 March 2023), www.bsa.org/policy-filings/ai-developers-and-deployers-an-important-distinction (accessed 11 March 2024).

Buiten 2024: Miriam Buiten, *Product Liability for Defective AI*, 57 Eur. J. Law Econ. 239-273 (2024), doi.org/10.1007/s10657-024-09794-z.

Buiten et al. 2023: Miriam Buiten, Alexandre de Streel & Martin Peitz, *The Law and Economics of AI liability*, 48 CLSR 105794 (2023), doi.org/10.1016/j.clsr.2023.105794.

Dheu et al. 2022: Orian Dheu, Charlotte Ducuing, & Jan De Bruyne, *The Commission's Proposals for Adapting Liability Rules to the Digital Age. Part 1: The AI Liability Directive*, KU Leuven CiTiP Blog (3 November 2022), www.law.kuleuven.be/citip/blog/the-commissions-proposals-for-adapting-liability-rules-to-the-digital-age-part-1-the-ai-liability-directive (accessed 11 March 2024).

Ebers et al. 2021: Martin Ebers et al., *The European Commission's Proposal for an Artificial Intelligence Act: A Critical Assessment by Members of the Robotics and AI Law Society (RAILS)*, 4(4) J 589 (2021), doi.org/10.3390/j4040043.

Geistfeld 2017: Mark Geistfeld, *A Roadmap for Autonomous Vehicles: State Tort Liability, Automobile Insurance, and Federal Safety Regulation*, 105 Cal. L. Rev. 10 (2017).

Smuha et al. 2021: Nathalie A. Smuha et al., *How the EU Can Achieve Legally Trustworthy AI: A Response to the European Commission's Proposal for an Artificial Intelligence Act*, SSRN (5 August 2021), papers.ssrn.com/sol3/papers.cfm?abstract_id=3899991 (accessed 11 March 2024), doi.org/10.2139/ssrn.3899991.

Wagner 2022: Gerhard Wagner, *Liability Rules for the Digital Age: Aiming for the Brussels Effect*, 13(3) JETL 191 (2022).

Wagner 2019: Gerhard Wagner, *Robot Liability in Liability for Artificial Intelligence and the Internet of Things*, 27-62 (Sebastian Lohsse, Reiner Schulze & Dirk Staudenmayer eds, 2019).

Zech 2020: Herbert Zech, *Verhandlungen des 73. Deutschen Juristentages Hamburg 2020/Bonn 2022 Bd. I: Gutachten Teil A – Entscheidungen digitaler autonomer Systeme: Empfehlen sich Regelungen zu Verantwortung und Haftung?* (2020).

ARTICLE 2(4) Definition: User

Miriam C. Buiten

Article 2. Definitions

For the purposes of this Directive, the following definitions shall apply: ...
(4) 'user' means a user as defined in [Article 3(4) of the AI Act]; ...

Recitals

(15) Consistency with [the AI Act] should also be ensured. It is therefore appropriate for this Directive to use the same definitions in respect of AI systems, providers and users. In addition, this Directive should only cover claims for damages when the damage is caused by an output or the failure to produce an output by an AI system through the fault of a person, for example the provider or the user under [the AI Act]. There is no need to cover liability claims when the damage is caused by a human assessment followed by a human act or omission, while the AI system only provided information or advice which was taken into account by the relevant human actor. In the latter case, it is possible to trace back the damage to a human act or omission, as the AI system output is not interposed between the human act or omission and the damage, and thereby establishing causality is not more difficult than in situations where an AI system is not involved.

(17) The large number of people usually involved in the design, development, deployment and operation of high-risk AI systems, makes it difficult for injured persons to identify the person potentially liable for damage caused and to prove the conditions for a claim for damages. To allow injured persons to ascertain whether a claim for damages is well-founded, it is appropriate to grant potential claimants a right to request a court to order the disclosure of relevant evidence before submitting a claim for damages. Such disclosure should only be ordered where the potential claimant presents facts and information sufficient to support the plausibility of a claim for damages and it has made a prior request to the provider, the person subject to the obligations of a provider or the user to disclose such evidence at their disposal about specific high-risk AI systems that are suspected of having caused damage which has been refused. Ordering disclosure should lead to a reduction of unnecessary litigation and avoid costs for the possible litigants caused by claims which are unjustified or likely to be unsuccessful. The refusal of the provider, the person subject to the obligations of a provider

or the user prior to the request to the court to disclose evidence should not trigger the presumption of non-compliance with relevant duties of care by the person who refuses such disclosure.

(19) National courts should be able, in the course of civil proceedings, to order the disclosure or preservation of relevant evidence related to the damage caused by high-risk AI systems from persons who are already under an obligation to document or record information pursuant to [the AI Act], be they providers, persons under the same obligations as providers, or users of an AI system, either as defendants or third parties to the claim. There could be situations where the evidence relevant for the case is held by entities that would not be parties to the claim for damages but which are under an obligation to document or record such evidence pursuant to [the AI Act]. It is thus necessary to provide for the conditions under which such third parties to the claim can be ordered to disclose the relevant evidence.

(26) This Directive covers the fault constituting non-compliance with certain listed requirements laid down in [Chapters 2 and 3] of [the AI Act] for providers and users of high-risk AI systems, the non-compliance with which can lead, under certain conditions, to a presumption of causality. The AI Act provides for full harmonization of requirements for AI systems, unless otherwise explicitly laid down therein. It harmonises the specific requirements for high-risk AI systems. Hence, for the purposes of claims for damages in which a presumption of causality according to this Directive is applied, the potential fault of providers or persons subject to the obligations of a provider pursuant to [the AI Act] is established only through a non-compliance with such requirements. Given that in practice it may be difficult for the claimant to prove such non-compliance when the defendant is a provider of the AI system, and in full consistency with the logic of [the AI Act], this Directive should also provide that the steps undertaken by the provider within the risk management system and the results of the risk management system, i.e. the decision to adopt or not to adopt certain risk management measures, should be taken into account in the determination of whether the provider has complied with the relevant requirements under the AI Act referred to in this Directive. The risk management system put in place by the provider pursuant to [the AI Act] is a continuous iterative process run throughout the lifecycle of the high-risk AI system, whereby the provider ensures compliance with mandatory requirements meant to mitigate risks and can, therefore, be a useful element for the purpose of the assessment of this compliance. This Directive also covers the cases of users' fault, when this fault consists in non-compliance with certain specific requirements set by [the AI Act]. In addition, the fault of users of high-risk AI systems may be established following non-compliance with other duties of care laid down in Union or national law, in light of Article [26 (2)] of [the AI Act].

(29) The application of the presumption of causality is meant to ensure for the injured person a similar level of protection as for situations where AI is not involved and where causality may therefore be easier to prove. Nevertheless, alleviating the burden of proving causation is not always appropriate under this Directive where the defendant is not a professional user but rather a person using the AI system for its private activities. In such circumstances, in order to balance interests between the injured person and the non-professional user, it needs to be taken into account whether such non-

> professional users can add to the risk of an AI system causing damage through their behaviour. If the provider of an AI system has complied with all its obligations and, in consequence, that system was deemed sufficiently safe to be put on the market for a given use by non-professional users and it is then used for that task, a presumption of causality should not apply for the simple launch of the operation of such a system by such non-professional users. A non-professional user that buys an AI system and simply launches it according to its purpose, without interfering materially with the conditions of operations, should not be covered by the causality presumption laid down by this Directive. However, if a national court determines that a non- professional user materially interfered with the conditions of operation of an AI system or was required and able to determine the conditions of operation of the AI system and failed to do so, then the presumption of causality should apply, where all the other conditions are fulfilled. This could be the case, for example, when the non- professional user does not comply with the instructions of use or with other applicable duties of care when choosing the area of operation or when setting performance conditions of the AI system. This is without prejudice to the fact that the provider should determine the intended purpose of an AI system, including the specific context and conditions of use, and eliminate or minimise the risks of that system as appropriate at the time of the design and development, taking into account the knowledge and expertise of the intended user.

RELATED ARTICLES

Article 3 (Disclosure of evidence and rebuttable presumption of non-compliance); Article 4 (Rebuttable presumption of a causal link in the case of fault).

RELATED LAWS

AI Act; AI Act Commission Proposal; AI Act Council Proposal.

COMMENTARY

1 Purpose

The purpose of the AI Liability Directive (AILD) is to contribute to the functioning of the internal market by laying down uniform requirements for some aspects of non-contractual civil liability for damages by involved artificial intelligence (AI) systems.[1] Article 2(4) of the AILD aims to clarify the definition of 'user' that should apply under the Directive.

1. AILD, 11.

2 Analysis

The definition of user in the AILD aligns with the AI Act's definition of user[2] to ensure consistency.[3] The initial AI Act proposal addressed providers and users. The AI Act definition of 'user' has changed during the legislative process. The original version of the AI Act defined a user as:[4]

> any natural or legal person, public authority, agency or other body using an AI system under its authority, except where the AI system is used in the course of a personal, non-professional activity.

The Council version removed the last part of the definition, effectively including consumers.[5] The Parliament version of the AI Act coined users as deployers, given that the term could create confusion, as in most cases, users are not responsible for the compliance of certain products.[6] The final version of the AI Act addresses the 'deployer' and defines it as:[7]

> any natural or legal person, public authority, agency or other body using an AI system under its authority, except where the AI system is used in the course of a personal non-professional activity.

Due to AI development's complex and demanding nature, the deployers of AI systems will outnumber those who produce and provide high-risk AI systems.[8] The phrase 'a personal non-professional activity' in the AI Act's definition of deployers is designed to exclude consumers from this category. The AI Act assigns monitoring responsibilities to providers and deployers, specifically excluding end users or consumers.[9] However, aligning the AI Act's term 'deployer' with the addressees of the AILD is problematic. While the AI Act shields AI end users, including consumers, from deployment-related responsibilities, they may still be liable for negligence under national tort law. This liability could arise from actions such as neglecting safety measures or improper use of AI devices.[10]

The AILD aims to harmonize liability rules for AI-related harm that AI producers cannot reasonably avoid.[11] However, adopting the AI Act's term for users in the AILD does not work, as the two legislations serve different purposes. The AI Act focuses on product safety, including responsibilities for compliance, while the AILD complements

2. *Ibid.*, Art. 2(3) notes that 'provider' means a provider as defined in AIA, Art. 3(3).
3. AILD, Rec. 15; Madiega 2023.
4. AIA, Art. 3(4).
5. AI Act Council Proposal, Art. 3(4).
6. *See also* Demircan 2023; De Bruyne et al. 2023; The use of the term deployer rather than user was also proposed by Haataja & Bryson 2022, 3.
7. AIA, Art. 3(4).
8. Demircan 2023.
9. Haataja & Bryson 2022, 8-9.
10. Spindler 2019.
11. *See, e.g.*, Commission Q&A 2022, question 9; Schütte et al. 2021; Hacker 2023.

the New Product Liability Directive (NPLD)by holding non-producers accountable for AI-related harm, specifically targeting end users not covered by the NPLD.[12]

Instead of mirroring the AI Act, the AILD should align the boundaries of its 'user' term with the 'manufacturer' concept defined in the NPLD to create a coherent liability framework. These scope-related challenges highlight the complexities of formulating a consistent yet balanced technology-based regulatory framework.[13]

Formulating the term 'user' or 'deployer' in the final version of the AILD requires careful evaluation. These concepts should be aligned with the concept of 'manufacturer' in the NPLD.[14] The goal of the AILD is to establish harmonized rules for claims against those not serving as the manufacturers of AI. Consequently, the term 'user' should encompass all potential defendants in civil liability claims who are not the manufacturer.

One approach is to adopt the term 'deployer' but define it, as suggested in the Parliament Draft Report, as the person 'who decides on the use of the AI system, exercises control over the risk, and benefits from its operation'.[15] This definition closely corresponds to that of the 'frontend operator' in the Parliament Resolution.[16] However, for clarity, it may be preferable to eliminate the vague expression 'control over the risk' and instead emphasize the user's choice to deploy or use the AI system.

BIBLIOGRAPHY

Reports and Recommendations

Parliament Draft Report 2020: Parliament, *Draft Report with Recommendations to the Commission on a Civil Liability Regime for Artificial Intelligence* (2020/2014(INL)), PE650.556v01-00 (27 April 2020).

Parliament Resolution 2020: Parliament, *Resolution with Recommendations on a Civil Liability for Artificial Intelligence* (2020/2014(INL)), P9_TA-PROV(2020)0276 (20 October 2020).

Academic Writings

Buiten 2019: Miriam Buiten, *Towards Intelligent Regulation of Artificial Intelligence*, 10(1) EJRR 41 (2019), doi.org/10.1017/err.2019.8.

De Bruyne et al. 2023: Jan De Bruyne, Orian Dheu & Charlotte Ducuing, *The European Commission's Approach to Extra-Contractual Liability and AI: An Evaluation of the AI Liability Directive and the Revised Product Liability Directive*, 51 CLSR 105894 (2023), doi.org/10.1016/j.clsr.2023.105894.

12. NPLD, Art. 7 holds manufacturers liable for defective products.
13. Buiten 2019.
14. NPLD, Art. 4(11) defines 'manufacturer' as any natural or legal person who develops, manufactures or produces a product or has a product designed or manufactured, or who markets that product under its name or trademark or who develops, manufactures or produces a product for its own use. Insofar as this definition overlaps with 'provider' in the AIA, this term could also be used (*see also* Buiten, Art. 2(3), in this volume).
15. Parliament Draft Report 2020, para. 11.
16. Parliament Resolution 2020, para. 12.

Demircan 2023: Muhammed Demircan, *Deployers of High-Risk AI Systems: What Will Be Your Obligations under the EU AI Act?*, Kluwer Competition Law Blog (2 June 2023), competitionlawblog.kluwercompetitionlaw.com/2023/06/02/deployers-of-high-risk-ai-systems-what-will-be-your-obligations-under-the-eu-ai-act (accessed 11 March 2024).

Haataja & Bryson 2022: Meeri Haataja & Joanna J. Bryson, *Reflections on the EU's AI Act and How We Could Make It Even Better*, TechREG Chronicle (March 2022).

Hacker 2023: Philipp Hacker, *The European AI Liability Directives: Critique of a Half-Hearted Approach and Lessons for the Future*, 51 CLSR 105871 (2023), doi.org/10.1016/j.clsr.2023.105871.

Schütte et al. 2021: Béatrice Schütte, Lotta Majewski & Katri Havu, *Damages Liability for Harm Caused by Artificial Intelligence: EU Law in Flux*, 69 Helsinki Legal Studies Research Paper 16 (2021), doi.org/10.2139/ssrn.3897839.

Spindler 2019: Gerald Spindler, *User Liability and Strict Liability in the Internet of Things and for Robots*, 128 (Sebastian Lohsse, Rainer Schulze & Dirk Staudenmayer eds, 2019).

Others

Commission Q&A 2022: Commission, *Questions and Answers on the Revision of the Product Liability Directive* (28 September 2022), ec.europa.eu/commission/presscorner/detail/en/qanda_22_5791 (accessed 11 March 2024).

Madiega 2023: Tambiama Madiega, *Briefing Artificial Intelligence Liability Directive*, European Parliamentary Research Service (February 2023), www.europarl.europa.eu/RegData/etudes/BRIE/2023/739342/EPRS_BRI(2023)739342_EN.pdf (accessed 11 March 2024).

ARTICLE 2(5) Definition: Claim for Damages

Florence Danis, Gert-Jan Hendrix & Jasper Bellon

Article 2. Definitions

For the purposes of this Directive, the following definitions shall apply: ...

(5) 'claim for damages' means a non-contractual fault-based civil law claim for compensation of the damage caused by an output of an AI system or the failure of such a system to produce an output where such an output should have been produced; ...

Recitals

(7) The purpose of this Directive is to contribute to the proper functioning of the internal market by harmonising certain national non-contractual fault-based liability rules, so as to ensure that persons claiming compensation for damage caused to them by an AI system enjoy a level of protection equivalent to that enjoyed by persons claiming compensation for damage caused without the involvement of an AI system. This objective cannot be sufficiently achieved by the Member States because the relevant internal market obstacles are linked to the risk of unilateral and fragmented regulatory measures at national level. Given the digital nature of the products and services falling within the scope of this Directive, the latter is particularly relevant in a cross-border context.

(15) Consistency with [the AI Act] should also be ensured. It is therefore appropriate for this Directive to use the same definitions in respect of AI systems, providers and users[1]. In addition, this Directive should only cover claims for damages when the damage is caused by an output or the failure to produce an output by an AI system through the fault of a person, for example the provider or the user under [the AI Act]. There is no need to cover liability claims when the damage is caused by a human assessment followed by a human act or omission, while the AI system only provided information or advice which was taken into account by the relevant human actor. In the latter case, it is possible to trace back the damage to a human act or omission, as the AI system output

1. At the time when the AILD came out, the draft AIA referred to 'users' of high-risk AI systems. This was changed in the final version of the AIA to 'deployers'. References in this article to 'users' of high-risk AI systems should therefore be understood as 'deployers'.

is not interposed between the human act or omission and the damage, and thereby establishing causality is not more difficult than in situations where an AI system is not involved.

RELATED ARTICLES

Article 1 (Subject matter and scope); Article 3 (Disclosure of evidence and rebuttable presumption of non-compliance); and Article 4 (Rebuttable presumption of a causal link in the case of fault).

RELATED LAWS

AI Act; Product Liability Directive; New Product Liability Directive; Antitrust Damages Directive.

COMMENTARY

1 Purpose

Article 2(5) sets out a definition for the concept of 'claim for damages'.

This is one of the core concepts defining the scope of the provisions of the AI Liability Directive (AILD). Indeed, only (potential) claimants in the context of claims for damages can benefit from the mechanisms easing the burden of proof introduced by the AILD. As such, the precise meaning of 'claim for damages' is of the essence to determine whether any given (potential) claimant may enjoy those benefits or not.

2 Analysis

2.1 Introduction

Article 2(5) defines the concept of 'claim for damages' and forms part of a general article only containing definitions of terms utilized throughout the AILD. The definitions in Article 2 follow those of the AI Act to ensure consistency, which is of course a practice to be commended.[2] The concept of 'claim for damages' is, however, not utilized in the AI Act and is therefore not defined there. This is not surprising considering the fact that the AI Act is meant to encompass only a general legislative framework for artificial intelligence (AI), with the element of liability related to AI being organized in the AILD, albeit to a limited extent.

The precise meaning of the concept of 'claim for damages' is of particular importance to determine the scope of the provisions of the AILD. The disclosure of evidence mechanism of Article 3, for example, applies only in the context of a claim for

2. AILD, Rec. 15; *see also* AILD, 12.

damages, or, if such a claim has not yet been initiated, when the potential claimant is at least able to show the plausibility of a claim for damages.[3] Similarly, the rebuttable presumption set out in Article 4 applies only when national courts are 'applying liability rules to a claim for damages'.[4]

The definition of 'claim for damages' set out in Article 2(5) of the AILD is rather dense, consisting of several components. This means that a given (potential) claim must fulfil multiple cumulative conditions to be considered a 'claim for damages' under the AILD. Indeed, it must qualify as:

- a non-contractual claim;
- a fault-based civil law claim; and
- a claim for compensation for the damage caused by an output of an AI system or the failure of such a system to produce an output where such an output should have been produced.

The definition of 'claim for damages' is being used to determine – and more specifically, to limit – the scope of the AILD and thus of the new mechanisms easing the burden of proof introduced by the Directive.

In doing so, the AILD sets itself apart from certain previous pieces of legislation such as the Antitrust Damages Directive. The Antitrust Damages Directive includes certain measures easing the burden of proof similar to those set out in the AILD. However, the concept 'claim for damages' is defined much more broadly in Article 2(5) of that Directive, being 'a claim for compensation for harm caused by an infringement of competition law'.

Indeed no reference is made to (and therefore no scope limitation is added concerning) the nature of the claim, as opposed to the definition in the AILD which limits 'claims for damages' to 'non-contractual fault-based civil law claims'. In addition, concerning the required cause of the harm, the definition in the Antitrust Damages Directive makes only a generic reference to 'harm caused by an infringement of competition law' as opposed to the definition in the AILD which refers to a specific set of facts ('damage caused by an output of an AI system or the failure of such a system to produce an output where such an output should have been produced').

In what follows, the three main components of the definition of 'claim for damages' in the AILD will be discussed in turn.

2.2 *Assessment of the Various Components of the Definition*

2.2.1 *Non-Contractual Claim*

First of all, to qualify as a 'claim for damages' under the AILD, a (potential) claim must qualify as 'non-contractual'.

3. *See* Danis, Hendrix & Bellon on *Art. 3*, in this volume.
4. *See* De Bruyne & Schollaert on *Art. 4*, in this volume.

According to the European Parliamentary Research Service, a non-contractual claim (for compensation of damage) is a compensation claim 'irrespective of a contractual link between the victim and the liable person'.[5] This stands opposite to contractual (compensation) claims which are based on a legally qualified relationship – i.e., generally a contract – that exists between the parties before the damage occurs.[6]

This relatively straightforward theoretical distinction can cause issues in practice. This is particularly the case when a party to a contract incurs damage due to the actions or negligence of its counterparty to the contract which may constitute both a breach of contract and a non-contractual fault. That situation raises the question of which type of compensation claim the damage-incurring party can introduce: can they only base their compensation claim on the provisions of the contract, or can they opt to base their claim on the relevant rules concerning non-contractual liability? If a choice can indeed be made, can both avenues be pursued at the same time?

Different Member States have adopted different solutions. In many jurisdictions, contractual liability claims compete with non-contractual claims, providing (potential) claimants with a choice as to the legal basis of their claim.[7] In others, such as France, Romania or Hungary, contractual liability claims in principle exclude alternative claims based on non-contractual liability (although certain exceptions usually exist).[8] To make the matter more complex, the solution adopted in a given Member State may itself evolve over time, such as in Belgium, where competing contractual and non-contractual claims were traditionally not possible but will soon be possible, following the adoption of a new legislation on extracontractual liability regime.

What does this difference in national rules mean for the application of the AILD? As mentioned, the benefits of the AILD apply only in the context of (potential) non-contractual liability claims. As a result, claimants faced with damage caused by a counterparty to a contract may be deprived of these benefits depending on what the national law applicable to their situation provides concerning the possibility of opting for the application of the (national) rules on non-contractual liability to their claim. In a jurisdiction where they can opt to file a non-contractual claim against their counterparty, the provisions of the AILD can be applied if they indeed choose the non-contractual route. In a jurisdiction where claimants are forced to opt for the route of contractual liability, however, claimants would be barred from relying on and benefitting from, the AILD.

One of the objectives of the AILD is reducing legal uncertainty, in particular for businesses trading across borders as they risk being faced with different rules in different jurisdictions.[9] Unfortunately, in view of the above, an unintended consequence of limiting the concept of 'claim for damages' to non-contractual claims may

5. Madiega 2023, 5.
6. *See, e.g.*, Bertolini 2020, 10.
7. Karner et al. 2020, 20-21.
8. *Ibid.*
9. *See, e.g.*, AILD, Recs 7-9; *see also* AILD, 2: 'Businesses will have difficulties to predict how the existing liability rules will be applied, and thus to assess and insure their liability exposure. The effect will be magnified for businesses trading across borders, as the uncertainty will cover different jurisdictions.'

under certain circumstances actually be an *increase* in legal uncertainty, as businesses will experience difficulties in predicting which liability rules will apply.

2.2.2 *Fault-Based Civil Law Claim*

Second, to qualify as a 'claim for damages', the relevant (potential) non-contractual claim must also qualify as a 'fault-based civil law claim'.

In the words of the Policy Department for Citizens' Rights and Constitutional Affairs (in a study requested by the Parliament's Committee on Legal Affairs):[10]

> fault-based liability ... establishes the duty to compensate damages upon the subject who negligently failed to maintain a desired standard of behaviour, causing damages.

Fault-based claims usually require proving the existence of a fault of the liable party, the existence of damage, and a causal link between the fault and the damage.[11] Fault-based liability is common to all Member States (although the precise rules may differ) and is usually considered to be the general standard.[12]

Generally speaking, two other avenues for non-contractual liability claims exist in the European Union (EU):[13]

- strict liability, which is liability independent of fault, or in other words, liability assigned to a person for certain risks without the need to prove a fault;[14] and
- product liability, i.e., the liability of a producer for defective products.[15]

Interestingly, as part of its starting position concerning the AILD, the Parliament recommended a strict liability regime for high-risk autonomous AI systems.[16] This proposal was not adopted: by limiting the definition of 'claim for damages' to fault-based claims, claims on the basis of strict liability or product liability are excluded from the benefits of the AILD.

Certain types of (sometimes strict) product liability are, however, already harmonized at the EU level by means of the Product Liability Directive (PLD). A revamping of the PLD is part of the legislative package on AI which also includes the AI Act and the AILD.[17]

Finally, the addition of 'civil law' to the definition of 'claim for damages' appears to simply be intended to exclude criminal liability from the scope of the AILD.[18] The Commission did expressly note in its proposal for the AILD that the provisions of the

10. Bertolini 2020, 10.
11. Madiega 2023, 2; Dheu et al. 2022; Buiten et al. 2023, 3.
12. Bertolini 2020, 10; Buiten et al. 2023, 3.
13. Madiega 2023, 2-3.
14. *Ibid.*, at 2.
15. *Ibid.*, at 3.
16. Parliament Resolution 2020, No. 14.
17. AILD, 2.
18. *Ibid.*, at 11.

Directive may apply to state liability. It presumably chose to make this explicit because state liability is approached in different ways by Member States, not always being based on the relevant state's (default) rules on non-contractual liability.[19]

2.2.3 *Claim for Compensation of Damage Caused by an Output of an AI System or the Failure of Such a System to Produce an Output*

Finally, the (potential) non-contractual fault-based civil law claim concerned must also qualify as a:

> claim for compensation of the damage caused by an output of an AI system or the failure of such a system to produce an output where such an output should have been produced.

It is to be noted, first of all, that the concept of 'damage' is not defined in the AILD. One of the Commission's concerns in drafting its proposal for the Directive appears to have been that the measures therein needed to be able to 'fit without friction in existing civil liability systems'.[20] This would not have been the case, according to the Commission, if the Directive would have defined fundamental concepts like 'fault' or 'damage' as the meaning thereof varies across Member States.[21] It nevertheless remains true that not providing a definition of such concepts at the EU level limits the harmonising effect of the Directive. This is particularly the case considering that the rules on which kinds of damage are to be remedied vary widely between Member States.[22]

Second, Recital 15 to the AILD deserves particular attention in this context. The relevant part of this Recital reads as follows:

> In addition, this Directive should only cover claims for damages when the damage is caused by an output or the failure to produce an output by an AI system through the fault of a person, for example, the provider or the user under the AI Act. *There is no need to cover liability claims when the damage is caused by a human assessment followed by a human act or omission, while the AI system only provided information or advice* which was taken into account by the relevant human actor. *In the latter case, it is possible to trace back the damage to a human act or omission,* as the AI system output is not interposed between the human act or omission and the damage, *and thereby establishing causality is not more difficult than in situations where an AI system is not involved.* (*emphasis added*).

It follows that the precise wording of the definition of 'claim for damages' appears to be intended to exclude from the scope of the AILD those situations in which a human act or omission has intervened between the output of the AI system and the damage when this intervention can be considered to have caused the damage.

However, this may cause quite some uncertainty as the Recital does not address the question of when damage should be considered 'caused by a human assessment'.

19. Wagner 2022, 222.
20. AILD, 11.
21. *Ibid.*
22. Karner et al. 2020, 22.

In particular, doubt arises as to whether (potential) claimants are supposed to be able to rely on the measures introduced by the AILD in case the damage could be considered to be partially caused by both the AI system and the subsequent human intervention, which may in fact often be the case. More generally, and as for the concept of 'damage', the AILD does not define the fundamental concept of causality. Various aspects of causation are, however, treated differently across Member States. The standard of proof, for example, ranges from a likelihood just exceeding 50% in some Member States to near certainty in others.[23] Cases of causal uncertainty (where multiple events could have caused the damage) are treated very differently as well, with some Member States attributing the damage to all potential tortfeasors jointly and severally, whereas other Member States require that these potential tortfeasors acted jointly, and still others, strive to find the essential cause.[24]

It follows that it is unclear when (potential) claimants will be able to rely on the measures implemented by the AILD in situations where a human assessment may or may not have 'caused' the damage after receiving input from an AI system and that the answer to this question is likely to differ depending on the applicable national law. It is therefore also uncertain which degree of 'human assessment' may lead to the loss of the benefit of these measures. It is possible that in some jurisdictions it will be accepted – due to the national rules concerning causality or due to judicial interpretation – that a relatively formal human assessment or review suffices to break the causal link between the output of the AI system and the damage, leading to the inapplicability of the measures set out in the AILD. In a worst-case scenario, such interpretation risks leading to circumvention through the implementation of an almost formal human review.[25]

The above illustrates, in any event, once again that not defining or detailing fundamental concepts (such as damage and causality) at the EU level, even if done for valid reasons, limits the harmonising effect of the AILD and introduces a certain level of legal uncertainty.

BIBLIOGRAPHY

Reports and Recommendations

Bertolini 2020: Andrea Bertolini, *Study: Artificial Intelligence and Civil Liability*, Parliament, Policy Department for Citizens' Rights and Constitutional Affairs (July 2020), www.europarl.europa.eu/RegData/etudes/STUD/2020/621926/IPOL_STU(2020)621926_EN.pdf (accessed 11 March 2024).

Karner et al. 2020: Ernst Karner, Bernhard A. Koch & Mark A. Geistfeld, *Comparative Law Study on Civil Liability for Artificial Intelligence*, Commission, Directorate-General for Justice and Consumers (November 2020), data.europa.eu/doi/10.2838/77360 (accessed 11 March 2024).

23. *Ibid.*, 24-25.
24. *Ibid.*, at 36.
25. Hacker 2023, 13.

Madiega 2023: Tambiama Madiega, *Briefing: Artificial Intelligence Liability Directive*, Parliament, European Parliamentary Research Service (February 2023), www.europarl.europa.eu/RegData/etudes/BRIE/2023/739342/EPRS_BRI(2023)739342_EN.pdf (accessed 11 March 2024).

Parliament Resolution 2020: Parliament Resolution of 20 October 2020 with recommendations to the Commission on a civil liability regime for artificial intelligence (2020/2014(INL)), OJ. C. 404 (6 October 2021).

Academic Writings

Buiten et al. 2023: Miriam Buiten, Alexandre De Streel & Martin Peitz, *The Law and Economics of AI Liability*, 48 Computer Law & Security Review (2023), doi.org/10.1016/j.clsr.2023.105794.

Dheu et al. 2022: Orjan Dheu, Charlotte Ducuing & Jan De Bruyne, *The Commission's Proposals for Adapting Liability Rules to the Digital Age. Part 1: The AI Liability Directive*, CiTiP (3 November 2022), www.law.kuleuven.be/citip/blog/the-commissions-proposals-for-adapting-liability-rules-to-the-digital-age-part-1-the-ai-liability-directive (accessed 11 March 2024).

Hacker 2023: Philipp Hacker, *The European AI Liability Directives: Critique of a Half-Hearted Approach and Lessons for the Future*, 51 Computer Law & Security Review (2023), doi.org/10.1016/j.clsr.2023.105871.

Wagner 2022: Gerhard Wagner, *Liability Rules for the Digital Age: Aiming for the Brussels Effect*, 13 Journal of European Tort Law 3 (2022).

ARTICLE 2(6) Definition: Claimant

Sonja Dürager

Article 2. Definitions

(6) 'claimant' means a person bringing a claim for damages that:
  (a) has been injured by an output of an AI system or by the failure of such a system to produce an output where such an output should have been produced;
  (b) has succeeded to or has been subrogated to the right of an injured person by virtue of law or contract; or
  (c) is acting on behalf of one or more injured persons, in accordance with Union or national law. ...

Recitals

(15) Consistency with [the AI Act] should also be ensured. It is therefore appropriate for this Directive to use the same definitions in respect of AI systems, providers and users. In addition, this Directive should only cover claims for damages when the damage is caused by an output or the failure to produce an output by an AI system through the fault of a person, for example the provider or the user under [the AI Act]. There is no need to cover liability claims when the damage is caused by a human assessment followed by a human act or omission, while the AI system only provided information or advice, which was taken into account by the relevant human actor. In the latter case, it is possible to trace back the damage to a human act or omission, as the AI system output is not interposed between the human act or omission and the damage, and thereby establishing causality is not more difficult than in situations where an AI system is not involved.

RELATED ARTICLE

Article 6 (Amendment to Article 6 (Amendment to Directive (EU) 2020/1828)).

RELATED LAWS

Representative Actions Directive.

COMMENTARY

1 Purpose

This provision clarifies the active legitimation of an injured party in a claims process and further introduces the possibility for class action.

2 Analysis

2.1 Damage

Article 2(6)(a) of the AI Liability Directive (AILD) clarifies that a plaintiff only has a claim for damages if the condition is fulfilled within the meaning of Article 2(5) of the AILD that the relevant damage was caused by the output of an artificial intelligence (AI) system or the failure to produce n output.

There is no need to cover liability claims when the damage is caused by a human assessment followed by a human act or omission, while the AI system only provided information or advice, which was taken into account by the relevant human actor (Recital 15).

This restriction is consistent because there are also special challenges in AI systems when it comes to proving the link between the action or omission of the tortfeasor and the output of the AI. At the same time, it also provides for facilitations in proving the causal link (Article 4).

2.2 Subrogation

Article 2(6)(b) of the AILD provides that claims for damages can be brought not only by the injured person but also by persons who have succeeded in or have been subrogated into the injured person's rights. Subrogation is the assumption by a third party (such as an insurance company) of another party's legal right to collect a debt or damages. Thus, one person is entitled to enforce the rights of another for their own benefit. Subrogation would also cover the heirs of a deceased victim.

This clarification of the legitimization to assert a claim by a third party is very important, as this is not regulated throughout the European Union (EU) and it therefore differs nationally whether only the directly injured party or also a third party who has only suffered indirect damage (e.g., insurance) can claim compensation. The AILD only provides that if the directly injured party does not suffer any financial disadvantage because a third party had to bear the economic risk due to a special legal relationship with the injured party (subrogation), this third party is also entitled to claim compensation.

2.3 *Representative Actions*

Article 2(6)(c) provides that an action for damages can also be brought by someone acting on behalf of one or more injured parties, in accordance with Union or national law. This provision aims to give more possibilities to persons injured by an AI system to have their claims assessed by a court, even in cases where individual actions may seem too costly or too cumbersome to bring, or where joint actions may entail a benefit of scale.

With Article 6 of the AILD, a new point 67 has been added in Annex I to the Representative Actions Directive in order to make clear that against infringements by traders of the provisions under the AILD representative actions can be brought by consumer organizations.[1]

1. *See* Ferreres Comella, *Art. 6*, in this volume.

ARTICLE 2(7) Definition: Potential Claimant

Sonja Dürager

Article 2. Definitions

(7) 'potential claimant' means a natural or legal person who is considering but has not yet brought a claim for damages;

Recitals

(17) The large number of people usually involved in the design, development, deployment and operation of high-risk AI systems, makes it difficult for injured persons to identify the person potentially liable for damage caused and to prove the conditions for a claim for damages. To allow injured persons to ascertain whether a claim for damages is well-founded, it is appropriate to grant potential claimants a right to request a court to order the disclosure of relevant evidence before submitting a claim for damages. Such disclosure should only be ordered where the potential claimant presents facts and information sufficient to support the plausibility of a claim for damages and it has made a prior request to the provider, the person subject to the obligations of a provider or the user to disclose such evidence at their disposal about specific high-risk AI systems that are suspected of having caused damage which has been refused. Ordering disclosure should lead to a reduction of unnecessary litigation and avoid costs for the possible litigants caused by claims which are unjustified or likely to be unsuccessful. The refusal of the provider, the person subject to the obligations of a provider or the user prior to the request to the court to disclose evidence should not trigger the presumption of non-compliance with relevant duties of care by the person who refuses such disclosure.

RELATED ARTICLE

Article 3 (Disclosure of evidence and rebuttable presumption of non-compliance).

RELATED LAWS

Austria

Austrian Code of Civil Procedure (ACCP): Law of 1 August 1895 on the judicial procedure in civil disputes (Code of Civil Procedure – ZPO), as amended by the Federal Law Gazette I No. 77/2023. www.ris.bka.gv.at/GeltendeFassung.wxe?Abfrage=Bundesnormen&Gesetzesnummer=10001699 (accessed 5 May 2024).

RELATED CASE LAW

Austria

Court of Appeal Innsbruck 2021: Court of Appeal Innsbruck, judgment of 24 August 2021, 4R141/21y, www.ris.bka.gv.at/Dokument.wxe?Abfrage=Justiz&Dokumentnummer=JJT_20210824_OLG0819_00400R00141_21Y0000_000&Suchworte=RI0100083+384*+zpo* (accessed 5 May 2024).

COMMENTARY

1 Purpose

The main obstacle for claimants to enforce claims against the use of an artificial intelligence (AI) system is the need to demonstrate and prove the damaging effects. This is why the AI Liability Directive (AILD) introduces the term 'potential claimant'. This legal term is important to harmonize enforcement options because the national codes of civil procedure have different provisions on the plaintiff's burden of proof and not all Member States provide for a right to obtain evidence, which claim could be based on procedural (e.g., through pre-trial procedure) or substantive law. Ordering disclosure should lead to a reduction of unnecessary litigation and avoid costs for the possible litigants caused by claims, which are unjustified or likely to be unsuccessful.[1]

2 Legal Background

2.1 National

Sections 384 et seq. of the ACCP provide for the independent preservation of evidence procedure, which is carried out before any main proceedings are initiated.

Pursuant to section 384(1) of the ACCP, an application may be made to preserve evidence at any stage of the legal dispute if it is to be feared that the evidence would otherwise be lost, or its use made more difficult. According to section 384(2), such taking of evidence (inspection, examination of witnesses and experts) may, however, also be ordered without the requirements of paragraph 1 being met if the current

1. *See* AILD, Rec. 17.

condition of an object is to be determined and the applicant has a legal interest in this determination. The provision of section 384(2) of the ACCP is therefore to be understood as meaning that the preservation of evidence can also be authorized without proof of danger within the meaning of paragraph 1 if there is only a legal interest in establishing the current condition. This provision seeks to authorize the establishment of facts that may affect the applicant's legal position.[2]

As the results of the proceedings to preserve evidence help to clarify civil law positions in advance, the preservation of evidence also has components that avoid litigation. Hence, the provision has the same intention as the European legislator has pursued with the definition of a potential claimant (*see* Recital 17).

3 Analysis

In complex AI systems, it can be very difficult for the injured party to identify potential tortfeasors among the multitude of underlying tools and corresponding actors.[3] As a potential plaintiff, the injured party therefore already has the opportunity to enforce the claim for disclosure of the relevant evidence in court in order to be able to conclusively bring the action against the defendant with active legitimacy.

As a consequence, the AILD prescribes that the Member States shall ensure that national courts are empowered, upon the request of a potential claimant to order the disclosure of such evidence from those persons (Article 3(1)). The potential claimant must previously ask the provider or deployer of the AI system to disclose the relevant evidence out of court and can enforce this claim in court if it is rejected by the potential tortfeasor. In support of that request, the potential claimant must present facts and evidence sufficient to support the plausibility of a claim for damages. This ultimately ensures that information must only be provided in such events, where it is only possible to derive a claim under the AILD from the information provided by the potential claimant.

2. Court of Appeal Innsbruck 2021.
3. *See* AILD, Rec. 17.

ARTICLE 2(8) Definition: Defendant

Miriam C. Buiten

Article 2. Definitions

For the purposes of this Directive, the following definitions shall apply: ...
(8) 'defendant' means the person against whom a claim for damages is brought;
...

Recitals

(19) National courts should be able, in the course of civil proceedings, to order the disclosure or preservation of relevant evidence related to the damage caused by high-risk AI systems from persons who are already under an obligation to document or record information pursuant to [the AI Act], be they providers, persons under the same obligations as providers, or users of an AI system, either as defendants or third parties to the claim. There could be situations where the evidence relevant for the case is held by entities that would not be parties to the claim for damages but which are under an obligation to document or record such evidence pursuant to [the AI Act]. It is thus necessary to provide for the conditions under which such third parties to the claim can be ordered to disclose the relevant evidence.

(20) To maintain the balance between the interests of the parties involved in the claim for damages and of third parties concerned, the courts should order the disclosure of evidence only where this is necessary and proportionate for supporting the claim or potential claim for damages. In this respect, disclosure should only concern evidence that is necessary for a decision on the respective claim for damages, for example only the parts of the relevant records or data sets required to prove non-compliance with a requirement laid down by [the AI Act]. To ensure the proportionality of such disclosure or preservation measures, national courts should have effective means to safeguard the legitimate interests of all parties involved, for instance the protection of trade secrets within the meaning of Directive (EU) 2016/943 of the European Parliament and of the Council[[1]] and of confidential information, such as information related to public or national security. In respect of trade secrets or alleged trade secrets which the court has identified as confidential within the meaning of Directive (EU) 2016/943, national courts

1. [Trade Secrets Directive].

should be empowered to take specific measures to ensure the confidentiality of trade secrets during and after the proceedings, while achieving a fair and proportionate balance between the trade-secret holder's interest in maintaining secrecy and the interest of the injured person. This should include measures to restrict access to documents containing trade secrets and access to hearings or documents and transcripts thereof to a limited number of people. When deciding on such measures, national courts should take into account the need to ensure the right to an effective remedy and to a fair trial, the legitimate interests of the parties and, where appropriate, of third parties, and any potential harm to either party or, where appropriate, to third parties, resulting from the granting or rejection of such measures. Moreover, to ensure a proportionate application of a disclosure measure towards third parties in claims for damages, the national courts should order disclosure from third parties only if the evidence cannot be obtained from the defendant.

(21) While national courts have the means of enforcing their orders for disclosure through various measures, any such enforcement measures could delay claims for damages and thus potentially create additional expenses for the litigants. For injured persons, such delays and additional expenses may make their recourse to an effective judicial remedy more difficult. Therefore, where a defendant in a claim for damages fails to disclose evidence at its disposal ordered by a court, it is appropriate to lay down a presumption of non-compliance with those duties of care which that evidence was intended to prove. This rebuttable presumption will reduce the duration of litigation and facilitate more efficient court proceedings. The defendant should be able to rebut that presumption by submitting evidence to the contrary.

(22) In order to address the difficulties to prove that a specific input for which the potentially liable person is responsible had caused a specific AI system output that led to the damage at stake, it is appropriate to provide, under certain conditions, for a presumption of causality. While in a fault-based claim the claimant usually has to prove the damage, the human act or omission constituting fault of the defendant and the causality link between the two, this Directive does not harmonise the conditions under which national courts establish fault. They remain governed by the applicable national law and, where harmonised, by applicable Union law. Similarly, this Directive does not harmonise the conditions related to the damage, for instance what damages are compensable, which are also regulated by applicable national and Union law. For the presumption of causality under this Directive to apply, the fault of the defendant should be established as a human act or omission which does not meet a duty of care under Union law or national law that is directly intended to protect against the damage that occurred. Thus, this presumption can apply, for example, in a claim for damages for physical injury when the court establishes the fault of the defendant for non-complying with the instructions of use which are meant to prevent harm to natural persons. Non-compliance with duties of care that were not directly intended to protect against the damage that occurred do not lead to the application of the presumption, for example a provider's failure to file required documentation with competent authorities would not lead to the application of the presumption in claims for damages due to physical injury. It should also be necessary to establish that it can be considered reasonably likely, based on the circumstances of the case, that the fault has influenced the output produced by the AI system or the failure of the AI system to

produce an output. Finally, the claimant should still be required to prove that the output or failure to produce an output gave rise to the damage.

(28) The presumption of causality could also apply to AI systems that are not high-risk AI systems because there could be excessive difficulties of proof for the claimant. For example, such difficulties could be assessed in light of the characteristics of certain AI systems, such as autonomy and opacity, which render the explanation of the inner functioning of the AI system very difficult in practice, negatively affecting the ability of the claimant to prove the causal link between the fault of the defendant and the AI output. A national court should apply the presumption where the claimant is in an excessively difficult position to prove causation, since it is required to explain how the AI system was led by the human act or omission that constitutes fault to produce the output or the failure to produce an output which gave rise to the damage. However, the claimant should neither be required to explain the characteristics of the AI system concerned nor how these characteristics make it harder to establish the causal link.

(29) The application of the presumption of causality is meant to ensure for the injured person a similar level of protection as for situations where AI is not involved and where causality may therefore be easier to prove. Nevertheless, alleviating the burden of proving causation is not always appropriate under this Directive where the defendant is not a professional user but rather a person using the AI system for its private activities. In such circumstances, in order to balance interests between the injured person and the non-professional user, it needs to be taken into account whether such non-professional users can add to the risk of an AI system causing damage through their behaviour. If the provider of an AI system has complied with all its obligations and, in consequence, that system was deemed sufficiently safe to be put on the market for a given use by non-professional users and it is then used for that task, a presumption of causality should not apply for the simple launch of the operation of such a system by such non-professional users. A non-professional user that buys an AI system and simply launches it according to its purpose, without interfering materially with the conditions of operations, should not be covered by the causality presumption laid down by this Directive. However, if a national court determines that a non-professional user materially interfered with the conditions of operation of an AI system or was required and able to determine the conditions of operation of the AI system and failed to do so, then the presumption of causality should apply, where all the other conditions are fulfilled. This could be the case, for example, when the non-professional user does not comply with the instructions of use or with other applicable duties of care when choosing the area of operation or when setting performance conditions of the AI system. This is without prejudice to the fact that the provider should determine the intended purpose of an AI system, including the specific context and conditions of use, and eliminate or minimise the risks of that system as appropriate at the time of the design and development, taking into account the knowledge and expertise of the intended user.

(30) Since this Directive introduces a rebuttable presumption, the defendant should be able to rebut it, in particular by showing that its fault could not have caused the damage.

RELATED ARTICLES

Article 3 (Disclosure of evidence and rebuttable presumption of non-compliance); Article 4 (Rebuttable presumption of a causal link in the case of fault).

RELATED LAWS

AI Act; Trade Secrets Directive; New Product Liability Directive; Digital Services Act.

COMMENTARY

1 Purpose

The purpose of the AI Liability Directive (AILD) is to contribute to the functioning of the internal market by laying down uniform requirements for some aspects of non-contractual civil liability for damages by involved artificial intelligence (AI) systems.[2] Article 2(8) of the AILD aims to clarify the definition of 'defendant' that should apply under the Directive.

2 Analysis

The AILD grants specific rights to individuals affected by AI, complementing the AI Act, which primarily concentrates on establishing rules for AI development and deployment.[3] In the context of the AILD, a defendant refers to the person against whom a claim for damages is brought.[4] The AILD encompasses both providers[5] and users[6] of AI as addressees of the Directive and, consequently, possible 'defendants'. Notably, certain provisions in the AILD are directed at defendants in a general sense, while others specifically target either providers or users.[7] The AILD addresses defendants in non-contractual civil liability claims. For a claimant to seek damages under the AILD, they must demonstrate non-compliance with specific European Union (EU) or national obligations relevant to the harm caused by an AI system.[8] The AILD defines a 'claim for damages' as a non-contractual, fault-based civil law claim seeking compensation for harm caused by an output of an AI system or the failure of the system to produce an expected output.[9]

2. AILD, 11.
3. A person is 'affected' if they are subject to the adverse effects of an AI system. *See also* Schuett 2023; Hacker 2023.
4. AILD, Art. 2(8).
5. As defined in *ibid.*, Art. 2(3) (*see also* Buiten, *Art. 2(3)* in this volume).
6. As defined in *ibid.*, Art. 2(4) (*see also* Buiten, *Art. 2(4)* in this volume).
7. De Bruyne et al. 2023.
8. AILD, Art. 4(1)(a).
9. *Ibid.*, Arts 1(2) and 2(5).

The term 'defendant' encompasses anyone bound by a duty of care in EU or national law that intends to prevent harm caused by an AI system.[10] These duties include but are not limited to duties on providers and users as outlined in the Act. The nature and parties subject to these obligations depend on various laws. The definition of 'defendant' is thus ultimately determined by EU and national law that lays down duties of care and determines who has a right to claim damages. National rules that limit the scope of damages claims are relevant here, such as rules on fault, causality and protected interests.

The term 'defendant' has a broader scope than the addressees of other directives, such as the New Product Liability Directive (NPLD).[11] Unlike the NPLD, which focuses on manufacturers and entities in the supply chain, the AILD aims to prevent liability gaps by encompassing anyone capable of causing harm through AI systems.[12] The broader definition of 'defendant' in the AILD seeks to include all possible contributors to harm through AI, aligning with the directive's goal of preventing gaps in liability and compensation.[13] 'Defendants' may encompass a range of entities involved in AI systems. Liability claims related to AI-related harm may involve not only manufacturers, providers, and developers but also deployers, professional users, operators, and consumers of AI systems.[14] The AILD recognizes that the term 'defendant' can apply to a diverse set of people or entities.[15] While the NPLD may primarily cover cases involving harm caused by AI providers,[16] the AILD covers providers or manufacturers who are the defendant in claims on grounds other than the defect of the product.[17] The AILD does not impact the provisions outlined in the Digital Services Act (DSA), including the exemption from liability for disseminating illegal user-generated content under the conditions of the DSA.[18] This limitation suggests that intermediary services may, in practice, not be 'defendants' under the AILD, at least for harm arising from user-generated content that involves the algorithmic moderation systems of these services.

10. *Ibid.*, Art. 4(1)(a).
11. NPLD, Art. 7 addresses the liability of manufacturers for defective products, limiting the possible defendants under the NPLD to manufacturers.
12. AILD, Explanatory Memorandum, 3: 'The Product Liability Directive covers producer's no-fault liability for defective products, leading to compensation for certain types of damages, mainly suffered by individuals. This proposal covers national liability claims mainly based on the fault of any person with a view of compensating any type of damage and any type of victim. They complement one another to form an overall effective civil liability system.'
13. *Ibid.*, Rec. 8, and Explanatory Memorandum, 4, 6 and 7.
14. Madiega, 2023, 5; Dheu et al. 2022.
15. AILD, Rec. 17: 'The large number of people usually involved in the design, development, deployment and operation of high-risk AI systems, makes it difficult for injured persons to identify the person potentially liable for damage caused and to prove the conditions for a claim for damages.'
16. Given that the NPLD concerns liability for defective products of manufacturers (Art. 7).
17. AILD, Rec. 11.
18. *Ibid.*, Rec. 12.

BIBLIOGRAPHY

Academic Writings

De Bruyne et al. 2023: Jan De Bruyne, Orian Dheu & Charlotte Ducuing, *The European Commission's Approach to Extra-Contractual Liability and AI: An Evaluation of the AI Liability Directive and the Revised Product Liability Directive*, 51 Computer Law & Security Review, 105894 (2023), doi.org/10.1016/j.clsr.2023.105894.

Dheu et al. 2022: Orian Dheu, Charlotte Ducuing, & Jan De Bruyne, *The Commission's Proposals for Adapting Liability Rules to the Digital Age. Part 1: The AI Liability Directive*, KU Leuven CiTiP Blog (3 November 2022), www.law.kuleuven.be/citip/blog/the-commissions-proposals-for-adapting-liability-rules-to-the-digital-age-part-1-the-ai-liability-directive (accessed 12 March 2024).

Hacker 2023: Philipp Hacker, *The European AI Liability Directives: Critique of a Half-Hearted Approach and Lessons for the Future*, 51 CLSR, 105871 (2023), doi.org/10.1016/j.clsr.2023.105871.

Schuett 2023: Jonas Schuett, *Risk Management in the Artificial Intelligence Act*, 15 European Journal of Risk Regulation 367-385 (2024), doi.org/10.1017/err.2023.1.

Other

Madiega 2023: Tambiama Madiega, *Briefing Artificial Intelligence Liability Directive*, European Parliamentary Research Service (February 2023), www.europarl.europa.eu/RegData/etudes/BRIE/2023/739342/EPRS_BRI(2023)739342_EN.pdf (accessed 12 March 2024).

ARTICLE 2(9) Definition: Duty of Care

Jan De Bruyne & Victor Schollaert

Article 2. Definitions

(9) 'duty of care' means a required standard of conduct, set by national or Union law, in order to avoid damage to legal interests recognised at national or Union law level, including life, physical integrity, property and the protection of fundamental rights.

Recitals

(15) Consistency with [the AI Act] should also be ensured. It is therefore appropriate for this Directive to use the same definitions in respect of AI systems, providers and [deployers]. In addition, this Directive should only cover claims for damages when the damage is caused by an output or the failure to produce an output by an AI system through the fault of a person, for example the provider or the [deployer] under [the AI Act]. There is no need to cover liability claims when the damage is caused by a human assessment followed by a human act or omission, while the AI system only provided information or advice which was taken into account by the relevant human actor. In the latter case, it is possible to trace back the damage to a human act or omission, as the AI system output is not interposed between the human act or omission and the damage, and thereby establishing causality is not more difficult than in situations where an AI system is not involved.

(22) In order to address the difficulties to prove that a specific input for which the potentially liable person is responsible had caused a specific AI system output that led to the damage at stake, it is appropriate to provide, under certain conditions, for a presumption of causality. While in a fault-based claim the claimant usually has to prove the damage, the human act or omission constituting fault of the defendant and the causality link between the two, this Directive does not harmonise the conditions under which national courts establish fault. They remain governed by the applicable national law and, where harmonised, by applicable Union law. Similarly, this Directive does not harmonise the conditions related to the damage, for instance what damages are compensable, which are also regulated by applicable national and Union law. For the presumption of causality under this Directive to apply, the fault of the defendant should be established as a human act or omission which does not meet a duty of care under Union law

or national law that is directly intended to protect against the damage that occurred. Thus, this presumption can apply, for example, in a claim for damages for physical injury when the court establishes the fault of the defendant for non-complying with the instructions of use which are meant to prevent harm to natural persons. Non-compliance with duties of care that were not directly intended to protect against the damage that occurred do not lead to the application of the presumption, for example a provider's failure to file required documentation with competent authorities would not lead to the application of the presumption in claims for damages due to physical injury. It should also be necessary to establish that it can be considered reasonably likely, based on the circumstances of the case, that the fault has influenced the output produced by the AI system or the failure of the AI system to produce an output. Finally, the claimant should still be required to prove that the output or failure to produce an output gave rise to the damage.

(24) In areas not harmonised by Union law, national law continues to apply and fault is established under the applicable national law. All national liability regimes have duties of care, taking as a standard of conduct different expressions of the principle how a reasonable person should act, which also ensure the safe operation of AI systems in order to prevent damage to recognised legal interests. Such duties of care could for instance require [deployers] of AI systems to choose for certain tasks a particular AI system with concrete characteristics or to exclude certain segments of a population from being exposed to a particular AI system. National law can also introduce specific obligations meant to prevent risks for certain activities, which are applicable irrespective whether AI is used for that activity, for example traffic rules or obligations specifically designed for AI systems, such as additional national requirements for [deployers] of high risk AI systems pursuant to [Article 26 (3) of the AI Act]. This Directive neither introduces such requirements nor affects the conditions for establishing fault in case of breach of such requirements.

(25) Even when fault consisting of a non-compliance with a duty of care directly intended to protect against the damage that occurred is established, not every fault should lead to the application of the rebuttable presumption linking it to the output of the AI. Such a presumption should only apply when it can be considered reasonably likely, from the circumstances in which the damage occurred, that such fault has influenced the output produced by the AI system or the failure of the AI system to produce an output that gave rise to the damage. It can be for example considered reasonably likely that the fault has influenced the output or failure to produce an output, when that fault consists in breaching a duty of care in respect of limiting the perimeter of operation of the AI system and the damage occurred outside the perimeter of operation. On the contrary, a breach of a requirement to file certain documents or to register with a given authority, even though this might be foreseen for that particular activity or even be applicable expressly to the operation of an AI system, could not be considered as reasonably likely to have influenced the output produced by the AI system or the failure of the AI system to produce an output.

RELATED ARTICLES

Article 2 (Definitions); Article 3 (disclosure of evidence and rebuttable presumption of non-compliance); Article 4 (rebuttable presumption of a causal link in the case of fault).

RELATED LAWS

International

AI Convention.

EU

AI Act; AI Act Commission Proposal; AI Act Council Proposal; AI Act Parliament Amendments; Resolution 2015/2103: Resolution (EU) 2015/2103 of the European Parliament of 16 February 2017 with recommendations to the Commission on Civil Law Rules on Robotics; Directive 2019/770: Directive (EU) 2019/770 of the European Parliament and of the Council of 20 May 2019 on certain aspects concerning contracts for the supply of digital content and digital services, OJ. L. 136/1 (22 May 2019); Resolution 2020/2014: Resolution 2020/2014 of the European Parliament of 20 October 2020 with recommendations to the Commission on a civil liability regime for artificial intelligence; New Product Liability Directive; Permanent Representatives Committee 2024: Permanent Representatives Committee of 26 January 2024 on 'Proposal for a Regulation of the European Parliament and of the Council laying down harmonised rules on artificial intelligence (Artificial Intelligence Act) and amending certain Union legislative acts'; several other legal acts rely on the concept of duty of care/due diligence, though in a different context. Some examples: (1) Proposal for a Directive of the European Parliament and of the Council on Corporate Sustainability Due Diligence and amending Directive (EU) 2019/1937, COM/2022/71 final; and (2) Digital Services Act.

National

Belgium: Legislative proposal houdende boek 6 'buitencontractuele aansprakelijkheid' van het Burgerlijk Wetboek, *Parl.St.* Kamer 2022-23, nr. 3213/001 & 3213/005 (8 March 2023).

France: Décret n° 2021-873 du 29 juin 2021 portant application de l'ordonnance n° 2021-443 du 14 avril 2021 relative au régime de responsabilité pénale applicable en cas de circulation d'un véhicule à délégation de conduite et à ses conditions d'utilisation (29 June 2021).

Germany: Gesetz zur Änderung des Straßenverkehrsgesetzes und des Pflichtversicherungsgesetzes - Gesetz zum autonomen Fahren (21 July 2021).

RELATED CASE LAW

Tort liability is to a large extent still determined by national law. As such, there may be several national cases further elaborating on the 'duty of care' and fault-based liability in general. It would, however, take us too far to discuss all these cases.[1] Considering

1. Wagner concludes in this regard that '[t]hese terminological ambiguities pay tribute to the many uncertainties and contradictions in legal doctrine regarding the relationship between the concepts of fault, negligence, and breach of the duty of care, for example in the German or the French law of delict' (Wagner 2022, 225).

that the AILD has not yet entered into force, there is no case law on the meaning of the concept 'duty of care' as relied upon in the Directive. As such, this will need to be clarified in the future. The concept of duty of care as relied upon in the AILD should, however, not be confused with the notion of the duty of care or diligence as developed by the CJEU.[2]

COMMENTARY

1 Purpose

The purpose of this provision is to define the notion of 'duty of care'. As it is a concept used in different articles of the AI Liability Directive (AILD), it was deemed necessary to define it.

2 Legal Background

2.1 International

There are no international instruments specifically dealing with liability for artificial intelligence (AI), and with the duty of care more particularly. Of importance, however, is that several instruments refer to accountability/liability and cover procedural aspects that are of importance in the allocation of liability.

Paragraph 42 of the UNESCO Recommendation, for instance, stipulates that:

> the ethical responsibility and liability for the decisions and actions based in any way on an AI system should always ultimately be attributable to AI actors corresponding to their role in the life cycle of the AI system.

Paragraph 43 further mentions that:

> [a]ppropriate oversight, impact assessment, audit and due diligence mechanisms, including whistle-blowers' protection, should be developed to ensure accountability for AI systems and their impact throughout their life cycle.

More importantly, according to paragraph 67:[3]

> Member States should develop, review and adapt, as appropriate, regulatory frameworks to achieve accountability and responsibility for the content and outcomes of AI systems at the different phases of their life cycle. Member States should, where necessary, introduce liability frameworks or clarify the interpretation of existing frameworks to ensure the attribution of accountability for the outcomes and the functioning of AI systems. Furthermore, when developing regulatory frameworks, Member States should, in particular, take into account that ultimate responsibility and accountability must always lie with natural or legal persons and that AI systems should not be given legal personality themselves.

2. *See in this regard, e.g.*, Hofmann 2020.
3. UNESCO Recommendation.

Similar concerns were also acknowledged in the feasibility study issued by the Council of Europe's Ad hoc Committee on Artificial Intelligence (CAHAI) within the Council of Europe. Paragraph 112 stipulates that:

> [p]ersons – including public and private organisations – designing, developing, deploying or evaluating AI systems must take responsibility for these systems, and they should be held accountable whenever legal norms based on the principles mentioned above are not respected or any unjust harm occurs to end-users or to others.

Contracting parties have to take appropriate measures to ensure this, for instance, by imposing civil or criminal liability when the design, development and use of AI applications infringe on human rights or negatively affect the democratic process and the rule of law. More importantly, Member States must ensure that:[4]

> those who might be negatively impacted by AI systems have an effective and accessible remedy against the developers or deployers of AI systems who are responsible. The availability of such remedy should be clearly communicated to them, with special attention to those who are marginalised or in vulnerable situations. Effective remedies should involve redress for any harm suffered, and may include measures under civil, administrative, or, where appropriate, criminal law.

Article 9 of the AI Convention – as adopted by the Council of Europe – stipulates that:[5]

> [e]ach Party shall adopt or maintain measures to ensure accountability and responsibility for adverse impacts on human rights, democracy and the rule of law resulting from activities within the lifecycle of artificial intelligence systems.

2.2 *European Union*

It has already been mentioned that tort liability is not harmonized at the European Union (EU) level. There are, however, some soft law frameworks that are relevant. For instance, the Principles of European Tort Law deal with the notion of fault.[6] According to Article 4:101, a person is liable on the basis of fault for intentional or negligent violation of the required standard of conduct.[7] Article 4:102 further stipulates that the required standard of conduct is that of the reasonable person in the circumstances, and depends, in particular, on the nature and value of the protected interest involved, the dangerousness of the activity, the expertise to be expected of a person carrying it on, the foreseeability of the damage, the relationship of proximity or special reliance between those involved, as well as the availability and the costs of precautionary or

4. CAHAI 2020, 38, paras 112-113.
5. CAI 2023, 6; AI Convention, 4.
6. *See* Koch 2005.
7. *See* EGTL 2024.

alternative methods. Rules which prescribe or forbid certain conduct have to be considered when establishing the required standard of conduct.[8] Article 4:103 deals with the duty to protect others from damage. It stipulates that a:[9]

> duty to act positively to protect others from damage may exist if law so provides, or if the actor creates or controls a dangerous situation, or when there is a special relationship between parties or when the seriousness of the harm on the one side and the ease of avoiding the damage on the other side point towards such a duty.

In recent years, several initiatives with regard to liability for damage involving AI have been taken or discussed at the EU level. Without going into detail, we will provide a high-level overview allowing us to better understand the substantive provisions of the AILD.[10] One should, however, be aware that several other EU frameworks are relevant in the context of liability involving AI as well. The application of the Product Liability Directive, for instance, has been heavily debated in an AI context (e.g., the notion of software as a product, 'defective' AI).[11] Moreover, consumer protection legislation could be relevant in an AI context as well. An example is the Digital Content Directive, which includes remedies when there is a lack of conformity and provisions on liability (including a reversal of the burden of proof).

The focus on AI liability was first covered by the Parliament report on civil law rules for robots in 2017. It urged the Commission to consider a legislative instrument that would deal with the liability for damage caused by autonomous systems and robots, thereby evaluating the feasibility of a strict liability or a risk management approach.[12] This was followed by a report issued by an expert group set up by the Commission on the 'Liability or Artificial Intelligence and Other Emerging Digital Technologies' in November 2019. The report explored the main liability challenges posed to current tort law by AI. It concluded that liability regimes 'in force in the Member States ensure at least basic protection of victims whose damage is caused by the operation of such new technologies'.[13] However, the specific characteristics of AI systems, such as their complexity, self-learning abilities, opacity and limited predictability, may make it more difficult to offer victims a claim for compensation in all cases where this seems justified. The report stressed that the allocation of liability may be unfair or inefficient. It contains several recommendations to remedy potential gaps in EU and national liability regimes.[14] The notion of 'duty of care' was also identified on several occasions. According to provision [16], for instance, operators of emerging digital technologies need to comply with an 'adapted range of duties of care', including with regard to:

8. *See ibid. See for an extensive discussion* Hinteregger 2023.
9. *See* EGTL 2024.
10. *See more extensively* De Bruyne & Dheu 2023, 30-34.
11. *See e.g., the many contributions* in Lohsse et al. 2019; Buiten 2024.
12. Resolution 2015/2103. Note that several reports have also been published upon request by European institutions (e.g., Bertolini 2020).
13. Expert Group on Liability and New Technologies 2019, 3.
14. *See in this regard also* Bertolini & Episcopo 2021, 644.

(1) choosing the right system for the right task and skills;
(2) monitoring the system; and
(3) maintaining the system.

Provision [17] in turn stipulates that producers, whether or not they incidentally also act as operators, need to (1) design, describe and market products in a way that effectively enables operators to comply with the applicable duties and (2) adequately monitor the product after putting it into circulation.[15]

The Commission subsequently issued a White Paper on AI in 2020. It had two main building blocks, namely an 'ecosystem of trust' and an 'ecosystem of excellence'.[16] More importantly, the White Paper was accompanied by a report on safety and liability (Report). The Report identified several points that needed further attention, such as clarifying the scope of the Product Liability Directive or assessing procedural aspects.[17] In October 2020, the Parliament adopted a Resolution with recommendations to the Commission on a civil liability regime for AI. It favours strict liability for operators of high-risk AI systems and fault-based liability for operators of low-risk AI systems, with a reversal of the burden of proof.[18] More specifically, it mentions that all activities, devices or processes driven by AI systems that cause harm or damage but are not listed in the Annex to the proposed Regulation – a list of high-risk AI systems – should remain subject to fault-based liability but:[19]

> believes that the affected person should nevertheless benefit from a presumption of fault on the part of the operator, who should be able to exculpate itself by proving it has abided by its duty of care.

In April 2021, the Commission issued the proposal for the AI Act,[20] which was followed by the adoption of the Council's general approach in December 2022[21] and the Parliament's negotiating position in June 2023.[22] The AI Act was published in the Official Journal in July 2024. The AI Act is of importance for liability involving AI, not only because of the risk-based approach and potential sanctions in that regard, but especially as it imposes obligations upon several parties, such as the providers and deployers of high-risk AI systems.[23] Those obligations will be important to assess the potential liability of such parties, for instance, when determining whether one of these parties committed a fault (i.e., violation of a specific legal norm in the AI Act or negligence).[24] In September 2022, the Commission eventually published two proposals that aim to adapt (tort) liability rules to the digital age, the circular economy and the impact of the global value chain. The AILD contains rules on the disclosure of

15. Commission AI/IoT/R 2020, 6-7 & 44-45.
16. Commission AI 2020, 2-3.
17. Commission AI/IoT/R 2020.
18. Resolution 2020/2014.
19. *Ibid.*, No. 20, 112.
20. AI Act Commission Proposal.
21. AI Act Council Proposal.
22. AI Act Parliament Amendments.
23. *See* Arts 8-28 in particular.
24. De Bruyne et al. 2022, 407-408.

information and the alleviation of the burden of proof in relation to damage caused by AI systems. The revised Product Liability Directive substantially modifies the current product liability regime by including software within its scope, integrating new circumstances to assess the product's defectiveness and introducing provisions regarding presumptions of defectiveness and causation.[25]

2.3 National

As mentioned above, liability is to a large extent still national. For instance, the notion of fault – which includes/refers to the concept of duty of care – is not harmonized at the EU level.[26] Wagner concludes in this regard that:[27]

> [t]hese terminological ambiguities [between fault and duty of care] pay tribute to the many uncertainties and contradictions in legal doctrine regarding the relationship between the concepts of fault, negligence, and breach of the duty of care, for example in the German or the French law of delict.

Member States may have relevant provisions on liability that could be relied upon in an AI context. This can be either the application of 'general'/'common' rules (e.g., on the burden of proof or other presumptions in procedural law) or sector-specific provisions (e.g., self-driving cars). Reference can, for instance, be made to the German Autonomous Driving Act[28] or to the French Decree on automated vehicles' conditions of use and automated road transport systems' commissioning.[29] The concept of the duty of care has also already been given a lot of attention at the national level[30] as well as in different sectors such as climate change,[31] the financial domain[32] or corporate responsibility.[33]

2.4 Case Law

As mentioned above, liability and procedural law is to a large extent still national. It is conceivable that national case law also exists on the concept of the duty of care and the further modalities. Against this background, we will not cover all these potential cases.[34]

25. NPLD.
26. Widmer 2005.
27. Wagner 2022, 225.
28. Gesetz zur Änderung des Straßenverkehrsgesetzes und des Pflichtversicherungsgesetzes – Gesetz zum autonomen Fahren 2021. *See for a discussion* Ebers 2022.
29. Décret n° 2021-873 du 29 juin 2021 portant application de l'ordonnance n° 2021-443 du 14 avril 2021 relative au régime de responsabilité pénale applicable en cas de circulation d'un véhicule à délégation de conduite et à ses conditions d'utilisation.
30. *See, e.g.,* Hinteregger 2023. *Also see* the relevant chapters on fault-based liability in van Dam 2013. Widmer 2005.
31. *See, e.g.,* Kysar 2023.
32. *See, e.g.,* Busch & van Dam 2019.
33. *See, e.g.,* Bright et al. 2020.
34. *See more in detail, e.g.,* Winiger et al. 2011.

3 Analysis

The Commission published two proposals in September 2022 that aim to adapt (tort) liability rules to the digital age, the circular economy and the impact of the global value chain. The AI Liability does not only include a disclosure obligation but also a rebuttable presumption of a causal link between the fault of the defendant and the output produced by the AI system or the failure of the AI system to produce an output. By doing so, the Directive:[35]

> aims to provide an effective basis for claiming compensation in connection with the fault consisting in the lack of compliance with a duty of care under Union or national law.

This presumption only applies when three conditions are met. One of these requirements relates to the fault, which needs to be demonstrated by the claimant or can be presumed following Article 3(5) of the AILD.[36] We will first discuss the notion of a fault under the AILD and the duty of care more specifically (section 3.1). We will then assess some of the remaining challenges (section 3.2) and summarize the main findings (section 3.3).

3.1 Fault in the AILD and the Duty of Care

The AILD uses the concept of 'duty of care' on several occasions. Article 4(1)(a), for instance, stipulates that the fault of the defendant or of a person for whose behaviour the defendant is responsible consists of a 'non-compliance with a duty of care laid down in Union or national law directly intended to protect against the damage that occurred'. Considering that tort law is still to a large extent national,[37] the reliance on this concept in EU legislation is rather surprising.[38] Article 2(9) of the AILD defines the duty of care as:

> a required standard of conduct, set by national or Union law, in order to avoid damage to legal interests recognised at national or Union law level, including life, physical integrity, property and the protection of fundamental rights.

The AILD acknowledges that all Member States' liability regimes are familiar with duties of care, 'taking as a standard of conduct different expressions of the principle

35. AILD, Art. 4(1)(a), *see also* 13.
36. AILD also contains a rebuttable presumption of non-compliance. Where a defendant in a claim for damages fails to disclose or preserve evidence at its disposal as ordered by a court, a presumption of non-compliance with duties of care is presumed which that evidence was intended to prove. In this regard, it has already been argued that '[m]ost often, the claimant will have to resort to the disclosure of evidence proceedings under Article 3 AILD Proposal to demonstrate this (negligent) breach of duty' (Hacker 2023, 22). *See more extensively* commentary on Art. 3 in this volume.
37. *See extensively* Wagner 2022, 232-234.
38. De Bruyne et al. 2023, 8.

how a reasonable person should act'.[39] This also ensures the safe operation of AI systems in order to prevent damage to recognized legal interests. Such duties of care could, for instance:[40]

> require [deployers] of AI systems to choose for certain tasks a particular AI system with concrete characteristics or to exclude certain segments of a population from being exposed to a particular AI system.

Hacker in this regard argues that such a duty of care may arise from either statutory or case law, as the source of the legal obligation is of no importance.[41]

The AILD contains specific provisions for *providers*, persons *subject to the obligations of a provider* or *users/deployer*[42] of a *high-risk* AI system. In other words, when high-risk AI systems are at stake, the qualification of the defendant becomes important.[43] The condition of fault (Article 4(1)(a)) is met *only* if the claimant demonstrates that a *provider* of a high-risk AI system or an individual *subject to the obligations of a provider* has failed to comply with any of the following requirements laid down in the AI Act, taking into account the steps undertaken in and the results of the risk management system provided for in the AI Act:[44]

- the AI system is a system which makes use of techniques involving the training of models with data and which was not developed on the basis of training, validation and testing data sets that meet the quality criteria referred to in Article 10(2) to (4) of the AI Act;[45]
- the AI system was not designed and developed in a way that meets the transparency requirements laid down in Article 13 of the AI Act;[46]
- the AI system was not designed and developed in a way that allows for an effective oversight by natural persons during the period in which the AI system is in use pursuant to Article 14 of the AI Act;[47]

39. AILD, Rec. 24.
40. *Ibid.*
41. Hacker 2023, 22.
42. Note that the final AIA does no longer mention 'user' but 'deployer' defined as 'any natural or legal person, public authority, agency or other body using an AI system under its authority except where the AI system is used in the course of a personal non-professional activity' (AIA, Art. 3(4)).
43. Hacker identifies different 'cases' in this regard (Hacker 2023, 22-24).
44. AILD, Art. 4(2).
45. For example, training, validation and testing datasets shall be relevant, sufficiently representative, and to the best extent possible, free of errors and complete in view of the intended purpose (AIA, Art. 10(3)).
46. For instance, high-risk AI systems shall be designed and developed in such a way to ensure that their operation is sufficiently transparent to enable deployers to interpret the system's output and use it appropriately. They also need to be accompanied by instructions for use in an appropriate digital format or otherwise that include concise, complete, correct and clear information that is relevant, accessible and comprehensible to deployers (AIA, Art. 13(1)-13(2)).
47. Supervision is aimed at preventing or minimizing the risks to health, safety, or fundamental rights posed by high-risk AI systems (AIA, Art. 14(2)).

- the AI system was not designed and developed so as to achieve, in the light of its intended purpose, an appropriate level of accuracy, robustness and cybersecurity pursuant to Article 15 and Article 16, point (a), of the AI Act;[48] or
- the necessary corrective actions were not immediately taken to bring the AI system in conformity with the obligations laid down in Chapter III, section 2 of the AI Act or to withdraw or recall the system, as appropriate, pursuant to Article 16, point (j), and Article 20 of the AI Act.

The AILD states that the steps undertaken in and the results of the risk management system provided for in the AI Act should be taken into account when establishing the fault.[49] However, it is unclear what specific weight should be attributed to those steps and results within the framework of the risk management system (Article 9 of the AI Act).[50] Some also note that it is a rather 'surprising point' that prohibited AI systems under the AI Act 'have no role to play' in the AILD.[51] The provision is problematic from another point of view as well because of using the term 'only'. It may indeed imply that claimants can benefit from the rebuttable presumption solely in case of a violation of the relevant/listed AI Act requirements, assuming of course that they comply with Article 4(1)(b) and (c) to benefit from it. This *a priori* excludes any other – potentially relevant – legal ground for tort law, whether in EU or national law.[52] In this regard, Wagner even concludes that it is 'irritating that a conclusive catalogue of duties, apparently meant to exclude the establishment of further duties of care under national tort law, is put in place particularly for manufacturers of high-risk systems', which in addition 'seems difficult to justify'.[53]

In the case of a liability claim against a *user/deployer* of a high-risk AI system, the fault (cf. Article 4(1)(a)) is presumed if the claimant demonstrates that the user/deployer:[54]

- did not comply with its obligations to use or monitor the AI system in accordance with the accompanying instructions of use or, where appropriate, suspend or interrupt its use pursuant to Article 26 of the AI Act;[55] or

48. Among other things, high-risk AI systems need to be resilient as regards errors, faults or inconsistencies that may occur within the system or the environment in which the system operates, in particular due to their interaction with natural persons or other systems (AIA, Art. 15(4)).
49. AILD, Art. 4(2).
50. Spindler 2023, 39; Spindler 2022, 703.
51. Wagner 2022, 227. *See also* Hacker 2023, 25.
52. De Bruyne et al. 2023, 8.
53. Wagner 2022, 226-227. At the same time, he concludes that the obligation to ensure 'accuracy, robustness, and cybersecurity' of high-risk AI systems (*see* AIA, Art. 15) may be a ground to establish a standard of care in tort law.
54. AILD, Art. 4(3).
55. There is an obligation to suspend the use of an AI system if its use in accordance with the instructions of use may result in the AI system presenting a risk to health or safety or to the protection of fundamental rights of persons (AIA, Art. 26(5)).

- exposed the AI system to input data under its control which is not relevant in view of the system's intended purpose pursuant to Article 26(4) of the Act.[56]

3.2 *The Problematic Notion of the 'Duty of Care'*

The AILD does not explicitly define the notion of fault 'to grant leeway to Member States continuing their traditional tort law regimes'.[57] Implicitly, however, it is mentioned that a fault refers to the:[58]

> non-compliance with a duty of care laid down in Union or national law directly intended to protect against the damage that occurred.

As such, a substantive violation of the AI Act is required. In some cases, however, the violation does not relate to the AI Act itself but is more situated in the procedural law domain. Article 5(5), for instance, stipulates that where a defendant fails to comply with an order by a national court in a claim for damages to disclose or to preserve evidence at its disposal, a national court is allowed to presume the defendant's non-compliance with a relevant duty of care.[59] Although the AILD does not intend to undermine the national definitions of fault,[60] the requirement of a 'duty of care' is problematic for several reasons. These relate to the problematic relationship between the fault and a 'duty of care' as used in the AILD (section 3.2.1), the restrictions with regard to the concept of fault due to its embedment in national law (section 3.2.2), and the unclarity as to what exactly is covered by the duty of care under the AILD (section 3.2.3). We will illustrate these challenges by relying on concepts of domestic law considering that tort law is still regulated under national law. The reference to and inclusion of national law is, therefore, key in evaluating the fitness of the AILD. We selected Belgium tort law due to its characteristics that may be difficult to reconcile with some of the core provisions in the AILD.[61] Moreover, Belgian tort law is in the process of being reformed/modernized with the adoption of Book 6 of the Civil Code on extra-contractual liability.[62] As such, its inclusion in our analysis is topical and the results can likely be extrapolated to other countries.[63]

---

56. The deployer needs to ensure that input data is relevant and sufficiently representative in view of the intended purpose of the high-risk AI system, to the extent the deployer exercises control over the input data (AIA, Art. 26(4)).
57. Hacker 2023, 13.
58. A fault is indeed the violation of this duty (*see* AILD, Art. 4(1)(a)).
59. Hacker 2023, 13.
60. AILD, Art. 1(3)(d) mentions that the Dir. will not affect 'how fault is defined, other than in respect of what is provided for in Articles 3 and 4'. *Also see* AILD, Rec. 24.
61. De Bruyne et al. 2023, 2.
62. *See in this regard* Legislative proposal of 8 Mar. 2023.
63. De Bruyne et al. 2023, 2.

3.2.1 *The Relationship Between 'Fault' and 'Duty of Care' under the AILD*

The relationship between the notions of 'fault' and 'duty of care' under the AILD, and especially in Article 4, is unclear and raises interpretation issues. Article 4(1) refers to the presumption of causal link following a fault committed by a defendant, by violating a duty of care under EU and national law directly intended to protect against the damage that occurred. This is a rather broad scope. Article 4(2) by contrast uses the term 'only'. This may imply that claimants can benefit from the rebuttable presumption solely in case of a violation of the relevant/listed AI Act requirements by the providers, assuming of course that the former comply with Article 4(1)(b) and (c) to benefit from it. As such, this a priori seems to exclude any other - potentially relevant - legal ground for tort law, whether in EU or national law.[64]

More importantly, in many EU countries, a fault consists of either negligence or the violation of a statutory rule.[65] Belgian law, for example, traditionally recognizes two types of wrongdoings, namely the breach of the standard of care or a violation of a specific legal rule of conduct.[66] It is unclear whether both forms of fault fall under the definition of 'duty of care' in the AILD. It is indeed the case that the *definiens* - the defining element - appears to refer more to the violation of a specific rule of conduct, but the *definiendum* - the term being defined - seems to indicate a violation of the standard of care. Therefore, Article 2(9) gives the impression that it applies both to a breach of a standard of care by referring to the 'duty of care' and to the violation of specific legal rule of conduct by mentioning 'a required standard of conduct, set by national or Union law'. According to Hacker, there is nothing in the wording of the definition or in the recitals of the AILD that suggests that only statutory law could establish a relevant 'duty of care'.[67] Wagner, however, concludes that a 'breach of the duty of care and fault mean the same' in the AILD. The drafters of the AILD 'did not attempt to harmonise this area of European tort law' due to the many 'uncertainties and contradictions in legal doctrine regarding the relationship between the concepts of fault, negligence, and breach of the duty of care'.[68]

Let us illustrate these theoretical findings with some provisions in the AILD itself. Article 4(1) refers to the presumption of causal link following a fault committed by a defendant, by violating a duty of care under EU and national law directly intended to protect against the damage that occurred. This is a rather broad scope. By contrast, Article 4(2) and (3), that specifically deal with providers, persons subject to the latter's obligations or deployers of high-risk AI systems could be interpreted in two different ways. On the one hand, these provisions could be read as requiring *solely/merely* a failure to comply with the relevant requirements in the AI Act. There is no need to additionally establish negligence to attribute a fault. On the other hand, they could be read as a mere rephrasing of the general standard of care. In other words, the standard

64. *Ibid.*, at 8.
65. *See also* Wagner 2022, 232-233.
66. Court of Cassation 24 May 2018, nr. C.17.0504.N; Vansweevelt & Weyts 2009, 126.
67. Hacker 2023, 22.
68. Wagner 2022, 225.

of care is 'packaged' within a specific behavioural norm. In those cases, when rules of conduct are not sufficiently specific, an assessment of the behaviour against the duty of care still takes place.[69] Although it is rather unclear and hard to picture concretely, this interpretation is seemingly supported not only by Article 4(2) that requires to 'take into account the steps undertaken in and the results of the risk management system pursuant to [the AI Act]' but also by the risk-based nature of the AI Act requirements that read as a spectrum rather than as black-or-white requirements.

3.2.2 The Remaining Importance and Challenges of National Law

Article 1(3)(d) of the AILD mentions that the Directive will not affect 'how fault is defined, other than in respect of what is provided for in Articles 3 and 4'. A fault under Belgian law (and by extension other jurisdictions in the EU) consists of both a subjective and an objective element. The (currently still applicable) subjective component requires that the fault can be attributed to the free will of the person who has committed it ('imputability') and that this person generally possesses the capacity to control and assess the consequences of his conduct ('culpability').[70] The AILD, however, does not seem to address the subjective element. This raises the question of whether the notion of 'fault', as referred to in Articles 3 and 4, *requires* such a subjective element to be present and/or *allows* for national law to require this.[71] The objective component of a fault refers to the wrongful behaviour in itself. Belgian law traditionally recognizes two types of wrongdoings, namely a violation of a specific legal rule of conduct[72] and the breach of a standard of care.[73] Under Belgian law, a violation of a standard of care requires that it was reasonably foreseeable for the defendant that their conduct could result in some kind of damage.[74] This means that a provider of a high-risk AI system would commit a fault when they could reasonably foresee that a violation of a duty of care following provisions of the AI Act would result in damage. However, it is unclear whether the notion of a 'duty of care' as relied upon in the AILD also includes this requirement of foreseeability or, instead, whether it is left to national (case) law to determine the additional modalities under which a violation of a 'duty of care' could be established.[75]

69. Dubuisson 2010, 20. Wagner also elaborates on the difference between the breach of statutory duty as a separate tort or merging the statutory norm into the general standard of care (Wagner 2022, 232-234).
70. *See, e.g.,* Court of Cassation 3 Oct. 1994, Arr.Cass. 1994, 807; Vansweevelt & Weyts 2009, 147-148; Jocqué 2007; Kruithof 2018, 53-56; Stijns 2013, 48 & 58; De Bruyne et al. 2023, 9. *See in this regard also* Art. 6(6) and 6(7) in Book 6 of the Belgian Civil Code on extra-contractual liability.
71. De Bruyne et al. 2023, 9.
72. *See, e.g.,* Court of Cassation 3 Oct. 1994, Arr.Cass. 1994, 807; Court of Cassation 10 Apr. 2014, Arr.Cass. 2014, 962. This is also true when the illegal act or omission would be considered non-negligent (*see, e.g.,* Court of Cassation 6 Jun. 2011, Arr.Cass. 2011, 1478).
73. *See, e.g.,* Court of Cassation 25 Nov. 2002, Arr.Cass. 2002, 2543; Bocken et al. 2014, 90-92.
74. Kruithof 2018, 49 with references; Bocken et al. 2014, 91; Vansweevelt & Weyts 2009, 134-137. *See in this regard also* Art. 6(7) in Book 6 of the Civil Code on extra-contractual liability.
75. De Bruyne et al. 2023, 9.

In addition to the fact that the content of a duty of care will ultimately have to be determined by judges, a more conceptual issue may arise as well in some countries, such as Belgium. That is because the existence of a *generally applicable positive duty* of care has already been contested, for instance, in Belgium. Kruithof concludes that Belgian case law and scholarship commonly agree that no breach of a 'pre-existing' duty is required for a fault to be established under extracontractual liability. As noted by Kruithof, what is usually referred to as the generally required level or the duty of care:[76]

> is therefore more properly qualified not as a legal duty or obligation, but merely a standard of behaviour serving as the yardstick for judging whether an act is negligent or not for purposes of establishing liability.

However, Article 4(1)(a) seems to equate the 'fault' with the non-compliance with a duty of care to avoid damage, thereby implicitly endorsing the view that the duty of care consists of a standalone obligation. This does not necessarily fit well in the Belgian (and by extension potentially other national) tort law framework(s), and may thus cause interpretation issues and fragmentation.[77] In other words, the question arises whether it means that not all violated standards of conduct qualify as fault under the AILD. After all, not all standards of conduct are motivated by the intention to prevent damage.

3.2.3 *What Is Covered by the Fault/Duty of Care under the AILD?*

A final concern that has already been flagged in scholarship relates to the restrictions of the types of fault that are covered by the AILD. The AILD only covers claims for damages when the damage is caused by (the failure to produce) an output by an AI system through the fault of a person, for example, the provider or deployer under the AI Act. The drafter did not deem it required to cover liability claims when the damage is caused by a human assessment followed by a human act or omission, while the AI system only provided information or advice which was taken into account by the relevant human actor. In such a case, it is possible to trace back the damage to a human act or omission. The AI system output is not interposed between the human act or omission and the damage. As a consequence, establishing causality is not more difficult than in situations where an AI system is not involved.[78] Hacker, however, identifies two problems with this restriction. On the one hand, it will induce people to blindly follow the advice given by an AI system,[79] while at the same time having to comply with the requirement of human oversight under the AI Act.[80] On the other hand, it remains uncertain whether the claims regarding causality underpinning the AILD are convincing as the question arises 'whether it is really equally difficult to prove causality

76. Kruithof 2018, 47 with references.
77. De Bruyne et al. 2023, 8-9.
78. AILD, Rec. 15.
79. Hacker 2023, 13.
80. *See* AIA, Art. 14.

and non-compliance in cases of human intervention with and without AI involvement'.[81]

Second, the standard of conduct in the AILD aims at avoiding 'damage to legal interests recognised at national or Union law level, including life, physical integrity, property and the protection of fundamental rights'.[82] This provision may eventually not align with the concept of damage as used in various Member States. It is, for example, not in line with the Belgian concept of damage. According to current Belgian law, damage consists of an *injury* to an interest.[83] In the upcoming legal reform of Belgian liability law (*see* Book 6 of the Belgian law), damage is defined as 'the economic and non-economic *consequences* of the injury to a personal legally protected interest'[84] (own translation). Logically, damage to interests cannot exist. That is because the concept of 'interest' is indispensable in/connected to the definition of damage itself. However, the definition of a 'duty of care' in the AILD implies that one could still 'suffer damage' to certain interests. The question then arises as to what is meant by the word 'damage', as it cannot mean the same as the concept used in Belgium.[85] Moreover, the definition provides a list of recognized interests as examples, including rights (e.g., the right to life, physical integrity, property and fundamental rights). However, interests and rights are two distinct concepts. An interest can be protected by a right, but it is not a right itself. The infringement of a right is, therefore, not seen as damage but qualified as a fault, according to many Belgian authors.[86] For example, if a person willingly destroys a computer through the use of an AI system, such behaviour qualifies as a violation of the property right. The damage resulting from this action is, for instance, the loss of the economic value of the computer.[87]

3.3 Conclusions

In this article, we discussed the concept of the duty of care as relied upon in the AILD. We first discussed the definition given in the AILD. It refers to the standard of conduct, set by national or Union law, in order to avoid damage to legal interests recognized at the national or Union law level, including life, physical integrity, property and the protection of fundamental rights. We then discussed some remaining challenges

81. Hacker 2023, 13-14.
82. AILD, Art. 2(9).
83. *See, e.g.*, Court of Cassation 16 Jan. 1939, Pas. 1939, 25; Court of Cassation 28 Oct. 1942, Pas. 1942, 261; Court of Cassation 2 May 1955, Arr.Cass. 1955, 725; Court of Cassation 4 Sep. 1972, Arr.Cass. 1973, 1; Court of Cassation 17 Oct. 2016, nr. C.09.0414.F, RGAR 2017, 15389; Court of Cassation 17 Oct. 2016, nr. C.11.0062.F, RGAR 2017, 15388, n. Guy Haarscher; Court of Cassation 13 Apr. 2018, nr. C.13.0302.F, JLMB 2018, 1076; Court of Cassation 5 Jun. 2020, nr. C.19.0396.F, TBBR 2022, 338, n. Victor Schollaert; Dirix 1984, 25; Bocken et al. 2014, 92; Schollaert 2023a, 378.
84. Legislative proposal 8 Mar. 2023 houdende boek 6 'buitencontractuele aansprakelijkheid' van het Burgerlijk Wetboek, *Parl.St.* Kamer 2022-23, nr. 3213/001 & 3213/005; *See* Schollaert 2023b, 378-379; *See also* Schollaert 2023a, 380-381.
85. Schollaert & De Bruyne 2023.
86. Bocken 2000, 198; Vansweevelt & Weyts 2009, 141; Dubuisson et al. 2009, 47; Weyts 2011, 180; Verjans 2013, 526; Isgour 2017, 99-100; Kruithof 2018, 46; Schollaert 2021, 518-521.
87. *See* Léonard 2013, 979.

related to his definition, such as the unclear relationship with the concept of 'fault' as used in the AILD as well as the remaining importance of national Law for the interpretation and application of different concepts (e.g., damage, foreseeability). It is also important to follow up on evolutions with regard to the AI Act considering that the AILD relies on different concepts used within the former framework.

BIBLIOGRAPHY

Reports and Recommendations

Bertolini 2020: Andrea Bertolini, *Artificial Intelligence and Civil Liability. Legal Affairs*, Parliament (July 2020).

CAHAI 2020: Council of Europe's Ad Hoc Committee on AI (December 2020), *Feasibility Study*, rm.coe.int/cahai-2020-23-final-eng-feasibility-study-/1680a0c6da (accessed 11 April 2024).

CAI 2023: CAI, *Draft Framework Convention on Artificial Intelligence, Human Rights, Democracy and the Rule of Law*, 6 (December 2023), rm.coe.int/cai-2023-28-draft-framework-convention/1680ade043 (accessed 11 April 2024).

Commission AI 2020: European Commission, *White Paper on Artificial Intelligence: A European Approach to Excellence and Trust* (February 2020), commission.europa.eu/document/download/d2ec4039-c5be-423a-81ef-b9e44e79825b_en?filename=commission-white-paper-artificial-intelligence-feb2020_en.pdf (accessed 11 April 2024).

Commission AI/IoT/R 2020: European Commission, *Report on the Safety and Liability Implications of Artificial Intelligence, the Internet of Things and Robotics* (February 2020), eur-lex.europa.eu/legal-content/en/TXT/?uri=CELEX%3A52020DC0064 (accessed 11 April 2024).

Expert Group on Liability and New Technologies 2019: Expert Group on Liability and New Technologies – New Technology Formation, *Liability for Artificial Intelligence and Other Emerging Digital Technologies* (November 2019), op.europa.eu/en/publication-detail/-/publication/1c5e30be-1197-11ea-8c1f-01aa75ed71a1/language-en (accessed 11 April 2024).

UNESCO Recommendation.

Academic Writings

Bertolini & Episcopo 2021: Andrea Bertolini & Francesca Episcopo, *The Expert Group's Report on Liability for Artificial Intelligence and Other Emerging Digital Technologies: A Critical Assessment*, 12 EJRR 644 (2021), doi.org/10.1017/err.2021.30.

Bocken 2000: Hubert Bocken, *Nog iets over inbreuk op recht?* 183 (Herman Cousy, Eric Dirix, Sophie Stijns, Jules Stuyck & Dirk Van Gerven eds, 2000).

Bocken et al. 2014: Hubert Bocken, Ingrid Boone & Marc Kruithof, *Inleiding tot het schadevergoedingsrecht. Buitencontractueel aansprakelijkheidsrecht en andere schadevergoedingsstelsels* (2014).

Bright et al. 2020: Claire Bright et al., *Toward a Corporate Duty for Lead Companies to Respect Human Rights in Their Global Value Chains?* 22 Business and Politics 667 (2020), doi.org/10.1017/bap.2020.15.

Buiten 2024: Miriam Buiten, *Product Liability for Defective AI*, 57 European Journal of Law and Economics 239-273 (2024), doi.org/10.1007/s10657-024-09794-z.

Busch & van Dam 2019: Danny Busch & Cees van Dam, *A Bank's Duty of Care* (2019).

De Bruyne & Dheu 2023: Jan De Bruyne & Orian Dheu, *Liability for Damage Caused by Artificial Intelligence: Some Food for Thought and Current Proposals* (Philip Morgan ed., 2023).

De Bruyne et al. 2023: Jan De Bruyne, Orian Dheu & Charlotte Ducuing, *The European Commission's Approach to Extra-Contractual Liability and AI: An Evaluation of the AI Liability Directive and the Revised Product Liability Directive*, 51 CLSR 1 (2023), doi.org/10.1016/j.clsr.2023.105894.

De Bruyne et al. 2022: Jan De Bruyne, Elias Van Gool & Thomas Gils, *Tort Law and Damage Caused by AI Systems* (Jan De Bruyne & Cedric Vanleenhove eds, 2022).

Dirix 1984: Eric Dirix, *Het Begrip Schade* (1984).

Dubuisson et al. 2009: Bernard Dubuisson et al., *La Responsabilité Civile. Chronique de Jurisprudence 1996-2007. Volume 1: Le Fait Générateur et le Lien Causal* (2009).

Dubuisson 2010: Bernard Dubuisson, *Responsabilité Contractuelle et Responsabilité Aquilienne. Comparaison n'est pas Raison* 1 (Sophie Stijns & Patrick Wery eds, 2010).

Ebers 2022: Martin Ebers, *Civil Liability for Autonomous Vehicles in Germany*, SSRN (5 February 2022), papers.ssrn.com/sol3/papers.cfm?abstract_id=4027594 (accessed 11 April 2024), doi.org/10.2139/ssrn.4027594.

EGTL 2024: European Group on Tort Law, www.egtl.org/PETLEnglish.html (accessed 11 April 2024).

Hacker 2023: Philipp Hacker, *The European AI Liability Directives: Critique of an Half-Hearted Approach and Lessons for the Future*, 51 CLSR 1 (2023), doi.org/10.1016/j.clsr.2023.105871.

Hinteregger 2023: Monika Hinteregger, *Art 4:102 Principles of European Tort Law. An Objective or Subjective Standard of Fault: Does the Difference Really Matter?*, 14 JETL 1 (2023), doi.org/10.1515/jetl-2023-0005.

Hofmann 2020: Herwig C.H. Hofmann, *The Duty of Care in EU Public Law: A Principle Between Discretion and Proportionality*, 13 Review of European Administrative Law 87 (2020), doi.org/10.7590/187479820x15930701852265.

Isgour 2017: Marc Isgour, *La réparation des atteintes au droit à la vie privée et au droit à l'honneur* 81 (René Robaye ed., 2017).

Jocqué 2007: Geert Jocqué, *Bewustzijn en subjectieve verwijtbaarheid, in Aansprakelijkheid, aansprakelijkheidsverzekering en andere schadevergoedingssystemen*, XXXIIIste Postuniversitaire cyclus Willy Delva 2006-2007, Mechelen (Kluwer, 2007), 1-101.

Koch 2005: Bernhard A. Koch, *The 'European Group on Tort Law' and Its 'Principles of European Tort Law'*, 53 The American Journal of Comparative Law 189 (2005), doi.org/10.1093/ajcl/53.1.189.

Kruithof 2018: Marc Kruithof, *Tort Law in Belgium* (2018).

Kysar 2023: Douglas A. Kysar, *The Duty of Climate Care*, Yale Law School, SSRN (27 October 2023), papers.ssrn.com/sol3/papers.cfm?abstract_id=4578011 (accessed 15 April 2024).

Léonard 2013: Thierry Léonard, *Faute extra-contractuelle et juridictions commercial es: principes et plaidoyer pour un retour à une vision unitaire de la faute*, 10 TBH 951 (2013).

Lohsse 2019: Sebastian Lohsse, *Liability for Artificial Intelligence and the Internet of Things* (Sebastian Lohsse, Reiner Schulze & Dirk Staudenmayer eds, 2019).

Schollaert 2021: Victor Schollaert, *Is de inbreuk op een recht absoluut dan wel relatief onrechtmatig?*, 445 NJW 514 (2021).

Schollaert 2023a: Victor Schollaert, *Het tweeledige schadebegrip in het wetsvoorstel houdende boek 6 'Buitencontractueele aansprakelijkheid' van het Burgerlijk Wetboek*, 8 TBBR 377 (2023).

Schollaert 2023b: Victor Schollaert, *Het nieuwe buitencontractueel aansprakelijkheidsrecht. Een verkennende analyse*, 482 NJW 374 (2023).

Schollaert & De Bruyne 2023: Victor Schollaert & Jan De Bruyne, *Voorstel Richtlijn AI-aansprakelijkheid: verkennende analyse vanuit Belgisch perspectief*, 486 NJW 574 (2023).

Spindler 2023: Gerard Spindler, *Different Approaches for Liability of Artificial Intelligence: Pros and Cons – the New Proposal of the EU Commission on Liability for Defective Products and AI Systems*, SSRN (15 January 2023), papers.ssrn.com/sol3/papers.cfm?abstract_id=4354468 (accessed 15 April 2024), doi.org/10.2139/ssrn.4354468.

Spindler 2022: Gerald Spindler, *Die Vorschläge der EU-Kommission zu einer neuen Produkthaftung und zur Haftung von Herstellern und Betreibern Künstlicher Intelligenz Die haftungsrechtliche Einordnung von Software als Produkt nach Unionsrecht: endlich*, 11 CR 689 (2022).

Stijns 2013: Sophie Stijns, *Verbintenissenrecht: Boek 1bis* (2013).

van Dam 2013: Cees van Dam, *European Tort Law* (2013).

Vansweevelt & Weyts 2009: Thierry Vansweevelt & Britt Weyts, *Handboek Buitencontractueel Aansprakelijkheidsrecht* (2009).

Verjans 2013: Elisabeth Verjans, *Buitencontractuele aansprakelijkheid voor schending van persoonlijkheidsrechten*, 14 RW 522 (2013-14).

Wagner 2022: Gerhard Wagner, *Liability Rules for the Digital Age: Aiming for the Brussels Effect*, 13 JETL 191 (2022).

Weyts 2011: Britt Weyts, *Punitieve elementen in het buitencontractueel aansprakelijkheidsrecht* 173 (Stefan Rutten ed., Intersentia 2011).

Widmer 2005: Pierre Widmer, *Unification of Tort Law Fault* (2005).

Winiger et al. 2011: Benedict Winiger et al., *Digest of European Tort Law. Volume 2: Essential Cases on Damage* (2011).

Others

Court of Cassation 16 January 1939, Pas. 1939, 25.

Court of Cassation 28 October 1942, Pas. 1942, 261.

Court of Cassation 2 May 1955, Arr.Cass. 1955, 725.

Court of Cassation 4 September 1972, Arr.Cass. 1973, 1.
Court of Cassation 3 October 1994, Arr.Cass. 1994, 807.
Court of Cassation 25 November 2002, Arr.Cass. 2002, 2543.
Court of Cassation 6 June 2011, Arr.Cass. 2011, 1478.
Court of Cassation 10 April 2014, Arr.Cass. 2014, 962.
Court of Cassation 17 October 2016, nr. C.09.0414.F, RGAR 2017, 15389.
Court of Cassation 17 October 2016, nr. C.11.0062.F, RGAR 2017, 15388, note Guy Haarscher.
Court of Cassation 13 April 2018, nr. C.13.0302.F, JLMB 2018, 1076.
Court of Cassation 24 May 2018, nr. C.17.0504.N.
Court of Cassation 5 June 2020, nr. C.19.0396.F, TBBR 2022, 338, note Victor Schollaert.

ARTICLE 3 Disclosure of Evidence and Rebuttable Presumption of Non-compliance

Florence Danis, Gert-Jan Hendrix & Jasper Bellon

Article 3. Disclosure of evidence and rebuttable presumption of non-compliance

1. Member States shall ensure that national courts are empowered, either upon the request of a potential claimant who has previously asked a provider, a person subject to the obligations of a provider pursuant to [Article 24 or Article 28(1) of the AI Act][1] or a user[2] to disclose relevant evidence at its disposal about a specific high-risk AI system that is suspected of having caused damage, but was refused, or a claimant, to order the disclosure of such evidence from those persons.

   In support of that request, the potential claimant must present facts and evidence sufficient to support the plausibility of a claim for damages.
2. In the context of a claim for damages, the national court shall only order the disclosure of the evidence by one of the persons listed in paragraph 1, if the claimant has undertaken all proportionate attempts at gathering the relevant evidence from the defendant.
3. Member States shall ensure that national courts, upon the request of a claimant, are empowered to order specific measures to preserve the evidence mentioned in paragraph 1.
4. National courts shall limit the disclosure of evidence to that which is necessary and proportionate to support a potential claim or a claim for damages and the preservation to that which is necessary and proportionate to support such a claim for damages.

1. The AILD was based on the initial proposal of the AIA that underwent various changes subsequent to the publication of the AILD. For instance, the references to the draft AIA, Arts 24 and 28(1) are made to Arts that have now been included as AIA, Arts 25(3) and 25(1), respectively.
2. At the time when the AILD came out, the draft AIA referred to 'users' of high-risk AI systems. This was changed in the final version of the AIA to 'deployers'. References in this article to 'users' of high-risk AI systems should therefore be understood as 'deployers'.

In determining whether an order for the disclosure or preservation of evidence is proportionate, national courts shall consider the legitimate interests of all parties, including third parties concerned, in particular in relation to the protection of trade secrets within the meaning of Article 2(1) of Directive (EU) 2016/943 and of confidential information, such as information related to public or national security.

Member States shall ensure that, where the disclosure of a trade secret or alleged trade secret which the court has identified as confidential within the meaning of Article 9(1) of Directive (EU) 2016/943 is ordered, national courts are empowered, upon a duly reasoned request of a party or on their own initiative, to take specific measures necessary to preserve confidentiality when that evidence is used or referred to in legal proceedings.

Member States shall also ensure that the person ordered to disclose or to preserve the evidence mentioned in paragraphs 1 or 2 has appropriate procedural remedies in response to such orders.

5. Where a defendant fails to comply with an order by a national court in a claim for damages to disclose or to preserve evidence at its disposal pursuant to paragraphs 1 or 2, a national court shall presume the defendant's non-compliance with a relevant duty of care, in particular in the circumstances referred to in Article 4(2) or (3), that the evidence requested was intended to prove for the purposes of the relevant claim for damages.

   The defendant shall have the right to rebut that presumption.

Recitals

(3) When an injured person seeks compensation for damage suffered, Member States' general fault-based liability rules usually require that person to prove a negligent or intentionally damaging act or omission ('fault') by the person potentially liable for that damage, as well as a causal link between that fault and the relevant damage. However, when AI is interposed between the act or omission of a person and the damage, the specific characteristics of certain AI systems, such as opacity, autonomous behaviour and complexity, may make it excessively difficult, if not impossible, for the injured person to meet this burden of proof. In particular, it may be excessively difficult to prove that a specific input for which the potentially liable person is responsible had caused a specific AI system output that led to the damage at stake.

(10) To ensure proportionality, it is appropriate to harmonise in a targeted manner only those fault-based liability rules that govern the burden of proof for persons claiming compensation for damage caused by AI systems. This Directive should not harmonise general aspects of civil liability which are regulated in different ways by national civil liability rules, such as the definition of fault or causality, the different types of damage that give rise to claims for damages, the distribution of liability over multiple tortfeasors, contributory conduct, the calculation of damages or limitation periods.

(13) Other than in respect of the presumptions it lays down, this Directive does not harmonise national laws regarding which party has the burden of proof or which degree of certainty is required as regards the standard of proof.

(14) This Directive should follow a minimum harmonisation approach. Such an approach allows claimants in cases of damage caused by AI systems to invoke more favourable rules of national law. Thus, national laws could, for example, maintain reversals of the burden of proof under national fault-based regimes, or national no-fault liability (referred to as 'strict liability') regimes of which there are already a large variety in national laws, possibly applying to damage caused by AI systems.

(16) Access to information about specific high-risk AI systems that are suspected of having caused damage is an important factor to ascertain whether to claim compensation and to substantiate claims for compensation. Moreover, for high risk AI systems, [the AI Act] provides for specific documentation, information and logging requirements, but does not provide a right to the injured person to access that information. It is therefore appropriate to lay down rules on the disclosure of relevant evidence by those that have it at their disposal, for the purposes of establishing liability. This should also provide an additional incentive to comply with the relevant requirements laid down in the AI Act to document or record the relevant information.

(17) The large number of people usually involved in the design, development, deployment and operation of high-risk AI systems, makes it difficult for injured persons to identify the person potentially liable for damage caused and to prove the conditions for a claim for damages. To allow injured persons to ascertain whether a claim for damages is well-founded, it is appropriate to grant potential claimants a right to request a court to order the disclosure of relevant evidence before submitting a claim for damages. Such disclosure should only be ordered where the potential claimant presents facts and information sufficient to support the plausibility of a claim for damages and it has made a prior request to the provider, the person subject to the obligations of a provider or the user to disclose such evidence at their disposal about specific high-risk AI systems that are suspected of having caused damage which has been refused. Ordering disclosure should lead to a reduction of unnecessary litigation and avoid costs for the possible litigants caused by claims which are unjustified or likely to be unsuccessful. The refusal of the provider, the person subject to the obligations of a provider or the user prior to the request to the court to disclose evidence should not trigger the presumption of non-compliance with relevant duties of care by the person who refuses such disclosure.

(18) The limitation of disclosure of evidence as regards high-risk AI systems is consistent with [the AI Act], which provides certain specific documentation, record keeping and information obligations for operators involved in the design, development and deployment of high-risk AI systems. Such consistency also ensures the necessary proportionality by avoiding that operators of AI systems posing lower or no risk would be expected to document information to a level similar to that required for high-risk AI systems under [the AI Act].

(19) National courts should be able, in the course of civil proceedings, to order the disclosure or preservation of relevant evidence related to the damage caused by high-risk AI systems from persons who are already under an obligation to document or record information pursuant to [the AI Act], be they providers, persons under the same obligations as providers, or users of an AI system, either as defendants or third parties to the claim. There could be situations where the evidence relevant for the case is held by entities that would not be parties to the claim for damages but which are under an obligation to document or record such evidence pursuant to [the AI Act]. It is thus necessary to provide for the conditions under which such third parties to the claim can be ordered to disclose the relevant evidence.

(20) To maintain the balance between the interests of the parties involved in the claim for damages and of third parties concerned, the courts should order the disclosure of evidence only where this is necessary and proportionate for supporting the claim or potential claim for damages. In this respect, disclosure should only concern evidence that is necessary for a decision on the respective

claim for damages, for example only the parts of the relevant records or data sets required to prove non-compliance with a requirement laid down by [the AI Act]. To ensure the proportionality of such disclosure or preservation measures, national courts should have effective means to safeguard the legitimate interests of all parties involved, for instance the protection of trade secrets within the meaning of Directive (EU) 2016/943 of the European Parliament and of the Council[3] and of confidential information, such as information related to public or national security. In respect of trade secrets or alleged trade secrets which the court has identified as confidential within the meaning of Directive (EU) 2016/943, national courts should be empowered to take specific measures to ensure the confidentiality of trade secrets during and after the proceedings, while achieving a fair and proportionate balance between the trade-secret holder's interest in maintaining secrecy and the interest of the injured person. This should include measures to restrict access to documents containing trade secrets and access to hearings or documents and transcripts thereof to a limited number of people. When deciding on such measures, national courts should take into account the need to ensure the right to an effective remedy and to a fair trial, the legitimate interests of the parties and, where appropriate, of third parties, and any potential harm to either party or, where appropriate, to third parties, resulting from the granting or rejection of such measures. Moreover, to ensure a proportionate application of a disclosure measure towards third parties in claims for damages, the national courts should order disclosure from third parties only if the evidence cannot be obtained from the defendant.

(21) While national courts have the means of enforcing their orders for disclosure through various measures, any such enforcement measures could delay claims for damages and thus potentially create additional expenses for the litigants. For injured persons, such delays and additional expenses may make their recourse to an effective judicial remedy more difficult. Therefore, where a defendant in a claim for damages fails to disclose evidence at its disposal ordered by a court, it is appropriate to lay down a presumption of non-compliance with those duties of care which that evidence was intended to prove. This rebuttable presumption will reduce the duration of litigation and facilitate more efficient court proceedings. The defendant should be able to rebut that presumption by submitting evidence to the contrary.

RELATED ARTICLE

Article 2 (Definitions).

RELATED LAWS

AI Act (Article 25(1) and 25(3)); Representative Actions Directive; Trade Secrets Directive; Antitrust Damages Directive; IP Enforcement Directive; and New Product Liability Directive.

3. [Trade Secrets Directive].

RELATED CASE LAW

Aeris (Case T-628/17): Case T-628/17, *Aeris Invest Sàrl v. European Commission and Single Resolution Board*, 1 June 2022, ECLI:EU:T:2022:315.
Bayer CropScience (Case C-499/18): Case C-499/18, *Bayer CropScience AG and Bayer AG v. European Commission*, 6 May 2021, ECLI:EU:C:2021:367.
Cruciano Siragusa (Case C-206/13): Case C-206/13, *Cruciano Siragusa v. Regione Sicilia – Soprintendenza Beni Culturali e Ambientali di Palermo*, 6 March 2014, ECLI:EU:C:2014:126.
Exportslachterijen van Oordegem BVBA (Case C-2/93): Case C-2/93, *Exportslachterijen van Oordegem BVBA v. Belgische Dienst voor Bedrijfsleven en Landbouw and Generale Bank NV.*, 2 June 1994, ECLI:EU:C:1994:223.
Italy (Case C-611/17): Case C-611/17, *Italian Republic v. Council of the European Union*, 30 April 2019, ECLI:EU:C:2019:332.
Paccar (Case C-163/21): Case C-163/21, *AD v. PACCAR Inc and Others*, 10 November 2022, ECLI:EU:C:2022:863.
RegioJet (Case C-57/21): Case C-57/21, *RegioJet a.s. v. České drďhy a.s.*, 12 January 2023, ECLI:EU:C:2023:6.

COMMENTARY

1 Purpose

From the earliest stages of the process which led up to the AI Liability Directive (AILD), difficulties were identified for victims of harm in uncovering whether any losses that they suffer are caused by artificial intelligence (AI) systems or not.[4] Those difficulties are generally deemed to result from various properties of AI systems,[5] which include:

- *Opacity*: for the average person, an AI system will be a so-called black box, meaning the operation of the system and the processes it goes through are difficult to understand or follow.[6] As a result, the average person is unable to understand how the AI system's algorithms reach a certain outcome.[7] Absent such understanding, victims are unable to assess whether an AI system reaches a correct or desirable outcome, even when knowing the system's inputs and output.
- *Complexity*: most AI systems will not operate in isolation, but will rather be embedded into other applications or devices. This will result in a complex interplay of various systems and components, making it difficult for victims to assess why the combined system's outcome is incorrect or not as desired.[8]

4. Evas 2018, 22; Expert Group 2019, 55; Commission 2020, 14; Parliament 2020, 6; Bertolini 2020, 91.
5. Expert Group 2019, 43.
6. *Ibid.*, at 33.
7. Commission 2020, 9 and 16.
8. *Ibid.*, at 9.

- *Autonomy*: as opposed to most other systems and devices, AI systems can usually operate without much human involvement, and may even have self-learning capabilities which allow them to alter their initial algorithms on the basis of external input.[9] This creates a lack of control and visibility for users over the performance by AI systems of their tasks and makes it difficult to assess whether an AI system is adequately performing.

Taken together, those properties are likely to cause difficulties for victims to assess the proper functioning of an AI system on various levels, and may hence make it more difficult for victims to exercise a claim.[10] Given the opacity and complexity of AI systems, victims may not be aware that a system has caused harm in the first place, or they may not be able to assess which of various interoperating systems has caused harm. In addition, even when victims are correctly able to identify the AI system which caused them harm, they may not be able to prove the facts which gave rise to that harm, in the absence of a record of the AI system's input, output, and/or functioning. Finally, even if victims have all of this information available, their lack of technical expertise or familiarity with the functioning of the AI system at stake may prevent them from being able to assess or explain to a court how the AI system caused their harm.

During the Commission's assessment process for rules on liability for AI, concerns were raised that this information asymmetry could lead to a liability gap – that is to say, there is a risk that not all victims of harm caused by AI systems are compensated. After all, some potential claimants may be unaware of the (extent of the) AI system's involvement in their harm and may therefore decide against bringing a claim, whereas others may bring a claim but see it dismissed for failure to reach the applicable evidentiary threshold.[11]

To mitigate that liability gap, the Parliament originally proposed far-reaching substantive and procedural rules to regulate liability for AI systems in its resolution of 20 October 2020, including a strict liability regime and thirty-year limitation periods for physical harm caused by high-risk AI systems as well as a requirement for producers of all AI systems to cooperate with and provide information to victims of harm caused by AI systems.

In the AILD, the Commission has taken a more cautious approach. However, it has decided to retain a form of the disclosure obligation originally suggested by the Parliament in Article 3 of the Directive. The goal of that disclosure obligation is to close the liability gap and ensure that victims of harm caused by AI systems do not face excessive hurdles when seeking compensation.[12] To achieve this, the Commission has taken a balanced approach, as it has subjected the disclosure obligation to various requirements and conditions on the side of the (potential) claimant, thus aiming to protect providers of AI systems from an overload of (baseless) litigation.

9. *Ibid.*, at 9 and 16.
10. Ziosi et al. 2023, 4; Schollaert & De Bruyne 2023, 579.
11. Dheu et al. 2023, 2.
12. Hacker 2023, 6.

2 Analysis

2.1 The Right of a (Potential) Claimant to Disclosure

The core of Article 3 of the AILD lies in its first and second paragraphs, which require that Member States adopt rules empowering national courts to order the disclosure of evidence about a specific high-risk AI system that is suspected of having caused damage. That disclosure mechanism applies both in the case of fault-based liability claims and strict liability claims.[13]

The purpose of the mechanism is to ensure that (potential) claimants are able to obtain sufficient information to assess whether they have a claim for damages and/or to exercise that claim by meeting their burden of proof.[14] As is noted in Recital 13 to the Directive, the purpose of disclosure is therefore not to shift the burden of proof to the defendant. It is still up to national law to decide which party has the burden of proof – if it lies with the (potential) claimant, then that claimant will still need to prove its claim on the basis of the evidence disclosed as well as any other evidence it has available.

The AILD has been criticized as not fully remedying the information asymmetry identified in the preparatory works for the Directive. After all, while it allows victims of harm caused by a high-risk AI system to access relevant information, it does not contain an express mechanism to ensure that the victim will also understand or be able to interpret the information provided.[15] For instance, the Directive does not require that the evidence disclosed is provided in a readable or understandable format, and would therefore seem to leave open the possibility that the disclosing party provides large quantities of technical data and logs which are difficult to understand for the (potential) claimant.

However, similar disclosure mechanisms included in previous European Union (EU) Directives on other topics have also not expressly included rules on the format in which evidence is to be disclosed. Nonetheless, in relation to the disclosure mechanism in the Antitrust Damages Directive (which relates to damages claims for competition infringements), the Court of Justice of the European Union (CJEU) held that:[16]

> from a practical point of view, ... for the claimant to be provided only with unprocessed, pre-existing and possibly very numerous documents would correspond only imperfectly with its request, whereas that provision must, on the contrary, be applied effectively so as to provide injured parties with tools that are capable of compensating for the information asymmetry between the parties to a dispute.

Consequently, the CJEU held that subject to similar requirements of relevance, proportionality, and necessity as included in Article 3 of the AILD, defendants could be required under the Antitrust Damages Directive to comply with disclosure requests by creating *ex novo* evidence by compiling or classifying information, knowledge, or data

13. *Ibid.*, at 17.
14. Dheu et al. 2023, 4.
15. *Ibid.*, at 5; Schollaert & De Bruyne, 580.
16. *Paccar* (Case C-163/21), para. 61.

in their possession. Given the broad similarities between the disclosure mechanism in that Directive and the mechanism in Article 3 of the AILD, it is likely that the same applies to defendants under Article 3.

At the same time, the Directive follows a minimum harmonization approach, and Member States are therefore free to adopt and include additional rules and requirements to frame the disclosure obligation in their national transposition measures.[17] National legislation may therefore provide requirements that information is provided in an understandable manner or that the disclosing party provides instructions on how to interpret data and logs disclosed. National courts may also fall back on more general measures, including, as available under national law, the appointment of a court expert, a reversal of the burden of proof, or witness examinations.

The imposition of such further requirements by national legislation may also be prompted by the transposition of other recent EU legislative initiatives, which did decide to address the need to have evidence that is easily accessible or easily understandable. This is, for instance, the case of the New Product Liability Directive (NPLD) (Article 8(5)).

The right for (potential) claimants to disclosure under the AILD complements the AI Act's provisions on the creation and retention of certain data on AI systems. For instance, the AI Act requires operators involved in the design, development and deployment of high-risk AI systems to create and keep up-to-date technical documentation (Articles 11 and 18), put in place record-keeping capabilities which record logs ensuring a level of traceability of the AI system's functioning throughout its lifecycle (Articles 12 and 19) and quality management policies, procedures and instructions (Article 17). Through the right to disclosure in the AILD, (potential) claimants can have access to that information and can use it to hold providers of AI systems liable. However, the right to disclosure is not limited to data, logs and records which are required under the AI Act, and information which the (potential) defendant is not required to create or keep on the basis of the AI Act is also eligible for disclosure.

The right to disclosure is not an absolute or unconditional right and therefore does not allow a request for disclosure by each and any interested party. Rather, Member States are only required to allow disclosure requests by a claimant or a potential claimant (both of which are defined terms in Article 2(6) and 2(7) of the AILD). While the term 'claimant' is rather broad and includes not only the person injured by the AI system but also anyone who has succeeded or been subrogated to the rights of that person (such as an insurer) or anyone acting on behalf of an injured person, it would not necessarily capture all parties to a dispute. For instance, where a defendant against a claim for damages believes it is not liable because the harm it is requested to indemnify was caused by an AI system rather than by its own actions, it is unclear whether that defendant will be able to obtain disclosure of information in relation to that AI system. This will rather depend on whether, in each national system, that defendant would have a claim against the AI system provider (such as a hold harmless claim).

17. AILD, Rec. 14.

However, even for (potential) claimants, various conditions apply before they are able to obtain disclosure of relevant information.

2.1.1 *The Request for Disclosure Must Be Brought Against the Provider or User of a High-Risk AI System*

The AILD only makes disclosure available if the request by the (potential) claimant is directed against one of the following persons involved in the operation of the AI system:

- a provider of high-risk AI systems;
- the manufacturer of a product to which one of the legal acts listed in section 1 of Annex I, to the AI Act apply, in any of the following circumstances:
  - it placed the high-risk AI system on the market together with the product under its name or trademark; or
  - it put the high-risk AI system into service under its name or trademark after the product was placed on the market.[18]
- any distributor, importer, user or other third party in any of the following circumstances:
  - they put their name or trademark on a high-risk AI system already placed on the market or put into service (without prejudice to contractual arrangements stipulating that the distributor, importer, user or other third party does not assume the obligations of a provider of high-risk AI systems);
  - they made a substantial modification to a high-risk AI system that has already been placed on the market or has already been put into service in such a way that it remains a high-risk AI system;
  - they modified the intended purpose of an AI system, including a general-purpose AI system, which has not been classified as high-risk and has already been placed on the market or put into service in such a way that the AI system concerned becomes a high-risk AI system.[19]
- a user of high-risk AI systems.

Recital 17 of the AILD indicates that the purpose of including such broad categories was to capture all of the persons people usually involved in the design, development, deployment and operation of high-risk AI systems, i.e., all of the persons which under the AI Act would have duties to create or retain data, logs, and other records on the AI systems concerned. As such, the goal is to ensure that potential claimants have access to all information necessary for them to assess whether they have a claim for damages.

At the same time, this condition also restricts the right to disclosure of matters involving high-risk AI systems. High-risk AI systems are defined in Article 2(2) of the AILD as any AI system referred to in Article 6 of the AI Act.

18. AIA, Art. 25(3).
19. *Ibid.*, Art. 25(1).

2.1.2 The Request Relates to Relevant Evidence

The information, data, or logs which the (potential) claimant is requesting disclosure of must be deemed 'relevant evidence' by the national court. While it will be up to national courts to interpret what constitutes 'relevant' evidence, that relevance requirement should be seen in light of the Directive's aim to ensure that potential claimants can obtain evidence to ascertain whether a claim for damages is well-founded. That is to say, the goal of the right to disclosure is not only to assist claimants who already have good arguments that they have a well-founded claim (but are unable to evidence it) but also to provide victims of harm caused by high-risk AI systems with sufficient information to assess whether or not they have a claim for damages in the first place and, if so, against which person or in relation to which high-risk AI system.[20]

As such, the relevance requirement is not intended as a high threshold but is likely intended to set a reasonable minimum bound which documents must attain before they fall within the scope of the right of disclosure. In our view, the relevance requirement then requires that the national court assesses whether, if the evidence to be disclosed demonstrates what the (potential) claimant argues it will demonstrate, a (potential) claim against the defendant could be well-founded. If, however, the information the (potential) claimant is seeking disclosure of could not be used for assessing whether a (potential) claim is well-founded even if it demonstrates what the (potential) claimant argues it will demonstrate, the evidence is likely irrelevant.

The relevance requirement does not require preliminary evidence on the part of the (potential) claimant that the evidence will demonstrate what the (potential) claimant argues it will – the point of disclosure is precisely to allow the (potential) claimant to uncover whether the information points towards liability. Nor does the relevance requirement call for evidence that a claim for damages will turn out to be well-founded. That assessment of the likelihood that there is a claim for damages is rather set by Article 3(1), second paragraph, which requires facts and evidence sufficient to support the plausibility of a claim for damages – but only for potential claimants, and not for claimants.

In our view, a court could then decide to dismiss a claim for disclosure if the underlying claim for damages would need to be dismissed in any event, for instance, because it is time-barred, or if the evidence requested is unrelated to an incident for which the (potential) claimant may seek compensation.

2.1.3 The Request Relates to Evidence at the Disposal of the Defendant

A request for disclosure must relate to documents which the defendant has at its disposal. Given their obligations under the AI Act to create and retain a variety of records, reports, data and logs, providers of high-risk AI systems as well as persons who have the same obligations as those imposed on providers will have a range of

20. AILD, Recs 16 and 17.

relevant information available.[21] Likewise, users of high-risk AI systems also have the obligation under the AI Act to retain certain automatically generated logs (to the extent they are under their control).[22]

However, the legal obligations imposed on those potential defendants to create and retain that information do not guarantee that it will also actually be available. Potential defendants may fail to create and retain the necessary information in breach of the AI Act or may lose that information for reasons outside their control. This has prompted some discussion on whether Article 3(1) of the AILD should clarify that (potential) claimants more broadly have a right to disclosure of information which defendants should legally have at their disposal.[23]

However, the Directive was not amended to reflect this concern, and on a plain reading Article 3(1) therefore does not grant (potential) claimants a right to obtain disclosure of evidence from defendants which they do not have at their disposal, even if they were legally required to retain that evidence. The practical consequence of this is that the presumption of non-compliance set out in Article 3(5) likely does not apply if the defendant did not have the evidence requested at its disposal prior to a disclosure or preservation order being issued. This potential gap in the protection of (potential) claimants will therefore need to be filled by national legislation, which can provide for broader rules on disclosure (since the AILD follows a minimum harmonization approach) or which may shift or alleviate the burden of proof for the claimant in that situation.[24]

However, the notion of being at the defendant's disposal should be interpreted broadly. In its judgment of 10 November 2022, the CJEU held that the disclosure requirement under the Antitrust Damages Directive could also create the creation *ex novo* by a defendant of records, by compiling or classifying information.[25] This was despite the fact that the Antitrust Damages Directive contains a similar criterion that information should be 'in the control' of a defendant.[26] The recitals to the NPLD, which contains a disclosure mechanism similar to the AILD, confirms that this possibility to require the creation *ex novo* of records also applies to the NPLD.[27] As such, it is likely that also under the AILD, information which the defendant does not have on hand but which it is able to create should also be considered within the scope of the disclosure mechanism.

21. AIA, Arts 11, 12, 17, 18, and 19.
22. *Ibid.*, Art. 26(6).
23. Hacker 2023, 19.
24. Karner et al. 2020.
25. *Paccar* (Case C-163/21), para. 61.
26. Antitrust Damages Directive, Art. 5(1).
27. NPLD, Rec. 20: 'It is therefore necessary to facilitate claimants' access to evidence to be used in legal proceedings, while ensuring that such access is limited to that which is necessary and proportionate, and that confidential information and trade secrets are protected. Such evidence should also include documents that have to be created ex novo by the defendant by compiling or classifying the available evidence.'

2.1.4 *The Request Relates to Evidence About a Specific High-Risk AI System That Is Suspected of Having Caused Damage*

To successfully request disclosure, a (potential) claimant will also need to show that the documents, data, logs or records which would be disclosed relate to a specific high-risk AI system that is suspected of having caused damage. The application of this criterion differs between potential claimants and claimants, with a higher threshold applying for potential claimants.

For potential claimants (i.e., persons who are considering but have not yet brought a claim for damages), Article 3(1), paragraph 2, of the AILD requires the presentation of facts and evidence sufficient to support the plausibility of a claim for damages. There is no precise definition of that 'plausible' standard,[28] and it is somewhat of a departure from similar disclosure mechanisms in other EU directives, which mostly require that a potential claimant put forward only reasonably available evidence or facts.[29] This new 'plausible' standard has also been used in the NPLD, which requires the injured person claiming compensation and seeking disclosure of relevant evidence to present facts and evidence sufficient to support the plausibility of the claim for compensation (Article 8(1)).

The purpose of this requirement is to protect potential defendants from fishing expeditions – that is to say, requests for disclosure by persons who do not suspect they have been harmed by a high-risk AI system but would rather use the right to disclosure to gain information from potential defendants for other purposes. Courts should therefore dismiss claims when it is clear that the party requesting disclosure is seeking information for purposes other than a claim for damages, for instance, because an actual or potential competitor wants insight into the defendant's data.[30]

That being said, the threshold for potential claimants to evidence the plausibility of their claim is still rather low, and national courts should only assess whether at first sight it appears reasonable for the potential claimant to assume, on the basis of the information available to it, that it may have a claim for damages against the defendant. After all, Recital 17 to the AILD clarifies that the purpose of the disclosure mechanism is to 'allow injured persons to ascertain whether a claim for damages is well-founded', that is, to allow persons who are unsure whether they have a claim for damages to gain more information to assess their potential claim. If the threshold for potential claims were set too high, the disclosure mechanism could no longer serve that purpose. After all, the facts and evidence which the potential claimant provides in support of the plausibility of its potential claim may very be limited.[31] Without access to information on the operation of a high-risk AI system, it is likely that the potential claimant will only

28. Ziosi et al. 2023, 5.
29. *See, for instance,* IP Enforcement Directive, Art. 6 (which requires 'reasonably available evidence sufficient to support its claims'); Antitrust Damages Directive, Art. 5 (which requires 'reasonably available facts and evidence sufficient to support the plausibility of its claim for damages'); and Representative Actions Directive, Art. 18 (which requires 'reasonably available evidence sufficient to support a representative action').
30. Hacker 2023, 19; Schollaert & De Bruyne 2023, 580.
31. Hacker 2023, 19.

be able to prove the fact that it has suffered harm and/or that it used a high-risk AI system.

The plausible claim for damages which the potential claimant is required to evidence does not need to be against the party from whom disclosure is requested. Rather, the claim for damages which the potential claimant purports to have may be against a third party provided the evidence the potential claimant is seeking disclosure of is at the disposal of the party against which the claim for disclosure is made and is relevant for that claim for damages against a third party.[32] However, such a request for disclosure against a third party will likely only be proportionate in accordance with Article 3(4) if the potential defendant does not have the evidence requested at its disposal.[33]

Claimants (i.e., persons who have brought a claim for damages), however, do not need to evidence that their claim is plausible, but will only need to show that the high-risk AI system at issue 'is suspected of having caused damage'. In our view, that threshold appears to be even lower than the 'plausibility' threshold and only seems to require that a claim for damages has been brought in relation to that high-risk AI system which does not seem clearly ill-founded.

2.1.5 *The (Potential) Claimant Has Attempted to Obtain the Evidence from the Defendant*

Litigating disclosure requests requires the expenditure of resources both on the part of the parties and of the courts. As such, both claimants and potential claimants are expected to first undertake efforts to obtain disclosure of relevant information from the (potential) defendant without going to court. However, the condition applies differently to potential claimants and claimants.

Potential claimants are required under Article 3(1), first paragraph, of the AILD to evidence that they have previously asked the defendant for the relevant evidence which they are seeking to have disclosed and that this request was refused, although the defendant had such relevant at its disposal. Since the purpose of this requirement is to provide the defendant the opportunity to disclose the evidence without going through litigation, a refusal should be understood as any conduct on the part of the defendant other than the voluntary disclosure to the potential claimant of the information, data, logs and records requested at its disposal. As such, a failure by the defendant to respond to a request for voluntary disclosure by a reasonable deadline or a partial disclosure could constitute a refusal. If this were not the case, the potential claimant would be unable to request disclosure absent an express refusal, which would greatly detract from his right to refusal under the AILD.

A claimant, however, is required under Article 3(2) of the AILD to undertake all proportionate attempts at gathering the relevant evidence from the defendant. It is

32. AILD, Rec. 19.
33. *Ibid.*, Rec. 20.

unclear from the wording of the AILD and its recitals what other actions a claimant could be asked to take other than a request for voluntary disclosure. What is more, it would be counterintuitive for a claimant, who has already brought a claim for damages, to have to expend more effort to obtain voluntary disclosure from a defendant than a potential claimant, who only needs to ask for voluntary disclosure under Article 3(1), first paragraph, of the AILD.

2.2 Evidence Preservation Measures

A request for disclosure requires that the (potential) claimant first attempts to get voluntary disclosure by a defendant. This will put the defendant on notice of the (potential) claimant's intention to bring a claim for damages and/or a request for the disclosure of certain documents, data, logs or records. In addition, proceedings to obtain forced disclosure by court order may take some time. As a result, there is a risk that relevant evidence is lost or destroyed between the moment where the (potential) claimant first initiates the disclosure process and an actual order for disclosure, either because of bad faith on the part of the defendant, short document retention periods in the defendant's internal policies, or causes outside the defendant's control.

To mitigate this risk, Article 3(3) of the AILD requires Member States to implement rules which allow national courts to take specific measures to preserve evidence. Only claimants are able to request such measures. This may partially detract from the usefulness of this provision, as defendants may act in bad faith once either: (1) a potential claimant asks for voluntary disclosure evidence or files a claim for the production of evidence; or (2) a claimant files its claim for damages. This risk may be mitigated by national law. For instance, some national systems may allow for an ex parte application for the production of evidence even if there has not been a prior request for voluntary disclosure.

The AILD leaves it up to the Member States to decide how courts should be requested. As such, it could be envisaged that the claimant can ask for evidence preservation measures in the context of the proceedings already pending in relation to its claim for damages, or in separate proceedings. Member States are therefore free to allow evidence preservation orders to be asked in ex parte proceedings. Such ex parte proceedings would further reduce the risk that a defendant acting in bad faith would destroy evidence, as it would not be aware of the request for evidence preservation prior to a preservation order.

Likewise, the AILD does not specify what measures could be ordered by a national court. As such, measures could take many forms and can be tailored to the specific situation. Member States could, for instance, allow the granting of measures requiring the defendant to suspend its ordinary document destruction policies or to keep relevant data, logs, and records in a segregated location. Moreover, Member States could also order that evidence is turned over to a third party pending the adjudication of the disclosure request.

2.3 Limits to the Disclosure and Preservation of Evidence

The obligation for a defendant to disclose data, logs, records, or other documents it holds on high-risk AI systems is far-reaching and may allow unwanted insight into the defendant's business and technical processes. For that reason, Article 3 of the AILD has set clear conditions for the exercise of the right to disclosure. Article 3(4) additionally sets limits to document disclosure and preservation orders.

2.3.1 The Proportionality and Necessity Test

First, Article 3(4) requires national courts to limit the disclosure and preservation of evidence to that which is necessary and proportionate to support a potential claim or a claim for damages. Where the 'relevancy' requirement set out in Article 3(1), first paragraph, of the AILD sets the lower bound which documents must at least attain before disclosure can be requested, the 'necessary and proportionate' requirement sets the upper bound for document disclosure and preservation: regardless of whether documents are relevant to a (potential) claim for damages, no disclosure can be ordered if that disclosure is not 'necessary and proportionate'. Such requirements can be found, for instance, in the provisions of the NPLD dealing with disclosure requests (Article 8(4)).

The principle of proportionality is a general principle of EU law.[34] It entails that a measure must not exceed what is necessary and appropriate in order to achieve the desired aim[35] and that the disadvantages caused must not be disproportionate to the aims pursued.[36] As such, the requirement of proportionality expresses a relationship between the objectives pursued and the means of achieving those objectives.[37] A measure is necessary when the legitimate objective pursued cannot be achieved by a measure that is just as appropriate but less restrictive.[38]

It is therefore important to identify the objectives pursued by the AILD as well as the potential disadvantages of granting a disclosure or preservation measure since the proportionality and necessity of any order will need to be assessed against those objectives and potential disadvantages. Recital 20 to the AILD clarifies that national courts should in that regard take into account:[39]

> the right to an effective remedy and to a fair trial, the legitimate interests of the parties and, where appropriate, of third parties, and any potential harm to either party or, where appropriate, to third parties.

34. *Cruciano Siragusa* (Case C-206/13), para. 34.
35. *Exportslachterijen van Oordegem BVBA* (Case C-2/93), para. 20.
36. *Aeris* (Case T-628/17), para. 176; *Bayer CropScience* (Case C-499/18), para. 166; *Italy* (Case C-611/17), para. 55.
37. Opinion of AG Pikamäe (9 Dec. 2021), Case C-184/20, *OT v. Vyriausioji tarnybines etikos komisija*, para. 55.
38. *Ibid.*
39. NPLD, Rec. 32 contains a similar disclosure mechanism and similar protections for confidential information and trade secrets, refers to the same criteria.

Article 3(4), second paragraph, furthermore requires national courts to consider as a legitimate interest of the defendant the protection of his trade secrets within the meaning of Article 2(1) of the Trade Secrets Directive and of confidential information.[40] As such, disclosure or preservation orders relating to evidence which constitutes a trade secret are not prohibited outright but are subject to a heightened level of scrutiny. This is also made clear by the fact that Article 3(4), third paragraph, requires Member States to empower national courts to impose protective measures for evidence which constitutes a trade secret – meaning such information is then at least subject to disclosure in the first place. National courts will need to weigh the risk and difficulties of disclosing trade secrets against, for instance, the evidence already available for the (potential) claimant or other evidence which the defendant may disclose and which does not constitute a trade secret.[41]

A good example of how the proportionality and necessity test is to be applied is offered by Article 5(3) of the Antitrust Damages Directive, which contains a disclosure mechanism for claimants who bring a claim for damages for the infringement of competition law, and which likewise requires national courts to only order proportionate disclosure. Recital 23 to that Directive clarifies that disclosure requests would 'not be deemed to be proportionate where they refer to the generic disclosure of documents' and refers to the 'requesting party's duty to specify the items of evidence or the categories of evidence as precisely and narrowly as possible'.[42]

In a judgment of 12 January 2023, the CJEU similarly held that the principle of proportionality prevents 'fishing expeditions', that is to say, requests for the disclosure of generic categories of documents.[43]

Recital 20 to the AILD also goes in that direction and indicates that:[44]

> disclosure should only concern evidence that is necessary for a decision on the respective claim for damages, for example only the parts of the relevant records or data sets required to prove non-compliance with a requirement laid down by [the AI Act].

The AILD therefore also prohibits blanket requests for information,[45] meaning requests for disclosure will need to be adequately circumscribed, and (potential) claimants will have to specify precisely which evidence they are seeking disclosure of. National courts should then only order disclosure of the parts of the evidence which relate to the (potential) claim.[46] The specificity with which a request or an order for disclosure or preservation can be delineated should of course be assessed with due regard to the

40. Under that Directive, a 'trade secret' is 'information which meets all of the following requirements: (a) it is secret in the sense that it is not, as a body or in the precise configuration and assembly of its components, generally known among or readily accessible to persons within the circles that normally deal with the kind of information in question; (b) it has commercial value because it is secret; (c) it has been subject to reasonable steps under the circumstances, by the person lawfully in control of the information, to keep it secret'.
41. Wagner 2023, 38.
42. Antitrust Damages Directive, Rec. 23.
43. *RegioJet* (Case C-57/21), para. 127.
44. AILD, Rec. 20.
45. Dheu et al. 2023, 5.
46. Schollaert & De Bruyne 2023, 581.

oftentimes limited view which both the (potential) claimant and the national court will have on the evidence available and the facts of the matter.

2.3.2 *Protective Measures for the Disclosure and Use of Trade Secrets*

A second limit imposed by Article 3(4) requires Member States to empower national courts to take specific measures necessary to preserve confidential trade secrets when evidence is used or referred to. National courts should be able to do so of their own motion or at the duly reasoned request of a party.

It will be up to national law to decide which specific measures should be allowed, although such measures can take a wide range of shapes and forms. For instance, national law could in our view allow that the evidence is only shown in court (potentially at a hearing behind closed doors) with no copies made available to other parties or is not shown to the (potential) claimant but only to a court expert or the court, or that the court imposes confidentiality obligations on the (potential) claimant.

2.3.3 *Procedural Remedies for Defendant*

Finally, Article 3(4), fourth paragraph, of the AILD also requires that Member States make available appropriate procedural remedies for defendants who have been ordered to disclose or preserve the relevant evidence.

This requirement shows the fundamental tension between the (potential) claimant and the defendant's interests which underlies the AILD. On the one hand, Recital 21 states the Directive's aim to 'reduce the duration of litigation and facilitate more efficient court proceedings' to ensure that victims of harm caused by high-risk AI systems are able to obtain compensation quickly.[47] The procedural remedies for defendants which Article 3(4), fourth paragraph, requires will, on the other hand, result in longer proceedings.

For a procedural remedy against a disclosure order to be efficient, defendants will need to be able to defer disclosure until their remedies have been exhausted. If disclosure is required pending the exercise of a remedy, (potential) claimants will become aware of the content of evidence and will potentially have copies – a situation which cannot be rolled back.

2.4 *Presumption of Defendant's Non-Compliance with a Relevant Duty of Care*

While national procedural law can ensure proper enforcement of disclosure or preservation orders in a variety of ways (such as penalty payments or seizure of relevant evidence), enforcing such an order is likely a costly and time-consuming matter for the (potential) claimant.[48] To remedy this, Article 3(5) of the AILD requires

47. AILD, Rec. 21.
48. *Ibid.*; Hacker 2023, 21.

national courts to presume the non-compliance with a relevant duty of care of a defendant who has not disclosed or preserved evidence at its disposal following an order to that effect. A similar presumption of non-compliance for failure to produce the requisite evidence is also included in the NPLD.[49]

The presumption of non-compliance only arises when the defendant does not comply with a disclosure or preservation order by a national court. It is not triggered merely by a refusal by the defendant to voluntarily disclose or preserve evidence following a request by a (potential) claimant to do so prior to a request for disclosure or preservation being brought before a national court.[50]

At first sight, it may appear that the scope of the presumption in Article 3(5) and the obligation to disclose in Article 3(1) is different.[51] The only entities required to disclose are providers or users of high-risk AI systems as well as any persons who have the same obligations as a provider, whereas the presumption of non-compliance applies more broadly to a 'defendant'. However, the presumption of non-compliance only applies to defendants who have failed to comply with a disclosure or preservation order. Pursuant to Article 3(1) and 3(2), such an order can only be made against providers or users of high-risk AI systems as well as any persons who have the same obligations as a provider. That requirement therefore aligns the parties to whom the presumption may apply with the parties against whom a disclosure or preservation order can be given.

The presumption set by Article 3(5) of the Directive is rebuttable, meaning the defendant is able to put forward evidence or arguments to convince the national court that it did comply with a relevant duty of care. As a result, the presumption of non-compliance should be seen as a shift in the burden of proof: rather than requiring the claimant to produce evidence of a breach of the duty of care – which it can no longer do given the defendant's failure to comply with the disclosure or preservation order – it will be up to the defendant to prove that it did comply with the relevant duties of care.

However, national courts will have to be careful when assessing the evidence presented by the defendant to rebut the presumption. Given the information asymmetry between the claimant and defendant, it is possible that the defendant will only give a partial view of the data, logs, and records it has available to the extent that they support its case. To rebut that presumption, the defendant should therefore provide credible and non-circumstantial evidence which clearly demonstrates that it complied with its duty of care.

BIBLIOGRAPHY

Reports and Recommendations

Bertolini 2020: Andrea Bertolini, *Study: Artificial Intelligence and Civil Liability*, European Parliament, Policy Department for Citizens' Rights and Constitutional

49. NPLD, Art. 9(2)(a).
50. Hacker 2023, 18; Schollaert & De Bruyne 2023, 580.
51. Dheu et al. 2023, 5.

Affairs (July 2020), www.europarl.europa.eu/RegData/etudes/STUD/2020/621926/IPOL_STU(2020)621926_EN.pdf (accessed 22 April 2024).

Commission 2020: Commission, *Report on the Safety and Liability Implications of Artificial Intelligence, the Internet of Things and Robotics*, COM(2020) 64 final.

Evas 2018: Tatjana Evas, *A Common EU Approach to Liability Rules and Insurance for Connected and Autonomous Vehicles. European Added Value Assessment*, European Parliament, European Parliamentary Research Service (February 2018), www.europarl.europa.eu/RegData/etudes/STUD/2018/615635/EPRS_STU(2018)615635_EN.pdf (accessed 22 April 2024).

Expert Group 2019: Expert Group on Liability and New Technologies – New Technologies Formation, *Liability for Artificial Intelligence and Other Emerging Digital Technologies*, Commission, Directorate-General for Justice and Consumers (November 2019), op.europa.eu/en/publication-detail/-/publication/1c5e30be-1197-11ea-8c1f-01aa75ed71a1/language-en (accessed 22 April 2024).

Karner et al. 2020: Ernst Karner, Bernhard A. Koch & Mark A. Geistfeld, *Comparative Law Study on Civil Liability for Artificial Intelligence*, Commission, Directorate-General for Justice and Consumers (November 2020), data.europa.eu/doi/10.2838/77360 (accessed 22 April 2024).

Academic Writings

Dheu et al. 2023: Orjan Dheu, Charlotte Ducuing & Jan De Bruyne, *The European Commission's Approach to Extra-Contractual Liability and AI: An Evaluation of the AI Liability Directive and the Revised Product Liability Directive*, 51 Computer Law & Security Review (2023), doi.org/10.1016/j.clsr.2023.105894.

Hacker 2023: Philipp Hacker, *The European AI Liability Directives: Critique of a Half-Hearted Approach and Lessons for the Future*, 51 Computer Law & Security Review (2023), doi.org/10.1016/j.clsr.2023.105871.

Schollaert & De Bruyne 2023: Victor Schollaert & Jan De Bruyne, *Voorstel Richtlijn AI-aansprakelijkheid. Verkennende analyse vanuit Belgisch prespectief*, Nieuw Juridisch Weekblad 574-587 (2023).

Wagner 2023: Gerhard Wagner, *Liability Rules for the Digital Age: Aiming for the Brussels Effect*, SSRN (14 April 2023).

Ziosi et al. 2023: Marta Ziosi et al., *The EU AI Liability Directive (AILD): Bridging Information Gaps*, SSRN (16 June 2023, revised 8 January 2024), papers.ssrn.com/sol3/papers.cfm?abstract_id=4470725 (accessed 22 April 2024).

Other

Parliament 2020: Parliament Resolution of 20 October 2020 with recommendations to the Commission on a civil liability regime for artificial intelligence (2020/2014 (INL)), OJ. C. 404 (6 October 2021).

ARTICLE 4 Rebuttable Presumption of a Causal Link in the Case of Fault

Jan De Bruyne & Victor Schollaert

Article 4. Rebuttable presumption of a causal link in the case of fault

1. Subject to the requirements laid down in this Article, national courts shall presume, for the purposes of applying liability rules to a claim for damages, the causal link between the fault of the defendant and the output produced by the AI system or the failure of the AI system to produce an output, where all of the following conditions are met:
   (a) the claimant has demonstrated or the court has presumed pursuant to Article 3(5), the fault of the defendant, or of a person for whose behaviour the defendant is responsible, consisting in the non-compliance with a duty of care laid down in Union or national law directly intended to protect against the damage that occurred;
   (b) it can be considered reasonably likely, based on the circumstances of the case, that the fault has influenced the output produced by the AI system or the failure of the AI system to produce an output;
   (c) the claimant has demonstrated that the output produced by the AI system or the failure of the AI system to produce an output gave rise to the damage.
2. In the case of a claim for damages against a provider of a high-risk AI system subject to the requirements laid down in [Sections] 2 and 3 of [Chapter] III of [the AI Act] or a person subject to the provider's obligations pursuant to [the AI Act], the condition of paragraph 1 letter (a) shall be met only where the complainant has demonstrated that the provider or, where relevant, the person subject to the provider's obligations, failed to comply with any of the following requirements laid down in those chapters, taking into account the steps undertaken in and the results of the risk management system pursuant to [Article 9 and Article 16 point (a) of the AI Act]:
   (a) the AI system is a system which makes use of techniques involving the training of models with data and which was not developed on the basis of training, validation and testing data sets that meet the quality criteria referred to in [Article 10(2) to (4) of the AI Act];
   (b) the AI system was not designed and developed in a way that meets the transparency requirements laid down in [Article 13 of the AI Act];

(c) the AI system was not designed and developed in a way that allows for an effective oversight by natural persons during the period in which the AI system is in use pursuant to [Article 14 of the AI Act];
(d) the AI system was not designed and developed so as to achieve, in the light of its intended purpose, an appropriate level of accuracy, robustness and cybersecurity pursuant to [Article 15 and Article 16, point (a), of the AI Act]; or
(e) the necessary corrective actions were not immediately taken to bring the AI system in conformity with the obligations laid down in [Chapter III, Section 2 of the AI Act] or to withdraw or recall the system, as appropriate, pursuant to [Article 16, point (j), and Article 20 of the AI Act].

3. In the case of a claim for damages against a [deployer] of a high-risk AI system subject to the requirements laid down in [Sections 2 and 3 of Chapter III of the AI Act], the condition of paragraph 1 letter (a) shall be met where the claimant proves that the [deployer]:
   (a) did not comply with its obligations to use or monitor the AI system in accordance with the accompanying instructions of use or, where appropriate, suspend or interrupt its use pursuant to [Article 26 of the AI Act]; or
   (b) exposed the AI system to input data under its control which is not relevant in view of the system's intended purpose pursuant to [Article 26(4) of the AI Act].
4. In the case of a claim for damages concerning a high-risk AI system, a national court shall not apply the presumption laid down in paragraph 1 where the defendant demonstrates that sufficient evidence and expertise is reasonably accessible for the claimant to prove the causal link mentioned in paragraph 1.
5. In the case of a claim for damages concerning an AI system that is not a high-risk AI system, the presumption laid down in paragraph 1 shall only apply where the national court considers it excessively difficult for the claimant to prove the causal link mentioned in paragraph 1.
6. In the case of a claim for damages against a defendant who used the AI system in the course of a personal, non-professional activity, the presumption laid down in paragraph 1 shall apply only where the defendant materially interfered with the conditions of the operation of the AI system or if the defendant was required and able to determine the conditions of operation of the AI system and failed to do so.
7. The defendant shall have the right to rebut the presumption laid down in paragraph 1.

Recitals

(3) When an injured person seeks compensation for damage suffered, Member States' general fault-based liability rules usually require that person to prove a negligent or intentionally damaging act or omission ('fault') by the person potentially liable for that damage, as well as a causal link between that fault and the relevant damage. However, when AI is interposed between the act or omission of a person and the damage, the specific characteristics of certain AI systems, such as opacity, autonomous behaviour and complexity, may make it excessively difficult, if not impossible, for the injured person to meet this burden of proof. In particular, it may be excessively difficult to prove that a specific input for which the potentially liable person is responsible had caused a specific AI system output that led to the damage at stake.

(10) To ensure proportionality, it is appropriate to harmonise in a targeted manner only those fault-based liability rules that govern the burden of proof for

persons claiming compensation for damage caused by AI systems. This Directive should not harmonise general aspects of civil liability which are regulated in different ways by national civil liability rules, such as the definition of fault or causality, the different types of damage that give rise to claims for damages, the distribution of liability over multiple tortfeasors, contributory conduct, the calculation of damages or limitation periods.

(21) While national courts have the means of enforcing their orders for disclosure through various measures, any such enforcement measures could delay claims for damages and thus potentially create additional expenses for the litigants. For injured persons, such delays and additional expenses may make their recourse to an effective judicial remedy more difficult. Therefore, where a defendant in a claim for damages fails to disclose evidence at its disposal ordered by a court, it is appropriate to lay down a presumption of non-compliance with those duties of care which that evidence was intended to prove. This rebuttable presumption will reduce the duration of litigation and facilitate more efficient court proceedings. The defendant should be able to rebut that presumption by submitting evidence to the contrary.

(22) In order to address the difficulties to prove that a specific input for which the potentially liable person is responsible had caused a specific AI system output that led to the damage at stake, it is appropriate to provide, under certain conditions, for a presumption of causality. While in a fault-based claim the claimant usually has to prove the damage, the human act or omission constituting fault of the defendant and the causality link between the two, this Directive does not harmonise the conditions under which national courts establish fault. They remain governed by the applicable national law and, where harmonised, by applicable Union law. Similarly, this Directive does not harmonise the conditions related to the damage, for instance what damages are compensable, which are also regulated by applicable national and Union law. For the presumption of causality under this Directive to apply, the fault of the defendant should be established as a human act or omission which does not meet a duty of care under Union law or national law that is directly intended to protect against the damage that occurred. Thus, this presumption can apply, for example, in a claim for damages for physical injury when the court establishes the fault of the defendant for non-complying with the instructions of use which are meant to prevent harm to natural persons. Non-compliance with duties of care that were not directly intended to protect against the damage that occurred do not lead to the application of the presumption, for example a provider's failure to file required documentation with competent authorities would not lead to the application of the presumption in claims for damages due to physical injury. It should also be necessary to establish that it can be considered reasonably likely, based on the circumstances of the case, that the fault has influenced the output produced by the AI system or the failure of the AI system to produce an output. Finally, the claimant should still be required to prove that the output or failure to produce an output gave rise to the damage.

(23) Such a fault can be established in respect of non-compliance with Union rules which specifically regulate high-risk AI systems like the requirements introduced for certain high-risk AI systems by [the AI Act], requirements which may be introduced by future sectoral legislation for other high-risk AI systems [...] or duties of care which are linked to certain activities and which are applicable irrespective whether AI is used for that activity. At the same time, this Directive neither creates nor harmonises the requirements or the liability of entities whose activity is regulated under those legal acts, and therefore

does not create new liability claims. Establishing a breach of such a requirement that amounts to fault will be done according to the provisions of those applicable rules of Union Law, since this Directive neither introduces new requirements nor affects existing requirements. For example, the exemption of liability for providers of intermediary services and the due diligence obligations to which they are subject pursuant to [the Digital Services Act] are not affected by this Directive. Similarly, the compliance with requirements imposed on online platforms to avoid unauthorised communication to the public of copyright protected works is to be established under Directive (EU) 2019/790 on copyright and related rights in the Digital Single Market and other relevant Union copyright law.

(24) In areas not harmonised by Union law, national law continues to apply and fault is established under the applicable national law. All national liability regimes have duties of care, taking as a standard of conduct different expressions of the principle how a reasonable person should act, which also ensure the safe operation of AI systems in order to prevent damage to recognised legal interests. Such duties of care could for instance require [deployers] of AI systems to choose for certain tasks a particular AI system with concrete characteristics or to exclude certain segments of a population from being exposed to a particular AI system. National law can also introduce specific obligations meant to prevent risks for certain activities, which are applicable irrespective whether AI is used for that activity, for example traffic rules or obligations specifically designed for AI systems, such as additional national requirements for [deployers] of high risk AI systems pursuant to [Article 26(3) of the AI Act]. This Directive neither introduces such requirements nor affects the conditions for establishing fault in case of breach of such requirements.

(25) Even when fault consisting of a non-compliance with a duty of care directly intended to protect against the damage that occurred is established, not every fault should lead to the application of the rebuttable presumption linking it to the output of the AI. Such a presumption should only apply when it can be considered reasonably likely, from the circumstances in which the damage occurred, that such fault has influenced the output produced by the AI system or the failure of the AI system to produce an output that gave rise to the damage. It can be for example considered reasonably likely that the fault has influenced the output or failure to produce an output, when that fault consists in breaching a duty of care in respect of limiting the perimeter of operation of the AI system and the damage occurred outside the perimeter of operation. On the contrary, a breach of a requirement to file certain documents or to register with a given authority, even though this might be foreseen for that particular activity or even be applicable expressly to the operation of an AI system, could not be considered as reasonably likely to have influenced the output produced by the AI system or the failure of the AI system to produce an output.

(26) This Directive covers the fault constituting non-compliance with certain listed requirements laid down in [Chapter III, Sections 2 and 3 of the AI Act] for providers and [deployers] of high-risk AI systems, the non-compliance with which can lead, under certain conditions, to a presumption of causality. The AI Act provides for full harmonisation of requirements for AI systems, unless otherwise explicitly laid down therein. It harmonises the specific requirements for high-risk AI systems. Hence, for the purposes of claims for damages in which a presumption of causality according to this Directive is applied, the potential fault of providers or persons subject to the obligations of a provider pursuant to [the AI Act] is established only through a noncompliance with

such requirements. Given that in practice it may be difficult for the claimant to prove such non-compliance when the defendant is a provider of the AI system, and in full consistency with the logic of [the AI Act], this Directive should also provide that the steps undertaken by the provider within the risk management system and the results of the risk management system, i.e., the decision to adopt or not to adopt certain risk management measures, should be taken into account in the determination of whether the provider has complied with the relevant requirements under the AI Act referred to in this Directive. The risk management system put in place by the provider pursuant to [the AI Act] is a continuous iterative process run throughout the lifecycle of the high-risk AI system, whereby the provider ensures compliance with mandatory requirements meant to mitigate risks and can, therefore, be a useful element for the purpose of the assessment of this compliance. This Directive also covers the cases of [deployers'] fault, when this fault consists in noncompliance with certain specific requirements set by [the AI Act]. In addition, the fault of [deployers] of high-risk AI systems may be established following non-compliance with other duties of care laid down in Union or national law, in light of [Article 26(3) of the AI Act].

(27) While the specific characteristics of certain AI systems, like autonomy and opacity, could make it excessively difficult for the claimant to meet the burden of proof, there could be situations where such difficulties do not exist because there could be sufficient evidence and expertise available to the complainant to prove the causal link. This could be the case, for example, in respect of high-risk AI systems where the claimant could reasonably access sufficient evidence and expertise through documentation and logging requirements pursuant to [the AI Act]. In such situations, the court should not apply the presumption.

(28) The presumption of causality could also apply to AI systems that are not high-risk AI systems because there could be excessive difficulties of proof for the claimant. For example, such difficulties could be assessed in light of the characteristics of certain AI systems, such as autonomy and opacity, which render the explanation of the inner functioning of the AI system very difficult in practice, negatively affecting the ability of the claimant to prove the causal link between the fault of the defendant and the AI output. A national court should apply the presumption where the claimant is in an excessively difficult position to prove causation, since it is required to explain how the AI system was led by the human act or omission that constitutes fault to produce the output or the failure to produce an output which gave rise to the damage. However, the claimant should neither be required to explain the characteristics of the AI system concerned nor how these characteristics make it harder to establish the causal link.

(29) The application of the presumption of causality is meant to ensure for the injured person a similar level of protection as for situations where AI is not involved and where causality may therefore be easier to prove. Nevertheless, alleviating the burden of proving causation is not always appropriate under this Directive where the defendant is not a professional [deployer] but rather a person using the AI system for its private activities. In such circumstances, in order to balance interests between the injured person and the non-professional [deployer], it needs to be taken into account whether such non-professional [deployers] can add to the risk of an AI system causing damage through their behaviour. If the provider of an AI system has complied with all its obligations and, in consequence, that system was deemed sufficiently safe to be put on the market for a given use by non-professional

[deployers] and it is then used for that task, a presumption of causality should not apply for the simple launch of the operation of such a system by such non-professional [deployers]. A non-professional [deployer] that buys an AI system and simply launches it according to its purpose, without interfering materially with the conditions of operations, should not be covered by the causality presumption laid down by this Directive. However, if a national court determines that a nonprofessional [deployer] materially interfered with the conditions of operation of an AI system or was required and able to determine the conditions of operation of the AI system and failed to do so, then the presumption of causality should apply, where all the other conditions are fulfilled. This could be the case, for example, when the nonprofessional [deployer]does not comply with the instructions of use or with other applicable duties of care when choosing the area of operation or when setting performance conditions of the AI system. This is without prejudice to the fact that the provider should determine the intended purpose of an AI system, including the specific context and conditions of use, and eliminate or minimise the risks of that system as appropriate at the time of the design and development, taking into account the knowledge and expertise of the intended [deployer].

(30) Since this Directive introduces a rebuttable presumption, the defendant should be able to rebut it, in particular by showing that its fault could not have caused the damage.

RELATED ARTICLES

Article 1 (Subject matter and scope); Article 2 (Definitions); Article 3 (Disclosure of evidence and rebuttable presumption of non-compliance).

RELATED LAWS

International

AI Convention.

EU

AI Act; AI Act Commission Proposal; DSA; PLD; Resolution 2015/2103: Resolution (EU) 2015/2103 of the European Parliament of 16 February 2017 with recommendations to the Commission on Civil Law Rules on Robotics; Digital Content Directive; Resolution 2020/2014 of the European Parliament of 20 October 2020 with recommendations to the Commission on a civil liability regime for artificial intelligence; NPLD; Draft Compromise AI Act 2023: Draft Compromise Amendments on the Draft Report Proposal (EU) of the European Parliament of 16 May 2023 for a regulation of the European Parliament and of the Council on harmonized rules on Artificial Intelligence (Artificial Intelligence Act) and amending certain Union Legislative Acts; Permanent Representatives Committee 2024: Permanent Representatives Committee of 26 January 2024 on 'Proposal for a Regulation of the European Parliament and of the Council laying down harmonised rules on artificial intelligence (Artificial Intelligence Act) and amending certain Union legislative acts'.

National

France: Décret n° 2021-873 du 29 juin 2021 portant application de l'ordonnance n° 2021-443 du 14 avril 2021 relative au régime de responsabilité pénale applicable en cas de circulation d'un véhicule à délégation de conduite et à ses conditions d'utilisation (29 June 2021).

Germany: Gesetz zur Änderung des Straßenverkehrsgesetzes und des Pflichtversicherungsgesetzes – Gesetz zum autonomen Fahren (21 July 2021).

Germany: Beschluss des Bundesrates 486/22 (16 December 2022).

RELATED CASE LAW

There is not yet any case law on this specific provision. Note, however, that non-contractual civil liability is not harmonized at the European Union (EU) level. As such, there may be case law in the Member States covering procedural elements that are relevant for damage involving AI.

COMMENTARY

1 Purpose

A wide-accepted procedural rule is that each party has to prove its claims and contentions (*actori incumbit probatio*).[1] A claimant will thus have to prove the fault, the damage and the causal link between that fault and the damage.[2] Existing research and policy documents show that the application of this procedural rule can be challenging when accidents involve artificial intelligence (AI) systems considering that such technologies can be complex and inaccessible.[3] AI can be 'interposed' between the fault of a person and the actual damage.[4] Some AI algorithms are not easily understandable and interpretable but come in the form of 'black boxes' that evolve through self-learning. Victims are, therefore, confronted with the increasingly demanding task of trying to identify and prove AI systems as their source of harm.[5] Most parties will not have access to the necessary information to build a case in court (*see* information asymmetry).[6] The specific characteristics of certain AI systems, such as opacity, autonomous behaviour and complexity, may make it excessively difficult, if not impossible, for the injured person to prove that the specific input provided (or not

1. The analysis in this part is based on previous research on the proposal including De Bruyne et al. 2023; Dheu & De Bruyne 2023; Schollaert & De Bruyne 2023.
2. AILD, Rec. 3.
3. *See, e.g.*, Expert Group on Liability and New Technologies 2019; Commission AI/IoT/R 2020, 13; Hacker 2023, 20 with further references; Dheu & De Bruyne 2023, 265-270 with further references. *See* in the context of product liability Koch et al. 2022; CERRE 2021, 55-56. *Also see* AILD, Recs 3-7.
4. AILD, Rec. 3.
5. *See, e.g.*, Expert Group on Liability and New Technologies 2019, 33; Dheu & De Bruyne 2023, 266.
6. Commission AI 2020, 13.

provided) by a potentially liable person to the AI system caused a specific output that led to the damage at stake.[7]

The complexities regarding the burden of proof can be illustrated with a simple example. Consider that a company is developing vehicles with autonomous systems. Suppose that such a vehicle runs a red light thereby causing damage. Ignoring that red light could be the result of the developer's (negligent) reliance on a flawed dataset (e.g., with a certain underrepresentation) while training the system. A victim may not have access to that dataset, let alone prove that the cause of the damage is rooted in the use of a poor/deficient dataset for which the developers remain responsible (also *see* Article 10 of the AI Act on data quality). In other words, it can be very difficult for the victim of the accident to prove that the ignorance of the red light is caused by the developer's input, i.e., the use of a flawed dataset or any other potential negligent act.[8] Against this background, the proposal for the AI Liability Directive (AILD) introduces a rebuttable presumption of a causal link between the fault of a defendant and the (lack of) output produced by the AI system. This presumption only applies when certain strict conditions are met. As will be shown in the following parts, the application of these conditions can be challenging.[9]

2 Legal Background

2.1 International

Although there are no legal frameworks at the international level that deal with liability for damage involving AI, some provisions are relevant. Paragraph 42 of the UNESCO Recommendation, for instance, stipulates that:

> the ethical responsibility and liability for the decisions and actions based in any way on an AI system should always ultimately be attributable to AI actors corresponding to their role in the life cycle of the AI system.

Paragraph 43 further mentions that:

> [a]ppropriate oversight, impact assessment, audit and due diligence mechanisms, including whistle-blowers' protection, should be developed to ensure accountability for AI systems and their impact throughout their life cycle.

More importantly, according to paragraph 67:[10]

> Member States should develop, review and adapt, as appropriate, regulatory frameworks to achieve accountability and responsibility for the content and outcomes of AI systems at the different phases of their life cycle. Member States should, where necessary, introduce liability frameworks or clarify the interpretation of existing frameworks to ensure the attribution of accountability for the

7. AILD, Rec. 3.
8. *See in this regard also* Hacker 2023, 22.
9. *See extensively* Dheu & De Bruyne 2023 with further references.
10. UNESCO Recommendation.

> outcomes and the functioning of AI systems. Furthermore, when developing regulatory frameworks, Member States should, in particular, take into account that ultimate responsibility and accountability must always lie with natural or legal persons and that AI systems should not be given legal personality themselves.

Similar concerns were also acknowledged in the feasibility study issued by the Council of Europe's Ad hoc Committee on Artificial Intelligence (CAHAI) within the Council of Europe. Paragraph 112 stipulates that:

> [p]ersons – including public and private organisations – designing, developing, deploying or evaluating AI systems must take responsibility for these systems, and they should be held accountable whenever legal norms based on the principles mentioned above are not respected or any unjust harm occurs to end-users or to others.

Contracting parties have to take appropriate measures to ensure this, for instance, by imposing civil or criminal liability when the design, development and use of AI applications infringe on human rights or negatively affect the democratic process and the rule of law. More importantly, Member States must ensure that:[11]

> those who might be negatively impacted by AI systems have an effective and accessible remedy against the developers or deployers of AI systems who are responsible. The availability of such remedy should be clearly communicated to them, with special attention to those who are marginalized or in vulnerable situations. Effective remedies should involve redress for any harm suffered, and may include measures under civil, administrative, or, where appropriate, criminal law.

Article 9 of the Convention on AI – as adopted by the Council of Europe – stipulates that:[12]

> [e]ach Party shall adopt or maintain measures to ensure accountability and responsibility for adverse impacts on human rights, democracy and the rule of law resulting from activities within the lifecycle of AI systems.

2.2 European Union

In recent years, several initiatives with regard to liability for damage involving AI have been taken or discussed at the EU level. Without going into detail, we will provide a high-level overview allowing us to better understand the substantive provisions of the AILD.[13] One should, however, be aware that several other EU frameworks are relevant in the context of liability involving AI. The application of the Product Liability Directive (PLD), for instance, has been heavily debated in an AI-context (e.g., the notion of software as a product, 'defective' AI).[14] Moreover, consumer protection legislation

11. CAHAI 2020, 38, paras 112-113.
12. CAI 2022; AI Convention, 4.
13. *See more extensively* De Bruyne & Dheu 2023, 30-34.
14. *See, e.g.*, the many contributions in Lohsse et al. 2019; Buiten 2024.

could also be relevant in an AI-context. An example is the Digital Content Directive, which includes remedies when there is a lack of conformity.

The focus on AI liability was first covered by the Parliament report on civil law rules for robots in 2017. It urged the Commission to consider a legislative instrument that would deal with the liability for damage caused by autonomous systems and robots, thereby evaluating the feasibility of a strict liability or a risk management approach.[15] This was followed by a report issued by an expert group set up by the Commission on the 'Liability or Artificial Intelligence and Other Emerging Digital Technologies' in November 2019. The report explored the main liability challenges posed to current tort law by AI. It concluded that liability regimes:[16]

> in force in the Member States ensure at least basic protection of victims whose damage is caused by the operation of such new technologies.

However, the specific characteristics of AI systems, such as their complexity, self-learning abilities, opacity and limited predictability, may make it more difficult to offer victims a claim for compensation in all cases where this seems justified. The report stressed that the allocation of liability may be unfair or inefficient. It contains several recommendations to remedy potential gaps in EU and national liability regimes.[17]

The Commission subsequently issued a White Paper on AI in 2020. It had two main building blocks, namely an 'ecosystem of trust' and an 'ecosystem of excellence'.[18] More importantly, the White Paper was accompanied by a report on safety and liability (Report). The Report identified several points that needed further attention, such as clarifying the scope of the PLD or assessing procedural aspects.[19] In October 2020, the Parliament adopted a Resolution with recommendations to the Commission on a civil liability regime for AI. It favours strict liability for operators of high-risk AI systems and fault-based liability for operators of low-risk AI systems, with a reversal of the burden of proof.[20] In April 2021, the Commission issued the proposal for the AI Act,[21] which was followed by the adoption of the Council's general approach in December 2022[22] and the Parliament's negotiating position in June 2023.[23] The AI Act was published in the Official Journal in July 2024. The AI Act is of importance for liability involving AI, not only because of the risk-based approach and potential sanctions in that regard, but especially as it imposes obligations upon several parties, such as the providers and deployers of high-risk AI systems.[24] Those obligations will be

15. Resolution 2015/2103. Note that several reports have also been published upon request by European institutions (e.g., Bertolini 2020).
16. Expert Group on Liability and New Technologies 2019, 3.
17. *See in this regard also* Bertolini & Episcopo 2021, 644.
18. Commission AI 2020, 2-3.
19. Commission AI/IoT/R 2020.
20. Resolution 2020/2014.
21. AI Act Commission Proposal.
22. AI Act Council Proposal.
23. AI Act Parliament Amendments.
24. *See* Arts 8-27 in particular.

important to assess the potential liability of such parties, for instance, when determining whether one of these parties committed a fault (i.e., violation of a specific legal norm in the AI Act or negligence).[25]

In September 2022, the Commission eventually published two proposals that aim to adapt (tort) liability rules to the digital age, the circular economy and the impact of the global value chain. The AILD contains rules on the disclosure of information and the alleviation of the burden of proof in relation to damage caused by AI systems. The revised PLD substantially modifies the current product liability regime by including software within its scope, integrating new circumstances to assess the product's defectiveness and introducing provisions regarding presumptions of defectiveness and causation.[26]

2.3 National

As mentioned above, liability and procedural law is to a large extent still national. In other words, Member States may have relevant provisions on liability that could be relied upon in an AI-context. This can be either the application of 'general'/'common' rules (e.g., on the burden of proof or other presumptions in procedural law) or sector-specific provisions (e.g., self-driving cars). Reference can, for instance, be made to the German Autonomous Driving Act[27] or to the French Decree on automated vehicles' conditions of use and automated road transport systems' commissioning.[28]

2.4 Case Law

As mentioned above, liability and procedural law is to a large extent still national. It is conceivable that national case law also exists to remedy the 'vulnerable' position of claimants in certain situations. Against this background, we will not cover all these potential cases.

3 Analysis

As already mentioned above, the application of 'traditional' procedural rules (*see actori incumbit probatio*) can be challenging when accidents involve AI systems. Previous studies have already unravelled the liability issues arising from AI's distinctive features, such as its autonomy, complexity, lack of transparency and opacity.[29]

25. De Bruyne et al. 2022, 407-408.
26. NPLD.
27. Gesetz zur Änderung des Straßenverkehrsgesetzes und des Pflichtversicherungsgesetzes – Gesetz zum autonomen Fahren 2021. *See for a discussion* Ebers 2022.
28. Décret n° 2021-873 du 29 juin 2021 portant application de l'ordonnance n° 2021-443 du 14 avril 2021 relative au régime de responsabilité pénale applicable en cas de circulation d'un véhicule à délégation de conduite et à ses conditions d'utilisation.
29. *See, e.g.*, Expert Group on Liability and New Technologies 2019, 32-34 *as reported in* Dheu & De Bruyne 2023, 265.

Existing liability rules were framed decades ago based on even older concepts and 'incorporating a primarily anthropocentric and monocausal model'[30] of causing damage. The adequacy of these existing liability rules 'may thus be questionable when applied to AI'.[31] Moreover, many actors are involved in the supply chain of AI systems (*see* the 'many hands' problem).[32] This can lead to uncertainty as to whom will or should eventually be held liable, and especially who to target when damage occurs. Persons having suffered harm involving AI systems may not have adequate access to the information and, therefore, evidence to prove their case in court. They may have less successful claims compared to damage involving 'traditional' products.[33] Litigation could become burdensome and expensive for victims, leaving them 'without effective access to justice'.[34]

It is, however, important that victims of accidents involving AI are not confronted with a lower level of protection compared to other (traditional) products and/or services for which they would get compensation under national law.[35] Otherwise, the societal acceptance of those AI systems could be hampered, resulting in 'hesitance to use them'.[36] Against this background, several suggestions have already been implemented to remedy the 'vulnerable' position of potential victims/claimants.[37] The report on liability and AI issued by the Expert Group acknowledges that the national court has already found ways to alleviate the burden of proving causation if the claimant is in a 'weak' position (e.g., prima facie evidence, the *res ipsa loquitur* theory or lowering the standard of proof).[38] The Commission eventually proposed to include a presumption of causality in the case of a fault in the AILD. After a general discussion of the presumption of causality (section 3.1), we will delve into some specific application conditions (section 3.2). We then address some remaining challenges with regard to the presumption itself (section 3.3) and summarize the main findings in a conclusion (section 3.4).

3.1 General

Article 4(1) contains a rebuttable presumption of a causal link between the fault of the defendant and the output produced by the AI system or the failure of the AI system to produce an output. By doing so, the Directive:[39]

30. *Ibid.*
31. *Ibid.*
32. *See, e.g.*, MSI-AUT 2019, 62-64.
33. Commission AI 2020, 13 *as reported in* Dheu & De Bruyne 2023, 265.
34. Expert Group on Liability and New Technologies 2019, 35 *as reported in* Dheu & De Bruyne 2023, 265-266.
35. *See also* UNESCO Recommendation; and CAHAI 2020.
36. Commission AI/IoT/R 2020, 13.
37. *See, e.g.*, Expert Group on Liability and New Technologies 2019, 4, 29-30 & 48-52; Wagner 2019, 47; De Meeus 2019, 152; De Bruin 2016, 495; Koch et al. 2022, 44. *Also see* the many references Hacker 2023, 20.
38. Expert Group on Liability and New Technologies 2019, 50-51 with references.
39. AILD, Art. 4(1)(a), *see also* p. 13.

> aims to provide an effective basis for claiming compensation in connection with the fault consisting in the lack of compliance with a duty of care under Union or national law.

However, this presumption only applies when three conditions are met. It has in this regard already been argued that these requirements are so stringent that they would make it impossible to truly alleviate the burden of proof for the victim.[40]

First, the *fault* must be demonstrated by the claimant, or this fault must be presumed following Article 3(5) of the AILD.[41] This fault must consist in:[42]

> the non-compliance with a duty of care laid down in Union or national law directly intended to protect against the damage that occurred.

Hacker argues that such a duty may arise from either statutory or case law, as the source of the legal obligation is of no importance.[43] The requirement of a 'duty of care', however, can be problematic in certain jurisdictions.[44] Article 1(3)(d) of the AILD mentions that the Directive will not affect 'how fault is defined, other than in respect of what is provided for in Articles 3 and 4'.[45] The notion of 'fault' as used in the AILD raises some questions and, more generally, establishing the fault of a defendant remains 'particularly difficult in the context of AI systems'.[46] A fault under Belgian law (and by extension other jurisdictions), for instance, consists of both a subjective and an objective component. The (currently still applicable) subjective component requires that the fault can be attributed to the free will of the person who has committed it ('imputability') and that this person generally possesses the capacity to control and assess the consequences of his conduct ('culpability').[47] Such subjective element does, however, not seem to be addressed in the AILD. This raises the question of whether the notion of 'fault', as referred to in Articles 3 and 4, requires such a subjective element to be present and/or allows for national law to require this.[48] The objective component of a fault refers to the wrongful behaviour in itself, such as a violation of a specific legal rule of conduct[49] or the breach of a standard of care.[50] Under Belgian law, a violation

40. *See, e.g.*, Hacker 2023, 24-25; Nawaz 2022.
41. The Directive also contains a rebuttable presumption of non-compliance. Where a defendant in a claim for damages fails to disclose or preserve evidence at its disposal as ordered by a court, a presumption of non-compliance with duties of care is presumed which that evidence was intended to prove. In this regard, it has already been argued that '[m]ost often, the claimant will have to resort to the disclosure of evidence proceedings under Art. 3 AILD Proposal to demonstrate this (negligent) breach of duty' (Hacker 2023, 22). *See more extensively* Danis, Hendrix & Bellon on Art. 3, in this volume.
42. AILD, Art. 4(1)(a).
43. Hacker 2023, 22.
44. *See more extensively* De Bruyne & Schollaert on Art. 2(9), in this volume.
45. *Also see* AILD, Rec. 22.
46. *See, e.g.*, EDPS 2023, 10; Duffourc & Gerke 2023, 4; De Bruyne et al. 2023, 7.
47. *See, e.g.*, Court of Cassation 3 Oct. 1994, Arr.Cass. 1994, 807; Vansweevelt & Weyts 2009 147-148; Stijns 2013 48 & 58. *See in this regard also* Belgian Civil Code, new Book 6 on extra-contractual liability, Art. 6.5, 6.6, 6.7 and 6.8.
48. De Bruyne et al. 2023, 9; Hacker 2023, 22.
49. *See, e.g.*, Court of Casación 3 Oct. 1994, Arr.Cass. 1994, 807; Court of Cassation 10 Apr. 2014, Arr.Cass. 2014, 962. This is also true when the illegal act or omission would be considered non-negligent (*see, e.g.*, Court of Cassation 6 Jun. 2011, Arr.Cass. 2011, 1478).

of a standard of care requires that it was reasonably foreseeable for the defendant that their conduct could result in some kind of damage.[51] A provider of a high-risk AI system would thus commit a fault when they could reasonably foresee that a violation of a duty of care following provisions of the AI Act would result in damage. However, it is unclear whether the notion of a 'duty of care' as relied upon in the AILD also includes this requirement of foreseeability or, instead, whether it is left to national (case) law to determine the additional modalities under which a violation of a 'duty of care' could be established.[52]

The presumption of causality only applies if the fault of the defendant is established as a human act or omission, which does not meet a duty of care under Union law or national law that is directly 'intended to protect' against the damage that occurred (Article 4(1)(a)). The presumption will, for example, apply:[53]

> in a claim for damages for physical injury when the court establishes the fault of the defendant for non-complying with the instructions of use which are meant to prevent harm to natural persons.

By contrast, it will not apply when there is a lack of compliance with duties of care that were not directly intended to protect against the damage that occurred. An example would be the provider's failure to file the necessary documentation with the competent authorities.[54] This requirement refers to the relative wrongfulness or the theory of a *Normzweck* or *Schutznorm*, which limits liability in case of a breach of a duty of care to losses that the violated duty was intended or serves to prevent. Some European liability regimes are familiar with this principle (e.g., Dutch[55] and German[56] civil liability law). This, however, is by no means the case in all European countries.[57] In Belgium, for instance, the principle of relative unlawfulness does not exist.[58] The traditional requirements of fault-based liability – violation of statutory rule, causality and damage – are sufficient to obtain compensation. There is no need to take into account the purpose or the protective scope of the violated norm.[59] The AILD now introduces relative wrongfulness in all Member States. It introduces this (in a targeted manner) by applying the presumption of causality only in cases where the violated norm aims to protect against the suffered damage.

It is unclear whether only the type of damage must fall within the protective scope of the violated norm (i.e., the material aspect of the doctrine of relativity) or also

50. *See, e.g.*, Court of Cassation 25 Nov. 2002, Arr.Cass. 2002, 2543; Bocken et al. 2014, 90-92.
51. *See, e.g.*, Kruithof 2018, 49 with references; Bocken et al. 2014, 91. *See in this regard also* Belgian Civil Code, new Book 6 on extra-contractual liability, Art. 6.
52. De Bruyne et al. 2023, 9. *Also see* De Bruyne & Schollaert on Art. 2(9), in this volume.
53. AILD, Rec. 22.
54. *Ibid.*
55. *See* Dutch Civil Code, 6:163; Lindenbergh 2008.
56. German Civil Code, §823(2); Kötz & Wagner 2021, 91-100.
57. *See in general* van Dam 2013; Giliker 2017.
58. Court of Cassation 4 Nov. 2010, *Arr.Cass.* 2010, 2678; Court of Cassation 13 Jan. 2022, *NJW* 2023, 702, n. Schollaert.
59. *See* Schollaert 2021, 514-527.

the specific victim (i.e., the personal aspect of the doctrine of relativity).[60] The question may arise whether only 'primary victims' are eligible or if 'secondary victims' are also considered within the AILD. If, for instance, an autonomous vehicle hits a person thereby leading to severe injuries, the question arises whether only that person's damage would fall within the scope of the AILD, or whether the latter's partner's emotional distress would also be covered. Moreover, no attention is given to the hurdle of determining which types of damage may fall within the protective scope of a norm. Determining the protective scope of a specific norm is eventually to a large extent left to the independent judgment of individual judges,[61] potentially opening the door to a further fragmented application of the AILD. That is because existing research shows that a historical analysis of legislation may not always provide any substantial insights as legislators typically do not contemplate liability questions during the enactment of laws.[62] This may also be the case for the AILD as there is no specific guidance on the application and interpretation of the concept 'intended to protect'.

Second, it must be considered *reasonably likely*, based on the circumstances, that the fault has *influenced* the output produced by the AI system or the failure of the AI system to produce an output.[63] This means that not every fault can lead to the application of the rebuttable presumption related to the AI's output. For example, it can be considered reasonably likely that the fault has influenced the (failure to produce an) output when that fault consisted of breaching a duty of care in respect of limiting the perimeter of operation of the AI system and the damage occurred outside the perimeter of operation. A breach of a requirement to file certain documents or to register with a given authority, in turn, cannot be considered reasonably likely to have influenced the output produced by the AI system or the failure to do so.[64] In any case, this assessment has to be made on a case-by-case basis and may require the involvement of machine learning experts in the legal procedure.[65] This second requirement is criticized as a source of legal uncertainty and potential diffuse effects in EU Member States due to its vague wording.[66] In any case, the requirement of relativity as discussed in the previous paragraphs should not be confused with the second condition for the presumption of causation under the AILD. The fact that it must be considered reasonably likely, based on the circumstances, that the fault influenced the output generated by the AI system or the failure of the AI system to generate output,[67] is different from the requirement that the damage must fall within the protective scope of the violated norm.[68]

Lastly, the claimant must demonstrate that the output produced by the AI system or the failure of the AI system to produce an output gave rise to the *damage*.[69] In the

60. Limpens 1965.
61. Lindenbergh 2008.
62. *See* the extensive research by Spier in his conclusions under HR 7 May 2004, *NJ* 2006, 281, n. Hijma, and HR 13 Apr. 2007, *NJ* 2008, 576, n. Vranken. *Also see* Verheij 2019, 43.
63. AILD, Art. 4(1)(b).
64. *Ibid.*, Rec. 25.
65. Hacker 2023, 22.
66. De Bruyne et al. 2023, 7.
67. AILD, Art. 4(1)(b).
68. *Ibid.*, Rec. 25.
69. *Ibid.*, Art. 4(1)(c) and Rec. 22.

example of the autonomous car, the victim will still have to prove that ignoring the red light caused the damage. This is a fairly straightforward example. There are, however, circumstances in which the proof of damage may be more challenging. Consider, for instance, proving that the output of an AI system entails discrimination and has caused non-pecuniary (moral) damage. At the same time, some scholars also conclude that the requirement to prove damage can be rather easily met as it often directly affects the (assets of the) claimant.[70]

3.2 *Specific Conditions*

The rebuttable presumption of causation discussed in the previous section applies to *all* types of *defendants*. This means that the presumption is not only applicable to providers, persons subject to the obligations of a provider, or [deployers] but also to other actors. For example, consider backend service providers/operators that provide software updates and do not necessarily qualify as providers.[71] However, the AILD contains specific provisions for *providers*, *persons subject to the obligations of a provider* or *deployers/users*[72] of a *high-risk* AI system. In other words, when high-risk AI systems are at stake, the qualification of the defendant becomes important.[73]

The condition of fault (Article 4(1)(a)) is met *only* if the claimant demonstrates that a *provider* of a high-risk AI system or an individual *subject to the obligations of a provider* has failed to comply with any of the following requirements laid down in the AI Act, taking into account the steps undertaken in and the results of the risk management system provided for in the AI Act:[74]

- the AI system is a system which makes use of techniques involving the training of models with data and which was not developed on the basis of training, validation and testing data sets that meet the quality criteria referred to in Article 10(2) to (4) of the AI Act;[75]
- the AI system was not designed and developed in a way that meets the transparency requirements laid down in Article 13 of the AI Act;[76]

70. Hacker 2023, 22.
71. *See in particular* on the liability of backend and frontend operators: Resolution 2020/2014.
72. Note that the final AIA does no longer mention 'user' but 'deployer' defined as 'any natural or legal person, public authority, agency or other body using an AI system under its authority except where the AI system is used in the course of a personal non-professional activity' (AIA, Art. 3(4)).
73. Hacker identifies different 'cases' in this regard (Hacker 2023, 22-24).
74. AILD, Art. 4(2).
75. For example, training, validation and testing datasets shall be relevant, sufficiently representative, and to the best extent possible, free of errors and complete in view of the intended purpose (AIA, Art. 10(3)).
76. For instance, high-risk AI systems shall be designed and developed in such a way to ensure that their operation is sufficiently transparent to enable deployers to interpret the system's output and use it appropriately. They also need to be accompanied by instructions for use in an appropriate digital format or otherwise that include concise, complete, correct and clear information that is relevant, accessible and comprehensible to deployers (AIA, Art. 13(1)-13(2)).

- the AI system was not designed and developed in a way that allows for an effective oversight by natural persons during the period in which the AI system is in use pursuant to Article 14 of the AI Act;[77]
- the AI system was not designed and developed so as to achieve, in the light of its intended purpose, an appropriate level of accuracy, robustness and cyber-security pursuant to Article 15 and Article 16, point (a), of the AI Act;[78] or
- the necessary corrective actions were not immediately taken to bring the AI system in conformity with the obligations laid down in Chapter III, section 2 of the AI Act or to withdraw or recall the system, as appropriate, pursuant to Article 16, point (j), and Article 20 of the AI Act.

The AILD states that the steps undertaken in and the results of the risk management system provided for in the AI Act should be taken into account when establishing the fault.[79] However, it is unclear what specific weight should be attributed to those steps and results within the framework of the risk management system (Article 9 of the AI Act).[80] Some also note that it is a rather 'surprising point' that prohibited AI systems under the AI Act 'have no role to play' in the AILD.[81] The provision is problematic from another point of view as well because of using the term 'only'. It may indeed 'imply that claimants can benefit from the rebuttable presumption solely in case of a violation of the relevant/listed AI Act requirements, assuming of course that they comply with Article 4(1)(b) and (c) to benefit from it. As such, this *a priori* excludes any other – potentially relevant – legal ground for tort law, whether in EU or national law'.[82] In this regard, Wagner even concludes that it is 'irritating that a conclusive catalogue of duties, apparently meant to exclude the establishment of further duties of care under national tort law, is put in place particularly for manufacturers of high-risk systems', which in addition 'seems difficult to justify'.[83]

In the case of a liability claim against a *user/deployer* of a high-risk AI system, the fault (*see* Article 4(1)(a)) is presumed if the claimant demonstrates that the deployer:[84]

77. Supervision is aimed at preventing or minimizing the risks to health, safety, or fundamental rights posed by high-risk AI systems (AIA, Art. 14(2)).
78. Among other things, high-risk AI systems need to be resilient as regards errors, faults or inconsistencies that may occur within the system or the environment in which the system operates, in particular due to their interaction with natural persons or other systems (AIA, Art. 15(4)).
79. AILD, Art. 4(2).
80. Spindler 2023, 39; Spindler 2022, 703.
81. Wagner 2022, 227; *Also see* Hacker 2023, 25.
82. De Bruyne et al. 2023, 8.
83. Wagner 2022, 226-227. At the same time, however, he concludes that the obligation to ensure 'accuracy, robustness, and cybersecurity' of high-risk AI systems (*see* AIA, Art. 15) may be a ground to establish a standard of care in tort law.
84. AILD, Art. 4(3).

- did not comply with its obligations to use or monitor the AI system in accordance with the accompanying instructions of use or, where appropriate, suspend or interrupt its use pursuant to Article 26 of the AI Act;[85] or
- exposed the AI system to input data under its control which is not relevant in view of the system's intended purpose pursuant to Article 26(4) of the Act.[86]

Hacker, however, points out that this provision has some shortcomings. That is because the obligations to monitor the AI system in accordance with Article 26 of the AI Act are generally only violated after the AI system has produced its output.[87] The actions a deployer takes in fulfilling their monitoring obligation to prevent damage from the previously gathered AI output naturally have no effect on that same output. In such cases, it is easy for a deployer to demonstrate that the output would have been produced even without the violated monitoring obligation(s). In other words, 'irrespective of any oversight, the output of the AI system would have been the same'.[88] In this context, a presumption would be useful for the injured party only between the output of the AI system and the damage, not between the fault of a person and the output of the AI system. Such a presumption takes into account the fact that the deployer's monitoring obligation can only have an impact after output has been produced by an AI system.[89] Pursuant to Article 4(3)(b), a deployer feeding irrelevant data to an AI system in view of the system's intended purpose also triggers the presumption of causality. This provision lacks accuracy. It is the insertion of incorrect/biased data that is susceptible to have contributed to an output which is contested by the victim should be considered a violation of the duty of care by a deployer. In other words, the mere introduction of irrelevant data as such should not result in the application of the assumption.[90] It should also be noted that the word 'only' is not included for users/deployers of high-risk AI systems. As a consequence, it may be supplemented by additional duties of care developed under national tort law, and have a broader scope of application as the duties imposed on deployers by the AI Act are so limited.[91]

3.3 The Limitations of the Presumption of Causality

The previous sections discussed the circumstances under which the presumption of causality applies. As mentioned, the presumption only covers the causal link between the fault of the defendant and the output produced by the AI system or the failure of the

85. There is an obligation to suspend the use of an AI system if its use in accordance with the instructions of use may result in the AI system presenting a risk to health or safety or to the protection of fundamental rights of persons (AIA, Art. 26(5)).
86. The deployer needs to ensure that input data is relevant and sufficiently representative in view of the intended purpose of the high-risk AI system, to the extent the deployer exercises control over the input data (AIA, Art. 26(4)).
87. *See in this regard also* AIA, Art. 14(4)(d) and (e).
88. Hacker 2023, 23.
89. *Ibid.*
90. European Chambers 2023, 7.
91. Wagner 2022, 227; Polat 2023, 116.

AI system to produce an output. The presumption is formulated to assist the injured party in determining whether the breach of duty caused the 'misconduct' of the AI system.[92] The evidentiary rules regarding the damage and fault remain unaffected by the AILD.[93] For example, the claimant still needs to demonstrate that the AI developer committed a fault, such as inadequately training the AI system. Moreover, the concept of causality is not defined in the AILD and is shaped differently in Member States.[94] For example, the traditionally accepted theory in Belgium is the doctrine of the equivalence of conditions.[95] Under this rule, courts are required to accept legal causality between a fact and the incurred damage if it has been established that the invoked fact was necessary in the given circumstances for the damage to occur (the so-called *conditio sine qua non* or but-for test). A fact that *in concreto* was necessary for the harm to occur is a cause even if a later intervening fact was also necessary. Moreover, a fact that was necessary for the damage to occur the way it did is a cause even if the damage was not a necessary consequence, not a normal consequence or not a foreseeable consequence of the fact.[96] As opposed to other countries, Belgian law only assesses factual causation without adding the additional layer/test of legal causation (e.g., proximate cause, foreseeability).[97] All of these elements show that the victim of an AI-related damage could still face some difficulties in proving the liability of the defendant, depending on national law.[98] A potential reversal of the burden of proof – and thus the presumption of causality – should, however, be carefully addressed.[99] It may have an impact on innovation[100] and could significantly 'alter the current distribution of risks to the detriment of the manufacturers'.[101] One of the risks with a reversal of the burden of proof resides in the possibility for litigants to engage in 'excessive or abusive litigation'.[102] As such, a reversal could foster a 'claims culture',[103] as it would encourage 'spurious claims'.[104] Therefore, several mitigation factors are included in AILD to 'maintain the balance between the interests of the parties involved in the claim for damages'.[105]

92. *Ibid.*, 226.
93. AILD, Rec. 22; Wagner 2022, 225-226.
94. *See* AILD, Rec. 10.
95. *See extensively* Vansweevelt & Weyts 2009, 763-873 with further references; Fagnart 2006, n. 3. *See*, however, Kruithof 2015 concluding that another rule can better describe Belgian positive law on causation in civil liability. Art. 6(18) of the new Belgian Civil Code would continue to depart from the *conditio sine qua non test*. Nevertheless, it would contain an exception for situations in which the relationship between the fact leading to the damage and the suffered damage is so remote that it would be 'manifestly unreasonable' to impose liability on the defendant.
96. Kruithof 2018, 126 with references.
97. Bocken et al. 2014, 64-65. *See*, however, the new Art. 6.18.
98. De Bruyne et al. 2023, 9.
99. *Ibid.*, at 7.
100. De Bruin 2016, 495.
101. CERRE 2021, 55-56 with further references.
102. Schütte et al. 2021, 26.
103. De Bruin 2016, 495.
104. Commission 2006, 9.
105. AILD, Rec. 20. *See extensively* Dheu & De Bruyne 2023, 274-275.

Article 4(4), for instance, establishes an exception to the presumption of causality specifically for high-risk AI systems where 'the defendant demonstrates that sufficient evidence and expertise is reasonably accessible for the claimant to prove the causal link'. This possibility can induce defendants to comply with their disclosure obligations, 'with measures set by the AI Act to ensure a high level of transparency of the AI or with documenting and recording requirements'.[106] A court will eventually have to assess whether the evidence and expertise are 'reasonably' accessible, which is a matter of interpretation.[107] A question that arises is whether this includes hiring (potentially expensive) AI experts as forensic witnesses. Hacker eventually concludes that this cannot be entirely ruled out, but relies on Recitals 21 and 27 to show that it may be unlikely.[108]

Article 4(5) of the AILD contains specific provisions for AI systems that are *not* a high-risk AI system. In the case of a claim for damages concerning a non-high-risk AI system, the presumption of causality only applies where the national court considers it excessively difficult for the claimant to prove the causal link. By doing so, Article 4(5) tightens the 'requirements needed to trigger the presumption of causation again'.[109] Recital 28 stipulates that such difficulties are to be assessed in light of the characteristics of certain AI systems, such as autonomy and opacity:

> which render the explanation of the inner functioning of the AI system, very difficult in practice, negatively affecting the ability of the claimant to prove the causal link between the fault of the defendant and the AI output.

The assumed lower risk of the non-high-risk AI system therefore leads to higher demands on the claimant. Such a rule, however, is not justified where non-high-risk systems are 'as opaque and individually risky' as high-risk systems.[110]

Moreover, in cases where the defendant uses the AI system in the course of a personal non-professional activity, Article 4(6) provides that the presumption of causality should only apply if the defendant has materially interfered with the conditions of the operation of the AI system[111] or if the defendant was required and able to determine the conditions of operation of the AI system and failed to do so.[112] The presumption against consumers does not apply when the consumer simply launches and uses the AI system as described in the instructions for use and according to the intended purpose. In other words, any routine operation of an AI system by consumers excludes the causality presumption.[113] This condition is justified by the need to balance the interests of injured persons and non-professional deployers, by exempting from the application of the presumption of causality the cases in which non-professional

106. *See* AILD, 13.
107. *Ibid.*, Rec. 27.
108. Hacker 2023, 24.
109. Wagner 2022, 228.
110. Hacker 2023, 23.
111. Consider an AI-based lawnmower being used on a gravel path and kicking up a stone that injures a pedestrian (Hacker 2023, 24).
112. Consider a consumer who knows and is contractually obliged to use an AI system only in certain weather conditions but decided to use it in adverse weather conditions anyway.
113. Hacker 2023, 24-25.

deployers do not add risk through their behaviour.[114] Article 2(4) defines the concept of user/deployer and refers to the relevant articles in the AI Act, which in turn defines a deployer as the natural or legal person who uses the AI system in the course of a professional activity.[115] Wagner, therefore, concludes that Article 4(6) of the AILD is actually 'redundant' as the proposal does not cover deployers that operate an AI system in the context of a personal, non-professional activity.[116]

A more general way to rebut the burden of proof is included in Article 4(7). It provides that the defendant has the right to rebut the causality presumption following Article 4(1) of the AILD. The coordination between all these different provisions is not clear.[117] Moreover, the application of this provision can be challenging due to the black-box nature of AI systems.[118]

3.4 Conclusion

The AILD has been introduced to remedy the 'vulnerable' position of the claimants/victims. It does so by introducing a disclosure requirement as well as a presumption of causality between the 'fault' of a defendant and the output or lack of output generated by the AI system. Our analysis has shown that several challenges remain with regard to the application of the presumption of causality as well as with the interpretation of the different requirements (e.g., 'fault'). From a more general point of view, one may wonder whether the AILD sufficiently and appropriately tackles existing gaps. The AILD introduces a horizontal liability regime but there is a risk that additional unclarities and legal uncertainty arise. This is especially the case as it relies on concepts that are not (yet) harmonized. As such, clarity will be needed – and hopefully provided – during the coming years, thereby especially considering the interplay with the AI Act.

BIBLIOGRAPHY

Reports and Recommendations

Bertolini 2020: Andrea Bertolini, *Artificial Intelligence and Civil Liability. Legal Affairs*, Parliament (July 2020), www.europarl.europa.eu/RegData/etudes/STUD/2020/621926/IPOL_STU(2020)621926_EN.pdf (accessed 11 April 2024).

CAHAI 2020: Council of Europe's Ad Hoc Committee on AI, *Feasibility Study* (December 2020), rm.coe.int/cahai-2020-23-final-eng-feasibility-study-/1680a0c6da (accessed 11 April 2024).

CAI 2023: CAI, *Draft Framework Convention on Artificial Intelligence, Human Rights, Democracy and the Rule of Law* 6 (December 2023), rm.coe.int/cai-2023-28-draft-framework-convention/1680ade043 (accessed 11 April 2024).

114. *See* AILD, 14 as discussed in De Bruyne et al. 2023, 7.
115. *See* AIA, Art. 3(4).
116. Wagner 2022, 228.
117. *See* AILD, 14; De Bruyne et al. 2023, 7.
118. Orgalim 2023, 3.

CERRE 2021: Centre on Regulation in Europe, *EU Liability Rules for the Age of Artificial Intelligence* (March 2021), cerre.eu/wp-content/uploads/2021/03/CERRE_EU-liability-rules-for-the-age-of-Artificial-Intelligence_March2021.pdf (accessed 11 April 2024).

Commission AI 2020: European Commission, *White Paper on Artificial Intelligence: A European Approach to Excellence and Trust* (February 2020), commission.europa.eu/document/download/d2ec4039-c5be-423a-81ef-b9e44e79825b_en?filename=commission-white-paper-artificial-intelligence-feb2020_en.pdf (accessed 11 April 2024).

Commission AI/IoT/R 2020: European Commission, *Report on the Safety and Liability Implications of Artificial Intelligence, the Internet of Things and Robotics* (February 2020), eur-lex.europa.eu/legal-content/en/TXT/?uri=CELEX%3A52020DC0064 (accessed 11 April 2024).

Commission 2006: Commission of the European Communities, *Third Report on the Application of Council Directive on the Approximation of Laws, Regulations and Administrative Provisions of the Member States Concerning Liability For Defective Products 85/374/EEC of 25 July 1985, Amended by Directive 1999/34/EC of the European Parliament and of the Council of 10 May 1999* (September 2006), eur-lex.europa.eu/legal-content/EN/TXT/PDF/?uri=CELEX:52006DC0496 (accessed 11 April 2024).

Council 2022: Council of the European Union, *General Approach, 'Proposal for a Regulation of the European Parliament and of the Council Laying Down Harmonised Rules on Artificial Intelligence (Artificial Intelligence Act) and Amending Certain Union Legislative Acts'* (November 2022).

EDPS 2023: European Data Protection Supervisor, *Opinion 42/2023 on the Proposals for Two Directives on AI Liability Rules* (October 2023), edps.europa.eu/data-protection/our-work/publications/opinions/2023-10-11-edps-opinion-422023-two-directives-ai-liability-rules_en (accessed 11 April 2024).

EPRS 2023: European Parliamentary Research Service, *Briefing: EU Legislation in Progress: Artificial Intelligence Liability Directive* (February 2023), www.europarl.europa.eu/RegData/etudes/BRIE/2023/739342/EPRS_BRI(2023)739342_EN.pdf (accessed 11 April 2024).

European Chambers 2023: Association of European Chambers of Commerce and Industry, *European Commission's Proposal for an Artificial Intelligence Liability Directive* (2 March 2023), www.eurochambres.eu/wp-content/uploads/2023/03/230301-Eurochambres-position-on-the-European-Commissions-proposal-for-an-Artificial-Intelligence-Liability-Directive-AILD.pdf (accessed 11 April 2024).

Expert Group on Liability and New Technologies 2019: Expert Group on Liability and New Technologies – New Technology Formation, *Liability for Artificial Intelligence and Other Emerging Digital Technologies* (November 2019), op.europa.eu/en/publication-detail/-/publication/1c5e30be-1197-11ea-8c1f-01aa75ed71a1/language-en (accessed 11 April 2024).

MSI-AUT 2019: Expert Committee on human rights dimensions of automated data processing and different forms of artificial intelligence (MSI-AUT) (Council of

Europe), *Responsibility and AI* (September 2019), rm.coe.int/responsabili ty-and-ai-en/168097d9c5 (accessed 11 April 2024).

Orgalim 2023: Orgalim, *Orgalim Comments on the Legislative Proposal for a Directive on AI liability* (7 March 2023), orgalim.eu/position-papers/legal-orgalim-com ments-legislative-proposal-directive-ai-liability (accessed 11 April 2024).

UNESCO Recommendation.

Academic Writings

Ampovska 2023: Marija Ampovska, *An Overview of the Proposal for the AI Liability Directive in the EU*, Eprints (18 October 2023), eprints.ugd.edu.mk/32457 (accessed 11 April 2024).

Bertolini & Episcopo 2021: Andrea Bertolini & Francesca Episcopo, *The Expert Group's Report on Liability for Artificial Intelligence and Other Emerging Digital Technologies: A Critical Assessment*, 12 EJRR 3 (2021), doi.org/10.1017/err.2021.30.

Bocken et al. 2014: Hubert Bocken, Ingrid Boone & Marc Kruithof, *Inleiding tot het schadevergoedingsrecht* (2014).

Buiten 2024: Miriam Buiten, *Product Liability for Defective AI*, 57 European Journal of Law and Economics 239-273 (2024), doi.org/10.1007/s10657-024-09794-z.

De Bruin 2016: Roeland De Bruin, *Autonomous Intelligent Cars on the European Intersection of Liability and Privacy*, 7 EJRR 3 (2016), doi.org/10.1017/s1867299x00006036.

De Bruyne & Dheu 2023: Jan De Bruyne & Orian Dheu, *Liability for Damage Caused by Artificial Intelligence: Some Food for Thought and Current Proposals* (Philip Morgan ed., 2023).

De Bruyne et al. 2023: Jan De Bruyne, Orian Dheu & Charlotte Ducuing, *The European Commission's Approach to Extra-Contractual Liability and AI: An Evaluation of the AI Liability Directive and the Revised Product Liability Directive*, 51 CLSR 1 (2023), doi.org/10.1016/j.clsr.2023.105894.

De Bruyne et al. 2022: Jan De Bruyne, Elias Van Gool & Thomas Gils, *Tort Law and Damage Caused by AI Systems* (Jan De Bruyne & Cedric Vanleenhove eds, 2022).

De Meeus 2019: Charlotte De Meeus, *The Product Liability Directive at the Age of the Digital Industrial Revolution: Fit for Innovation?*, 8 EuCML 4 (2019).

Dheu & De Bruyne 2023: Orian Dheu & Jan De Bruyne, *Artificial Intelligence and Tort Law: A 'Multi-faceted' Reality*, 31 ERPL 2/3 (2023), doi.org/10.54648/erpl2023021.

Duffourc & Gerke 2023: Mindy Dufourc & Sara Gerke, *The Proposed EU Directives for AI Liability Leave Worrying Gaps Likely to Impact Medical AI*, 6 NPJ Digit Med 1 (2023), doi.org/10.1038/s41746-023-00823-w.

Ebers 2022: Martin Ebers, *Civil Liability for Autonomous Vehicles in Germany*, SSRN (5 February 2022), papers.ssrn.com/sol3/papers.cfm?abstract_id=4027594 (accessed 11 April 2024), doi.org/10.2139/ssrn.4027594.

Fagnart 2006: Jean-Luc Fagnart, *Petite Navigation Dans Les Méandres de la Causalité*, RGAR 14.080 (2006).

Giliker 2017: Paula Giliker, *Research Handbook on EU Tort Law* (2017).

Hacker 2023: Philipp Hacker, *The European AI Liability Directives: Critique of an Half-Hearted Approach and Lessons for the Future*, 51 CLSR 1 (2023), doi.org/10.1016/j.clsr.2023.105871.

Koch et al. 2022: Bernhard Koch et al., *Response of the European Law Institute to the Public Consultation on Civil Liability: Adapting Liability Rules to the Digital Age and Artificial Intelligence*, 13 JETL 1 (2022), doi.org/10.1515/jetl-2022-0002.

Kötz & Wagner 2021: Hein Kötz & Gerhard Wagner, *Deliktsrecht* (2021).

Kruithof 2018: Marc Kruithof, *Tort Law in Belgium* (2018).

Kruithof 2015: Marc Kruithof, *Oorzaak of aanleiding? Geen causaal verband zonder causale bijdrage* (Thierry Vansweevelt & Britt Weyts eds, Intersentia 2015).

Limpens 1965: Jean Limpens, *La Théorie de la Relativité Aquillienne en Droit Comparé* 559 (Libraire Dalloz ed., 1965).

Lindenbergh 2008: Siewert Lindenbergh, *De betrekkelijkheid van de geschonden norm een verweer dat dwingt tot keuzes*, TPR 907 (2008).

Lohsse et al. 2019: Sebastian Lohsse, *Liability for Artificial Intelligence and the Internet of Things* (Sebastian Lohsse, Reiner Schulze & Dirk Staudenmayer eds, 2019).

Nawaz 2022: Samar Nawaz, *The Proposed EU AI Liability Rules: Ease or Burden?*, European Law Blog (7 November 2022), europeanlawblog.eu/2022/11/07/the-proposed-eu-ai-liability-rules-ease-or-burden (accessed 11 April 2024).

Polat 2023: Cemre Polat, *A Critical Appraisal of the Proposal for an AI Liability Directive: Is It Fit for Its Own Purpose?*, 3 GPR 114 (2023).

Schollaert 2021: Victor Schollaert, *Is de inbreuk op een recht absoluut dan wel relatief onrechtmatig?*, 445 NJW 514 (2021).

Schollaert & De Bruyne 2023: Victor Schollaert & Jan De Bruyne, *Voorstel Richtlijn AI-aansprakelijkheid. Verkennende analyse vanuit Belgisch perspectief*, 486 NJW 574 (2023).

Schütte et al. 2021: Béatrice Schütte, Lotta Majewski & Katri Havu, *Damages Liability for Harm Caused by Artificial Intelligence: EU Law in Flux*, SSNR (January 2021), papers.ssrn.com/sol3/papers.cfm?abstract_id=3897839 (accessed 11 April 2024), doi.org/10.2139/ssrn.3897839.

Stijns 2013: Sophie Stijns, *Verbintenissenrecht: Boek 1bis* (2013).

Spindler 2023: Gerard Spindler, *Different Approaches for Liability of Artificial Intelligence: Pros and Cons – the New Proposal of the EU Commission on Liability for Defective Products and AI Systems*, SSRN (15 January 2023), papers.ssrn.com/sol3/papers.cfm?abstract_id=4354468 (accessed 11 April 2024), doi.org/10.2139/ssrn.4354468.

Spindler 2022: Gerald Spindler, *Die Vorschläge der EU-Kommission zu einer neuen Produkthaftung und zur Haftung von Herstellern und Betreibern Künstlicher Intelligenz Die haftungsrechtliche Einordnung von Software als Produkt nach Unionsrecht: endlich*, 11 CR 689 (2022).

van Dam 2013: Cees Van Dam, *European Tort Law* (2013).

Vansweevelt & Weyts 2009: Thierry Vansweevelt & Britt Weyts, *Handboek Buitencontractueel Aansprakelijkheidsrecht* (2009).

Verheij 2019: Albert Verheij, *Onrechtmatige daad* 43 (2019).

Wagner 2022: Gerhard Wagner, *Liability Rules for the Digital Age: Aiming for the Brussels Effect*, 13 JETL 191 (2022).
Wagner 2019: Gerhard Wagner, *Robot Liability* (Sebastian Lohsse, Reiner Schulze & Dirk Staudenmayer eds, 2019).

Others

Court of Cassation 3 October 1994, *Arr.Cass.* 1994.
Court of Cassation 25 November 2002, *Arr.Cass.* 2002, 2543.
Court of Cassation 4 November 2010, *Arr.Cass.* 2010, 2678.
Court of Cassation 6 June 2011, *Arr.Cass.* 2011, 1478
Court of Cassation 10 April 2014, *Arr.Cass.* 2014, 962.
Court of Cassation 13 January 2022, *NJW* 2023, 702, note Victor Schollaert.
HR 7 May 2004, *NJ* 2006, 281, note Jacob Hijma.
HR 13 April 2007, *NJ* 2008, 576, note Jan Vranken.
Belgian Civil Code.
Dutch Civil Code.
German Civil Code.

ARTICLE 5 Evaluation and Targeted Review

Jan De Bruyne & Victor Schollaert

Article 5. Evaluation and targeted review

1. By [DATE five years after the end of the transposition period], the Commission shall review the application of this Directive and present a report to the Parliament, to the Council and to the European Economic and Social Committee, accompanied, where appropriate, by a legislative proposal.
2. The report shall examine the effects of Articles 3 and 4 on achieving the objectives pursued by this Directive. In particular, it should evaluate the appropriateness of no-fault liability rules for claims against the operators of certain AI systems, as long as not already covered by other Union liability rules, and the need for insurance coverage, while taking into account the effect and impact on the roll-out and uptake of AI systems, especially for SMEs.
3. The Commission shall establish a monitoring programme for preparing the report pursuant to paragraphs 1 and 2, setting out how and at what intervals the data and other necessary evidence will be collected. The programme shall specify the action to be taken by the Commission and by the Member States in collecting and analysing the data and other evidence. For the purposes of that programme, Member States communicate the relevant data and evidence to the Commission, by [31 December of the second full year following the end of the transposition period] and by the end of each subsequent year.

Recitals

(31) It is necessary to provide for a review of this Directive [five years] after the end of the transposition period. In particular, that review should examine whether there is a need to create no-fault liability rules for claims against the operator, as long as not already covered by other Union liability rules in particular Directive 85/374/EEC, combined with a mandatory insurance for the operation of certain AI systems, as suggested by the Parliament.[1] In accordance with the principle of proportionality, it is appropriate to assess such a need in the light of relevant technological and regulatory developments in the coming years, taking into account the effect and impact on the roll-out and uptake of AI systems, especially for SMEs. Such a review should consider, among others, risks involving damage to important legal values like

1. [Resolution 2020/2014].

> life, health and property of unwitting third parties through the operation of AI-enabled products or services. That review should also analyse the effectiveness of the measures provided for in this Directive in dealing with such risks, as well as the development of appropriate solutions by the insurance market. To ensure the availability of the information necessary to conduct such a review, it is necessary to collect data and other necessary evidence covering the relevant matters.

RELATED ARTICLES

Article 3 (Disclosure of evidence and rebuttable presumption of non-compliance); Article 4 (Rebuttable presumption of a causal link in the case of fault).

RELATED LAWS

International

IMO CLC 1969: International Maritime Organization, *International Convention on Civil Liability for Oil Pollution Damage (CLC)*, treaties.un.org/doc/Publication/UNTS/Volume%20973/volume-973-I-14097-English.pdf (accessed 19 July 2024); AI Convention.

EU

AI Act; AI Act Commission Proposal; AI Act Council Proposal; AI Act Parliament Amendments; Resolution 2015/2103: Resolution (EU) 2015/2103 of the European Parliament of 16 February 2017 with recommendations to the Commission on Civil Law Rules on Robotics; Resolution 2020/2014: Resolution (EU) 2020/2014 of the European Parliament of 20 October 2020 with recommendations to the Commission on a civil liability regime for artificial intelligence; New Product Liability Directive; Draft Compromise AI Act 2023: Draft Compromise Amendments on the Draft Report Proposal (EU) of the European Parliament of 16 May 2023 for a regulation of the European Parliament and of the Council on harmonised rules on Artificial Intelligence (Artificial Intelligence Act) and amending certain Union Legislative Acts; Permanent Representatives Committee 2024: Permanent Representatives Committee of 26 January 2024 on 'Proposal for a Regulation of the European Parliament and of the Council laying down harmonised rules on artificial intelligence (Artificial Intelligence Act) and amending certain Union legislative acts'.

National

France: Décret n° 2021-873 du 29 juin 2021 portant application de l'ordonnance n° 2021-443 du 14 avril 2021 relative au régime de responsabilité pénale applicable en cas de circulation d'un véhicule à délégation de conduite et à ses conditions d'utilisation (29 June 2021).

Germany: Gesetz zur Änderung des Straßenverkehrsgesetzes und des Pflichtversicherungsgesetzes – Gesetz zum autonomen Fahren (21 July 2021).

COMMENTARY

1 Purpose

Liability for damage involving artificial intelligence (AI) has already attracted much attention in academic scholarship.[2] Several policy initiatives have been taken at the European Union (EU) level as well.[3] It should, however, be noted that the law of tort of 'EU Member States is largely non-harmonised',[4] with some exceptions (e.g., product liability). Suggestions have, therefore, been made to adapt existing liability regimes in Member States.[5] The AI Liability Directive (AILD) takes into account the differences between national legal traditions,[6] thereby echoing the findings of the Expert Group on Liability and New Technologies, which concluded that the 'landscape of *strict liability* in Europe is quite varied' (*emphasis added*).[7] Against this background, the AILD introduces disclosure requirements and a rebuttable presumption of a causal link between the fault of a defendant and the (lack of) output produced by the AI system.[8] This presumption only applies when certain strict conditions are met. One requirement, for instance, is the fault of a defendant which consists of a non-compliance with a duty of care laid down in Union or national law directly intended to protect against the damage that occurred.[9] Arguably, the choice for a fault-based liability regime is based on the situation/reality as it was before September 2022. This, however, can change during the coming years. The AILD considered that the kind of products and services equipped with AI systems that could affect the public at large and have an impact on legal rights (e.g., the right to life, health and property), and therefore could be subject to a strict liability regime, were not yet widely available on the market in September 2022.[10] The impact of the launch of ChatGPT in November 2022 may already shed a different light on that conclusion. A monitoring programme is, therefore, put in place to provide the Commission with information on incidents involving

2. *See, e.g.*, the many contributions in Lohsse et al. 2019 and in Lohsse et al. 2023; Schütte et al. 2021, 26; Beckers & Teubner 2022, 208; Geistfeld et al. 2022; Dheu & De Bruyne 2023, 261-298 with further references. Authors have also been working on AI liability in different domains, such as autonomous vehicles (e.g., Steege et al. 2024) or healthcare (e.g., Griffin 2021, 65-106).
3. *See, e.g.*, Expert Report 2019. Note that several reports have also been published upon request by European institutions (e.g., Bertolini 2020).
4. Expert Report 2019, 15.
5. *See, e.g.*, De Bruyne et al. 2022.
6. AILD, 14.
7. Expert Report 2019, 26.
8. *See extensively* De Bruyne et al. 2023, 9; Hacker 2023, 22.
9. *See* AILD, Art. 4(1)(a).
10. *Ibid.*, Art. 14. *See*, however, the case of a Belgian man who committed suicide in Mar. 2023 following interactions with an AI-powered chatbot (El Atillah 2023).

AI systems. The targeted review will assess whether additional measures would be needed, such as introducing a strict liability regime and/or mandatory insurance.[11]

2 Legal Background

2.1 International

There are no specific international provisions on (strict or fault-based) liability for damage involving AI at the international level. Yet, reference to liability is made in several instruments, which may be relied upon to establish either a strict, fault-based or more 'tailored' liability regime.

Paragraph 42 of the UNESCO Recommendation, for instance, stipulates that:

> the ethical responsibility and liability for the decisions and actions based in any way on an AI system should always ultimately be attributable to AI actors corresponding to their role in the life cycle of the AI system.

Paragraph 43 further mentions that:

> [a]ppropriate oversight, impact assessment, audit and due diligence mechanisms, including whistle-blowers' protection, should be developed to ensure accountability for AI systems and their impact throughout their life cycle.

More importantly, according to paragraph 67:[12]

> Member States should develop, review and adapt, as appropriate, regulatory frameworks to achieve accountability and responsibility for the content and outcomes of AI systems at the different phases of their life cycle. Member States should, where necessary, introduce liability frameworks or clarify the interpretation of existing frameworks to ensure the attribution of accountability for the outcomes and the functioning of AI systems. Furthermore, when developing regulatory frameworks, Member States should, in particular, take into account that ultimate responsibility and accountability must always lie with natural or legal persons and that AI systems should not be given legal personality themselves.

Similar concerns were also acknowledged in the feasibility study issued by the Council of Europe's Ad hoc Committee on Artificial Intelligence (CAHAI) within the Council of Europe. Paragraph 112 stipulates that:

> [p]ersons – including public and private organisations – designing, developing, deploying or evaluating AI systems must take responsibility for these systems, and they should be held accountable whenever legal norms based on the principles mentioned above are not respected or any unjust harm occurs to end-users or to others.

Contracting parties have to take appropriate measures to ensure this, for instance, by imposing civil or criminal liability when the design, development and use of AI

11. Expert Report 2019, 26.
12. UNESCO Recommendation.

applications infringes human rights or negatively affect the democratic process and the rule of law. More importantly, Member States must ensure that:[13]

> those who might be negatively impacted by AI systems have an effective and accessible remedy against the developers or deployers of AI systems who are responsible. The availability of such remedy should be clearly communicated to them, with special attention to those who are marginalized or in vulnerable situations. Effective remedies should involve redress for any harm suffered, and may include measures under civil, administrative, or, where appropriate, criminal law.

Article 9 of the Convention on AI – as adopted by the Council of Europe – also stipulates that:[14]

> [e]ach Party shall adopt or maintain measures to ensure accountability and responsibility for adverse impacts on human rights, democracy and the rule of law resulting from activities within the lifecycle of artificial intelligence systems.

Although establishing a liability regime at the international level is not straightforward, the International Convention on Civil Liability for Oil Pollution Damage (CLC) illustrates that it can be possible after all. The Convention places the liability on the owner of the ship from which the polluting oil escaped or was discharged. Subject to a number of specific exceptions, this liability is strict. The shipowner is normally entitled to limit his liability to an amount determined by the size of the ship.[15] One could rely on the context of that convention to also draft potential international (liability) rules for damage involving AI.

2.2 European Union

In recent years, several initiatives with regard to liability for damage involving AI have been taken or discussed at the EU level.[16]

The focus on AI liability was first covered by the Parliament report on civil law rules for robots in 2017. It urged the Commission to consider a legislative instrument that would deal with the liability for damage caused by autonomous systems and robots, thereby evaluating the feasibility of a strict liability or a risk management approach. The strict liability requires only proof that damage has occurred and the 'establishment of a causal link between the harmful functioning of the robot'[17] – whatever that may mean – and the incurred damage. The risk management approach does not focus on the person who acted negligently, but instead on the person 'who is able, under certain circumstances, to minimize risks and deal with negative impacts'[18]

13. CAHAI 2020 38, paras 112-113.
14. AI Convention, 4.
15. IMO CLC 1969. *See for more information also* IMO Conventions (undated).
16. *See in this regard, e.g.*, CERRE 2021; Novelli et al. 2024.
17. Resolution 2015/2103, para. 54.
18. *Ibid.*, para. 55.

(*see* concept of the cheapest cost avoider).[19] It also calls for the Commission to consider an obligatory insurance scheme as well as the creation of a compensation fund.[20] This was followed by a report issued by an expert group set up by the Commission on the 'Liability or Artificial Intelligence and Other Emerging Digital Technologies' in November 2019. The report explored the main liability challenges posed to current tort law by AI. It concluded that liability regimes 'in force in the Member States ensure at least basic protection of victims whose damage is caused by the operation of such new technologies'.[21] However, the specific characteristics of AI systems, such as their complexity, self-learning abilities, opacity and limited predictability, may make it more difficult to offer victims a claim for compensation in all cases where this seems justified. The report stressed that the allocation of liability may be unfair or inefficient. It contains several recommendations to remedy potential gaps in EU and national liability regimes.[22]

The Commission subsequently issued a White Paper on AI in 2020. It had two main building blocks, namely an 'ecosystem of trust' and an 'ecosystem of excellence'.[23] More importantly, the White Paper was accompanied by a Report on safety and liability. The Report identified several points that needed further attention, such as clarifying the scope of the Product Liability Directive (PLD) or assessing procedural aspects.[24] In October 2020, the Parliament adopted a Resolution with recommendations to the Commission on a civil liability regime for AI. It favours strict liability for operators of high-risk AI systems and fault-based liability for operators of low-risk AI systems, with a reversal of the burden of proof.[25] In April 2021, the Commission issued the proposal for the AI Act,[26] which was followed by the adoption of the Council's general approach in December 2022[27] and the Parliament's negotiating position in June 2023.[28] The AI Act was published in July 2024. The AI Act is of importance for liability involving AI, not only because of the risk-based approach and potential sanctions in that regard, but especially as it imposes obligations upon several parties, such as the providers and deployers of high-risk AI systems.[29] Those obligations will be important to assess the potential liability of such parties, for instance, when determining whether one of these parties committed a fault (i.e., violation of a specific legal norm in the AI Act or negligence).[30]

In September 2022, the Commission eventually published two proposals that aim to adapt (tort) liability rules to the digital age, the circular economy and the impact of the global value chain. The AILD contains rules on the disclosure of information and

19. Calabresi 1970.
20. Resolution 2015/2103, para. 59.
21. Expert Report 2019, 3.
22. *Ibid. See in this regard also* Bertolini & Episcopo 2021, 644.
23. Commission AI 2020, 2-3.
24. Commission AI/IoT/R 2020.
25. Resolution 2020/2014.
26. AI Act Commission Proposal.
27. AI Act Council Proposal.
28. AI Act Parliament Amendments.
29. *See* Arts 8-27 in particular.
30. De Bruyne et al. 2022.

the alleviation of the burden of proof in relation to damage caused by AI systems. The revised PLD substantially modifies the current product liability regime by including software within its scope, integrating new circumstances to assess the product's defectiveness and introducing provisions regarding presumptions of defectiveness and causation.[31]

2.3 National

Liability law is to a large extent still national. In other words, Member States may have relevant provisions on liability that could be relied upon in an AI-context. This can be either the application of 'general'/'common' rules (e.g., strict or fault-based) or sector-specific provisions (e.g., self-driving cars). Reference can, for instance, be made to the German Autonomous Driving Act[32] or to the French Decree on automated vehicles' conditions of use and automated road transport systems' commissioning.[33]

2.4 Case Law

Liability law is to a large extent still national. It is conceivable that national case law exists on strict or fault-based liability that can be relevant to AI. Taking this into account, we will not cover all these potential cases.

3 Analysis

Article 5 assigns the Commission the task of reviewing the application of the AILD. This is a 'usual mandate for evaluation and targeted review after five years of the expiration of the transposition deadline'.[34] Although the European Data Protection Supervisor (EDPS) acknowledges 'the difficulty of establishing new liability rules in a constantly evolving area like AI',[35] it nevertheless points out that a review after only five years is relatively long. A shorter review period could help to achieve a:[36]

> timely understanding of the extent to which the natural persons who have suffered damages caused by an AI system have an effective access to compensation.

Hacker already suggested that an update of the AILD based on this article should also cover harm inflicted by the use of a prohibited AI system.[37] The Commission does not only have to examine the effects of Articles 3 and 4 on achieving the objectives pursued by the AILD but – rather unusual – should also evaluate the:[38]

31. NPLD.
32. Germany (*Gesetz*). *See for a discussion* Ebers 2022.
33. France (*Décret*).
34. Wagner 2022, 241.
35. EDPS 2023, 11.
36. *Ibid.*
37. Hacker 2023, 25.
38. AILD, Art. 5(2); Wagner 2022, 241-242.

> appropriateness of no-fault liability rules for claims against the operators of certain AI systems ... and the need for insurance coverage.

Based on the initial impact assessment conducted by the Commission, a 'staged approach' was relied upon in the AILD. The first stage consisted of measures to ease the burden of proof for victims (*see* Article 4 on the rebuttably presumption of causality). The second stage includes a review mechanism to re-assess, in particular, the need for harmonizing strict liability for AI use cases with a particular risk profile potentially coupled with a mandatory insurance.[39] As such, the Commission did not immediately opt for a system of strict liability in the AILD, fearing that it could have a deterring effect on innovation[40] and because many respondents considered it disproportionate.[41] The AILD's reliance on a fault-based liability regime coupled with a rebuttable presumption could thus be changed if/once a strict liability regime turns out to be more appropriate.[42]

In this regard, it should be noted that both fault-based liability as well as strict liability have benefits.[43] It is, therefore, not surprising that there has already been much research on the modalities of a liability regime for damage involving AI.[44] Some scholars, for instance, favour a strict liability regime for operators of AI.[45] The *Bureau Européen des Unions de Consommateurs* (BEUC) is also clear when concluding that a fault-based approach makes it 'very difficult, if not impossible, for consumers to benefit from their right to compensation for damages'.[46] The choice for a strict liability regime has already been acknowledged in supranational initiatives as well. The AILD, for instance, explicitly refers to the Resolution of the Parliament of 20 October 2020.[47] That Resolution contains recommendations to the Commission on a civil liability regime for AI. It contains a proposal for a regulation on liability for the operation of AI systems. It

39. AILD, 9.
40. *Ibid.*, 6: 'The proposal does not lead to a reversal of the burden of proof, to avoid exposing providers, operators and users of AI systems to higher liability risks, which may hamper innovation and reduce the uptake of AI-enabled products and services.' *Also see* Expert Report 2019, 27: 'A factor which any legislator considering the introduction of strict liability will have to take into account is the effect that such introduction may have on the advancement of the technology, as some may be more hesitant to actively promote technological research if the risk of liability is considered a deterrent'; Van Uytsel 2021, 84: 'Knowing that there will be always a liability imposed on the manufacturer, innovation could chill. The financial burden may be just too heavy to take the risks of innovation.'
41. AILD, 8: 'Strict liability was considered disproportionate by most business respondents. Harmonisation of the easing of the burden of proof gained more support, particularly among SMEs. However, businesses cautioned against a complete shift of the burden of proof. Therefore, the preferred policy option was developed and refined in light of feedback received from stakeholders throughout the impact assessment process to strike a balance between the needs expressed and concerns raised by all relevant stakeholder groups.'
42. *See more generally on strict liability* van Dam 2007, 255-265. Note that this approach is in contrast with the expansion of strict liability in the PLD (Spindler 2022, 703).
43. *See, e.g.*, Dheu & De Bruyne 2023, 261-298 with further references; Spindler 2022, 41-96.
44. *See* the many references *supra* n. 2.
45. *See, e.g.*, Zech 2021, 152; Wendehors 2020, 150. On applying strict liability to autonomous vehicle accidents, *see* Bertolini & Riccaboni 2021, 281; Rosenberg 2017, 205.
46. BEUC 2023, 5.
47. AILD, Rec. 31; Resolution 2020/2014.

imposes strict liability for operators of high-risk AI systems that cause damage.[48] The report issued by the Expert Group also discusses strict liability for damage involving AI. It concludes that strict liability for the operation of computers, software or the like is so far 'widely unknown in Europe', even though there are some limited examples 'where countries provide for the liability of the operator of some (typically narrowly defined) computer system'.[49] Eventually, it states that:[50]

> [s]trict liability is an appropriate response to the risks posed by emerging digital technologies, if, for example, they are operated in non-private environments and may typically cause significant harm.

According to the report, strict liability should lie with the person who is in control of the risk connected with the operation of emerging digital technologies and who benefits from their operation. If there are two or more operators, in particular:[51]

(1) the person primarily deciding on and benefitting from the use of the relevant technology (the so-called frontend operator); and
(2) the person continuously defining the features of the relevant technology and providing essential and ongoing backend support (the so-called backend operator), strict liability should lie with the one who has more control over the risks of the operation.

Other scholars, however, are more reluctant towards the option of strict liability for operators[52] or developers/producers[53,54]

According to the principle of proportionality, the need for a strict liability regime and insurance coverage should be assessed again in light of technological and regulatory developments in the coming years. The effect and impact on the roll-out and uptake of AI systems, especially for small and medium-sized enterprises (SMEs), should thereby be considered. Such a review needs to take into account risks involving damage to important legal values (e.g., life, health and property of unwitting third parties) through the operation of AI-enabled products or services. That review should analyse the effectiveness of the measures provided for in the AILD in dealing with such risks, as well as the development of appropriate solutions by the insurance market. It is necessary to collect data and other necessary evidence covering the relevant matters to ensure the availability of the information necessary to conduct the review. As such, it is conceivable that reports and articles will be published in the coming years further analysing the application of different liability regimes in an AI-context.[55]

48. Resolution 2020/2014.
49. Expert Report 2019, 26.
50. *Ibid.*, at 39.
51. *Ibid.*
52. *See, e.g.*, Wagner 2022, 241-242.
53. *See, e.g.*, Hacker 2023, 30.
54. *See more in generally* Diamantis 2024.
55. AILD, Rec. 31. Wagner concludes that '[w]hile it is true that strict liability irrespective of defect should be considered for a future world dominated by AI systems, ... the current state of technical development does not justify such a radical step' (Wagner 2022, 241).

Several scholars have already expressed their concerns about the AILD and suggested some future options.[56] For instance, Hacker writes that the:[57]

> artificial distinction between the supposedly strict liability under the PLD and the fault-based framework under the AILD Proposal is, to a large extent, artificial and should be given up.

Instead:[58]

> a coherent and unified framework for AI liability is needed which addresses the main risks, facilitates enforcement, and prevents confusion on the part of consumers and other affected persons concerning their rights to compensation.

Against this background, he develops a framework, *inter alia,* including 'truly strict liability' for economic operators and professional users of high-risk AI systems. With regard to so-called foundation models, strict liability needs to be 'tailored to their high-risk deployments'. Whereas SMEs as well as non-high-risk AI systems should be subject to rebuttable presumptions of fault and causality to prevent overdeterrence, consumers using AI should face fault-based liability with a limited presumption of causality.[59] The reliance on a 'tailored-based' liability regime indeed seems appropriate in certain complex settings or ecosystems.[60]

In addition to strict liability which has already been covered by different scholars, a potential review should also assess the insurance coverage for damage involving AI.[61] References to insurance aspects are not new either. Already in 2017, the Parliament indicated that a 'possible solution to the complexity of allocating responsibility for damage caused by increasingly autonomous robots could be an obligatory insurance scheme', as is the case for vehicles. As opposed to the insurance system for road traffic in which the insurance covers human acts and failures, 'an insurance system for robotics should consider all potential responsibilities in the chain'.[62]

An insurance system could be supplemented by a fund in order to ensure that reparation can be made for damage in cases where no insurance cover exists.[63] At the same time, however, an obligatory insurance scheme cannot be considered the only answer to the problem of how to allocate liability. It cannot completely replace clear and fair liability rules.[64] In any case, questions on insurance in the AI-context will likely emerge in the coming years. It has in this regard already been argued that companies are best placed to carry out a comprehensive risk assessment to evaluate the need for insurance coverage.[65] The European Association of Co-operative Banks (EACB) holds

56. *See, e.g.*, De Bruyne et al. 2023.
57. Hacker 2023, 30.
58. *Ibid.*
59. *Ibid.*, 30-33.
60. *See, e.g.*, in the context of third-party certifiers: De Bruyne 2019.
61. *See in this regard, e.g.*, Lior 2022, 467; Amankwah 2022, 449-476.
62. Resolution 2015/2103, para. 57.
63. *Ibid.*, para. 58.
64. Expert Report 2019, 30-31.
65. Orgalim 2023, 4. In this regard, some car manufacturers already provide insurances (e.g., Tesla Insurance).

the view that mandatory insurance is not the preferred policy option. This is because compelling insurance companies to provide AI insurance would significantly impact the risk management and pricing of AI insurance products. The EACB is sceptical about the notion that such insurance would enhance innovation in the EU. Instead, it asserts that it could undermine the adoption of AI. The EACB believes that the decision to offer AI insurance, along with its conditions and pricing, should remain at the discretion of insurance companies. It is worth considering that insurance companies might willingly choose to offer AI insurance without it being mandatory.[66]

In any case, the Commission will have to establish a monitoring programme for preparing the review setting out how and at what intervals data and other necessary evidence will be collected. The programme needs to specify the action to be taken by the Commission and by the Member States in collecting and analysing the data and other evidence.[67] The monitoring mechanism can cover different types of data and evidence including:[68]

(1) reporting and information sharing by Member States regarding the application of measures to ease the burden of proof in national judicial or out-of-court settlement procedures;
(2) information collected by the Commission or market surveillance authorities under the AI Act or other relevant instruments;
(3) information and analyses supporting the evaluation of the AI Act and the reports to be prepared by the Commission on the implementation of that Act; and
(4) information and analyses supporting the assessment of relevant future policy measures under the 'old approach' safety legislation to ensure that products placed on the Union market meet high health, safety and environmental requirements.

BIBLIOGRAPHY

Reports and Recommendations

Bertolini 2020: Andrea Bertolini, *Artificial Intelligence and Civil Liability. Legal Affairs,* Parliament (July 2020), www.europarl.europa.eu/RegData/etudes/STUD/2020/621926/IPOL_STU(2020)621926_EN.pdf (accessed 12 April 2024).

BEUC 2023: BEUC, *Proposal for an AI Liability Directive: BEUC Position Paper* (May 2023), www.beuc.eu/sites/default/files/publications/BEUC-X-2023-050_Proposal_for_an_AI_Liability_Directive.pdf (accessed 12 April 2024).

CAI 2023: Council of Europe's Committee on Artificial Intelligence, *Draft Framework Convention on Artificial Intelligence, Human Rights, Democracy and the Rule of*

66. EACB 2022, 5.
67. AILD, Art. 5(3).
68. NPLD, 10.

Law (December 2023), rm.coe.int/cai-2023-28-draft-framework-convention/1680ade043 (accessed 12 April 2024).

CAHAI 2020: Council of Europe's Ad Hoc Committee on AI, *Feasibility Study* (December 2020), rm.coe.int/cahai-2020-23-final-eng-feasibility-study-/1680a0c6da (accessed 12 April 2024).

CERRE 2021: Centre on Regulation in Europe, *EU Liability Rules for the Age of Artificial Intelligence* (March 2021), cerre.eu/wp-content/uploads/2021/03/CERRE_EU-liability-rules-for-the-age-of-Artificial-Intelligence_March2021.pdf (accessed 12 April 2024).

Commission AI 2020: European Commission, *White Paper on Artificial Intelligence: A European Approach to Excellence and Trust* (February 2020), commission.europa.eu/document/download/d2ec4039-c5be-423a-81ef-b9e44e79825b_en?filename=commission-white-paper-artificial-intelligence-feb2020_en.pdf (accessed 12 April 2024).

Commission AI/IoT/R 2020: European Commission, *Report on the Safety and Liability Implications of Artificial Intelligence, the Internet of Things and Robotics* (February 2020), eur-lex.europa.eu/legal-content/en/TXT/?uri=CELEX%3A52020DC0064 (accessed 12 April 2024).

Council 2022: Council of the European Union, *General Approach, 'Proposal for a Regulation of the European Parliament and of the Council Laying Down Harmonised Rules On Artificial Intelligence (Artificial Intelligence Act) and Amending Certain Union Legislative Acts'* (November 2022).

EACB 2022: European Association of Co-operative Banks, *EACB Position Paper on a Proposal for a Directive on Adapting Non-Contractual Civil Liability Rules to Artificial Intelligence (The AI Liability Directive)* (November 2022), ec.europa.eu/info/law/better-regulation/have-your-say/initiatives/13601-Artificial-intelligence-liability-rules/F3362246_en (accessed 12 April 2024).

EDPS 2023: European Data Protection Supervisor, *Opinion 42/2023 on the Proposals for Two Directives on AI Liability Rules* (October 2023), edps.europa.eu/data-protection/our-work/publications/opinions/2023-10-11-edps-opinion-422023-two-directives-ai-liability-rules_en (accessed 12 April 2024).

Expert Report 2019: Expert Group on Liability and New Technologies – New Technology Formation, *Liability for Artificial Intelligence and Other Emerging Digital Technologies* (November 2019), op.europa.eu/en/publication-detail/-/publication/1c5e30be-1197-11ea-8c1f-01aa75ed71a1/language-en (accessed 12 April 2024).

IMO Conventions (undated): International Maritime Organization, *International Convention on Civil Liability for Oil Pollution Damage (CLC)*, www.imo.org/en/About/Conventions/Pages/International-Convention-on-Civil-Liability-for-Oil-Pollution-Damage-(CLC).aspx (accessed 12 April 2024).

Orgalim 2023: Orgalim, *Orgalim Comments on the Legislative Proposal for a Directive on AI Liability*, Orgalim (March 2023), orgalim.eu/position-papers/legal-orgalim-comments-legislative-proposal-directive-ai-liability (accessed 12 April 2024).

UNESCO Recommendation.

Academic Writings

Amankwah 2022: Jeffrey Amankwah, *Insurance Underwriting on the Basis of Telematics: Segmentation and Profiling* (Jan De Bruyne & Cedric Vanleenhove eds, 2022).

Beckers & Teubner 2022: Anna Beckers & Gunther Teubner, *Three Liability Regimes for Artificial Intelligence: Algorithmic Actants, Hybrids, Crowds* (2022).

Bertolini & Episcopo 2021: Andrea Bertolini & Francesca Episcopo, *The Expert Group's Report on Liability for Artificial Intelligence and Other Emerging Digital Technologies: A Critical Assessment*, 12 EJRR 3 (2021), doi.org/10.1017/err.2021.30.

Bertolini & Riccaboni 2021: Andrea Bertolini & Massimo Riccaboni, *Grounding the Case for a European Approach to the Regulation of Automated Driving: The Technology-Selection Effect of Liability Rules*, 51 European Journal of Law and Economics 281 (2021), doi.org/10.1007/s10657-020-09671-5.

Calabresi 1970: Guido Calabresi, *The Costs of Accidents: A Legal and Economic Analysis* (1970).

De Bruyne 2019: Jan De Bruyne, *Third-Party Certifiers* (2019).

De Bruyne et al. 2023: Jan De Bruyne, Orian Dheu & Charlotte Ducuing, *The European Commission's Approach to Extra-Contractual Liability and AI: An Evaluation of the AI Liability Directive and the Revised Product Liability Directive*, 51 CLSR 1 (2023), doi.org/10.1016/j.clsr.2023.105894.

De Bruyne et al. 2022: Jan De Bruyne, Elias Van Gool & Thomas Gils, *Tort Law and Damage Caused by AI Systems*, 407-408 (Jan De Bruyne & Cedric Vanleenhove eds, Intersentia 2022).

Dheu & De Bruyne 2023: Orian Dheu & Jan De Bruyne, *Artificial Intelligence and Tort Law: A 'Multi-faceted' Reality*, 31 ERPL 2/3 (2023), doi.org/10.54648/erpl20 23021.

Diamantis 2024: Mihailis Diamantis, *Reasonable AI: A Negligence Standard*, SSRN (January 2024), ssrn.com/abstract=4609545 (accessed 12 April 2024), doi.org/10.2139/ssrn.4609545.

Ebers 2022: Martin Ebers, *Civil Liability for Autonomous Vehicles in Germany*, SSRN (February 2022), papers.ssrn.com/sol3/papers.cfm?abstract_id=4027594 (accessed 12 April 2024), doi.org/10.2139/ssrn.4027594.

El Atillah 2023: Imane El Atillah, *Man Ends His Life after an AI Chatbot 'Encouraged' Him to Sacrifice Himself to Stop Climate Change*, Euronews (2023), www.euronews.com/next/2023/03/31/man-ends-his-life-after-an-ai-chatbot-encouraged-him-to-sacrifice-himself-to-stop-climate- (accessed 24 April 2024).

Geistfeld et al. 2022: Mark Geistfeld et al., *Civil Liability for Artificial Intelligence and Software* (2022).

Griffin 2021: Frank Griffin, *Artificial Intelligence and Liability in Health Care*, 31 Health Matrix: Journal of Law-Medicine 1, 65-106 (2021).

Hacker 2023: Philipp Hacker, *The European AI Liability Directives: Critique of An Half-Hearted Approach and Lessons for the Future*, 51 CLSR 1 (2023), doi.org/10.1016/j.clsr.2023.105871.

Lior 2022: Anat Lior, *Insuring AI: The Role of Insurance in Artificial Intelligence Regulation*, 35 Harvard Journal of Law & Technology 2 (2022).

Lohsse et al. 2023: *Liability for AI. Münster Colloquia on EU Law and the Digital Economy VII* (Sebastian Lohsse, Reiner Schulze & Dirk Staudenmayer eds, Nomos 2023).

Lohsse et al. 2019: *Liability for Artificial Intelligence and the Internet of Things* (Sebastian Lohsse, Reiner Schulze & Dirk Staudenmayer eds, Nomos 2019).

Novelli et al. 2024: Claudio Novelli et al., *Generative AI in EU Law: Liability, Privacy, Intellectual Property, and Cybersecurity*, SSRN (March 2024), papers.ssrn.com/sol3/papers.cfm?abstract_id=4694565&download=yes (accessed 12 April 2024), doi.org/10.2139/ssrn.4821952.

Rosenberg 2017: Adam Rosenberg, *Strict Liability: Imagining a Legal Framework for Autonomous Vehicles*, 20 Tulane Journal of Technology and Intellectual Property (2017).

Schütte et al. 2021: Béatrice Schütte, Lotta Majewski & Katri Havu, *Damages Liability for Harm Caused by Artificial Intelligence: EU Law in Flux*, SSRN (January 2021), papers.ssrn.com/sol3/papers.cfm?abstract_id=3897839 (accessed 12 April 2024), doi.org/10.2139/ssrn.3897839.

Spindler 2023: Gerald Spindler, *Different Approaches for Liability of Artificial Intelligence: Pros and Cons* (Sebastian Lohsse, Reiner Schulze & Dirk Staudenmayer eds, Nomos 2023).

Spindler 2022: Gerald Spindler, *Die Vorschläge der EU-Kommission zu einer neuen Produkthaftung und zur Haftung von Herstellern und Betreibern Künstlicher Intelligenz Die haftungsrechtliche Einordnung von Software als Produkt nach Unionsrecht: endlich*, 11 CR 689 (2022).

Steege et al. 2024: Hans Steege et al., *Autonomous Vehicles and Civil Liability in a Global Perspective* (2024).

van Dam 2007: Cees van Dam, *European Tort Law*, 255-265 (2007).

Van Uytsel 2021: Steven Van Uytsel, *Different Liability Regimes for Autonomous Vehicles: One Preferable Above the Other?* (Steven Van Uytsel & Danilo Vasconcellos Vargas eds, Springer 2021).

Wagner 2022: Gerhard Wagner, *Liability Rules for the Digital Age: Aiming for the Brussels Effect*, 13 JETL 191 (2022).

Wendehors 2020: Christiane Wendehors, *Strict Liability for AI and Other Emerging Technologies*, 11 JETL 2 (2020), doi.org/10.1515/jetl-2020-0140.

Zech 2021: Herbert Zech, *Liability for AI: Public Policy Considerations*, 22 ERA Forum (2021), doi.org/10.1007/s12027-020-00648-0.

ARTICLE 6 Amendment to Directive (EU) 2020/1828

Alejandro Ferreres Comella

Article 6. Amendment to Directive (EU) 2020/1828

In Annex I to Directive (EU) 2020/1828[1], the following point (67) is added:

> "(67) Directive (EU) .... /.... of the European Parliament and of the Council of ... on adapting non-contractual civil liability rules to artificial intelligence (AI Liability Directive) (OJ L ..., ..., p. ...).".

RELATED ARTICLES

Article 2 (Definitions); Article 3 (Disclosure of evidence and rebuttable presumption of non-compliance); Article 4 (Rebuttable presumption of a causal link in the case of fault).

RELATED LAWS

EU

Representative Actions Directive (RAD).

National

Denmark: Implementation Act, 20 April 2023.
Germany: Verbandsklagenrichtlinienumsetzungsgesetz (VRUG), 29 September 2023.
Hungary: Act LXI, 19 December 2022.
Ireland: Representative Actions Act, 11 July 2023.
Italy: Legislative Decree No. 28, 10 March 2023 (arising from Law No. 127, 4 August 2022).

1. [Representative Actions Directive].

Portugal: Decree-Law 114-A/2023, 5 December 2023 (*Decreto-Lei n.º 114-A/2023, de 5 de dezembro*).

Slovakia: Act on Actions for the Protection of the Collective Interests of Consumers and on Amendments and Additions to Certain Acts, 21 June 2023.

COMMENTARY

1 Purpose

The addition of the AI Liability Directive (AILD) to the directives and regulations listed in Annex I of the RAD means that collective redress will be available to claim damages arising from infringements of the AILD. The RAD requires Member States to ensure that certain qualified entities can seek collective injunctive and redress measures on behalf of a group or class of consumers that have been damaged by the infringement of European Union (EU) laws by businesses.[2]

2 Legal Background

2.1 International

The collective redress mechanism to be provided in compliance with the RAD is different than the traditional United States (US) class actions, in that legal standing to bring collective actions is not granted to individual members of the class but to a third party, a legal entity that meets certain requirements related to its representativeness of consumers' general interests.

In this regard, the RAD defines the collective redress actions which it covers as 'representative actions' (as opposed to the 'class actions' name which is used under the more liberal US collective redress system).

2.2 European Union

The collective redress mechanism set out in the RAD is subject to the damages having been caused to consumers, i.e., within a consumption activity. Therefore, in those cases in which the affected individuals are interacting with businesses for professional purposes or on a professional basis, collective redress will not be available to them. However, the RAD allows Member States to extend the applicability of the collective redress mechanisms set out in it to cover damages caused to businesses and individuals within their professional activities.

The RAD does not include provisions for every procedural aspect of collective redress actions. It is for each Member State to decide on these, provided that they meet

2. *See* RAD, Art. 4.

the minimum requirement to allow an effective collective redress mechanism for consumers.[3]

Therefore, the elements which will determine the magnitude of collective redress actions – also in the context of artificial intelligence (AI) liability claims – are the following:

2.2.1 Opt-In Versus Opt-Out

Collective redress actions are much facilitated under opt-out systems. There are two reasons for this.

First, opt-out systems make it possible to achieve a higher aggregation of underlying claims (and therefore, a larger aggregate claim amount). This is so because in opt-out collective redress systems, consumers that are members of the group or class will be bound by the final decision issued because of the legal action unless they have expressly opted not to be represented members of the class or group. In opt-in systems, the members of the group or class need to expressly confirm their consent to be represented in the collective action so that the decision will therefore be binding for them. Therefore, opt-out collective redress actions will usually result in larger claim amounts since represented consumers are bound by the outcome of the collective claim unless they expressly opt out.

Second, opt-out systems are better to remove barriers to access to justice. Thus, where the amount of the damages related to the underlying individual claims is not significant, there may not be enough incentive for every represented consumer to actively engage in the collective actions through available opt-in mechanisms; and therefore, a practical barrier to access to justice arises. Opt-out systems facilitate collective actions in those cases. In general, third-party funders can also operate better in the context of opt-out systems, which permit a much higher aggregate amount of claimed damages and thus guarantee a sufficient return on third parties' investment. At the same time, the fact that third-party funding is made more available also facilitates collective redress.

2.2.2 Qualified Entities

The strictness of the requirements which consumer associations or other entities must meet to bring collective redress actions and the potential use of litigation vehicles by third-party funders.

Under the RAD, Member States shall make certification of consumer associations and any other legal entities as qualified entities to bring collective redress actions subject to meeting certain criteria. These criteria are that the entity is a non-profit, independent from any businesses, has the purpose of defending consumers' general interests and has a proven track record in this activity. As a matter of fact, the latter is the only material and measurable requirement set out in the RAD. The other more

3. *See ibid.*, Rec. 12.

formal requirements can be easily met by entities by merely including their non-profit purpose and independence from business in their by-laws and/or internal governance regulations.

However, when defining requirements for qualified entities allowed to bring cross-border collective redress actions within the EU, the Directive sets out that the minimum track record in the defence of consumers' general interests that those entities will have to prove will be just twelve months.[4]

It is obvious that this twelve-month period can be easily demonstrated by entities – consumer associations, in most Member States – that are formed by third-party funders or their intermediaries, and which may very well be used as mere litigation vehicles by third-party funders.[5]

Most Member States have taken the non-exacting requirements set out in the RAD – including the need to prove a minimum of just twelve months' track record in the defence of consumers' general interests – to also apply for local consumer associations or other legal entities to bring national collective redress legal actions. As discussed above, this may contribute to facilitating third-party funding of these types of lawsuits in the Member States.

2.2.3 *Commonality Requirement*

The degree of similarity between underlying individual claims which the resulting rules require to certify the collective redress action.

For collective redress to be effective, it must be possible to issue a decision on the defendant's liability in a sole proceeding disregarding the relevant individual factual circumstances or legal issues applicable to each underlying represented consumer. This prerequisite is known as the commonality requirement.

In the US case law, the commonality requirement is understood to be satisfied if one or more questions of fact or law affect all or a substantial number of the class members. Thus, the commonality requirement does not require that all the questions of law and facts raised by the complaint are common, but it is sufficient that the common issues are preponderant. In the United Kingdom (UK), analysis of the commonality requirement is embedded in the suitability analysis, in that this analysis requires the assessment, among other circumstances, of whether collective proceedings are an appropriate means for the fair and efficient resolution of the common issues and whether it is possible to determine in respect of any person whether that person is or is not a member of the class.[6]

Legal presumptions on the existence of fault or negligence and/or causation may facilitate satisfaction of the commonality requirement. For example, the fraud-on-the-market theories applicable to securities litigation have facilitated the certification of class actions in that litigation context. The underlying presumption is that since stock

4. *See ibid.*, Art. 4(3).
5. *See* Ferreres Comella 2023.
6. *See Walter Hugh Merricks CBE v. Mastercard Incorporation & Ors* [2021] CAT 28.

prices incorporate material information, material fraudulent statements will affect stock prices.[7]

There is no European case law on the commonality requirement yet, and the legislation which is being passed in the Member States to transpose the RAD is not specific enough in that respect.

2.2.4 *Protection of Consumers*

Finally, as mentioned above, the RAD requires that Member States set out at least one effective and efficient mechanism for collective redress actions for *consumers* (i.e., in those cases in which harm has been caused to consumers as a result of the infringement by a business of certain regulations and directives listed in an Annex to the Directive itself whose infringement can cause harm to consumers). Therefore, the RAD does not request Member States to include collective redress mechanisms for individuals not acting as consumers, or for businesses. However, a certain few Member States – e.g., Portugal[8] – do not subject the applicability of collective redress mechanisms to the fact that represented members of the class or group are consumers, and therefore, collective redress legal actions are also available to individuals not acting as consumers and businesses.

3 Analysis

It is noteworthy that Recitals of the AILD do not discuss the reason why EU legislators have decided to add the AILD to Annex I of the RAD. Only the Explanatory Memorandum of the Directive, when discussing its Article 2 (Definitions), explains that:

> Article 2(6)(c) provides that an action for damages can also be brought by someone acting on behalf of one or more injured parties, in accordance with Union or national law. This provision aims to give more possibilities to persons injured by an AI system to have their claims assessed by the court, even in cases where the individual actions may seem too costly or too cumbersome to bring, or where joint actions may entail a benefit for scale. To enable victims of damage caused by AI systems to enforce their rights in relation to this Directive through representative actions, Article 6 amends Annex I to Directive (EU) 2020/1828.

In those Member States in which collective redress rules are based on an opt-in system, those AI liability cases in which the value of each underlying individual claim is not significant may still be difficult to litigate through collective redress actions, since the level of aggregation that plaintiffs may achieve is not significant enough. Therefore, it may also be more difficult to access third-party funding, as explained above.

Additionally, collective redress actions will not be applicable to those cases in which damages arising from the output or the failure to produce an output through AI

7. *See* US Supreme Court decisions in *Basic v. Levison*, 485 US 224 (1988), *Erica P John Fund, Inc v. Halliburton Co*, 563 US 804 (2011), or *Goldman Sachs Group v. Arkansas Teacher Retirement System*, 141 S.Ct. 1951 (2021).
8. *See Lei Ação Popular No. 83/95*, 31 May 1995.

are caused to businesses or individuals who have used the AI concerned for professional – i.e., not private – purposes. This is unless the procedure of the Member State where the damage is claimed allows for collective redress claims beyond consumer protection cases.

It remains to be seen whether the legal presumptions on fault and on causation set forth in Articles 3 and 4 of the AILD will facilitate claimants' compliance with the commonality requirement as a matter of fact. In this regard, Article 4(1) sets forth that the presumption of the existence of fault and causal link is subject to the plaintiff proving that:

(1) the defendant failed to disclose or to preserve evidence at its disposal which was intended to prove the lack of compliance by the defendant of duties of care/obligations set forth in Article 4(2);
(2) it is likely that the fault has influenced the output produced by the AI system or the failure of the AI system to produce an output; and
(3) the output produced or the failure to produce the output gave rise to the damage.

While the circumstances referred to in (1) and (2) can be proven on a common basis (i.e., for all the represented members of the class or group of consumers), proving that the output produced or that the failure to produce it caused the damage will in many cases require specific evidence on the underlying individual cases. Going back to the example of the autonomous car referred to in the commentary on Article 4 of the AILD, the circumstances in which the accident involving the autonomous car took place can only be assessed on an individual basis. In general, it will be difficult to meet the commonality requirement in those cases in which AI liability involves personal injury.

This will also be the case in other types of damaging events in which causation may be assessed on a common basis, but where the actuality and amount of the damages caused must also be considered on an individual basis.

This is so, for example, in a case in which it is claimed that the output of an AI system entails gender discrimination and is alleged to have caused harm. The assessment of the discriminatory effect might be analysed on a common (general) basis (e.g., through statistical data derived from the class or group of consumers itself). However, the existence and quantification of the financial damages and the causal link of those with gender discrimination coming from the use of AI may require an assessment of the specific circumstances of the underlying cases.

If the damages claimed are non-material (known as *moral damages* in many Member States), it may be understood that commonality is satisfied provided that the applicable law in the Member States allows moral damages to be claimed on a general basis – i.e., without the need to prove the specific circumstances that support the claim for moral damages in each underlying case – and assigning a common value to these.

However, this approach by the Member States may be inconsistent with the case law of the Court of Justice of the European Union (CJEU) on non-material damages in certain cases, namely in right to data protection/privacy cases. For example, when dealing with the possibility for individuals to seek compensation for non-material damages under Article 82(1) of the General Data Protection Regulation (GDPR), the CJEU has stated that:[9]

> the person seeking compensation on the basis of that provision is required to establish not only the infringement of provisions of that regulation, but also that that infringement caused him or her material or non-material damage.

This reference to the need to prove that the data protection infringement caused non-material damages specifically to the claimant – 'caused him or her' – may suggest that specific evidence on each individual case is required to award non-material/moral damages compensation. It remains to be seen whether this approach will be widely applied by the CJEU to non-material damages claims in other regulatory contexts, namely in AI liability.

BIBLIOGRAPHY

Case Law

CJEU

MediaMarktSaturn (Case C-687/21): Case C-687/21, *BL v. MediaMarktSaturn Hagen-Iserlohn GmbH*, 25 January 2024, ECLI:EU:C:2024:72.

UK

Walter Hugh Merricks CBE v. Mastercard Incorporation & Ors [2021] CAT 28.

US

Basic v. Levison, 485 US 224 (1988).
Erica P John Fund, Inc v. Halliburton Co, 563 US 804 (2011).
Goldman Sachs Group v. Arkansas Teacher Retirement System, 141 S.Ct. 1951 (2021).

Reports and Recommendations

Commission AILD Explanatory Memorandum 2022: Commission, *Explanatory Memorandum: Proposal for a Directive of the Parliament and of the Council on Adapting Non-contractual Civil Liability Rules to Artificial Intelligence (AI Liability Directive)*, COM(2022) 496 final 2022/0303 (COD) (Brussels, 28 September 2022).
Commission Recommendation 2013: Commission, *Commission Recommendation of 11 June 2013 on Common Principles for Injunctive and Compensatory Collective Redress Mechanisms in the Member States Concerning Violation of Rights Granted under the Union Law*, OJ. L. 201, 60-65 (26 July 2013), data.europa.eu/eli/reco/2013/396/oj (accessed 1 June 2024).

9. *See MediaMarktSaturn* (Case C-687/21), para. 61.

Academic Writings

Aguilera Morales et al. 2021: Marien Aguilera Morales et al., *Algunas ideas sobre la transposición de la Directiva 2020/1828 relativa a las acciones de representación para la protección de los intereses colectivos de los consumidores*, La Ley No. 9938/2021 (2021).

Ferreres Comella 2023: Alejandro Ferreres Comella, *La legitimación activa y la financiación de litigios en el Anteproyecto de Ley de Acciones de Representación*, Almacén de Derecho (28 February 2023), almacendederecho.org/53368-2 (accessed 1 June 2024).

Marina 2023: Federico Marina, *European Collective Redress and Data Protection: Challenges and Opportunities*, Rivista di Diritto di Media (June 2023).

Ogunleye 2022: Ifejesu Ogunleye, *AI's Redress Problem: Recommendations to Improve Consumer Protection from Artificial Intelligence*, Centre for Long-Term Cybersecurity, UC Berkeley (August 2022).

ARTICLE 7 Transposition

Ceyhun Necati Pehlivan

Article 7. Transposition

1. Member States shall bring into force the laws, regulations and administrative provisions necessary to comply with this Directive by [two years after the entry into force] at the latest. They shall forthwith communicate to the Commission the text of those provisions.

   When Member States adopt those provisions, they shall contain a reference to this Directive or be accompanied by such a reference on the occasion of their official publication. Member States shall determine how such reference is to be made.
2. Member States shall communicate to the Commission the text of the main provisions of national law which they adopt in the field covered by this Directive.

Recitals

(31) It is necessary to provide for a review of this Directive [five years] after the end of the transposition period. In particular, that review should examine whether there is a need to create no-fault liability rules for claims against the operator, as long as not already covered by other Union liability rules in particular Directive 85/374/EEC, combined with a mandatory insurance for the operation of certain AI systems, as suggested by the European Parliament.[1] In accordance with the principle of proportionality, it is appropriate to assess such a need in the light of relevant technological and regulatory developments in the coming years, taking into account the effect and impact on the roll-out and uptake of AI systems, especially for SMEs. Such a review should consider, among others, risks involving damage to important legal values like life, health and property of unwitting third parties through the operation of AI-enabled products or services. That review should also analyse the effectiveness of the measures provided for in this Directive in

1. [European Parliament resolution of 20 Oct. 2020 with recommendations to the Commission on a civil liability regime for AI (2020/2014(INL)) – OJ. C. 404, 107 (6 Oct. 2021)].

dealing with such risks, as well as the development of appropriate solutions by the insurance market. To ensure the availability of the information necessary to conduct such a review, it is necessary to collect data and other necessary evidence covering the relevant matters.

(32) Given the need to make adaptations to national civil liability and procedural rules to foster the rolling-out of AI-enabled products and services under beneficial internal market conditions, societal acceptance and consumer trust in AI technology and the justice system, it is appropriate to set a deadline of not later than [two years after the entry into force] of this Directive for Member States to adopt the necessary transposition measures.

(33) In accordance with the Joint Political Declaration of 28 September 2011 of Member States and the Commission on explanatory documents,[2] Member States have undertaken to accompany, in justified cases, the notification of their transposition measures with one or more documents explaining the relationship between the components of a directive and the corresponding parts of national transposition instruments. With regard to this Directive, the legislator considers the transmission of such documents to be justified,

RELATED ARTICLES

Article 5 (Evaluation and targeted review); Article 8 (Entry into force); Article 9 (Addressees).

RELATED LAWS

TFEU (Articles 258, 260 and 288).

RELATED CASE LAW

Commission v. France (Case C-304/02): Case C-304/02, *Commission of the European Communities v. French Republic*, 12 July 2005, ECLI:EU:C:2005:444.

Commission v. Ireland (Case C-374/11): Case C-374/11, *European Commission v. Ireland*, 19 December 2012, ECLI:EU:C:2012:827.

Francovich v. Italy (Joined Cases C-6/90 and C-9/90): Joined Cases C-6/90 and C-9/90, *Andrea Francovich and Danila Bonifaci and others v. Italian Republic*, 19 November 1991, ECLI:EU:C:1991:428.

Marshall v. Southampton Health Authority (Case C-152/84): Case C-152/84, *M. H. Marshall v. Southampton and South-West Hampshire Area Health Authority (Teaching)*, 26 February 1986, ECLI:EU:C:1986:84.

Van Duyn v. Home Office (Case C-41/74): Case C-41/74, *Yvonne van Duyn v. Home Office*, 4 December 1974, ECLI:EU:C:1974:133.

2. [OJ. C. 369, 14 (17 Dec. 2011)].

COMMENTARY

1 Purpose

The term 'transposition' is commonly associated with European Union (EU) directives.[3] It refers to the process of incorporating them into the national laws of Member States.

Transposition of EU directives into national law is a critical process that underpins the functioning of the EU as a legal and political entity. As discussed below, directives are legislative acts that require Member States to achieve specific results, but they leave the choice of form and methods to the national authorities. This process allows the EU to harmonize laws across Member States while respecting their individual legal systems and cultural differences.

Accordingly, the purpose of this provision is to set out the Member States' obligation to transpose the AI Liability Directive (AILD) into their national law. Article 7 sets forth the terms applicable to such transposition in accordance with EU law. This is a standard Article for EU directives.

2 Analysis

2.1 Transposition of EU Directive

The AILD is an EU directive. Directives, similar to regulations, decisions, recommendations, and opinions, are part of the EU's secondary legislation.[4]

In accordance with Article 288, third paragraph of the Treaty on the Functioning of the EU (TFEU), directives are binding as to the objectives to be achieved.[5] National authorities are nevertheless free to choose the form and the means that they deem most appropriate to achieve those policy objectives.[6] Under Article 7(1) of the AILD, Member States must, at their choice, adopt 'laws, regulations and administrative provisions necessary to comply with [the AI Liability Directive]' within the transposition period.

Unlike a regulation, such as the AI Act, which is directly applicable in Member States after its entry into force, a directive, such as the AILD, is not directly applicable in Member States. Directives must therefore first be transposed into national law before they become applicable in each Member State.

3. EU decisions can also have transposition deadlines for the addressees.
4. Treaties are considered in the EU as primary law, such as the founding treaties, the TFEU and the TEU. Primary law sets out the division of competences between the EU and the Member States.
5. Regulations and decisions are also binding (TFEU, Art. 288, paras 2 and 4), as opposed to recommendations and opinions that have no binding force (TFEU, Art. 288, para. 5).
6. TFEU, Art. 288, para. 3; EUR-Lex 2021.

2.2 *Deadline for Transposition*

Each EU directive specifies a deadline by which the Member States are required to transpose the provisions into its national legislation, which is generally within two years after the entry into force. Consistent with this, Article 7(1) of the AILD requires transposition by 'two years after the entry into force at the latest'. Such a two-year term is common for EU directives.

Recital 32 of the AILD explains that it is appropriate to provide the Member States with a two-year transposition period considering:

> the need to make adaptations to national civil liability and procedural rules to foster the rolling-out of artificial intelligence (AI)-enabled products and services under beneficial internal market conditions, societal acceptance and consumer trust in AI technology and the justice system.

The objectives of building and maintaining societal and consumer trust in AI technology and the judicial system mentioned in Recital 32 above are also stated in Recital 5:

> To reap the economic and societal benefits of AI and promote the transition to the digital economy, it is necessary to adapt in a targeted manner certain national civil liability rules to those specific characteristics of certain AI systems. Such adaptations should contribute to societal and consumer trust and thereby promote the roll-out of AI. Such adaptations should also maintain trust in the judicial system, by ensuring that victims of damage caused by the involvement of AI have the same effective compensation as victims of damage caused by other technologies.

The two-year transposition period starts from the date of entry into force of the AILD. In accordance with Article 8, the entry into force occurs on the twentieth day following that of its publication in the Official Journal of the EU.[7]

2.3 *Communication to the Commission*

By the aforementioned transposition deadline, Article 7(1), the second sentence, also requires the Member States to communicate to the Commission the text of such national transposition measures incorporating the provisions of the Directive into their legislation. This is to allow the Commission to ensure that the AILD is transposed into national Member State law properly and in a timely manner, as further discussed below.

As mentioned in Recital 33, Member States agreed, under the Joint Political Declaration of 28 September 2011, that:[8]

> the information they supply to the Commission as regards the transposition of directives in national law 'must be clear and precise' and 'must indicate unequivocally the laws, regulations and administrative provisions', or any other provisions of national law, as well as, where relevant, the jurisprudence of national courts, by

7. *See* the next commentary on *Art. 8*, in this volume.
8. AILD, Rec. 33.

> means of which the Member States consider that they have satisfied the various requirements imposed on them by the directive.[9]

The Declaration further states that:[10]

> In justified cases, Member States undertake to accompany the notification of transposition measures with one or more explanatory documents, which can take the form of correlation tables or other documents serving the same purpose.

The latter is only applicable in 'justified cases'. The last sentence of Recital 33 of the AILD confirms that, in relation to this Directive, 'the legislator considers the transmission of such documents to be *justified' (emphasis added)*. Therefore, Member States must provide the Commission with such documents to demonstrate that their national transposition measures properly address and achieve the objectives set out by the AILD.

In this regard, the Commission's Explanatory Memorandum to the AILD states that when communicating such national transposition measures to the Commission:[11]

> Member States should also provide explanatory documents which give sufficiently clear and precise information and state, for each provision of this Directive, the national provision(s) ensuring its transposition.

Such documentation is considered to be:[12]

> necessary to enable the Commission to identify, for each provision of the Directive requiring transposition, the relevant part of national transposition measures creating the corresponding legal obligation in the national legal order, whatever the form chosen by the Member States.

Accordingly, the aim of the Member States' obligation to communicate their national transposition measures to the Commission and provide sufficient explanatory documentation, is to allow the Commission to monitor and ensure the appropriate and timely transposition of the AILD into the Member State national legal system.

As part of its monitoring activity, as further discussed below, the Commission publishes the 'Single Market and Competitiveness Scoreboard' (Scoreboard), which measures the performance and results of the EU market in different policy areas and, as such, provides an overview of how well the internal market is functioning.[13] A key indicator in the Scoreboard is the so-called transposition deficit, which shows the gap between the number of Single Market directives adopted by the EU and the number of directives transposed by each Member State. In other words, it is the percentage of Single Market directives not yet completely notified to the Commission out of the total number of directives that should have been notified by the deadline.[14] For instance, as

9. *See Commission v. Ireland* (Case C-427/07), para. 107 and the case law cited therein.
10. Joint Political Declaration 2011.
11. Explanatory Memorandum to the AILD.
12. *Ibid.*
13. Commission Scoreboard (undated).
14. Commission Transposition (undated).

of 5 December 2023, the average EU transposition deficit of Single Market directives was at 0.7%.[15]

In addition to this transposition communication obligation under Article 7(1) of the AILD, Member States are also required to communicate to the Commission the text of the 'main provisions of national law that they adopt in the field covered by [the AI Liability Directive]' in accordance with Article 7(2).

Accordingly, the Member States' communication obligation goes beyond the mere transposition of the AILD into their national legislation. They must not only communicate to the Commission the national measures transposing the AILD into their legislation (Article 7(1)) but also other relevant national provisions that may be adopted in relation to the liability rules related to AI (Article 7(2)).

2.4 Failure to Transpose

Often referred to as the 'guardian of the treaties', the Commission is responsible for, among other things, monitoring the transposition process for the directives in the Member States and overseeing the application of EU law under the supervision of the Court of Justice of the European Union (CJEU).

As such, when a Member State communicates its national transposition measures to the Commission, the latter will examine whether such measures taken by the Member State are adequate and meet the objectives set by the directive, and ensure that the transposition has been carried out by the applicable deadline.

Where a Member State fails to transpose a directive on time and communicate to the Commission what measures it has taken to this end, or has taken measures but the Commission considers them to be incomplete or incorrect, the Commission may initiate a formal infringement procedure against that Member State under Article 258 of the TFEU.

Before launching such a formal infringement procedure, the Commission may also decide to engage in an informal bilateral dialogue called 'EU Pilot' with the Member State. This mechanism is not a mandatory step preceding an infringement procedure but is used when the issue is likely to be resolved through informal dialogue between the Commission and the Member State.[16]

Where the issue is not resolved following a formal infringement procedure, then the Commission may refer the case to the CJEU under Article 260(3) of the TFEU. In such a case, the Commission may propose that the CJEU impose a financial penalty, either a lump sum and/or a daily payment, on the defaulting Member State.

If the CJEU finds that the Member State has failed to fulfil an obligation under EU law, the Member State is required to comply with the judgment under Article 260(1) of the TFEU.

Where the Member State fails to comply with this obligation, the Commission may again bring the Member State before the CJEU, which, in this case, has the

15. *Ibid.*
16. Commission EU Pilot (undated).

additional power of imposing financial sanctions on it under Article 260(2) TFEU. Accordingly, the CJEU may impose on the Member State a lump sum for the failure to comply in the past and/or a periodic penalty payment that is effective until compliance is achieved.[17]

In conclusion, appropriate and timely transposition of the AILD by the Member States under Article 7 will be monitored by the Commission. Where a Member State fails to do so, the Commission is empowered to take action against that Member State under the TFEU.

2.5 *Protection of Individuals for Incorrect or Lack of Transposition*

As a general rule, a directive only takes effect once transposed. However, where a directive has not been transposed correctly or in due course, as discussed above, it can still have direct effects when the following conditions are met, as per the case law of the CJEU:[18]

- the transposition into national law has not taken place or has been done incorrectly;
- the terms of the directive are unconditional and sufficiently clear and precise; and
- the terms of the directive give rights to individuals.

In such a case, individuals may rely on the directive against a Member State in national courts. Individuals are also entitled, under certain conditions, to obtain compensation from the state for directives that have not been properly transposed or whose transposition has been delayed.[19]

Conversely, an individual may not rely on making a claim against another individual with respect to the direct effect of a directive that has not been transposed.[20]

2.6 *Reference to the Directive*

In accordance with Article 7(1), second paragraph, when Member States adopt national transposition provisions, the latter must contain a reference to the AILD or be accompanied by such a reference on the occasion of their official publication. Again, Member States are free to decide on how such reference is to be made.

This requirement is outlined in many directives and is a critical aspect of ensuring transparency, accountability, and clarity in the legal obligations deriving from EU directives.

17. *Commission v. France* (Case C-304/02); *Commission v. Ireland* (Case C 374/11).
18. EUR-Lex 2022.
19. *Ibid.*, and the case law cited therein, *e.g.*, *Francovich v. Italy* (Joined Cases C-6/90 and C-9/90).
20. *Ibid.*, and the case law cited therein, *e.g.*, *Van Duyn v. Home Office* (Case C-41/74) for 'vertical direct effect'; and *Marshall v. Southampton Health Authority* (Case C-152/84) for 'horizontal direct effect'. *See also* the commentary on *Art. 9* in this volume, s. 2.1.

First, including a reference to a directive makes it easier for the Commission to monitor and enforce the implementation of EU law at the national level. It provides a clear basis for evaluating whether national laws faithfully transpose the directive's requirements.

Second, by referencing the EU directive in the national laws or regulations that transpose the directive, Member States provide clear links between EU law and national law. This transparency helps legal practitioners, companies, and individuals understand the origin of certain legal obligations and how they relate to broader EU objectives.

Third, the reference helps maintain consistency in the application of EU law across different Member States. By explicitly acknowledging the directive, Member States ensure that the national measures are seen within the context of the EU-wide goals the directive aims to achieve.

Finally, it helps to provide legal certainty about which national laws are implementing EU directives. This is especially crucial for sectors regulated by multiple layers of legislation.

BIBLIOGRAPHY

Other

Commission EU Pilot (undated): Commission, *EU Pilot*, Single Market Scoreboard (undated), single-market-scoreboard.ec.europa.eu/enforcement-tools/eu-pilot_en#:~:text=EU%20Pilot%20is%20a%20mechanism,non%2Dcompliance%20with%20EU%20law. (accessed 5 July 2024).

Commission Scoreboard (undated): Commission, *The Single Market and Competitiveness Scoreboard*, Single Market Scoreboard (undated), single-market-scoreboard.ec.europa.eu/home_en (accessed 5 July 2024).

Commission Transposition (undated): Commission, *Transposition*, Single Market Scoreboard (undated), single-market-scoreboard.ec.europa.eu/enforcement-tools/transposition_en#:~:text=The%20transposition%20deficit%20is%20the,been%20notified%20by%20the%20deadline (accessed 5 July 2024).

EUR-Lex 2022: Publications Office of the European Union (EUR-Lex), *European Union Directives* (16 March 2022), eur-lex.europa.eu/EN/legal-content/summary/european-union-directives.html (accessed 5 July 2024).

EUR-Lex 2021: Publications Office of the European Union (EUR-Lex), *The European Union's Secondary Law* (2 December 2021), eur-lex.europa.eu/EN/legal-content/summary/the-european-union-s-secondary-law.html (accessed 5 July 2024).

Explanatory Memorandum to the AI Liability Directive.

Joint Political Declaration 2011: Joint Political Declaration of 28 September 2011 of Member States and the Commission on explanatory documents, SL C 369 (17 December 2011).

ARTICLE 8 Entry into Force

Ceyhun Necati Pehlivan

Article 8. Entry into force

This Directive shall enter into force on the twentieth day following that of its publication in the Official Journal of the European Union.

Recitals

(32) Given the need to make adaptations to national civil liability and procedural rules to foster the rolling-out of AI-enabled products and services under beneficial internal market conditions, societal acceptance and consumer trust in AI technology and the justice system, it is appropriate to set a deadline of not later than [two years after the entry into force] of this Directive for Member States to adopt the necessary transposition measures.

RELATED ARTICLES

Article 7 (Transposition).

RELATED LAWS

TFEU (Articles 289 and 297); Council Regulation 216/2013: Council Regulation (EU) No. 216/2013 of 7 March 2013 on the electronic publication of the Official Journal of the European Union, OJ. L. 69 (13 March 2013).

RELATED CASE LAW

Public.Resource.Org (Case C-588/21 P), AG Opinion: Case C-588/21 P, *Public.Resource.Org and Right to Know v. Commission and Others*, Opinion of Advocate General Laila Medina, 22 June 2023, ECLI:EU:C:2023:509.

Skoma-Lux (Case C-161/06): Case C-161/06, *Skoma-Lux sro v. Celní ředitelství Olomouc*, 11 December 2007, ECLI:EU:C:2007:773.

COMMENTARY

1 Purpose

The purpose of this provision is to determine the date of entry into force of the AI Liability Directive (AILD).

The entry into force of European Union (EU) directives constitutes a critical juncture in the lifecycle of EU lawmaking. This phase not only marks the beginning of legal obligations under EU directives but also sets the stage for their transposition into national law by the Member States, as discussed below.

EU directives commonly specify an entry into force date to establish a clear timeline for when the directives begin to have legal effect and to provide a structured framework for their implementation. It provides legal certainty to Member States, businesses, and individuals about when the provisions of the directive start to apply. This clear demarcation helps all stakeholders prepare for and adapt to the changes required by the directive.

Also, a common entry into force date ensures that all Member States start applying the directive's provisions simultaneously, fostering uniformity in how the law is applied across the EU. This is particularly important for directives that impact the single market, such as the AILD, as it helps maintain a level playing field.

The date of entry into force of the AILD represents the date when the Directive has legal existence in the EU legal order, setting a timeline for Member States to comply with its provisions by transposing it into their national legislation which is different from the date of applicability. As discussed below and in the previous commentary on Article 7 of the AILD, directives must first be transposed into national law before they become applicable in each Member State.

2 Analysis

2.1 Transposition of EU Directive

The AILD is an EU directive. Directives, similar to regulations, decisions, recommendations, and opinions, are part of the EU's secondary legislation.[1]

Unlike a regulation, such as the AI Act, which is directly applicable in Member States after its entry into force, a directive, such as the AILD, is not directly applicable in Member States. Directives must therefore first be transposed into national law before they become applicable in each Member State.[2]

1. Treaties are considered in the EU as primary law, such as the founding treaties, the TFEU and the TEU. Primary law sets out the division of competences between the EU and the Member States.
2. *See* the previous commentary on *Art. 7*, in this volume.

The entry into force date is crucial as it marks the beginning of the period within which Member States are obligated to enact national legislation that aligns with the directive. This date is essential for maintaining the synchronicity and coordination needed in the multi-level governance system of the EU.

Article 7(1) of the AILD requires transposition by 'two years after the entry into force at the latest'.[3] Such a two-year transposition term is common for EU directives.

2.2 *Entry into Force*

The aforementioned transposition period starts from the date of entry into force of the AILD.

In relation to entry into force, Article 297(1), paragraph 3 of the Treaty on the Functioning of the EU (TFEU) sets forth that:

> Legislative acts shall be published in the Official Journal of the European Union. They shall enter into force on the date specified in them or, in the absence thereof, on the twentieth day following that of their publication.

Legislative acts include regulations, directives, and decisions that are adopted by an 'ordinary' or 'special' legislative procedure under Article 289 of the TFEU.

The main characteristic of the 'ordinary legislative procedure' is the adoption of legislation jointly by the Parliament and the Council, on a proposal made by the Commission. The ordinary legislative procedure is the default procedure and is used for the majority of EU legislation.

Conversely, the 'special legislative procedure' means that the Council is the only legislator, instead of being a co-legislator together with the Parliament on an ordinary legislative procedure. The special legislative procedure is only used when the EU treaties expressly provide so.

According to its header, the AILD is expected to be adopted, following the Commission's proposal, by the Parliament and the Council 'acting in accordance with the ordinary legislative procedure'. The AILD will therefore be a legislative act referred to in Article 297(1) of the TFEU, as discussed above.

Article 8 of the AILD specifies the date of entry into force of the Directive: 'on the twentieth day following that of its publication in the Official Journal of the European Union'. This twenty-day period expressly set out in the AILD is also the same as the default period of time that would apply to such a legislative act, should the Directive be silent on the date of its entry into force, in accordance with Article 297(1) of the TFEU.

2.3 *Publication in the Official Journal of the EU*

As discussed in the previous section, the AILD will enter into force twenty days after publication in the Official Journal of the EU (OJEU).

3. *Ibid.*

The OJEU is the official publication through which the EU disseminates its legal documents to Member States and the public. It is published every day[4] in all official languages of the EU, ensuring that EU citizens and stakeholders have access to the laws and policies that affect them in their own language.[5]

The OJEU plays a central role in the accessibility of EU law. For directives, publication in the OJEU also formally announces the directive to the Member States and the public. This publication is essential for transparency and starts the clock on the timeline for transposition.

The publication of EU legislation in the OJEU is also a crucial step for the legislation to become legally binding. Directives themselves become legally binding on the Member States to which they are addressed from the date they enter into force. This date often follows shortly after their publication in the OJEU.

The Court of Justice of the European Union (CJEU) concluded in *Skoma-Lux* that EU law must be accessible to EU citizens:[6]

> In accordance with the principle of legal certainty, [EU] rules must enable the persons concerned to identify precisely the scope of the obligations which they are subject to, which can only be guaranteed by the proper publication of those rules in the official language of the addressee.

Accordingly, the CJEU ruled that:[7]

> EU regulations or directives do not have legal effects vis-à-vis individuals if they are not properly published in the OJEU in the language of a Member State, 'even though those persons could have learned of that legislation by other means'.

Since 1 July 2013, the electronic edition of the OJEU published on EUR-Lex is authentic and produces legal effects in accordance with Council Regulation 216/2013. The paper version no longer has any legal value, except when OJEU cannot be published online due to unforeseen disruption to IT systems.

The OJEU consists of two main series:[8]

(1) L series: legislation, including regulations, directives, decisions, recommendations, and opinions.
(2) C series: information and notices, containing reports and announcements, such as the judgments of the CJEU and the General Court.

The AILD will be published in the L series of the OJEU.

As discussed above, the OJEU is published in all the official EU languages. The AILD will therefore be available in all the twenty four official languages.

4. The OJEU is published Monday to Friday inclusive, and on Saturdays, Sundays and public holidays only in urgent cases.
5. The 24 official languages of the EU are: Bulgarian, Croatian, Czech, Danish, Dutch, English, Estonian, Finnish, French, German, Greek, Hungarian, Irish, Italian, Latvian, Lithuanian, Maltese, Polish, Portuguese, Romanian, Slovak, Slovenian, Spanish and Swedish.
6. *Skoma-Lux* (Case C-161/06).
7. *Public.Resource.Org* (Case C-588/21 P), AG Opinion, para. 56.
8. EUR-Lex (undated).

BIBLIOGRAPHY

Other

EUR-Lex (undated): Publications Office of the European Union (EUR-Lex), *Official Journal of the European Union* (undated), eur-lex.europa.eu/EN/legal-content/glossary/official-journal-of-the-european-union.html (accessed 5 July 2024).

ARTICLE 9 Addressees

Ceyhun Necati Pehlivan

Article 9. Addressees

This Directive is addressed to the Member States.

Recitals

(32) Given the need to make adaptations to national civil liability and procedural rules to foster the rolling-out of AI-enabled products and services under beneficial internal market conditions, societal acceptance and consumer trust in AI technology and the justice system, it is appropriate to set a deadline of not later than [two years after the entry into force] of this Directive for Member States to adopt the necessary transposition measures.

RELATED ARTICLES

Article 7 (Transposition); Article 8 (Entry into force).

RELATED LAWS

TFEU (Articles 288 and 289).

RELATED CASE LAW

Marshall v. Southampton Health Authority (Case C-152/84): Case C-152/84, *M. H. Marshall v. Southampton and South-West Hampshire Area Health Authority (Teaching)*, 26 February 1986, ECLI:EU:C:1986:84.

COMMENTARY

1 Purpose

The purpose of this provision is to determine the addressees of the AI Liability Directive (AILD), which are the Member States.

The explicit mention of addressees in European Union (EU) directives serves primarily to provide clarity and legal certainty. This specification ensures that both the Member States and the Commission (and other EU institutions) are aware of who is obliged to act under the terms of the directive. It delineates responsibilities and creates a clear legal expectation for compliance, which is essential for maintaining the rule of law within the EU. This is fundamental in a Union where not all directives apply universally across all Member States due to various opt-outs or specific provisions, as discussed below.

The identification of addressees also enhances the ability of the EU to monitor and enforce compliance. It provides a foundation for the Commission to initiate infringement proceedings against non-compliant states effectively.[1] This enforcement mechanism is crucial for upholding the integrity of the EU's legal system and ensures that the directives' objectives are achieved across the EU, contributing to a more cohesive and integrated European legal order.

2 Analysis

2.1 EU Directives Are Addressed to Member State(s)

The AILD is an EU directive. Directives, similar to regulations, decisions, recommendations, and opinions, are part of the EU's secondary legislation.[2]

Unlike regulations, which have direct applicability, directives require transposition into national law.[3] A critical aspect of these directives is the specification of their addressees - typically the Member States - which is integral to the directive's successful implementation and enforcement.

In accordance with Article 288, paragraph 3 of the Treaty on the Functioning of the EU (TFEU):

> A directive shall be binding, as to the result to be achieved, *upon each Member State to which it is addressed,* but shall leave to the national authorities the choice of form and methods. (*emphasis added*).

From this paragraph, it is understood that an EU directive can only be *addressed to Member States*. Directives require the Member States to achieve a particular result

1. Regarding the Commission's monitoring activity, *see* the commentary on *Art. 7* in this volume, s. 2.3.
2. Treaties are considered in the EU as primary law, such as the founding treaties, the TFEU and the TEU. Primary law sets out the division of competences between the EU and the Member States.
3. *See* the commentary on *Art. 7* in this volume, s. 2.1.

without dictating the means of achieving that result. Companies and individuals cannot be the addressees of a directive. Article 9 of the AILD also states that it is 'addressed to the Member States'.

Conversely, for example, Article 288, paragraph 4 of the TFEU sets out that '[a] decision which specifies those to whom it is addressed shall be binding only on them'. Thus, the addressees of a decision are not specified or limited to the Member States; they may be addressed to one or several Member States, companies or individuals.[4] For instance, where the Commission decides to impose a fine on a company for abusing its dominant market position, it addresses its decision to that company.[5] Such a decision would only be binding on that company.

Furthermore, according to Article 288, paragraph 3 of the TFEU, the *binding force* of a directive only applies to the Member State to which it is addressed. This principle was decisively affirmed in the Court of Justice of the European Union's (CJEU's) seminal case *Marshall v. Southampton Health Authority*, where the CJEU held that while directives can have a direct effect, meaning that individuals can rely on them in disputes with the state (or state bodies), directives cannot impose obligations directly on individuals. This is because directives are addressed to Member States, and not to private parties. The CJEU ruled that it is up to the Member States to implement directives into national law, which then can impose obligations on individuals. Once a directive is transposed into the national law of a Member State, it becomes part of the legal framework that companies and individuals must comply with.

Marshall v. Southampton Health Authority helped solidify the conditions under which the direct effect of directives could be invoked, distinguishing between vertical direct effect (against state entities) and ruling out horizontal direct effect (between private parties).[6]

Directives serve as a tool for harmonizing laws across the EU while allowing flexibility in how laws are implemented to reflect different national contexts. They do not directly address companies or individuals but create obligations for them through national legislation once they are transposed. This indirect method ensures that while the EU can set common objectives, the specific legal environments of the Member States are respected.

Finally, in principle, directives are only binding upon *each Member State to whom* they are addressed, which can be one, several or all of them. Nevertheless, in practice, directives are typically addressed to all of the Member States, with the exception of directives adopted under specific circumstances.[7] Article 9 also refers to *all* of the Member States.

4. EUR-Lex 2021.
5. *Ibid.*
6. *See also* the commentary on *Art. 7* in this volume, s. 2.4.
7. There are specific circumstances under which EU directives and regulations might be binding only on some Member States. *First*, enhanced cooperation allows a group of at least nine EU Member States to implement measures in a certain area within the EU's structures, even if all Member States do not agree to participate. This mechanism is used as a last resort when the EU as a whole cannot reach agreement. Directives and regulations issued under this framework apply only to those countries participating in the enhanced cooperation. For example, the EU's provisions on the unitary patent system only apply to participating Member States under

In conclusion, the common practice of specifying addressees in EU directives is more than a mere formal requirement; it is a pivotal component that enhances the directive's effectiveness and ensures that EU law is integrated smoothly into the national laws of the Member States. This practice ultimately leads to legal alignment under relevant articles.

BIBLIOGRAPHY

Other

EUR-Lex 2021: Publications Office of the European Union (EUR-Lex), *European Union decisions* (26 July 2021), eur-lex.europa.eu/EN/legal-content/summary/europe an-union-decisions.html (accessed 6 July 2024).

---

enhanced cooperation (Regulation (EU) No. 1257/2012 of the European Parliament and of the Council of 17 Dec. 2012 implementing enhanced cooperation in the area of the creation of unitary patent protection). *Second*, some EU Member States have negotiated opt-outs from certain areas of EU policy, which means that directives related to these policies do not apply to them. These opt-outs are usually part of the treaty agreements. For example, the UK (before Brexit) had opt-outs in areas such as the eurozone and Schengen Agreement; or Denmark has an opt-out from the Common Security and Defence Policy. *Third*, when new countries join the EU, transitional arrangements might temporarily exempt them from certain directives until they fully integrate with EU standards and practices. For example, newer EU members might have temporary exemptions from certain environmental or agricultural directives until they can fully comply with EU standards. Similarly, directives such as the Free Movement of Workers Directive 2004/38/EC were not fully applicable to the new Member States until the end of the transitional period, allowing old Member States to temporarily restrict labour movement from these countries. *Fourth*, occasionally, directives themselves include specific provisions that apply only to certain Member States. This could be due to particular conditions or agreements during the negotiation phase of the directive. For example, directives that pertain to regions with specific economic or environmental conditions that do not exist in all Member States. For instance, the Water Framework Directive 2000/60/EC allows for specific adaptations based on regional and local conditions, thus not uniformly applying the same provisions to all Member States. *Fifth*, in some cases, temporary derogations (exemptions) are granted to Member States from certain directives due to extraordinary circumstances such as natural disasters or severe economic crises. For example, temporary financial exemptions granted during economic crises to allow more flexibility in budgetary policies. Each of these scenarios represents a nuanced approach to EU law application, reflecting the diverse and often complex nature of governance across multiple countries with varying needs and capabilities.

Index

A

Accessibility, 65, 68, 143, 147, 181, 205, 408
Accountability / accountable, 4, 5, 7, 8, 10-13, 16, 17, 19, 36, 43-45, 57, 59, 60, 66-68, 72, 94, 136, 137, 140, 141, 143, 145, 155, 158, 285, 312, 313, 356-379, 403
Accuracy, 4, 44, 63, 136, 192-193, 195, 232, 234, 240, 245, 246, 319, 350, 365, 366
Adverse effect, 43, 154, 249
Agency/agencies, 20-21, 62
Agriculture, 181
AI Act, 3-13, 37-38, 51-75, 93-109, 165-177, 203-204, 275-276
AI Advisory Forum, 65, 73
AI Board, 74, 119, 135, 167
AI Convention, 9-11, 35-47
AI Liability Directive, 217-414
AI literacy, 144
AI model, 14, 15, 69, 81, 83, 88-90, 92, 93, 100, 109, 110, 144, 145, 147-151, 154, 156, 172, 173, 174, 181, 183, 193, 196-198, 201, 232, 259, 268, 269, 276
AI Office, 17, 68, 74, 100, 119, 121, 126, 143, 145, 146, 150, 167, 168, 170, 173, 204
AI system, 37, 41-47, 61-68, 128-131, 133-142, 144, 154-155, 230-250, 257-271, 292-293, 337, 340-341
AILD, 317-324
Algorithm, 11, 19, 22, 24, 34, 42, 43, 64, 84, 118, 128, 137, 149, 154, 182, 196, 222-224, 243, 262, 264, 307, 333, 334
ALTAI, 60, 73, 75
Anonymization, 182, 186-190, 192, 202
Anonymous, 186, 335
Anthropomorphizing, 41
Anti-competitive, 168, 169, 175
API, 183
Apulia, 13
Auditability, 64, 67, 73, 74
Auditing, 16, 42
Authorised / Authorized representative, 123, 125-127, 139, 155
Autonomous / autonomy, 41-42, 261-263
Availability, 45, 82, 86-91, 106-107, 171, 205, 313, 357, 376, 379, 383, 398
Aviation, 58, 134

B

Behavioural identification, 72
Benchmark, 9, 53, 148, 149
Best practices, 68, 74, 148
Bias, 11, 15, 20, 21, 23, 34, 41, 43, 63, 65, 117, 137, 158, 192, 193, 240, 249, 270, 366

Biden, 14-17, 19, 25, 93, 118, 131, 221
Big Data, 24, 181-184, 186-188
Biometric data, 23, 60, 143, 240
Biometric identification, 61, 96, 120-122, 132, 133, 138, 235, 240, 241, 270
Black box, 41, 172, 196, 232-234, 243, 250, 251, 333, 369
Border control, 135, 236-238, 246, 248
Brussels Effect, 127
Burden of proof, 219, 260, 271, 288, 289, 300, 314-316, 330, 335, 336, 339, 346, 350, 353, 356, 358, 359, 361, 367, 369, 380-382, 385
Burdensome, 360

C

CAHAI, 34, 47, 56, 269, 313, 357, 378
CAI, 34, 35, 49, 50, 56, 268
California, 118
Canada, 22, 35, 222
Causal link, 349-369
Causality, 366-369
CE marking, 125, 139, 140, 142, 152, 234
Charter, 14, 53, 59, 72, 122, 133, 176, 200, 224, 226, 229, 238, 240, 245, 249
ChatGPT, 22, 105, 110, 118, 181, 182, 377
China, 22-25
Chinese State Council, 118
Civil liability, 227, 233, 275, 283, 285, 292, 306, 311, 315, 330, 351, 354, 355, 358, 362, 376, 380, 382, 389, 398, 400, 405, 411
CJEU, 175, 176, 184, 185, 202, 312, 335, 339, 344, 394, 395, 402, 403, 408, 413
Claim, 287-293
Claimant, 295-301, 335-342
Clearview, 105
Codes of conduct, 12, 13, 52, 60, 61, 65, 66, 68, 75, 122
Common Crawl, 90
Compensation, 268, 269, 287-290, 292-293, 296, 306, 307, 314, 317, 330, 331, 334, 338, 340, 345, 350, 351, 358, 360-362, 380-382, 384, 394, 395, 400, 403
Competent authority, 42, 135, 139-142, 145-147, 150, 155, 168, 304, 310, 351, 362
Competition, 165-177
Complaint, 21-22, 45, 74, 120, 166, 170, 171, 236, 246, 392
Compliance, 11, 14, 22, 25, 37, 39, 44, 64, 72, 74, 94, 100, 105, 108, 109, 119, 122, 123, 125, 126, 138-142, 145-147, 150-152, 154, 156-158, 165, 167, 170, 193, 195, 274, 282, 284, 317, 352, 353, 361, 362, 390, 394, 412
Compliance monitoring, 74
Computing power, 16, 86-91, 100, 107, 110, 188
Confidential information, 173, 303, 330, 332, 344
Conformity assessment, 119, 124-126, 134, 139, 140, 153, 157, 158, 231
Consent, 24, 197-198, 221, 391
Constitutional, 39, 40, 291
Consumer, 393
Consumer trust, 398, 400, 405, 411
Controller, 104, 184, 185, 187, 189, 191, 193, 194
Copyright, 25, 42, 146, 147, 151, 166, 168, 172-174, 269, 352
Corrective, 137, 141, 142, 150, 319, 350, 365
Council of Europe, 9-11, 33-50, 268-269
Court, 34, 171, 174, 184, 219, 223, 225-227, 240, 242, 247, 250,

258, 268, 273, 274, 281-283, 289, 297, 299-301, 303-305, 309, 310, 320, 329-332, 334-336, 338, 340-346, 349, 350
Criminal, 10, 15, 43, 117, 132, 135, 142, 219, 236, 245, 291, 313, 357, 378, 379
Criminal liability, 291, 313, 357, 378
Criminal offences, 132, 135, 236, 245
Critical, 13, 15, 16, 18, 34, 45, 59-61, 67, 72, 110, 118, 134, 138, 143, 148-150, 153, 189, 191, 235, 237, 238, 240-242, 244, 270, 399, 403
Critical infrastructure, 15, 16, 18, 134, 138, 235, 237, 238, 241-242
Cyber, 19, 118
Cybersecurity, 4, 12, 15, 19-21, 44, 63, 150, 241, 319, 350, 365

D

Damage, 287-293, 296, 340-341
Damage caused, 219, 226, 233, 258, 268, 269, 273, 274, 281, 282, 287-290, 292-293, 299, 303, 314, 316, 330, 331, 351, 358, 359, 379, 381, 384, 393, 400
Damages, 287-293, 296, 340-341
Data accuracy, 192-193, 195
Data Act, 82, 106, 205
Data collection, 23, 24, 37, 186, 196, 200, 226
Data governance, 7, 14, 63, 65, 94, 104-106, 136, 166
Data Governance Act / DGA, 82, 105, 106
Data management, 105, 137, 152, 153
Data minimization, 104, 182, 189, 191, 192, 200
Data mining, 173, 226
Data privacy, 34, 40, 44, 153, 169, 182, 190
Data protection, 44, 152-153, 165-177, 181-183
Data protection authorities, 105, 199
Data protection impact assessment / DPIA, 23, 104, 138, 152
Data retention, 16, 225, 336, 342
Data sharing, 105, 106
Data subject, 103, 184-186, 188, 189, 193, 195-203, 205
Decision-making, 4, 11, 34, 42, 45, 62, 64, 125, 128, 135, 136, 172, 222, 239, 240, 249, 250, 263, 270
Declaration of conformity, 125, 126, 139, 140
Deep fake, 143
Defendant, 303-307, 338-339, 341-342, 345
Delegated acts, 129, 146, 149, 237, 239
Democracy, 33-50
Deployer, 124
Design, 4-6, 9, 16, 17, 21, 34, 37, 42, 44, 55, 56, 64, 65, 68, 69, 73, 81, 86, 99, 100, 103, 105, 108, 118, 119, 121, 125, 127, 129, 136, 137, 142, 144, 147, 148, 152, 154, 156, 189, 192, 193, 202, 203, 205, 225, 228, 229, 242, 244-247, 258-261, 264, 268, 269, 273, 275-278, 281, 284, 299, 305, 310, 313, 315, 318, 319, 331, 336, 337, 350, 352, 354, 357, 364, 365, 378
Digital economy, 5, 24, 25, 56, 107, 109, 219, 258, 400
Digital infrastructure, 134, 235, 241
Digital Markets Act / DMA, 82, 106-107
Digital service, 82, 154, 311
Digital Services Act / DSA, 82, 107-109, 119, 121, 153-154, 158, 307, 311, 352, 354
Digital strategy, 120
Dignity, 7, 8, 11, 35, 40-42, 49, 53, 229, 238, 243, 244, 268

Disability, 40, 48, 65, 68, 73, 143, 238, 240, 242
Disclosure, 329-346
Disclosure of evidence, 219, 220, 228, 257, 269, 274, 283, 288, 303, 329-346, 354
Discrimination, 10, 13, 15, 18-21, 23, 43-44, 137, 242, 244, 278, 364, 394
Distribution, 39, 147, 277, 330, 351, 367
Distributor, 99, 123, 125, 137, 140-142, 152, 155, 337
Downstream provider, 146, 170, 171
Due diligence, 125, 219, 311, 312, 352, 356, 378
Duties of care / duty of care, 274, 282, 283, 299, 304, 305, 307, 310, 314, 317-319, 331, 332, 346, 351-353, 362, 365, 366, 394

E

ECHR, 9, 41, 44, 48, 223, 224, 226, 229, 240, 245
Economic / economy, 5, 7, 13, 24, 25, 53, 56, 107, 109, 182, 219, 222, 258, 315, 317, 359, 380, 400
EDPB, 204, 206
Effective judicial remedy, 155, 304, 332, 351
Elections, 18, 41, 48, 66, 135, 237, 249
Emotion recognition, 91, 98, 134, 138, 143, 235, 241, 270
Enforcement / enforcing, 154-157, 168, 170, 175, 244-245, 304, 332, 345, 351
Equal treatment, 43
Ethics, 7-9, 57-69
Ethics guidelines, 42, 51, 53, 54, 57-69, 72, 94, 166
EU Institution Data Protection Regulation, 143
EUR, 100, 154-156, 408
Evaluation, 8, 16, 18, 22, 43, 136, 145, 149-150, 156, 225, 239, 243, 269, 285, 375-385
Evidence, 329-346
Ex-ante, 18, 45, 67, 69, 73, 74, 192, 261
Excessive, 156, 260, 270, 305, 330, 334, 350, 353, 355, 367, 368
Excessively difficult, 260, 305, 330, 350, 353, 355, 368
Executive Order, 14-17, 93, 118, 131, 148, 149, 221
Explainability, 5, 8, 42, 64, 258
Explanatory Memorandum, 4, 38, 95, 232, 393, 401
Exploitation, 66, 133, 174, 241
Ex-post, 45, 68, 121, 261
Extraterritorial, 23, 127, 173, 174

F

Facial recognition, 11, 23, 72, 91, 93, 98, 118, 122, 132
Failure, 292-293, 402-403
Fair, 5, 21, 41, 44, 48, 55, 56, 86, 99, 109, 167, 170, 195, 225, 226, 238, 245, 249, 304, 332, 343, 384, 392
Fairness, 4, 5, 8, 18, 20, 23, 26, 53, 60, 65, 94, 107, 155, 156, 166
Fake news, 24, 91
Fault, 291-292, 317-324, 349-369
Fault of the defendant, 304, 305, 309, 310, 317, 349, 351, 353, 360, 362, 366, 368
Fault-based liability, 220, 227, 233, 248, 251, 275, 287, 291, 311, 315, 330, 335, 350, 358, 362, 377, 378, 380, 381, 382, 384
Financial institutions, 244
Floating point operations / FLOP, 86-89, 100, 148, 149
Foreseeability, 49, 313, 322, 325, 362, 367
Foreseeable risks, 205, 226, 322, 362, 367
Foundation model, 11, 15, 19, 98, 121, 122, 259, 384

Fragmented, 287, 363
France, 33, 55, 121, 290, 311, 355, 376
FTC, 21-22
Fundamental right, 175-176
Fundamental rights impact assessment / FRIA, 62, 73, 74, 121, 133, 138

G

G20, 4-7, 56
G7, 11, 13
Gatekeeper, 107, 139
GDPR, 103-105, 181-206
Gender equality, 10, 33, 44, 48, 68, 238
Generative AI (generative AI), 5, 6, 11, 12, 16, 19, 24-26, 49, 93, 107, 118, 121, 145, 192, 196, 222, 258
Germany, 55, 121, 311, 355, 377, 389
Google, 20, 56, 92, 93, 144, 169
Governance, 1-206
GPAI, 144-152, 155-156
GPT, 21, 22, 88, 89, 93, 100, 105, 110, 118, 144, 148, 149, 181, 182, 377
Guiding principles, 11-14, 205, 206

H

Harm, 6, 8, 9, 15, 16, 18, 35, 38, 52, 53, 57, 58, 60, 62, 63, 70, 73, 94, 132, 133, 135, 150, 155, 167, 229, 230-233, 238-240, 243, 244, 245, 250, 251, 261, 264, 270, 275, 277, 278, 284, 285, 289, 304, 306, 307, 310, 313-315, 332-336, 338, 341, 343, 345, 351, 355, 357, 360, 362, 367, 378, 379, 381, 383, 393, 394
Harmful, 20, 24, 99, 123, 154, 158, 165, 205, 229, 237, 270, 379
Harmonization, 33, 134, 231-234, 282, 336, 339
Harmonize67, 95-96, 121, 143, 146, 147, 150, 151, 155, 158, 205, 231, 247, 275, 284, 285, 291, 300, 313, 316, 354, 355, 369, 399
Healthcare, 18, 117, 181, 199, 232, 235, 236, 243, 244, 251
High-impact, 147-149, 151, 156
High-risk, 61-68, 133-142, 230-250, 267-271, 337, 340-341
High-risk AI systems, 61-68, 133-142, 230-250, 267-271, 337, 340-341
Hiroshima, 4, 11-13
HLEG, 51-57
HLEG Guidelines, 51-53, 55, 57-70, 73-75, 94, 166, 167, 221
HUDERIA, 35
Human activity, 136, 250
Human agency, 49, 62, 94
Human assessment, 250, 257, 267, 273, 281, 287, 292, 293, 295, 296, 309, 323
Human dignity, 7, 8, 11, 35, 41-42, 45, 49, 229, 238, 243, 244, 268
Human oversight, 8, 18, 42, 45, 62, 104, 137, 157, 158, 323
Human resource, 124
Human review, 143, 250, 293
Human rights, 33-50
Human trafficking, 40, 248

I

IBM, 20, 56
Importer, 99, 123, 125, 139-141, 152, 155, 337
Independent oversight, 11, 22
Information asymmetry44, 334, 335, 346, 355
Injured, 219, 260, 273, 281, 282, 295-297, 299, 301, 304, 305, 330-332, 335, 336, 340, 350, 351, 353, 355, 366, 367, 368, 393
Innovation, 44

Input, 6, 54, 57, 84, 85, 94, 99, 104, 106, 129, 130, 137, 142, 192, 204, 205, 206, 228, 258, 259, 263, 268, 276, 293, 304, 309, 320, 330, 333, 334, 350, 351, 355, 356, 366
Instructions, 51, 124, 137, 139, 140, 283, 304, 305, 310, 319, 336, 350, 351, 354, 362, 366, 368
Insurance, 18, 62, 135, 224, 235, 244, 270, 296, 375, 376, 378, 380, 382-385, 397, 398
Intellectual property / IP, 12, 145, 172-176, 238
Intended purpose, 6, 124, 137, 138, 204, 238, 277, 283, 305, 319, 320, 337, 350, 354, 365, 366, 368
Intermediary, 108, 109, 307, 352, 392
Interpretability, 42
Italy, 22, 105, 121, 389

J

Japan, 11, 13, 14, 22, 35, 55, 167, 222
Judicial remedy, 74, 155, 304, 332, 351
Judiciary, 40, 41, 48

K

Key requirements, 60, 61, 65-69, 73, 75, 166

L

Labelling, 64, 140, 144
Large language model / LLM, 22, 88, 121, 149, 183
Law enforcement, 39, 41, 96, 120, 122, 128, 132, 133, 135, 142, 143, 168, 171, 174, 175, 223, 228, 236-238, 241, 244-245
Legal professionals, 41
Legitimate interest, 42, 197-203, 303, 304, 330, 332, 343, 344
Liability, 217-414
Lifecycle, 6, 10, 12, 13, 16, 22, 35-37, 39-46, 49, 66, 137, 140, 141, 221, 274, 282, 313, 336, 353, 357, 379, 406
Litigation, 155, 172, 230, 231, 243, 273, 281, 299-301, 304, 331, 332, 334, 341, 345, 351, 360, 367, 391, 392
Lodge a complaint, 74, 166, 170
Logging / logs, 64, 138, 139, 331, 335-343, 346, 353

M

Machinery, 82, 134, 231
Making available, 276
Malfunction, 137, 241
Manipulation, 40-42, 48, 49, 62, 66, 143, 190
Manufacturer, 123-125, 152, 168, 251, 277, 278, 285, 307, 319, 337, 365, 367
Market surveillance, 74, 100, 119, 120, 126, 136, 137, 139, 140, 142, 166, 385
Market surveillance authorities (MSA), 74, 100, 120, 126, 137, 139, 166-168, 170, 385
Medical, 90, 128, 132, 134, 181, 199, 231-234, 236, 243, 244, 251
Medical devices, 128, 134, 231
Member State, 412-414
Meta, 20, 89, 93, 144, 169, 172
Microsoft, 20, 171
Migration, 135, 224, 236-238, 246-248
Military, 81, 91, 96, 120, 128, 228, 229
Misinformation, 6, 40, 81, 118, 143
Mitigation, 12, 15, 16, 18, 42, 45, 66, 154, 268, 367
Monitoring, 6, 8, 9, 13, 18, 37, 42, 71, 74, 119, 124, 135, 137-139, 152, 157, 158, 235, 242, 243, 284, 315, 366, 375, 377, 385, 401, 402

N

National courts, 219, 274, 282, 283, 289, 301, 303-305, 309, 320, 329-332, 335, 336, 338, 340, 342-346, 349, 350, 353, 354, 360, 368, 400, 403
National law, 244-245, 322-323
National security, 10, 15, 19, 24, 39-40, 72, 117, 120, 128, 225, 228, 229, 241, 303, 330, 332
Negotiations, 35, 39, 46, 48, 50, 57, 66, 98, 121, 122, 171, 237
Netherlands, the, 34, 92, 223-226
Neural networks, 84, 85, 144, 196
New Legislative Framework / NLF, 66, 134
New York, 22, 118
Non-compliance, 100, 119, 127, 141, 156, 157, 167, 220, 225, 257, 264, 274, 282, 299, 303, 306, 310, 317, 320, 323, 324, 331, 332, 339, 344, 346, 349, 351-353, 361, 376, 377
Non-discrimination, 8, 10, 35, 40, 43-44, 48, 49, 52, 94, 166, 168, 170, 229, 243, 244, 246
Non-personal data, 205
Non-professional, 128, 229, 283, 284, 305, 350, 353, 354, 368, 369
Notified bodies, 119, 140, 155
NPLD / New Product Liability Directive, 227, 229-233, 244, 250-252, 275, 277, 278, 285, 307, 311, 332, 336, 339, 340, 343, 346, 354, 376
Nudging, 72, 239
Nvidia, 20, 87-89, 91

O

OECD, 4-7
OECD AI Principles, 4-7, 25, 26, 221, 258
OECD Recommendation, 258, 264
Official Journal, 93, 100, 122, 156, 315, 358, 400, 405, 497, 407-408
Omission, 167, 257, 263, 267, 273, 281, 287, 288, 292, 295, 296, 304, 305, 309, 323, 330, 350, 351, 353, 362
Opacity, 232, 249, 258, 260, 305, 314, 330, 333, 334, 353, 355, 358, 359, 368, 380
OpenAI, 20-22, 88-90, 92, 93, 110, 118, 144, 148, 181, 182
Open-source, 90, 92, 98, 100, 121, 128, 147-148, 232
Output, 292-293
Oversight, 8, 10, 11, 16, 18, 22, 25, 35, 42, 45, 62, 73, 74, 94, 104, 137, 147, 151, 154-158, 167, 261, 312, 318, 323, 350, 356, 365, 366, 378

P

Packaging, 140
Parliament, 97-98, 120-121
Pattern, 12, 109, 136, 144, 188, 242, 250
Personal data, 8, 12, 23, 33, 35, 44, 103, 104, 143, 152, 153, 157, 182-186, 188-195, 197, 200-205, 225, 238, 240
Personal identifier, 182, 184-190
Physical injury, 304, 310, 351, 362
Placed on the market, 64, 126, 128, 136, 140, 141, 228-230, 261, 276, 277, 337
Placing on the market, 231, 239, 276-277
Policy recommendations, 51, 52, 55, 57, 70-75
Policymaking, 11, 59, 75, 268
Political, 41, 48, 60, 98, 121, 132, 167, 224, 237, 249, 250, 398-400
Post-market monitoring, 119, 157, 158
Post-remote biometric identification, 122
Potential harm, 9, 133, 304, 332, 343
Predictions, 6, 41, 42, 99, 129, 131, 228, 234, 258, 259, 276

Preparatory work, 60, 75, 335
Preservation, 274, 282, 300, 301, 303, 329-332, 339, 342-346
Presumption of causality, 264, 268, 274, 282, 283, 304, 305, 309, 351-354, 360, 362, 366-369, 382, 384
Presumption of conformity, 67, 146, 150
Principled-based, 71
Privacy by design, 192, 202
Private life, 41, 49, 199, 225, 226
Procedural, 10, 45, 122, 136, 155, 156, 168, 245, 250, 300, 312, 315, 316, 320, 330, 334, 345, 355, 358, 359, 380, 390, 398, 400, 405, 411
Procedural remedies, 330, 345
Proceedings, 99, 155, 199, 245, 249, 274, 282, 300, 301, 303, 304, 330-332, 342, 345, 351, 392, 412
Processing operations, 194, 195
Processor, 104, 185, 225
Product liability, 227, 232, 291, 316, 359, 377, 381
Product Liability Directive / PLD, 227, 251, 252, 275, 277-278, 291, 314-316, 354, 357-359, 380, 381, 384
Product safety, 66, 71, 101, 153, 166-167, 176, 278, 284
Profiling, 4, 72, 135, 136, 201, 202, 222, 236, 245, 250
Prohibited AI, 61, 72, 75, 96, 97, 99, 101, 128, 240, 319, 365, 381
Prohibited practices, 62, 72, 119, 122, 132-134, 136, 174
Proof, 50, 97, 219, 260, 271, 288, 289, 293, 300, 301, 305, 314-316, 330, 335, 336, 339, 346, 350, 353, 356, 358, 359-361, 364, 367, 369, 379, 380-381, 385
Proportionality / proportionate, 8, 60, 68, 71, 72, 131, 133, 156, 269, 303, 304, 329-332, 335, 341, 343-345, 350, 375, 383, 397
Prosecution, 135, 142, 236, 245
Provider, 123-124, 136-137, 142-143, 145-146, 150-152, 273-278, 337
Pseudonymization, 188-190, 192, 202, 225, 249
Public safety, 4, 21, 147, 225
Publicly accessible, 22, 120, 122, 133, 147, 183, 196, 197, 203
Purpose limitation, 193-195
Putting into service, 231, 239, 276-277

Q

Quality management, 74, 124, 157, 158, 336

R

Radio equipment, 134
Railway, 134
Real-time remote biometric identification, 96, 120, 122, 132
Rebuttable, 329-369
Rebuttable presumption, 329-369
Recall, 45, 68, 103, 141, 319, 350, 365
Recording, 64, 184, 368
Record-keeping, 68, 125, 336
Referendum, 66, 135, 237, 249
Regulatory sandbox, 44, 97, 100, 119, 120
Regulatory standards, 139-141
Remedy, 8, 10, 45, 74, 107, 155, 175, 220, 230, 233, 237, 238, 242-245, 249-251, 292, 304, 313, 314, 330, 332, 335, 343, 345, 351, 357-360, 369, 379, 380
Remote biometric identification system, 96, 120, 122, 132, 138, 235, 240, 241, 270
Reporting, 12, 13, 15, 20, 22, 25, 46, 47, 67, 137, 142, 148, 149, 155, 269, 385

Representative action, 297, 332, 389, 390, 393
Responsibility, 7, 8, 10, 23, 35, 38, 43, 45, 57, 66, 126, 137, 140, 141, 154, 166, 195, 228, 233, 244, 260, 263, 277, 312, 313, 316, 356, 357, 378, 379, 384
Right of access, 40
Right to explanation, 64, 172
Right to privacy, 8, 9, 44, 49
Rights of children, 40, 73
Rights to remedies, 45
Risk management, 6, 12, 13, 15-17, 19, 67, 105, 136, 150, 152-154, 237, 274, 282, 314, 318, 319, 322, 349, 353, 358, 364, 365, 379, 385
Risk-based, 12, 68, 70-73, 95, 96, 99, 119, 131, 132, 193, 197, 203, 205, 222, 269, 315, 322, 358, 380
Robustness, 5, 44, 59, 62-63, 94, 166, 245, 319, 350, 365
Rule of law, 33-50

S

Safety, 62-63, 134, 166-167, 231-234
Safety component, 125, 134, 230-235, 238, 241, 242
Sandbox, 44, 97, 100, 119, 120
Scientific research, 128, 229
Scope, 123-128, 219-252
Scraping, 98, 132, 183, 196, 203
Search engine, 107, 108, 153, 154
Secrecy, 304, 332
Sectorial legislation, 134
Sensitive, 18, 23, 41, 42, 142, 143, 146, 151, 184, 187, 201-203, 235, 240, 241, 270
Serious incident, 67, 137, 150
Singapore, 55, 118
Small and medium-sized enterprises (SME), 65, 98, 100, 154, 158, 375, 383, 384, 397
Social control, 43, 229
Social scoring, 4, 8, 61, 96, 120, 132
Society, 5, 7, 11, 12, 14, 15, 20, 23, 24, 34, 35, 44, 48-50, 52-53, 55, 57, 58, 62, 65, 66, 70, 73, 91, 92, 95, 105, 110, 159, 165, 168, 203, 205, 219, 223, 225, 226
Spain, 121, 248
Special categories of personal data, 201, 204, 240
Speech recognition, 91, 259
Stakeholder participation, 72
Stakeholders, 6, 11, 13, 14, 42, 46, 47, 50, 53-57, 60, 65, 68, 70, 72-75, 118, 119, 123, 144, 154, 156, 157-159, 268, 406, 408
Standards, 4, 9-13, 15, 16, 25, 26, 34, 44, 47-49, 54, 56, 64, 67, 72, 119, 127, 136-142, 146, 147, 150, 151, 153, 154, 157, 158, 182, 185, 191, 195, 196, 200, 202, 203, 219, 220, 223, 231, 233, 234, 242, 247, 258, 261-263, 291, 293, 309, 310, 313, 314, 317, 321, 322-324, 330, 340, 352, 360-362, 399
State of the art, 84, 91, 93, 107, 146, 149, 150, 173, 183, 205
Subject matter, 46, 170, 219-252, 288, 354
Substantial modification, 124, 277, 337
Suitability, 392
Surveillance, 4, 8, 11, 18, 40, 74, 100, 118-120, 126, 136, 137, 139, 140, 142, 166, 245
Systemic risk, 67, 100, 132, 145-152, 154, 269-271

T

Targeted review, 220, 375-385
Technical documentation, 64, 68, 88, 125, 126, 139, 145-147, 269, 336
Technical robustness, 62-63, 94, 166

Technical solutions, 68
Technical specifications, 44
Testing, 10, 16, 18, 37, 39, 63, 97, 100, 120, 128, 137, 145, 150, 166, 167, 183, 229, 318, 349, 364
Testing data, 318, 349, 364
Testing in real-world, 128
TEU, 228
TFEU, 169-171, 176, 398, 399, 402, 403, 405, 407, 411-413
Threats of harm, 72
Toy, 134, 231
Traceability, 64, 73, 137, 138, 140, 142, 336
Trade secret, 146, 151, 173, 303, 304, 306, 330, 332, 344, 345
Trademark, 123-125, 139, 276, 277, 337
Training, 181-206
Training data, 25, 43, 85, 90, 147, 151, 172, 174, 181-184, 186, 190, 192-201, 203-205
Transparency, 42, 63-65, 142-144, 195-197
Transport, 18, 90, 117, 140-142, 181, 219, 316, 359, 381
Transpose / transposition, 62, 251, 397-404, 406, 413
Trustworthy AI, 57-74

U

UGAI, 3, 4, 26
UK, 11, 14, 118, 392
UN, 13, 14, 25, 26, 220, 223, 240
UN Charter, 14
Unacceptable risk, 72, 96, 132-133
UNESCO, 7-9
Union harmonization legislation, 231-234
Union law, 67, 101, 166, 168, 173, 219, 244, 309, 310, 321, 324, 351, 352, 362, 395
Urgency, 133
US, 14-22, 25, 52, 91-93, 118, 127, 131, 148, 221, 222, 390, 392
User, 281-285, 337

V

Vehicle, 125, 134, 316, 356, 359, 363, 381, 384, 391, 392
Very large online platforms, 108, 121, 153, 154
Victim, 10, 34, 133, 135, 232-234, 236, 241, 245, 264, 290, 296, 314, 333-335, 338, 345, 355, 356, 358, 360, 361, 363, 364, 366, 367, 369, 380, 382, 393, 400
Voluntary, 12, 19-20, 25, 38, 51, 52, 60, 61, 65, 66, 68, 75, 122, 171, 177, 341, 342
Von Der Leyen, 57
Vulnerable groups, 68

W

White House, 14-17
White Paper, 3, 57, 94-96, 315, 358, 380
Withdrawal, 168, 198, 252, 319, 350, 365

www.ingramcontent.com/pod-product-compliance
Lightning Source LLC
Chambersburg PA
CBHW071236230926
51849CB00001B/118
* 9 7 8 9 4 0 3 5 0 5 4 9 7 *